Introduction

WHY THIS DIRECTORY IS NEEDED

Each year, more than 19 million Americans will head off to college and graduate school. Many of them are going to experience sticker shock. According to the College Board, undergraduates at a private four-year college can pay $34,000 or more, Graduate students can expect even higher charges; it can cost $100,000+ to complete some master's and doctoral degrees.

To help students pay for their postsecondary studies, a number of print and online sources have been developed that identify funding opportunities. While many of these listings have been general in nature, a number have described, in depth, scholarships available to students based on personal characteristics: gender, ethnicity, military affiliation, and economic level, to name just a few. Surprisingly, despite the fact that Christian students represent a major segment of the college population, no source—other than *Money for Christian College Students*—has focused on the billions of dollars in aid that's been set aside exclusively to support Christian undergraduate and graduate students.

The general financial aid directories—even the thorough ones like *Kaplan Scholarships* and *Peterson's Scholarships, Grants & Prizes*—include only a couple dozen programs open specifically to Christian college students. And, the Internet sites that have listed funding for Christian students—while providing some assistance—have generally proved to be lacking in detail, out of date, and/or incomplete in their coverage.

That's why this updated edition of *Money for Christian College Students* is so important. Now, in just one place, Christian students (along with the counselors and librarians trying to serve them) can have current and detailed information about the 850 biggest and best scholarships, fellowships, awards, loans, grants, and other funding opportunities available specifically to help them pay for their undergraduate or graduate degree (secular or religious) at public, nondenominational private, or Christian schools.

Money for Christian College Students makes it easy to find out about the billions of dollars available to support undergraduate and graduate study, research, creative activities, future projects, and travel. There's no other source, in print or online, like it. Perhaps that's why Sources for Students calls this a "ground-breaking directory" and Kaplan Educational Centers labels it a "must-have guide."

WHAT'S INCLUDED?

Money for Christian College Students is unique in many ways. Not only does it provide the most comprehensive coverage of funding opportunities (850 entries) open specifically to Christian students working on an undergraduate or graduate degree, but it also offers the most informative program descriptions (on the average, more than twice the detail found in any other source).

In addition, the directory focuses exclusively on funding set aside for Christians working on a secular or religious undergraduate or graduate degree at any type of postsecondary institution. If a program doesn't support study, training, research, or creative activities for these students, it is not covered here.

Third, only the biggest and best funding programs are described in this book. To be listed here, a program has to offer Christian undergraduate or graduate students at least $500 per year. The majority of programs go way beyond that, with many paying $20,000 or more annually, or covering the full cost of college attendance.

Fourth, you can take the money awarded by these funding programs to any number of locations. Unlike many of the print or online listings, which often include scholarships available only to students enrolled at one specific school, all of the entries in this book are "portable" (although some portability may be restricted by other program parameters). Another plus: many of the programs listed here have never been covered in other financial aid resources. So, even if you have checked elsewhere, you will want to look at *Money for Christian College Students* for additional leads.

Fifth, unlike other funding directories, which tend to follow a straight alphabetical arrangement, this one divides entries by educational level (undergraduates and graduate students), to facilitate your search for appropriate programs. The same convenience is offered in the indexes, where sponsoring organization, geographic focus, subject, denominational affiliation, and deadline date entries point out opportunities for either undergraduate or graduate students.

Further, we have tried to anticipate all the ways you might wish to search for funding; we've organized the volume so you can identify programs not only by educational level, but by program title, sponsor, subject field, where you live, where you want to go to school, religious affiliation, and when you plan to apply for funding. In addition, we've included all the information you will need to decide if a program is right for you: purpose, eligibility requirements, financial data, duration, special features, limitations, number awarded, and application date. You even get fax numbers, toll-free numbers, e-mail addresses, and web sites (when available), along with complete contact information, to make your requests for applications proceed smoothly.

Finally, we've included all types of funding in our listing:

- *Scholarships.* Programs that support secular or religious study and training for Christian students at the undergraduate level in the United States. Usually no return of service or repayment is required.

- *Fellowships.* Programs that support secular or religious study and training for Christian students at the graduate level in the United States. Usually no return of service or repayment is required.

- *Grants.* Programs that provide funding to Christian students to support innovative efforts, projects, creative activities, or research at the postsecondary level (from a 2-year degree through the doctorate) in the United States. Usually no return of service or repayment is required.

- *Awards.* Competitions, prizes, and honoraria granted to Christian undergraduate or graduate students in recognition of personal accomplishments, research results, creative writing, or other achievements. Prizes received solely as the result of entering contests are excluded.

- *Loans.* Programs that provide money to Christian undergraduate or graduate students for study, training, research, or other activities in the United States which eventually must be repaid—with or without interest.

- *Forgivable Loans.* Sometimes called scholarship/loans, fellowship/loans, or loans-for-service, these are loans that convert to scholarships or fellowships (provided the recipients meet specified service requirements). If these requirements are not met, however, the money awarded must be repaid (often with interest).

WHAT'S EXCLUDED?

The focus of *Money for Christian College Students* is on portable programs aimed specifically at undergraduate or graduate students who are affiliated with denominations "professing belief in Jesus as Christ or based on the life and teachings of Jesus." These students may be beginning, continuing, or returning to their postsecondary studies. They may be studying any subject (secular or religious) at any type of college or university (secular or religious). While the directory is intended to be the most current and comprehensive source of information on available funding, there are some programs we've specifically excluded from the listing:

SAMPLE ENTRY

(1) **[591]**

(2) **HARVEY FELLOWS PROGRAM**

(3) Mustard Seed Foundation
Attn: Harvey Fellows Program
7115 Leesburg Pike, Suite 304
Falls Church, VA 22043
(703) 524-5620   Fax: (703) 524-5643
Web: msfdn.org/scholarships

(4) **Summary** To provide financial aid to Christian students to attend prestigious graduate schools in the United States or abroad and to prepare for careers in "strategic occupations where Christians appear to be underrepresented."

(5) **Eligibility** This program is open to American and foreign students. The most competitive applicants are those whose intended vocational fields are demonstrated to have a significant impact on society and to be of high priority for Christian involvement. Vocations that are not considered a priority for this scholarship include: work within a church or religious organization; civil service; elementary and secondary education; general business; homemaking; farming; nonprofit relief and economic development; military service; private practice law or medicine; clinical psychology or counseling; social work; professional sports; and other fields that traditionally have attracted a higher percentage of Christians.

(6) **Financial data** Each fellow is awarded an annual $16,000 stipend. Funds must be used at a "premier" graduate degree program, subject to approval by the selection committee. Fellows may use their stipends for tuition, living expenses, research tools or travel, studio space, professional conferences, and interview travel.

(7) **Duration** 1 year; may be renewed up to 2 additional years.

(8) **Additional information:** Recipients must attend 1 of the top 5 institutions (anywhere in the world) in their field of study. Christian colleges and small liberal arts schools are excluded, because, according to the sponsors, they "have not yet found" any that are "nationally acknowledged in professional publications or national rankings as top five institutions."

(9) **Number awarded** Varies each year. Recently, 33 were awarded.

(10) **Deadline** October of each year.

DEFINITION

(1) **Entry number:** Consecutive number that is assigned to the program descriptions and used to identify the entry in the index.

(2) **Program title:** Title of scholarship, fellowship, loan, forgivable loan, grant, award, or other funding opportunity.

(3) **Sponsoring organization:** Name, address, and telephone number, toll-free number, fax number, e-mail address, and/or web site (when information was supplied) for organization sponsoring the program.

(4) **Summary:** Identifies the major program requirements; read the rest of the entry for additional detail.

(5) **Eligibility:** Qualifications required of applicants and factors considered in the selection process.

(6) **Financial data:** Financial details of the program, including fixed sum, average amount, or range of funds offered, expenses for which funds may and may not be applied, and cash-related benefits supplied (e.g., room and board).

(7) **Duration:** Period for which support is provided; renewal prospects.

(8) **Additional information:** Any benefits, features, restrictions, or limitations (generally non-monetary) associated with the program.

(9) **Number of awards:** Total number of recipients each year or other specified period.

(10) **Deadline:** The month by which applications must be submitted.

- *Programs not focused on Christian students:* Only money set aside primarily or exclusively for undergraduate or graduate students affiliated with denominations that accept some or all of the core tenets of Christianity are described here. Funding opportunities offered to students with a less direct connection to Christianity (or none at all) have been excluded. You can find information on those, and thousands of other programs, in Reference Service Press's other award-winning financial aid publications (some are listed on the inside front cover of this directory), in general financial resources at the library, at bookstores, and online.

- *Programs that do not accept applications from U.S. citizens or residents:* If a program is open only to foreign nationals for study in their own country or excludes Americans from applying, it is not covered.

- *Funding not aimed at incoming, currently-enrolled, or returning students:* If a program is open to Christians but is not specifically intended for undergraduate or graduate students (e.g., a contest open to Christians of any age, a research grant for Christian postdoctorates, a scholarship to attend a Christian high school), it is not covered here.

- *Individual school-based programs:* The directory identifies portable programs (ones that can be used at any number of schools). Financial aid administered by individual schools solely for the benefit of their incoming or continuing students is not covered. Write directly to or visit the Internet sites of the schools you are considering, to get information on their offerings.

- *Money for study or research outside the United States:* Since there are comprehensive and up-to-date directories that describe available funding for study and research abroad (see *Financial Aid for Research and Creative Activities Abroad* and *Financial Aid for Study and Training Abroad,* both published by Reference Service Press), only programs that support study or research in the United States are covered here.

- *Very restrictive programs:* In general, programs are excluded if they are open only to a limited geographic area (less than a state), are available to a very limited membership group (e.g., a local union or a tightly targeted organization), or offer very limited financial support (under $500).

- *Programs that did not respond to our research inquiries:* Programs are included in *Money for Christian College Students* only if the sponsors responded to our research requests for up-to-date information or posted up-to-date information on their web sites (for more detail on our data collection procedures, see below).

WHAT'S UPDATED?

The preparation of each new edition of *Money for Christian College Students* involves extensive updating and revision. To make sure that the information included here is both reliable and current, the editors at Reference Service Press 1) reviewed and updated all relevant programs currently in our funding database and 2) searched exhaustively for new program leads in a variety of sources, including directories, news reports, newsletters, annual reports, and sites on the Internet. Since we only include program descriptions that are written directly from information supplied by the sponsoring organization in print or online (no information is ever taken from secondary sources), we first check the appropriate web site; if current information is not available there, we then send up to four collection letters (followed by up to three telephone inquiries, if necessary) to each sponsor identified in the process. Despite our best efforts, however, some sponsoring organizations still failed to respond by the fourth quarter of 2011 and, as a result, their programs are not included in this edition of the directory.

The 2012-2014 edition of *Money for Christian College Students* completely revises and updates the previous (second) edition. Programs that have ceased operation have been dropped. Similarly, programs that have broadened their scope and no longer focus on or relate to Christian students have also been removed from the listing. Profiles of continuing programs have been rewritten to reflect current requirements; over 80 percent of the continuing programs reported substantive changes in their locations, deadlines, or benefits since the previous edition was issued. In addition, more than 350 new entries have been added. The result is a listing of 850 scholarships, fellowships, traineeships, grants, loans, and other funding opportunities available specifically to Christian undergraduates and graduate students.

HOW THE DIRECTORY IS ORGANIZED

Money for Christian College Students is divided into two sections: 1) a detailed list of funding opportunities open to Christian students working on an undergraduate or graduate degree; and 2) a set of indexes to help you pinpoint available funding programs.

Funding for Christian Students Working on a Postsecondary Degree. The first section of the directory describes 850 scholarships, fellowships, grants, loans, loans-for-service, awards, and other funding opportunities available specifically to Christian students working on an undergraduate or graduate degree. These programs are sponsored by more than 375 different agencies, organizations, foundations, educational associations, and religious groups. All subject fields (secular and religious) are represented, as are all types of postsecondary institutions.

To help you focus your search, the entries in this section are grouped into two main categories:

- **Undergraduates.** Described here are 404 scholarships, grants, awards, loans, scholarship/loans, and other funding opportunities available to Christians that support study, training, research, or creative activities on the undergraduate level. These programs are open to college-bound high school seniors, high school graduates, currently-enrolled college students, and students returning to college after an absence.

- **Graduate Students.** Described here are 446 fellowships, grants, awards, loans, fellowship/loans, and other funding opportunities available to Christians that support post-baccalaureate study, training, research, and creative activities. Funding is available for all graduate-level degrees: master's, doctoral, and professional, both secular and religious (although many programs funded on the graduate level are for religious study).

Entries in each of the two subsections appear alphabetically by program title. Each program entry has been designed to provide a concise profile that, as the sample on page 7 illustrates, includes information (when available) on organization address and telephone numbers (including fax and toll-free numbers), e-mail address and web site, purpose, eligibility, money awarded, duration, special features, limitations, number of awards, and application deadline.

Indexes. To help you find the aid you need, we have constructed six indexes; these will let you access the listings by sponsoring organization, residency, tenability, subject field, religious affiliation, and deadline date. These indexes use a word-by-word alphabetical arrangement. Note: numbers in the index refer to entry numbers, not to page numbers in the book.

Sponsoring Organization Index. This index makes it easy to identify agencies that offer funding to Christian students working on an undergraduate or graduate degree in a secular or religious field. More than 375 sponsoring organizations are listed alphabetically, word by word. In addition, we've used a code to help you identify the intended recipients of the funding programs sponsored by these organizations: U = Undergraduates; G = Graduate Students.

Residency Index. Some programs listed in this book are restricted to residents of a particular state or region. Others are open to Christian students wherever they live. This index helps you identify programs available only to residents in your area as well as programs that have no residency restrictions.

Tenability Index. Some programs in this book can be used only in specific cities, counties, states, or regions. Others may be used anywhere in the United States (or even abroad). Use this index to find out what programs are available to support your studies in a particular geographic area.

Subject Index. Refer to this index when you want to identify funding opportunities for Christian students working on an undergraduate or graduate degree in a specific secular or religious field.

Denomination Index. You can target funding opportunities by religious affiliation in this index: Baptist, Episcopalian, Methodist, Presbyterian, Roman Catholic, and a dozen more.

Calendar Index. Since most financial aid programs have specific deadline dates, some may have closed by the time you begin to look for funding. You can use the Calendar Index to identify which programs are still open. This index is arranged by student group (undergraduates and graduate students) and divided by month during which the deadline falls. Filing dates can and quite often do vary from year to year; consequently, the dates in this index should be viewed as only approximations after mid-2014.

HOW TO USE THE DIRECTORY

Here are some tips to help you get the most out of the financial aid listings in *Money for Christian College Students:*

To Locate Funding by Educational Level. If you want to get an overall picture of the kind of funding that is available to Christian students to support either undergraduate or graduate study, turn to the appropriate category in the first section of the guide and browse through the listings there. Originally, we also intended to subdivide these two chapters by focus (secular and religious). Once the compilation was complete, however, it became clear that many of the programs provided funding for both types of study on the undergraduate level and primarily for religious studies on the graduate level. Thus, further subdivision (beyond educational level) would have been unnecessarily repetitious.

To Find Information on a Particular Financial Aid Program. If you know the name and degree focus of a particular financial aid program, then go directly to the appropriate category in the first section of the directory, where you'll find program profiles arranged alphabetically by title.

To Browse Quickly Through the Listings. Turn to the listings in the educational section that relates to you (undergraduates or graduate students) and read the "Summary" field in each entry. In seconds, you'll know if this is an opportunity that might apply to you. If it is, read the rest of the information in the entry to make sure you meet all of the program requirements before writing or going online for an application form. Remember: don't apply if you don't qualify!

To Locate Financial Aid Programs Sponsored by a Particular Organization. The Sponsoring Organization Index makes it easy to determine which groups are providing funding to Christian undergraduate and graduate students (more than 375 are listed here), as well as to identify specific financial aid programs offered by a particular sponsor. Each entry number in the index is coded to indicate educational level (undergraduates and graduate students), to help you target appropriate entries.

To Locate Financial Aid Based on Residency or Where You Want to Study/Conduct Your Research. Use the Residency Index to identify funding that has been set aside for Christian students in your area. If you are looking for funding to support activities in a particular city, county, state, or region, turn to the Tenability Index. Both of these indexes are subdivided by educational level (undergraduates and graduate students), to help you identify the funding that's right for you. When using these indexes, always check the listings under the term "United States," since the programs indexed there have no geographic restrictions and can be used in any area.

To Locate Financial Aid for Study or Research in a Specific Subject Field. Look at the Subject Index first if you are interested in identifying available funding for a degree in a particular secular or religious field. As part of your search, be sure to check the listings in the index under the "General programs" heading; that term identifies programs supporting activities in any field (although they may be restricted in other ways). Each index entry indicates whether the funding is available to undergraduates or to graduate students.

To Locate Financial Aid by Religious Affiliation. In this book, we have described hundreds of financial aid programs available primarily or exclusively to Christian students interested in working on an undergraduate or graduate degree. You can use this index to look for leads by specific denomination. In addition, you should also check the "Protestant" (if appropriate) and "Christianity" entries (where you will find a number of funding opportunities that can be used by students belonging to any Christian denomination, although the programs may be restricted in other ways).

To Locate Financial Aid by Deadline Date. If you are working with specific time constraints and want to weed out financial aid programs whose filing dates you won't be able to meet, you can turn first to the Calendar Index and check the program references listed under the appropriate group (undergraduates and graduate students) and month. But, to identify every relevant financial aid program, regardless of filing dates, go to the first section and read through all the entries in the chapter that matches your degree focus.

PLANS TO UPDATE THE DIRECTORY

This is the third revised and updated edition of *Money for Christian College Students.* The next edition will cover the years 2014-2016 and will be released mid-2014.

OTHER RELATED PUBLICATIONS

Money for Christian College Students is one of more than two dozen financial aid titles published by Reference Service Press on an annual or biennial basis. Some of these titles are listed on the inside front cover of this directory. For more information on those and other award-winning financial aid directories, you can 1) write to Reference Service Press's marketing department at 5000 Windplay Drive, Suite 4, El Dorado Hills, CA 95762; 2) call us at (916) 939-9620; 3) fax us at (916) 939-9626; 4) send us an e-mail at info@rspfunding.com; or 5) visit our web site: www.rspfunding.com.

ACKNOWLEDGEMENTS

A debt of gratitude is owed all the organizations that contributed information to *Money for Christian College Students.* Their generous cooperation has helped to make this third edition of the publication a current and comprehensive survey of funding available to Christian undergraduate and graduate students.

ABOUT THE AUTHOR

Dr. Gail Ann Schlachter has worked for more than three decades as a library administrator, a library educator, and an administrator of library-related publishing companies. Among the reference books to her credit are the biennially-issued *College Student's Guide to Merit and Other No-Need Funding* (named by *Choice* as one of the outstanding reference titles of the year) and two award-winning bibliographic guides: *Minorities and Women: A Guide to Reference Literature in the Social Sciences* (which also was chosen as an "Outstanding Reference Book of the Year" by *Choice)* and *Reference Sources in Library and Information Services* (which won the first Knowledge Industry Publications "Award for Library Literature"). She was the reference book review editor for *RQ* (now *Reference and User Services Quarterly)* for 10 years, is a past president of the American Library Association's Reference and User Services Association, is the former editor-in-chief of the *Reference and User Services Association Quarterly,* and is currently serving her fifth term on the American Library Association's governing council. In recognition of her outstanding contributions to reference service, Dr. Schlachter has been named the "Alumna of the Year" by the University of Wisconsin School of Library and Information Studies and has been awarded both the Isadore Gilbert Mudge Citation and the Louis Shores/Oryx Press Award.

Dr. R. David Weber taught history and economics at Los Angeles Harbor College (in Wilmington, California) for many years and continues to teach history as an emeritus professor. During his years of full-time teaching there, and at East Los Angeles College, he directed the Honors Program and was frequently chosen the "Teacher of the Year." He has written several critically-acclaimed reference works, including *Dissertations in Urban History* and the three-volume *Energy Information Guide.* With Gail Schlachter, he is the author of Reference Service Press's award-winning *High School Senior's Guide to Merit and Other No-Need Funding* and two dozen other financial aid titles, including *Money for Graduate Students in the Arts & Humanities* and *Financial Aid for the Disabled and Their Families,* which was selected as one of the "Best Reference Books of the Year" by *Library Journal.*

Money for Christian College Students

Undergraduates ●

Graduate Students ●

Undergraduates

Listed alphabetically by program title are 404 scholarships, loans, forgivable loans, awards, grants and other funding opportunities available to Christian college students that support undergraduate study, training, research, and creative activities in either secular or religious fields.

[1]
ABC UNDERGRADUATE SCHOLARSHIPS

American Baptist Churches USA
National Ministries
Attn: Office of Financial Aid for Studies
P.O. Box 851
Valley Forge, PA 19482-0851
(610) 768-2067   Toll Free: (800) ABC-3USA, ext. 2067
Fax: (610) 768-2453
E-mail: Financialaid.Web@abc-usa.org
Web: www.nationalministries.org

Summary   To provide financial assistance to undergraduate students who are members of American Baptist-related churches.

Eligibility   This program is open to students planning to enroll as a full-time freshman at a college or university in the United States or Puerto Rico. Applicants must be U.S. citizens who have been a member of a church affiliated with American Baptist Churches USA for at least 1 year. Along with their application, they must submit a 500-word essay on the gifts they believe God has given them. Preference is given to students attending a college or university affiliated with American Baptist Churches USA and to dependents of American Baptist pastors. Students receiving assistance from other American Baptist scholarship programs are not eligible.

Financial data   Stipends range from $500 to $1,000 per year. Funds are paid directly to the recipient's school and credited towards tuition.

Duration   1 year; may be renewed if the recipient maintains a GPA of 2.75 or higher.

Number awarded   Varies each year.

Deadline   May of each year.

[2]
ACT SIX SCHOLARSHIPS

Act Six
c/o Northwest Leadership Foundation
717 Tacoma Avenue South, Suite A
Tacoma, WA 98402
(253) 272-0771   Fax: (253) 272-0719
E-mail: info@actsix.org
Web: www.actsix.org

Summary   To provide financial assistance to residents of Washington and Oregon who come from diverse backgrounds and are interested in attending designated private faith-based universities in those states.

Eligibility   This program is open to residents of Washington and Oregon who are high school seniors or recent graduates and planning to enter college as freshmen. Applicants must come from diverse, multicultural backgrounds. They must be planning to attend 1 of the following institutions: George Fox University (Newberg, Oregon), Gonzaga University (Spokane, Washington), Heritage University (Yakima, Washington), Northwest University (Kirkland, Washington), Pacific Lutheran University (Tacoma, Washington), Trinity Lutheran College (Everett, Washington), Warner Pacific College (Portland, Oregon), or Whitworth University (Spokane, Washington). Students are not required to identify as Christians, but they must be interested in engaging in a year-long exploration and discussion of Christian perspectives on leadership, diversity, and reconciliation. Ethnicity and family income are considered as factors in selecting an intentionally diverse group of scholars, but there are no income restrictions and students from all ethnic backgrounds are encouraged to apply.

Financial data   The program makes up the difference between any other assistance the student receives and full tuition. For recipients who demonstrate financial need in excess of tuition, awards cover some or all of the cost of room and board, books, travel, and personal expenses.

Duration   1 year; may be renewed.

Additional information   Information on the Oregon program is available c/o Portland Leadership Foundation, 809 North Russell, Suite 203, Portland, OR 97227, (503) 281-3757, E-mail: oregon@actsix.org.

Number awarded   Varies each year. Recently, 48 scholarships were awarded to the Washington schools and 21 to the Oregon schools.

Deadline   October of each year.

[3]
AHEPA UNDERGRADUATE SCHOLARSHIPS

American Hellenic Educational Progressive Association
Attn: AHEPA Educational Foundation
1909 Q Street, N.W., Suite 500
Washington, DC 20009
(202) 232-6300   Fax: (202) 232-2140
E-mail: Admin@ahepa.org
Web: ahepa.org

Summary   To provide financial assistance for college to students with a connection to the American Hellenic Educational Progressive Association (AHEPA) who have been active in Greek Orthodox youth activities.

Eligibility   This program is open to 1) active members of the AHEPA family (the Order of AHEPA, Daughters of Penelope, Sons of Pericles, or Maids of Athena); or 2) children of members of those organizations and of Greek descent. Applicants must be enrolled or planning to enroll full time at a college or university. High school seniors and college freshmen must submit official high school transcripts that include SAT or ACT scores and a GPA of 3.0 or higher; college sophomores and juniors must submit their most recent college transcript. Selection is based primarily on academic achievement, although consideration is also given to AHEPA affiliation, extracurricular activities, community service, and Greek Orthodox youth activities; special consideration is given to applicants who can demonstrate financial need.

Financial data   Stipends range up to $2,000.

Duration   1 year.

Additional information   This program includes the following named scholarships: the George Chirgotis Scholarship, the George and Helen Constantine Scholarship, the Sam Dakis Scholarship, the George Leber Scholarship, the Gus County Scholarship, the Dr. John C. Yavis Scholarship, the Archbishop Demetrios Scholarship, the P.A. Margaronis Scholarship, the Nick Cost Scholarship, and the Chris Gustav Rallis Scholarship.

Number awarded   Varies each year.

Deadline   March of each year.

[4]
AILEEN C. AND CARSON F. SINCLAIR SCHOLARSHIPS

Florida United Methodist Foundation
Attn: Scholarship Committee
450 Martin Luther King Jr. Avenue
P.O. Box 3549
Lakeland, FL 33802-3549
(863) 904-2970, ext. 7103
Toll Free: (866) 363-9673, ext. 7103
Fax: (863) 904-0169   E-mail: Foundation@fumf.org
Web: www.fumf.org/InfoForIndividuals/Sinclair_Scholarship

Summary   To provide financial assistance for college to high school seniors in Florida who are members of a United Methodist Church and planning to attend college in the state.

Eligibility   This program is open to seniors graduating from high schools in Florida who have been full and active members of a United Methodist Church for at least 1 year. Applicants must have been admitted either to a college or university in Florida or to a United Methodist college or university in any state. They must be in the top 10% of their graduating class and have a GPA of 3.0 or higher. Along with their application, they must submit an essay describing their church, community, and school leadership; their leadership activities; and their educational plans and goals. Selection is based on academic achievement, church involvement, and community service; financial need is not considered.

Financial data   The stipend is $3,000 per year.

Duration   1 year; may be renewed up to 3 additional years, provided that the recipient makes adequate progress toward a bachelor's degree, maintains a GPA of 3.0 or higher, and remains an active church and community leader.

Additional information   This program was established in 2001.

Number awarded   2 each year.

Deadline   March of each year.

[5]
AL SHACKLEFORD AND DAN MARTIN UNDERGRADUATE SCHOLARSHIP

Baptist Communicators Association
Attn: Scholarship Committee
1519 Menlo Drive
Kennesaw, GA 30152
(770) 425-3728 E-mail: office@baptistcommunicators.org
Web: www.baptistcommunicators.org/about/scholarship.cfm

Summary   To provide financial assistance to undergraduate students who are working on a college degree to prepare for a career in Baptist communications.

Eligibility   This program is open to undergraduate students who are majoring in communications, English, journalism, or public relations and have a GPA of 2.5 or higher. Their vocational objective must be in Baptist communications. Along with their application, they must submit a statement explaining why they desire to receive this scholarship.

Financial data   The stipend is $1,000.

Duration   1 year; recipients may reapply.

Additional information   This program was established in 1988.

Number awarded   1 each year.

Deadline   December of each year.

[6]
ALAN COMPTON AND BOB STANLEY MINORITY AND INTERNATIONAL SCHOLARSHIP

Baptist Communicators Association
Attn: Scholarship Committee
1715-K South Rutherford Boulevard, Suite 295
Murfreesboro, TN 37130
(615) 904-0152   E-mail: bca.office@comcast.net
Web: www.baptistcommunicators.org/about/scholarship.cfm

Summary   To provide financial assistance to minority and international students who are working on an undergraduate degree to prepare for a career in Baptist communications.

Eligibility   This program is open to undergraduate students of minority or international origin. Applicants must be majoring in communications, English, journalism, or public relations with a GPA of 2.5 or higher. Their vocational objective must be in Baptist communications. Along with their application, they must submit a statement explaining why they want to receive this scholarship.

Financial data   The stipend is $1,000.

Duration   1 year; recipients may reapply.

Additional information   This program was established in 1996.

Number awarded   1 each year.

Deadline   December of each year.

[7]
ALBERT BAKER FUND STUDENT FINANCIAL AID

Albert Baker Fund
777 Campus Commons Road, Suite 165
Sacramento, CA 95825-8309
(916) 643-9999   Toll Free: (800) 269-0388
Fax: (916) 568-1372 E-mail: admin@albertbakerfund.org
Web: www.albertbakerfund.org/financial-aid/us-canada

Summary   To provide financial aid and loans to undergraduate, graduate, and vocational students in the United States and Canada who are Christian Scientists.

Eligibility   This program is open to students who are Christian Scientists and members of The Mother Church (the First Church of Christ, Scientist in Boston, Massachusetts) or a branch church. Applicants must be enrolled or planning to enroll at least half time as an undergraduate or graduate student at an accredited college, university, or accredited vocational school in the United States or Canada. They must have a GPA of 2.5 or higher and be able to demonstrate financial need. U.S. or Canadian citizenship is required.

Financial data   Financial aid is provided in the form of grants and loans (amount not specified). For loans, interest rates are fixed at 3%; they must be repaid within 10 years.

Duration   1 year; may be renewed.

Number awarded   Varies each year. Recently, the program awarded $370,000 in grants and $515,000 in loans to 557 North American students (including 407 undergraduates, 71 graduate students, and 79 vocational students).

Deadline   February, May, September, or November of each year.

[8]
ALBERT R. MURDOCH MINISTERIAL SCHOLARSHIP

Nebraska United Methodist Foundation
100 West Fletcher Avenue, Suite 100
Lincoln, NE 68521-3848
(402) 323-8844   Toll Free: (877) 495-5545
Fax: (402) 323-8840   E-mail: info@numf.org
Web: www.numf.org/special_programs/scholarships.html

Summary To provide financial assistance to upper-division and seminary students at schools in any state who are preparing for Methodist ministry in Nebraska.

Eligibility This program is open to full-time students in the junior or senior year of undergraduate study or the first year of seminary at a college, university, or theological school in any state accredited by the United Methodist Board of Higher Education. Applicants must be planning to become pastors in the Nebraska Annual Conference of the United Methodist Church. They must have a cumulative GPA of 2.5 or higher. Along with their application, they must submit a 1-page statement of their career plans and financial need, a current academic transcript, and 2 letters of recommendation.

Financial data The stipend is approximately $700.

Duration 1 year; may be renewed.

Number awarded 1 each year.

Deadline June of each year.

[9]
ALEXANDER CHRISTIAN FOUNDATION OF INDIANA SCHOLARSHIPS

Alexander Christian Foundation of Indiana
312 East Main Street, Suite B
P.O. Box 246
Greenfield, IN 46140-0246
(317) 467-1223   E-mail: Judith@acfindiana.org
Web: www.acfindiana.org/awards.html

Summary To provide financial assistance to members of the Christian Church or Church of Christ (Independent) in Indiana who are preparing for a church-related vocation at a school in any state.

Eligibility This program is open to members of the Christian Church or Church of Christ (Independent) in Indiana who are candidates for a church-related vocation or currently working full time on an appropriate undergraduate or graduate degree. Applicants must be attending or planning to attend a college or seminary in any state affiliated with the Christian Churches/Churches of Christ. Students currently enrolled at Christian colleges must have a GPA of 3.0 or higher. Along with their application, they must submit an essay of 500 to 1,000 words on "Why I Desire to Serve Christ in a Church-Related Vocation." Selection is based on that essay, evaluations of the applicant's character and motivation by their home church minister and an elder of their church, and transcripts.

Financial data Stipends range from $1,250 to $2,000 per year.

Duration 1 year; may be renewed for 3 additional years of undergraduate study or 1 additional year of graduate study, provided the recipient remains enrolled full time, continues to attend an approved college or seminar, maintains a GPA of 3.0 or higher, and pursues a church-related vocation.

Additional information This program was established in 1964. Church-related vocations include preaching ministry, youth ministry, missions ministry, music ministry, and children's ministry.

Number awarded Varies each year.

Deadline February of each year.

[10]
ALEXANDER CHRISTIAN FOUNDATION OF NEBRASKA SCHOLARSHIP

Alexander Christian Foundation of Nebraska
P.O. Box 5145
Lincoln, NE 68505
(402) 467-9101
Web: www.acfnebraska.com/scholarship.html

Summary To provide financial assistance to members of the Christian Church or Church of Christ in Nebraska who are preparing for a church-related or other profession at a school in any state.

Eligibility This program is open to members of the Christian Church or Church of Christ in Nebraska who are interested in serving in a full-time church-related vocation or in a nontraditional form of ministry (e.g., medical, teaching, engineering, missions, business). Applicants must submit an essay of 300 to 500 words on how they have served Christ in the past and how they plan to serve Christ in the future. Selection is based on that essay, high school and/or college transcripts, letters of recommendation, and financial need.

Financial data The stipend is $500.

Duration 1 year.

Number awarded Varies each year.

Deadline March of each year.

[11]
ALEXANDER CHRISTIAN FOUNDATION OF OREGON SCHOLARSHIPS

Alexander Christian Foundation of Oregon
4742 Liberty Road South
PMB 112
Salem, OR 97302-5000
(503) 364-7573 E-mail: alexanderfoundation@yahoo.com
Web: www.acfo-online.org

Summary To provide financial assistance to members of the Christian Church or Church of Christ (Independent) in Oregon who are preparing for a church-related vocation at a school in any state.

Eligibility This program is open to members of the Christian Church or Church of Christ (Independent) in Oregon who are candidates for a church-related vocation or currently working on an appropriate degree. Applicants must be attending or planning to attend a school in any state affiliated with the Christian Churches/Churches of Christ. Along with their application, they must submit an essay of 500 to 1,000 words on "Why I Desire to Serve Christ in a Church-Related Vocation." Selection is based on that essay, evaluations of the applicant's character and motivation by their home church minister and an elder of their church, and transcripts. An interview may be required.

Financial data The stipend is $500 per year.

Duration 1 year; may be renewed up to 3 additional years.

Additional information This program began in 1993. Church-related vocations include preaching ministry, youth ministry, missions ministry, music ministry, counseling ministry, and education ministry.

Number awarded Varies each year.

Deadline March of each year.

[12]
ALICE J. MCGIVEN ENDOWMENT FUND SCHOLARSHIP

Iowa United Methodist Foundation
2301 Rittenhouse Street
Des Moines, IA 50321
(515) 974-8927
Web: www.iumf.org/umscholarships.html

Summary To provide financial assistance to high school seniors in Iowa who plan to attend a United Methodist college in the state to prepare for a career in the ministry.

Eligibility This program is open to graduating high school seniors in Iowa who plan to attend a United Methodist college in the state. Applicants must be preparing to enter the ministry or do missionary work. Financial need is considered in the selection process.

Financial data The stipend is $1,300.

Duration 1 year.

Number awarded 1 each year.

Deadline March of each year.

[13]
ALICE W. LOCKMILLER SCHOLARSHIPS

Florida United Methodist Foundation
Attn: Scholarship Committee
450 Martin Luther King Jr. Avenue
P.O. Box 3549
Lakeland, FL 33802-3549
(863) 904-2970, ext. 7103
Toll Free: (866) 363-9673, ext. 7103
Fax: (863) 904-0169   E-mail: Foundation@fumf.org
Web: www.fumf.org

Summary To provide financial assistance to students who have a connection to the United Methodist Church (UMC) in Florida and are currently attending college, university, or seminary.

Eligibility This program is open to students currently enrolled full time at a junior college, senior college, university, seminary, or other institution for educational or occupational training beyond the high school level. Applicants must be members or the children of members of a UMC church within the boundaries of the Florida Annual Conference. First consideration is given to students attending institutions related to the UMC in Florida. Second consideration is given to students attending institutions related to the UMC outside Florida. Third consideration is given to students attending all other institutions. Along with their application, they must submit an essay describing their church, community, and school leadership and involvement and their educational plans and goals. Selection is based on academic achievement, church involvement, and community service; financial need is not considered.

Financial data A stipend is awarded (amount not specified).

Duration 1 year.

Number awarded 1 or more each year.

Deadline March of each year.

[14]
ALL-AMERICAN FEMALE NATIONAL ATHLETE OF THE YEAR

SportQuest Ministries, Inc.
Attn: All-American Program
770 North High School Road
P.O. Box 53433
Indianapolis, IN 46253-0433
(317) 270-9495   Fax: (317) 244-0495
Web: www.allamericanaward.org/atp.html

Summary To provide financial assistance for college to outstanding female Christian high school athletes.

Eligibility This program is open to female high school sophomores, juniors, and seniors who are currently a varsity-level athlete in 1 or more sports. Applicants must be a committed follower of Christ. They must have a grade point average of "C" or higher. Along with their application, they must submit 1-paragraph essays on 1) how they have used, or would like to use, their athletic ability to share their faith and/or to influence others positively; and 2) how and when they accepted Jesus Christ as their personal Lord and Savior and what their personal relationship with Him means to them. Selection is based on those essays, GPA, SAT and/or ACT scores, athletic accomplishments, church and community involvement, essays, and references.

Financial data The award is a $500 scholarship.

Duration 1 year.

Number awarded 1 each year.

Deadline February of each year.

[15]
ALL-AMERICAN MALE NATIONAL ATHLETE OF THE YEAR

SportQuest Ministries, Inc.
Attn: All-American Program
770 North High School Road
P.O. Box 53433
Indianapolis, IN 46253-0433
(317) 270-9495   Fax: (317) 244-0495
Web: www.allamericanaward.org/atp.html

Summary To provide financial assistance for college to outstanding male Christian high school athletes.

Eligibility This program is open to male high school sophomores, juniors, and seniors who are currently a varsity-level athlete in 1 or more sports. Applicants must be a committed follower of Christ. They must have a grade point average of "C" or higher. Along with their application, they must submit 1-paragraph essays on 1) how they have used, or would like to use, their athletic ability to share their faith and/or to influence others positively; and 2) how and when they accepted Jesus Christ as their personal Lord and Savior and what their personal relationship with Him means to them. Selection is based on those essays, GPA, SAT and/or ACT scores, athletic accomplishments, church and community involvement, essays, and references.

Financial data The award is a $500 scholarship.

Duration 1 year.

Number awarded 1 each year.

Deadline February of each year.

[16]
ALLAN JEROME BURRY SCHOLARSHIP

United Methodist Church
Attn: General Board of Higher Education and Ministry
Office of Loans and Scholarships
1001 19th Avenue South
P.O. Box 340007
Nashville, TN 37203-0007
(615) 340-7344   Fax: (615) 340-7367
E-mail: umscholar@gbhem.org
Web: www.gbhem.org/loansandscholarships

Summary To provide financial assistance to undergraduate students attending schools affiliated with the United Methodist Church.

Eligibility This program is open to U.S. citizens and permanent residents who have been active, full members of a United Methodist Church for at least 3 years prior to applying. Applicants must be enrolled full time at a college or university related to the United Methodist Church and be nominated by their campus ministry unit or college chaplain. They must have a GPA of "B+" or higher and be able to document financial need. Selection is based on academic performance, leadership skills, and participation in the activities of the Methodist campus ministry or chaplaincy program at their institution.

Financial data The stipend ranges from $500 to $1,200.

Duration 1 year.

Number awarded 1 each year.

Deadline January of each year.

[17]
ALLIE L. SILLS MEMORIAL FUND

Synod of the Northeast
Attn: Student Loan/Scholarship Programs
5811 Heritage Landing Drive
East Syracuse, NY 13057-9360
(315) 446-5990, ext. 215
Toll Free: (800) 585-5881, ext. 215
Fax: (315) 446-3708   E-mail: SynodOffice@Synodne.org
Web: www.synodne.org

Summary To provide interest-free loans for college or graduate school to Presbyterian students.

Eligibility This program is open to Presbyterians who are or will be attending a postsecondary institution in the United States or Canada on a full-time basis. Institutions may include but are not limited to: 2-year and 4-year colleges, community colleges and other 2-year programs, nondegree professional or technical training programs, or seminary studies leading to an M.Div. or master's of religious education. Graduate work, other than for those 2 master's degrees, is not supported. Applicants must submit an essay of 400 to 500 words on why they should be considered for a loan, their reasons for wanting to pursue a college or seminary education, their extracurricular activities and interests (school, church, and community), and the role their faith will take in fulfilling their academic goals. Preference is given to applicants from Jefferson County, New York and then to the areas that make up the Northern New York Presbytery.

Financial data Loans are normally made in the $500 to $2,500 range; there is an individual lifetime maximum of $10,000 for undergraduate students or $20,500 for seminary students. No interest is charged.

Duration 1 year; may be renewed. Loans must be repaid as soon as the student is financially able to do so.

Number awarded Varies each year.

Deadline March of each year.

[18]
AME CHURCH PREACHER'S KID SCHOLARSHIP

African Methodist Episcopal Church
Connectional Ministers' Spouses, Widows and Widowers Organization
c/o Jennifer Green, Scholarship Committee Chair
2386 S.W. 102nd Avenue
Miramar, FL 33025-6509
E-mail: ConnMSWAWOPk@aol.com
Web: www.amemswwpk.org/pr01.htm

Summary To provide financial assistance for college to children of ministers in the African Methodist Episcopal (AME) Church.

Eligibility This program is open to dependent children under 21 years of age whose parent or legal guardian is an AME minister. Applicants must be a member of the AME Church, have a satisfactory score on the SAT or ACT, rank in the top 50% of their high school class, and have a cumulative GPA of 2.5 or higher. Along with their application, they must submit a 300-word essay on how the AME Church has made a difference in their life and what they will do to support their church. Their minister parent must be a member of the Connectional AME Ministers' Spouses, Widows and Widowers Organization.

Financial data The scholarship stipend is $2,500. Book awards are $500.

Duration 1 year.

Number awarded Varies each year. Recently, the program awarded 1 scholarship for districts 14-20 (which serve Africa and the Caribbean) and 4 book awards for districts 1-20 (which includes districts 1-13 that serve the United States).

Deadline April of each year.

[19]
AMELIA KEMP MEMORIAL SCHOLARSHIP

Women of the Evangelical Lutheran Church in America
Attn: Scholarships
8765 West Higgins Road
Chicago, IL 60631-4101
(773) 380-2736   Toll Free: (800) 638-3522, ext. 2736
Fax: (773) 380-2419   E-mail: emily.hansen@elca.org
Web: www.elca.org

Summary To provide financial assistance to lay women of color who are members of Evangelical Lutheran Church of America (ELCA) congregations and who wish to study on the undergraduate, graduate, professional, or vocational school level.

Eligibility This program is open to ELCA lay women of color who are at least 21 years of age and have experienced an interruption of at least 2 years in their education since high school. Applicants must have been admitted to an educational institution to prepare for a career in other than a church-certified profession. U.S. citizenship is required.

Financial data The maximum stipend is $1,000.

Duration Up to 2 years.

Number awarded Varies each year, depending upon the funds available.

Deadline February of each year.

[20]
AMERICAN BAPTIST CHURCHES OF NEW JERSEY UNDERGRADUATE EMERGING SCHOLAR AWARDS

American Baptist Churches of New Jersey
Attn: Scholar Awards Committee
3752 Nottingham Way, Suite 101
Trenton, NJ 08690-3802
(609) 587-8700   Fax: (609) 587-7474
Web: www.abcnj.net

Summary To provide financial assistance to undergraduate students at colleges in any state who are members of American Baptist Churches of New Jersey (ABCNJ).

Eligibility This program is open to members of churches that are in covenant with ABCNJ. Applicants must be working on or planning to work on an associate or bachelor's degree at a college or university in any state. Along with their application, they must submit a 1-page essay on the topic, "Living Out my Faith in a College Setting." Financial need is not considered in the selection process.

Financial data Stipends range from $200 to $500.

Duration 1 year.

Number awarded 15 each year: 1 at $500, 1 at $400, 1 at $300, and 12 at $200.

Deadline July of each year.

[21]
AMERICAN BAPTIST WOMEN'S MINISTRIES OF COLORADO STUDENT GRANTS

American Baptist Churches of the Rocky Mountains
Attn: American Baptist Women's Ministries
9085 East Mineral Circle, Suite 170
Centennial, CO 80112
(303) 988-3900   E-mail: web@abcrm.org
Web: www.abcrm.org

Summary To provide financial assistance to women who are members of churches affiliated with the American Baptist Churches (ABC) USA in Colorado, New Mexico, and Utah and interested in attending an ABC college or seminary in any state.

Eligibility This program is open to women older than 26 years of age who are active members of churches cooperating with ABC in Colorado, New Mexico, or Utah. Applicants must be enrolled or planning to enroll at an ABC college, university, or seminary in any state. Along with their application, they must submit a personal letter describing their Christian experience; their participation in the life of their church, school, and community; and their goals for the future. Selection is based on academic performance, Christian participation in church and school, and financial need.

Financial data A stipend is awarded (amount not specified). Funds are sent directly to the recipient's school.

Duration 1 year; recipients may reapply.

Number awarded 1 or more each year.

Deadline March of each year.

[22]
AMERICAN BAPTIST WOMEN'S MINISTRIES OF MASSACHUSETTS SCHOLARSHIP PROGRAM

American Baptist Women's Ministries of Massachusetts
c/o Penny Mulloy, Scholarship Committee Chair
27 Ox Road
Billerica, MA 01821-4439
(978) 667-7496   E-mail: pennymulloy@gmail.com
Web: www.abwmofma.org

Summary To provide financial assistance to American Baptist women in Massachusetts interested in church-related vocations.

Eligibility This program is open to women who intend to offer Christian service in their chosen vocation, have been active members of an American Baptist Church in Massachusetts for at least 1 year prior to submitting an application, and are able to supply satisfactory references. They must be nominated by their pastor. Applicants should include a written statement of faith and a separate letter of life purpose that clearly indicates how they intend to serve in the Christian community after their education is completed. Selection is based on dedication, need, and scholastic ability.

Financial data A stipend is awarded (amount not specified).

Duration 1 year; may be renewed.

Additional information Of the scholarships awarded, 2 are designated as the Lenore S. Bigelow Scholarships, for graduate study at Andover Newton Theological School in Newton Centre, Massachusetts and/or Colgate-Rochester Divinity School in Rochester, New York. An interview with the committee or designated members is required of first-time applicants.

Number awarded Varies each year.

Deadline April of each year.

[23]
AMERICAN BAPTIST WOMEN'S MINISTRIES OF MICHIGAN SCHOLARSHIP GIRLS

American Baptist Churches of Michigan
Attn: American Baptist Women's Ministries of Michigan
4578 South Hagadorn Road
East Lansing, MI 48823-5355
(517) 332-3594   Toll Free: (800) 632-2953
Fax: (517) 332-3186   E-mail: mawilliams@abc-mi.org
Web: www.abc-mi.org/?q=node/38

Summary To provide financial assistance to female members of American Baptist Churches of Michigan who interested in attending a college or seminary in any state.

Eligibility This program is open to female members of American Baptist Churches of Michigan who are entering or attending an accredited college, nursing school, or seminary in any state. The school does not need to have an affiliation with American Baptist Churches, but applicants must be able to demonstrate that their lives and chosen vocations will glorify God as they minister in this world.

Financial data Stipends range from $700 to $800.

Duration 1 year.

Number awarded Varies each year; recently, 2 of these scholarships were awarded.

Deadline February of each year.

[24]
AMERICAN BAPTIST WOMEN'S MINISTRIES OF NEW YORK STATE SCHOLARSHIPS

American Baptist Women's Ministries of New York State
Attn: Scholarship Committee
5865 East Seneca Turnpike
Jamesville, NY 13078
(315) 469-4236   Fax: (315) 492-2369
E-mail: isingram@rochester.rr.com
Web: www.abwm-nys.org/M_M/scholarship.html

Summary To provide financial assistance to women who are members of American Baptist Churches in New York and interested in attending college in any state.

Eligibility This program is open to women who are residents of New York and active members of an American Baptist Church. Applicants must be enrolled or planning to enroll full time at a college or university in any state. While in college, they must maintain Christian fellowship, preferably with the American Baptist Church (although any Protestant church or campus ministry is acceptable). Along with their application, they must submit a 1-page essay on an event that occurred in their life during the past year and how it has impacted their faith. Women may be of any age; graduate students are considered on an individual basis. Financial need is considered in the selection process.

Financial data A stipend is awarded (amount not specified).

Duration 1 year.

Number awarded Varies each year.

Deadline February of each year.

[25]
AMERICAN BAPTIST WOMEN'S MINISTRIES OF PENNSYLVANIA AND DELAWARE STUDENT LOANS

American Baptist Churches of Pennsylvania and
    Delaware
Attn: American Baptist Women's Ministries
106 Revere Lane
Coatesville, PA 19320
Toll Free: (800) 358-6999   Fax: (610) 466-2013
Web: www.abcopad.com/abwm/ABWMOPADIndexnew.htm

Summary To provide loans to students who are members of churches affiliated with the American Baptist Churches of Pennsylvania and Delaware and interested in attending college, seminary, or graduate school in any state.

Eligibility This program is open to members of churches affiliated with the American Baptist Churches of Pennsylvania and Delaware or the Philadelphia Baptist Association. Applicants must be enrolled or planning to enroll full time at a college, graduate school, or special vocational training institution in any state; study at a seminary is eligible if it prepares students for church-related vocations in American Baptist Churches. They may be of any age.

Financial data The maximum loan is $1,500 per year.

Duration 1 year; may be renewed, to a maximum $5,250 in loans to each student. Loans must be repaid within 5 years,

with interest of 1% during the first year, 2% during the second year, 3% during the third year, 4% during the fourth year, and 5% during the fifth year.

Additional information This program was established in 1959.

Number awarded Varies each year; recently, approximately 30 students were receiving loans through this program.

Deadline Applications may be submitted at any time.

[26]
AMERICAN BAPTIST WOMEN'S MINISTRIES OF WISCONSIN YOUTH SCHOLARSHIP

American Baptist Women's Ministries of Wisconsin
c/o Lois A. Horsman, Scholarship Committee Chair
P.O. Box 68
Wyocena, WI 53969
(608) 429-2483
Web: www.abcofwi.org/abwinfo.htm

Summary To provide financial assistance to members of American Baptist Churches in Wisconsin who are interested in attending a college in any state that is affiliated with the denomination.

Eligibility This program is open to residents of Wisconsin who are attending or planning to attend an American Baptist college in any state as an undergraduate student. Applicants must have been an active member of an American Baptist Church in Wisconsin for the preceding 12 months.

Financial data A stipend is awarded (amount not specified).

Duration 1 year.

Number awarded 1 or more each year.

Deadline Deadline not specified.

[27]
AMOS GENTRY BULLARD FAMILY FUND SCHOLARSHIP

North Carolina Baptist Foundation, Inc.
Attn: Denominational Relations Committee
201 Convention Drive
Cary, NC 27511-4257
(919) 380-7334   Toll Free: (800) 521-7334
Fax: (919) 460-6334
Web: www.ncbaptistfoundation.org

Summary To provide financial assistance to children of members of churches affiliated with the North Carolina Baptist State Convention who are interested in attending a college or seminary in any state.

Eligibility This program is open to residents of North Carolina who are members or children of members of churches affiliated with the Baptist State Convention. Applicants must have been accepted for enrollment at an accredited college, university, or seminary in any state to prepare for a career in full-time Christian ministry. Along with their application, they must submit a 100-word essay on why they should be chosen for this scholarship, including their reasons and ambitions for wishing to continue their education. Financial need is also considered in the selection process.

Financial data A stipend is awarded (amount not specified).

Duration 1 year.

Number awarded   1 or more each year.
Deadline   January of each year.

[28]
ANNIE B. AND L. ESSEX MOSELEY SCHOLARSHIP FUND

Synod of the Mid-Atlantic
Attn: Finance and Scholarship Committee
3218 Chamberlayne Avenue
P.O. Box 27026
Richmond, VA 23261-7026
(804) 342-0016   Toll Free: (800) 743-7670
Fax: (804) 355-8535
Web: www.synatlantic.org/scholarships/right.html

Summary   To provide financial assistance to African Americans who are members of Presbyterian churches within designated presbyteries throughout Virginia and interested in attending college in any state.

Eligibility   This program is open to members of racial ethnic groups, preferably African Americans, who are active members of churches within the presbyteries of Eastern Virginia, James, and Peaks. Applicants must be a graduate or a graduating senior of a public school who are accepted or enrolled at an accredited college, university, or presbytery technical institute program in any state. Selection is based on academic achievement and financial need.

Financial data   A stipend is awarded (amount not specified).

Duration   1 year; nonrenewable.

Additional information   This fund was established in 1988.

Number awarded   1 or more each year.

Deadline   February of each year.

[29]
ANTHONY J. LABELLA ENDOWED SCHOLARSHIPS

Knights of Columbus
Attn: Department of Scholarships
P.O. Box 1670
New Haven, CT 06507-0901
(203) 752-4332   Fax: (203) 772-2696
E-mail: info@kofc.org
Web: www.kofc.org/un/en/scholarships/endowed.html

Summary   To provide financial assistance to freshmen entering Catholic colleges and universities.

Eligibility   Eligible are students entering their freshman year in a program leading to a bachelor's degree at a Catholic college or university in the United States; applicants must be members in good standing of the Columbian Squires or Knights of Columbus, or the child of a member, or the child of a deceased member who was in good standing at the time of death. Selection is based on secondary school record, class rank, and aptitude test scores.

Financial data   The stipend is $1,500 per year.

Duration   1 year; may be renewed up to 3 additional years upon evidence of satisfactory academic performance.

Additional information   This program was established in 1997.

Number awarded   1 or more each year, depending on the availability of funds.
Deadline   February of each year.

[30]
ARFORA UNDERGRADUATE SCHOLARSHIP FOR WOMEN

Association of Romanian Orthodox Ladies Auxiliaries of North America
Attn: Scholarship Committee
222 Orchard Park Drive
New Castle, PA 16105
(724) 652-4313   E-mail: adelap@verizon.net
Web: www.arfora.org/scholarships.htm

Summary   To provide financial assistance to women who are members of a parish of the Romanian Orthodox Episcopate of America and currently enrolled in college.

Eligibility   This program is open to women who have been voting communicant members of a parish of the Romanian Orthodox Episcopate of America for at least 1 year or are daughters of a communicant member. Applicants must have completed at least 1 year of undergraduate study at a college or university. Along with their application, they must submit a 300-word statement describing their personal goals; high school, university, church, and community involvement; honors and awards; and why they should be considered for this award. Selection is based on academic achievement, character, worthiness, and participation in religious life.

Financial data   The stipend is $1,000.

Duration   1 year; nonrenewable.

Additional information   This scholarship was first awarded in 1994. The Association of Romanian Orthodox Ladies Auxiliaries (ARFORA) was established in 1938 as a women's organization within the Romanian Orthodox Episcopate of America.

Number awarded   1 or more each year.

Deadline   May of each year.

[31]
ARIZONA EASTERN STAR TRAINING AWARDS FOR RELIGIOUS LEADERSHIP

Order of the Eastern Star-Grand Chapter of Arizona
4600 North 24th Street
Phoenix, AZ 85016
(602) 954-9413
Web: azoes.com

Summary   To provide financial assistance to residents of Arizona who are attending a college or seminary in any state to prepare for a career in Christian or Jewish religious service.

Eligibility   This program is open to residents of Arizona who are members of a Christian church or of the Jewish faith. Applicants must have declared their intention to devote their life to full-time religious service as a minister, missionary, director of religious education, director of church music, or youth director. They must have completed at least 2 full years of study at a college or seminary in any state. Selection is based primarily on financial need, although GPA (at least 3.0) and courses taken for credit instead of for grade (at least 75% of courses must have been taken for grade).

Financial data A stipend is awarded (amount not specified).

Duration 1 year.

Number awarded Varies each year.

Deadline June or December of each year.

[32]
ARKANSAS BAPTIST FOUNDATION MEDICAL MISSIONS SCHOLARSHIP

Arkansas Baptist Foundation
10117 Kanis Road
Little Rock, AR 72205-6220
(501) 376-0732   Toll Free: (800) 798-0969
Fax: (501) 376-3831   E-mail: info@abf.org
Web: www.abf.org/individuals_scholarships.htm

Summary To provide financial assistance to members of Southern Baptist churches in Arkansas who are interested in attending a college, seminary, or medical school in any state to prepare for a career as a medical missionary.

Eligibility This program is open to members of Southern Baptist churches in Arkansas who are attending or planning to attend a college, seminary, or medical school in any state. Applicants must be preparing for a vocation or an appointment with the International Mission Board or North American Mission Board of the Southern Baptist Convention as a medical missionary.

Financial data A stipend is awarded (amount not specified).

Duration 1 year; recipients may reapply.

Number awarded Varies each year.

Deadline February of each year.

[33]
ARKANSAS CONFERENCE ETHNIC LOCAL CHURCH CONCERNS SCHOLARSHIPS

United Methodist Church-Arkansas Conference
Attn: Committee on Ethnic Local Church Concerns
800 Daisy Bates Drive
Little Rock, AR 72202
(501) 324-8045   Toll Free: (877) 646-1816
Fax: (501) 324-8018   E-mail: mallen@arumc.org
Web: www.arumc.org

Summary To provide financial assistance to ethnic minority Methodist students from Arkansas who are interested in attending college or graduate school in any state.

Eligibility This program is open to ethnic minority undergraduate and graduate students who are active members of local congregations affiliated with the Arkansas Conference of the United Methodist Church (UMC). Applicants must be currently enrolled in an accredited institution of higher education in any state. Along with their application, they must submit a transcript (GPA of 2.0 or higher) and documentation of participation in local church activities. Preference is given to students attending a UMC-affiliated college or university.

Financial data The stipend is $500 per semester ($1,000 per year) for undergraduates or $1,000 per semester ($2,000 per year) for graduate students.

Duration 1 year; may be renewed.

Number awarded 1 or more each year.

Deadline September of each year.

[34]
ARKANSAS CONFERENCE MERIT SCHOLARSHIP

United Methodist Church-Arkansas Conference
Attn: Board of Higher Education and Campus Ministry
800 Daisy Bates Drive
Little Rock, AR 72202
(501) 324-8045   Toll Free: (877) 646-1816
Fax: (501) 324-8018   E-mail: conference@arumc.org
Web: www.arumc.org

Summary To provide financial assistance to Methodist students from Arkansas who are attending a Methodist-related college or university in any state.

Eligibility This program is open to residents of Arkansas who have been members of a United Methodist Church (UMC) for at least 1 year. Applicants must be full-time undergraduate students at a United Methodist-related college or university in any state. They must be able to demonstrate a record of involvement in their local church or United Methodist campus ministry. Along with their application, they must submit a statement that includes their philosophy of life, religious development, and what influenced them in selecting their career goal.

Financial data The stipend is $500.

Duration 1 year.

Number awarded 1 or more each year.

Deadline April of each year.

[35]
ARMENIAN CHURCH OF AMERICA EASTERN DIOCESE SCHOLARSHIPS

Diocese of the Armenian Church of America
Attn: Director of Mission Parishes
630 Second Avenue
New York, NY 10016-4806
(212) 686-0710   Fax: (212) 686-0245
Web: www.armenianchurch-ed.net

Summary To provide financial assistance to Armenian Americans who are active in their local church and are undergraduates at a 4-year college.

Eligibility Eligible to apply are Armenian American undergraduates at 4-year colleges and universities who are active in their local church and have assumed leadership roles in their local community. Applicants must be able to demonstrate financial need. Preference is given to students who have been active in the Armenian Church (e.g., ACYOA, altar servers, Sunday or Armenian teachers, choir members). In addition to a completed application, students must submit a recommendation from their parish priest or parish council.

Financial data The stipends average $1,000 each.

Duration 1 year.

Additional information A number of named scholarships are offered through this program: Adrina Movsesian Scholarship, Armine Dikijian Journalism Scholarship, Mabel Fenner Scholarship, and the George Holopigian Memorial Fund (the largest fund providing scholarships through the Diocese).

Number awarded Varies each year; recently, 32 of these scholarships were awarded.

Deadline June of each year.

[36]
ASSOCIATION OF BRETHREN CARING MINISTRIES NURSING SCHOLARSHIPS

Church of the Brethren
Attn: Caring Ministries
1451 Dundee Avenue
Elgin, IL 60120-1694
(847) 742-5100, ext. 300   Toll Free: (800) 323-8039
Fax: (847) 742-6103
Web: www.brethren.org

Summary To provide financial assistance to members of the Church of the Brethren working on an undergraduate or graduate degree in nursing.

Eligibility This program is open to students who are members of the Church of the Brethren or employed in a Church of the Brethren agency. Applicants must be enrolled in a L.P.N., R.N., or graduate program in nursing. Along with their application, they must submit 1) a statement describing their reasons for wanting to enter nursing or continue their nursing education, including something of their aspirations for service in the profession; and 2) a description of how the scholarship will assist them in reaching their educational and career goals.

Financial data The stipend is $2,000 for R.N. and graduate nurse candidates or $1,000 for L.P.N. candidates.

Duration 1 year. Recipients are eligible for only 1 scholarship per degree.

Number awarded Varies each year.

Deadline March of each year.

[37]
ASSOCIATION OF EPISCOPAL COLLEGES SCHOLARSHIPS

Association of Episcopal Colleges
Attn: Episcopal Schools Scholarship Committee
815 Second Avenue
New York, NY 10017
(212) 716-6149   Fax: (212) 986-5039
E-mail: office@cuac.org
Web: cuac.anglicancommunion.org/aec.cfm

Summary To provide financial assistance to seniors graduating from Episcopal high schools and planning to attend an Episcopal college or university.

Eligibility This program is open to seniors graduating from high schools that are members of the National Association of Episcopal Schools. Applicants must be planning to enroll at their choice of 9 Episcopal colleges and universities. They must have been active Episcopalians both in their school and in their home parish. Selection is based on academic achievement during the junior and senior years of high school, leadership, and commitment to worship and community life in school and parish; community service and social justice outreach are especially recognized.

Financial data The stipend is $1,200 per year.

Duration 1 year; may be renewed up to 3 additional years.

Additional information The Episcopal colleges and universities are Bard College (Annandale-on-Hudson, New York), Clarkson College (Omaha, Nebraska), Hobart and William Smith Colleges (Geneva, New York), Kenyon College (Gambier, Ohio), St. Augustine College (Chicago, Illinois), St. Augustine's College (Raleigh, North Carolina), St. Paul's College (Lawrenceville, Virginia), the University of the South (Sewanee, Tennessee), and Voorhees College (Denmark, South Carolina).

Number awarded 1 each year.

Deadline December of each year.

[38]
BALTIMORE-WASHINGTON CONFERENCE SCHOLARSHIPS

United Methodist Church-Baltimore-Washington
  Conference
Attn: Joint Scholarship Coordinating Task Force
11711 East Market Place
Fulton, MD 20759
(410) 309-3484   Toll Free: (800) 492-2525, ext. 484
Fax: (410) 309-9794
Web: www.bwcumc.org/content/college-scholarships

Summary To provide financial assistance for college to Methodists from the Baltimore-Washington Conference.

Eligibility This program is open to full-time undergraduate students who are members of a United Methodist Church in the Baltimore-Washington Conference. Applicants must submit a brief statement on the following topic: "How have I responded to God's call in my life and how do I see myself responding to God's call in the future (through my career and service)?" Selection is based on academic merit, indication of Christian commitment, past and future service to the United Methodist Church, and financial need.

Financial data Stipends range from $500 to $1,000 per year.

Duration 1 year; recipients may reapply.

Number awarded Varies each year. Recently, 48 of these scholarships were awarded.

Deadline June of each year.

[39]
BAPTIST FOUNDATION OF ALABAMA SCHOLARSHIPS

Baptist Foundation of Alabama
Attn: Client Services
7650 Halcyon Summit Drive
P.O. Box 241227
Montgomery, AL 36124-1227
(334) 394-2000   Fax: (334) 394-2039
E-mail: scholarship@tbfa.og
Web: www.tbfa.org/scholarship.html

Summary To provide financial assistance to members of Baptist churches in Alabama who are interested in attending a college or seminary in any state.

Eligibility This program is open to full-time students who are affiliated with a Southern Baptist church in Alabama. Applicants must be attending or planning to attend a college or seminary in any state and have a GPA of 2.0 or higher.

Financial data A stipend is awarded (amount not specified).

Duration 1 year.

Number awarded 1 or more each year.

Deadline March of each year.

[40]
BAPTIST FOUNDATION OF COLORADO SCHOLARSHIPS

Colorado Baptist General Convention
Attn: Baptist Foundation of Colorado
7393 South Alton Way
Centennial, CO 80112-2302
(303) 771-2480, ext. 224
Toll Free: (888) 771-2480, ext. 224
E-mail: dlohrey@cbgc.org
Web: www.baptistfoundationofcolorado.org

Summary To provide financial assistance to members of Southern Baptist churches in Colorado who are interested in attending a college or seminary in any state to prepare for a career in ministry.

Eligibility This program is open to students who are members of Colorado Baptist General Convention home churches. Applicants must be enrolled full time at a Southern Baptist college, university, or seminary in any state to prepare for a church-related vocation. They must have a GPA of 3.0 or higher and be able to demonstrate financial need. Undergraduates must be at least sophomores; seminary students must have completed at least 15 credit hours of study. Along with their application, they must submit 1-paragraph statements that 1) describe their salvation experience, and 2) describe the church-related vocation they are pursuing and why they feel God's call to that vocation.

Financial data A stipend is awarded (amount not specified).

Duration 1 year; may be renewed.

Number awarded Varies each year.

Deadline March of each year.

[41]
BAPTIST FOUNDATION OF ILLINOIS SCHOLARSHIPS

Illinois Baptist State Association
Attn: Baptist Foundation of Illinois
3085 Stevenson Drive
P.O. Box 19247
Springfield, IL 62794-9247
(217) 391-3123   Fax: (217) 585-1029
E-mail: dougmorrow@ibsa.org
Web: www.ibsa.org/ministries/baptistfoundation

Summary To provide financial assistance to Southern Baptists from Illinois who are interested in attending a college or seminary in any state.

Eligibility This program is open to students enrolled or planning to enroll full time at an accredited college, university, or seminary in any state. Applicants must have been an active member for at least 1 year of a church affiliated with the Illinois Baptist State Association. They must be able to demonstrate financial need and the potential for Christian leadership and service. Along with their application, they must submit a statement of personal Christian testimony, including a description of their life and attitudes before they met Christ, how they realized they needed Christ in their life, how they became a Christian, what being a Christian means to them today, and how they might use their vocation as a means to share a Christian witness. Selection is based on academic ability; leadership and participation in church, school, and

community activities; vocational clarity; character; and financial need.

Financial data Recently, stipend amounts averaged approximately $1,500.

Duration 1 year.

Number awarded Varies each year. Recently, 33 of these scholarships, with a total value of $49,000, were awarded.

Deadline February of each year.

[42]
BAPTIST GENERAL ASSOCIATION OF VIRGINIA ACHIEVEMENT SCHOLARSHIPS

Baptist General Association of Virginia
Virginia Baptist Missionary Board
Attn: Shared Ministry Assistant
2828 Emerywood Parkway
Richmond, VA 23294
(804) 915-2439   Toll Free: (800) ALL-BGAV, ext. 6225
Fax: (804) 672-2051   E-mail: scholarships@vbmb.org
Web: www.vbmb.org/Services/Scholarship/default.cfm

Summary To provide financial assistance to Baptist residents of Virginia interested in attending college in any state.

Eligibility This program is open to students enrolled or planning to enroll full time in a nonministerial undergraduate program at an accredited college or university in any state. Applicants must have been active members of a cooperating church of the Baptist General Association of Virginia (BGAV) for at least 1 year. They must have been involved with the Chaplain's Office, Baptist Collegiate Ministry, or other Christian ministries on or off campus and be able to demonstrate the potential for Christian leadership. Selection is based on academic ability, Christian service, community service, character, demonstrated leadership, and financial need.

Financial data The stipend is $1,000 per year.

Duration 1 year; recipients may reapply, provided they maintain a GPA of 3.0 or higher.

Number awarded 1 or more each year.

Deadline March of each year.

[43]
BAPTIST GENERAL ASSOCIATION OF VIRGINIA MINISTERIAL EDUCATION FUNDS

Baptist General Association of Virginia
Virginia Baptist Missionary Board
Attn: Shared Ministry Assistant
2828 Emerywood Parkway
Richmond, VA 23294
(804) 915-2439   Toll Free: (800) ALL-BGAV, ext. 6225
Fax: (804) 672-2051   E-mail: scholarships@vbmb.org
Web: www.vbmb.org/Services/Scholarship/default.cfm

Summary To provide financial assistance to Baptist residents of Virginia interested in attending a college or seminary in any state to prepare for a career in ministry.

Eligibility This program is open to students enrolled or planning to enroll at an accredited college, university, or seminary in any state. Applicants must have been active members of a cooperating church of the Baptist General Association of Virginia (BGAV) for at least 1 year. They must be called and committed to religious service as a local church minister, missionary, chaplain, or denominational servant. Preference is given to applicants from Virginia Baptist backgrounds and who plan their ministries in and through Virginia Baptist channels. Students working on an advanced degree beyond the master's level are not eligible. Selection is based on academic ability, Christian service, community service, vocational clarity, BGAV commitment, and financial need.

Financial data   The stipend ranges up to $5,000 per year.

Duration   1 year. Full-time students are eligible for up to 4 years of undergraduate study and up to 4 years at the graduate level. Part-time students are eligible for up to 6 years of undergraduate study and up to 6 years at the graduate level.

Additional information   Recipients are expected to participate in a practical ministry experience of approximately 2 to 6 hours per week under a mentor approved by the BGAV.

Number awarded   1 or more each year.

Deadline   March of each year.

[44]
BAPTIST LIFE SCHOLARSHIP GRANTS

Baptist Life Association
Attn: Scholarship Committee
8555 Main Street
Buffalo, NY 14221-7494
(716) 633-4393   Toll Free: (800) 227-8543
Fax: (716) 633-4916
E-mail: memberservice@baptistlife.org
Web: www.baptistlife.org/benefits.html

Summary   To provide financial assistance for college or graduate school to insured members of Baptist Life.

Eligibility   This program is open to full-time undergraduate and graduate students who have been insured members of Baptist Life for at least 2 years. Applicants must submit a pastoral reference and a statement of personal testimony that provides information about their interests, hobbies, strengths, or any other item that will help the committee get to know them and their walk with God. Selection is based on those submissions, academic achievement, and financial need.

Financial data   The stipend is $1,000.

Duration   1 year; may be renewed up to 3 additional years.

Number awarded   Several each year.

Deadline   May of each year.

[45]
BEALL SCHOLARSHIP

Presbyterian Church (USA)
Attn: Office of Financial Aid for Studies
100 Witherspoon Street, Room M-052
Louisville, KY 40202-1396
(502) 569-5224   Toll Free: (888) 728-7228, ext. 5224
Fax: (502) 569-8766   E-mail: finaid@pcusa.org
Web: www.pcusa.org/financialaid/programs/beall.htm

Summary   To provide financial assistance to female Presbyterian residents of designated southeastern states who are interested in studying the arts at a school in any state.

Eligibility   This program is open to women who are members of the Presbyterian Church (USA) between 16 and 36 years of age. Applicants must be residents of Alabama, Florida, Georgia, Kentucky, Louisiana, Mississippi, North Carolina, South Carolina, Tennessee, or Virginia. They must be enrolled or planning to enroll full time at a college or university in any state to major in the arts. Selection is based on academic standing (GPA of 2.5 or higher) and financial need.

Financial data   Stipends range up to $5,000 per year, depending upon the financial need of the recipient.

Duration   1 year; may be renewed up to 3 additional years.

Number awarded   1 or more each year.

Deadline   June of each year.

[46]
BERNICE F. ELLIOTT MEMORIAL SCHOLARSHIP

Baptist Convention of New Mexico
Attn: Missions Mobilization Team
5325 Wyoming Boulevard, N.E.
P.O. Box 94485
Albuquerque, NM 87199-4485
(505) 924-2315   Toll Free: (800) 898-8544
Fax: (505) 924-2320   E-mail: cpairett@bcnm.com
Web: www.bcnm.com

Summary   To provide financial assistance to women who are Southern Baptists from New Mexico and interested in attending a college or seminary in any state.

Eligibility   This program is open to women college and seminary students who are members of churches affiliated with the Baptist Convention of New Mexico. Preference is given to applicants who are committed to full-time Christian service, have a background in the Woman's Missionary Union, and can demonstrate financial need.

Financial data   A stipend is awarded (amount not specified).

Duration   1 year; may be renewed.

Number awarded   1 or more each year.

Deadline   March of each year.

[47]
BESSIE BARROW MEMORIAL FOUNDATION SCHOLARSHIPS

Baptist Convention of Maryland/Delaware
Attn: United Baptist Women of Maryland, Inc.
10255 Old Columbia Road
Columbia, MD 21046
(410) 290-5290   Toll Free: (800) 466-5290
E-mail: gparker@bcmd.org
Web: bcmd.org/wmu

Summary   To provide financial assistance to women who are members of Baptist churches associated with an affiliate of United Baptist Women of Maryland and interested in working on an undergraduate degree at a college in any state.

Eligibility   This program is open to women who are enrolled or planning to enroll full time at an accredited college or university in any state to work on an undergraduate degree in any field. Applicants must be a member in good standing of a Baptist church associated with an affiliate of United Baptist Women of Maryland. They must have a grade point average of "C" or higher and be able to demonstrate financial need. Along with their application, they must submit brief statements on their Christian experience, school activities, church and community activities, and career goals.

Financial data   A stipend is awarded (amount not specified).

Duration   1 year.

Number awarded   Varies each year.

Deadline   June of each year.

[48]
BETTY ANN LIVINGSTON SCHOLARSHIP

United Methodist Higher Education Foundation
Attn: Scholarships Administrator
1001 19th Avenue South
P.O. Box 340005
Nashville, TN 37203-0005
(615) 340-7385   Toll Free: (800) 811-8110
Fax: (615) 340-7330
E-mail: umhefscholarships@gbhem.org
Web: www.umhef.org/receive.php?id=endowed_funds

Summary To provide financial assistance to Methodist high school seniors who plan to study designated fields in college.

Eligibility This program is open to graduating high school seniors who are planning to enroll full time in a degree program at an accredited institution and major in pre-law, medicine, public policy, literature, or a related field. Applicants must have been active, full members of a United Methodist Church for at least 1 year prior to applying. They must have a GPA of 3.0 or higher and be able to demonstrate financial need. Along with their application, they must submit a 200-word essay on their involvement and/or leadership responsibilities in their church, school, and community within the last 3 years. Preference is given to members of Macedonia United Methodist Church in Macedonia, Ohio. U.S. citizenship or permanent resident status is required.

Financial data A stipend is awarded (amount not specified).

Duration 1 year; may be renewed.

Additional information This program was established in 2008.

Number awarded Varies each year. Recently, 3 of these scholarships were awarded.

Deadline May of each year.

[49]
BILLIE HOLDER MEMORIAL SCHOLARSHIP

New Mexico Baptist Foundation
5325 Wyoming Boulevard, N.E.
P.O. Box 16560
Albuquerque, NM 87191-6560
(505) 332-3777   Toll Free: (877) 841-3777
Fax: (505) 332-2777   E-mail: foundation@nmbf.com
Web: www.bcnm.com

Summary To provide financial assistance to members of Southern Baptist churches in New Mexico attending college in any state.

Eligibility This program is open to students attending college in any state who have a GPA of 2.5 or higher and are able to demonstrate financial need. Applicants must be members of Southern Baptist churches in New Mexico and able to provide a letter of recommendation from their pastor.

Financial data A stipend is awarded (amount not specified).

Duration 1 year.

Number awarded 1 or more each year.

Deadline April of each year.

[50]
BISHOP JOHN J. DOUGHERTY SCHOLARSHIPS

Knights of Columbus-New Jersey State Council
Attn: Executive Secretary
172 Main Street
West Orange, NJ 07052
(973) 736-5632   Fax: (973) 736-7170
E-mail: ExecutiveSecretary@njkofc.org
Web: njkofc.org

Summary To provide financial assistance to high school seniors who are relatives of members of the Knights of Columbus in New Jersey and planning to attend college in any state.

Eligibility This program is open to seniors graduating from high schools in New Jersey who are the children, siblings, or grandchildren of members of the Knights of Columbus. Applicants must be planning to enroll at a college or university in any state. They are not required to be attending a Catholic high school or entering a Catholic college.

Financial data The stipend is $1,000.

Duration 1 year.

Number awarded Up to 4 each year.

Deadline February of each year.

[51]
BISHOP JOSEPH B. BETHEA SCHOLARSHIPS

United Methodist Church
Attn: General Board of Higher Education and Ministry
Office of Loans and Scholarships
1001 19th Avenue South
P.O. Box 340007
Nashville, TN 37203-0007
(615) 340-7344   Fax: (615) 340-7367
E-mail: umscholar@gbhem.org
Web: www.gbhem.org/loansandscholarships

Summary To provide financial assistance for college to African American Methodist students from the southeastern states.

Eligibility This program is open to full-time undergraduate students at accredited colleges and universities who have been active, full members of a United Methodist Church for at least 1 year prior to applying. Applicants must be African Americans and members of Black Methodists for Church Renewal in the Southeastern Jurisdiction (which covers Alabama, Florida, Georgia, Kentucky, Mississippi, North Carolina, South Carolina, Tennessee, and Virginia). They must have a GPA of 2.8 or higher and be able to demonstrate financial need. U.S. citizenship or permanent resident status is required.

Financial data A stipend is awarded (amount not specified).

Duration 1 year; recipients may reapply.

Number awarded 1 or more each year.

Deadline April of each year.

[52]
BISHOP LANCE WEBB SCHOLARSHIP/LOAN GRANT

United Methodist Church-Iowa Annual Conference
Attn: Board of Ordained Ministry
2301 Rittenhouse Street
Des Moines, IA 50321-3101
(515) 283-1991   Fax: (515) 974-8950
Web: www.iaumc.org/forms/detail/93

Summary To provide forgivable loans to upper-division students preparing for ordained ministry under the Iowa Annual Conference of the United Methodist Church (UMC).

Eligibility This program is open to college juniors and seniors in Iowa who are inquiring candidates for ministry through a District Committee on Ordained Ministry in the Iowa Annual Conference of the UMC. Applicants must be enrolled full time at a college or university in any state accredited by the UMC University Senate and have a GPA of 3.0 or higher. They must be planning to attend an accredited graduate school of theology. Along with their application, they must submit an essay on how they are called to ministry and the type of ministry they see themselves offering to Christ and His church.

Financial data The maximum annual loan is $1,500. Loans are forgiven at the rate of 1 year of service in full-time ministry in the United Methodist Church for each year of support received.

Duration 1 year.

Number awarded 1 or more each year.

Deadline May or November of each year.

[53]
BISHOP T. LARRY KIRKLAND SCHOLARSHIP OF EXCELLENCE

African Methodist Episcopal Church
Fifth Episcopal District Lay Organization
400 Corporate Pointe, Suite 300
Culver City, CA 90230
(424) 750-3065   Fax: (424) 750-3067
E-mail: AmecEpiscopal5@aol.com
Web: www.amec5th.net/scholarship_of_excellence.aspx

Summary To provide financial assistance to members of African Methodist Episcopal (AME) churches in its Fifth Episcopal District who are attending college in any state.

Eligibility This program is open to residents of the AME Fifth Episcopal District (Alaska, Arizona, California, Colorado, Idaho, Kansas, Missouri, Montana, Nebraska, Nevada, New Mexico, North Dakota, Oregon, South Dakota, Utah, Washington, and Wyoming) who are currently enrolled at an accredited institution of higher learning in any state. Applicants must have been a member of an AME church for at least 12 months and have been an active member of its Lay Organization, another lay-sponsored program, the Young People's Department (YPD), the Missionary Society, or a missionary-sponsored program. They must have a GPA of 2.5 or higher. Along with their application, they must submit a 500-word personal essay that describes their long-range plans, community and church involvement, accomplishments or special awards, challenges they have faced, and how they responded. Selection is based on that essay, academic

record, letters of recommendation, accomplishments, and level of participation in church activities.

Financial data The stipend is $1,500.

Duration 1 year.

Number awarded 1 each year.

Deadline May of each year.

[54]
BOARD HIGHER EDUCATION ON CAMPUS MINISTRY SCHOLARSHIP

United Methodist Church-Oklahoma Conference
Attn: Campus Ministry Office
1501 N.W. 24th Street
Oklahoma, OK 73106-3635
(405) 530-2013   Toll Free: (800) 231-4166, ext. 2013
Fax: (405) 525-4164   E-mail: lmachalek@okumc.org
Web: www.okumcministries.org

Summary To provide financial assistance to undergraduate and graduate Methodist students from Oklahoma who plan to attend college, graduate school, or seminary in any state.

Eligibility This program is open to undergraduate and graduate students who are members of congregations affiliated with the Oklahoma Conference of the United Methodist Church. Applicants must be enrolled or planning to enroll as a full-time student at a college, university, graduate school, or seminary in any state. Selection is based on academic excellence, participation in church activities, and financial need.

Financial data The stipend is $500.

Duration 1 year.

Number awarded 1 or more each year.

Deadline April of each year.

[55]
BOHNETT MEMORIAL FOUNDATION SCHOLARSHIPS

Violet R. and Nada V. Bohnett Memorial Foundation
Attn: Jamie Bohnett, Director
7981 168th Avenue, N.E., Suite 220
Redmond, WA 98052
(425) 883-0208   Fax: (425) 883-2729
E-mail: jnbohnett@aol.com
Web: www.bohnettmemorialfoundation.org

Summary To provide financial assistance for college or graduate school in any field to students in selected western states who are "people of faith."

Eligibility This program is open to undergraduate and graduate students who "profess a genuine faith in Jesus Christ" and are interested in addressing the needs of fragile families today. Applicants must have demonstrated a pattern of volunteer service in their church or community. Preference is given to residents of western Washington, but residents of California, Colorado, and Hawaii are also eligible.

Financial data Stipends range from $1,000 to $1,500.

Duration 1 year.

Number awarded Several each year.

Deadline Deadline not specified.

[56]
BOWEN CHARITABLE TRUST SCHOLARSHIPS

West Virginia Baptist Convention
1019 Juliana Street
P.O. Box 1019
Parkersburg, WV 26102-1019
(304) 422-6449   Fax: (304) 485-0940
Web: bowentrust.org

Summary To provide financial assistance to undergraduate and graduate students from West Virginia who are preparing for a career of vocational ministry within the American Baptist Church USA.

Eligibility This program is open to undergraduate and graduate students who are preparing to dedicate their lives to Christian service in vocational ministry, including as a pastor, associate/assistant pastor, minister of Christian education, music, worship, youth, pastoral care, or family life, Christian counselor, or chaplain. Scholarships are granted in the following order of priority: 1) members of Calvary Baptist Church in Charleston, West Virginia and/or First Baptist Church of Clendenin, West Virginia; 2) members of other churches in the Kanawha Valley Association of the West Virginia Baptist Convention; 3) members of other churches in the West Virginia Baptist Convention; 4) members of the Mount Lebanon Baptist Church in Mount Lebanon, Pennsylvania; and 5) members of other American Baptist USA churches. Preference is also given to students at Alderson Broaddus College (Philippi, West Virginia) and Eastern University or Palmer Seminary (Philadelphia, Pennsylvania). Applicants must submit documentation of financial need and an essay on their call to ministry.

Financial data A stipend is awarded (amount not specified). Funding does not exceed the cost of tuition, housing, meals, books, and fees for a student living on campus in campus housing.

Duration 1 year; may be renewed for the maximum number of years for the course of study.

Number awarded Varies each year.

Deadline Applications may be submitted at any time, but they must be received at least 90 days prior to the beginning of the school term for which funding is requested.

[57]
CALIFORNIA STATE COUNCIL KNIGHTS OF COLUMBUS ACADEMIC SCHOLARSHIPS

Knights of Columbus-California State Council
15808 Arrow Boulevard, Suite A
Fontana, CA 92335
(909) 434-0460   E-mail: state.office@kofc-ca.org
Web: kofc-ca.org/?t=t_csc_studentscholarships2

Summary To provide financial assistance to members of the Knights of Columbus and their families in California who are interested in attending college in any state.

Eligibility This program is open to 1) members of the Knights of Columbus in a California council; 2) spouses and children of Knights of Columbus members in a California council; 3) spouses and children of deceased members who were in good standing with a California council at the time of death; 4) members of a California Columbian Squires Circle; and 5) former members of a California Columbian Squires Circle who are either current members in good standing or

sons of Knights of Columbus members in good standing in a California council. Applicants must be high school seniors or current undergraduates attending or planning to attend a college or university (public or private) in any state. Along with their application, they must submit transcripts, SAT and/or ACT scores, a personal statement, and 3 letters of recommendation.

Financial data The stipend is $1,000.

Duration 1 year.

Number awarded 7 each year.

Deadline February of each year.

[58]
CALIFORNIA-NEVADA ANNUAL CONFERENCE AWARD FOR SCHOLASTIC EXCELLENCE

United Methodist Church-California-Nevada Annual
    Conference
Attn: Board of Higher Education and Campus Ministry
1276 Halyard Drive
P.O. Box 980250
West Sacramento, CA 95798-0250
(916) 374-1528   Fax: (916) 372-5544
E-mail: sharis@calnevumc.org
Web: www.cnumc.org/forms/detail/343

Summary To provide financial assistance to members of United Methodist Church (UMC) congregations in its California-Nevada Annual Conference who are interested in attending a college in any state that is affiliated with the denomination.

Eligibility This program is open to residents of northern California and Nevada who have been members of a UMC congregation for at least 1 year. Applicants must be enrolled or planning to enroll full time at a UMC college or university in any state. Along with their application, they must submit brief essays describing 1) their participation in projects and activities of their church, community, or education and service clubs; and 2) their philosophy of life and religious development and what influenced them in selecting their career goal. Selection is based on academic record, church involvement, special vocational preparation for ministry or other service, and financial need.

Financial data Stipends range from $500 to $1,000.

Duration 1 year.

Number awarded Varies each year.

Deadline April of each year.

[59]
CAMPBELL TRUST STUDENT LOAN PROGRAM

Florida United Methodist Foundation, Inc.
Attn: Scholarship Committee
450 Martin Luther King Jr. Avenue
P.O. Box 3549
Lakeland, FL 33802-3549
(863) 904-2970   Toll Free: (866) 363-9673
Fax: (863) 904-0169   E-mail: Foundation@fumf.org
Web: www.fumc.org/InfoForIndividuals/StudentLoans

Summary To provide educational loans to Methodist college and seminary students from Florida.

Eligibility This program is open to Methodist students enrolled full time at a junior college, senior college, university, seminary, or other postsecondary institution for educational or occupational training. First priority is given to Florida residents attending institutions related to the United Methodist Church in Florida. Second priority is given to Florida residents attending institutions related to the United Methodist Church outside of Florida. Third priority is given to Florida residents attending non-church-related institutions. Final priority is given to non-Florida residents attending church-related institutions.

Financial data The amount of the loan depends on the availability of funds and the number of approved applicants.

Duration 1 year.

Number awarded Varies each year.

Deadline July of each year for fall term; November of each year for spring term.

[60]
CATHOLIC FINANCIAL LIFE COLLEGE SCHOLARSHIPS

Catholic Financial Life
Attn: Fraternal Department
1100 West Wells Street
P.O. Box 3211
Milwaukee, WI 53201-3211
(414) 273-6266   Toll Free: (800) 927-2547
Fax: (414) 278-6535
E-mail: service@catholicfinanciallife.org
Web: www.catholicfinanciallife.org

Summary To provide financial assistance to members of Catholic Financial Life who are interested in attending college in any state.

Eligibility This program is open to financial members of Catholic Financial Life who are younger than 23 years of age and enrolled full time at a 2- or 4-year college or university in any state. Applicants must have been the primary insured on a life insurance certificate or spousal rider for at least 1 year. They must have performed at least 10 service hours during the preceding year for a branch or chapter of Catholic Financial Life, the Society of St. Vincent de Paul, or other nonprofit organization. Preference is given to students whose service has been with Catholic Financial Life or the Society of St. Vincent de Paul and who have performed more than the minimum number of hours. Financial need is not considered in the selection process.

Financial data The stipend is $1,000 for students at 4-year colleges and universities or $500 for students at community colleges or technical schools.

Duration 1 year; nonrenewable.

Additional information Catholic Financial Life, formerly Catholic Knights of America, operates in Arkansas, California, Connecticut, Indiana, Iowa, Louisiana, Maine, Massachusetts, Michigan, Minnesota, Missouri, New Hampshire, New Mexico, North Dakota, Ohio, Pennsylvania, Rhode Island, Texas, Vermont, and Wisconsin.

Number awarded Varies each year.

Deadline March of each year.

[61]
CHAMPIONS FOR CHRIST SCHOLARSHIPS

Champions for Christ Foundation, Inc.
P.O. Box 786
Greenville, SC 29602-0786
(864) 294-0800   E-mail: contact@championsforchrist.us
Web: www.championsforchrist.us

Summary To provide financial assistance to students interested in working on an undergraduate or graduate degree to prepare for full time Christian ministry.

Eligibility This program is open to high school seniors, undergraduates, and graduate students "who have surrendered their lives to full-time Christian service." Applicants must submit a letter of recommendation from their pastor, a personal statement of their salvation experience and call to the ministry, and a statement of doctrinal beliefs. Financial need is considered in the selection process.

Financial data A stipend is awarded (amount not specified).

Duration 1 year; may be renewed.

Number awarded Varies each year.

Deadline June of each year for fall term; October of each year for winter or spring term; March of each year for summer term.

[62]
CHARLES ZARIGIAN, ESQ. MEMORIAL AWARD

Armenian Students' Association
Attn: Scholarship Committee
333 Atlantic Avenue
Warwick, RI 02888
(401) 461-6114   Fax: (401) 461-6112
E-mail: headasa@aol.com
Web: www.asainc.org/national/scholarships.shtml

Summary To provide financial assistance to students of Armenian ancestry, especially those working on an undergraduate or graduate degree in law, teaching, or Christian ministry.

Eligibility This program is open to undergraduate and graduate students of Armenian descent who have completed at least the first year of college; preference is given to those working on a degree in law, teaching, or Christian ministry. Applicants must be enrolled full time at a 4-year college or university or a 2-year college and planning to transfer to a 4-year institution in the following fall. They must be a U.S. citizen or have appropriate visa status to study in the United States. Along with their application, they must submit a 300-word essay about themselves, including their future plans. Financial need is considered in the selection process.

Financial data The stipends range from $500 to $2,500.

Duration 1 year.

Additional information There is a $15 application fee.

Number awarded 1 each year.

Deadline March of each year.

[63]
CHARLESTON HEIGHTS BAPTIST CHURCH SCHOLARSHIP

Woman's Missionary Union
Attn: WMU Foundation
100 Missionary Ridge
Birmingham, AL 35242
(205) 408-5525   Toll Free: (877) 482-4483
Fax: (205) 408-5508   E-mail: wmufoundation@wmu.org
Web: www.wmufoundation.com

Summary To provide financial assistance for undergraduate or graduate study to the dependent children of Southern Baptist missionaries, especially those from South Carolina.

Eligibility This program is open to Southern Baptist students who are working on an undergraduate or graduate degree in any field. Applicants must be dependents of international missionaries who are under appointment of the North American Mission Board (NAMB) of the Southern Baptist Convention. Preference is given to missionaries from South Carolina.

Financial data A stipend is awarded (amount not specified).

Duration 1 year.

Number awarded Varies each year.

Deadline January of each year.

[64]
CHEA SUPPORT NETWORK SCHOLARSHIP

Christian Home Educators Association of California, Inc.
Attn: Scholarship
12440 East Firestone Boulevard, Suite 311
P.O. Box 2009
Norwalk, CA 90651-2009
(562) 864-CHEA   Fax: (562) 864-3747
E-mail: CHEAinfo@cheaofca.org
Web: www.cheaofca.org

Summary To provide financial assistance children of members of the Christian Home Educators Association of California (CHEA) who plan to attend college in any state.

Eligibility This program is open to children of CHEA members between 17 and 19 years of age who have been privately home schooled (not enrolled in a public school program) with their parents teaching them at home at least 51% of the time and at least 51% of the academic subjects for each of the past 4 years. Applicants must have been members of 1 or more support network member groups for at least the past 2 years. They must have been accepted by a community college, college, university, or career/vocational school in any state. Along with their application, they must submit a letter of recommendation from their support group or PSP leader, a letter of recommendation from a pastor or church elder, a letter of recommendation from their parents or legal guardians, a 1-page statement on their personal Christian faith and conversion, a 1-page essay about home education, transcripts, a list of courses taken during the past 4 years, SAT or ACT scores, and a letter of acceptance from the institution they plan to attend. Financial need is not considered.

Financial data The stipend is $1,000.

Duration 1 year.

Number awarded 1 each year.

Deadline February of each year.

[65]
CHILDREN OF MISSIONARIES SCHOLARSHIPS

Presbyterian Church (USA)
Attn: Office of Financial Aid for Studies
100 Witherspoon Street, Room M-052
Louisville, KY 40202-1396
(502) 569-5224   Toll Free: (888) 728-7228, ext. 5224
Fax: (502) 569-8766   E-mail: finaid@pcusa.org
Web: www.pcusa.org

Summary To provide financial assistance for college or graduate school to children of Presbyterian missionaries.

Eligibility This program is open to students whose parents are engaged in active service as foreign missionaries for the Presbyterian Church (USA). Applicants must be full-time undergraduate or graduate students at an accredited institution in the United States and have a GPA of 2.5 or higher. They must be able to demonstrate financial need. U.S. citizenship or permanent resident status and membership in the PCUSA are also required.

Financial data Stipends range up to $1,500 per year, depending upon the financial need of the recipient.

Duration 1 year; may be renewed up to 3 additional years.

Number awarded Varies each year.

Deadline June of each year.

[66]
CHRISTIAN COLLEGE LEADERS SCHOLARSHIPS

Foundation for College Christian Leaders
2658 Del Mar Heights Road
PMB 266
Del Mar, CA 92014
(858) 481-0848   E-mail: LMHays@aol.com
Web: www.collegechristianleader.com

Summary To provide financial assistance for college to Christian students from California, Oregon, and Washington.

Eligibility This program is open to entering or continuing undergraduate students who reside or attend college in California, Oregon, or Washington. Applicants must have a GPA of 3.0 or higher, be able to document financial need (parents must have a combined income of less than $60,000), and be able to demonstrate Christian testimony and Christian leadership. Selection is based on identified leadership history, academic achievement, financial need, and demonstrated academic, vocational, and ministry training to further the Kingdom of Jesus Christ. Special consideration is given to minority students.

Financial data A stipend is awarded (amount not specified).

Duration 1 year; may be renewed.

Additional information The foundation, formerly known as the Eckmann Foundation, was founded in 1988.

Deadline May of each year.

[67]
CHRISTIAN CONNECTOR UNDERGRADUATE SCHOLARSHIP

Christian Connector, Inc.
627 24 1/2 Road, Suite D
Grand Junction, CO 81501
(970) 256-1610   Toll Free: (800) 667-0600
Web: www.christianconnector.com

Summary To provide financial assistance to high school seniors and transfer students interested in attending a Christ-centered Christian college or Bible college.

Eligibility This program is open to students planning to enroll for the first time at a Christ-centered Christian college or Bible college. Schools that are members of the CCCU, NACCAP, or AABC automatically qualify. Students currently enrolled at a Christian college or Bible college are not eligible. Applicants enter the competition by registering online with the sponsoring organization, providing personal information and indicating the colleges they are considering attending. The recipient of the scholarship is selected in a random drawing.

Financial data The award is $2,500. Funds are sent directly to the winner's school.

Duration The award is presented annually.

Number awarded 1 each year.

Deadline May of each year.

[68]
CHRISTIAN MISSIONARY SCHOLARSHIPS

Christian Missionary Scholarship Foundation
3230 Lake Drive S.E.
Grand Rapids, MI 49546
(616) 526-7731   Fax: (616) 526-6777
E-mail: info@ christianmissionaryscholarship.org
Web: www.christianmissionaryscholarship.org

Summary To provide financial assistance to the children of Christian missionaries who are attending selected Christian colleges.

Eligibility This program is open to students attending or planning to attend Calvin College (Grand Rapids, Michigan), Dordt College (Sioux Center, Iowa), Hope College (Holland, Michigan), Kuyper College (Grand Rapids, Michigan), Trinity Christian College (Palos Heights, Illinois), or Wheaton College (Wheaton, Illinois). Applicants must be the children of Christian missionaries. They must submit brief statements on what they believe to be the essential truths of Christianity, how those beliefs have impacted their life and their personal journey of faith, a significant and/or important experience they have had during the last year and how it has affected their personal growth, their probable career and professional goals, how they selected those goals and how they relate to and support their vision of their future after college, and how they plan to participate actively in and sacrifice for the financial support of their college education.

Financial data A stipend is awarded (amount not specified).

Duration 1 year; may be renewed up to 3 additional years.

Additional information Recipients are required to earn half of their annual room and board expense, maintain a reasonable GPA, and live a faithful Christian life.

Number awarded Up to 100 each year.

Deadline February of each year.

[69]
CHRISTIAN VOCATION/WALLINGFORD SCHOLARSHIPS

First Presbyterian Church
Attn: Scholarship Fund Program
709 South Boston Avenue
Tulsa, OK 74119-1629
(918) 584-4701   Fax: (918) 584-5233
E-mail: TBriscoe@firstchurchtulsa.org
Web: www.firstchurchtulsa.org/scholarships.htm

Summary To provide financial assistance to Presbyterian students interested in preparing for a religion-related career.

Eligibility To be eligible for this program, students must be communicant members of the Presbyterian Church (USA), be pursuing a Christian vocation field of study at an accredited institution, and have a GPA of 2.0 or higher. Priority is given first to members of the First Presbyterian Church (in Tulsa), second to applicants in the Presbytery of Eastern Oklahoma, third to applicants in the Synod of the Sun (Arkansas, Louisiana, Oklahoma, and Texas), and fourth to members of the Presbyterian Church at large. Selection is based on academic merit, academic or career intent, church or religious involvement, and financial need.

Financial data Stipends range from $500 to $2,000. Funds are paid directly to the recipient's school.

Duration 1 year; recipients may reapply.

Additional information This program was established in 1988.

Number awarded Several each year.

Deadline April of each year.

[70]
CLINICAL EDUCATOR SCHOLARSHIPS

Evangelical Lutheran Church in America
Division for Ministry
Attn: Ministries in Chaplaincy, Pastoral Counseling, and
   Clinical Education
8765 West Higgins Road
Chicago, IL 60631-4195
(773) 380-2876   Toll Free: (800) 638-3522, ext. 2876
Fax: (773) 380-2829   E-mail: Theresa.Duty@elca.org
Web: www.elca.org

Summary To provide financial assistance to members of the Evangelical Lutheran Church in America (ELCA) interested in preparing for certification as educators in pastoral care and counseling ministries.

Eligibility This program is open to active members of ELCA congregations (either lay or ordained) who are preparing to become CPE supervisors, pastoral counseling educators, or other certified clinical ministry educators. Applicants must be ecclesiastically endorsed or in the process of seeking Ministries in Chaplaincy, Pastoral Counseling, and Clinical Education (MCPCCE) endorsement. All training positions/programs must comply with the Inter-Lutheran Coordinating Committee (ILCC) document, "Ministries in Chaplaincy, Pastoral Counseling and Clinical Education, Endorsement Standards and Procedures, Call Criteria and Program Guidelines" (2006 edition). They must submit 1) a statement of the nature of the training program and how it fits into both long- and short-range goals for their ministry; 2) a statement of acceptance and contract from a training supervisor; 3) a statement explaining financial need; 4) supervisory and self-evaluations from previous clinical education programs, including units of CPE and/or pastoral counseling training experiences; and 5) if presently serving in a ministry under call, a letter stating the extent to which financial support and/or compensatory time will be provided by the congregation or employing organization for this training.

Financial data   Grants up to $3,000 per year are awarded.

Duration   1 year; may be renewed.

Number awarded   Varies each year.

Deadline   March or September of each year.

[71]
CLINT AND MARGE HAWKINS MEMORIAL CHRISTIAN EDUCATION FUND FOR YOUTH

Missouri United Methodist Foundation
Attn: Scholarships
111 South Ninth Street, Suite 230
P.O. Box 1076
Columbia, MO 66205-1076
(573) 875-4168   Toll Free: (800) 332-8238
Fax: (573) 875-4595   E-mail: foundation@mumf.org
Web: www.mumf.org/view_page.php?page=20

Summary   To provide financial assistance to members of United Methodist churches in Missouri who are interested in attending college in any state.

Eligibility   This program is open to United Methodist residents of Missouri who are high school seniors or current college students. Applicants must submit a letter of recommendation from their pastor indicating that they are full members of the United Methodist Church and of suitable character to be considered for a scholarship. They must also submit high school or college transcripts, a 1-page statement describing their course of study and goals for the future, and a photograph.

Financial data   The stipend is $1,000.

Duration   1 year.

Number awarded   Up to 4 each year.

Deadline   March of each year.

[72]
COLLEGE AND UNIVERSITY MERIT SCHOLARS PROGRAM

United Methodist Higher Education Foundation
Attn: Scholarships Administrator
1001 19th Avenue South
P.O. Box 340005
Nashville, TN 37203-0005
(615) 340-7385   Toll Free: (800) 811-8110
Fax: (615) 340-7330
E-mail: umhefscholarships@gbhem.org
Web: www.umhef.org/receive.php?id=foundation_merit

Summary   To provide financial assistance to undergraduate students attending colleges and universities affiliated with the United Methodist Church.

Eligibility   This program is open to freshmen, sophomores, juniors, and seniors at United Methodist-related 4-year colleges and universities and to freshmen and sophomores at 2-year colleges. Nominees must have been active members of the United Methodist Church for at least 1 year prior to application. They must be planning to enroll full time and have a

GPA of 3.0 or higher. Financial need is considered in the selection process. U.S. citizenship or permanent resident status is required.

Financial data   The stipend is $1,000.

Duration   1 year; nonrenewable.

Additional information   Students may obtain applications from their school.

Number awarded   420 each year: 1 to a member of each class at each school.

Deadline   Nominations from schools must be received by August of each year.

[73]
COLORADO EASTERN STAR TRAINING AWARDS FOR RELIGIOUS LEADERSHIP

Order of the Eastern Star-Grand Chapter of Colorado
2445 South Quebec Street, Suite B
Denver, CO 80231
(303) 759-5936   Fax: (303) 759-3924
E-mail: grchapcoestar@qwestoffice.net
Web: www.oes-colorado.org/estarl.html

Summary   To provide financial assistance to residents of Colorado who are attending college in any state to prepare for a career in religious service.

Eligibility   This program is open to residents of Colorado who have completed at least 2 years of college and are enrolled full time at a college, university, or seminary in any state. Applicants must be preparing for a career in religious service as a minister, missionary, director of church music, director of religious education, or youth leadership.

Financial data   The stipend is $1,000 per year.

Duration   1 year; recipients may reapply.

Number awarded   Varies each year. Recently, 6 of these scholarships were awarded.

Deadline   April of each year.

[74]
CONNECTICUT EAGLE SCOUT OF THE YEAR SCHOLARSHIP

American Legion
Department of Connecticut
287 West Street
P.O. Box 208
Rocky Hill, CT 06067
(860) 721-5942   E-mail: deptadj@ctlegion.necoxmail.com
Web: www.ct.legion.org/?programs

Summary   To recognize and reward, with scholarships for college in any state, Eagle Scouts who are members of a troop associated with the American Legion in Connecticut or a son or grandson of a member of the Legion in the state.

Eligibility   Applicants for this award must be either 1) a registered, active member of a Boy Scout Troop, Varsity Scout Team, or Venturing Crew chartered to an American Legion Post, Auxiliary Unit, or Sons of the American Legion Squadron in Connecticut, or 2) a registered active member of a Boy Scout Troop, Varsity Scout Team, or Venturing Crew and also the son or grandson of a member of the American Legion or American Legion Auxiliary in Connecticut. Candidates must also 1) have received the Eagle Scout Award; 2) be active members of their religious institution and have received the appropriate religious emblem; 3) have demonstrated practical citizenship in church, school, Scouting, and community; 4) be at least 15 years of age and enrolled in high school; and 5) submit at least 4 letters of recommendation, including 1 each from leaders of their religious institution, school, community, and Scouting. They must be planning to attend college in any state.

Financial data The stipend is $1,000, presented in the form of a savings bond which the recipient may use whenever he attends college.

Duration The award is presented annually.

Number awarded 1 each year.

Deadline February of each year.

[75]
CONNECTICUT EASTERN STAR TRAINING AWARDS FOR RELIGIOUS LEADERSHIP

Order of the Eastern Star-Grand Chapter of Connecticut
c/o Nancy A. Watson, Scholarship Committee Chair
48 Elderkin Crossing
Norwich, CT 06360
(860) 887-1128   E-mail: nawatson@snet.net
Web: www.ctoes.com/CT_OES/oes_info.htm

Summary To provide financial assistance to residents of Connecticut who are attending college or graduate school in any state to work on a degree related to religious leadership or religious music.

Eligibility This program is open to residents of Connecticut who are preparing for a career in religion as a minister, missionary, church musician or organist, director of religious education, director of youth leadership, or other related position. Applicants must be enrolled at a college or university in any state and working on an associate, bachelor's, master's, or doctoral degree. They must be able to demonstrate financial need (family adjusted gross income less than $50,000 per year). Along with their application, they must submit a brief statement or summary of their plans as those relate to their educational and religious leadership career objectives and long-term goals.

Financial data A stipend is awarded (amount not specified).

Duration 1 year.

Number awarded 1 or more each year.

Deadline February of each year.

[76]
CONNECTICUT STATE COUNCIL KNIGHTS OF COLUMBUS SCHOLARSHIPS

Knights of Columbus-Connecticut State Council
c/o James W. Ciaglo, Jr., Scholarship Chair
565 Old Hartford Road
Colchester, CT 06415
E-mail: jwciaglo@snet.net
Web: www.kofc-ct-state.org/Programs.html

Summary To provide financial assistance to residents of Connecticut who are members or children of members of the Knights of Columbus and entering a college in any state.

Eligibility This program is open to residents of Connecticut who are 1) a member of the Knights of Columbus; 2) a child of either a member in good standing or a deceased member who was in good standing at the time of his death; or 3) a member of the Columbian Squires. Applicants must be enter-

ing the freshman year as a full-time student at an accredited college or university in any state to work on a bachelor's degree. Along with their application, they must submit transcripts, SAT and/or ACT scores, 2 letters of recommendation, and an autobiographical statement that includes their educational objectives and goals. Selection is based on academic excellence, extracurricular activities, and church and community activities.

Financial data A stipend is awarded (amount not specified).

Duration 1 year.

Number awarded 1 or more each year.

Deadline February of each year.

[77]
CONTINUING EDUCATION FOR ADULT WOMEN SCHOLARSHIP

American Baptist Women's Ministries of Wisconsin
c/o Lois A. Horsman, Scholarship Committee Chair
P.O. Box 68
Wyocena, WI 53969
(608) 429-2485
Web: www.abcofwi.org/abwinfo.htm

Summary To provide financial assistance to adult female members of American Baptist Churches in Wisconsin who are interested in attending college in any state.

Eligibility This program is open to adult women who are residents of Wisconsin and attending or planning to attend college in any state. Applicants must have been an active member of an American Baptist Church in Wisconsin for the preceding 3 years. The college does not need to be affiliated with the American Baptist Churches USA.

Financial data A stipend is awarded (amount not specified).

Duration 2 or 4 years.

Number awarded 1 or more each year.

Deadline Deadline not specified.

[78]
CONVENCION BAUTISTA HISPANA DE TEXAS SCHOLARSHIP

Baptist General Convention of Texas
Attn: Hispanic Education Initiative
333 North Washington
Dallas, TX 75246-1798
(214) 828-5279   Fax: (214) 828-5284
E-mail: lou.merryman@texasbaptists.org
Web: texasbaptists.org

Summary To provide financial assistance to Hispanic members of Baptist churches in Texas who are interested in attending college in any state.

Eligibility This program is open to members of congregations affiliated with the Baptist General Convention of Texas who are currently participating in an Hispanic-related ministry. Applicants must be enrolled or planning to enroll at a college or university in any state. They may be of any age and be participating in their youth, singles, and/or adults group at church. Along with their application, they must submit essays of 5 to 7 sentences on any 2 of the following: 1) why they are pursuing higher education; 2) in what ways education will help them serve Christ in their church; or 3) what their challenges are in working toward higher education.

Financial data The stipend is $1,000 per year.

Duration 1 year; may be renewed up to 3 additional years.

Number awarded 1 or more each year.

Deadline June of each year.

[79]
COOK SCHOLARSHIP AWARDS

South Carolina United Methodist Foundation
P.O. Box 5087
Columbia, SC 29250-5087
(803) 771-9125   Fax: (803) 771-9135
E-mail: scumf@bellsouth.net
Web: www.umcsc.org/scholarships.html

Summary To provide financial assistance to Methodist students from South Carolina who are attending college or graduate school in any state to prepare for a career in Christian service.

Eligibility This program is open to members of United Methodist Churches in South Carolina and to persons affiliated with the South Carolina Conference of the United Methodist Church (UMC). Applicants must be enrolled in an undergraduate, graduate, or professional degree program at an accredited college, university, or theological school in any state approved by the UMC University Senate. They must be preparing for a career in full-time Christian service. Selection is based on their understanding of their ministry and its future direction, promise for ministry in the church, and financial need.

Financial data The stipend is at least $500.

Duration 1 year.

Additional information This scholarship was established by the South Carolina Conference of the United Methodist Church in 1989.

Number awarded 1 or more each year.

Deadline March of each year.

[80]
COOPER FUND GRANTS

United Methodist Church-Mississippi Conference
Attn: Office of Ministerial Services
321 Mississippi Street
Jackson, MS 39201
(601) 354-0515, ext. 32   Toll Free: (866) 647-7486
E-mail: scumbest@mississippi-umc.org
Web: www.mississippi-umc.org/pages/detail/779

Summary To provide financial assistance to upper-division and graduate students from Mississippi who are preparing for full-time professional ministry within the United Methodist Church (UMC) at a school in any state.

Eligibility This program is open to residents of Mississippi who are either 1) juniors or seniors at an accredited college or university in any state, or 2) enrolled at an accredited seminary in any state. Applicants must be planning to enter the full-time professional ministry (ordained, elder, deacon, music, education) of the UMC. They must be able to demonstrate financial need.

Financial data The stipend is $1,000.

Duration 1 year.

Additional information This program was established in 1906.

Number awarded 4 each year: 2 to undergraduates and 2 to seminary students.

Deadline May of each year.

[81]
COOPERATIVE BAPTIST FELLOWSHIP OF FLORIDA SCHOLARSHIPS

Cooperative Baptist Fellowship of Florida
Attn: Chair, Scholarship Team
217 Hillcrest Street
P.O. Box 2556
Lakeland, FL 33806-2556
(863) 682-6802   Toll Free: (888) 241-CBFF
Fax: (863) 683-5797   E-mail: contact@floridacbf.org
Web: www.floridacbf.org/fl/scholarships.htm

Summary To provide financial assistance for college, seminary, or graduate school to members of the Cooperative Baptist Fellowship (CBF) of Florida.

Eligibility This program is open to CBF members in Florida, including both clergy and laity. Applicants must be proposing to participate in an official educational endeavor that will enhance their ministry. The activity may be overtly religious or secular as long as the recipient will use the education to enhance a ministry within the Baptist community of faith. Applications are accompanied by 2 brochures, entitled "Where Do I Belong?" and "Why It Matters Where You Serve the Lord." Applicants must submit their reaction to those brochures. They must also demonstrate financial need. Priority is given to students in master's or doctoral programs at accredited institutions.

Financial data A stipend is awarded (amount not specified).

Duration 1 year.

Number awarded 1 or more each year.

Deadline April of each year.

[82]
DAKOTAS CONFERENCE MERIT AWARD PROGRAM

United Methodist Church-Dakotas Conference
Attn: Office of Leadership Development
1331 West University Avenue
P.O. Box 460
Mitchell, SC 57301-0460
(605) 996-6552   Fax: (605) 996-1766
Web: www.dakotasumc.org/Contents/Scholarships.aspx

Summary To provide financial assistance to members of the United Methodist Church (UMC) in its Dakotas Conference who are interested in attending a college in any state that is affiliated with the denomination.

Eligibility This program is open to members of UMC congregations in North and South Dakota who are enrolled or planning to enroll at a UMC college or university in any state. Each church in the Dakotas Conference may nominate 1 student for this award. Applicants must demonstrate exceptional promise or achievement.

Financial data A stipend is awarded (amount not specified).

Duration 1 year.

Additional information Funding for this is provided from the proceeds of the Student Day Offering.

Number awarded 1 or more each year.

Deadline November of each year.

[83]
DAVID AND MARY CROWLEY SCHOLARSHIP

Baptist Convention of New York
Attn: BCNY Foundation
6538 Baptist Way
East Syracuse, NY 13057
(315) 433-1001   Toll Free: (800) 552-0004
Fax: (315) 433-1026   E-mail: cmeyer@bcnysbc.org
Web: www.bcnysbc.org/bcnyfoundation.html

Summary To provide financial assistance to members of churches in the Baptist Convention of New York who are interested in additional education.

Eligibility This program is open to members in good standing of churches in the Baptist Convention of New York. Applicants must be seeking education through the Southern Baptist Convention schools associated with the Cooperative Program. Along with their application, they must submit 1) an essay in which they share their goals for the future and how a degree in higher education will help them achieve those goals; and 2) an autobiography that includes their conversion experience, call to Christian service (for those planning a religious vocation), and plans to fulfill this calling. Financial need is also considered in the selection process.

Financial data A stipend is awarded (amount not specified).

Duration 1 year; may be renewed up to 3 additional years.

Number awarded 1 or more each year.

Deadline February of each year.

[84]
DAVID W. SELF SCHOLARSHIP

United Methodist Church
Attn: General Board of Discipleship
Division on Ministries with Young People
P.O. Box 340003
Nashville, TN 37203-0003
(615) 340-7184   Toll Free: (877) 899-2780, ext. 7184
Fax: (615) 340-7063   E-mail: youngpeople@gbod.org
Web: www.gbod.org/youngpeople/grants/grants.htm

Summary To provide financial assistance to Methodist high school seniors who wish to prepare for a church-related career.

Eligibility This program is open to graduating high school seniors who have been active members of a United Methodist Church for at least 1 year. Applicants must have been admitted to an accredited college or university to prepare for a church-related career. They must have maintained at least a "C" average throughout high school and be able to demonstrate financial need. Along with their application, they must submit brief essays on their participation in church projects and activities, a leadership experience, the role their faith plays in their life, the church-related vocation to which God is calling them, and their extracurricular interests and activities. U.S. citizenship or permanent resident status is required.

Financial data The stipend is $1,000.

Duration 1 year; nonrenewable.

Additional information This scholarship was first awarded in 1997. Recipients must enroll full time in their first year of undergraduate study.

Number awarded 2 each year.

Deadline May of each year.

[85]
DEATLEY SCHOLARS AWARD

Wisconsin United Methodist Foundation
750 Windsor Street, Suite 305
P.O. Box 620
Sun Prairie, WI 53590-0620
(608) 837-9582   Toll Free: (888) 903-9863
Fax: (608) 837-2492   E-mail: wumf@wumf.org
Web: www.wumf.org/grantsFF/grantsScholars.html

Summary To provide financial assistance to Methodist high school seniors from Wisconsin who are interested in attending college in any state to major in a service-oriented field.

Eligibility This program is open to graduating high school seniors who are members of United Methodist Churches affiliated with the Wisconsin Conference. Applicants must be planning to enroll at a 4-year college or university in any state to major in a service-oriented field. Along with their application, they must submit an essay that describes their personal situation and vocational goals, church-related activities and involvement, school and community involvement, and financial plan for funding their education, including any special financial needs.

Financial data Stipends range from $500 to $1,000.

Duration 1 year.

Number awarded 1 or more each year.

Deadline March of each year.

[86]
DEGENRING SCHOLARSHIP FUND

American Baptist Women's Ministries of New Jersey
36-10 Garden View Terrace
East Windsor, NJ 08520
Web: www.abwminnj.org/custom.html

Summary To provide financial assistance to Baptist women in New Jersey who are interested in attending college in any state to prepare for a career in Christian service.

Eligibility This program is open to Baptist women in New Jersey who are at least sophomores at postsecondary institutions in any state and preparing for a career involving Christian work. Applicants must be members of an American Baptist church in New Jersey. Selection is based on financial need and career goals.

Financial data The amount awarded varies, depending upon the need of the recipient and her career goals in Christian work.

Duration 1 year.

Number awarded 1 or more each year.

Deadline February of each year.

[87]
DESERT SOUTHWEST UNITED METHODIST FOUNDATION SCHOLARSHIPS

Desert Southwest United Methodist Foundation
Attn: Executive Director
1550 East Meadowbrook Avenue
Phoenix, AZ 85014-4040
(602) 266-6956, ext. 203   Toll Free: (800) 229-8622
Fax: (602) 265-1524   E-mail: Lucille@dsumf.org
Web: www.dsumf.org/scholarships.htm

Summary To provide financial assistance for college or graduate school to members of Methodist Churches within the Desert Southwest Conference.

Eligibility This program is open to active members of congregations that are affiliated with the United Methodist Church Desert Southwest Conference, which serves Arizona and southern Nevada. Applicants must be 1) enrolled in a seminary or school of religion that is accredited by the United Methodist Church University Senate; 2) enrolled in a college or university within the boundaries of the Desert Southwest Conference; or 3) majoring in elementary education. They must submit essays on 1) their recent past, current, and anticipated future non-ordained involvement in their church; 2) their immediate and long-term goals; 3) their plan for their ordained or licensed Christian ministry; and 4) their financial need.

Financial data A stipend is awarded (amount not specified).

Duration 1 year.

Number awarded Varies each year.

Deadline June of each year for fall semester; December of each year for spring semester.

[88]
DEVELOPMENTAL DISABILITIES CAREER AWARENESS AWARDS FOR LUTHERAN STUDENTS IN HIGH SCHOOL

Bethesda Lutheran Communities
Attn: Coordinator, Bethesda Institute
600 Hoffmann Drive
Watertown, WI 53094
(920) 261-3050   Toll Free: (800) 369-4636, ext. 4449
Fax: (920) 262-6513
E-mail: Bethesda.institute@mailblc.org
Web: bethesdalutherancommunities.org/youth/scholarships

Summary To recognize and reward seniors in high school who are Lutherans and have been involved in service to people with developmental disabilities.

Eligibility This award is available to active communicant members of a Lutheran congregation who are seniors in high school and have a GPA of 3.0 or higher. Applicants must have an interest in a career in the field of developmental disabilities. They must submit 1) documentation that they have completed, within the past 2 calendar years, at least 25 hours of contact with a person who has a developmental disability in either a family, community, or church setting; 2) a 100-word summary for each of 2 interviews of developmental disabilities professionals (social worker, psychologist, teacher, vocational or rehabilitation specialist, etc.); 3) 4 letters of reference; and 4) an official high school transcript.

Financial data The award is $500.

Duration The awards are presented annually.

Number awarded 2 each year.

Deadline April of each year.

[89]
DEVELOPMENTAL DISABILITIES SCHOLASTIC EXCELLENCE AWARD FOR LUTHERAN STUDENTS IN COLLEGE OR UNIVERSITY

Bethesda Lutheran Communities
Attn: Coordinator, Bethesda Institute
600 Hoffmann Drive
Watertown, WI 53094
(920) 261-3050   Toll Free: (800) 369-4636, ext. 4449
Fax: (920) 262-6513
E-mail: Bethesda.institute@mailblc.org
Web: bethesdalutherancommunities.org/youth/scholarships

Summary To provide financial assistance to undergraduates who are Lutherans and interested in preparing for a career in an area of service to people with developmental disabilities.

Eligibility Applicants must be active communicant members of a Lutheran congregation; be classified as a sophomore or junior at a college or university (not necessarily a Lutheran college); have an overall GPA of 3.0 or higher; and be interested in preparing for a career in the field of developmental disabilities. Along with their application, they must submit 1) an essay of 250 to 300 words on the career they are planning in the field of developmental disabilities and how that career choice would impact the lives of people with developmental disabilities; 2) 4 letters of recommendation; 3) an official college transcript; and 4) documentation that they have completed at least 100 hours of volunteer and/or paid service to people who are developmentally disabled within the past 2 calendar years. Financial need is not considered in the selection process.

Financial data The stipend is $3,000.

Duration 1 year.

Number awarded 2 each year.

Deadline April of each year.

[90]
DISTANCE LEARNING SCHOLARSHIP

Christian Connector, Inc.
627 24 1/2 Road, Suite D
Grand Junction, CO 81501
(970) 256-1610   Toll Free: (800) 667-0600
Web: www.christianconnector.com

Summary To provide financial assistance to students interested in working on an undergraduate or graduate degree from a Christ-centered distance learning program.

Eligibility This program is open to students planning to enroll through a distance learning program at a Christ-centered Christian college, Bible college, seminary, or Christian graduate school. Schools that are members of the CCCU, NACCAP, or AABC automatically qualify. Applicants enter the competition by registering online with the sponsoring organization, providing personal information and information about the distance learning program they are considering. The recipient of the scholarship is selected in a random drawing.

Financial data The award is $1,000. Funds are sent directly to the winner's school.

Duration The award is presented annually.
Number awarded 1 each year.
Deadline May of each year.

[91]
DOLLARS FOR SCHOLARS PROGRAM

United Methodist Higher Education Foundation
Attn: Scholarships Administrator
1001 19th Avenue South
P.O. Box 340005
Nashville, TN 37203-0005
(615) 340-7385   Toll Free: (800) 811-8110
Fax: (615) 340-7330
E-mail: umhefscholarships@gbhem.org
Web: www.umhef.org/receive.php?id=dollars_for_scholars

Summary To provide financial assistance to students at Methodist colleges, universities, and seminaries whose home churches agree to contribute to their support.

Eligibility The Double Your Dollars for Scholars program is open to students attending or planning to attend a United Methodist-related college, university, or seminary as a full-time student. Applicants must have been an active, full member of a United Methodist Church for at least 1 year prior to applying. Their home church must nominate them and agree to contribute to their support. Many of the United Methodist colleges and universities have also agreed to contribute matching funds for a Triple Your Dollars for Scholars Program, and a few United Methodist conference foundations have agreed to contribute additional matching funds for a Quadruple Your Dollars for Scholars Program. Awards are granted on a first-come, first-served basis. Some of the awards are designated for Hispanic, Asian, and Native American (HANA) students funded by the General Board of Higher Education and Ministry.

Financial data The sponsoring church contributes $1,000 and the United Methodist Higher Education Foundation (UMHEF) contributes a matching $1,000. Students who attend a participating United Methodist college or university receive an additional $1,000 for the Triple Your Dollars for Scholars Program, and those from a participating conference receive a fourth $1,000 increment for the Quadruple Your Dollars for Scholars Program.

Duration 1 year; may be renewed as long as the recipients maintain satisfactory academic progress as defined by their institution.

Additional information Currently, participants in the Double Your Dollars for Scholars program include 2 United Methodist seminaries and theological schools, 1 professional school, 19 senior colleges and universities, and 1 2-year college. The Triple Your Dollars for Scholars program includes an additional 11 United Methodist seminaries and theological schools, 73 senior colleges and universities, and 5 2-year colleges (for a complete list, consult the UMHEF). The conference foundations participating in the Quadruple Your Dollars for Scholars Program are limited to the Alabama-West Florida United Methodist Foundation, the Mississippi United Methodist Foundation (for students at Millsaps College or Rust College), the Missouri United Methodist Foundation (for students at Saint Paul School of Theology or Central Methodist University), the Nashville Area United Methodist Foundation, the North Carolina United Methodist Foundation (for students at Louisburg College, Methodist University, or North Carolina

Wesleyan College), the North Georgia United Methodist Foundation, the Oklahoma United Methodist Foundation (for students at Oklahoma City University) the United Methodist Foundation of Arkansas (for students at Hendrix College or Philander Smith College), the United Methodist Foundation of South Indiana, and the United Methodist Foundation of Western North Carolina.

Number awarded 350 each year, including 25 designated for HANA students.

Deadline Local churches must submit applications in March of each year for senior colleges, universities, and seminaries or May of each year for 2-year colleges.

[92]
DORA AMES LEE LEADERSHIP DEVELOPMENT FUND

United Methodist Church
General Board of Global Ministries
Attn: United Methodist Committee on Relief
475 Riverside Drive, Room 1522
New York, NY 10115
(212) 870-3871   Toll Free: (800) UMC-GBGM
E-mail: jyoung@gbgm-umc.org
Web: gbgm-umc.org/health/doralee.cfm

Summary To provide financial assistance to Methodists and other Christians of Asian or Native American descent who are preparing for a career in a health-related field.

Eligibility This program is open to undergraduate and graduate students who are U.S. citizens of Asian American or Native American descent. Applicants must be professed Christians, preferably United Methodists. They must be attending a college or university to enter or continue in a health-related field. Financial need is considered in the selection process.

Financial data The stipend is $2,000.

Duration 1 year.

Additional information This program was established in 1980.

Number awarded 5 each year.

Deadline June of each year.

[93]
DOREENE CATER SCHOLARSHIP

First United Methodist Church of the Saint Cloud Region
Attn: Scholarship Committee
302 Fifth Avenue South
St. Cloud, MN 56301
(320) 251-0804   Fax: (320) 251-0878
E-mail: fumc@fumc-stcloud.org
Web: www.fumc-stcloud.org/education

Summary To provide financial assistance to members of United Methodist Churches in the Minnesota Conference who are interested in preparing for a career in an area that will benefit people and the environment.

Eligibility This program is open to members of United Methodist Churches in the Minnesota Conference who are interested in a career in such areas as education, medicine, environmental sciences, seminary education, and social service. Applicants must be entering at least their sophomore year. They must submit 2 letters of reference and transcripts of previous work.

Financial data Stipends range from $500 to $1,500, depending on the need of the recipient and the number of applicants.

Duration 1 year; may be renewed.

Number awarded Varies each year.

Deadline May of each year.

[94]
DR. CHESTER A. MCPHEETERS SCHOLARSHIP

United Methodist Higher Education Foundation
Attn: Scholarships Administrator
1001 19th Avenue South
P.O. Box 340005
Nashville, TN 37203-0005
(615) 340-7385   Toll Free: (800) 811-8110
Fax: (615) 340-7330
E-mail: umhefscholarships@gbhem.org
Web: www.umhef.org/receive.php?id=endowed_funds

Summary To provide financial assistance to undergraduate and graduate Methodist students who are preparing for ministry.

Eligibility This program is open to full-time undergraduate and graduate students who are preparing for a career as a minister in the United Methodist Church. Applicants must have been active, full members of a United Methodist Church for at least 1 year prior to applying and be attending or planning to attend a seminary or theological school affiliated with that denomination. They must have a GPA of 3.0 or higher and be able to demonstrate financial need. Along with their application, they must submit a 200-word essay on their involvement and/or leadership responsibilities in their church, school, and community within the last 3 years. U.S. citizenship or permanent resident status is required.

Financial data The stipend is at least $1,000 per year.

Duration 1 year; recipients may reapply.

Number awarded Varies each year. Recently, 4 of these scholarships were awarded.

Deadline May of each year.

[95]
DR. CLAUDE AND JEANNIE CONE CENTURY FUND

New Mexico Baptist Foundation
5325 Wyoming Boulevard, N.E.
P.O. Box 16560
Albuquerque, NM 87191-6560
(505) 332-3777   Toll Free: (877) 841-3777
Fax: (505) 332-2777   E-mail: foundation@nmbf.com
Web: www.bcnm.com

Summary To provide financial assistance to members of Southern Baptist churches in New Mexico who are interested in attending designated Baptist institutions.

Eligibility This program is open to members of Southern Baptist churches in New Mexico who are enrolled at Wayland Baptist University (Plainview, Texas), Southwestern Baptist Theological Seminary (Fort Worth, Texas), or Golden Gate Baptist Theological Seminary (Mill Valley, California). Applicants must have a GPA of 2.5 or higher and be able to demonstrate financial need.

Financial data A stipend is awarded (amount not specified).

Duration 1 year.

Number awarded 1 or more each year.

Deadline June of each year.

[96]
DWAIN MARROW SCHOLARSHIP

New Mexico Baptist Foundation
5325 Wyoming Boulevard, N.E.
P.O. Box 16560
Albuquerque, NM 87191-6560
(505) 332-3777   Toll Free: (877) 841-3777
Fax: (505) 332-2777   E-mail: foundation@nmbf.com
Web: www.bcnm.com

Summary To provide financial assistance to members of Southern Baptist churches in New Mexico who are interested in attending a college or seminary in any state.

Eligibility This program is open to members of Southern Baptist churches in New Mexico who are enrolled at an accredited a college or seminary in any state in response to a call to full-time ministry. Applicants must have a GPA of 2.0 or higher and be able to demonstrate financial need.

Financial data A stipend is awarded (amount not specified).

Duration 1 year.

Number awarded 1 or more each year.

Deadline June of each year.

[97]
E. CRAIG BRANDENBURG SCHOLARSHIP

United Methodist Church
Attn: General Board of Higher Education and Ministry
Office of Loans and Scholarships
1001 19th Avenue South
P.O. Box 340007
Nashville, TN 37203-0007
(615) 340-7344   Fax: (615) 340-7367
E-mail: umscholar@gbhem.org
Web: www.gbhem.org/loansandscholarships

Summary To provide financial assistance to mature Methodist students who are working on an undergraduate or graduate degree to change their profession or continue study after interruption.

Eligibility This program is open to full-time undergraduate and graduate students who are 35 years of age or older. Applicants must have been active, full members of a United Methodist Church for at least 1 year prior to applying. They must 1) be able to demonstrate special need because of a change of profession or vocation, interruption of study, or resumption of education; 2) have a GPA of 2.5 or higher; and 3) be U.S. citizens or permanent residents. Preference is given to applicants attending United Methodist colleges, universities, or seminaries.

Financial data Stipends range from $500 to $2,000.

Duration 1 year; recipients may reapply.

Number awarded Varies each year.

Deadline February of each year.

[98]
EAGLE SCOUT OF THE YEAR

American Legion
Attn: Americanism and Children & Youth Division
700 North Pennsylvania Street
P.O. Box 1055
Indianapolis, IN 46206-1055
(317) 630-1202   Fax: (317) 630-1223
E-mail: acy@legion.org
Web: www.legion.org/programs/resources/scholarships

Summary To recognize and reward, with college scholarships, Eagle Scouts who are members of a troop associated with the American Legion or are the son or grandson of a member of the Legion.

Eligibility Applicants for this award must be either 1) a registered, active member of a Boy Scout Troop, Varsity Scout Team, or Venturing Crew chartered to an American Legion Post, Auxiliary Unit, or Sons of the American Legion Squadron, or 2) a registered active member of a Boy Scout Troop, Varsity Scout Team, or Venturing Crew and also the son or grandson of a member of the American Legion or American Legion Auxiliary. They must also 1) have received the Eagle Scout Award; 2) be active members of their religious institution and have received the appropriate religious emblem; 3) have demonstrated practical citizenship in church, school, Scouting, and community; 4) be at least 15 years of age and enrolled in high school; and 5) submit at least 4 letters of recommendation, including 1 each from leaders of their religious institution, school, community, and Scouting.

Financial data The Scout of the Year receives $10,000; each runner-up receives $2,500.

Duration The awards are presented annually; recipients are eligible to receive their scholarships immediately upon graduation from an accredited high school and must utilize the award within 4 years of their graduation date.

Additional information The recipients may use the scholarships at any school of their choice, provided it is accredited for education above the high school level and located within the United States or its possessions.

Number awarded 1 Scout of the Year and 3 runners-up are selected each year.

Deadline Nominations must be received by the respective department headquarters by the end of February of each year and by the national headquarters before the end of March.

[99]
EASTERN ORTHODOX COMMITTEE ON SCOUTING SCHOLARSHIP

Boy Scouts of America
Attn: Eastern Orthodox Committee on Scouting
862 Guy Lombardo Avenue
Freeport, NY 11520
(516) 868-4050   Fax: (516) 868-4052
Web: eocs.org/?page_id=21

Summary To provide financial assistance for college to Boy or Girl Scouts of Eastern Orthodox religious background.

Eligibility This program is open to registered members of a Boy or Girl Scout unit who have received the Eagle Scout Award for boys or the Gold Award for girls, are active members of an Eastern Orthodox Church, and have received the

Alpha Omega Religious Award. Applicants must have demonstrated practical citizenship in their church, school, Scouting unit, and community and be enrolled in the final year of an accredited high school. They must be planning to attend an accredited 4-year college or university. Selection is based on academic achievement and involvement in church, school, community, and Scouting.

Financial data Stipends are $1,000 or $500.

Duration 1 year.

Number awarded 2 each year: 1 each at $1,000 and $500.

Deadline April of each year.

[100]
EASTERN STAR TRAINING AWARDS FOR RELIGIOUS LEADERSHIP

Order of the Eastern Star
Attn: Right Worthy Grand Secretary
1618 New Hampshire Avenue, N.W.
Washington, DC 20009-2549
(202) 667-4737   Toll Free: (800) 648-1182
Fax: (202) 462-5162   E-mail: easternstar@rcn.com
Web: www.easternstar.org

Summary To provide financial assistance for college to individuals who are willing to dedicate their lives to full-time religious service.

Eligibility In general, awards are made to applicants preparing for leadership in various fields of religious service, including ministers, missionaries, directors of church music, directors of religious education, and counselors of youth leadership. They need not be affiliated with the Masonic Fraternity or the Order of the Eastern Star. Specific eligibility is determined by each Grand Jurisdiction (state or province) and each chapter under jurisdiction of the General Grand Chapter.

Financial data The amounts are determined by each jurisdiction or committee on the basis of funds available, number of applicants, and needs of the individual. Funds are paid directly to the recipient's school and may be used, as needed, for books, tuition, board, or medical aid.

Duration 1 year; may be renewed.

Additional information This program was established in 1952.

Number awarded Varies each year.

Deadline Deadlines vary by jurisdiction or committee; check with the unit in your area for details.

[101]
ECL CAREER IN TEACHING SCHOLARSHIPS

American Baptist Churches of the Rocky Mountains
Attn: American Baptist Women's Ministries
9085 East Mineral Circle, Suite 170
Centennial, CO 80112
(303) 988-3900   E-mail: web@abcrm.org
Web: www.abcrm.org

Summary To provide financial assistance to women who are members of churches affiliated with the American Baptist Churches (ABC) USA in Colorado, New Mexico, and Utah and interested in attending college in Colorado to prepare for a career as a teacher.

Eligibility This program is open to women under 26 years of age who are active members of churches cooperating with ABC in Colorado, New Mexico, or Utah. Applicants must be enrolled or planning to enroll full time at a 4-year college or university in Colorado. They must be preparing for a career in teaching. Along with their application, they must submit a personal letter describing their Christian experience; their participation in the life of their church, school, and community; and their goals for the future. Selection is based on academic performance, Christian participation in church and school, and financial need.

Financial data The stipend is $1,000 per year.

Duration 1 year; recipients may reapply.

Number awarded 1 or more each year.

Deadline March of each year.

[102]
ED E. AND GLADYS HURLEY FOUNDATION GRANTS

Ed E. and Gladys Hurley Foundation
Bank of America, N.A., Trustee
Attn: Jenae Guillory
901 Main Street, 19th Floor
Dallas, TX 75202-3714

Summary To provide financial assistance to undergraduate and graduate students in Texas who are interested in becoming Protestant ministers or who wish to pursue religious education.

Eligibility This program is open to undergraduate and graduate students who are preparing for a career as a Protestant minister, missionary, or other religious worker. Applicants may be residents of any state, but they must be attending a college or university in Texas. They must be able to demonstrate financial need and above-average grades.

Financial data The stipend is $1,000 per year.

Duration 1 year.

Number awarded Varies each year. Recently, 87 of these grants were awarded.

Deadline April of each year.

[103]
ED VANLANDINGHAM MUSIC SCHOLARSHIP

Kansas-Nebraska Convention of Southern Baptists
Attn: Kansas-Nebraska Southern Baptist Foundation
5410 S.W. Seventh Street
Topeka, KS 66606-2398
(785) 228-6800   Toll Free: (800) 984-9092
Fax: (785) 273-4992   E-mail: beckyholt@kncsb.org
Web: www.kncsb.org/ministry/article/foundation_funds

Summary To provide financial assistance to Southern Baptists from Kansas and Nebraska who are interested in preparing for a career as a church musician.

Eligibility This program is open to members of churches in the Kansas-Nebraska Convention of Southern Baptists who are attending or planning to attend a college or university in any state. Applicants must have declared church music as their vocation.

Financial data A stipend is awarded (amount not specified).

Duration 1 year.

Number awarded 1 or more each year.

Deadline May of each year.

[104]
EDITH A. GORSUCH SCHOLARSHIP

Center for Scholarship Administration, Inc.
Attn: Wells Fargo Accounts
4320 Wade Hampton Boulevard, Suite G
Taylors, SC 29687
Toll Free: (866) 608-0001
E-mail: sallyking@bellsouth.net
Web: www.csascholars.org/gorsuch/index.php

Summary To provide financial assistance to undergraduate students enrolled at designated universities in Pennsylvania and preparing for a career in Christian ministry, law, or medicine.

Eligibility This program is open to residents of any state currently enrolled as full-time undergraduates at Bryn Mawr College, Lafayette College, Swarthmore College, or Widener University. Applicants must be preparing for a profession in Christian ministry, law, or medicine. They must have a cumulative GPA of 2.0 or higher and be able to demonstrate "high personal character, academic ability and achievement." Selection is based on academic merit and community service.

Financial data A stipend is awarded (amount not specified).

Duration 1 year; recipients may reapply.

Number awarded Several each year.

Deadline April of each year.

[105]
EDITH M. ALLEN SCHOLARSHIPS

United Methodist Church
Attn: General Board of Higher Education and Ministry
Office of Loans and Scholarships
1001 19th Avenue South
P.O. Box 340007
Nashville, TN 37203-0007
(615) 340-7344   Fax: (615) 340-7367
E-mail: umscholar@gbhem.org
Web: www.gbhem.org/loansandscholarships

Summary To provide financial assistance to Methodist students who are African American and working on an undergraduate or graduate degree in specified fields.

Eligibility This program is open to full-time undergraduate and graduate students at Methodist colleges and universities (preferably Historically Black United Methodist colleges) who have been active, full members of a United Methodist Church for at least 3 years prior to applying. Applicants must be African Americans working on a degree in education, social work, medicine, and/or other health professions. They must have at least a "B+" average and be recognized as a person whose academic and vocational contributions will help improve the quality of life for others.

Financial data A stipend is awarded (amount not specified).

Duration 1 year; recipients may reapply.

Number awarded Varies each year.

Deadline April of each year.

[106]
EDWIN G. AND LAURETTA M. MICHAEL SCHOLARSHIP

Christian Church (Disciples of Christ)
Attn: Disciples Home Missions
130 East Washington Street
P.O. Box 1986
Indianapolis, IN 46206-1986
(317) 713-2652   Toll Free: (888) DHM-2631
Fax: (317) 635-4426   E-mail: mail@dhm.disciples.org
Web: www.discipleshomemissions.org

Summary To provide financial support to ministers' wives whose basic education was interrupted to enable their husbands to complete their theological education.

Eligibility This program is open to ministers' wives who are working on an undergraduate degree and whose husbands have completed their basic theological education, are employed full time in ministry, and hold standing in the ministry of the Christian Church (Disciples of Christ). Primary consideration is given to ministers' wives who will be in institutions of higher education accredited by 1 of the major regionally accrediting bodies for secondary schools and colleges. Evidence of financial need is required.

Financial data The stipend is $1,000 per year.

Duration 1 year.

Number awarded A limited number are awarded each year.

Deadline March of each year.

[107]
ELIZABETH LOWNDES SCHOLARSHIP

Woman's Missionary Union
Attn: WMU Foundation
100 Missionary Ridge
Birmingham, AL 35242
(205) 408-5525   Toll Free: (877) 482-4483
Fax: (205) 408-5508   E-mail: wmufoundation@wmu.org
Web: www.wmufoundation.com

Summary To provide financial assistance to college seniors who are the children of Southern Baptist missionaries.

Eligibility This program is open to Southern Baptist students who are graduating college seniors, have maintained at least a 3.0 GPA in college, and have demonstrated scholarship, leadership, and character while in college. Applicants must be dependents of North American or international missionaries who are under appointment of the North American Mission Board (NAMB) of the Southern Baptist Convention.

Financial data A stipend is awarded (amount not specified).

Duration 1 year.

Number awarded Varies each year.

Deadline February of each year.

[108]
ELLA TACKWOOD FUND

United Methodist Higher Education Foundation
Attn: Scholarships Administrator
1001 19th Avenue South
P.O. Box 340005
Nashville, TN 37203-0005
(615) 340-7385   Toll Free: (800) 811-8110
Fax: (615) 340-7330
E-mail: umhefscholarships@gbhem.org
Web: www.umhef.org/receive.php?id=endowed_funds

Summary To provide financial assistance to Methodist undergraduate and graduate students at Historically Black Colleges and Universities of the United Methodist Church.

Eligibility This program is open to students enrolling as full-time undergraduate and graduate students at the Historically Black Colleges and Universities of the United Methodist Church. Applicants must have been active, full members of a United Methodist Church for at least 1 year prior to applying. They must have a GPA of 2.5 or higher and be able to demonstrate financial need. Along with their application, they must submit a 200-word essay on their involvement and/or leadership responsibilities in their church, school, and community within the last 3 years. U.S. citizenship or permanent resident status is required.

Financial data The stipend is at least $1,000 per year.

Duration 1 year; nonrenewable.

Additional information This program was established in 1985. The qualifying schools are Bennett College for Women, Bethune-Cookman College, Claflin University, Clark Atlanta University, Dillard University, Huston-Tillotson College, Meharry Medical College, Paine College, Philander Smith College, Rust College, and Wiley College.

Number awarded Varies each year. Recently, 3 of these scholarships were awarded.

Deadline May of each year.

[109]
ELMER AND KATHRYN HARVEY SCHOLARSHIP

Wisconsin United Methodist Foundation
750 Windsor Street, Suite 305
P.O. Box 620
Sun Prairie, WI 53590-0620
(608) 837-9582   Toll Free: (888) 903-9863
Fax: (608) 837-2492   E-mail: wumf@wumf.org
Web: www.wumf.org/grantsFF/grantsScholars.html

Summary To provide financial assistance to Methodists from Wisconsin who are interested in attending college in any state to prepare for service in ministry or education.

Eligibility This program is open to members of United Methodist Churches affiliated with the Wisconsin Conference who are enrolled or planning to enroll at a 4-year college or university in any state. Applicants must be preparing for a career of service in ministry or education. Along with their application, they must submit an essay that describes their personal situation and vocational goals, church-related activities and involvement, school and community involvement, and financial plan for funding their education, including any special financial needs.

Financial data Stipends range from $500 to $1,000.

Duration 1 year.

Additional information This program was established in 2006.

Number awarded 1 or more each year.

Deadline March of each year.

[110]
EMIL SLAVIK MEMORIAL SCHOLARSHIP

Slovak Catholic Sokol
Attn: Membership Memorial Scholarship Fund
205 Madison Street
P.O. Box 899
Passaic, NJ 07055-0899
(973) 777-2605   Toll Free: (800) 886-7656
Fax: (973) 779-8245 E-mail: life@slovakcatholicsokol.org
Web: www.slovakcatholicsokol.org

Summary To provide financial assistance to members of the Slovak Catholic Sokol who are working on a degree in specified fields at a college or graduate school in any state.

Eligibility This program is open to members of the Slovak Catholic Sokol who have completed at least 1 semester of college and are currently enrolled full time as an undergraduate or graduate student at an accredited college, university, or professional school in any state. Applicants must have been a member for at least 5 years, have at least $3,000 permanent life insurance coverage, have both parents who are members, and have at least 1 parent who is of Slovak descent. They must be working on a degree in the liberal arts, the sciences, pre-law, pre-medicine, or business.

Financial data The stipend is $2,500 per year.

Duration 1 year; may be renewed 1 additional year.

Additional information Slovak Catholic Sokol was founded as a fraternal benefit society in 1905. It is licensed to operate in the following states: Connecticut, Illinois, Indiana, Massachusetts, Michigan, New Jersey, New York, Ohio, Pennsylvania, and Wisconsin.

Number awarded 1 each year.

Deadline March of each year.

[111]
EMILY S. GARRISON NURSING SCHOLARSHIP

United Methodist Church-Greater New Jersey Conference
Conference Board of Higher Education and Ministry
Attn: Scholarship Committee
1001 Wickapecko Drive
Ocean, NJ 07712-4733
(732) 359-1040   Toll Free: (877) 677-2594, ext. 1040
Fax: (732) 359-1049   E-mail: Lperez@gnjumc.org
Web: www.gnjumc.org/grants_loans_and_scholarship

Summary To provide financial assistance to members of United Methodist Churches in New Jersey who are attending college in any state to prepare for a career in nursing.

Eligibility This program is open to members of congregations affiliated with the Greater New Jersey Conference of the United Methodist Church. Applicants must be enrolled in a program in any state leading to a bachelor's degree in nursing to prepare for a nursing career. Along with their application, they must submit a statement on why they wish to be considered for this scholarship, including information on their financial need and Christian commitment.

Financial data A stipend is awarded (amount not specified).

Duration 1 year.

Additional information This program is sponsored by Greater New Jersey Conference United Methodist Women.

Number awarded 1 each year.

Deadline March of each year.

[112]
EMMETT J. DOERR MEMORIAL DISTINGUISHED SCOUT SCHOLARSHIP

Boy Scouts of America
Attn: National Catholic Committee on Scouting
1325 West Walnut Hill Lane
P.O. Box 152079
Irving, TX 75015-2079
(972) 580-2114   E-mail: nccs@scouting.org
Web: www.nccs-bsa.org/business/EJDscholarship.php

Summary To provide financial assistance for college to Catholic Boy Scouts, Varsity Scouts, and Venturers.

Eligibility This program is open to registered, active members of a Boy Scout troop, Varsity Scout team, or Venturing crew who have received the Eagle Scout or Silver Award and have also earned the Ad Altare Dei or Pope Pius XII Religious Award. Applicants must be practicing Catholics and high school seniors who plan to attend a college or university. They must provide service to their home parish and have held or currently hold a leadership role in a school or community organization other than scouting.

Financial data The stipend is $2,000. Funds are paid directly to an accredited institution of higher learning.

Duration 1 year; nonrenewable.

Number awarded 5 each year.

Deadline February of each year.

[113]
EPISCOPAL DIOCESE OF BETHLEHEM/ GRESSLE FUND

Episcopal Diocese of Bethlehem
Attn: Archdeacon Howard Stringfellow
333 Wyandotte Street
Bethlehem, PA 18015
(610) 691-5655, ext. 222
Toll Free: (800) 358-5655 (within PA)
E-mail: archdeacon@diobeth.org
Web: www.diobeth.org

Summary To provide financial assistance to residents of Pennsylvania who are sons of Episcopal clergy and interested in working on a degree at a college in any state.

Eligibility Applicants must be 1) residents of 1 of the 5 dioceses of Pennsylvania; 2) sons of an Episcopal priest; 3) younger than 20 years of age; and 4) interested in working on a degree at a college in any state. The clergy parent must live in the Commonwealth of Pennsylvania and must be canonically resident in 1 of its dioceses. Preference is given to sons of clergy in the diocese of Bethlehem; only when surplus funds are available can scholarships be awarded to sons of clergy in the other 4 Pennsylvania dioceses. Financial need is considered in the selection process.

Financial data Stipends up to $1,500, depending on need, are available.

Duration 1 year; may be renewed until the recipient reaches the age of 20.

Number awarded   Varies each year.

Deadline   May of each year.

[114]
ERNEST I. AND EURICE MILLER BASS SCHOLARSHIP

United Methodist Higher Education Foundation
Attn: Scholarships Administrator
1001 19th Avenue South
P.O. Box 340005
Nashville, TN 37203-0005
(615) 340-7385   Toll Free: (800) 811-8110
Fax: (615) 340-7330
E-mail: umhefscholarships@gbhem.org
Web: www.umhef.org/receive.php?id=endowed_funds

Summary   To provide financial assistance to undergraduate Methodist students, especially those who are preparing for a career in ministry or other religious vocation.

Eligibility   This program is open to undergraduate students who are enrolled or planning to enroll full time in a degree program at an accredited institution. Applicants must have been active, full members of a United Methodist Church for at least 1 year prior to applying. They must have a GPA of 2.5 or higher and be able to demonstrate financial need. Along with their application, they must submit a 200-word essay on their involvement and/or leadership responsibilities in their church, school, and community within the last 3 years. Preference is given to 1) students preparing for ministry or other religious vocations, and 2) students enrolled or planning to enroll at a United Methodist-related college or university. U.S. citizenship or permanent resident status is required.

Financial data   The stipend is at least $1,000 per year.

Duration   1 year; recipients may reapply.

Number awarded   Varies each year. Recently, 47 of these scholarships were awarded.

Deadline   May of each year.

[115]
ETHEL SNYDER BOOK SCHOLARSHIP

United Methodist Church-Greater New Jersey Conference
Conference Board of Higher Education and Ministry
Attn: Scholarship Committee
1001 Wickapecko Drive
Ocean, NJ 07712-4733
(732) 359-1040   Toll Free: (877) 677-2594, ext. 1040
Fax: (732) 359-1049   E-mail: Lperez@gnjumc.org
Web: www.gnjumc.org/grants_loans_and_scholarship

Summary   To provide financial assistance to daughters of United Methodist clergy from New Jersey who are interested in attending college in any state.

Eligibility   This program is open to daughters of clergy affiliated with the Greater New Jersey Conference of the United Methodist Church. Applicants must be attending or planning to attend a college or university in any state and studying in the field of their choice. Along with their application, they must submit a statement on why they wish to be considered for this scholarship, including information on their financial need and Christian commitment.

Financial data   The stipend is $500.

Duration   1 year.

Number awarded   1 each year.

Deadline   March of each year.

[116]
FANNIE V. WARD SCHOLARSHIP

Order of the Eastern Star-Grand Chapter of Texas
Attn: Education Committee
1503 West Division Street
Arlington, TX 76012
(817) 265-6263
Web: www.grandchapteroftexasoes.org/scholar_forms.asp

Summary   To provide financial assistance to residents of Texas interested in attending college or graduate school in any state, especially those planning to prepare for a career in religious service.

Eligibility   This program is open to residents of Texas who are high school seniors or graduates already enrolled at an accredited college, university, or seminary in any state. Applicants must be interested in working on an undergraduate or graduate degree in any field, although the program especially encourages applications from those planning to prepare for a full-time career as a minister, missionary, director of religious education, Christian youth worker, or church music director. Along with their application, they must submit an essay describing their plans for the future, reasons for applying for the scholarship, and financial status. Undergraduates must be enrolled full time.

Financial data   The stipend is $1,000.

Duration   1 year; nonrenewable.

Number awarded   1 or more each year.

Deadline   February of each year.

[117]
FANNIE WILDER EDUCATIONAL FUND SCHOLARSHIP

Center for Scholarship Administration, Inc.
Attn: Wachovia Accounts
4320 Wade Hampton Boulevard, Suite G
Taylors, SC 29687
Toll Free: (866) 608-0001
E-mail: wachoviascholars@bellsouth.net
Web: www.wachoviascholars.com/wilder/index.php

Summary   To provide financial assistance to women from Georgia who plan to attend college in any state.

Eligibility   This program is open to female residents of Georgia who have a cumulative GPA of 2.5 or higher. Applicants must be attending or planning to attend an accredited 4-year college or university in any state. Selection is based on academic ability, educational goals, career ambitions, and financial need.

Financial data   A stipend is awarded (amount not specified).

Duration   1 year; may be renewed up to 3 additional years or until completion of a bachelor's degree (whichever comes first).

Number awarded   1 or more each year.

Deadline   April of each year.

[118]
FATHER JOSEPH GEARY SCHOLARSHIP

Knights of Columbus-California State Council
15808 Arrow Boulevard, Suite A
Fontana, CA 92335
(909) 434-0460   E-mail: state.office@kofc-ca.org
Web: kofc-ca.org/?t=t_csc_studentscholarships2

Summary To provide financial assistance to members of the Columbian Squires in California who are interested in attending college in any state.

Eligibility This program is open to 1) members of a California Columbian Squires Circle; and 2) former members of a California Columbian Squires Circle who are either current members in good standing or sons of Knights of Columbus members in good standing in a California council. Applicants must be high school seniors or current undergraduates attending or planning to attend a college or university (public or private) in any state. Along with their application, they must submit transcripts, SAT and/or ACT scores, a personal statement, and 3 letters of recommendation.

Financial data The stipend is $1,000.

Duration 1 year.

Number awarded 1 each year.

Deadline February of each year.

[119]
FATHER KREWITT SCHOLARSHIP AWARD

Catholic Kolping Society of America
Attn: Office of the National Administrator
1223 Van Houten Avenue
P.O. Box 4907
Clifton, NJ 07015-4907
(201) 666-1169   Toll Free: (877) 659-7237
Fax: (201) 666-5262   E-mail: patfarkas@optonline.net
Web: www.kolping.org/scholar.htm

Summary To provide financial assistance for college to members of the Catholic Kolping Society of America and their dependents.

Eligibility This program is open to members, children of members, and grandchildren of members who are attending college. Applicants must submit an essay (500 to 1,000 words) on a Christian topic that changes annually; recently, applicants were invited to write on the topic, "What would you like to see as your vision of Kolping USA in the future?"

Financial data The award is $1,000.

Duration The competition is held annually.

Additional information This program was established in 1978.

Number awarded 1 each year.

Deadline February of each year.

[120]
FAYE AND ROBERT LETT SCHOLARSHIP

American Baptist Churches of Ohio
Attn: Ohio Baptist Education Society
136 Galway Drive North
P.O. Box 288
Granville, OH 43023-0288
(740) 587-0804   Fax: (740) 587-0807
E-mail: pastorchris@neo.rr.com
Web: www.abc-ohio.org

Summary To provide funding to African American upper-division and graduate students from Ohio who are interested in preparing for the Baptist ministry at a college or seminary in any state.

Eligibility This program is open to African American residents of Ohio who have completed at least 2 years of study at an accredited college or university in any state and are interested in continuing their education as an upper-division or seminary student. Applicants must 1) hold active membership in a church affiliated with the American Baptist Churches of Ohio or a church dually-aligned with the American Baptist Churches of Ohio; 2) be in the process of preparing for a professional career in Christian ministry (such as a local church pastor, church education, youth or young adult ministries, church music, specialized ministry, chaplaincy, ministry in higher education, or missionary service); 3) be committed to working professionally within the framework of the American Baptist Churches USA; and 4) acknowledge a personal commitment to the Gospel of Jesus Christ, an understanding of the Christian faith, and a definite call to professional Christian ministry as a life work. Financial need must be demonstrated.

Financial data Stipends generally range from $1,000 to $1,500 a year.

Duration 1 year.

Additional information This program was established in 1990.

Number awarded 1 or more each year.

Deadline March of each year.

[121]
FELLOWSHIP OF UNITED METHODISTS IN MUSIC AND WORSHIP ARTS SCHOLARSHIPS

The Fellowship of United Methodists in Music and
    Worship Arts
Attn: Executive Director
P.O. Box 24787
Nashville, TN 37202-4787
(615) 749-6875   Toll Free: (800) 952-8977
Fax: (615) 749-6874   E-mail: fummwa@aol.com
Web: fummwa.affiniscape.com

Summary To provide financial assistance to Methodist and other selected Christian students who are working on an academic degree in music or the worship arts.

Eligibility This program is open to full-time students entering or enrolled at an accredited college, university, or school of theology. Applicants must be studying sacred music, worship, or the arts related to worship. They must have been members of the United Methodist Church (UMC) for at least 1 year immediately before applying. Members of other Christian denominations are also eligible if they have been employed in the UMC for at least 1 year. Applicants must be able to demonstrate exceptional artistic or musical talents, leadership abilities, and outstanding promise of future usefulness to the church in an area of worship and/or music.

Financial data The stipend is $1,000.

Duration 1 year.

Number awarded 1 or more each year.

Deadline February of each year.

[122]
FIRST CATHOLIC SLOVAK LADIES ASSOCIATION COLLEGE SCHOLARSHIPS

First Catholic Slovak Ladies Association
Attn: Director of Fraternal Scholarship Aid
24950 Chagrin Boulevard
Cleveland, OH 44122-5634
(216) 464-8015   Toll Free: (800) 464-4642
Fax: (216) 464-9260   E-mail: info@fcsla.com
Web: www.fcsla.com/scholarship.shtml

Summary To provide financial assistance to college students who are members of the First Catholic Slovak Ladies Association.

Eligibility This program is open to students working on a bachelor's degree at accredited colleges and universities in the United States or Canada; full-time students working on a 2-year associate degree are also eligible. Applicants must have been beneficial members of the First Catholic Slovak Ladies Association for at least 3 years on a $1,000 legal reserve certificate, a $5,000 term certificate, or an annuity certificate. Along with their application, they must submit an autobiographical essay of approximately 500 words that includes a statement of their goals and objectives. Selection is based on academic standing (50%), financial need (20%), family membership in the association (15%), leadership (10%), and extenuating circumstances (5%).

Financial data The stipend is $1,250.

Duration 1 year; recipients may receive only 1 college scholarship, but they may later apply for a graduate scholarship.

Number awarded 117 each year: 58 for freshmen, 27 for sophomores, 16 for juniors, and 16 for seniors.

Deadline February of each year.

[123]
FIRST FREEDOM STUDENT COMPETITION

First Freedom Center
Attn: Student Competition Coordinator
1301 East Main Street
Richmond, VA 23219-3629
(804) 643-1786   Fax: (804) 644-5024
E-mail: competition@firstfreedom.org
Web: firstfreedom.org/education/students.html

Summary To recognize and reward high school students who submit outstanding essays or videos on religious freedom.

Eligibility This competition is open to students in grades 9-12 in public, private, parochial, and home schools in the United States and U.S. territories, along with U.S. students attending high schools overseas, students attending American high schools overseas, foreign exchange students in the United States, and legal aliens and visitors studying in the United States. GED students under 20 years of age are also

eligible. Applicants must be interested in submitting an essay (from 750 to 1,450 words) or a video (from 3 to 5 minutes in play length) on a topic that changes annually but relates to freedom of religion. Selection of the winning essay is based on knowledge of subject matter and historical accuracy (20 points), analysis and interpretation of the topic (15 points), use of supporting evidence (15 points), grammatical conventions (20 points), organization and clarity (15 points), and originality and creativity (15 points). Selection of the winning essay is based on knowledge of subject matter and historical accuracy (20 points), analysis and interpretation of the topic (15 points), use of supporting evidence (15 points), organization and clarity (15 points), originality and creativity (15 points), video quality (15 points), and video script (5 points).

Financial data The prizes are $2,500.

Duration The competition is held annually.

Number awarded 2 each year: 1 for an essay and 1 for a video.

Deadline November of each year.

[124]
FIRST NATIONAL BANK OF AMHERST CENTENNIAL EDUCATIONAL SCHOLARSHIPS

Community Foundation of Western Massachusetts
Attn: Scholarship Department
1500 Main Street, Suite 2300
P.O. Box 15769
Springfield, MA 01115
(413) 732-2858   Fax: (413) 733-8565
E-mail: scholar@communityfoundation.org
Web: www.communityfoundation.org

Summary To provide financial assistance for undergraduate study to residents of designated towns in Massachusetts and to graduate students at designated institutions in the state.

Eligibility This program is open to 1) high school seniors from Northampton, Hadley, and Amherst (Massachusetts), and 2) students working on an undergraduate degree at the University of Massachusetts, Amherst College, or Hampshire College. Applicants must submit their most recent academic transcript and documentation of financial need.

Financial data Stipend amounts vary, but they are capped at a cumulative total of $4,000 for community college students or $8,000 for other schools. Funds are paid directly to the student's institution.

Duration 1 year; recipients may reapply.

Number awarded Varies each year. Recently, 4 of these scholarships were awarded.

Deadline March of each year.

[125]
FIRST PRESBYTERIAN CHURCH SCHOLARSHIP FUND

First Presbyterian Church
Attn: Scholarship Fund Program
709 South Boston Avenue
Tulsa, OK 74119-1629
(918) 584-4701   Fax: (918) 584-5233
E-mail: TBriscoe@firstchurchtulsa.org
Web: www.firstchurchtulsa.org/scholarships.htm

Summary To provide financial assistance to Presbyterian students interested in working on an undergraduate or graduate degree in any field.

Eligibility To be eligible for this program, students must be communicant members of the Presbyterian Church (USA), be working on an undergraduate or graduate degree at an accredited institution, and have at least a 2.0 GPA. Priority is given first to members of the First Presbyterian Church (in Tulsa), second to applicants in the Presbytery of Eastern Oklahoma, third to applicants in the Synod of the Sun (Arkansas, Louisiana, Oklahoma, and Texas), and fourth to members of the Presbyterian Church at large. Selection is based on academic merit, academic or career intent, church or religious involvement, and financial need.

Financial data Stipends range from $500 to $2,000. Funds are paid directly to the recipient's school.

Duration 1 year; recipients may reapply.

Additional information This program was established in 1988. It includes the following named funds (each of which includes additional restrictions): the Harry Allen Scholarship Fund, the Ethel Frances Crate Scholarship Fund, the Elsa Everett Scholarship Fund, the Cydna Ann Huffstetler Scholarship Fund, and the Clarence Warren Scholarship Fund.

Number awarded Varies each year. Recently, this program awarded 12 unrestricted scholarships and another 14 scholarships with various restrictions.

Deadline April of each year.

[126]
FLEMING FAMILY FOUNDATION SCHOLARSHIPS

Fleming Family Foundation
Attn: Randy Fleming, President
P.O. Box 410
Springfield, NE 68059
(402) 210-4885　　　　　　　Fax: (402) 253-2208
E-mail: auctioneer_32@msn.com
Web: www.umcneb.org/pages/detail/114

Summary To provide financial assistance to Methodists from Nebraska interested in entering full-time Christian service by working on an undergraduate or graduate degree at a school in any state.

Eligibility This program is open to residents of Nebraska who are members of a congregation of the United Methodist Church (UMC). Applicants must be attending or planning to attend a college or university in any state to work on an undergraduate or graduate degree as preparation for a career in full-time Christian service. Along with their application, they must submit brief essays on 1) their participation in the life of their school, community, church, and similar organizations; 2) what influenced them in selecting their college and their career goals; 3) where they see themselves professionally after graduation; and 4) their financial need.

Financial data The stipend is $1,000.

Duration 1 year.

Number awarded Varies each year.

Deadline May of each year.

[127]
FLORIDA BAPTIST FOUNDATION STUDENT LOANS

Florida Baptist Foundation
Attn: Student Loan Committee
1320 Hendricks Avenue, Suite 2
Jacksonville, FL 32207
(904) 346-0325, ext. 221
Toll Free: (800) 780-0325, ext. 221
Fax: (904) 346-0414　　　　E-mail: info@floridabaptist.org
Web: www.floridabaptist.org/studentloans

Summary To provide academic loans for college or seminary to members of Southern Baptist churches in Florida.

Eligibility This loan program is open to residents of Florida who are members of a Southern Baptist church. Applicants must be enrolled (or planning to enroll) full time at 1) an accredited college or university in any state, or 2) a Southern Baptist seminary. They must submit a 1-page statement about themselves, their family, and their future plans. Selection is based on financial need, academic performance, Christian character, and church participation.

Financial data The maximum loan is $2,500 per year or $6,000 in a lifetime. Interest payments, at a rate based on the outstanding principal balance, are due monthly while the student is in school. Principal payments begin 6 months after completion of or leaving school and must be repaid within 48 months.

Duration 1 year; may be renewed.

Additional information Loans to selected seminary students are made from the Gross Loan Fund. Loans to other seminary students and undergraduates are made from the Cunningham Loan Fund.

Number awarded Varies each year. The Gross Loan Fund provides loans to 6 seminary students each year. The number of loans from the Cunningham Loan Fund varies.

Deadline Deadline not specified.

[128]
FLORIDA EAGLE SCOUT OF THE YEAR SCHOLARSHIPS

American Legion
Department of Florida
1912A Lee Road
P.O. Box 547859
Orlando, FL 32854-7859
(407) 295-2631　　　　　　　Fax: (407) 299-0901
E-mail: fal@fllegion.newsouth.net
Web: www.floridalegion.org

Summary To recognize and reward, with scholarships for college in any state, Eagle Scouts who are members of a troop associated with the American Legion in Florida or a son or grandson of a member of the Legion in the state.

Eligibility This program is open to Florida high school students who have earned the Eagle Scout award and religious emblem. Applicants must 1) be a registered, active member of a Boy Scout troop, Varsity Scout team, or Venturing Crew chartered to an American Legion Post or Auxiliary unit; or 2) be a registered active member of a duly chartered Boy Scout troop, Varsity Scout team, or Venturing Crew and the son or grandson of a Legionnaire or Auxiliary member. Applicants must be interested in attending a college or university in any state. They must be able to demonstrate practical citizenship in church, school, Scouting, and community.

Financial data The winner receives a $2,500 scholarship, first runner-up a $1,500 scholarship, second runner-up a $1,000 scholarship, and third runner-up a $500 scholarship.

Duration The awards are presented annually.

Number awarded 4 each year.

Deadline February of each year.

[129]
FLORIDA EASTERN STAR TRAINING AWARDS FOR RELIGIOUS LEADERSHIP

Order of the Eastern Star-Grand Chapter of Florida
Attn: Grand Secretary
P.O. Box 97
Bonifay, FL 32425-0097
(850) 547-9199　　　　　　　Fax: (850) 547-9299
E-mail: grandsecretary@floridaoes.org
Web: www.floridaoes.org

Summary To provide financial assistance to residents of Florida who are attending a college or seminary in any state to prepare for a career in religious leadership.

Eligibility This program is open to residents of Florida who are currently enrolled full time at an accredited college or seminary in any state. Applicants must be taking classes that will lead to a degree in a field of religious leadership, as a minister, missionary, director of religious education, Christian youth worker, or church music director. They must have a GPA of 2.0 or higher and a record of good moral character. Selection is based on academic record, character, leadership in Christian activities, citizenship, and financial need. Preference is given to students who are at least a junior in college.

Financial data A stipend is awarded (amount not specified).

Duration 1 year.

Number awarded 1 or more each year.

Deadline May of each year for fall semester; November of each year for spring semester.

[130]
FORREST AND SYBILLIA FUHR MEMORIAL SCHOLARSHIP

Alaska Baptist Foundation
1750 O'Malley Road
Anchorage, AK 99507
(907) 770-0581　　　Toll Free: (800) 883-9627 (within AK)
Fax: (907) 344-7044
E-mail: foundation@alaskabaptistfoundation.com
Web: www.alaskabaptistfoundation.com/fuhr-scholarship

Summary To provide financial assistance to members of Southern Baptist churches in Alaska who are interested in attending college in any state.

Eligibility This program is open to members of churches in good standing with the Alaska Baptist Convention who have been residents of Alaska for at least 2 years. Applicants must be attending or planning to attend an accredited college or university in any state. Financial need is considered in the selection process.

Financial data The stipend is $760 per year. Funds are paid directly to the school to be used for tuition, room and board, fees, and books.

Duration 1 year; may be renewed.

Number awarded 5 each year.

Deadline April of each year.

[131]
FOURTH DEGREE PRO DEO AND PRO PATRIA SCHOLARSHIP PROGRAM

Knights of Columbus
Attn: Department of Scholarships
P.O. Box 1670
New Haven, CT 06507-0901
(203) 752-4332　　　　　　　Fax: (203) 772-2696
E-mail: info@kofc.org
Web: www.kofc.org/un/en/scholarships/prodeo_us.html

Summary To provide financial assistance to entering freshmen at Catholic colleges and universities.

Eligibility Eligible are students entering their freshman year in a program leading to a baccalaureate degree at a Catholic college or university in the United States, including Catholic University of America; applicants must be members in good standing of the Columbian Squires or Knights of Columbus, or the son or daughter of a member, or the child of a deceased member who was in good standing at the time of death. Selection is based on secondary school record, class rank, and aptitude test scores.

Financial data The stipend is $1,500 per year.

Duration 1 year; may be renewed up to 3 additional years upon evidence of satisfactory academic performance.

Number awarded 62 each year, of which 12 are to attend Catholic University of America and 50 are to attend other Catholic institutions.

Deadline February of each year.

[132]
FRANCES NELSON SCHOLARSHIP

United Methodist Church-Greater New Jersey Conference
Conference Board of Higher Education and Ministry
Attn: Scholarship Committee
1001 Wickapecko Drive
Ocean, NJ 07712-4733
(732) 359-1040　　　　Toll Free: (877) 677-2594, ext. 1040
Fax: (732) 359-1049　　　　E-mail: Lperez@gnjumc.org
Web: www.gnjumc.org/grants_loans_and_scholarship

Summary To provide financial assistance to members of United Methodist Churches in New Jersey who are enrolled at a college in any state to prepare for a career in Christian service.

Eligibility This program is open to members of congregations affiliated with the Greater New Jersey Conference of the United Methodist Church. Applicants must be enrolled or planning to enroll in a program in any state to prepare them for full-time Christian service following graduation. Along with their application, they must submit a statement on why they wish to be considered for this scholarship, including information on their financial need and Christian commitment.

Financial data A stipend is awarded (amount not specified).

Duration 1 year. May be renewed up to 3 additional years upon reapplication; previous recipients are given priority.

Additional information This program is sponsored by Greater New Jersey Conference United Methodist Women.

Number awarded 1 each year.

Deadline March of each year.

[133]
FRANCIS P. MATTHEWS AND JOHN E. SWIFT EDUCATIONAL TRUST SCHOLARSHIPS

Knights of Columbus
Attn: Department of Scholarships
P.O. Box 1670
New Haven, CT 06507-0901
(203) 752-4332   Fax: (203) 772-2696
E-mail: info@kofc.org
Web: www.kofc.org/en/scholarships/matthews_swift.html

Summary To provide financial assistance at Catholic colleges or universities in any country to children of disabled or deceased veterans, law enforcement officers, or firemen who are/were also Knights of Columbus members.

Eligibility This program is open to children of members of the sponsoring organization who are high school seniors in any country planning to attend a 4-year Catholic college or university in their country. The parent must be a member of Knights of Columbus who 1) was serving in the military forces of their country and was killed by hostile action or wounded by hostile action, resulting within 2 years in permanent and total disability; 2) was a full-time law enforcement officer who became disabled or died as a result of criminal violence; or 3) was a fire fighter who became disabled or deceased in the line of duty.

Financial data The amounts of the awards vary but are designed to cover tuition, to a maximum of $25,000 per year, at the Catholic college or university of the recipient's choice in the country of their residence. Funds are not available for room, board, books, fees, transportation, dues, computers, or supplies.

Duration 1 year; may be renewed up to 3 additional years.

Additional information This program was established in 1944 to provide scholarships to the children of Knights who became totally and permanently disabled through service during World War II. It has been modified on many occasions, most recently in 2007 to its current requirements.

Number awarded Varies each year.

Deadline February of each year.

[134]
FRANK L. GOULARTE ENDOWED SCHOLARSHIPS

Knights of Columbus
Attn: Department of Scholarships
P.O. Box 1670
New Haven, CT 06507-0901
(203) 752-4332   Fax: (203) 772-2696
E-mail: info@kofc.org
Web: www.kofc.org/un/en/scholarships/endowed.html

Summary To provide financial assistance to freshmen entering Catholic colleges and universities.

Eligibility Eligible are students entering their freshman year in a program leading to a bachelor's degree at a Catholic college or university in the United States; applicants must be members in good standing of the Columbian Squires or Knights of Columbus, or the child of a member, or the child of a deceased member who was in good standing at the time of

death. Selection is based on secondary school record, class rank, financial need, and aptitude test scores.

Financial data The stipend is $1,500 per year.

Duration 1 year; may be renewed up to 3 additional years upon evidence of satisfactory academic performance.

Additional information This program was established in 2000.

Number awarded 1 or more each year, depending on the availability of funds.

Deadline February of each year.

[135]
FRANK WATTS SCHOLARSHIP

Watts Charity Association, Inc.
6245 Bristol Parkway, Suite 224
Culver City, CA 90230
(323) 671-0394   Fax: (323) 778-2613
E-mail: wattscharity@aol.com
Web: 4watts.tripod.com/id5.html

Summary To provide financial assistance to upper-division African Americans interested in preparing for a career as a minister.

Eligibility This program is open to U.S. citizens of African American descent who are enrolled full time as a college or university junior. Applicants must be studying to become a minister. They must have a GPA of 3.0 or higher, be between 17 and 24 years of age, and be able to demonstrate that they intend to continue their education for at least 2 years. Along with their application, they must submit 1) a 1-paragraph statement on why they should be awarded a Watts Foundation scholarship, and 2) a 1- to 2-page essay on a specific type of cancer, based either on how it has impacted their life or on researched information.

Financial data A stipend is awarded (amount not specified).

Duration 1 year.

Additional information Royce R. Watts, Sr. established the Watts Charity Association after he learned he had cancer in 2001.

Number awarded 1 each year.

Deadline May of each year.

[136]
FRED J. STUART SCHOLARSHIP OF EXCELLENCE

African Methodist Episcopal Church
Fifth Episcopal District Lay Organization
400 Corporate Pointe, Suite 300
Culver City, CA 90230
(424) 750-3065   Fax: (424) 750-3067
E-mail: AmecEpiscopal5@aol.com
Web: www.amec5th.net/scholarship_of_excellence.aspx

Summary To provide financial assistance to members of African Methodist Episcopal (AME) churches in its Fifth Episcopal District who are interested in attending college in any state.

Eligibility This program is open to residents of the AME Fifth Episcopal District (Alaska, Arizona, California, Colorado, Idaho, Kansas, Missouri, Montana, Nebraska, Nevada, New Mexico, North Dakota, Oregon, South Dakota, Utah, Washington, and Wyoming) who are graduating high school seniors or students currently enrolled at an accredited institution of higher learning in any state. Applicants must have been a member of an AME church for at least 12 months and have been an active member of its Lay Organization or other lay-sponsored programs. High school seniors must have a GPA of 3.0 or higher; students already enrolled in college must have a GPA of 2.5 or higher. Along with their application, they must submit a 250-word personal essay that describes their long-range plans, community and church involvement, accomplishments or special awards, challenges they have faced, and how they responded. Selection is based on that essay, academic record, letters of recommendation, accomplishments, and Lay Organization participation.

Financial data The stipend is $1,000.

Duration 1 year.

Number awarded 1 each year.

Deadline May of each year.

[137]
GENE ROGER AND MILDRED WIMBERLY KIZER SCHOLARSHIP

South Carolina United Methodist Foundation
P.O. Box 5087
Columbia, SC 29250-5087
(803) 771-9125   Fax: (803) 771-9135
E-mail: scumf@bellsouth.net
Web: www.umcsc.org/scholarships.html

Summary To provide financial assistance to Methodist students from South Carolina who are attending college or graduate school in any state to prepare for a career in Christian service.

Eligibility This program is open to residents of South Carolina who are preparing for full-time Christian service in the United Methodist Church (i.e., those ministries of the Church for which ordination, consecration, or certification is required). Applicants must be enrolled at a college, seminary, theological school, or graduate school in any state approved by the University Senate of the United Methodist Church. Preference is given to members of Indian Field, St. George, North, or Saint Andrews (Orangeburg) United Methodist Churches. Financial need is a significant factor in the selection process.

Financial data A stipend is awarded (amount not specified).

Duration 1 year.

Additional information This scholarship was established by the South Carolina Conference of the United Methodist Church in 1998.

Number awarded 1 or more each year.

Deadline April of each year.

[138]
GEORGE AND LYNNA GENE COOK SCHOLARSHIP

Lincoln Community Foundation
215 Centennial Mall South, Suite 100
Lincoln, NE 68508
(402) 474-2345   Toll Free: (888) 448-4668
Fax: (402) 476-8532   E-mail: lcf@lcf.org
Web: www.lcf.org/page29412.cfm

Summary To provide financial assistance for college to Nebraska residents who are members of the First Church of God, attending a college or university in any state, and preparing for a career in ministry or education.

Eligibility This program is open to Nebraska residents who are preparing for a career in ministry or education at a qualified college or university in any state. Applicants must be members of First Church of God congregations in Nebraska that are affiliated with the church body headquartered in Anderson, Indiana. They must have a GPA of 3.0 or higher and be either a graduating high school senior or a current college student. Preference is given to those who demonstrate financial need.

Financial data Stipends provided by the foundation generally range from $500 to $2,000.

Duration 1 year.

Number awarded 1 or more each year.

Deadline March of each year.

[139]
GEORGE AND NAOUMA GIOLES SCHOLARSHIP

Greek Orthodox Archdiocese of America
Attn: Office of the Chancellor
8 East 79th Street
New York, NY 10075
(212) 774-0513   Fax: (212) 774-0251
E-mail: scholarships@goarch.org
Web: www.goarch.org

Summary To provide financial assistance to high school seniors and current undergraduates who are of the Greek Orthodox faith and plan to study the sciences, business, or the arts.

Eligibility The program is open to high school seniors and current undergraduates who are enrolled or planning to enroll full time at an accredited college or university in the United States. Applicants must be of the Greek Orthodox faith, preferably of Greek descent, and U.S. citizens or permanent residents. They must have a GPA of 3.0 or higher and an SAT score of at least 1500 (or an equivalent score on the ACT). Preference is given to applicants who are orphans and to those who are interested in studying the sciences, business, or the arts (with at least 1 scholarship reserved for a student majoring in journalism). Along with their application, they must submit a 500-word essay on 1 of the following topics: 1) how their background as an orphan, or as a person of Greek descent, or as a Greek Orthodox Christian, has affected their life; 2) how Hellenes abroad, or Greek Orthodox Christians in the United States, can retain their religious and ethnic identity for generations to come; or 3) how they will use their Hellenic culture, their Greek Orthodox faith, and their planned studies to contribute to the betterment of humanity. Financial need is considered in the selection process.

Financial data The stipend is $1,500.

Duration 1 year.

Number awarded 5 each year, including 1 reserved for an applicant studying journalism.

Deadline April of each year.

[140]
GEORGE WRAY MEMORIAL SCHOLARSHIP FUND

San Antonio Area Foundation
Attn: Scholarship Funds Program Officer
110 Broadway, Suite 230
San Antonio, TX 78205
(210) 228-3759   Fax: (210) 225-1980
E-mail: buresti@ssafdn.org
Web: www.saafdn.org/NetCommunity/Page.aspx?pid=257

Summary To provide financial assistance to Judeo-Christian graduates of high schools in Texas who are attending college in any state to prepare for a career in the health care field.

Eligibility This program is open to graduates of high schools in Texas who are members of the Judeo-Christian faith. Applicants must be preparing for a career in the health care field; have a strong background in science; be in the upper 15% of their graduating class; and be able to demonstrate community service work, excellent moral character, and financial need. U.S. citizenship is required.

Financial data Stipends vary; recently, they averaged approximately $2,800.

Duration 1 year; may be renewed.

Number awarded Varies each year. Recently, 8 of these scholarships were awarded.

Deadline February of each year.

[141]
GEORGIA BAPTIST MINISTERIAL EDUCATION FUND

Georgia Baptist Convention
Attn: Education Commission
6405 Sugarloaf Parkway
Duluth, GA 30097
(770) 936-5240   Toll Free: (800) 746-4422, ext. 240
E-mail: pschildecker@gabaptist.org
Web: gabaptist.org

Summary To provide scholarship/loans to students at Georgia Baptist colleges who are planning to enter a church ministry vocation.

Eligibility This program is open to students attending 1 of the 3 Baptist colleges in Georgia. Applicants must be interested in preparing for a church ministry vocation, including the pastorate, missionary service, and church staff ministry; students considering bivocational ministry are also eligible. They must apply through the financial aid director at their college.

Financial data The amount of the assistance depends on the number of recipients and the availability of funds; recently, the maximum award was $564 per term. The funding is a grant to students eventually serving in a ministerial vocation. It must be repaid if the student does not enter a church-related vocation and continue in ministry for 3 years.

Duration 1 year; may be renewed.

Additional information The eligible colleges are Brewton-Parker College (Mount Vernon), Shorter University (Rome), and Truett-McConnell College (Cleveland).

Number awarded Varies each year. Recently, nearly 100 students received this assistance.

Deadline Deadline not specified.

[142]
GEORGIA BAPTIST STUDENT ACHIEVEMENT AWARDS

Georgia Baptist Convention
Attn: Education Commission
6405 Sugarloaf Parkway
Duluth, GA 30097
(770) 936-5240   Toll Free: (800) 746-4422, ext. 240
E-mail: pschildecker@gabaptist.org
Web: gabaptist.org

Summary To provide financial assistance to high school seniors who are members of Georgia Baptist churches interested in attending a Georgia Baptist college.

Eligibility This program is open to graduating high school seniors who are active members of churches affiliated with the Georgia Baptist Convention. Applicants must be interested in attending 1 of the 3 Baptist colleges in Georgia. They must be nominated by their pastor. Selection is based primarily on academic achievement, but extracurricular activities and church involvement are also considered.

Financial data The stipend is $1,000 per year.

Duration 4 years.

Additional information The eligible colleges are Brewton-Parker College (Mount Vernon), Shorter University (Rome), and Truett-McConnell College (Cleveland).

Number awarded 30 each year.

Deadline October of each year.

[143]
GERALD A. WIEWEL VOCATION SCHOLARSHIP

Western Catholic Union
510 Maine Street
P.O. Box 410
Quincy, IL 62306-0410
(217) 223-9721   Toll Free: (800) 223-4WCU
Fax: (217) 223-9726   E-mail: info@wculife.com
Web: www.westerncatholicunion.org/benefits.htm

Summary To provide financial assistance to members of Western Catholic Union (WCU) who are preparing for a religious vocation.

Eligibility This program is open to WCU members who are enrolled in a seminary or convent to prepare for a religious vocation. Applicants must submit a 500-word essay on why they are qualified to receive this grant, including a statement of their future goals and aspirations. Selection is based on that essay, academic achievement, religious activities, community involvement, and financial need.

Financial data The stipend is $1,000.

Duration 1 year.

Additional information Western Catholic Union was established in 1877 as a fraternal benefit society.

Number awarded 3 each year.

Deadline February of each year.

[144]
GERNENZ-SHURTLEFF SCHOLARSHIP

American Baptist Churches of the Great Rivers Region
Attn: Scholarship Committee
3940 Pintail Drive
P.O. Box 3786
Springfield, IL 62708
(217) 726-7366   Fax: (888) 922-2477
E-mail: grrabc@abcgrr.org
Web: www.abcgrr.org/ministries/scholarshipinformation.htm

Summary To provide financial assistance for college or seminary to members of American Baptist Churches in Illinois and Missouri.

Eligibility This program is open to members of American Baptist Churches of the Great Rivers Region, which covers Missouri and all of Illinois except for Cook, DuPage, and Lake counties. Applicants must be nominated by their pastor or other professional leader of their church and attending or planning to attend an accredited college, university, or seminary. College students may be majoring in any field, but all applicants must show evidence of potential for Christian service in the world today, regardless of their vocation. Financial need and potential for service are more important factors in the selection process than present academic standing.

Financial data The amount of the stipend varies each year.

Duration 1 year.

Number awarded Varies each year.

Deadline March of each year.

[145]
GIRL SCOUT ACHIEVEMENT AWARD

American Legion Auxiliary
8945 North Meridian Street
Indianapolis, IN 46260
(317) 569-4500   Fax: (317) 569-4502
E-mail: alahq@legion-aux.org
Web: www.legion-aux.org

Summary To provide financial assistance for college to members of the Girl Scouts.

Eligibility This program is open to Girl Scouts who have received the Gold Award; are high school juniors or seniors; are active members of a religious institution (and have received the appropriate religious emblem at the Cadette or Senior Scout level); have demonstrated practical citizenship in their religious institution, school, Girl Scouting, and community; and submit at least 4 letters of recommendation, with 1 letter required from a representative of each of the following: church, school, community, and Scout troop. Candidates must submit a 500-word essay describing their Gold Award project and explaining why they chose the project they did and how it made an impact on them and their community. They must be nominated at the local level; those selected at the state level compete at the national level.

Financial data The stipend is $1,000.

Duration 1 year; the award must be utilized within 1 year of high school graduation.

Number awarded 1 each year.

Deadline Applications must be submitted to a local American Legion Auxiliary Unit by March of each year.

[146]
GLOSTER B. CURRENT, SR. SCHOLARSHIP

United Methodist Church-New York Annual Conference
Attn: Gloster B. Current Scholarship Committee
c/o Rev. Dr. John E. Carrington
50 Ralph Road
New Rochelle, NY 10804
(917) 617-4360   Fax: (914) 235-7313
E-mail: johnecarrington@aol.com
Web: www.nyac.com/pages/detail/1725

Summary To provide financial assistance to Methodist undergraduate students of African descent from any state who are preparing for a career in public service.

Eligibility This program is open to members of United Methodist Church (UMC) congregations in any state who are of African descent. Applicants must be enrolled or planning to enroll at an accredited institution of higher education in any state to work on an undergraduate degree in a field of public service (e.g., the ministry, social work, health care, or government service). They must be between 16 and 25 years of age and have a GPA of at least "C" in high school and/or 2.75 or higher in college. Along with their application, they must submit a 1-page essay on their interest in a career of public service. Selection is based on academic record, leadership potential, a letter of recommendation from a UMC local pastor, and financial need.

Financial data The stipend is $1,000.

Duration 1 year; nonrenewable.

Additional information This program was established in 2003.

Number awarded 1 or more each year.

Deadline April of each year.

[147]
GOLDEN CROSS HEALTH CARE SCHOLARSHIP

United Methodist Church-South Carolina Conference
Attn: Connectional Ministries
4908 Colonial Drive
Columbia, SC 29203-6070
(803) 786-9486, ext. 313
Toll Free: (888) 678-6272, ext. 313
Fax: (803) 691-0220   E-mail: tfulmer@umcsc.org
Web: www.umcsc.org/scholarships2.html

Summary To provide financial assistance to members of United Methodist Churches in South Carolina who are working on a degree in nursing or other health care field at a school in any state.

Eligibility This program is open to members of United Methodist Churches in South Carolina who have completed at least 1 semester of work on a degree in nursing at a school in any state. Students enrolled in such programs as physical therapy or medical technology may also be considered, if funding is available. Preference is given to undergraduates who are applying for the first time. Applicants must have a grade point average of "C" or better and be able to demonstrate financial need. Along with their application, they must submit a brief statement on why they want to be a nurse.

Financial data A stipend is awarded (amount not specified).

Duration 1 year.

Number awarded 1 or more each year.

Deadline July of each year for fall semester; November of each year for spring semester; April of each year for summer.

[148]
GRANT K. PULEN SCHOLARSHIP

The Fellowship of United Methodists in Music and
  Worship Arts-Florida Chapter
c/o Luke Nash
5836-4 Queen Elizabeth Way
Fort Myers, FL 33907
E-mail: bigluke@peganet.com
Web: www.floridafellowship.org/scholarship.htm

Summary To provide financial assistance to undergraduate students majoring in music who are members of a United Methodist Church in Florida.

Eligibility This program is open to high school seniors and current undergraduate students who are majoring in music. Applicants must have been a member of a United Methodist Church in the Florida Conference for at least 1 year prior to applying. Preference is given to applicants currently active in religious and music activities in churches, schools, or other organizations. Selection is based on health, emotional stability, Christian character, talent, leadership ability, promise of future usefulness to the Methodist Church, transcripts, 3 letters of recommendation, and financial need.

Financial data The stipend is $1,500 per year.

Duration 1 year; may be renewed.

Number awarded 1 each year.

Deadline May of each year.

[149]
GREATER NEW JERSEY CONFERENCE
EDUCATIONAL SOCIETY LOANS

United Methodist Church-Greater New Jersey Conference
Conference Board of Higher Education and Ministry
Attn: Scholarship Committee
1001 Wickapecko Drive
Ocean, NJ 07712-4733
(732) 359-1040   Toll Free: (877) 677-2594, ext. 1040
Fax: (732) 359-1049   E-mail: Lperez@gnjumc.org
Web: www.gnjumc.org/grants_loans_and_scholarship

Summary To provide loans for college to United Methodist undergraduate and seminary students from New Jersey who are preparing for ministry at a school in any state.

Eligibility This program is open to active members of United Methodist Churches affiliated with the Greater New Jersey Conference. Applicants must be enrolled as undergraduate or seminary students at a school in any state and planning to enter the Christian ministry of the conference. Selection is based on academic achievement, financial need, and participation in church activities.

Financial data Loans up to $2,000 per year are available.

Duration 1 year; may be renewed.

Number awarded Varies each year.

Deadline March of each year.

[150]
GREATER NEW JERSEY CONFERENCE MERIT
AWARDS

United Methodist Church-Greater New Jersey Conference
Conference Board of Higher Education and Ministry
Attn: Scholarship Committee
1001 Wickapecko Drive
Ocean, NJ 07712-4733
(732) 359-1040   Toll Free: (877) 677-2594, ext. 1040
Fax: (732) 359-1049   E-mail: Lperez@gnjumc.org
Web: www.gnjumc.org/grants_loans_and_scholarship

Summary To provide financial assistance to United Methodist students from New Jersey who are interested in attending a Methodist college in any state.

Eligibility This program is open to students who are members of United Methodist Churches affiliated with the Greater New Jersey Conference. Applicants must be attending or planning to attend a United Methodist college or university in any state. They must be nominated by their local church. Along with their application, they must submit a statement on why they wish to be considered for this scholarship, including information on their financial need and Christian commitment. Selection is based on academic achievement, church involvement, special vocational preparation for ministry or other service, and financial need.

Financial data A stipend is awarded (amount not specified).

Duration 1 year.

Number awarded Varies each year.

Deadline March of each year.

[151]
GREATER NEW JERSEY CONFERENCE TRUST
FUND SCHOLARSHIPS

United Methodist Church-Greater New Jersey Conference
Conference Board of Higher Education and Ministry
Attn: Scholarship Committee
1001 Wickapecko Drive
Ocean, NJ 07712-4733
(732) 359-1040   Toll Free: (877) 677-2594, ext. 1040
Fax: (732) 359-1049   E-mail: Lperez@gnjumc.org
Web: www.gnjumc.org/grants_loans_and_scholarship

Summary To provide financial assistance to Methodist students from New Jersey interested in working on an undergraduate degree at a school in any state.

Eligibility This program is open to undergraduate students at colleges and universities in any state who are members of congregations affiliated with the Greater New Jersey Conference of the United Methodist Church. Along with their application, they must submit a statement on why they wish to be considered for this scholarship, including information on their financial need and Christian commitment. Selection is based on academic achievement, financial need, and participation in church activities.

Financial data A stipend is awarded (amount not specified).

Duration 1 year.

Number awarded Varies each year.

Deadline March of each year.

[152]
HANA SCHOLARSHIPS

United Methodist Church
Attn: General Board of Higher Education and Ministry
Office of Loans and Scholarships
1001 19th Avenue South
P.O. Box 340007
Nashville, TN 37203-0007
(615) 340-7344   Fax: (615) 340-7367
E-mail: umscholar@gbhem.org
Web: www.gbhem.org/loansandscholarships

Summary   To provide financial assistance to upper-division and graduate Methodist students who are of Hispanic, Asian, Native American, Alaska Native, or Pacific Islander ancestry.

Eligibility   This program is open to full-time juniors, seniors, and graduate students at accredited colleges and universities in the United States who have been active, full members of a United Methodist Church (UMC) for at least 1 year prior to applying. Applicants must have at least 1 parent who is Hispanic, Asian, Native American, Alaska Native, or Pacific Islander. They must be able to demonstrate involvement in their Hispanic, Asian, or Native American (HANA) community in the UMC. Selection is based on that involvement, academic ability (GPA of at least 2.85 for undergraduates or 3.0 for graduate students), and financial need. U.S. citizenship or permanent resident status is required.

Financial data   The maximum stipend is $3,000 for undergraduates or $5,000 for graduate students.

Duration   1 year; recipients may reapply.

Number awarded   50 each year.

Deadline   March of each year.

[153]
HANDY SIMMONS SCHOLARSHIP

African Methodist Episcopal Church
Women's Missionary Society
c/o Mrs. Braunwin H. Camp
1250 Heritage Lakes Drive
Mableton, GA 30126
(770) 739-1069   E-mail: bhcamp@yahoo.com
Web: www.wmsscholarships.com

Summary   To provide financial assistance to members of African Methodist Episcopal (AME) churches who are interested in attending college.

Eligibility   This program is open to active members of AME churches and its Young People's Department (YPD). Applicants must be high school seniors or students currently working on an associate, technical, or bachelor's degree in any field. Along with their application, they must submit an essay of 500 to 1,000 words on a topic that changes annually but relates to Christian themes. Selection is based on that essay, academic performance, quality and level of church participation, leadership and extracurricular activities, letters of reference, and financial need.

Financial data   Stipends range from $300 to $1,000.

Duration   1 year.

Number awarded   1 or more each year.

Deadline   January of each year.

[154]
HAROLD O. LONG SCHOLARSHIP

American Baptist Churches of the Great Rivers Region
Attn: Scholarship Committee
3940 Pintail Drive
P.O. Box 3786
Springfield, IL 62708
(217) 726-7366   Fax: (888) 922-2477
E-mail: grrabc@abcgrr.org
Web: www.abcgrr.org/ministries/scholarshipinformation.htm

Summary   To provide financial assistance for college or seminary to members of American Baptist Churches in Illinois and Missouri.

Eligibility   This program is open to members of American Baptist Churches of the Great Rivers Region, which covers Missouri and all of Illinois except for Cook, DuPage, and Lake counties. Applicants must be entering or attending an American Baptist-related college, university, or seminary to prepare for full-time Christian ministry in the American Baptist Church. Selection is based on financial need and academic achievement. First priority is given to members of the First Baptist Church of Decatur, Illinois; second preference is given to members of American Baptist Churches in Area II (which covers the Illinois cities of Decatur, Jacksonville, Quincy, and Springfield); third preference is given to applicants from other churches in the Great Rivers region.

Financial data   The stipend is at least $1,000 per year.

Duration   1 year; may be renewed if the recipient maintains a GPA of 2.0 or higher.

Number awarded   Varies each year.

Deadline   March of each year.

[155]
HARRIET ALICEA SCHOLARSHIP FUND

United Methodist Church-Wisconsin Conference
Attn: Board of Higher Education and Campus Ministry
750 Windsor Street
P.O. Box 620
Sun Prairie, WI 53590-0620
(608) 837-7328   Toll Free: (888) 240-7328
Fax: (608) 837-8547
Web: www.wisconsinumc.org

Summary   To provide financial assistance to Native American and Hispanic members of United Methodist churches in Wisconsin interested in preparing for ministry at an institution in any state.

Eligibility   This program is open to Native American and Hispanic members of congregations of the United Methodist Church (UMC) in Wisconsin. Applicants must be involved in ministry leading toward licensed Local Pastor or Ordained Pastoral Ministry. They must be seeking funding for Lay Speaking School, Course of Studies, college expenses preparatory for seminary education, or seminary. Along with their application, they must submit a letter of recommendation from their pastor.

Financial data   The stipend is $500.

Duration   1 year.

Number awarded   1 or more each year.

Deadline   Deadline not specified.

[156]
HARRODSBURG BAPTIST FOUNDATION SCHOLARSHIPS

Harrodsburg Baptist Church
Attn: Harrodsburg Baptist Foundation
312 South Main Street
P.O. Box 286
Harrodsburg, KY 40330
(859) 734-2339   Fax: (859) 734-8384
E-mail: hbf1954@harrodsburgbaptistfoundation.org
Web: www.harrodsburgbaptist.org

Summary To provide financial assistance to Baptist upper-division and seminary students, especially those from selected areas of Kentucky.

Eligibility This program is open to members of Baptist churches who are full-time students working on a degree in a Christian vocational studies program, mainly as a Baptist minister or missionary. Students in a non-ministerial school must be classified as a junior or higher; graduate students must be attending an accredited seminary. First preference is given to members of Harrodsburg Baptist Church, second to members of other Baptist churches in Mercer County, Kentucky, third to members of other Kentucky Baptist churches, and fourth to other students. Applicants must submit information on their reasons for seeking this scholarship and their current financial situation. A personal interview is required.

Financial data The normal annual stipend is $1,200.

Duration 1 year; may be renewed until the student has 1) received a total of $4,800 from the fund; 2) completed a master's degree; or 3) received funds for 4 calendar years.

Additional information The foundation was organized in 1954.

Number awarded 1 or more each year.

Deadline Deadline not specified.

[157]
HARRY C. AND REBA C. RICKARD ENDOWMENT FUND SCHOLARSHIPS

Virginia United Methodist Foundation
10330 Staples Mill Road
P.O. Box 5060
Glen Allen, VA 23058-5606
(804) 521-1122   Toll Free: (800) 768-6040, ext. 122
Fax: (804) 521-1121   E-mail: Foundation@vaumc.org
Web: www.vaumc.org/Page.aspx?pid=1033

Summary To provide financial assistance to Methodists in Virginia who are interested in attending a college or university in any state to prepare for a church-related vocation.

Eligibility This program is open to members of United Methodist Churches in Virginia between 17 and 30 years of age who are graduating high school seniors, college undergraduates, or seminary students. Applicants must be attending or planning to attend a college or seminary in any state to prepare for a full-time church vocation. Along with their application, they must submit an essay of 1 to 2 pages on their career plans and their goals and hopes for ministry; the essay should include whether they plan to serve in a local church setting or in a church-related institution or agency.

Financial data The stipend is $1,000.

Duration 1 year.

Additional information This program was established in 2007.

Number awarded 5 each year.

Deadline March of each year.

[158]
HARRY R. KENDALL LEADERSHIP DEVELOPMENT SCHOLARSHIPS

United Methodist Church
General Board of Global Ministries
Attn: United Methodist Committee on Relief
475 Riverside Drive, Room 1522
New York, NY 10115
(212) 870-3871   Toll Free: (800) UMC-GBGM
E-mail: jyoung@gbgm-umc.org
Web: new.gbgm-umc.org/umcor/work/health/scholarships

Summary To provide financial assistance to African Americans who are Methodists or other Christians and preparing for a career in a health-related field.

Eligibility This program is open to undergraduate and graduate students who are U.S. citizens or permanent residents of African American descent. Applicants must be professed Christians, preferably United Methodists. They must be planning to enter a health care field or already be a practitioner in such a field. Financial need is considered in the selection process.

Financial data The stipend is $2,000.

Duration 1 year.

Additional information This program was established in 1980.

Number awarded Varies each year.

Deadline June of each year.

[159]
HARVESTERS SCHOLARSHIPS

Harvesters Scholarship Foundation
3642 Castle Rock Road
Diamond Bar, CA 91765
E-mail: HarvestersScholarship@hotmail.com
Web: www.harvestersscholarship.com

Summary To provide financial assistance to undergraduate and graduate students who are preparing for a career as a Christian missionary.

Eligibility This program is open to full-time students working on an undergraduate or master's degree at a college or university in Canada or the United States. Applicants must be responding to a call to become a missionary upon graduation. They must have a GPA of 3.0 or higher and a family income less than $60,000 per year. Along with their application, they must submit 1) verification that they are a born-again Christian, have accepted Jesus Christ as their personal savior, and have committed their whole life to serving the Lord, Jesus Christ and God, as a loyal servant; 2) a personal statement describing their calling, vision for ministry, and any specific desires (e.g., mission field); 3) letters of reference; and 4) documentation of financial status.

Financial data A stipend is awarded (amount not specified).

Duration 1 year; may be renewed.

Additional information Recipients must agree to participate in sharing or witnessing in events sponsored by the sponsoring foundation.

Number awarded 1 or more each year.

Deadline May of each year.

[160]
HAZEL STONE MEMORIAL SCHOLARSHIP

Jews for Jesus
60 Haight Street
San Francisco, CA 94102
(415) 864-2600   Fax: (415) 552-8325
E-mail: ruthrosen@jewsforjesus.org
Web: www.jewsforjesus.org

Summary To provide financial assistance to "Jewish women proclaiming Jesus" who are interested in going to a Bible college.

Eligibility This program is open to Jewish women who have committed their life to Jesus, are committed to going to a Bible college or seminary, are going to be committed to an evangelistic ministry after graduation, and are having difficulty meeting the cost of their education.

Financial data The amount awarded varies, depending upon the needs of the recipient.

Duration 1 year.

Number awarded 1 or more each year.

Deadline Deadline not specified.

[161]
HELEN MUNTEAN EDUCATION SCHOLARSHIP FOR WOMEN

Association of Romanian Orthodox Ladies Auxiliaries of
    North America
Attn: Scholarship Committee
222 Orchard Park Drive
New Castle, PA 16105
(724) 652-4313   E-mail: adelap@verizon.net
Web: www.arfora.org/scholarships.htm

Summary To provide financial assistance to women who are members of a parish of the Romanian Orthodox Episcopate of America and interested in working on a degree in education in college.

Eligibility This program is open to women who have been voting communicant members of a parish of the Romanian Orthodox Episcopate of America for at least 1 year or are daughters of a communicant member. Applicants must have completed at least 1 year of work on a baccalaureate degree in education at a college or university. Along with their application, they must submit a 300-word statement describing their personal goals; high school, university, church, and community involvement; honors and awards; and why they should be considered for this award. Selection is based on academic achievement, character, worthiness, and participation in religious life.

Financial data The stipend is $1,000.

Duration 1 year; nonrenewable.

Additional information The Association of Romanian Orthodox Ladies Auxiliaries (ARFORA) was established in 1938 as a women's organization within the Romanian Orthodox Episcopate of America.

Number awarded 1 or more each year.

Deadline May of each year.

[162]
HENRIETTA S. TREEN SCHOLARSHIP

Center for Scholarship Administration, Inc.
Attn: Wells Fargo Accounts
4320 Wade Hampton Boulevard, Suite G
Taylors, SC 29687
Toll Free: (866) 608-0001
E-mail: sallyking@bellsouth.net
Web: www.csascholars.org/treen/index.php

Summary To provide financial assistance to undergraduate students enrolled at designated universities in New Jersey and Pennsylvania and preparing for a career in Christian ministry, law, or medicine.

Eligibility This program is open to residents of any state currently enrolled as full-time undergraduates at Lehigh University, Lafayette College, Princeton University, Temple University, or University of Pennsylvania. Applicants must be preparing for a profession in Christian ministry, law, or medicine. They must have a cumulative GPA of 2.0 or higher and be able to demonstrate "high personal character, academic ability and achievement." Selection is based on academic merit and community service.

Financial data A stipend is awarded (amount not specified).

Duration 1 year; recipients may reapply.

Number awarded Several each year.

Deadline April of each year.

[163]
HENRY P. BRIDGES MINISTERS' TRUST

First Presbyterian Church
105 South Boone Street
Johnson City, TN 37604
(423) 926-5108   Fax: (423) 434-2751
E-mail: contact@fpcjc.org
Web: www.fpcjc.org

Summary To provide financial assistance to students intending to go into the Presbyterian ministry who reside in selected areas in the East and Southeast.

Eligibility Bridges scholarships are available to selected students intending to go into the Presbyterian ministry who reside in and are members of a Presbyterian church in the presbyteries located in east Tennessee, western North Carolina, Baltimore, District of Columbia, and New Castle, Delaware. They must attend either 1) Davidson College (Davidson, North Carolina) or Hampden-Sydney College (Hampden-Sydney, Virginia) or 2) 1 of the following Presbyterian theological seminaries: Columbia (Decatur, Georgia), Louisville (Louisville, Kentucky), McCormick (Chicago, Illinois), Princeton (Princeton, New Jersey), or Union (Richmond, Virginia). Selection is based on academic achievement, leadership ability, church involvement, and financial need.

Financial data The fund provides for living expenses, tuition, books, and other related needs.

Duration 1 year; may be renewed.

Additional information Application requests from Tennessee or North Carolina should be sent to the First Presbyterian Church in Johnson City. Application requests from

Maryland, District of Columbia, or Delaware should be made to: Bridges Scholarship Committee, Hancock Presbyterian Church, 17 East Main Street, P.O. Box 156, Hancock, MD 21750, (301) 678-5510. Funds have been awarded since 1957.

Number awarded Varies each year.

Deadline March of each year.

[164]
HIGHER EDUCATION AND LEADERSHIP MINISTRIES (HELM) FELLOWS

Christian Church (Disciples of Christ)
Attn: Higher Education and Leadership Ministries
11477 Olde Cabin Road, Suite 310
St. Louis, MO 63141-7130
(314) 991-3000   Fax: (314) 991-2957
E-mail: helm@helmdisciples.org
Web: www.helmdisciples.org/aid/undergrad.htm

Summary To provide financial assistance for college to members of the Christian Church (Disciples of Christ) who are interested in taking a leadership role in the church.

Eligibility This program is open to high school seniors and transfers from community college who plan to be a full-time student at a 4-year college or university in the United States or Canada. Applicants must be a participating member of a congregation of the Christian Church (Disciples of Christ) who express a commitment to serve the church as a clergy or lay leader. Some preference is given to students attending colleges and universities related to the Christian Church (Disciples of Christ).

Financial data The stipend is $2,000 per year.

Duration 1 year; may be renewed up to 3 additional years, provided the recipient has a GPA of 2.5 or higher after the first semester of undergraduate work, 2.8 or higher after 3 semesters, and 3.0 or higher after 5 semesters.

Additional information This program began in 2001. Fellows must attend annual leadership conferences and hold summer internships at Disciples of Christ churches and the office of the Higher Education and Leadership Ministries (HELM). They also must agree to assist in the leadership of a ministry activity or program on or near their campus, under the mentorship of a campus minister or chaplain.

Number awarded Approximately 7 each year.

Deadline March of each year.

[165]
HILBURN PRINE STUDENT LOAN PROGRAM

Florida United Methodist Foundation, Inc.
Attn: Scholarship Committee
450 Martin Luther King Jr. Avenue
P.O. Box 3549
Lakeland, FL 33802-3549
(863) 904-2970   Toll Free: (866) 363-9673
Fax: (863) 904-0169   E-mail: Foundation@fumf.org
Web: www.fumc.org/InfoForIndividuals/StudentLoans

Summary To provide educational loans to Methodist students from Florida who are preparing for a church-related career at a college or seminary in any state.

Eligibility This program is open to members of congregations affiliated with the Florida Conference of the United Methodist Church. Applicants must be full-time students

attending a junior college, senior college, university, seminary, or other postsecondary institution in any state and working on a degree in a Christian educational field. Those fields are not limited to pastoral ministry or directors of Christian education but include children and youth counselors, teachers, youth coordinators, children and youth directors associated with Christian schools, local after-school programs, or camping ministries.

Financial data The amount of the loan depends on the availability of funds and the number of approved applicants.

Duration 1 year.

Number awarded Varies each year.

Deadline July of each year for fall term; November of each year for spring term.

[166]
HISPANIC LEADERSHIP DEVELOPMENT FUND

United Methodist Church
General Board of Global Ministries
Attn: United Methodist Committee on Relief
475 Riverside Drive, Room 1522
New York, NY 10115
(212) 870-3871   Toll Free: (800) UMC-GBGM
E-mail: jyoung@gbgm-umc.org
Web: new.gbgm-umc.org/umcor/work/health/scholarships

Summary To provide financial assistance to Methodists and other Christians of Hispanic descent who are preparing for a career in a health-related field.

Eligibility This program is open to undergraduate and graduate students who are U.S. citizens or permanent residents of Hispanic descent. Applicants must be professed Christians, preferably United Methodists. They must be working on an undergraduate or graduate degree to enter or continue in a health-related field. Financial need is considered in the selection process.

Financial data The stipend is $2,000.

Duration 1 year.

Additional information This program was established in 1986.

Number awarded Varies each year.

Deadline June of each year.

[167]
HISPANIC SCHOLARSHIP FUNDS

American Baptist Churches USA
National Ministries
Attn: Hispanic Ministries
P.O. Box 851
Valley Forge, PA 19482-0851
(610) 768-2421   Toll Free: (800) ABC-3USA, ext. 2421
Fax: (610) 768-2453
E-mail: Salvador.Orellana@abc-usa.org
Web: www.nationalministries.org

Summary To provide financial assistance to Hispanic Americans who are interested in preparing for or furthering a church career in the American Baptist Church (ABC).

Eligibility This program is open to Hispanic American members of the ABC or its recognized institutions who demonstrate financial need. They must be enrolled on at least a two-thirds basis at an accredited institution, working on an undergraduate degree or first professional degree in a seminary. Applicants must be currently serving or planning to serve in a vocation with the church or with its recognized institutions. They must be U.S. citizens who have been a member of an American Baptist Church for at least 1 year.

Financial data The stipends range from $500 to $3,000 per year.

Duration 1 year; may be renewed.

Deadline May of each year.

[168]
HOCUTT MEMORIAL SCHOLARSHIP

Woman's Missionary Union
Attn: WMU Foundation
100 Missionary Ridge
Birmingham, AL 35242
(205) 408-5525   Toll Free: (877) 482-4483
Fax: (205) 408-5508   E-mail: wmufoundation@wmu.org
Web: www.wmufoundation.com

Summary To provide financial assistance to undergraduate or graduate students preparing for a career in Baptist missions.

Eligibility This program is open to Southern Baptist undergraduate and graduate students who are preparing for a career as a chaplain or in U.S. based Baptist missions. Applicants may be seeking funding for academic preparation, internships designed to develop their abilities to serve in the chaplaincy or missions field, or for formal continuing education programs related to the chaplaincy or missions.

Financial data A stipend is awarded (amount not specified).

Duration 1 year.

Number awarded Varies each year.

Deadline January of each year.

[169]
HONOR U CONTINUING EDUCATION SCHOLARSHIPS

Degree of Honor Foundation
400 Robert Street North, Suite 1600
St. Paul, MN 55101-2029
(651) 228-7600   Toll Free: (800) 947-5812
Fax: (651) 224-7446
Web: www.degreeofhonor.com/pages/Scholar.html

Summary To provide financial assistance to college student members of Degree of Honor.

Eligibility This program is open to students of any age who have been insured with Degree of Honor for at least 2 years and have completed at least 2 years of higher education after high school with a GPA of 2.75 or higher. Applicants must submit an affirmation of their acceptance of Christian beliefs and values and demonstration of high moral character; information on their Degree of Honor and other community service activities; a statement of what they enjoy most about volunteer involvement; a list of hobbies, talents, or interests; an essay on their anticipated areas of study and career goals; and a description of their leadership qualities and positions held.

Financial data The stipend is $500.

Duration 1 year.

Additional information This program began in 1989. Degree of Honor is a fraternal insurance society licensed to operate in 23 states: Arkansas, Arizona, California, Colorado, Illinois, Indiana, Iowa, Michigan, Minnesota, Missouri, Montana, Nebraska, North Dakota, Ohio, Oklahoma, Oregon, Pennsylvania, South Dakota, Tennessee, Texas, Washington, West Virginia, and Wisconsin.

Number awarded Varies each year; recently, 3 of these scholarships were awarded.

Deadline March of each year.

[170]
HONOR U SCHOLARSHIPS

Degree of Honor Foundation
400 Robert Street North, Suite 1600
St. Paul, MN 55101-2029
(651) 228-7600   Toll Free: (800) 947-5812
Fax: (651) 224-7446
Web: www.degreeofhonor.com/pages/Scholar.html

Summary To provide financial assistance to high school senior members of Degree of Honor who wish to attend college.

Eligibility This program is open to graduating high school seniors who have been insured with Degree of Honor for at least 2 years and have a GPA of 2.75 or higher. Additional funding is provided to students who have also completed the Fraternal Heart (or "Teens With a Heart") Program. Applicants must submit an affirmation of their acceptance of Christian beliefs and values and demonstration of high moral character; information on their Degree of Honor and other community service activities; a statement of what they enjoy most about their volunteer involvement; a list of hobbies, talents, or interests; an essay on their anticipated areas of study and career goals; and a description of their leadership qualities and positions held.

Financial data The stipend is $1,000. Recipients of Teens With a Heart Scholarships are awarded an additional $500 scholarship.

Additional information This program began in 1959. Degree of Honor is a fraternal insurance society licensed to operate in 23 states: Arkansas, Arizona, California, Colorado, Illinois, Indiana, Iowa, Michigan, Minnesota, Missouri, Montana, Nebraska, North Dakota, Ohio, Oklahoma, Oregon, Pennsylvania, South Dakota, Tennessee, Texas, Washington, West Virginia, and Wisconsin.

Number awarded Varies each year; recently, 10 students received these scholarships, including 1 who received a Teens With a Heart Scholarship.

Deadline March of each year.

[171]
HOOD MEMORIAL SCHOLARSHIP

United Methodist Church-Arkansas Conference
Attn: Board of Higher Education and Campus Ministry
800 Daisy Bates Drive
Little Rock, AR 72202
(501) 324-8045   Toll Free: (877) 646-1816
Fax: (501) 324-8018   E-mail: conference@arumc.org
Web: www.arumc.org

Summary To provide financial assistance to Methodist students from Arkansas preparing for Christian service in ministry at a college or seminary in any state.

Eligibility This program is open to residents of Arkansas who have been members of a United Methodist Church (UMC) for at least 1 year. Applicants must be full-time undergraduate or graduate students at an accredited college, university, or seminary in any state approved by the UMC University Senate and preparing for full-time Christian service in ministry. They must be able to demonstrate financial need and a record of involvement in their local church, Wesley Foundation, and/or United Methodist campus ministry and with their community. Along with their application, they must submit a statement that includes their philosophy of life, their religious development, and what influenced them in selecting their career goal.

Financial data The stipend is $1,000 per year.

Duration 1 year; may be renewed.

Number awarded 1 or more each year.

Deadline April of each year.

[172]
HUBERT TRUST SCHOLARSHIP

Baptist Medical Dental Fellowship
4209 Royal Avenue
Oklahoma City, OK 73108-2033
(405) 606-7027   Fax: (405) 609-3203
E-mail: bmdf@bmdf.org
Web: www.bmdf.org/scholarships

Summary To provide funding to health professions students interested in conducting a project anywhere in the world under the supervision of a medical missionary affiliated with Baptist Medical Dental Fellowship (BMDF).

Eligibility This program is open to health professions students interested in conducting a short-term mission project in response to global humanitarian needs. Although applicants are not required to be members of BMDF, they are expected to support its goal of sharing the Gospel of Jesus Christ through each of its health care missions projects. Examples of projects they may propose to conduct include assisting hospitals in immunization campaigns, conducting public health seminars, assisting with medical or dental clinics, or establishing nutritional rehabilitation centers. Along with their application, they must submit a description of the proposed project that includes why the project is important to them, how the experience will expand their world awareness, and why the project will enhance their personal and professional life.

Financial data The amount of the grant depends on the merits of the proposal.

Duration Most projects should be completed within 4 months.

Number awarded Varies each year.

Deadline Applications may be submitted at any time.

[173]
IDAHO EASTERN STAR TRAINING AWARDS FOR RELIGIOUS LEADERSHIP

Order of the Eastern Star-Grand Chapter of Idaho
c/o Eleanor Rupp, ESTARL Central Committee Chair
4589 Aspen Way
Post Falls, ID 83854
(208) 773-7650
Web: www.idahooes.org

Summary To provide financial assistance to residents of Idaho who are attending a college or seminary in any state to prepare for a career in religious service.

Eligibility This program is open to residents of Idaho who are entering their junior or senior year at an accredited college or university or a seminary in any state. Applicants must be preparing for a full-time career as a minister, missionary, director of religious education, Christian youth worker, or church music director. Along with their application, they must submit a personal letter explaining their goals and reasons for applying for this award.

Financial data A stipend is awarded (amount not specified).

Duration 1 year.

Number awarded 1 or more each year.

Deadline March of each year.

[174]
ILLINOIS EASTERN STAR TRAINING AWARDS FOR RELIGIOUS LEADERSHIP

Order of the Eastern Star-Grand Chapter of Illinois
P.O. Box 317
Macon, IL 62544
(217) 764-3326   Fax: (217) 764-5462
E-mail: gc@illoes.org
Web: www.illoes.org/Charities.htm

Summary To provide financial assistance to residents of Illinois who are attending a college or seminary in any state to prepare for a career in religious service.

Eligibility This program is open to residents of Illinois who are enrolled at an accredited college, university, or seminary in any state. Applicants must be preparing for a full-time career as a minister, missionary, director of religious education, Christian youth worker, or church music director. Along with their application, they must submit a brief statement on their vocational goals after completion of higher education and their involvement in community services.

Financial data A stipend is awarded (amount not specified).

Duration 1 year.

Number awarded 1 or more each year.

Deadline March of each year.

[175]
INDIANA BAPTIST FOUNDATION SCHOLARSHIPS

State Convention of Baptists in Indiana
Attn: Indiana Baptist Foundation
900 North High School Road
P.O. Box 24189
Indianapolis, IN 46224
(317) 481-2400, ext. 238   Toll Free: (800) 444-5424
Fax: (317) 241-9875   E-mail: ray.barrett@ibflegacy.org
Web: www.inbaptistfoundation.com

Summary To provide financial assistance for college, seminary, or graduate school in any state to members of Southern Baptist churches in Indiana.

Eligibility This program is open to Indiana Southern Baptists who are preparing for a religious or other vocation at a college, seminary, or graduate school in any state. Doctoral candidates are not eligible. Applicants must submit an endorsement by an Indiana Southern Baptist church and a statement describing God's leadership in their choice of profession, area of study, or school selection. Financial need is the most important factor considered in the selection process.

Financial data The stipend is $1,000.

Duration 1 year; may be renewed.

Number awarded Varies each year.

Deadline February of each year.

[176]
INDIANA EAGLE SCOUT OF THE YEAR SCHOLARSHIPS

American Legion
Department of Indiana
777 North Meridian Street
Indianapolis, IN 46204
(317) 630-1264   Fax: (317) 630-1277
Web: www.indlegion.org/boy_scouts.htm

Summary To recognize and reward, with scholarships for college in any state, Eagle Scouts who are members of a troop associated with the American Legion in Indiana or a son or grandson of a member of the Legion in the state.

Eligibility Applicants for this award must be either 1) a registered, active member of a Boy Scout Troop, Varsity Scout Team, or Venturing Crew chartered to an Indiana American Legion Post, Auxiliary Unit, or Sons of the American Legion Squadron, or 2) a registered active member of an Indiana Boy Scout Troop, Varsity Scout Team, or Venturing Crew and also the son or grandson of a member of the American Legion or American Legion Auxiliary. Candidates must also 1) have received the Eagle Scout Award; 2) be active members of their religious institution and have received the appropriate religious emblem; 3) have demonstrated practical citizenship in church, school, Scouting, and community; 4) be at least 15 years of age and enrolled in high school; and 5) submit at least 4 letters of recommendation, including 1 each from leaders of their religious institution, school, community, and Scouting. They must be planning to attend college in any state.

Financial data District winners receive $200 scholarships; the state winner receives a $1,000 scholarship.

Duration The awards are presented annually.

Number awarded 12 each year: 1 state winner and 11 district winners.

Deadline January of each year.

[177]
INDIANA EASTERN STAR TRAINING AWARDS FOR RELIGIOUS LEADERSHIP

Order of the Eastern Star-Grand Chapter of Indiana
Attn: Jonny Beeler, Grand Secretary
890 Red Skelton Circle
Franklin, IN 46131
(317) 736-4487   E-mail: indianaoes@embarqmail.com
Web: farrandtel.com/oes-indiana/awardmenub.htm

Summary To provide financial assistance to residents of Indiana who are attending a college or seminary in any state to prepare for a career in Christian service.

Eligibility This program is open to residents of Indiana who have completed at least 1 year of study at a college, university, or seminary in any state. Applicants must "wish to devote

their lives to God's Service" as a minister, missionary, evangelist, director of religious education, director of youth leadership, director of church choir, director of youth choir, or church musician. Selection is based on character, leadership in Christian activities, citizenship, and financial need.

Financial data A stipend is awarded (amount not specified).

Duration 1 year.

Number awarded Varies each year.

Deadline February of each year.

[178]
INDIANA MERIT SCHOLARSHIPS

United Methodist Church-Indiana Conference
Attn: Associate Director of Youth, Young Adult and
  Campus Ministries
301 Pennsylvania Parkway, Suite 300
Indianapolis, IN 46280
(317) 924-1321   Fax: (317) 735-4228
E-mail: brian.durand@inumc.org
Web: www.inumc.org/pages/detail/161

Summary To provide financial assistance to members of United Methodist churches in the Indiana Conference who plan to attend a Methodist college in any state.

Eligibility This program is open to full, active members of a United Methodist Church in the Indiana Conference. Applicants must be enrolled or planning to enroll at an institution of higher education in any state recognized as United Methodist by the University Senate. They must be nominated by their pastor. Selection is based on merit, defined as academic achievement and expression of Christian faith through 1) participation in home church, campus ministry, and/or community service, and 2) vocational preparation for service to humanity.

Financial data A stipend is awarded (amount not specified).

Duration 1 year.

Number awarded Varies each year.

Deadline Deadline not specified.

[179]
INEZ R. IRONS SCHOLARSHIP

United Methodist Church-Greater New Jersey Conference
Conference Board of Higher Education and Ministry
Attn: Scholarship Committee
1001 Wickapecko Drive
Ocean, NJ 07712-4733
(732) 359-1040   Toll Free: (877) 677-2594, ext. 1040
Fax: (732) 359-1049   E-mail: Lperez@gnjumc.org
Web: www.gnjumc.org/grants_loans_and_scholarship

Summary To provide financial assistance to sons of United Methodist clergy from New Jersey who are interested in attending college in any state.

Eligibility This program is open to sons of clergy affiliated with the Greater New Jersey Conference of the United Methodist Church. Applicants must be attending or planning to attend a college or university in any state and studying in the field of their choice. Along with their application, they must submit a statement on why they wish to be considered for this scholarship, including information on their financial need and Christian commitment.

Financial data The stipend is $500.
Duration 1 year.
Number awarded 1 each year.
Deadline March of each year.

[180]
INEZ TURNER BYRD MEMORIAL SCHOLARSHIP
Alabama-West Florida United Methodist Foundation, Inc.
170 Belmont Drive
P.O. Box 8066
Dothan, AL 36304
(334) 793-6820   Fax: (334) 794-6480
E-mail: foundation@alwfumf.org
Web: www.alwfumf.org
Summary To provide financial assistance for college to students from the Alabama-West Florida Conference of the United Methodist Church who are interested in preparing for a career in service to society.
Eligibility This program is open to members of United Methodist Churches within the Alabama-West Florida Conference. Applicants must be enrolled or planning to enroll in college in order to prepare for a career of service that "will provide for the mental, spiritual, and/or physical enhancement of society." They must submit 1) an essay on why they feel they should receive this scholarship and 2) documentation of financial need.
Financial data The stipend is $500.
Duration 1 year.
Number awarded 2 each year.
Deadline June of each year.

[181]
IOKDS HEALTH CAREERS SCHOLARSHIPS
International Order of the King's Daughters and Sons
Attn: Director, Health Careers Scholarship Department
34 Vincent Avenue
P.O. Box 1040
Chautauqua, NY 14722-1040
(716) 357-4951   Fax: (716) 357-3762
E-mail: iokds5@windstream.net
Web: www.iokds.org/scholarship.html
Summary To provide financial assistance to Christian and other students preparing for careers in medicine, dentistry, pharmacy, physical and occupational therapy, and selected medical technologies.
Eligibility This program is open to U.S. or Canadian citizens who are enrolled full time at an accredited college or university and studying medicine, dentistry, nursing, pharmacy, physical or occupational therapy, or medical technology. Applicants in undergraduate programs must be in at least the third year of college. Nursing students must have completed their first year of schooling. Students seeking M.D. or D.D.S. degrees must be in at least the second year of medical or dental school. Pre-med students are not eligible. Preference is given to students of Christian background. Selection is based on personal statistics, educational background, financial statement, and a statement from the applicant describing the reason for choosing the field of training and future plans.
Financial data The stipend is $1,000 per year.
Duration 1 year; may be renewed up to 2 additional years.

Additional information This program began in 1976.
Number awarded Varies each year. Recently, 43 of these scholarships were awarded.
Deadline March of each year.

[182]
IOWA EAGLE SCOUT OF THE YEAR SCHOLARSHIP
American Legion
Department of Iowa
720 Lyon Street
Des Moines, IA 50309-5481
(515) 282-5068   Toll Free: (800) 365-8387
Fax: (515) 282-7583   E-mail: programs@ialegion.org
Web: www.ialegion.org/eagle_scout_of_the_year.htm
Summary To recognize and reward, with scholarships for college in any state, Eagle Scouts who are members of a troop associated with the American Legion in Iowa or a son or grandson of a member of the Legion.
Eligibility Applicants for this award must be either 1) a registered, active member of a Boy Scout Troop, Varsity Scout Team, or Venturing Crew chartered to an Iowa American Legion Post, Auxiliary Unit, or Sons of the American Legion Squadron, or 2) a registered active member of an Iowa Boy Scout Troop, Varsity Scout Team, or Venturing Crew and also the son or grandson of a member of the American Legion or American Legion Auxiliary. Candidates must also 1) have received the Eagle Scout Award; 2) be active members of their religious institution and have received the appropriate religious emblem; 3) have demonstrated practical citizenship in church, school, Scouting, and community; 4) be at least 15 years of age and enrolled in high school; and 5) submit at least 4 letters of recommendation, including 1 each from leaders of their religious institution, school, community, and Scouting. They must be planning to attend college in any state.
Financial data The first-place winner receives a $2,000 scholarship, second a $1,500 scholarship, and third a $1,000 scholarship. All awards must be used for payment of tuition at the recipient's college or university.
Duration The awards are presented annually.
Number awarded 3 each year.
Deadline January of each year.

[183]
IOWA EASTERN STAR TRAINING AWARDS FOR RELIGIOUS LEADERSHIP
Order of the Eastern Star-Grand Chapter of Iowa
c/o Nancy L. Niday, Grand Secretary
303 1/2 East Marion Street
P.O. Box 72
Knoxville, IA 50138
(641) 842-2720   Toll Free: (866) 484-2071
Fax: (641) 842-3678   E-mail: iowaoes@iowatelecom.net
Web: www.iowaeasternstar.org/EASTARL.html
Summary To provide financial assistance to residents of Iowa interested in attending a college or seminary in any state to prepare for a religious career.
Eligibility This program is open to residents of Iowa who have completed at least 3 years of postsecondary education at a college or university in any state. Applicants must be

interested in continuing their education at their current school or at a postgraduate institution to prepare for a career in full-time Christian service, including minister, missionary, director of church music, church youth leader, and religious educator. They must be able to demonstrate financial need. Along with their application, they must submit a short statement that includes why they should receive this award and what use they expect to make of the training.

Financial data A stipend is awarded (amount not specified).

Duration 1 year.

Number awarded Varies each year.

Deadline April of each year.

[184]
IOWA UNITED METHODIST CHURCH SCHOLARSHIPS

Iowa United Methodist Foundation
2301 Rittenhouse Street
Des Moines, IA 50321
(515) 974-8927
Web: www.iumf.org/umscholarships.html

Summary To provide financial assistance to members of United Methodist Church (UMC) congregations in Iowa who are interested in attending a UMC-affiliated college in the state.

Eligibility This program is open to members of UMC congregations in Iowa who are planning to attend a UMC-affiliated college in the state as a first-time student (including high school seniors and undergraduates transferring from other colleges). Applicants must be planning to work on a degree as a full-time student. Along with their application, they must submit a letter of nomination from the administrative board or council and a personal statement of their church involvement. Financial need is not considered in the selection process.

Financial data The stipend is $1,000.

Duration 1 year.

Additional information This program is supported by the Iowa Annual Conference of the UMC and administered by the Iowa United Methodist Foundation.

Number awarded 25 each year.

Deadline March of each year.

[185]
IOWA UNITED METHODIST FOUNDATION GENERAL SCHOLARSHIPS

Iowa United Methodist Foundation
2301 Rittenhouse Street
Des Moines, IA 50321
(515) 974-8927
Web: www.iumf.org/otherscholarships.html

Summary To provide financial assistance to members of United Methodist Church (UMC) congregations in Iowa interested in studying at UMC-affiliated colleges in Iowa or a UMC seminary.

Eligibility This program is open to high school seniors, college students, vocational/technical students, seminarians, and graduate students who are members of Iowa UMC congregations. Applicants must be attending or planning to attend a UMC college in Iowa or a UMC seminary in any state. Financial need is considered in the selection process.

Financial data The stipend is $520.

Duration 1 year.

Additional information This program is supported by small undesignated gifts to the Iowa United Methodist Foundation.

Number awarded 2 each year.

Deadline March of each year.

[186]
IRA L. AND MARY L. HARRISON MEMORIAL SCHOLARSHIP

Baptist Convention of New Mexico
Attn: Missions Mobilization Team
5325 Wyoming Boulevard, N.E.
P.O. Box 94485
Albuquerque, NM 87199-4485
(505) 924-2315   Toll Free: (800) 898-8544
Fax: (505) 924-2320   E-mail: cpairett@bcnm.com
Web: www.bcnm.com

Summary To provide financial assistance to Native American Southern Baptist students from New Mexico who are attending designated colleges or Baptist seminaries.

Eligibility This program is open to undergraduate and seminary students who are Native American members of churches affiliated with the Baptist Convention of New Mexico. Applicants must have a GPA of 2.0 or higher and be able to demonstrate financial need. Undergraduates must be attending Wayland Baptist University at its main campus in Plainview, Texas or at its New Mexico external campuses in Clovis or Albuquerque. Graduate students must be attending 1 of the 6 Southern Baptist seminaries: Southeastern Baptist Theological Seminary (Wake Forest, North Carolina); Southern Baptist Theological Seminary (Louisville, Kentucky); Southwestern Baptist Theological Seminary (Fort Worth, Texas); New Orleans Baptist Theological Seminary (New Orleans, Louisiana); Midwestern Baptist Theological Seminary (Kansas City, Missouri); or Golden Gate Baptist Theological Seminary (Mill Valley, California).

Financial data A stipend is awarded (amount not specified).

Duration 1 year; may be renewed.

Number awarded 1 or more each year.

Deadline June of each year for fall semester; November of each year for spring semester.

[187]
IRENE S. WISCHER EDUCATIONAL FOUNDATION SCHOLARSHIPS

Irene S. Wischer Educational Foundation
c/o ETS Scholarship & Recognition Programs
P.O. Box 6730
Princeton, NJ 08541
(609) 771-7878   E-mail: SRP-CSR@ets.org
Web: www.frostbank.com

Summary To provide financial assistance to residents of Texas, especially Christians, who are interested in attending college or graduate school in any state.

Eligibility This program is open to U.S. citizens who have been residents of Texas for at least 12 consecutive months. Preference is given to Christians who attend church regularly. Applicants must be attending or planning to attend an accredited college, university, graduate school, vocational/technical school, or trade school in any state. They must be able to demonstrate academic potential and ability, good character, and financial need. Along with their application, they must submit 3 letters of recommendation, including 1 from a member of clergy at their church.

Financial data Stipends range up $10,000 per year, depending on the need of the recipient.

Duration 1 year; may be renewed up to 3 additional years.

Additional information This program, established in 2007, is administered by Frost National Bank, with operational management by ETS Scholarship & Recognition Programs.

Number awarded 1 or more each year.

Deadline January of each year.

[188]
ITALIAN CATHOLIC FEDERATION COLLEGE SCHOLARSHIP PROGRAM

Italian Catholic Federation
8393 Capwell Drive, Suite 110
Oakland, CA 94621
(510) 633-9058   Toll Free: (888) ICF-1924
Fax: (510) 633-9758   E-mail: info@icf.org
Web: www.icf.org/scholarships.html

Summary To provide financial assistance to high school seniors in selected states who are of Italian Catholic heritage and are interested in going to college.

Eligibility This program is open to high school seniors who live within Catholic Dioceses in Arizona, California, Nevada, and Illinois and are baptized Roman Catholics of Italian descent (or whose non-Italian Catholic parents, grandparents, or guardians are members of the Italian Catholic Federation). Applicants must have a GPA of 3.2 or higher and have been accepted at an accredited college, university, junior college, or technical school in any state. They must submit a 150-word personal statement explaining their Italian origin (or federation membership affiliation of their non-Italian Catholic parents, grandparents, or guardians), why their Roman Catholic faith is important to them, and their plans for the future. Selection is based on scholastic achievement, financial need, leadership role, faculty recommendations and character references, and extracurricular activities.

Financial data The stipend is $400 for the first year, $500 for the second year, $600 for the third year, and $1,000 for the fourth year.

Duration First-year scholarship recipients become automatically eligible to receive an advanced scholarship for up to 3 additional years, if they maintain at least a 3.2 GPA. Applications for these advanced scholarships are sent directly to first-year recipients.

Number awarded Varies each year; recently, 178 first-year and 46 second-, third-, and fourth-year scholarships were awarded, totaling $99,400.

Deadline March of each year.

[189]
J.A. KNOWLES MEMORIAL SCHOLARSHIP

United Methodist Church
Attn: General Board of Higher Education and Ministry
Office of Loans and Scholarships
1001 19th Avenue South
P.O. Box 340007
Nashville, TN 37203-0007
(615) 340-7344   Fax: (615) 340-7367
E-mail: umscholar@gbhem.org
Web: www.gbhem.org/loansandscholarships

Summary To provide financial assistance to undergraduate and graduate students attending schools in Texas affiliated with the United Methodist Church.

Eligibility This program is open to U.S. citizens and permanent residents who have been active, full members of a United Methodist Church in Texas for at least 1 year prior to applying. Applicants must be attending a Texas college or university related to the United Methodist Church. They must have a GPA of 2.5 or higher and be enrolled as a full-time undergraduate or graduate student. Financial need is considered in the selection process.

Financial data The stipend is $1,000.

Duration 1 year.

Number awarded 50 each year.

Deadline May of each year.

[190]
JACOBSEN FUND SCHOLARSHIPS

Jacobsen Scholarship Fund
1400 Foothill Drive, Suite 25
Salt Lake City, UT 84108
(801) 592-7314
Web: www.jacobsenscholarshipfund.com

Summary To provide financial assistance for college to members of the Church of Jesus Christ of Latter-day Saints (LDS).

Eligibility This program is open to worthy and active members of the LDS who are enrolled or planning to enroll full time at an accredited postsecondary institution in any state. Applicants must have a GPA of 2.75 or higher and be able to demonstrate financial need. U.S. citizenship is required.

Financial data Awards are equal to the full-time undergraduate resident tuition, plus a standardized amount for books, supplies, and fees. All funds are paid directly to the student's institution.

Duration 1 semester; may be renewed up to 7 additional semesters, provided the recipient continues to demonstrate financial need and activity in the LDS church.

Number awarded Varies each year.

Deadline May of each year for fall semester; October of each year for winter semester.

[191]
JAMYE COLEMAN WILLIAMS AND JOSEPH C. MCKINNEY SCHOLARSHIPS

African Methodist Episcopal Church
Connectional Lay Organization
c/o Evelyn Welch Graham
2910 Fourth Avenue South
St. Petersburg, FL 33712
(727) 327-9927   E-mail: verne764@aol.com
Web: www.connectionallay-amec.org

Summary To provide financial assistance to members of the African Methodist Episcopal (AME) Church who are interested in attending a college or university, especially those interested preparing for leadership in the denomination.

Eligibility This program is open to members of AME churches who are working on or planning to work on a bachelor's degree at a college or university. Applicants must submit a 500-word essay on why they want to attend college. Preference is given to students who desire to serve the AME Church in a leadership capacity. Selection is based on academic record, qualities of leadership, extracurricular activities and accomplishments, reference letters, and financial need.

Financial data The stipend is $1,500. Funds are sent directly to the student's college or university.

Duration 1 year.

Number awarded 2 each year.

Deadline May of each year.

[192]
JANE FRYER MCCONAUGHY MEMORIAL SCHOLARSHIP PROGRAM

Elkhart County Community Foundation
Attn: Scholarship Coordinator
101 South Main Street
P.O. Box 2932
Elkhart, IN 46515-2932
(574) 295-8761   Fax: (574) 389-7497
E-mail: shannon@elkhartccf.org
Web: www.elkhartccf.org/scholarships/index.xpl

Summary To provide financial assistance to undergraduate and graduate students who are Indiana residents or enrolled at colleges in the state and preparing for a career in the ministry, missionary service, or teaching.

Eligibility This program is open to Indiana residents attending college in any state and residents of any state attending college in Indiana. Applicants must be enrolled as undergraduate or graduate students obtaining training required for the ministry, missionary service, or the teaching profession. Priority is given to seminary students and students training for missionary services. Selection is based on career goals, academic record, and financial need.

Financial data Stipends range from $500 to $1,500.

Duration 1 year.

Number awarded 2 to 6 each year.

Deadline February of each year.

[193]
JANE LORING JONES SCHOLARSHIPS

American Baptist Churches of the Rocky Mountains
Attn: American Baptist Women's Ministries
9085 East Mineral Circle, Suite 170
Centennial, CO 80112
(303) 988-3900   E-mail: web@abcrm.org
Web: www.abcrm.org

Summary To provide financial assistance to women who are members of churches affiliated with the American Baptist Churches (ABC) USA in Colorado, New Mexico, and Utah and interested in attending an ABC college in any state.

Eligibility This program is open to women under 26 years of age who are active members of churches cooperating with ABC in Colorado, New Mexico, or Utah. Applicants must be enrolled or planning to enroll full time at an ABC college or university in any state. They are not required to enter Christian service as a vocation, but they must have a real desire to prepare themselves for Christian leadership in the home, church, and community. Along with their application, they must submit a personal letter describing their Christian experience; their participation in the life of their church, school, and community; and their goals for the future. Selection is based on academic performance, Christian participation in church and school, and financial need. Preference is given to women entering their first or second year at an ABC school.

Financial data The stipend is $2,000 per year.

Duration 1 year; recipients may reapply.

Number awarded 1 or more each year.

Deadline March of each year.

[194]
JANE WALKER SCHOLARSHIP

United Methodist Church-Alabama-West Florida Conference
Attn: Commission on the Status and Role of Women
100 Interstate Park Drive, Suite 120
Montgomery, AL 36109
(334) 356-8014   Toll Free: (888) 873-3127
Fax: (334) 356-8029   E-mail: awfcrc@awfumc.org
Web: www.awfumc.org

Summary To provide financial assistance to female residents of the Alabama-West Florida Conference of the United Methodist Church (UMC) who are undergraduate or seminary students preparing for a church-related career.

Eligibility This program is open to women who are residents of the Alabama-West Florida Conference of the UMW and who affirm, represent, and advocate women's leadership in the church. Applicants must be accepted or enrolled at an approved UMC seminary or working on an undergraduate degree in Christian education at an approved UMC institution in any state. They must be a candidate for ministry or preparing for a UMC church-related career. Along with their application, they must submit a 500-word essay on why they are preparing for full-time Christian ministry and how they can promote the cause of women through this ministry. Financial need is also considered in the selection process.

Financial data The stipend is $1,000.

Duration 1 year.

Number awarded 1 each year.

Deadline May of each year.

[195]
JANET V. STEWART SCHOLARSHIP

Iowa United Methodist Foundation
2301 Rittenhouse Street
Des Moines, IA 50321
(515) 974-8927
Web: www.iumf.org/umscholarships.html

Summary To provide financial assistance to high school seniors and current college student who are members of an Iowa United Methodist Church and interested in attending a church-affiliated college in the state.

Eligibility This program is open to seniors graduating from high schools in Iowa and recent graduates of those schools who are members of a United Methodist Church congregation. Applicants must be enrolled or planning to enroll full time at an Iowa college affiliated with the United Methodist Church. Financial need is considered in the selection process.

Financial data The stipend is $2,000.

Duration 1 year.

Number awarded 11 each year.

Deadline March of each year.

[196]
JANIE CREE BOSE ANDERSON SCHOLARSHIPS

Kentucky Woman's Missionary Union
Attn: Scholarships
13420 Eastpoint Centre Drive
P.O. Box 436569
Louisville, KY 40253-6569
(502) 489-3534   Toll Free: (866) 489-3534 (within KY)
Fax: (502) 489-3566   E-mail: kywmu@kybaptist.org
Web: kywmu.org/scholarships

Summary To provide financial assistance to female Baptists from Kentucky who are attending a college or seminary in any state to prepare for Christian service.

Eligibility This program is open to women who are active members of churches affiliated with the Kentucky Baptist Convention or the General Association of Baptists in Kentucky. Applicants must be attending an accredited college, university, or seminary in any state as a full-time student. They must have a GPA of 2.7 or higher and be preparing for Christian service. Along with their application, they must submit a brief essay on how they became a Christian and their career goals.

Financial data Stipends range from $400 to $700.

Duration 1 year.

Number awarded 1 or more each year.

Deadline January of each year.

[197]
JANIE ROBINSON THOMASON MEMORIAL SCHOLARSHIP FUND

United Methodist Church-South Carolina Conference
Attn: Board of Higher Education and Campus Ministry
4908 Colonial Drive
Columbia, SC 29203-6070
(803) 786-9486   Toll Free: (888) 678-6272
Fax: (803) 691-0220
Web: www.umcsc.org/scholarships2.html

Summary To provide financial assistance to Methodist students from South Carolina who are interested in attending college in any state.

Eligibility This program is open to residents of South Carolina who have been a member and regular attendee of a United Methodist Church for at least 1 year. Preference is given to members of St. Paul United Methodist Church (Clover, South Carolina) and of churches in the Rock Hill District. Applicants must be enrolled or planning to enroll at a college or university in any state and major in any field. Students at 2-year institutions are eligible if they provide evidence of intent to transfer to a 4-year college or university. Along with their application, they must submit a personal statement that describes their participation in projects and activities of church, school, and/or community; official college or high school transcripts; a letter of recommendation from their pastor; a statement regarding their financial need; and a general statement that may include their philosophy of life, faith development, and what influenced them in selecting their career goal.

Financial data The stipend is $750.

Duration 1 year.

Additional information This program was established in 1996.

Number awarded 1 or more each year.

Deadline March of each year.

[198]
J.D. WILLIAMS SCHOLARSHIP

African Methodist Episcopal Church
Connectional Lay Organization
c/o Evelyn Welch Graham
2910 Fourth Avenue South
St. Petersburg, FL 33712
(727) 327-9927   E-mail: verne764@aol.com
Web: www.connectionallay-amec.org

Summary To provide financial assistance to members of the African Methodist Episcopal (AME) Church who are interested in attending a college or university affiliated with the denomination.

Eligibility This program is open to members of AME churches who are working on or planning to work on a bachelor's degree in any field at an AME college or university. Applicants must submit a 500-word essay on the importance of a college education in the 21st century. Selection is based on that essay, academic achievement, quality of church involvement, leadership, extracurricular activities, and reference letters.

Financial data The stipend is $2,500. Funds are sent directly to the student.

Duration 1 year.

Number awarded 1 or more each year.

Deadline May of each year.

[199]
JERI SUE HOLLENBACH BAUMAN SCHOLARSHIP

New Mexico Baptist Foundation
5325 Wyoming Boulevard, N.E.
P.O. Box 16560
Albuquerque, NM 87191-6560
(505) 332-3777   Toll Free: (877) 841-3777
Fax: (505) 332-2777   E-mail: foundation@nmbf.com
Web: www.bcnm.com

Summary To provide financial assistance for college to members of Southern Baptist churches in New Mexico.

Eligibility This program is open to members of Southern Baptist churches in New Mexico who are enrolled full time at an accredited college or university. Members of other evangelical churches may also be considered. Preference is given to students attending New Mexico colleges or universities.

Financial data A stipend is awarded (amount not specified).

Duration 1 year.

Number awarded 1 or more each year.

Deadline April of each year.

[200]
JEROME J. JUNK MEMORIAL SCHOLARSHIPS

Knights of Columbus-California State Council
15808 Arrow Boulevard, Suite A
Fontana, CA 92335
(909) 434-0460   E-mail: state.office@kofc-ca.org
Web: kofc-ca.org/?t=t_csc_studentscholarships2

Summary To provide financial assistance to members of the Knights of Columbus and their families in California who are interested in attending a religious vocational school in any state.

Eligibility This program is open to 1) members of the Knights of Columbus in a California council; 2) spouses and children of Knights of Columbus members in a California council; 3) spouses and children of deceased members who were in good standing with a California council at the time of death; 4) members of a California Columbian Squires Circle; and 5) former members of a California Columbian Squires Circle who are either current members in good standing or sons of Knights of Columbus members in good standing in a California council. Applicants must be attending or planning to attend a postsecondary school in any state to prepare for a religious vocation. Along with their application, they must submit transcripts, SAT and/or ACT scores, a personal statement, and 3 letters of recommendation.

Financial data The stipend is $1,000.

Duration 1 year.

Number awarded 3 each year.

Deadline February of each year.

[201]
JESSICA POWELL LOFTIS SCHOLARSHIP FOR ACTEENS

Woman's Missionary Union
Attn: WMU Foundation
100 Missionary Ridge
Birmingham, AL 35242
(205) 408-5525   Toll Free: (877) 482-4483
Fax: (205) 408-5508   E-mail: wmufoundation@wmu.org
Web: www.wmufoundation.com

Summary To provide financial assistance for college or other activities to female high school seniors who have been active in the Southern Baptist Convention's Acteens (Academic/Events/Training).

Eligibility This program is open to female high school seniors who are members of a Baptist church and active in Acteens. Applicants must 1) be planning to attend college and have completed Quest for Vision in the MissionsQuest program or StudiAct; 2) have been an Acteen for at least 1 year and be planning to attend an Acteens event; or 3) be an Acteens leader who is pursuing academic or leadership training to lead an Acteens group. Along with their application, they must submit an essay listing their major accomplishments and missions activities.

Financial data A stipend is awarded (amount not specified).

Duration 1 year.

Additional information This program was established in 1995 by Woman's Missionary Union, an Auxiliary to Southern Baptist Convention.

Number awarded 1 or more each year.

Deadline February of each year.

[202]
JESSIE AND PHYLLIS ALLEN MEMORIAL SCHOLARSHIP

New Mexico Baptist Foundation
5325 Wyoming Boulevard, N.E.
P.O. Box 16560
Albuquerque, NM 87191-6560
(505) 332-3777   Toll Free: (877) 841-3777
Fax: (505) 332-2777   E-mail: foundation@nmbf.com
Web: www.bcnm.com

Summary To provide financial assistance for college to members of Southern Baptist churches in New Mexico.

Eligibility This program is open to college students who are members of churches affiliated with the Baptist Convention of New Mexico. First preference is given to former members of Lesbia Baptist Church, second to residents of Quay County, and third to other New Mexico students.

Financial data A stipend is awarded (amount not specified).

Duration 1 year.

Number awarded 1 or more each year.

Deadline April of each year.

[203]
JOE ALLMAN SCHOLARSHIP

Japanese American Citizens League-Arizona Chapter
5414 West Glenn Drive
Glendale, AZ 85301-2628
E-mail: arizonajacl@gmail.com
Web: www.jaclaz.org

Summary   To provide financial assistance to graduating high school seniors in Arizona who are of Japanese heritage.

Eligibility   This program is open to graduating high school seniors in Arizona. Applicants or their parents must have been members of 1 of the following organizations for at least the preceding 3 years: Arizona Chapter of the Japanese American Citizens League (JACLA), the Phoenix Japanese Free Methodist Church, the Arizona Buddhist Church, a youth group of JACLA, a youth group of the Phoenix Free Methodist Church, or a youth group of the Arizona Buddhist Church. Financial need is not considered in the selection process. Special consideration is given to students currently involved in Scouting.

Financial data   A stipend is awarded (amount not specified).

Duration   1 year.

Additional information   Recipients must attend the association's scholarship awards banquet and accept the award in person; failure to do so results in forfeiture of the award.

Number awarded   1 each year.

Deadline   February of each year.

[204]
JOHN C. WRIGHT SCHOLARSHIP

United Methodist Higher Education Foundation
Attn: Scholarships Administrator
1001 19th Avenue South
P.O. Box 340005
Nashville, TN 37203-0005
(615) 340-7385   Toll Free: (800) 811-8110
Fax: (615) 340-7330
E-mail: umhefscholarships@gbhem.org
Web: www.umhef.org/receive.php?id=endowed_funds

Summary   To provide financial assistance to undergraduate and graduate Methodist students from Virginia who are interested in preparing for a career in ministry.

Eligibility   This program is open to undergraduate and graduate students who are studying theology to prepare for United Methodist ministry. Applicants must have been active, full members of a United Methodist Church in Virginia for at least 1 year prior to applying. They must have a GPA of 3.0 or higher and be able to demonstrate financial need. Along with their application, they must submit a 200-word essay on their involvement and/or leadership responsibilities in their church, school, and community within the last 3 years. U.S. citizenship or permanent resident status is required. Priority is given to Virginia residents who are enrolled or planning to enroll at 1) a United Methodist-related seminary or theological school; 2) a United Methodist-related liberal arts school and study theology; or 3) Virginia Wesleyan College in Norfolk, Virginia.

Financial data   The stipend is at least $1,000 per year.

Duration   1 year; recipients may reapply.

Additional information   The donor of this scholarship intended that recipients should repay it if they decide not to become ordained and give service in the United Methodist Church.

Number awarded   Varies each year. Recently, 2 of these scholarships were awarded.

Deadline   May of each year.

[205]
JOHN, KARL, ELIZABETH WURFFEL MEMORIAL FUND

Synod of the Northeast
Attn: Student Loan/Scholarship Programs
5811 Heritage Landing Drive
East Syracuse, NY 13057-9360
(315) 446-5990, ext. 215
Toll Free: (800) 585-5881, ext. 215
Fax: (315) 446-3708   E-mail: SynodOffice@Synodne.org
Web: www.synodne.org

Summary   To provide financial assistance to Presbyterians in the Synod of the Northeast who are interested in attending college or graduate school in any state.

Eligibility   This program is open to members of Presbyterian churches in the Synod of the Northeast (Connecticut, Maine, Massachusetts, New Hampshire, New Jersey, New York, Rhode Island, and Vermont) who are entering into a program in any state leading to 1) a 4-year baccalaureate degree, 2) a 3-year M.Div. degree, or 3) a 2-year Christian education degree. Applicants must submit an essay of 400 to 500 words on why they should be considered for this assistance, their reasons for wanting to pursue a college or seminary education, their extracurricular activities and interests (school, church, and community), and the role their faith will take in fulfilling their academic goals. Selection is based on financial need, academic potential, church and campus ministry involvement, community and mission involvement, and continued academic improvement.

Financial data   The stipend is $2,000 per year.

Duration   1 year; may be renewed up to 3 additional years.

Additional information   This program was established in 2000.

Number awarded   3 each year.

Deadline   March of each year.

[206]
JOHN W. MCDEVITT (FOURTH DEGREE) SCHOLARSHIPS

Knights of Columbus
Attn: Department of Scholarships
P.O. Box 1670
New Haven, CT 06507-0901
(203) 752-4332   Fax: (203) 772-2696
E-mail: info@kofc.org
Web: www.kofc.org/un/en/scholarships/mcdevitt.html

Summary   To provide financial assistance to entering freshmen at Catholic colleges and universities who have ties to the Knights of Columbus.

Eligibility   Eligible are students entering their freshman year in a program leading to a baccalaureate degree at a Catholic college or university in the United States; applicants must be members in good standing of the Knights of Columbus, or the wife, widow, son, or daughter of a current member or of a deceased member who was in good standing at the time of death. Selection is based on secondary school record, class rank, and aptitude test scores.

Financial data The stipend is $1,500 per year.

Duration 1 year; may be renewed up to 3 additional years upon evidence of satisfactory academic performance.

Number awarded Approximately 36 each year.

Deadline February of each year.

[207]
JORDAN SCHOLARSHIP FUND

International Council of Community Churches
21116 Washington Parkway
Frankfort, IL 60423-3112
(815) 464-5690   Fax: (815) 464-5692
E-mail: iccc60423@sbcglobal.net
Web: www.iccusa.com

Summary To provide financial assistance for college to members of a Community Church in good standing with the International Council of Community Churches.

Eligibility This program is open to high school seniors and older adults seeking to further their education who are in need of financial assistance. Applicants must be active members of a Community Church in good standing with the International Council of Community Churches. They must submit an application form, proof of financial need, 2 letters of recommendation (1 must be from a pastor of a member church), grade transcripts, and a statement of education and career goals.

Financial data The maximum stipend is $1,000.

Duration 1 year.

Additional information This fund was established in 1960 in memory of Ralph W. Jordan, the council's first treasurer, and his wife, Helen Moucey Jordan, a major national leader in the Women's Christian Fellowship.

Number awarded Several each year.

Deadline Deadline not specified.

[208]
J.S. REESE SHANKLIN SCHOLARSHIP

Baptist Convention of Maryland/Delaware
Attn: Woman's Missionary Union of Maryland/Delaware
10255 Old Columbia Road
Columbia, MD 21046
(410) 290-5290   Toll Free: (800) 466-5290
E-mail: gparker@bcmd.org
Web: bcmd.org/wmu

Summary To provide financial assistance to men who are members of Southern Baptist churches affiliated with the Baptist Convention of Maryland/Delaware and interested in attending a college or seminary in any state.

Eligibility This program is open to men who are active members of a Southern Baptist church/mission or Baptist student ministry affiliated with the Baptist Convention of Maryland/Delaware. Applicants must be enrolled or planning to enroll full time at 1) an accredited college or university in any state, or 2) a Southern Baptist seminary. They must have a grade point average of "C" or higher and be able to demonstrate financial need. Along with their application, they must submit a brief essay that includes a testimony of their salvation experience; their involvement in church, school, and community activities; and the kind of work God has called

them to do after completing their education, how they have come to believe God wants them in this work, and their plans to fulfill His call. Priority is given to applicants who are preparing for missionary service under the North American Mission Board or International Mission Board of the Southern Baptist Convention, career service with the Woman's Missionary Union (WMU), or work with the Men's Ministries.

Financial data The stipend is $375 per semester ($750 per year). Funds are paid directly to the recipient's school.

Duration 1 year; may be renewed for a total of 8 semesters of undergraduate study or 6 semesters of seminary master's degree work.

Number awarded Varies each year.

Deadline February of each year for fall semester or August of each year for spring semester.

[209]
JUDGE LEAH B. MCCARTNEY SCHOLARSHIP FUND

Missouri United Methodist Foundation
Attn: Scholarships
111 South Ninth Street, Suite 230
P.O. Box 1076
Columbia, MO 66205-1076
(573) 875-4168   Toll Free: (800) 332-8238
Fax: (573) 875-4595   E-mail: foundation@mumf.org
Web: www.mumf.org/view_page.php?page=20

Summary To provide financial assistance to members of United Methodist churches in Missouri who are interested in attending college in any state.

Eligibility This program is open to United Methodist residents of Missouri who are high school seniors or current college students. Applicants must submit a letter of recommendation from their pastor indicating that they are full members of the United Methodist Church and of suitable character to be considered for a scholarship. They must also submit high school or college transcripts, a statement describing their course of study and goals for the future, and a photograph.

Financial data The stipend is $2,000.

Duration 1 year.

Number awarded 2 each year.

Deadline March of each year.

[210]
JULIA C. PUGH SCHOLARSHIP

Woman's Missionary Union
Attn: WMU Foundation
100 Missionary Ridge
Birmingham, AL 35242
(205) 408-5525   Toll Free: (877) 482-4483
Fax: (205) 408-5508   E-mail: wmufoundation@wmu.org
Web: www.wmufoundation.com

Summary To provide financial assistance for undergraduate or graduate study to the dependent children of Southern Baptist missionaries.

Eligibility This program is open to Southern Baptist undergraduate and graduate students in any field who have significant financial need and do not qualify for regular scholarships. Applicants must be dependents of North American or international missionaries who are under appointment of the

North American Mission Board (NAMB) of the Southern Baptist Convention.

Financial data A stipend is awarded (amount not specified).

Duration 1 year.

Number awarded Varies each year.

Deadline February of each year.

[211]
JULIETTE M. ATHERTON SCHOLARSHIP FOR MINISTER'S SONS AND DAUGHTERS

Hawai'i Community Foundation
Attn: Scholarship Department
827 Fort Street Mall
Honolulu, HI 96813
(808) 537-6333   Toll Free: (888) 731-3863
Fax: (808) 521-6286
E-mail: scholarships@hcf-hawaii.org
Web: www.hawaiicommunityfoundation.org/scholarships

Summary To provide financial assistance the dependents of Protestants ministers in Hawaii who plan to attend college in any state.

Eligibility This program is open to the dependent sons or daughters of ordained and active Protestant ministers in an established denomination. Applicants must be residents of the state of Hawaii, able to demonstrate financial need, interested in enrolling full time at an accredited 2- or 4-year college or university in any state, and able to demonstrate academic achievement (GPA of 2.7 or higher). Along with their application, they must submit a short statement indicating their reasons for attending college, their planned course of study, their career goals, what community service means to them, their parent's current position, their parent's church/parish name, the denomination and place and date of ordination of their minister parent, and the name of the seminary attended by their minister parent.

Financial data The amounts of the awards depend on the availability of funds and the need of the recipient. Recently, the average value of all scholarships awarded by the foundation was $2,041.

Duration 1 year.

Number awarded Varies each year. Recently, 49 of these scholarships were awarded.

Deadline February of each year.

[212]
JULIETTE MATHER SCHOLARSHIP

Woman's Missionary Union
Attn: WMU Foundation
100 Missionary Ridge
Birmingham, AL 35242
(205) 408-5525   Toll Free: (877) 482-4483
Fax: (205) 408-5508   E-mail: wmufoundation@wmu.org
Web: www.wmufoundation.com

Summary To provide financial assistance to Southern Baptist undergraduate or graduate students preparing for a career in Christian ministry.

Eligibility This program is open to Southern Baptist undergraduate and graduate students who are preparing for a career in Christian ministry and service. They must be inter-

ested in preparing to become the Baptist leaders of the future.

Financial data A stipend is awarded (amount not specified).

Duration 1 year.

Number awarded Varies each year.

Deadline January of each year.

[213]
JULIUS S., JR. AND IANTHIA H. SCOTT ENDOWED SCHOLARSHIP

United Methodist Higher Education Foundation
Attn: Scholarships Administrator
1001 19th Avenue South
P.O. Box 340005
Nashville, TN 37203-0005
(615) 340-7385   Toll Free: (800) 811-8110
Fax: (615) 340-7330
E-mail: umhefscholarships@gbhem.org
Web: www.umhef.org/receive.php?id=endowed_funds

Summary To provide financial assistance to Methodist undergraduate students at designated Historically Black Colleges and Universities of the United Methodist Church.

Eligibility This program is open to students entering their sophomore year at the following Historically Black Colleges and Universities of the United Methodist Church: Wiley College, Paine College, or Philander Smith College. Applicants must have been active, full members of a United Methodist Church for at least 1 year prior to applying. They must have a GPA of 3.0 or higher and be able to demonstrate financial need. Along with their application, they must submit a 200-word essay on their involvement and/or leadership responsibilities in their church, school, and community within the last 3 years. U.S. citizenship or permanent resident status is required.

Financial data The stipend is at least $1,000 per year.

Duration 1 year; nonrenewable.

Additional information This program was established in 1999.

Number awarded 1 scholarship is awarded each year on a rotational basis among the 3 participating institutions.

Deadline May of each year.

[214]
KANETA FOUNDATION SCHOLARSHIP FUND

Hawai'i Community Foundation
Attn: Scholarship Department
827 Fort Street Mall
Honolulu, HI 96813
(808) 537-6333   Toll Free: (888) 731-3863
Fax: (808) 521-6286
E-mail: scholarships@hcf-hawaii.org
Web: www.hawaiicommunityfoundation.org/scholarships

Summary To provide financial assistance to residents of Hawaii who are members of a Christian church and interested in attending college in any state.

Eligibility This program is open to seniors graduating from high schools in Hawaii who are members of a Christian church. Applicants must be planning to attend a college or university in any state. They must be able to demonstrate academic achievement (GPA of 3.0 or higher and satisfactory

SAT or ACT scores), good moral character, and financial need. Along with their application, they must submit a short statement indicating their reasons for attending college, their planned course of study, their career goals, what community service means to them, a description of their family dynamics, a discussion of any adversities they have overcome, and their participation in community service activities.

Financial data The amounts of the awards depend on the availability of funds and the need of the recipient. Recently, the average value of all scholarships awarded by the foundation was $2,041.

Duration 1 year; may be renewed.

Number awarded Varies each year. Recently, 66 of these scholarships were awarded.

Deadline February of each year.

[215]
KANSAS EAGLE SCOUT OF THE YEAR SCHOLARSHIP

American Legion
Department of Kansas
1314 S.W. Topeka Boulevard
Topeka, KS 66612-1886
(785) 232-9315   Fax: (785) 232-1399
Web: www.ksamlegion.org

Summary To recognize and reward, with scholarships for college in the state, Eagle Scouts who are members of a troop associated with the American Legion in Kansas or a son or grandson of a member of the Legion in the state.

Eligibility Applicants for this award must be Kansas residents who are either 1) a registered, active member of a Boy Scout Troop, Varsity Scout Team, or Explorer Post sponsored by an American Legion Post or Auxiliary Unit or 2) a registered active member of a Boy Scout Troop, Varsity Scout Team, or Explorer Post and also the son or grandson of a member of the American Legion or American Legion Auxiliary. Candidates must also 1) be active members of their religious institution and have received the appropriate religious emblem; 2) have demonstrated practical citizenship in church, school, Scouting, and community; and 3) be at least 15 years of age and enrolled in high school. They must be planning to attend a college or university in Kansas.

Financial data The award is a $500 scholarship.

Duration This award is presented annually.

Number awarded 1 each year.

Deadline February of each year.

[216]
KANSAS-NEBRASKA CHRISTIAN HIGHER EDUCATION FUND

Kansas-Nebraska Convention of Southern Baptists
Attn: Kansas-Nebraska Southern Baptist Foundation
5410 S.W. Seventh Street
Topeka, KS 66606-2398
(785) 228-6800   Toll Free: (800) 984-9092
Fax: (785) 273-4992   E-mail: beckyholt@kncsb.org
Web: www.kncsb.org/ministry/article/foundation_funds

Summary To provide financial assistance to Southern Baptists from Kansas and Nebraska who are entering a college or seminary in any state affiliated with the denomination.

Eligibility This program is open to members of churches in the Kansas-Nebraska Convention of Southern Baptists. Applicants must be entering their first year at a Southern Baptist college, university, or seminary in any state.

Financial data A stipend is awarded (amount not specified).

Duration 1 year. Seminary students may reapply.

Number awarded 1 or more each year.

Deadline February of each year.

[217]
KATHY LOUDAT MUSIC SCHOLARSHIP

New Mexico Baptist Foundation
5325 Wyoming Boulevard, N.E.
P.O. Box 16560
Albuquerque, NM 87191-6560
(505) 332-3777   Toll Free: (877) 841-3777
Fax: (505) 332-2777   E-mail: foundation@nmbf.com
Web: www.bcnm.com

Summary To provide financial assistance to female members of Southern Baptist churches in New Mexico who are attending college in any state to prepare for a career in church music.

Eligibility This program is open to full-time female college, university, and seminary students who are preparing for a career in church music. Applicants must have a GPA of 3.0 or higher and be able to demonstrate financial need. They must be members of Southern Baptist churches in New Mexico or former members in good standing with the Southern Baptist Convention.

Financial data A stipend is awarded (amount not specified).

Duration 1 year.

Number awarded 1 or more each year.

Deadline April of each year.

[218]
KATINA JOHN MALTA SCHOLARSHIPS

Greek Orthodox Archdiocese of America
Attn: Office of the Chancellor
8 East 79th Street
New York, NY 10075
(212) 774-0513   Fax: (212) 774-0251
E-mail: scholarships@goarch.org
Web: www.goarch.org

Summary To provide financial assistance to high school seniors and current undergraduates who are of the Eastern Orthodox faith and plan to study the sciences, business, or the arts.

Eligibility The program is open to high school seniors and current undergraduates who are enrolled or planning to enroll full time at an accredited college or university in the United States. Applicants must be of the Eastern Orthodox faith (within a jurisdiction of the member churches of the Standing Conference of Canonical Orthodox Bishops in the Americas) and U.S. citizens or permanent residents. They must have an SAT score of at least 1500 (or an equivalent score on the ACT). Preference is given to applicants who are orphans and to those who are interested in studying the sciences, business, or the arts. Along with their application, they must submit a 1-page essay on their reasons for applying for this scholarship and how their planned studies will help them serve the Church and/or the community at large. Financial need is considered in the selection process.

Financial data The stipend ranges from $1,000 to $3,000.

Duration 1 year.

Number awarded Varies each year. Recently, 13 of these scholarships, with a value of $28,000, were awarded.

Deadline April of each year.

[219]
KEMPERS HISTORY SCHOLARSHIP

Iowa United Methodist Foundation
2301 Rittenhouse Street
Des Moines, IA 50321
(515) 974-8927
Web: www.iumf.org/umscholarships.html

Summary To provide financial assistance to students majoring in history at Iowa colleges affiliated with the United Methodist Church.

Eligibility This program is open to students enrolled full time at Iowa United Methodist-affiliated colleges. Applicants must exhibit a "Christian philosophy of history," be a good conveyor of ideas, and communicate well. Financial need is considered in the selection process, but it is not necessarily the determining factor.

Financial data The stipend is $1,300.

Duration 1 year.

Number awarded 1 each year.

Deadline March of each year.

[220]
KEN WILLIAMS SCHOLARSHIP

New Mexico Baptist Foundation
5325 Wyoming Boulevard, N.E.
P.O. Box 16560
Albuquerque, NM 87191-6560
(505) 332-3777   Toll Free: (877) 841-3777
Fax: (505) 332-2777   E-mail: foundation@nmbf.com
Web: www.bcnm.com

Summary To provide financial assistance to members of Southern Baptist churches in New Mexico who plan to attend college in any state.

Eligibility This program is open to members of Southern Baptist churches in New Mexico who are enrolled full time at an accredited college or university in any state. Applicants must have a GPA of 2.0 or higher and be able to demonstrate financial need.

Financial data A stipend is awarded (amount not specified).

Duration 1 year.

Number awarded 1 or more each year.

Deadline April of each year.

[221]
KEN YAMADA SCHOLARSHIP ENDOWMENT

United Methodist Higher Education Foundation
Attn: Scholarships Administrator
1001 19th Avenue South
P.O. Box 340005
Nashville, TN 37203-0005
(615) 340-7385   Toll Free: (800) 811-8110
Fax: (615) 340-7330
E-mail: umhefscholarships@gbhem.org
Web: www.umhef.org/receive.php?id=endowed_funds

Summary To provide financial assistance to Methodist students who are entering freshmen at Methodist-related colleges and universities.

Eligibility This program is open to students enrolling as full-time freshmen at United Methodist-related colleges and universities. Applicants must have been active, full members of a United Methodist Church for at least 1 year prior to applying. They must have a GPA of 3.0 or higher and be able to demonstrate financial need. Along with their application, they must submit a 200-word essay on their involvement and/or leadership responsibilities in their church, school, and community within the last 3 years. U.S. citizenship or permanent resident status is required.

Financial data The stipend is at least $1,000 per year.

Duration 1 year; nonrenewable.

Additional information This program was established in 2005.

Number awarded Varies each year. Recently, 2 of these scholarships were awarded.

Deadline May of each year.

[222]
KENTUCKY STATE MISSIONARIES' CHILDREN SCHOLARSHIPS

Kentucky Woman's Missionary Union
Attn: Scholarships
13420 Eastpoint Centre Drive
P.O. Box 436569
Louisville, KY 40253-6569
(502) 489-3534   Toll Free: (866) 489-3534 (within KY)
Fax: (502) 489-3566   E-mail: kywmu@kybaptist.org
Web: kywmu.org/scholarships

Summary To provide financial assistance for college or nursing school to children of Baptist mission personnel in Kentucky.

Eligibility This program is open to unmarried children of mission personnel employed by churches and associations related to the Missions Division of the Kentucky Baptist Convention. Applicants must have a GPA of 2.7 or higher and be enrolled or planning to enroll full-time at Campbellsville University, Cumberland College, Georgetown College, or a collegiate nursing program.

Financial data Stipends range from $250 to $500.

Duration 1 year.

Number awarded 1 or more each year.

Deadline January of each year.

[223]
KENTUCKY WMU ANNIVERSARY SCHOLARSHIPS

Kentucky Woman's Missionary Union
Attn: Scholarships
13420 Eastpoint Centre Drive
P.O. Box 436569
Louisville, KY 40253-6569
(502) 489-3534   Toll Free: (866) 489-3534 (within KY)
Fax: (502) 489-3566   E-mail: kywmu@kybaptist.org
Web: kywmu.org/scholarships

Summary   To provide financial assistance to students at Baptist colleges and universities in Kentucky who are preparing for Christian service.

Eligibility   This program is open to natives of Kentucky who are sophomores, juniors, or seniors at Baptist colleges and universities in the state. Applicants must be active members of churches affiliated with the Kentucky Baptist Convention or the General Association of Baptists in Kentucky, be enrolled full time, have a GPA of 2.7 or higher, be able to demonstrate financial need, and be preparing for full-time Christian service. They must apply through their college or university.

Financial data   Stipends range from $400 to $600.

Duration   1 year.

Additional information   This program was established in 1953. The Baptist institutions in Kentucky are Georgetown College, Cumberland College, and Campbellsville University.

Number awarded   12 each year.

Deadline   January of each year.

[224]
KITTRELL-ALLEN-ADAMS SCHOLARSHIP

African Methodist Episcopal Church
Second Episcopal District
c/o Jettie Williams, District Coordinator
905 Lira Drive
Fort Washington, MD 20744
(301) 203-6836

Summary   To provide financial assistance to members of the African Methodist Episcopal (AME) Church in its Second Episcopal District who are interested in attending college in any state.

Eligibility   This program is open to AME members in the Second Episcopal District, which includes the Conferences of Baltimore, Washington, Virginia, North Carolina, and Western North Carolina. Applicants must be graduating high school seniors or students already working on an undergraduate degree at a college or university in any state. Along with their application, they must submit an autobiographical essay of 1 to 2 pages that includes information about their future goals and family, school, church, and community involvements. Selection is based on that essay, high school grades and SAT scores, letters of recommendation, and financial need.

Financial data   A stipend is awarded (amount not specified).

Duration   1 year.

Number awarded   1 or more each year.

Deadline   July of each year.

[225]
KJT HIGH SCHOOL SCHOLARSHIPS

KJT Memorial Foundation
214 East Colorado
P.O. Box 297
La Grange, TX 78945
(979) 968-5877   Toll Free: (800) 245-8182
E-mail: info@kjtnet.org
Web: www.kjtnet.org/benefits.htm

Summary   To provide financial assistance to graduating high school seniors who are members of the Catholic Union of Texas (KJT) and interested in attending college in any state.

Eligibility   This program is open to graduating high school seniors who have been KJT-insured members for at least 1 year. Applicants must be planning to attend a college or university in any state. Selection is based on academic record, active participation in KJT, extracurricular activities, and applicants' individual merits.

Financial data   The stipend is $1,000; however, if any of the recipients enroll in a Catholic institution, they receive an additional $1,000.

Duration   1 year.

Additional information   KJT is the symbol for the Catholic Union of Texas. In Czech, it is Katolicka Jednota Texaskaa, hence KJT. This is a Texas fraternal benefit insurance organization. To be eligible for membership, applicants must be Catholic or a non-Catholic spouse or child of a KJT member.

Number awarded   10 each year.

Deadline   February of each year.

[226]
LAWRENCE AND DONNA TAYLOR SCHOLARSHIPS

Boone First United Methodist Church
703 Arden Street
Boone, IA 50036
(515) 432-4660   E-mail: bnfumc@mchsi.com
Web: www.boonefmc.org/TaylorEstateScholarships

Summary   To provide financial assistance to members of congregations affiliated with the World Methodist Council who are interested in attending college or graduate school to prepare for a church-related vocation.

Eligibility   This program is open to full-time students preparing for the ordained ministry or certification as director of Christian education, minister of Christian education, or associate in Christian education. Applicants must have been an active member of a congregation of a denomination within the World Methodist Council for at least 3 years. Selection is based on academic standing, leadership ability, character, Christian commitment, and financial need. Preference is given to graduate students.

Financial data   Stipends range from $375 to $3,000 per year. Payment is made directly to the recipient's school.

Duration   1 year; recipients may reapply.

Number awarded   1 or more each year.

Deadline   April of each year.

[227]
LEADERSHIP SCHOLARS PROGRAM

United Methodist Higher Education Foundation
Attn: Scholarships Administrator
1001 19th Avenue South
P.O. Box 340005
Nashville, TN 37203-0005
(615) 340-7385   Toll Free: (800) 811-8110
Fax: (615) 340-7330
E-mail: umhefscholarships@gbhem.org
Web: umls.umc.org

Summary To provide financial assistance to undergraduate Methodist students who are planning to enroll at a church-related institution in the Southeast.

Eligibility This program is open to students entering 1 of 36 participating United Methodist-related colleges and universities in the southeastern states as a full-time first-year student. Applicants must have been an active member of a United Methodist Church in any state for at least 1 year. Their local church must agree to provide at least $1,000 for their support in college. Along with their application, they must submit a statement from their pastor, youth minister, or Sunday school teacher describing their leadership skills and potential.

Financial data The local church must agree to provide a stipend of $1,000 and the participating college or university agrees to match that. In addition, the United Methodist Higher Education Foundation (UMHEF) has agreed to provide a limited number of $1,000 matching scholarships, so students may receive as much as $3,000.

Duration 1 year; nonrenewable.

Additional information This program was established in 2004 by the Jurisdictional Conference of the Southeastern Jurisdiction (SEJ) of the United Methodist Church. It is jointly administered by the UMHEF and the General Board of Higher Education and Ministry.

Number awarded Varies each year; the UMHEF provides matching funds for up to 100 students.

Deadline March of each year.

[228]
LEE FRANCES HELLER MEMORIAL AWARD

International Foundation for Gender Education
Attn: Transgender Scholarship and Education Legacy
  Fund
13 Felton Street
P.O. Box 540229
Waltham, MA 02454-0229
(781) 899-2212   Fax: (781) 899-5703
E-mail: carrie@tself.org
Web: www.tself.org

Summary To provide financial assistance to Christian transgender students who are working on an undergraduate or graduate degree in religious studies.

Eligibility This program is open to undergraduate and graduate students who are living full time in a gender or sex role that differs from that assigned to them at birth and who are "out and proud" about their transgender identity. Applicants must be Christians working on a degree in religious studies. They may be of any age or nationality, but they must be attending or planning to attend a college, university, trade school, or technical college in the United States or Canada. Along with their application, they must submit an essay that identifies their home congregation and indicates how their transgender identity and their involvement in the Christian church have related to each other. Selection is based on affirmation of transgender identity; demonstration of integrity and honesty; participation and leadership in community activities; service as a role model, mentor, colleague, or adviser for the transgender communities; and service as transgender role model, mentor, colleague, or adviser to non-transpeople in religious studies.

Financial data Stipends average $2,000. Funds are paid directly to the student.

Duration 1 year; nonrenewable.

Number awarded 1 each year.

Deadline January of each year.

[229]
LEMUEL C. SUMMERS SCHOLARSHIP

United Methodist Higher Education Foundation
Attn: Scholarships Administrator
1001 19th Avenue South
P.O. Box 340005
Nashville, TN 37203-0005
(615) 340-7385   Toll Free: (800) 811-8110
Fax: (615) 340-7330
E-mail: umhefscholarships@gbhem.org
Web: www.umhef.org/receive.php?id=endowed_funds

Summary To provide financial assistance to undergraduate and graduate Methodist students who are preparing for ministry.

Eligibility This program is open to full-time undergraduate, graduate, and professional students at United Methodist-related colleges, universities, seminaries, and theological schools. Applicants must have been active, full members of a United Methodist Church for at least 1 year prior to applying and be preparing for Christian ministry. They must have a GPA of 3.0 or higher and be able to demonstrate financial need. Along with their application, they must submit a 200-word essay on their involvement and/or leadership responsibilities in their church, school, and community within the last 3 years. U.S. citizenship or permanent resident status is required.

Financial data The stipend is at least $1,000 per year.

Duration 1 year; recipients may reapply.

Number awarded Varies each year. Recently, 5 of these scholarships were awarded.

Deadline May of each year.

[230]
LEONARD M. PERRYMAN COMMUNICATIONS SCHOLARSHIP FOR ETHNIC MINORITY STUDENTS

United Methodist Communications
Attn: Communications Resourcing Team
810 12th Avenue South
P.O. Box 320
Nashville, TN 37202-0320
(615) 742-5481   Toll Free: (888) CRT-4UMC
Fax: (615) 742-5485   E-mail: scholarships@umcom.org
Web: crt.umc.org/interior.asp?ptid=44&mid=10270

Summary To provide financial assistance to minority United Methodist college students who are interested in careers in religious communications.
Eligibility This program is open to United Methodist ethnic minority students enrolled in accredited institutions of higher education as juniors or seniors. Applicants must be interested in preparing for a career in religious communications. For the purposes of this program, "communications" is meant to cover audiovisual, electronic, and print journalism. Selection is based on Christian commitment and involvement in the life of the United Methodist church, academic achievement, journalistic experience, clarity of purpose, and professional potential as a religion communicator.
Financial data The stipend is $2,500 per year.
Duration 1 year.
Additional information The scholarship may be used at any accredited institution of higher education.
Number awarded 1 each year.
Deadline March of each year.

[231]
LOUISE REEP SCHOLARSHIP

Iowa United Methodist Foundation
2301 Rittenhouse Street
Des Moines, IA 50321
(515) 974-8927
Web: www.iumf.org/umscholarships.html

Summary To provide financial assistance to high school seniors who are members of an Iowa United Methodist Church planning to attend a church-affiliated college in the state.
Eligibility This program is open to seniors graduating from high schools in Iowa who are members of a United Methodist Church congregation. Applicants must be planning to enroll full time at an Iowa college affiliated with the United Methodist Church. Financial need is considered in the selection process.
Financial data The stipend is $1,750.
Duration 1 year.
Number awarded 2 each year.
Deadline March of each year.

[232]
LOUISIANA METHODIST MERIT SCHOLARSHIP

United Methodist Church-Louisiana Conference
Attn: Higher Education and Campus Ministry
527 North Boulevard
Baton Rouge, LA 70802-5700
(225) 346-1646   Toll Free: (888) 239-5286
Fax: (225) 383-2652   E-mail: lcumc@bellsouth.net
Web: www.la-umc.org

Summary To provide financial assistance to undergraduate and graduate students from Louisiana who are attending or planning to attend a United Methodist college or university in any state.
Eligibility This program is open to undergraduate and graduate students who are members of United Methodist Churches in Louisiana. Applicants must be attending or planning to attend an accredited United Methodist college or university in any state. A letter of nomination from their pastor or chair of higher education and campus ministry is required

and must describe their academic achievement; active involvement in church, school, civic, and community activities; and reasons why they merit the scholarship. Applicants must also submit a statement that describes their career goals and financial need.
Financial data The stipend is $1,000.
Duration 1 year.
Number awarded 2 each year.
Deadline March of each year.

[233]
LOYAL CHRISTIAN BENEFIT ASSOCIATION POSTSECONDARY SCHOOL SCHOLARSHIPS

Loyal Christian Benefit Association
Attn: Scholarship Committee
700 Peach Street
P.O. Box 13005
Erie, PA 16514-1305
(814) 453-4331   Toll Free: (888) 230-LCBA
Fax: (866) 588-3173   E-mail: outreach@lcbalife.org
Web: lcbalife.org

Summary To provide financial assistance for college to students who are benefit members of the Loyal Christian Benefit Association (LCBA).
Eligibility This program is open to LCBA benefit members and the natural or legally adopted children or grandchildren of benefit members. Applicants must be high school seniors, GED recipients, high school graduates of any age entering college for the first time, or full-time undergraduates entering their second, third, or fourth year at an accredited degree- or certificate-granting institution. They must have a GPA of 2.5 or higher. Selection is based on a random drawing. Students are given bonus entries for the drawing based on 1) their GPA (up to 5 bonus entries for a GPA up to 4.0); 2) years of continuous LCBA membership as a base insured (up to 5 bonus entries for each year of membership); and 3) acts of LCBA fraternal service as attested to by LCBA branch or national officers (up to 5 bonus entries for each act of service).
Financial data The stipend is $2,500 per year.
Duration Up to 4 years.
Number awarded 5 each year.
Deadline April of each year.

[234]
LUKE E. HART MEMORIAL SCHOLARSHIPS

Knights of Columbus-Missouri State Council
c/o J.Y. Miller, Scholarship Committee Chair
322 Second Street
Glasgow, MO 65254
(660) 338-2105   E-mail: j.y.miller@sbcglobal.net
Web: www.mokofc.org/youth.htm

Summary To provide financial assistance to members of the Missouri Council of the Knights of Columbus and their families who plan to attend a branch of the University of Missouri system.
Eligibility This program is open to residents of Missouri who are enrolled or planning to enroll at a branch of the University of Missouri in Columbia, St. Louis, Kansas City, or Rolla. Applicants must be a member of the Knights of Columbus; the child or wife of a member; the child or widow of a member who was in good standing at the time of his death; a

Squire or Columbus Girl in good standing; or a minor child whose legal guardian is a member. Along with their application, they must submit a 200-word statement explaining their goals for the future, their professional ambitions, and how this scholarship will help them to achieve their goals. Selection is based on Catholic citizenship, community service, scholarship, and financial need.

Financial data The stipend is $1,000.

Duration 1 year.

Additional information This program was originally established in 1971.

Number awarded 4 each year.

Deadline February of each year.

[235]
LUTHER H. BUTLER STUDENT LOAN FUND

North Carolina Baptist Foundation, Inc.
Attn: Denominational Relations Committee
201 Convention Drive
Cary, NC 27511-4257
(919) 380-7334   Toll Free: (800) 521-7334
Fax: (919) 460-6334
Web: www.ncbaptistfoundation.org

Summary To provide educational loans to undergraduate and graduate students at designated Baptist colleges and universities in North Carolina.

Eligibility This loan program is open to students at the following historically-Baptist institutions in North Carolina: Campbell University, Chowan College, Gardner-Webb University, Mars Hill College, Meredith College, or Wingate College. Preference is given to applicants of evangelical Christian faith or background and those seeking a church-related vocation. Selection is based on moral character; dedication to family, church, and community; and financial need. U.S. citizenship or legal resident status is required.

Financial data The maximum loan is $12,000 per year. The interest rate is equal to the prevailing rate charged, plus 2%. No interest is charged and repayment need not begin until 6 months after conclusion of studies. Loans must be repaid within 10 years.

Duration 1 year; may be renewed up to 3 additional years by undergraduates or up to 2 additional years by graduate students.

Additional information There is a $10 application fee.

Number awarded 1 or more each year.

Deadline January of each year.

[236]
LUTHERAN COMMUNITY FOUNDATION SCHOLARSHIP

Lutheran Community Foundation
Attn: Senior Associated, Donor Services
625 Fourth Avenue South, Suite 1500
Minneapolis, MN 55415
(612) 844-4110   Toll Free: (800) 365-4172
Fax: (800) 844-4109
E-mail: rebecca.westermeyer@thelcf.org
Web: www.thelcf.org

Summary To provide financial assistance to high school seniors who belong to a congregation that has an active

Lutheran Community Foundation (LCF) Organizational Fund and who plan to attend a Lutheran college.

Eligibility This program is open to graduating high school seniors who are members of a congregation that has an active LCF Organizational Fund. Applicants must be planning to enroll full time at an accredited Lutheran-affiliated college or university. They must have a GPA of 3.5 or higher and be able to demonstrate financial need. Along with their application, they must submit a 200-word essay on why they are uniquely qualified for this award and a 500-word essay related to the mission of the LCF.

Financial data The stipend is $5,000. Funds must be used for tuition, room and board, books, laboratory expenses, and/or other educational expenditures.

Duration 1 year.

Number awarded 1 each year.

Deadline May of each year.

[237]
MABEL BOLLE SCHOLARSHIP

American Baptist Churches of the Rocky Mountains
Attn: American Baptist Women's Ministries
9085 East Mineral Circle, Suite 170
Centennial, CO 80112
(303) 988-3900   E-mail: web@abcrm.org
Web: www.abcrm.org

Summary To provide financial assistance to members of churches affiliated with the American Baptist Churches (ABC) USA in Wyoming who are interested in attending an ABC college or seminary in any state.

Eligibility This program is open to active members of churches cooperating with ABC in Wyoming. Applicants must be enrolled or planning to enroll at an ABC college, university, or seminary in any state. They must be committed to full-time Christian service.

Financial data The stipend is $500.

Duration 1 year.

Number awarded 1 or more each year.

Deadline Deadline not specified.

[238]
MABEL D. RUSSELL BLACK COLLEGE FUND

United Methodist Higher Education Foundation
Attn: Scholarships Administrator
1001 19th Avenue South
P.O. Box 340005
Nashville, TN 37203-0005
(615) 340-7385   Toll Free: (800) 811-8110
Fax: (615) 340-7330
E-mail: umhefscholarships@gbhem.org
Web: www.umhef.org/receive.php?id=endowed_funds

Summary To provide financial assistance to Methodist undergraduate and graduate students at Historically Black Colleges and Universities of the United Methodist Church.

Eligibility This program is open to students enrolling as full-time undergraduate and graduate students at the Historically Black Colleges and Universities of the United Methodist Church. Applicants must have been active, full members of a United Methodist Church for at least 1 year prior to applying. They must have a GPA of 3.0 or higher and be able to demonstrate financial need. Along with their application, they must submit a 200-word essay on their involvement and/or leadership responsibilities in their church, school, and community within the last 3 years. U.S. citizenship or permanent resident status is required.

Financial data The stipend is at least $1,000 per year.

Duration 1 year; nonrenewable.

Additional information This program was established in 1978. The qualifying schools are Bennett College for Women, Bethune-Cookman College, Claflin University, Clark Atlanta University, Dillard University, Huston-Tillotson College, Meharry Medical College, Paine College, Philander Smith College, Rust College, and Wiley College.

Number awarded 1 each year.

Deadline May of each year.

[239]
MABEL HEIL SCHOLARSHIP

United Methodist Church-Wisconsin Conference
Attn: Board of Higher Education and Campus Ministry
750 Windsor Street
P.O. Box 620
Sun Prairie, WI 53590-0620
(608) 837-7328   Toll Free: (888) 240-7328
Fax: (608) 837-8547
Web: www.wisconsinumc.org

Summary To provide financial assistance to United Methodist women from Wisconsin who are interested in attending college or graduate school in any state.

Eligibility This program is open to women who are members of congregations affiliated with the Wisconsin Conference of the United Methodist Church and attending or planning to attend college or graduate school in any state. Applicants must submit an essay on why they consider themselves a worthy student and a letter of recommendation from their pastor or the president of the local United Methodist Women. Preference is given to women who are responsible for others and are returning to the employment field.

Financial data A stipend is awarded (amount not specified).

Duration 1 semester; recipients may reapply.

Number awarded 1 or more each year.

Deadline April of each year for the first semester; September of each year for the second semester.

[240]
MAE LASSLEY/OSAGE SCHOLARSHIPS

Osage Scholarship Fund
c/o Roman Catholic Diocese of Tulsa
P.O. Box 690240
Tulsa, OK 74169-0240
(918) 294-1904   Fax: (918) 294-0920
E-mail: sarah.jameson@dioceseoftulsa.org
Web: www.osagetribe.com

Summary To provide financial assistance to Osage Indians who are Roman Catholics attending college or graduate school.

Eligibility This program is open to Roman Catholics who are attending or planning to attend a college or university as a full-time undergraduate or graduate student. Applicants must be Osage Indians on the rolls in Pawhuska, Oklahoma and have a copy of their Certificate of Indian Blood (CIB) or Osage

tribal membership card. Selection is based on academic ability and financial need.

Financial data The stipend is $1,000 per year.

Duration 1 year; may be renewed if the recipient maintains full-time enrollment and a GPA of 2.5 or higher as an undergraduate or 3.0 or higher as a graduate student.

Number awarded Normally, 10 each year: 2 for students attending St. Gregory's University in Shawnee, Oklahoma as freshmen and 8 for any college or university.

Deadline April of each year.

[241]
MANDY COATS MEMORIAL SCHOLARSHIP

Arkansas Baptist Foundation
10117 Kanis Road
Little Rock, AR 72205-6220
(501) 376-0732   Toll Free: (800) 798-0969
Fax: (501) 376-3831   E-mail: info@abf.org
Web: www.abf.org/individuals_scholarships.htm

Summary To provide financial assistance to high school seniors in Arkansas who are members of a church or other Christian organization and planning to attend college in any state.

Eligibility This program is open to seniors graduating from high schools in Arkansas who plan to enroll full time at a college or university in any state. Applicants must be an active member of a church and/or other Christian organization. They must have a GPA of 2.0 or higher. Along with their application, they must submit a statement explaining why they are applying for this scholarship; how their educational desires fit into their life's plan; honors, achievements, and/or awards from their church, school, or community; work experience; the happiest moment of their life; and their most difficult life experience. An interview may be required. Preference is given to student-athletes who are active members of evangelical Christian churches and who show promise of becoming outstanding Christian citizens.

Financial data A stipend is awarded (amount not specified).

Duration 1 year; may be renewed, provided the recipient maintains a GPA of 2.0 or higher.

Additional information This scholarship was first awarded in 2005.

Number awarded 1 or more each year.

Deadline March of each year.

[242]
MARIO CUGIA ITALIAN STUDIES SCHOLARSHIP

Italian Catholic Federation
8393 Capwell Drive, Suite 110
Oakland, CA 94621
(510) 633-9058   Toll Free: (888) ICF-1924
Fax: (510) 633-9758   E-mail: info@icf.org
Web: www.icf.org/scholarships.html

Summary To provide financial assistance to college students from selected states who are of Italian Catholic heritage and are interested in studying Italian language, literature, or culture.

Eligibility This program is open to undergraduates who live within Catholic Dioceses in Arizona, California, Nevada, and Illinois and are baptized Roman Catholics of Italian descent (or whose non-Italian Catholic parents, grandparents, or guardians are members of the Italian Catholic Federation). Applicants must be entering their third year of study, have at least a 3.2 GPA, and be majoring in Italian language, Italian literature, or another area of Italian art, history, or culture. They must submit a 150-word personal statement explaining their Italian origin (or federation membership affiliation of their non-Italian Catholic parents, grandparents, or guardians), why their Roman Catholic faith is important to them, and their plans for the future. Selection is based on scholastic achievement, financial need, leadership role, faculty recommendations, character references, and extracurricular activities.

Financial data The stipend is $600 per year for third-year students or $1,000 for fourth-year students.

Duration 1 year; may be renewed for the fourth year of university study.

Additional information This program was established in 1998.

Number awarded Varies each year; recently, 20 of these scholarships were awarded, including both third-year and fourth-year students.

Deadline July of each year.

[243]
MARTHA WATSON STUDENT LOAN FUND

North Carolina Baptist Foundation, Inc.
Attn: Denominational Relations Committee
201 Convention Drive
Cary, NC 27511-4257
(919) 380-7334   Toll Free: (800) 521-7334
Fax: (919) 460-6334
Web: www.ncbaptistfoundation.org

Summary To provide educational loans to college and seminary students, especially those attending Baptist institutions.

Eligibility This loan program is open to U.S. citizens and legal residents who are attending or planning to attend a college, university, technical school, or seminary. Preference is given to 1) applicants of evangelical Christian faith or background; 2) those seeking a church-related vocation; 3) residents of North Carolina; 4) members of 3 named churches in Robeson County and their children; 5) blood relatives of Mrs. Fawn Watson; and 6) students who can demonstrate financial need.

Financial data The maximum loan is $3,000 per year for students attending a Baptist institution or $1,600 for students attending a non-Baptist institution. The interest rate is equal to the prevailing rate, up to a maximum of 12%. No interest is charged and repayment need not begin until 6 months after conclusion of studies. Loans must be repaid within 15 years.

Duration 1 year; may be renewed up to 3 additional years by undergraduates or up to 2 additional years by graduate students.

Additional information There is a $10 application fee.

Number awarded 1 or more each year.

Deadline January of each year.

[244]
MARY AND ORLIN TRAPP SCIENCE SCHOLARSHIP

Iowa United Methodist Foundation
2301 Rittenhouse Street
Des Moines, IA 50321
(515) 974-8927
Web: www.iumf.org/umscholarships.html

Summary To provide financial assistance to Catholic, Protestant, or other students majoring in science or mathematics at a United Methodist college in Iowa.

Eligibility Eligible to apply for this support are students who have completed at least 1 year at a United Methodist college in Iowa. They must be majoring in science (including chemistry, physics, biology, botany, and zoology) or mathematics. First consideration is given to members of the Protestant or Catholic church. Selection is based on academic record and a broad range of other attributes, including honesty, high moral character, ethics, integrity, initiative, leadership ability, and concern for community and peers; financial need is not considered.

Financial data The stipend is $1,000.

Duration 1 year.

Number awarded 2 each year.

Deadline March of each year.

[245]
MARY B. RHODES MEDICAL SCHOLARSHIP

Woman's Missionary Union
Attn: WMU Foundation
100 Missionary Ridge
Birmingham, AL 35242
(205) 408-5525   Toll Free: (877) 482-4483
Fax: (205) 408-5508   E-mail: wmufoundation@wmu.org
Web: www.wmufoundation.com

Summary To provide financial assistance to children of Southern Baptist missionaries who are working on a degree in a medical field.

Eligibility This program is open to Southern Baptist students who are working on a degree in a medical field, including nursing, dentistry, or pharmacy. Applicants must be planning to go into international missions work. They must be dependents of international missionaries who are under appointment of the North American Mission Board (NAMB) of the Southern Baptist Convention.

Financial data A stipend is awarded (amount not specified).

Duration 1 year.

Number awarded Varies each year.

Deadline February of each year.

[246]
MARY CATHRYN KENNINGTON SCHOLARSHIP

Order of the Eastern Star-Grand Chapter of Texas
Attn: Education Committee
1503 West Division Street
Arlington, TX 76012
(817) 265-6263
Web: www.grandchapteroftexasoes.org/scholar_forms.asp

Summary To provide renewable financial assistance to residents of Texas interested in attending college or graduate school in any state, especially those planning to prepare for a career in religious service.

Eligibility This program is open to residents of Texas who are high school seniors or graduates already enrolled at an accredited college, university, or seminary in any state. Applicants must be interested in working on an undergraduate or graduate degree in any field, although the program especially encourages applications from those planning to prepare for a full-time career as a minister, missionary, director of religious education, Christian youth worker, or church music director. They must have a GPA of 2.0 or higher. Along with their application, they must submit an essay describing their plans for the future, reasons for applying for the scholarship, and financial status. Undergraduates must be enrolled full time.

Financial data The stipend is $1,000 per year.

Duration 1 year; may be renewed, provided the recipient maintains a GPA of 2.0 or higher.

Number awarded 1 or more each year.

Deadline February of each year.

[247]
MARY CROWLEY MEMORIAL SCHOLARSHIP

Baptist Convention of New York
Attn: BCNY Foundation
6538 Baptist Way
East Syracuse, NY 13057
(315) 433-1001   Toll Free: (800) 552-0004
Fax: (315) 433-1026   E-mail: cmeyer@bcnysbc.org
Web: www.bcnysbc.org/bcnyfoundation.html

Summary To provide financial assistance to members of churches in the Baptist Convention of New York who are preparing for a vocation in full-time Christian service or other activities.

Eligibility This program is open to members in good standing of churches in the Baptist Convention of New York. First priority is given to students preparing for full-time Christian service as ministerial students, missionary candidates, or other church-related vocations in music, education, or youth. If funds are available, students not entering full-time Christian vocations are considered. Along with their application, they must submit 1) an essay in which they share their goals for the future and how a degree in higher education will help them achieve those goals; and 2) an autobiography that includes their conversion experience, call to Christian service (for those planning a religious vocation), and plans to fulfill this calling. Financial need is also considered in the selection process.

Financial data A stipend is awarded (amount not specified).

Duration 1 year; may be renewed up to 3 additional years.

Number awarded 1 or more each year.

Deadline February of each year.

[248]
MARY HILL DAVIS ETHNIC/MINORITY STUDENT SCHOLARSHIP PROGRAM

Baptist General Convention of Texas
Attn: Institutional Ministries Department
333 North Washington
Dallas, TX 75246-1798
(214) 828-5252   Toll Free: (888) 244-9400
Fax: (214) 828-5261   E-mail: institutions@bgct.org
Web: texasbaptists.org

Summary To provide financial assistance for college to ethnic minority residents of Texas who are members of Texas Baptist congregations.

Eligibility This program is open to members of Texas Baptist congregations who are of African American, Hispanic, Native American, Asian, or other intercultural heritage. Applicants must be attending or planning to attend a university affiliated with the Baptist General Convention of Texas to work on a bachelor's degree as preparation for service as a future lay or vocational ministry leader in a Texas Baptist ethnic/minority church. They must have been active in their respective ethnic/minority community. Along with their application, they must submit a letter of recommendation from their pastor and transcripts. Students still in high school must have a GPA of at least 3.0; students previously enrolled in a college must have at least a 2.0 GPA. U.S. citizenship or permanent resident status is required.

Financial data Stipends are $800 per semester ($1,600 per year) for full-time students or $400 per semester ($800 per year) for part-time students.

Duration 1 semester; may be renewed up to 7 additional semesters.

Additional information The scholarships are funded through the Week of Prayer and the Mary Hill Davis Offering for state missions sponsored annually by Women's Missionary Union of Texas. The eligible institutions are Baptist University of The Americas, Baylor University, Dallas Baptist University, East Texas Baptist University, Hardin Simmons University, Houston Baptist University, Howard Payne University, University of Mary Hardin Baylor, and Wayland Baptist University.

Number awarded Varies each year.

Deadline April of each year.

[249]
MASSACHUSETTS DIOCESAN SCHOLARSHIP FUND FOR CHILDREN OF CLERGY

Episcopal Diocese of Massachusetts
Attn: Office of Administration
138 Tremont Street
Boston, MA 02111
(617) 482-5800, ext. 1349
Toll Free: (800) 696-6079 (within MA)
Fax: (617) 482-8431   E-mail: dianep@diomass.org
Web: www.diomass.org

Summary To provide financial assistance to the children of Episcopal clergy in Massachusetts who are interested in attending college in any state.

Eligibility This program is open to the children of canonically resident and licensed Episcopal clergy in the Diocese of Massachusetts; the children of clergy widows and widowers are also eligible. Applicants must be enrolled or planning to enroll as undergraduate students at a college or university in any state. Selection is based primarily on financial need.

Financial data Small grants are awarded.

Duration 1 year; may be renewed until completion of an undergraduate degree, provided the recipient demonstrates adequate academic achievement and continuing financial need.

Number awarded Varies each year; recently, a total of $45,600 was available for this program.

Deadline May of each year.

[250]
MASTER'S FUND

Order of the Daughters of the King, Inc.
101 Weatherstone Drive, Suite 870
Woodstock, GA 30188
(770) 517-8552   Fax: (770) 517-8066
E-mail: dok1885@doknational.org
Web: www.doknational.org

Summary To provide financial assistance to members of the Daughters of the King who are seeking undergraduate or graduate training at a church-related school in the United States or abroad.

Eligibility This program is open to women who are communicants of the Episcopal church, autonomous churches of the Anglican communion, or churches in communion with the Episcopal church. Applicants must be at least 21 years of age, have at least 2 years of college education or its equivalent, and have letters of recommendation from their bishop/ rector, the dean or academic adviser of their school, and 3 church women who know them well. The program gives priority to women preparing for missionary or other church-related work, but applicants may be seeking training at an accredited college, university, or graduate school in the United States or abroad. They must be willing to give at least 2 years' service (at a suitable salary) to the church upon completion of their training. Along with their application, they must submit a 500-word statement on what they believe God is calling them to do. Individuals can apply, but nominations are welcome. Priority is given to members of the Daughters; nominees from the church's Executive Council, bishops, and clergy; and nominees from members of the Daughters.

Financial data Scholarships range from $500 to $700 per year; funds are granted for tuition only and the money is paid directly to the school.

Duration 1 year; may be renewed until completion of studies.

Additional information This program was established in 1922.

Number awarded Varies; up to 15 each year.

Deadline February, May, or September of each year.

[251]
MATTIE J.C. RUSSELL SCHOLARSHIP

Woman's Missionary Union
Attn: WMU Foundation
100 Missionary Ridge
Birmingham, AL 35242
(205) 408-5525   Toll Free: (877) 482-4483
Fax: (205) 408-5508   E-mail: wmufoundation@wmu.org
Web: www.wmufoundation.com

Summary To provide financial assistance for undergraduate or graduate study to the dependent children of Southern Baptist missionaries.

Eligibility This program is open to Southern Baptist students who are working on an undergraduate or graduate degree in any field. Applicants must be dependents of North American missionaries who are under appointment of the North American Mission Board (NAMB) of the Southern Baptist Convention.

Financial data A stipend is awarded (amount not specified).

Duration 1 year.

Number awarded Varies each year.

Deadline February of each year.

[252]
MAUD BYRD WINDHAM SCHOLARSHIP

Alabama-West Florida United Methodist Foundation, Inc.
170 Belmont Drive
P.O. Box 8066
Dothan, AL 36304
(334) 793-6820   Fax: (334) 794-6480
E-mail: foundation@alwfumf.org
Web: www.alwfumf.org

Summary To provide financial assistance for college to students from the Alabama-West Florida Conference of the United Methodist Church who are interested in preparing for a career in designated fields.

Eligibility This program is open to members of United Methodist Churches within the Alabama-West Florida Conference. Applicants must be enrolled or planning to enroll in college in order to prepare for a career in a church-related vocation, nursing, or medicine. They must submit an essay on why they feel they should receive this scholarship and documentation of financial need.

Financial data The stipend is $500.

Duration 1 year.

Number awarded 1 or more each year.

Deadline June of each year.

[253]
MAUDE DAVIS/JOSEPH C. MCKINNEY SCHOLARSHIP

African Methodist Episcopal Church
Second Episcopal District Lay Organization
c/o Dr. V. Susie Oliphant, District Coordinator
910 Luray Place
Hyattsville, MD 20783
(301) 559-9488   E-mail: vsfo@verizon.net

Summary To provide financial assistance to members of the African Methodist Episcopal (AME) Church in its Second

Episcopal District who are interested in attending college in any state.

Eligibility This program is open to AME members in the Second Episcopal District, which includes the Conferences of Baltimore, Washington, Virginia, North Carolina, and Western North Carolina. Applicants must be graduating high school seniors or college freshmen who are attending or planning to attend a college or university in any state to work on an undergraduate degree or certification. Along with their application, they must submit a high school transcript and SAT scores, 3 letters of recommendation, a 1-page biographical statement that includes career goals, and documentation of financial need.

Financial data A stipend is awarded (amount not specified).

Duration 1 year.

Number awarded Each of the 5 Conferences may award 1 or more of these scholarships each year.

Deadline June of each year.

[254]
MEL LARSON JOURNALISM SCHOLARSHIPS

Evangelical Press Association
Attn: Scholarships
P.O. Box 28129
Crystal, MN 55428
(763) 535-4793   Fax: (763) 535-4794
E-mail: director@epassoc.org
Web: www.epassoc.org

Summary To provide financial assistance to upper-division and graduate students interested in preparing for a career in Christian journalism.

Eligibility This program is open to entering juniors, seniors, and graduate students who have at least 1 year of full-time study remaining. Applicants must be majoring or minoring in journalism or communications, preferably with an interest in the field of Christian journalism. They must be enrolled at an accredited Christian or secular college or university in the United States or Canada and have a GPA of 3.0 or higher. Along with their application, they must submit a biographical sketch that includes their birth date, hometown, family, and something about the factors that shaped their interest in Christian journalism; a copy of their academic record; references from their pastor and from an instructor; samples of published writing from church or school publications; and an original essay (from 500 to 700 words) on the state of journalism today.

Financial data Stipends range from $1,000 to $2,500.

Duration 1 year.

Additional information This program includes the Mel Larson Memorial Scholarship.

Number awarded Varies each year: recently, 4 of these scholarships were awarded.

Deadline March of each year.

[255]
MELVIN KELLY AND MAYME DUBOSE MEDLOCK MINISTERIAL SCHOLARSHIP

South Carolina United Methodist Foundation
P.O. Box 5087
Columbia, SC 29250-5087
(803) 771-9125   Fax: (803) 771-9135
E-mail: scumf@bellsouth.net
Web: www.umcsc.org/scholarships.html

Summary To provide financial assistance to residents of South Carolina who are attending college or graduate school in any state to prepare for ordained Methodist ministry.

Eligibility This program is open to residents of South Carolina who are certified candidates for ordained ministry in the United Methodist Church (UMC). Applicants must be enrolled full time either as an undergraduate at an accredited college or university or as a graduate student at a seminary or theological school in any state approved by the University Senate of the United Methodist Church. Financial need may be considered in the selection process.

Financial data A stipend is awarded (amount not specified).

Duration 1 year.

Additional information This scholarship was established by the South Carolina Conference of the United Methodist Church in 2001.

Number awarded 1 or more each year.

Deadline April of each year.

[256]
METHODIST SEPTEMBER 11 MEMORIAL SCHOLARSHIPS

United Methodist Higher Education Foundation
Attn: Scholarships Administrator
1001 19th Avenue South
P.O. Box 340005
Nashville, TN 37203-0005
(615) 340-7385   Toll Free: (800) 811-8110
Fax: (615) 340-7330
E-mail: umhefscholarships@gbhem.org
Web: www.umhef.org/receive.php?id=sept_11_scholarship

Summary To provide financial assistance to Methodists and undergraduate and graduate students at Methodist institutions whose parent or guardian was disabled or killed in the terrorist attacks on September 11, 2001.

Eligibility This program is open to 1) students attending a United Methodist-related college or university in the United States, and 2) United Methodist students attending a higher education institution in the United States. All applicants must have lost a parent or guardian or had a parent or guardian disabled as a result of the September 11, 2001 terrorist attacks. They must be enrolled as full-time undergraduate or graduate students. U.S. citizenship or permanent resident status is required.

Financial data The stipend depends on the number of applicants.

Duration 1 year; may be renewed as long as the recipients maintain satisfactory academic progress as defined by their institution.

Number awarded Varies each year; a total of $30,000 is available for this program.

Deadline Applications may be submitted at any time.

[257]
MICHIGAN BAPTIST SCHOLARSHIP SOCIETY SCHOLARSHIPS

American Baptist Churches of Michigan
Attn: Michigan Baptist Scholarship Society
4578 South Hagadorn Road
East Lansing, MI 48823
(517) 332-3594   Toll Free: (800) 632-2953
Fax: (517) 332-3186   E-mail: mawilliams@abc-mi.org
Web: www.abc-mi.org/?q=node/865

Summary To provide financial assistance to members of American Baptist Churches of Michigan who are preparing for a professional church vocation.

Eligibility This program is open to members of American Baptist Churches of Michigan who are entering or attending an accredited college, university, or seminary. Applicants must be able to provide evidence of 1) God's call to a professional church vocation; 2) spiritual, personal, and academic maturity; and 3) financial need. Along with their application, they must submit an autobiographical essay of 2 to 3 pages describing their Christian experience, call to professional church vocation, and career goals. Preference is given to full-time students at institutions related to the American Baptist Church.

Financial data Stipends are at least $2,000 per year for seminary students and at least $1,000 per year for college students.

Duration 1 year; may be renewed if the recipient maintains full-time enrollment and a GPA of 2.5 or higher.

Number awarded Varies each year.

Deadline June of each year for support beginning in the first academic term; October of each year for support beginning in the second academic term.

[258]
MIDWEST CONFERENCE/J.D. WILLIAMS SCHOLARSHIP

African Methodist Episcopal Church
Midwest Conference
Attn: Lay Organization Scholarship Committee
c/o Nedra Locke
1023 West Elm Terrace, Number One
Olathe, KS 66061
Web: midwestconflay.org

Summary To provide financial assistance to high school seniors who are members of African Methodist Episcopal (AME) churches in its Midwest Conference and interested in attending college in any state.

Eligibility This program is open to high school seniors who are members of an AME church in the Midwest Conference (Kansas, Nebraska, and northwest Missouri). Applicants must be planning to attend a college, university, junior college, or vocational school in any state. They must have a GPA of 2.5 or higher and "a positive Christian attitude." Along with their application, they must submit an essay of 250 to 300 words on how this scholarship will aid them in the attainment of their educational goals. Selection is based on academic

record, reference letters, qualities of leadership, and extracurricular activities and accomplishments.

Financial data The stipend is $500.

Duration 1 year.

Number awarded 1 each year.

Deadline March of each year.

[259]
MIDWEST CONFERENCE WOMEN'S MISSIONARY SOCIETY YOUTH EDUCATION SCHOLARSHIP AWARD

African Methodist Episcopal Church
Midwest Conference
Attn: Women's Missionary Society
YES Scholarship Committee
P.O. Box 171488
Kansas City, KS 66117-0488
Web: www.midwestwms.org/ypd.html

Summary To provide financial assistance to members of African Methodist Episcopal (AME) churches in its Midwest Conference who are interested in attending college in any state.

Eligibility This program is open to high school seniors and students already enrolled at a college, university, junior college, or vocational school in any state. Applicants must be a member of an AME church and its Young People's Department (YPD) in the Midwest Conference (Kansas, Nebraska, and northwest Missouri).

Financial data A stipend is awarded (amount not specified).

Duration 1 year.

Number awarded 1 or more each year.

Deadline June of each year.

[260]
MINISTERIAL EDUCATION FUND OF THE EVANGELICAL METHODIST CHURCH

Evangelical Methodist Church
Attn: General Board of Ministerial Education
P.O. Box 17070
Indianapolis, IN 46217
(317) 780-8017   Fax: (317) 780-8078
E-mail: hq@emchurch.org
Web: emchurch.org/general-boards/ministerial-education

Summary To provide loans-for-service to college, Bible school, and seminary students preparing for ministry service in the Evangelical Methodist Church.

Eligibility This program is open to 1) undergraduate students enrolled in an accredited Christian college in the Wesleyan tradition who are majoring in Bible, pastoral ministry, Christian education, or missions; and 2) students enrolled in an accredited theological seminary in the Wesleyan tradition approved by the Board of Ministerial Education of the Evangelical Methodist Church. Applicants must be in process toward ordination as an Evangelical Methodist Elder as recommended by their home District Superintendent and Board of Ministerial Relations. They must be a member in good standing in an Evangelical Methodist Church. Students working on a degree beyond the M.Div. are not eligible.

Financial data The maximum loan amount varies each year and is greater for seminary students than for undergraduates. Funds are disbursed jointly to the student and the school, for payment of tuition only. For each year of full-time ministry service while under a call to an Evangelical Methodist Church or the Board of World Missions, after being ordained an elder, one-sixth of the debt is cancelled. If the recipient does not complete the process of ordination as an Elder or drops out of school, the loan is repayable at an interest rate of 6%. Years of service as a Member on Trial do not qualify toward repaying the loan debt. If an Elder withdraws or is discontinued from ministerial service, the balance of the unpaid loan becomes due and is repayable at 6% interest.

Duration   1 year; may be renewed, provided the recipient maintains a GPA of 2.0 or higher.

Number awarded   Varies each year.

Deadline   Deadline not specified.

[261]
MINNESOTA EASTERN STAR TRAINING AWARDS FOR RELIGIOUS LEADERSHIP

> Order of the Eastern Star-Grand Chapter of Minnesota
> Attn: Grand Secretary
> 11501 Masonic Home Drive
> Bloomington, MN 55437
> (952) 948-6800   E-mail: mngrsecoes@hotmail.com
> Web: www.mnoes.com

Summary   To provide financial assistance to residents of Minnesota who are attending a college or seminary in any state to prepare for a career in religious leadership in any denomination.

Eligibility   This program is open to full- and part-time students at colleges, universities, and seminaries in any state who have been residents of Minnesota for at least 1 year. Applicants must be preparing for a full-time religious career, including ordained ministry, missionary, youth ministry, director of religious education, music ministry, or other related profession. Along with their application, they must submit brief personal statements on the role of religion in today's living, how churches can become more effective, the ways in which they feel they can make a difference in people's lives, and their personal religious philosophy. Selection is based on character, scholarship, leadership, citizenship, and financial need.

Financial data   Stipends vary; the total award received by any single student may not exceed $10,000.

Duration   1 year; may be renewed.

Number awarded   1 or more each year.

Deadline   January of each year.

[262]
MINNESOTA GLBT LUTHERAN STUDENT AWARD

> Philanthrofund Foundation
> Attn: Scholarship Committee
> 1409 Willow Street, Suite 210
> Minneapolis, MN 55403-3251
> (612) 870-1806   Toll Free: (800) 435-1402
> Fax: (612) 871-6587   E-mail: info@PfundOnline.org
> Web: www.pfundonline.org/scholarships.html

Summary   To provide financial assistance to gay, lesbian, bisexual, and transgender students who are Lutherans, resi-

dents of Minnesota, and interested in attending college or graduate school in any state.

Eligibility   This program is open to Minnesota residents who are Lutherans and attending or planning to attend a Lutheran or other institution (college, university, or graduate school) in any state. Applicants must identify with or be involved with the gay, lesbian, bisexual, or transgender (GLBT) community. They must indicate how their GLBT identity and their involvement in the Lutheran church are related to each other. Selection is based on the applicant's 1) affirmation of GLBT identity or commitment to GLBT communities; 2) evidence of experience and skills in service and leadership; and 3) evidence of service and leadership in GLBT communities, including serving as a role model, mentor, and/or adviser.

Financial data   The stipend is $2,000. Funds must be used for tuition, books, fees, or dissertation expenses.

Duration   1 year.

Number awarded   1 or more each year.

Deadline   January of each year.

[263]
MIRIAM HOFFMAN SCHOLARSHIPS

> United Methodist Church
> Attn: General Board of Higher Education and Ministry
> Office of Loans and Scholarships
> 1001 19th Avenue South
> P.O. Box 340007
> Nashville, TN 37203-0007
> (615) 340-7344   Fax: (615) 340-7367
> E-mail: umscholar@gbhem.org
> Web: www.gbhem.org/loansandscholarships

Summary   To provide financial assistance to undergraduate and graduate Methodist students who are preparing for a career in music (including music education).

Eligibility   This program is open to undergraduate and graduate students who are enrolled full time and preparing for a career in music. Applicants must have been active, full members of a United Methodist Church for at least 1 year prior to applying and have a GPA of 2.5 or higher. Preference is given to students interested in music education or music ministry. U.S. citizenship or permanent resident status is required.

Financial data   The stipend is $1,000.

Duration   1 year; recipients may reapply.

Additional information   This program was established in 2001.

Number awarded   Varies each year. Recently, 12 of these scholarships were awarded.

Deadline   May of each year.

[264]
MISSISSIPPI BAPTIST CONVENTION MINISTERIAL AID PROGRAM

> Mississippi Baptist Convention
> Attn: Board of Ministerial Education
> P.O. Box 1832
> Madison, MS 39130-1843
> (601) 853-4436   E-mail: rcourtney53@comcast.net
> Web: www.mbcb.org/agencies/bme

Summary To provide scholarship/loans to undergraduate ministerial students from Mississippi attending Baptist colleges in the state.

Eligibility This program is open to active members of Southern Baptist churches that are contributing to the Mississippi Baptist Convention. Applicants must have made a public commitment to Southern Baptist ministry in the area of local church ministry, evangelism, North American missions, or international missions. They must be enrolled as full-time undergraduates at a Southern Baptist institution in Mississippi (Blue Mountain College, Mississippi College, or William Carey College), have and maintain a GPA of 2.0 or higher, and attend monthly meetings of their campus ministerial association. Along with their application, they must submit a brief description of their call to ministry and the work they feel called to do. An interview is required.

Financial data Recently, assistance for the full enrollment period averaged $5,960. Recipients must sign an agreement that obligates them to serve in a Southern Baptist ministry for a period of time no less than that for which they receive this assistance; if they fail to comply with the agreement, the ministerial aid becomes a loan which must be repaid.

Duration The full enrollment period is 26 months.

Additional information This program includes the following named scholarships (all held in trust by the Mississippi Baptist Foundation): the Therman V. Bryant Scholarship, the Carpenter-Gandy Scholarship, the William Clawson Scholarship, the Hardy R. Denham Scholarship, the Ernest Pinson Memorial Scholarship, and the William N. Washburn Scholarship.

Number awarded Approximately 275 each year.

Deadline September of each year.

[265]
MISSISSIPPI BAPTIST FOUNDATION COLLEGE SCHOLARSHIPS

Mississippi Baptist Foundation
Attn: MBF Scholarship Ministry
515 Mississippi Street
P.O. Box 530
Jackson, MS 39205-0530
(601) 292-3210   Toll Free: (800) 748-1651 (within MS)
Fax: (601) 968-0904
Web: www.msbaptistfoundation.org

Summary To provide financial assistance for college to members of Baptist churches in Mississippi, especially those who are interested in attending a Baptist institution in the state.

Eligibility This program is open to members in good standing of Baptist churches in Mississippi that are cooperating members of the Mississippi Baptist Convention. Applicants must submit a letter of recommendation from their pastor, documentation of financial need, and a brief summary of their life, including their Christian testimony, goals, and vocational and/or ministry pursuits. Preference is given to full-time students working on a bachelor's degree at 1 of the Mississippi Baptist colleges (Blue Mountain College, Mississippi College, or William Carey College). Graduate students are not eligible.

Financial data A stipend is awarded (amount not specified).

Duration 1 year; may be renewed if the recipient maintains a GPA of 2.5 or higher.

Additional information This program consists of a number of individual endowments, many of which specify a field of study, institution attended, and scholarship amount.

Number awarded Varies each year.

Deadline April of each year.

[266]
MISSISSIPPI CONFERENCE MERIT AWARD PROGRAM

United Methodist Church-Mississippi Conference
Attn: Committee on Higher Education and Campus Ministry
321 Mississippi Street
Jackson, MS 39201
(601) 354-0515, ext. 32   Toll Free: (866) 647-7486
E-mail: scumbest@mississippi-umc.org
Web: www.mississippi-umc.org/pages/detail/779

Summary To provide financial assistance to undergraduate and graduate students who are members of United Methodist Church (UMC) congregations in Mississippi and interested in attending an institution affiliated with the denomination in any state.

Eligibility This program is open to members of UMC congregations affiliated with the Mississippi Conference who are enrolled or planning to enroll at a UMC college or university in any state as an undergraduate or graduate student. Applicants must submit information on their financial need and their participation in organizations, programs, and their school, church, and community, including honors, awards, and leadership roles.

Financial data The stipend is $500.

Duration 1 year.

Number awarded 4 each year.

Deadline May of each year.

[267]
MISSISSIPPI UNITED METHODIST FOUNDATION SCHOLARSHIPS

Mississippi United Methodist Foundation
Attn: Executive Director
581 Highland Colony Parkway
P.O. Box 2415
Ridgeland, MS 39158-2415
(601) 948-8845   Toll Free: (800) 496-0975
Fax: (601) 360-0843   E-mail: info@ms-umf.org
Web: www.ms-umf.org

Summary To provide financial assistance for college or seminary to members of United Methodist Churches in Mississippi.

Eligibility This program is open to members of United Methodist Churches in Mississippi who are attending or planning to attend a college or seminary. The foundation administers a number of scholarship funds that have been established by particular congregations or individuals within the state. Each fund has different requirements. For further information, contact the foundation.

Financial data Stipends range up to $1,000.

Duration 1 year.

Number awarded Varies each year.

Deadline May of each year.

[268]
MISSOURI CONFERENCE STUDENT AID GRANTS

United Methodist Church-Missouri Conference
Attn: Board of Ordained Ministry
3601 Amron Court
Columbia, MO 65202
(573) 441-1770   Toll Free: (877) 736-1806
Fax: (573) 441-1780
E-mail: TMcManus@moumethodist.org
Web: www.moumethodist.org/pages/detail/851

Summary To provide financial assistance to undergraduate and seminary students who are preparing for ministry within the Missouri Conference of the United Methodist Church.

Eligibility This program is open to full- and part-time students at colleges and seminaries approved by the University Senate of the United Methodist Church (UMC). Applicants must have a working relationship with a district committee or team on ordained ministry in the Missouri Conference of the UMC. Undergraduates must be serving under appointment as a local pastor; seminarians must be certified candidates. Financial need is considered in the selection process.

Financial data A stipend is awarded (amount not specified). Both full- and part-time grants are available. Funds are paid jointly to the student and the institution.

Duration 1 year. Full-time grants may be renewed up to 3 additional years; part-time grants may be renewed up to 5 additional years.

Number awarded Varies each year.

Deadline June of each year.

[269]
MISSOURI STATE KNIGHTS OF COLUMBUS LADIES AUXILIARY SCHOLARSHIP

Knights of Columbus-Missouri State Council
c/o J.Y. Miller, Scholarship Committee Chair
322 Second Street
Glasgow, MO 65254
(660) 338-2105   E-mail: j.y.miller@sbcglobal.net
Web: www.mokofc.org/youth.htm

Summary To provide financial assistance to members of the Ladies Auxiliary of the Knights of Columbus in Missouri who are interested in attending college in the state.

Eligibility This program is open to residents of Missouri who are enrolled or planning to enroll at an accredited college, university, or trade school in the state. Applicants must be a member of the Ladies Auxiliary of the Knights of Columbus. Along with their application, they must submit a 200-word statement explaining their goals for the future, their professional ambitions, and how this scholarship will help them to achieve their goals. Selection is based on Catholic citizenship, community service, scholarship, and financial need.

Financial data The stipend is $1,000.

Duration 1 year.

Additional information This program was originally established in 1971.

Number awarded 1 each year.

Deadline February of each year.

[270]
MISSOURI STATE KNIGHTS OF COLUMBUS SCHOLARSHIPS

Knights of Columbus-Missouri State Council
c/o J.Y. Miller, Scholarship Committee Chair
322 Second Street
Glasgow, MO 65254
(660) 338-2105   E-mail: j.y.miller@sbcglobal.net
Web: www.mokofc.org/youth.htm

Summary To provide financial assistance to members of the Missouri Council of the Knights of Columbus and their families who plan to attend college in any state.

Eligibility This program is open to residents of Missouri who are enrolled or planning to enroll at an accredited college, technical school, or university in any state. Applicants must be a member of the Knights of Columbus; the child or wife of a member; the child or widow of a member who was in good standing at the time of his death; a Squire or Columbus Girl in good standing; or a minor child whose legal guardian is a member. Along with their application, they must submit a 200-word statement explaining their goals for the future, their professional ambitions, and how this scholarship will help them to achieve their goals. Selection is based on Catholic citizenship, community service, scholarship, and financial need.

Financial data The stipend is $1,000.

Duration 1 year.

Additional information This program was originally established in 1971.

Number awarded 3 each year.

Deadline February of each year.

[271]
MISSOURI STATE KNIGHTS OF COLUMBUS VOCATION SCHOLARSHIPS

Knights of Columbus-Missouri State Council
c/o J.Y. Miller, Scholarship Committee Chair
322 Second Street
Glasgow, MO 65254
(660) 338-2105   E-mail: j.y.miller@sbcglobal.net
Web: www.mokofc.org/youth.htm

Summary To provide financial assistance to residents of Missouri who plan to attend a college or seminary in any state to prepare for a religious vocation.

Eligibility This program is open to residents of Missouri who are enrolled or planning to enroll at an accredited college, university, or seminary in any state. Applicants must be preparing for a religious vocation with the approval of a Missouri Catholic diocese or a religious order in the state. Along with their application, they must submit a 200-word statement explaining their goals for the future, their professional ambitions, and how this scholarship will help them to achieve their goals. Selection is based on Catholic citizenship, community service, scholarship, and financial need.

Financial data The stipend is $1,000.

Duration 1 year.

Additional information This program was originally established in 1971. If no applications are received from individuals desiring to attend a seminary or be a postulant in a religious community, these scholarships may be awarded to applicants wishing to attend any accredited college or university, with preference to those attending a Catholic institution.

Number awarded 2 each year.

Deadline February of each year.

[272]
MISSOURI UNITED METHODIST FOUNDATION UNDERGRADUATE SCHOLARSHIPS

Missouri United Methodist Foundation
Attn: Scholarships
111 South Ninth Street, Suite 230
P.O. Box 1076
Columbia, MO 66205-1076
(573) 875-4168   Toll Free: (800) 332-8238
Fax: (573) 875-4595   E-mail: foundation@mumf.org
Web: www.mumf.org/view_page.php?page=20

Summary To provide financial assistance to members of United Methodist churches in Missouri who are interested in attending college in any state.

Eligibility This program is open to United Methodist residents of Missouri who are high school seniors or current college students. Applicants must submit a letter of recommendation from their pastor indicating that they are full members of the United Methodist Church and of suitable character to be considered for a scholarship. They must also submit high school or college transcripts, a statement describing their course of study and goals for the future, and a photograph.

Financial data The stipend is $1,000.

Duration 1 year.

Additional information This program includes support provided by the United Methodist Dollars for Scholars program, the Merrydelle May Scholarships, and the Mary Alice Reinhardt Scholarships.

Number awarded Varies each year. Recently, 47 of these scholarships were awarded.

Deadline March of each year.

[273]
MOTHER CARRIE SCHOLARSHIP

Iowa United Methodist Foundation
2301 Rittenhouse Street
Des Moines, IA 50321
(515) 974-8927
Web: www.iumf.org/otherscholarships.html

Summary To provide financial assistance for college to Iowa residents interested in preparing for a career in Christian service at a school in any state.

Eligibility This program is open to residents of Iowa who are graduating high school seniors or students already enrolled at a college, university, or community college in any state. Applicants must be preparing for a career in Christian service, particularly pastoral or diaconal ministry. Preference is given to members of Aldersgate United Methodist Church (in Urbandale, Iowa). Financial need is considered in the selection process.

Financial data The stipend is $1,000.

Duration 1 year.

Number awarded 1 each year.

Deadline March of each year.

[274]
MOUNT OLIVET FOUNDATION GRANTS

Mount Olivet United Methodist Church
Attn: Mount Olivet Foundation
1500 North Glebe Road
Arlington, VA 22207-2199
(703) 527-3934   Fax: (703) 524-8613
E-mail: scutshaw@mtolivet-umc.org
Web: www.mountolivetfoundation.org

Summary To provide financial assistance to undergraduate and graduate students, particularly Methodists.

Eligibility This program is open to undergraduate and graduate students, especially those already enrolled in a degree program. In the selection process, first preference is given to individuals connected to Mount Olivet United Methodist Church, second to members of a United Methodist Church in any state, third to residents of Arlington and northern Virginia, fourth to residents of the Washington, D.C. metropolitan area, and finally to residents of other areas. Financial need is considered in the selection process.

Financial data Stipends range from $500 to $1,500.

Duration 1 year.

Number awarded A limited number are awarded each year.

Deadline March, June, September, or December of each year.

[275]
MOUNT OLIVET FOUNDATION LOANS

Mount Olivet United Methodist Church
Attn: Mount Olivet Foundation
1500 North Glebe Road
Arlington, VA 22207-2199
(703) 527-3934   Fax: (703) 524-8613
E-mail: scutshaw@mtolivet-umc.org
Web: www.mountolivetfoundation.org

Summary To provide educational loans to undergraduate students, particularly Methodists.

Eligibility This program is open to high school seniors entering college for the first time. Applicants must be planning to enroll at least half time at a university, college, business school, technical school, or vocational school. They must be able to demonstrate financial need. In the selection process, first preference is given to individuals connected to Mouth Olivet United Methodist Church, second to members of a United Methodist Church in any state, third to residents of Arlington and northern Virginia, fourth to residents of the Washington, D.C. metropolitan area, and finally to residents of other areas.

Financial data Loans range from $1,000 to $5,000. Repayment must begin 6 months after the recipient completes the course of study or leaves school. Interest is charged at the rate of 1% until repayment begins and then 4% on the unpaid balance.

Duration 1 year; recipients may reapply.

Number awarded A limited number are awarded each year.

Deadline March, June, September, or December of each year.

[276]
MUSIC AND CHRISTIAN ARTS MINISTRY SCHOLARSHIP

African Methodist Episcopal Church
Attn: Christian Education Department
Music and Christian Arts Ministry
500 Eighth Avenue South
Nashville, TN 37203
Toll Free: (800) 525-7282   Fax: (615) 726-1866
E-mail: cedoffice@ameced.com
Web: www.ameced.com/music.shtml

Summary To provide financial assistance to members of African Methodist Episcopal (AME) churches who are interested in working on an undergraduate degree in music at a Black-related college in any state.

Eligibility This program is open to graduating high school seniors who are members of an AME congregation. Applicants must be planning to attend an AME-supported college or university or an Historically Black College or University (HBCU) in any state to study music. They must be planning to assume a music leadership position in a local AME church. Along with their application, they must submit a current high school transcript, 3 letters of recommendation (including 1 from their music teacher or director and 1 from their pastor), a 1-page essay on why they should be awarded this scholarship, and a CD or cassette recording of a musical performance. Selection is based on academic achievement, school involvement, music involvement and performance genre, community involvement, and other honors and awards.

Financial data The stipend is $2,000 per year. Funds are sent directly to the student upon proof of enrollment.

Duration 1 year; recipients may apply for 1 additional year if they earn a GPA of 3.3 or higher in their first year.

Number awarded 1 or more each year.

Deadline April of each year.

[277]
MYRTLE CREASMAN/MARY NORTHINGTON/ GENERAL TENNESSEE WMU SCHOLARSHIPS

Tennessee Baptist Convention
Attn: WMU Scholarships
5001 Maryland Way
P.O. Box 728
Brentwood, TN 37024-9728
(615) 373-2255   Toll Free: (800) 558-2090, ext. 2038
Fax: (615) 371-2014   E-mail: jferguson@tnbaptist.org
Web: www.tnbaptist.org/page.asp?page=92

Summary To provide financial assistance to members of Baptist churches in Tennessee who have been active in Baptist mission programs and are attending college in any state.

Eligibility This program is open to undergraduate students who are members and active participants in a Tennessee Baptist church and currently enrolled as full-time undergraduates at a college or university in any state. Applicants must show evidence of participation in Tennessee Baptist missions programs, Baptist collegiate ministries, and Tennessee Bap-

tist ministry. They must have a GPA of 2.6 or higher and be able to demonstrate financial need.

Financial data A stipend is awarded (amount not specified).

Duration 1 year.

Number awarded 1 or more each year.

Deadline January of each year.

[278]
NANETTE KIRBY MEMORIAL SCHOLARSHIPS

United Methodist Church-Louisiana Conference
Attn: Coordinator, Conference Board of Ordained Ministry
527 North Boulevard
Baton Rouge, LA 70802-5700
(225) 346-1646, ext. 230
Toll Free: (888) 239-5286, ext. 230
Fax: (225) 383-2652   E-mail: johneddd@bellsouth.net
Web: www.la-umc.org

Summary To provide financial assistance to Methodists from Louisiana who are attending a college or seminary in any state to prepare for a career in vocational service to the church.

Eligibility This program is open to members of United Methodist Churches in Louisiana who are enrolled or planning to enroll full time at a college, graduate school, or seminary in any state. Applicants may be working on an undergraduate degree with plans to enter a seminary or on a graduate or professional degree. They must be able to articulate vocational goals in service to the church. That may include ministry as an elder in full connection, deacon in full connection, licensed local pastor, diaconal minister, or certified lay professional in Christian education, music, youth, evangelism, camping/retreat ministries, spiritual formation, or older adult ministry. Along with their application, they must submit an essay on their vocational goals and plans for ministry.

Financial data The stipend is $1,000.

Duration 1 year.

Additional information This program was established in 2000.

Number awarded 2 each year.

Deadline February of each year.

[279]
NATIONAL JCDA SCHOLARSHIP

Catholic Daughters of the Americas
Attn: Scholarship Chair
10 West 71st Street
New York, NY 10023
(212) 877-3041   Fax: (212) 724-5923
E-mail: CDofANatl@aol.com
Web: www.catholicdaughters.org

Summary To provide financial assistance for college to members of the Junior Catholic Daughters of the Americas (JCDA).

Eligibility This program is open to students entering college who have been JCDA members for at least 2 years. Applicants must submit a 500-word essay on their Catholic values that were enhanced during their years as a JCDA member and that they will use in college. Financial need is not considered in the selection process.

Financial data The stipend is $1,000.

Duration 1 year.
Number awarded 1 each year.
Deadline April of each year.

[280]
NATIONAL PRESBYTERIAN COLLEGE SCHOLARSHIP

Presbyterian Church (USA)
Attn: Office of Financial Aid for Studies
100 Witherspoon Street, Room M-052
Louisville, KY 40202-1396
(502) 569-5224   Toll Free: (888) 728-7228, ext. 5224
Fax: (502) 569-8766   E-mail: finaid@pcusa.org
Web: www.pcusa.org

Summary To provide financial assistance to high school seniors planning to attend a Presbyterian college.

Eligibility This program is open to be high school seniors preparing to enroll as full-time incoming freshmen at a participating college related to the Presbyterian Church (USA). Applicants must be members of the PCUSA, have a GPA of 3.0 or higher, be U.S. citizens or permanent residents, and be able to demonstrate financial need. They must submit an essay (up to 500 words) on their career choice and the influence that informed their choice. Selection is based on that essay; personal qualities of character and leadership as reflected in contributions to church, school, and community; academic achievements; and recommendations from school and church officials.

Financial data Stipends range from $250 to $1,400 per year, depending upon the financial need of the recipient.

Duration 1 year; may be renewed up to 3 additional years, provided the recipient maintains of GPA of 3.0 or higher.

Number awarded Approximately 100 each year.

Deadline January of each year.

[281]
NATIONAL TEMPERANCE SCHOLARSHIP

United Methodist Higher Education Foundation
Attn: Scholarships Administrator
1001 19th Avenue South
P.O. Box 340005
Nashville, TN 37203-0005
(615) 340-7385   Toll Free: (800) 811-8110
Fax: (615) 340-7330
E-mail: umhefscholarships@gbhem.org
Web: www.umhef.org/receive.php?id=endowed_funds

Summary To provide financial assistance to undergraduate and graduate Methodist students at Methodist-related colleges and universities.

Eligibility This program is open to full-time undergraduate and graduate students at United Methodist-related colleges and universities. Applicants must have been active, full members of a United Methodist Church for at least 1 year prior to applying. They must have a GPA of 3.0 or higher and be able to demonstrate financial need. Along with their application, they must submit a 200-word essay on their involvement and/or leadership responsibilities in their church, school, and community within the last 3 years. U.S. citizenship or permanent resident status is required.

Financial data The stipend is at least $1,000 per year.

Duration 1 year; recipients may reapply.

Number awarded 1 each year.
Deadline May of each year.

[282]
NATIVE AMERICAN EDUCATION GRANTS

Presbyterian Church (USA)
Attn: Office of Financial Aid for Studies
100 Witherspoon Street, Room M-052
Louisville, KY 40202-1396
(502) 569-5776   Toll Free: (888) 728-7228, ext. 5776
Fax: (502) 569-8766   E-mail: finaid@pcusa.org
Web: www.pcusa.org

Summary To provide financial assistance to Native American students, especially members of the Presbyterian Church (USA), interested in continuing their college education.

Eligibility This program is open to Alaska Native and Native American students who have completed at least 2 years of full-time study at an accredited institution in the United States and have a GPA of 2.5 or higher. Applicants must be making satisfactory progress toward a degree, able to provide proof of tribal membership, U.S. citizens or permanent residents, recommended by their church pastor, and able to demonstrate financial need. Students from all faith traditions are encouraged to apply, but preference is given to members of the PCUSA.

Financial data Stipends range from $500 to $1,500 per year, depending upon the recipient's financial need.

Duration 1 year; may be renewed.

Number awarded Varies each year.

Deadline June of each year.

[283]
NEBRASKA EAGLE SCOUT OF THE YEAR SCHOLARSHIP

American Legion
Department of Nebraska
200 North 56th Street
P.O. Box 5205
Lincoln, NE 68505-0205
(402) 464-6338   Fax: (402) 464-6330
E-mail: nebraska@legion.org
Web: www.nebraskalegion.net/scholarships.htm

Summary To recognize and reward, with scholarships for college in any state, Eagle Scouts who are members of a troop associated with the American Legion in Nebraska or a son or grandson of a member of the Legion in the state.

Eligibility Applicants for this award must be either 1) a registered, active member of a Boy Scout Troop, Varsity Scout Team, or Venturing Crew chartered to an American Legion Post, Auxiliary Unit, or Sons of the American Legion Squadron in Nebraska, or 2) a registered active member of a Boy Scout Troop, Varsity Scout Team, or Venturing Crew and also the son or grandson of a member of the American Legion or American Legion Auxiliary in Nebraska. Candidates must also 1) have received the Eagle Scout Award; 2) be active members of their religious institution and have received the appropriate religious emblem; 3) have demonstrated practical citizenship in church, school, Scouting, and community; 4) be at least 15 years of age and enrolled in high school; and 5) submit at least 4 letters of recommendation, including 1 each from leaders of their religious institution, school, community, and Scouting. They must be planning to attend college in any state.

Financial data The award is a $500 scholarship.

Duration The award is presented annually.

Number awarded 1 each year.

Deadline February of each year.

[284]
NEBRASKA EASTERN STAR TRAINING AWARDS FOR RELIGIOUS LEADERSHIP

Order of the Eastern Star-Grand Chapter of Nebraska
Attn: ESTARL Program
P.O. Box 156
Fremont, NE 68026-0156
(402) 727-8644   Fax: (402) 727-7729
E-mail: nebraskaoes@msn.com
Web: www.neoes.org/estarl/index.htm

Summary To provide financial assistance to residents of Nebraska who are attending a college or seminary in any state to prepare for full-time Christian service.

Eligibility This program is open to residents of Nebraska who are preparing for a career in full-time Christian service. Applicants must be 1) enrolled at an accredited Bible college with a goal of ordination; 2) enrolled at an accredited seminary with a goal of ordination; 3) currently assigned to a parish and enrolled in a "Course of Study" program at an accredited seminary; or 4) current ordained clergy who are pursuing additional training to enhance their ministry or obtain additional degrees. Along with their application, they must submit a 1-page essay outlining their experiences and goals. There is no requirement of a Masonic affiliation, although preference may be given to Eastern Star members. Some consideration may be given to financial need.

Financial data A stipend is awarded (amount not specified).

Duration 1 year; recipients may reapply.

Number awarded 1 or more each year.

Deadline February of each year.

[285]
NEBRASKA UNITED METHODIST MERIT SCHOLARSHIPS

United Methodist Church-Nebraska Conference
Attn: Merit Scholarships
3333 Landmark Circle
Lincoln, NE 68504-4760
(402) 464-5994   Toll Free: (800) 435-6107
Fax: (402) 464-6203   E-mail: info@umcneb.org
Web: www.umcneb.org/pages/detail/114

Summary To provide financial assistance to Methodists from Nebraska interested in attending a college in any state that is affiliated with the denomination.

Eligibility This program is open to residents of Nebraska who are members of a congregation of the United Methodist Church (UMC). Applicants must be attending or planning to attend a UMC-related college or university in any state. Along with their application, they must submit a 1,000-word essay describing the major influences in their life and faith development, their passions in life, how they see themselves growing in faith, and what influenced them in selecting their college

and career goals. Selection is based on merit, defined as academic achievement and expression of Christian faith through 1) participation in home church, campus ministry, or community service; and 2) vocational preparation for service.

Financial data A stipend is awarded (amount not specified).

Duration 1 year.

Number awarded Varies each year.

Deadline April of each year.

[286]
NEW ENGLAND CONFERENCE SCHOLARSHIPS

United Methodist Church-New England Conference
Attn: Scholarship Committee
276 Essex Street
P.O. Box 249
Lawrence, MA 01842-0449
(978) 682-7676, ext. 221   Fax: (978) 682-8227
Web: www.neumc.org/forms/detail/1041

Summary To provide financial assistance to members of United Methodist churches within the New England Conference who are interested in attending college in any state.

Eligibility This program is open to high school seniors and students currently enrolled as college undergraduates or in a technical or trade school in any state. Applicants must be members of United Methodist Churches in the New England Conference and recommended by their local church. Financial need is considered in the selection process.

Financial data Stipends normally range from $200 to $600.

Duration 1 year.

Number awarded Varies each year.

Deadline April of each year.

[287]
NEW HAMPSHIRE CHARITABLE FOUNDATION STATEWIDE STUDENT AID PROGRAM

New Hampshire Charitable Foundation
37 Pleasant Street
Concord, NH 03301-4005
(603) 225-6641   Toll Free: (800) 464-6641
Fax: (603) 225-1700   E-mail: info@nhcf.org
Web: www.nhcf.org/page16960.cfm

Summary To provide scholarships or loans for undergraduate or graduate study in any state to Episcopal and other New Hampshire residents.

Eligibility This program is open to New Hampshire residents who are graduating high school seniors planning to enter a 4-year college or university, undergraduate students between 17 and 23 years of age working on a 4-year degree, or graduate students of any age. Applicants must be enrolled on at least a half-time basis at a school in New Hampshire or another state. Selection is based on financial need, academic merit, community service, school activities, and work experience. Priority is given to students with the fewest financial resources.

Financial data Awards range from $500 to $3,500 and average $1,800. Most are made in the form of grants (recently, 82% of all awards) or no-interest or low-interest loans.

Duration 1 year; approximately one-third of the awards are renewable.

Additional information Through this program, students submit a single application for more than 50 different scholarship and loan funds. Many of the funds have additional requirements, including field of study; residency in region, county, city, or town; graduation from designated high schools; and special attributes (e.g., of Belgian descent, employee of designated firms, customer of Granite State Telephone Company, disabled, suffering from a life-threatening or serious chronic illness, of Lithuanian descent, dependent of a New Hampshire police officer, dependent of a New Hampshire Episcopal minister, of Polish descent, former Sea Cadet or Naval Junior ROTC, or employed in the tourism industry). The Citizens' Scholarship Foundation of America reviews all applications; recipients are selected by the New Hampshire Charitable Foundation. A $20 application fee is required.

Number awarded Varies each year; approximately $700,000 is awarded annually.

Deadline April of each year.

[288]
NEW MEXICO CONFERENCE MERIT SCHOLARSHIPS

United Methodist Church-New Mexico Conference
Attn: Youth Ministries Conference Coordinator
11816 Lomas Boulevard, N.E.
Albuquerque, NM 87112
(505) 255-8786, ext. 110   Toll Free: (800) 678-8786
Fax: (505) 265-6184   E-mail: youthdir@nmconfum.com
Web: www.nmconfum.com

Summary To provide financial assistance to Methodists from New Mexico who are interested in attending a college in any state that is affiliated with the denomination.

Eligibility This program is open to members of congregations that are affiliated with the New Mexico Conference of the United Methodist Church (UMC). Applicants must be enrolled or planning to enroll at a UMC college or university in any state. They must be working on an undergraduate degree. The pastor or a lay leader of their congregation must submit a letter of nomination explaining why the students should receive this scholarship.

Financial data The stipend is $500.

Duration 1 year.

Number awarded 2 each year.

Deadline June of each year.

[289]
NEW MEXICO SINGING CHURCHMEN SCHOLARSHIP

Baptist Convention of New Mexico
Attn: Leadership Development Team
5325 Wyoming Boulevard, N.E.
P.O. Box 94485
Albuquerque, NM 87199-4485
(505) 924-2313   Toll Free: (800) 898-8544
Fax: (505) 924-2349   E-mail: mrobinson@bcnm.com
Web: www.bcnm.com

Summary To provide financial assistance to Southern Baptist students from New Mexico who are attending a college or seminary in any state to prepare for a career in music.

Eligibility This program is open to college and seminary students who are active members of churches affiliated with the Baptist Convention of New Mexico. Applicants must have experienced a call to vocational music ministry. They must be enrolled full time at the sophomore level or higher, have a GPA of 3.0 or higher, and be majoring in music.

Financial data A stipend is awarded (amount not specified).

Duration 1 year; may be renewed.

Number awarded 1 or more each year.

Deadline April of each year.

[290]
NEW YORK EAGLE SCOUT OF THE YEAR SCHOLARSHIP

American Legion
Department of New York
112 State Street, Suite 1300
Albany, NY 12207
(518) 463-2215   Toll Free: (800) 253-4466
Fax: (518) 427-8443   E-mail: info@nylegion.org
Web: www.ny.legion.org/scouting_.htm

Summary To recognize and reward, with scholarships for college in any state, Eagle Scouts who are members of a troop associated with the American Legion in New York or a son or grandson of a member of the Legion in the state.

Eligibility The New York nominee for American Legion Scout of the Year receives this award. Applicants must be either 1) registered, active members of a Boy Scout Troop or Varsity Scout Team sponsored by an American Legion Post in New York or Auxiliary Unit in New York, or 2) registered, active members of a duly chartered Boy Scout Troop or Varsity Scout Team and the sons or grandsons of American Legion or Auxiliary members. They must be active members of their religious institution; have received the appropriate religious emblem; have demonstrated practical citizenship in church, school, Scouting, and community; have received the Eagle Scout award; be between 15 and 19 years of age; be enrolled in high school; and be planning to attend college in any state.

Financial data The award is a $1,000 scholarship.

Duration The award is presented annually.

Number awarded 1 each year.

Deadline February of each year.

[291]
NMBF SCHOLARSHIP

New Mexico Baptist Foundation
5325 Wyoming Boulevard, N.E.
P.O. Box 16560
Albuquerque, NM 87191-6560
(505) 332-3777   Toll Free: (877) 841-3777
Fax: (505) 332-2777   E-mail: foundation@nmbf.com
Web: www.bcnm.com

Summary To provide financial assistance to members of Southern Baptist churches in New Mexico who plan to attend college in any state.

Eligibility This program is open to members of Southern Baptist churches in New Mexico who are enrolled at a college, university, or seminary in any state. Applicants must have a GPA of 2.5 or higher and be able to demonstrate financial need.

Financial data A stipend is awarded (amount not specified).

Duration 1 year.

Number awarded 1 or more each year.

Deadline April of each year.

[292]
NORMAN NICKERSON SCHOLARSHIP

New Mexico Baptist Foundation
5325 Wyoming Boulevard, N.E.
P.O. Box 16560
Albuquerque, NM 87191-6560
(505) 332-3777   Toll Free: (877) 841-3777
Fax: (505) 332-2777   E-mail: foundation@nmbf.com
Web: www.bcnm.com

Summary To provide financial assistance to members of Southern Baptist churches in New Mexico who are attending college in any state to prepare for a career in church music.

Eligibility This program is open to college and seminary students who are preparing for a career in church music. Applicants must have a GPA of 2.5 or higher and be able to demonstrate financial need. They must be members of Southern Baptist churches in New Mexico.

Financial data A stipend is awarded (amount not specified).

Duration 1 year.

Number awarded 1 or more each year.

Deadline April of each year.

[293]
NORTH CAROLINA BAPTIST SCHOLARSHIPS

Baptist State Convention of North Carolina
Attn: Scholarship Office
205 Convention Drive
P.O. Box 1107
Cary, NC 27512-1107
Toll Free: (800) 395-5102
E-mail: scholarships@ncbaptist.org
Web: www.ncbaptist.org/index.php?id=451

Summary To provide financial assistance to members of churches cooperating with the Baptist State Convention of North Carolina who are interested in attending a Baptist college in the state.

Eligibility This program is open to students enrolled or planning to enroll as full-time undergraduates at a Baptist college or university in North Carolina. Applicants must have been a member for at least 1 year of a church in friendly cooperation with the Baptist State Convention of North Carolina. Along with their application, they must submit 300-word essays on 1) their personal testimony, and 2) why the Cooperative Program is relevant to today's generation.

Financial data A stipend is awarded (amount not specified).

Duration 1 year; may be renewed for up to 3 additional years, provided the recipient maintains a GPA of 2.5 or higher.

Additional information The North Carolina Baptist institutions are Campbell University, Chowan University, Gardner-Webb University, Mars Hill College, and Wingate University.

Number awarded Varies each year. This program was established in 2008.

Deadline March of each year.

[294]
NORTH DAKOTA EASTERN STAR TRAINING AWARDS FOR RELIGIOUS LEADERSHIP

Order of the Eastern Star-Grand Chapter of North Dakota
1405 Third Street North
Fargo, ND 58102
(701) 364-0335   E-mail: ndoes4us@ndoes.org
Web: www.ndoes.org/Estarl.htm

Summary To provide financial assistance to residents of North Dakota who are attending a college or seminary in any state to prepare for a career in Christian service.

Eligibility This program is open to residents of North Dakota who are preparing for a career in Christian service as a minister, missionary, director of church music, director of religious education, youth leader, or other related position. Applicants must be enrolled full time at an accredited Bible college, university, or seminary in any state. Selection is based on character, scholarship, citizenship, and financial need.

Financial data A stipend is awarded (amount not specified). Funds are sent directly to the student's college or seminary.

Duration 1 year; recipients may reapply.

Number awarded 1 or more each year.

Deadline April of each year.

[295]
NORTHWEST BAPTIST FOUNDATION UNDERGRADUATE SCHOLARSHIPS

Northwest Baptist Convention
Attn: Northwest Baptist Foundation
3200 N.E. 109th Avenue
Vancouver, WA 98682
(360) 882-2250   Toll Free: (800) 594-2981
Fax: (360) 882-2252
Web: www.nwbaptistfdn.org/students.html

Summary To provide financial assistance for college to upper-division students affiliated with a Northwest Baptist Convention church.

Eligibility This program is open to members of churches affiliated with the Northwest Baptist Convention who are entering their junior or senior year at a college or university in any state. Applicants must have a GPA of 3.0 or higher. Along with their application, they must submit a current transcript, 2 letters of recommendation (including 1 from their pastor), and a brief statement on why they are seeking assistance and how they feel their course of study is preparing them for their life's work. Financial need is also considered in the selection process.

Financial data A stipend is awarded (amount not specified).

Duration 1 year; may be renewed.

Additional information The Northwest Baptist Convention serves Oregon, Washington, and northern Idaho.

Number awarded 1 or more each year.

Deadline January of each year.

[296]
NURSES' TRAINING GRANTS

Albert Baker Fund
777 Campus Commons Road, Suite 165
Sacramento, CA 95825
(916) 643-9999   Toll Free: (800) 269-0388
Fax: (916) 568-1372 E-mail: admin@albertbakerfund.org
Web: www.albertbakerfund.org

Summary To provide financial assistance to Christian Science nursing students.

Eligibility This program is open to high school seniors who are Christian Scientists and members of The Mother Church (the First Church of Christ, Scientist in Boston, Massachusetts) or a branch church. Applicants must be planning to enroll at a Christian Science nurses training facility and become enrolled in *The Christian Science Journal*. Along with their application, they must submit an essay on what Christian Science means to them. Financial need is also considered in the selection process.

Financial data A stipend is awarded (amount not specified).

Duration 1 year.

Number awarded 1 or more each year.

Deadline Deadline not specified.

[297]
O.D. LAMBIRTH MEMORIAL SCHOLARSHIP

Baptist Convention of New Mexico
Attn: Missions Mobilization Team
5325 Wyoming Boulevard, N.E.
P.O. Box 94485
Albuquerque, NM 87199-4485
(505) 924-2315   Toll Free: (800) 898-8544
Fax: (505) 924-2320   E-mail: cpairett@bcnm.com
Web: www.bcnm.com

Summary To provide financial assistance to Southern Baptist students from New Mexico interested in attending college in the state.

Eligibility This program is open to students who are members of churches affiliated with the Baptist Convention of New Mexico and attending or planning to attend a college in the state. Applicants must be able to demonstrate financial need and a GPA of 2.0 or higher.

Financial data A stipend is awarded (amount not specified).

Duration 1 year; may be renewed.

Number awarded 1 or more each year.

Deadline March of each year.

[298]
OHIO BAPTIST EDUCATION SOCIETY SCHOLARSHIPS

American Baptist Churches of Ohio
Attn: Ohio Baptist Education Society
136 Galway Drive North
P.O. Box 288
Granville, OH 43023-0288
(740) 587-0804   Fax: (740) 587-0807
E-mail: pastorchris@neo.rr.com
Web: www.abc-ohio.org

Summary To provide funding to upper-division and graduate Baptist students from Ohio who are interested in attending a college or seminary in any state.

Eligibility This program is open to residents of Ohio who have completed at least 2 years of study at an accredited college or university in any state and are interested in continuing their education as an upper-division or seminary student. Applicants must 1) hold active membership in a church affiliated with the American Baptist Churches of Ohio or a church dually-aligned with the American Baptist Churches of Ohio; 2) be in the process of preparing for a professional career in Christian ministry (such as a local church pastor, church education, youth or young adult ministries, church music, specialized ministry, chaplaincy, ministry in higher education, or missionary service); 3) be committed to working professionally within the framework of the American Baptist Churches USA; and 4) acknowledge a personal commitment to the Gospel of Jesus Christ, an understanding of the Christian faith, and a definite call to professional Christian ministry as a life work. Financial need must be demonstrated.

Financial data Stipends generally range from $1,000 to $1,500 a year.

Duration 1 year.

Additional information The Ohio Baptist Education Society has been supporting Baptist students since 1831. This program includes the Rev. Dr. Ralph and Joyce Lamb Memorial Scholarship (established in 2002) and the Rev. Robert E. and Gladys Ernst Scholarship (established in 2007).

Number awarded Varies; generally, 8 to 17 each year.

Deadline March of each year.

[299]
OHIO BAPTIST FOUNDATION SCHOLARSHIPS

Ohio Baptist Foundation
Attn: Director
9000 Antares Avenue
Columbus, OH 43240
(614) 827-1781   Fax: (614) 827-1860
E-mail: JackHelton@scbo.org
Web: www.ohiobaptistfoundation.org

Summary To provide financial assistance for college or seminary in any state to members of Southern Baptist churches in Ohio.

Eligibility This program is open to members of Southern Baptist churches in Ohio who are attending postsecondary educational institutions in any state. Applicants must be studying to become pastors, missionaries, music and children's ministers, doctors, nurses, or lawyers.

Financial data Stipends depend on the terms of the fund providing assistance.

Duration 1 year.

Additional information This program is comprised of 14 funds that provide assistance for specified programs of study. For details on each fund, contact the foundation.

Number awarded Varies each year.

Deadline Deadline not specified.

[300]
OHIO EASTERN STAR TRAINING AWARDS FOR RELIGIOUS LEADERSHIP

Order of the Eastern Star-Grand Chapter of Ohio
c/o Clifford Houk, ESTARL Committee Chair
12 Northwood Drive
Athens, OH 45701
E-mail: chouk@columbus.rr.com
Web: www.ohoes.org/projects.htm

Summary To provide financial assistance to residents of Ohio interested in attending a college or seminary in any state to prepare for a religious career.

Eligibility This program is open to residents of Ohio who have completed at least 2 years of postsecondary education at a college or university in any state. Applicants must be interested in continuing their education at their current school or at a postgraduate institution to prepare for a career in full-time Christian service as a minister, missionary, director of church music, director of youth leadership, or director of religious education. Students working on a doctoral degree are not eligible. Selection is based on scholarship, character, leadership qualities, evidence of self-help, and financial need. Preference is given to application who are already training in the religious field and need to continue their education.

Financial data A stipend is awarded (amount not specified).

Duration 1 year; recipients may reapply.

Number awarded Varies each year.

Deadline Deadline not specified.

[301]
OKLAHOMA CONFERENCE MERIT SCHOLARSHIPS

United Methodist Church-Oklahoma Conference
Attn: Campus Ministry Office
1501 N.W. 24th Street
Oklahoma, OK 73106-3635
(405) 530-2013   Toll Free: (800) 231-4166, ext. 2013
Fax: (405) 525-4164   E-mail: lmachalek@okumc.org
Web: www.okumcministries.org

Summary To provide financial assistance to undergraduate and graduate Methodist students from Oklahoma who plan to attend a Methodist institution in any state.

Eligibility This program is open to undergraduate and graduate students who are members of congregations affiliated with the Oklahoma Conference of the United Methodist Church. Applicants must be enrolled or planning to enroll as a full-time student at a United Methodist college, university, graduate school, or seminary in any state. Along with their application, they must submit a 1-page essay outlining their career goals. Selection is based on academic excellence, participation in church activities, and financial need.

Financial data The stipend is $600.

Duration 1 year.

Number awarded 1 or more each year.

Deadline April of each year.

[302]
OREGON EASTERN STAR TRAINING AWARDS FOR RELIGIOUS LEADERSHIP

Order of the Eastern Star-Grand Chapter of Oregon
c/o Elena Sipp
P.O. Box 102
Sumpter, OR 97877
(541) 894-2447
Web: www.oregonoes.org/scholarships/index.html

Summary To provide financial assistance to residents of Oregon who are attending college in any state to work on an undergraduate or graduate degree that will prepare them for a career in church service.

Eligibility This program is open to residents of Oregon who are attending a school in any state that is accredited by the Accrediting Association of Bible Colleges, American Association of Schools of Religious Education, American Association of Theological School, National Association of Schools of Music, or similar association. Applicants must be working on an undergraduate or graduate degree that will prepare them for a full-time church vocation. They must submit a letter of reference from a denominational leader who can describe their relationship or prospect for full-time church service. Financial need is considered in the selection process.

Financial data A stipend is awarded (amount not specified).

Duration 1 year.

Number awarded 1 or more each year.

Deadline April of each year.

[303]
OREGON-IDAHO CONFERENCE UMC ETHNIC MINORITY LEADERSHIP AWARDS

United Methodist Church-Oregon-Idaho Conference
Attn: Campus Ministries and Higher Education Ministry Team
1505 S.W. 18th Avenue
Portland, OR 97201-2524
(503) 226-7031   Toll Free: (800) J-WESLEY
Web: www.umoi.org/pages/detail/45

Summary To provide financial assistance to ethnic minority Methodists from Oregon and Idaho who are interested in attending a college or graduate school in any state.

Eligibility This program is open to members of ethnic minority groups (African American, Native American, Asian, Pacific Islander, or Hispanic) who have belonged to a congregation affiliated with the Oregon-Idaho Conference of the United Methodist Church (UMC) for at least 1 year. Applicants must be enrolled or planning to enroll full time as an undergraduate or graduate student at a 2- or 4-year college or university in any state. Along with their application, they must submit personal statements on 1) their faith development; and 2) where they sense God is calling the church in the present and future. Selection is based primarily on demonstrated leadership excellence and/or the potential for leadership excellence in the UMC and in community projects or activities, but other factors, including financial need, are also considered.

Financial data The stipend is $750.

Duration 1 year.

Number awarded 1 each year.

Deadline April of each year.

[304]
OREGON-IDAHO CONFERENCE UMC MERIT AWARDS

United Methodist Church-Oregon-Idaho Conference
Attn: Campus Ministries and Higher Education Ministry
  Team
1505 S.W. 18th Avenue
Portland, OR 97201-2524
(503) 226-7031   Toll Free: (800) J-WESLEY
Web: www.umoi.org/pages/detail/45

Summary To provide financial assistance to Methodists from Oregon and Idaho who are interested in attending a college or graduate school affiliated with the denomination in any state.

Eligibility This program is open to members of congregations affiliated with the Oregon-Idaho Conference of the United Methodist Church (UMC). Applicants must be enrolled or planning to enroll full time as an undergraduate or graduate student at a UMC college or university in any state. They must be nominated by their local church; each church may nominate only 1 member. Along with their application, they must submit a personal statement that includes their philosophy of life, religious development, and what influenced them in selecting their career goal. In the selection process, 35% of the weight is placed on demonstrated leadership excellence and/or the potential for leadership excellence in the UMC and in community projects or activities, but other factors, including financial need, are also considered.

Financial data The stipend is $750.

Duration 1 year.

Number awarded 1 each year.

Deadline April of each year.

[305]
OREGON-IDAHO CONFERENCE UMC UNDERGRADUATE LEADERSHIP AWARDS

United Methodist Church-Oregon-Idaho Conference
Attn: Campus Ministries and Higher Education Ministry
  Team
1505 S.W. 18th Avenue
Portland, OR 97201-2524
(503) 226-7031   Toll Free: (800) J-WESLEY
Web: www.umoi.org/pages/detail/45

Summary To provide financial assistance to Methodists from Oregon and Idaho who are interested in attending college in any state.

Eligibility This program is open to students who have belonged to a congregation affiliated with the Oregon-Idaho Conference of the United Methodist Church (UMC) for at least 1 year. Applicants must be enrolled or planning to enroll full time as an undergraduate student at a 2- or 4-year college or university in any state. Along with their application, they must submit personal statements on 1) their faith development; and 2) where they sense God is calling the church in

the present and future. In the selection process, 35% of the weight is placed on demonstrated leadership excellence and/or the potential for leadership excellence in the UMC and in community projects or activities, but other factors, including financial need, are also considered.

Financial data The stipend is $800.

Duration 1 year.

Number awarded 5 each year: 1 in each district of the Oregon-Idaho Conference.

Deadline April of each year.

[306]
ORPHAN'S COLLEGE SCHOLARSHIP

Catholic Financial Life
Attn: Member Services Department
1100 West Wells Street
P.O. Box 05900
Milwaukee, WI 53205-0900
(414) 273-6266   Toll Free: (800) 927-2547
Fax: (414) 278-6535
E-mail: service@catholicfinanciallife.org
Web: www.catholicfinanciallife.org

Summary To provide financial assistance to orphans who have ties to Catholic Financial Life and are interested in attending college in any state.

Eligibility This entitlement benefit is available to children who became orphaned and either 1) are financial members of Catholic Financial Life; or 2) have at least 1 parent who died while being a financial member of the society. They must be younger than 23 years of age and enrolled full time at a college or university in any state.

Financial data The stipend is $4,000 per year.

Duration This is an entitlement benefit and is paid up to 4 years of college.

Additional information Catholic Financial Life, formerly Catholic Knights of America, operates in Arkansas, California, Connecticut, Indiana, Iowa, Louisiana, Maine, Massachusetts, Michigan, Minnesota, Missouri, New Hampshire, New Mexico, North Dakota, Ohio, Pennsylvania, Rhode Island, Texas, Vermont, and Wisconsin.

Number awarded Varies each year.

Deadline Applications may be submitted at any time.

[307]
ORTHODOX DIVISION COLLEGE SCHOLARSHIPS

Loyal Christian Benefit Association
Attn: Orthodox Division
700 Peach Street
P.O. Box 13005
Erie, PA 16514-1305
(814) 453-4331   Toll Free: (888) 230-LCBA
Fax: (866) 588-3173   E-mail: outreach@lcbalife.org
Web: lcbalife.org/index.php?option=com_form&Itemid=367

Summary To provide financial assistance for college to members of the Orthodox Division of the Loyal Christian Benefit Association (LCBA).

Eligibility Applicants must have belonged to the division for at least 1 year and be the insured on a life insurance certificate of at least $1,000 or an annuity with a minimum deposit of at least $1,000. They must be accepted to or enrolled in an accredited institution as a full-time student in a degree or certificate program and have a GPA of 2.0 or higher. Along with their application, they must submit information on their extracurricular activities, academic honors or awards, involvement in church activities or volunteer work, and career plans or ambitions following their educational preparation. Selection is based on a random drawing from among eligible applicants.

Financial data The stipend is $1,000 per year.

Duration 1 year; recipients may reapply until completion of their initial degree or certificate.

Additional information This program began in 1980.

Number awarded 6 each year.

Deadline April of each year.

[308]
PAUL AND BETTY HONZIK SCHOLARSHIP

Hawai'i Community Foundation
Attn: Scholarship Department
827 Fort Street Mall
Honolulu, HI 96813
(808) 537-6333   Toll Free: (888) 731-3863
Fax: (808) 521-6286
E-mail: scholarships@hcf-hawaii.org
Web: www.hawaiicommunityfoundation.org/scholarships

Summary To provide financial assistance to residents of Hawaii who are members of a Presbyterian church and interested in attending a college or seminary in any state.

Eligibility This program is open to residents of Hawaii who are members of a Presbyterian church. Applicants must be attending or planning to attend a 4-year college or seminary in any state. They must be able to demonstrate academic achievement (GPA of 3.0 or higher), good moral character, and financial need. Along with their application, they must submit a short statement indicating their reasons for attending college, their planned course of study, their career goals, and what community service means to them.

Financial data The amounts of the awards depend on the availability of funds and the need of the recipient. Recently, the average value of all scholarships awarded by the foundation was $2,041.

Duration 1 year.

Additional information This program was established in 2005.

Number awarded Varies each year.

Deadline February of each year.

[309]
PEGGY WORTHY TOWNES ENDOWED SCHOLARSHIP

United Methodist Higher Education Foundation
Attn: Scholarships Administrator
1001 19th Avenue South
P.O. Box 340005
Nashville, TN 37203-0005
(615) 340-7385   Toll Free: (800) 811-8110
Fax: (615) 340-7330
E-mail: umhefscholarships@gbhem.org
Web: www.umhef.org/receive.php?id=endowed_funds

Summary To provide financial assistance to Methodist students who are entering freshmen at Methodist-related colleges and universities.

Eligibility This program is open to students enrolling as full-time freshmen at United Methodist-related colleges and universities. Applicants must have been active, full members of a United Methodist Church for at least 1 year prior to applying. They must have a GPA of 3.0 or higher and be able to demonstrate financial need. Along with their application, they must submit a 200-word essay on their involvement and/or leadership responsibilities in their church, school, and community within the last 3 years. U.S. citizenship or permanent resident status is required.

Financial data The stipend is at least $1,000.

Duration 1 year; nonrenewable.

Additional information This program was established in 2004.

Number awarded 1 each year.

Deadline May of each year.

[310]
PENNSYLVANIA EAGLE SCOUT OF THE YEAR AWARD

American Legion
Department of Pennsylvania
Attn: Scholarship Secretary
P.O. Box 2324
Harrisburg, PA 17105-2324
(717) 730-9100   Fax: (717) 975-2836
E-mail: hq@pa-legion.com
Web: www.pa-legion.com

Summary To recognize and reward Eagle Scouts who are members of a troop associated with the American Legion in Pennsylvania or a son or grandson of a member of the Legion.

Eligibility Applicants for this award must be either 1) a registered, active member of a Boy Scout Troop, Varsity Scout Team, or Venturing Crew chartered to a Pennsylvania American Legion Post, Auxiliary Unit, or Sons of the American Legion Squadron, or 2) a registered active member of a Pennsylvania Boy Scout Troop, Varsity Scout Team, or Venturing Crew and also the son, grandson, or great-grandson of a member of the American Legion or American Legion Auxiliary. Candidates must also 1) have received the Eagle Scout Award; 2) be active members of their religious institution and have received the appropriate religious emblem; 3) have demonstrated practical citizenship in church, school, Scouting, and community; 4) be at least 15 years of age and enrolled in high school; and 5) submit at least 4 letters of recommendation, including 1 each from leaders of their religious institution, school, community, and Scouting.

Financial data The award is a $1,000 savings bond.

Duration The award is presented annually.

Number awarded 1 each year.

Deadline February of each year.

[311]
PENNSYLVANIA EASTERN STAR TRAINING AWARDS FOR RELIGIOUS LEADERSHIP

Order of the Eastern Star-Grand Chapter of Pennsylvania
Attn: Grand Secretary
P.O. Box 8
Womelsdorf, PA 19567
(717) 361-5203
E-mail: grand secretary@paeasternstar.org
Web: www.paeasternstar.org/edscholarship.htm

Summary To provide financial assistance to members of the Order of the Eastern Star in Pennsylvania and their families who are interested in attending a college or seminary in any state to prepare for a religious career.

Eligibility This program is open to residents of Pennsylvania who are members of Eastern Star or their spouses, children, stepchildren, grandchildren, parents, or siblings. Applicants must have completed at least 1 year of study at an accredited school offering religious training in any state. They must have a cumulative GPA of 2.5 or higher and be able to demonstrate financial need. Preference is given to juniors and seniors in college and students in theological seminaries. Along with their application, they must submit 4 letters of recommendation, including 2 from ministers or church leaders, 1 from the religious body they wish to serve, and 1 from a professor or other academic person.

Financial data The stipend is $1,000 per year.

Duration 1 year; may be renewed 1 additional year.

Number awarded Varies each year.

Deadline February of each year.

[312]
PENNSYLVANIA STATE COUNCIL KNIGHTS OF COLUMBUS SCHOLARSHIPS

Knights of Columbus-Pennsylvania State Council
c/o Richard L. Corriveau, Scholarship Chair
114 Singer Road
New Freedom, PA 17349-9655
(717) 227-2728   E-mail: rickkorivo@verizon.net
Web: www.pakofc.us

Summary To provide financial assistance to high school seniors in Pennsylvania who are members or children of members of the Knights of Columbus and planning to attend college in any state.

Eligibility This program is open to seniors graduating from high schools in Pennsylvania who are practicing Catholics and planning to attend a college, university, or school of nursing (Catholic or non-Catholic) in any state. Applicants must be 1) a member of the Knights of Columbus in Pennsylvania who has been a member for at least 1 year; 2) the child of a member who has been a member for at least 1 year; 3) a child of a deceased member who was not in arrears at the time of his death; or 4) a qualified Columbian Squire. They must have taken the SAT and/or ACT examinations. Financial need is not considered in the selection process.

Financial data The stipend is $750 per year.

Duration 4 years.

Number awarded 20 each year.

Deadline December of each year.

[313]
PERCY J. JOHNSON ENDOWED SCHOLARSHIPS

Knights of Columbus
Attn: Department of Scholarships
P.O. Box 1670
New Haven, CT 06507-0901
(203) 752-4332   Fax: (203) 772-2696
E-mail: info@kofc.org
Web: www.kofc.org/un/en/scholarships/endowed.html

Summary To provide financial assistance to men starting their first year at a Catholic college or university.

Eligibility Eligible are male students entering their freshman year in a program leading to a bachelor's degree at a Catholic college or university in the United States; applicants must be members in good standing of the Columbian Squires or Knights of Columbus, or the son of a member, or the son of a deceased member who was in good standing at the time of death. Selection is based on secondary school record, class rank, financial need, and aptitude test scores.

Financial data The stipend is $1,500 per year.

Duration 1 year; may be renewed up to 3 additional years upon evidence of satisfactory academic performance.

Additional information This program was established in 1990.

Number awarded 1 or more each year, depending on the availability of funds.

Deadline February of each year.

[314]
POLISH ROMAN CATHOLIC UNION OF AMERICA EDUCATION FUND SCHOLARSHIPS

Polish Roman Catholic Union of America
Attn: Education Fund Scholarship Program
984 North Milwaukee Avenue
Chicago, IL 60622-4101
(773) 782-2600   Toll Free: (800) 772-8632
Fax: (773) 278-4595   E-mail: info@prcua.org
Web: www.prcua.org

Summary To provide financial assistance to undergraduate and graduate students of Polish heritage.

Eligibility This program is open to students enrolled full time as sophomores, juniors, and seniors in an undergraduate program or full or part time as a graduate or professional school students. Along with their application, they must submit brief statements on 1) the Polonian organization(s) that benefited from their membership and how; 2) the organized or other group(s) the benefited from their membership or service and how; and 3) how this scholarship will help them in working on their degree. Selection is based on academic achievement, Polonia involvement, and community service.

Financial data A stipend is awarded (amount not specified). Funds are paid directly to the institution.

Duration 1 year.

Additional information As funding is available, this program also provides awards from the following: the Stanley W. Marion Fund (for study of any field), the Jean C. Osajda Fund (for study of education), the Adele Szumilus Sularski Fund (for study of any field), and the Ann Kushel Fund (for study of religion).

Number awarded 1 or more each year.

Deadline May of each year.

[315]
POLISH ROMAN CATHOLIC UNION OF AMERICA EDUCATIONAL LOANS

Polish Roman Catholic Union of America
Attn: Secretary-Treasurer
984 North Milwaukee Avenue
Chicago, IL 60622-4101
(773) 782-2600   Toll Free: (800) 772-8632
Fax: (773) 278-4595   E-mail: info@prcua.org
Web: www.prcua.org/benefits/educationalloan.htm

Summary To provide loans for college to members of the Polish Roman Catholic Union of America (PRCUA).

Eligibility This program is open to active PRCUA members who have held at least $5,000 in permanent life insurance for at least 1 year. Applicants must be attending or planning to attend an accredited college or university as a full-time student.

Financial data The maximum loan is $1,000 per year. Funds may be used only for tuition and are issued jointly to the student and the school. No interest is charged while the student remains in school, but repayment must begin within 6 months of graduating or leaving school with interest at 5%.

Duration 1 year; may be renewed up to 3 additional years.

Number awarded Varies each year.

Deadline Deadline not specified.

[316]
POLISH ROMAN CATHOLIC UNION OF AMERICA STUDENT SCHOLARSHIP GRANTS

Polish Roman Catholic Union of America
Attn: President
984 North Milwaukee Avenue
Chicago, IL 60622-4101
(773) 782-2600   Toll Free: (800) 772-8632
Fax: (773) 278-4595   E-mail: info@prcua.org
Web: www.prcua.org/benefits/scholarship.htm

Summary To provide financial assistance for college or graduate school to members of the Polish Roman Catholic Union of America (PRCUA).

Eligibility This program is open to active PRCUA members who have held at least $5,000 in life insurance for at least 5 years, at least $15,000 in life insurance for at least 4 years, or at least $25,000 in life insurance for at least 3 years. Applicants must be enrolled as a full-time sophomore, junior, or senior in an undergraduate program or as a part- or full-time graduate or professional student. They must have a GPA of 2.5 or higher. Along with their application, they must submit a 500-word essay on "How I can use my degree to benefit my Polish heritage." Selection is based on that essay along with statements on 1) their career goals and how they plan to achieve those goals, 2) their educational and other accomplishments and why those accomplishments were important in their life, 3) educational organizations to which they belong, and 4) extracurricular activities. U.S. citizenship or permanent resident status is required.

Financial data A stipend is awarded (amount not specified). Funds are paid directly to the institution.

Duration 1 year; may be renewed up to 2 additional years.

Number awarded Varies each year.

Deadline June of each year.

[317]
POST-HIGH SCHOOL TUITION SCHOLARSHIPS

Catholic United Financial
3499 Lexington Avenue North
St. Paul, MN 55126-8098
(651) 490-0170, ext. 133   Toll Free: (800) 568-6670
Fax: (651) 490-0746   E-mail: caa@catholicunited.org
Web: www.catholicunitedfinancial.org

Summary To provide financial assistance to members of Catholic United Financial who are interested in attending college in any state.

Eligibility This program is open to applicants who have been members of Catholic United Financial for at least 2 years; are entering their freshman or sophomore year at a college, university, or technical school in any state; and will be working on a college degree. Selection is based on academic performance and financial need.

Financial data There are 2 categories of stipends: $500 for recipients who will be attending a Catholic college or university or $300 for recipients planning on attending a state college, university, community college, or technical school.

Duration 1 year; nonrenewable.

Additional information Catholic United Financial, formerly the Catholic Aid Association, is licensed to sell insurance in Iowa, Minnesota, North Dakota, South Dakota, and Wisconsin.

Number awarded Varies each year.

Deadline February of each year.

[318]
POWELL-DUFFELL SCHOLARSHIPS

Arkansas Baptist Foundation
10117 Kanis Road
Little Rock, AR 72205-6220
(501) 376-0732   Toll Free: (800) 798-0969
Fax: (501) 376-3831   E-mail: info@abf.org
Web: www.abf.org/individuals_scholarships.htm

Summary To provide financial assistance to members of Southern Baptist churches in Arkansas who are attending colleges or universities in the state to prepare for vocational Christian ministry.

Eligibility This program is open to members of churches affiliated with the Arkansas Baptist State Convention. Applicants must be entering their sophomore or junior year at an accredited Arkansas college or university. They must be preparing for vocational Christian ministry.

Financial data The stipend is $1,500 per year. Funds are paid to the recipient's institution.

Duration 1 year; sophomores may reapply.

Number awarded Varies each year.

Deadline February of each year.

[319]
PRESBYTERIAN CHURCH PARENT LOANS

Presbyterian Church (USA)
Attn: Office of Financial Aid for Studies
100 Witherspoon Street, Room M-052
Louisville, KY 40202-1396
(502) 569-5224   Toll Free: (888) 728-7228, ext. 5224
Fax: (502) 569-8766   E-mail: finaid@pcusa.org
Web: www.pcusa.org

Summary To provide educational loans to parents of students who are members of the Presbyterian Church (USA).

Eligibility This program is open to parents and legal guardians of students enrolled in an accredited institution of higher education. Applicants must be members of the PCUSA, U.S. citizens or permanent residents, able to demonstrate financial need, and able to give satisfactory evidence of financial reliability.

Financial data Loans may not exceed the actual cost of attendance, to a maximum of $5,000 per year. Funds are disbursed in 2 equal payments: first before start of fall semester and second at the beginning of spring semester. The maximum total loan is $20,000 per family. The interest rate varies but recently was 7%. Repayment begins 60 days after the second disbursement of funds and must be completed in 10 years.

Duration 1 year; may be renewed.

Number awarded Varies each year.

Deadline July of each year.

[320]
PRESBYTERIAN CHURCH UNDERGRADUATE/ GRADUATE LOAN PROGRAM

Presbyterian Church (USA)
Attn: Office of Financial Aid for Studies
100 Witherspoon Street, Room M-052
Louisville, KY 40202-1396
(502) 569-5224   Toll Free: (888) 728-7228, ext. 5224
Fax: (502) 569-8766   E-mail: finaid@pcusa.org
Web: www.pcusa.org

Summary To provide financial assistance in the form of loans to undergraduate and graduate students who are members of the Presbyterian Church (USA).

Eligibility This program is open to members of the PCUSA who are enrolled full time at an accredited institution. Applicants must be U.S. citizens or permanent residents making satisfactory progress toward an undergraduate or graduate degree. Both the student and a cosigner must give satisfactory evidence of financial reliability and demonstrate financial need.

Financial data Undergraduates may apply for up to $1,500 in the first year, $2,000 in the second year, $2,500 in the third year, or $3,000 in the fourth year. Graduate students may apply for up to $6,000, divided evenly between the number of academic years remaining. The maximum lifetime loans are $9,000 for undergraduates or $6,000 for graduate students. The interest rate varies but recently was 5.5%. No interest accrues while the student remains in school. Repayment begins 6 months after graduation or discontinuation of studies and must be completed in 10 years.

Duration 1 year; may be renewed by undergraduates for up to 4 years and by graduate students until completion of a degree.

Number awarded Varies each year.

Deadline July of each year.

[321]
PRISCILLA R. MORTON SCHOLARSHIPS

United Methodist Higher Education Foundation
Attn: Scholarships Administrator
1001 19th Avenue South
P.O. Box 340005
Nashville, TN 37203-0005
(615) 340-7385   Toll Free: (800) 811-8110
Fax: (615) 340-7330
E-mail: umhefscholarships@gbhem.org
Web: www.umhef.org/receive.php?id=endowed_funds

Summary To provide financial assistance to members of the United Methodist Church who are interested in working on an undergraduate, graduate, or professional degree.

Eligibility This program is open to undergraduate, graduate, and professional students who have been active, full members of a United Methodist Church for at least 1 year prior to applying. Applicants must have a GPA of 3.5 or higher and be able to demonstrate financial need. Along with their application, they must submit a 200-word essay on their involvement and/or leadership responsibilities in their church, school, and community within the last 3 years. U.S. citizenship or permanent resident status is required. Preference is given to students enrolled or planning to enroll full time at a United Methodist-related college, university, seminary, or theological school.

Financial data The stipend is at least $1,000 per year.

Duration 1 year; recipients may reapply.

Number awarded Varies each year. Recently, 21 of these scholarships were awarded.

Deadline May of each year.

[322]
R. QUINN PUGH EDUCATIONAL SCHOLARSHIP

Baptist Convention of New York
Attn: BCNY Foundation
6538 Baptist Way
East Syracuse, NY 13057
(315) 433-1001   Toll Free: (800) 552-0004
Fax: (315) 433-1026   E-mail: cmeyer@bcnysbc.org
Web: www.bcnysbc.org/bcnyfoundation.html

Summary To provide financial assistance to members of churches in the Baptist Convention of New York who are interested in attending college in any state.

Eligibility This program is open to members in good standing of churches in the Baptist Convention of New York. Applicants must be attending or planning to attend a postsecondary institution in any state. Along with their application, they must submit 1) an essay in which they share their goals for the future and how a degree in higher education will help them achieve those goals; and 2) an autobiography that includes their conversion experience, call to Christian service (for those planning a religious vocation), and plans to fulfill this calling. Financial need is also considered in the selection process.

Financial data A stipend is awarded (amount not specified).

Duration 1 year; may be renewed up to 3 additional years.

Number awarded 1 or more each year.

Deadline February of each year.

[323]
RACE RELATIONS MULTIRACIAL STUDENT SCHOLARSHIP

Christian Reformed Church
Attn: Office of Race Relations
2850 Kalamazoo Avenue, S.E.
Grand Rapids, MI 49560-0200
(616) 241-1691   Toll Free: (877) 279-9994
Fax: (616) 224-0803   E-mail: crcna@crcna.org
Web: www.crcna.org/pages/racerelations_scholar.cfm

Summary To provide financial assistance to undergraduate and graduate minority students interested in attending colleges related to the Christian Reformed Church in North America (CRCNA).

Eligibility Students of color in the United States and Canada are eligible to apply. Normally, applicants are expected to be members of CRCNA congregations who plan to pursue their educational goals at Calvin Theological Seminary or any of the colleges affiliated with the CRCNA. Students who have no prior history with the CRCNA must attend a CRCNA-related college or seminary for a full academic year before they are eligible to apply for this program. Students entering their sophomore year must have earned a GPA of 2.0 or higher as freshmen; students entering their junior year must have earned a GPA of 2.3 or higher as sophomores; students entering their senior year must have earned a GPA of 2.6 or higher as juniors.

Financial data First-year students receive $500 per semester. Other levels of students may receive up to $2,000 per academic year.

Duration 1 year.

Additional information This program was first established in 1971 and revised in 1991. Recipients are expected to train to engage actively in the ministry of racial reconciliation in church and in society. They must be able to work in the United States or Canada upon graduating and must consider working for 1 of the agencies of the CRCNA.

Number awarded Varies each year; recently, 31 students received a total of $21,000 in support.

Deadline March of each year.

[324]
RAYMOND R. DAVIS SCHOLARSHIP

African Methodist Episcopal Church
Third Episcopal District Lay Organization
c/o Kimberley Gordon Brooks, Director of Lay Activities
904 South Main Street
Urbana, OH 43078
(937) 925-2299   E-mail: kimberlysaponi@yahoo.com
Web: www.thirddistrictame.org/raydavis.htm

Summary To provide financial assistance to members of African Methodist Episcopal (AME) churches in its Third Episcopal District who are interested in attending college in any state.

Eligibility This program is open to members of Third Episcopal District AME churches (in Ohio, western Pennsylvania, and West Virginia). Applicants must be high school seniors or students already enrolled in a bachelor's degree program in any field at an accredited college or university in any state. Along with their application, they must submit an essay of 500 to 700 words on how they have demonstrated leadership abil-

ity in their school, community, and AME church. Selection is based on that essay, academic achievement, quality and level of church participation, leadership, extracurricular activities, honors, and letters of recommendation.

Financial data Stipends range from $500 to $1,000.

Duration 1 year.

Number awarded 1 or more each year.

Deadline February of each year.

[325]
RCA ETHNIC SCHOLARSHIP FUND

Reformed Church in America
Attn: Director of Operations and Support
475 Riverside Drive, Room 1814
New York, NY 10115
(212) 870-3071   Toll Free: (800) 722-9977, ext. 3017
Fax: (212) 870-2499   E-mail: mrich@rca.org
Web: www.rca.org/sslpage.aspx?&pid=2177

Summary To provide assistance to minority student members of the Reformed Church in America (RCA) who are interested in working on an undergraduate degree.

Eligibility This program is open to members of minority groups (American Indian, African American/Caribbean American, Hispanic, or Pacific/Asian American) who are attending or planning to attend a college or other institution of higher learning. Applicants must be member of the RCA congregation or attending an RCA institution. Priority is given to applicants who will be entering undergraduate colleges or universities and students currently enrolled in occupational training programs. Selection is based primarily on financial need.

Financial data Stipends range up to $500.

Duration 1 academic year; may be renewed until completion of an academic program.

Number awarded Several each year.

Deadline April of each year.

[326]
REV. BEVERLY E. BOND MEMORIAL SCHOLARSHIP

Jefferson United Methodist Church
Attn: Bond Memorial Scholarship
10328 Jefferson Highway
Baton Rouge, LA 70809
(225) 293-4440   Fax: (225) 293-6821
E-mail: staff@jeffersononline.org
Web: www.jeffersononline.org

Summary To provide financial assistance to Methodists in Louisiana who are preparing for a career as a minister, Christian educator, missionary, or other Christian service professional.

Eligibility This program is open to members of United Methodist Churches in Louisiana who are enrolled or planning to enroll at an accredited college or university supported by the United Methodist Church. Applicants must be planning or currently studying to become a minister, Christian educator, missionary, or other Christian service professional.

Financial data A stipend is awarded (amount not specified).

Duration 1 year.

Number awarded Varies each year.

Deadline May of each year.

[327]
REV. DR. KAREN LAYMAN GIFT OF HOPE: 21ST CENTURY SCHOLARS PROGRAM

United Methodist Church
Attn: General Board of Higher Education and Ministry
Office of Loans and Scholarships
1001 19th Avenue South
P.O. Box 340007
Nashville, TN 37203-0007
(615) 340-7344 Fax: (615) 340-7367
E-mail: umscholar@gbhem.org
Web: www.gbhem.org/loansandscholarships

Summary To provide financial assistance to undergraduate Methodist students who can demonstrate leadership in the church.

Eligibility This program is open to full-time undergraduate students at United Methodist institutions who have been active, full members of a United Methodist Church for at least 3 years prior to applying. Applicants must have a GPA of 3.0 or higher and be able to show evidence of leadership and participation in religious activities during college either through their campus ministry or through local United Methodist Churches in the city where their college is located. They must also show how their education will provide leadership for the church and society and improve the quality of life for others. U.S. citizenship, permanent resident status, or membership in the Central Conferences of the United Methodist Church is required. Financial need is considered in the selection process.

Financial data The stipend is $1,000.

Duration 1 year; recipients may reapply.

Additional information This program was established in 1999.

Number awarded Varies each year. Recently, 1,000 of these scholarships were awarded.

Deadline April of each year.

[328]
REV. RALPH KAPPLER MEMORIAL SCHOLARSHIP

United Methodist Church-Greater New Jersey Conference
Conference Board of Higher Education and Ministry
Attn: Scholarship Committee
1001 Wickapecko Drive
Ocean, NJ 07712-4733
(732) 359-1040 Toll Free: (877) 677-2594, ext. 1040
Fax: (732) 359-1049 E-mail: Lperez@gnjumc.org
Web: www.gnjumc.org/grants_loans_and_scholarship

Summary To provide financial assistance to Methodist students from New Jersey interested in working on an undergraduate degree at a school in any state.

Eligibility This program is open to students who are members of churches affiliated with the Greater New Jersey Conference of the United Methodist Church and working on an undergraduate degree at a college or university in any state. Applicants must be nominated by their church. Along with their application, they must submit a statement on why they wish to be considered for this scholarship, including information on their financial need and Christian commitment.

Financial data A stipend is awarded (amount not specified).

Duration 1 year.

Number awarded Varies each year.

Deadline March of each year.

[329]
RHODA D. HOOD MEMORIAL SCHOLARSHIP

Northwest Baptist Convention
Attn: Woman's Missionary Union
3200 N.E. 109th Avenue
Vancouver, WA 98682
(360) 882-2100 Fax: (360) 882-2295
Web: www.nwbaptist.org

Summary To provide financial assistance to women from the Northwest who are attending a college or seminary in any state to prepare for a career in vocational ministry, preferably with a Southern Baptist Convention church.

Eligibility This program is open to women who have been active members of a church affiliated with the Northwest Baptist Convention and a member of the Woman's Missionary Union within their church. Special consideration is given to children of ministers from the Northwest. Applicants must be attending or planning to attend an accredited college, university, or Southern Baptist seminary in any state with the intention of serving in a vocational ministry position through a church or denomination; priority is given to applicants going into a mission vocation affiliated with the Southern Baptist Convention. Along with their application, they must submit 1) a written account of their conversion experience and their call to vocational ministry; and 2) a written endorsement from their church.

Financial data A stipend is awarded (amount not specified).

Duration 1 year; may be renewed if the recipient maintains a GPA of 2.5 or higher.

Additional information The Northwest Baptist Convention serves Oregon, Washington, and northern Idaho.

Number awarded 1 or more each year.

Deadline May of each year for fall term; October of each year for spring term.

[330]
RHODE ISLAND EASTERN STAR TRAINING AWARDS FOR RELIGIOUS LEADERSHIP

Order of the Eastern Star-Grand Chapter of Rhode Island
c/o Kathryn Newman, Education and ESTARL Committee
19 Preston Drive
Warwick, RI 02886
(401) 921-0317 E-mail: knewman58@cox.net
Web: www.oesri.org/scholarships.html

Summary To provide financial assistance to residents of Rhode Island who are attending college or graduate school in any state to work on a degree related to religious service.

Eligibility This program is open to residents of Rhode Island who are preparing for a career in religious service as a minister, priest, church leader, director of church music, director of religious education, counselor of youth leadership, or other related fields. Applicants must be enrolled at a college or theological school in any state and working on an undergraduate or graduate degree. They must have a GPA of 2.25 or higher and be able to demonstrate financial need. Along with their application, they must submit an essay of 400 to 500 words on the most important issues their field is facing today.

Financial data A stipend is awarded (amount not specified).

Duration 1 year.

Number awarded Varies each year.

Deadline June of each year.

[331]
RICHARD S. SMITH SCHOLARSHIP

United Methodist Church
Attn: General Board of Discipleship
Division on Ministries with Young People
P.O. Box 340003
Nashville, TN 37203-0003
(615) 340-7184   Toll Free: (877) 899-2780, ext. 7184
Fax: (615) 340-7063   E-mail: youngpeople@gbod.org
Web: www.gbod.org

Summary To provide financial assistance to minority high school seniors who wish to prepare for a Methodist church-related career.

Eligibility This program is open to graduating high school seniors who are members of racial/ethnic minority groups and have been active members of a United Methodist Church for at least 1 year. Applicants must have been admitted to an accredited college or university to prepare for a church-related career. They must have maintained at least a "C" average throughout high school and be able to demonstrate financial need. Along with their application, they must submit brief essays on their participation in church projects and activities, a leadership experience, the role their faith plays in their life, the church-related vocation to which God is calling them, and their extracurricular interests and activities. U.S. citizenship or permanent resident status is required.

Financial data The stipend is $1,000.

Duration 1 year; nonrenewable.

Additional information This scholarship was first awarded in 1997. Recipients must enroll full time in their first year of undergraduate study.

Number awarded 2 each year.

Deadline May of each year.

[332]
ROBERT WALKER SCHOLARSHIPS IN CHRISTIAN JOURNALISM

Christian Life Missions
600 Rinehard Road
P.O. Box 952248
Lake Mary, FL 32795
(407) 333-0600   E-mail: Amy.condiff@strang.com
Web: www.christianlifemissions.com

Summary To provide financial assistance to undergraduate and graduate students interested in preparing for a career in Christian journalism.

Eligibility This program is open to undergraduate and graduate journalism students who have a GPA of 3.5 or higher. Applicants must submit a letter explaining their inter-

est and commitment to Christian journalism, a current resume, an official transcript, and 5 published works.

Financial data The stipend is $2,000 per year.

Duration 1 year; recipients may reapply.

Number awarded Up to 5 each year.

Deadline April of each year.

[333]
RUDY AND MICAELA CAMACHO SCHOLARSHIP

Baptist General Convention of Texas
Attn: Institutional Ministries Department
333 North Washington
Dallas, TX 75246-1798
(214) 828-5252   Toll Free: (888) 244-9400
Fax: (214) 828-5261   E-mail: institutions@bgct.org
Web: www.bgct.org

Summary To provide financial assistance for college to residents of Texas who are members of Texas Baptist Hispanic congregations.

Eligibility This program is open to members of Hispanic Baptist churches in Texas that are cooperating with the Baptist General Convention of Texas. Applicants must be working on or planning to work on a bachelor's degree at a 4-year college or university in Texas. They must have a GPA of 3.0 or higher on their high school or college transcript. Along with their application, they must submit 1-page essays on 1) how they became a Christian; 2) their church involvement; 3) their personal goals and aspirations; and 4) what they would like to contribute to the work of Hispanic Baptists in Texas.

Financial data The stipend is $1,000 per year.

Duration 1 year; may be renewed up to 3 additional years as long as the recipient remains active in their church and attends the Hispanic Baptist Convention of Texas annual meeting.

Number awarded Up to 2 each year.

Deadline April of each year.

[334]
RUMPLE MEMORIAL PRESBYTERIAN CHURCH SCHOLARSHIP ENDOWMENT

Watauga Community Foundation
c/o North Carolina Community Foundation
P.O. Box 2851
Hickory, NC 28603
(828) 328-1237   Toll Free: (888) 375-8117
Fax: (828) 328-3948
E-mail: mmanning@nccommunityfoundation.org
Web: www.nccommunityfoundation.org

Summary To provide financial assistance to residents of North Carolina who are preparing for a career of service to Presbyterian churches.

Eligibility This program is open to residents of North Carolina who are 1) candidates for ministry under supervision and care of their Presbytery; 2) enrolled at a Presbyterian school of Christian education to prepare for a career as a director of Christian education or in the mission field; or 3) accepted by a graduate school or seminary in preparation for a church vocation. Preference is given to members of Rumple Church and to graduates of the Blowing Rock Elementary School District. Financial need is considered in the selection process.

Financial data A stipend is awarded (amount not specified).

Duration 1 year.

Number awarded 1 or more each year.

Deadline Deadline not specified.

[335]
RUSCH-SHEPARD EDUCATIONAL SCHOLARSHIPS

Synod of the Trinity
Attn: Scholarships
3040 Market Street
Camp Hill, PA 17011-4599
(717) 737-0421, ext. 233
Toll Free: (800) 242-0534, ext. 233
Fax: (717) 737-8211   E-mail: mhumer@syntrinity.org
Web: www.syntrinity.org

Summary To provide financial assistance to children of clergy in the Presbyterian Synod of the Trinity who are interested in attending college in any state.

Eligibility This program is open to children of minimally-salaried clergy in the Synod of the Trinity of the Presbyterian Church (USA): all of Pennsylvania; West Virginia except for the counties of Berkeley, Grant, Hampshire, Hardy, Jefferson, Mineral, Morgan, and Pendleton; and the Ohio counties of Belmont, Harrison, Jefferson, Monroe, along with the southern sector of Columbiana. Applicants must be enrolled or planning to enroll full time at an accredited college or vocational school in any state. They must have total income of less than $85,000 for a family of 4. U.S. citizenship or permanent resident status is required.

Financial data A stipend is awarded (amount not specified).

Duration 1 year; recipients may reapply.

Number awarded Varies each year.

Deadline April of each year.

[336]
RUTH SPECHT SCHOLARSHIP

Iowa United Methodist Foundation
2301 Rittenhouse Street
Des Moines, IA 50321
(515) 974-8927
Web: www.iumf.org/umscholarships.html

Summary To provide financial assistance to high school seniors in Iowa who plan to attend a United Methodist college in the state.

Eligibility This program is open to graduating high school seniors in Iowa who plan to attend a United Methodist college in the state. Applicants must submit transcripts, 2 letters of recommendation (including 1 from a teacher or counselor and 1 from the pastor verifying that the student is a member of the United Methodist Church and describing their church involvement), and a financial statement.

Financial data The stipend is $1,725.

Duration 1 year.

Number awarded 1 each year.

Deadline March of each year.

[337]
SAMUEL ROBINSON AWARD

Presbyterian Church (USA)
Attn: Office of Financial Aid for Studies
100 Witherspoon Street, Room M-052
Louisville, KY 40202-1396
(502) 569-5224   Toll Free: (888) 728-7228, ext. 5224
Fax: (502) 569-8766   E-mail: finaid@pcusa.org
Web: www.pcusa.org

Summary To recognize and reward students in Presbyterian colleges who write essays on religious topics.

Eligibility Eligible are juniors and seniors enrolled full time in 1 of the 65 colleges related to the Presbyterian Church (USA). Applicants must successfully recite the answers to the Westminster Shorter Catechism and write a 2,000-word original essay on an assigned topic related to the Shorter Catechism.

Financial data Awards range from $200 to $1,000.

Duration 1 year; nonrenewable.

Number awarded 1 each year.

Deadline March of each year.

[338]
SARA HUTCHINGS CLARDY SCHOLARSHIP AWARDS

Japanese American Citizens League-Arizona Chapter
5414 West Glenn Drive
Glendale, AZ 85301-2628
E-mail: arizonajacl@gmail.com
Web: www.jaclaz.org

Summary To provide financial assistance to graduating high school seniors in Arizona who are of Japanese heritage.

Eligibility This program is open to graduating high school seniors in Arizona who have a GPA of 3.0 or higher. Applicants or their parents must have been members of 1 of the following organizations for at least the preceding 3 years: Arizona Chapter of the Japanese American Citizens League (JACLA), the Phoenix Japanese Free Methodist Church, the Arizona Buddhist Church, a youth group of JACLA, a youth group of the Phoenix Free Methodist Church, or a youth group of the Arizona Buddhist Church. Financial need is not considered in the selection process.

Financial data A stipend is awarded (amount not specified).

Duration 1 year.

Additional information Recipients must attend the association's scholarship awards banquet and accept the award in person; failure to do so results in forfeiture of the award.

Number awarded 4 each year.

Deadline February of each year.

[339]
SCHOLARSHIPS FOR CHILDREN OF CHRISTIAN BRETHREN COMMENDED WORKERS

Stewards Ministries
1101 Perimeter Drive, Suite 600
Schaumburg, IL 60173
(847) 842-0227   Toll Free: (800) 551-6505
Fax: (847) 517-2705
E-mail: info@stewardsministries.com
Web: www.stewardsministries.com/scholarships.html

Summary To provide financial assistance for college to children of full-time workers commended from Plymouth Brethren (Christian Brethren) assemblies.

Eligibility This program is open to unmarried undergraduate students who are dependent children of full-time workers commended from Plymouth Brethren (Christian Brethren) assemblies in the United States and Canada. Applicants must have a proven Christian testimony and character and be able to demonstrate financial need. Along with their application, they must submit an essay on their reasons to further their studies and their relationship with the Lord.

Financial data Stipends are $1,000 per year or $2,000 per year for students at Emmaus Bible College.

Duration 1 year; may be renewed up to 3 additional years.

Number awarded Varies each year.

Deadline May of each year.

[340]
SCHOLARSHIPS FOR ELCA SERVICE ABROAD

Women of the Evangelical Lutheran Church in America
Attn: Scholarships
8765 West Higgins Road
Chicago, IL 60631-4101
(773) 380-2736   Toll Free: (800) 638-3522, ext. 2736
Fax: (773) 380-2419   E-mail: emily.hansen@elca.org
Web: www.elca.org

Summary To provide financial assistance to lay women who are members of Evangelical Lutheran Church of America (ELCA) congregations and who wish to pursue postsecondary education for service abroad, either in general or in health fields.

Eligibility This program is open to ELCA lay women who are at least 21 years of age and have experienced an interruption of at least 2 years in their education since high school. Applicants must have been admitted to an academic institution to prepare for a career other than the ordained ministry. This program is available only to women studying for ELCA service abroad, either in general or in health professions associated with ELCA projects abroad. U.S. citizenship is required.

Financial data The stipend ranges from $800 to $1,000 per year.

Duration Up to 2 years.

Additional information This program includes the following named scholarships: the Belmer Scholarship, the Flora Prince Scholarship, the Kahler Scholarship, the Vickers/Raup Scholarship, and the Emma Wettstein Scholarship.

Number awarded Varies each year, depending upon the funds available.

Deadline February of each year.

[341]
SELMO BRADLEY SCHOLARSHIP

African Methodist Episcopal Church
Attn: Eleventh Episcopal District Lay Organization
101 East Union Street, Suite 301
Jacksonville, FL 32202
(904) 355-8262   Fax: (904) 356-1617
E-mail: eedlo@eedlo.org
Web: www.eedlo.org/scholarships.html

Summary To provide financial assistance to members of African Methodist Episcopal (AME) churches in Florida who are interested in attending college in any state.

Eligibility This program is open to seniors graduating from public or private high schools in Florida who are members of AME churches. Applicants must be planning to enroll full time at an institution of higher learning in any state: an AME-supported college, a Predominantly Black College or University, or an accredited trade school. They must have a GPA of 2.5 or higher. Along with their application, they must submit a 1-page essay on why a college education is important and a statement regarding their financial need.

Financial data A stipend is awarded (amount not specified).

Duration 1 year.

Number awarded 1 or more each year.

Deadline April of each year.

[342]
SHANNON FUND

Episcopal Diocese of Bethlehem
Attn: Archdeacon Howard Stringfellow
333 Wyandotte Street
Bethlehem, PA 18015
(610) 691-5655, ext. 222
Toll Free: (800) 358-5655 (within PA)
E-mail: archdeacon@diobeth.org
Web: www.diobeth.org

Summary To provide financial assistance to residents of Pennsylvania who are daughters of Episcopal clergy and interested in working on a degree at a college in any state.

Eligibility Applicants must be 1) residents of 1 of the 5 dioceses of Pennsylvania; 2) daughters of an Episcopal priest; 3) younger than 20 years of age; and 4) interested in working on a degree at a college in any state. The clergy parent must live in the Commonwealth of Pennsylvania and must be canonically resident in 1 of its dioceses. Preference is given to daughters of clergy in the diocese of Bethlehem; if there are surplus funds, then scholarships can be awarded to daughters of clergy in the other 4 Pennsylvania dioceses. Financial need is considered in the selection process.

Financial data Stipends up to $1,500, depending on need, are available.

Duration 1 year; may be renewed until the recipient reaches the age of 20.

Number awarded Varies each year.

Deadline April of each year.

[343]
SISTER THEA BOWMAN FOUNDATION KNIGHTS OF COLUMBUS SCHOLARSHIPS

Knights of Columbus
Attn: Department of Scholarships
P.O. Box 1670
New Haven, CT 06507-0901
(203) 752-4332   Fax: (203) 772-2696
E-mail: info@kofc.org
Web: www.kofc.org/un/en/scholarships/bowman.html

Summary   To provide financial assistance to African American high school seniors interested in attending a Catholic college.

Eligibility   This program is open to African American seniors graduating from high schools in the United States. Applicants must be planning to attend a Catholic college or university. They are not required to be the children of members of the Knights of Columbus.

Financial data   The stipend is $5,000 per year.

Duration   1 year; may be renewed up to 3 additional years.

Additional information   This program was established in 1996.

Number awarded   Scholarships are offered when funds are available.

Deadline   February of the year when available.

[344]
SLOVAK CATHOLIC SOKOL COLLEGE SCHOLARSHIP GRANTS

Slovak Catholic Sokol
Attn: Membership Memorial Scholarship Fund
205 Madison Street
P.O. Box 899
Passaic, NJ 07055-0899
(973) 777-2605   Toll Free: (800) 886-7656
Fax: (973) 779-8245 E-mail: life@slovakcatholicsokol.org
Web: www.slovakcatholicsokol.org

Summary   To provide financial assistance to members of the Slovak Catholic Sokol who are attending college or graduate school in any state.

Eligibility   This program is open to members of the Slovak Catholic Sokol who have completed at least 1 semester of college and are currently enrolled full time as an undergraduate or graduate student at an accredited college, university, or professional school in any state. Applicants must have been a member for at least 5 years, have at least $3,000 permanent life insurance coverage, and have at least 1 parent who is a member.

Financial data   The stipend is $1,000 per year.

Duration   1 year; may be renewed 1 additional year.

Additional information   Slovak Catholic Sokol was founded as a fraternal benefit society in 1905. It is licensed to operate in the following states: Connecticut, Illinois, Indiana, Massachusetts, Michigan, New Jersey, New York, Ohio, Pennsylvania, and Wisconsin. This program was established in 2003.

Number awarded   30 each year.

Deadline   March of each year.

[345]
SOUTH CAROLINA CHURCH RELATED VOCATIONAL SCHOLARSHIPS

South Carolina Baptist Convention
Attn: Collegiate Ministry Group
190 Stoneridge Drive
Columbia, SC 29210-8254
(803) 765-0030, ext. 4400
Toll Free: (800) 723-7242 (within SC)
Fax: (803) 799-1044   E-mail: CRVS@scbaptist.org
Web: www.scbcm.org/scholarships

Summary   To provide financial assistance to South Carolina Baptists who are attending a college or university in the state to prepare for a church-related vocation.

Eligibility   This program is open to residents of South Carolina who have been active members of a Southern Baptist church for at least 9 months prior to the beginning of an academic year. Applicants must be 1) enrolled full time at an accredited college or university in South Carolina; 2) recommended by their church; 3) able to demonstrate financial need; and 4) committed to a church-related vocation. They must agree to participate in a ministry-related practical experience approximately 2 to 6 hours per week under a designated supervisor. A personal interview is required.

Financial data   The stipend depends on the need of the recipient. Funds are sent directly to the school to be applied to tuition and academic fees.

Duration   1 year; recipients may reapply if they maintain full-time enrollment and a GPA of 2.0 or higher.

Number awarded   1 or more each year.

Deadline   March of each year.

[346]
SOUTH CAROLINA CONFERENCE MERIT SCHOLARSHIP

United Methodist Church-South Carolina Conference
Attn: Board of Higher Education and Campus Ministry
4908 Colonial Drive
Columbia, SC 29203-6070
(803) 786-9486   Toll Free: (888) 678-6272
Fax: (803) 691-0220
Web: www.umcsc.org/scholarships2.html

Summary   To provide financial assistance to residents of South Carolina who are interested in attending a Methodist college in any state.

Eligibility   This program is open to members of United Methodist Churches in South Carolina who are graduating high school seniors or graduates. Applicants must be enrolled or planning to enroll at a United Methodist Church college or university in any state and major in any field. Along with their application, they must submit a personal statement that describes their participation in projects and activities of church, school, and/or community; official college or high school transcripts; a letter of recommendation from their pastor; a statement regarding their financial need; and a general statement that may include their philosophy of life, faith development, and what influenced them in selecting their career goal. Selection is based on merit, but that is defined to include academic scholarship, church involvement, special vocational preparation for ministry or other service, and financial need.

Financial data The stipend ranges from $500 to $1,000.
Duration 1 year.
Number awarded 1 or more each year.
Deadline March of each year.

[347]
SOUTH CAROLINA WMU COLLEGE SCHOLARSHIPS

South Carolina Baptist Convention
Attn: Woman's Missionary Union
190 Stoneridge Drive
Columbia, SC 29210-8254
(803) 227-6209   Toll Free: (800) 723-7242 (within SC)
Fax: (803) 799-1044
E-mail: deannedeaton@scbaptist.org
Web: www.scwmu.org/article783.htm

Summary To provide financial assistance to high school seniors who have participated in youth activities of South Carolina Baptist churches and plan to attend college in any state.

Eligibility This program is open to seniors graduating from high schools in South Carolina and planning to attend a college or university in any state. Applicants must have completed at least 3 levels of MissionsQuest or Challengers Journey by their senior year and be currently active in an Acteens or Youth on Mission organization. Financial need is considered in the selection process.

Financial data The stipend is $1,000.

Duration 1 year; may be renewed, provided the recipient maintains satisfactory academic achievement and exercises Christian leadership on campus.

Number awarded Varies each year.

Deadline Deadline not specified.

[348]
SOUTH DAKOTA EASTERN STAR TRAINING AWARDS FOR RELIGIOUS LEADERSHIP

Order of the Eastern Star-Grand Chapter of South Dakota
c/o Carol Helms, ESTARL Committee Chair
P.O. Box 143
Buffalo, SD 57720
E-mail: helmscarol@hotmail.com
Web: www.oeshugs.com/ESTARL.html

Summary To provide financial assistance to residents of South Dakota who are interested in attending a college or seminary in any state to prepare for a career in religious service.

Eligibility This program is open to residents of South Dakota who are attending or planning to attend a college or seminary in any state. Applicants must be interested in preparing for a career in fields of religious service as a minister, missionary, director of church music, director of religious education, or counselor of youth leadership.

Financial data A stipend is awarded (amount not specified).

Duration 1 year; may be renewed.

Number awarded Varies each year.

Deadline Deadline not specified.

[349]
SPANISH BAPTIST CONVENTION OF NEW MEXICO SCHOLARSHIP

Baptist Convention of New Mexico
Attn: Missions Mobilization Team
5325 Wyoming Boulevard, N.E.
P.O. Box 94485
Albuquerque, NM 87199-4485
(505) 924-2315   Toll Free: (800) 898-8544
Fax: (505) 924-2320   E-mail: cpairett@bcnm.com
Web: www.bcnm.com

Summary To provide financial assistance to Hispanic Baptist students from New Mexico interested in attending a college or seminary in any state.

Eligibility This program is open to college and seminary students who are active members of churches affiliated with the Baptist Convention of New Mexico. Applicants must be of Hispanic background and committed to full-time Christian service. They must be attending a college or seminary in any state.

Financial data A stipend is awarded (amount not specified).

Duration 1 year; may be renewed.

Number awarded 1 or more each year.

Deadline April of each year.

[350]
SPORTQUEST ALL-AMERICAN FEMALE INDIANA STATE ATHLETE OF THE YEAR

SportQuest Ministries, Inc.
Attn: All-American Program
770 North High School Road
P.O. Box 53433
Indianapolis, IN 46253-0433
(317) 270-9495   Fax: (317) 244-0495
Web: www.allamericanaward.org/atp.html

Summary To provide financial assistance to outstanding female Christian high school athletes from Indiana who plan to attend college in any state.

Eligibility This program is open to female sophomores, juniors, and seniors who are currently a varsity-level athlete in 1 or more sports at high schools in Indiana. Applicants must be planning to attend a college or university in any state. They must be a committed follower of Christ and have a grade point average of "C" or higher. Along with their application, they must submit 1-paragraph essays on 1) how they have used, or would like to use, their athletic ability to share their faith and/or to influence others positively; and 2) how and when they accepted Jesus Christ as their personal Lord and Savior and what their personal relationship with Him means to them. Selection is based on those essays, GPA, SAT and/or ACT scores, athletic accomplishments, church and community involvement, essays, and references.

Financial data The award is a $500 scholarship.

Duration 1 year.

Number awarded 1 each year.

Deadline February of each year.

[351]
SPORTQUEST ALL-AMERICAN MALE INDIANA STATE ATHLETE OF THE YEAR

SportQuest Ministries, Inc.
Attn: All-American Program
770 North High School Road
P.O. Box 53433
Indianapolis, IN 46253-0433
(317) 270-9495   Fax: (317) 244-0495
Web: www.allamericanaward.org/atp.html

Summary To provide financial assistance to outstanding male Christian high school athletes from Indiana who plan to attend college in any state.

Eligibility This program is open to male sophomores, juniors, and seniors who are currently a varsity-level athlete in 1 or more sports at high schools in Indiana. Applicants must be planning to attend a college or university in any state. They must be a committed follower of Christ and have a grade point average of "C" or higher. Along with their application, they must submit 1-paragraph essays on 1) how they have used, or would like to use, their athletic ability to share their faith and/or to influence others positively; and 2) how and when they accepted Jesus Christ as their personal Lord and Savior and what their personal relationship with Him means to them. Selection is based on those essays, GPA, SAT and/or ACT scores, athletic accomplishments, church and community involvement, essays, and references.

Financial data The award is a $500 scholarship.

Duration 1 year.

Number awarded 1 each year.

Deadline February of each year.

[352]
ST. ANDREW BY-THE-SEA SCHOLARSHIPS

St. Andrew By-The-Sea United Methodist Church
Attn: Scholarship Committee
20 Pope Avenue
Hilton Head Island, SC 29928
(843) 785-4711   Fax: (843) 785-5716
E-mail: standrewbythesea@gmail.com
Web: www.hhiumc.com/scholarships

Summary To provide financial assistance to Methodists who are attending a college or seminary in any state to prepare for a career in religious service.

Eligibility This program is open to members of United Methodist Church (UMC) congregations in any state who have completed at least their freshman year of college. Applicants must be preparing for a career in ministry, Christian education, or church music. Seminary students are eligible if they intend to enter the ministry of the UMC. Selection is based on academic achievement, personal accomplishments, and financial need. Special consideration is given to graduates of Epworth Children's Home of Columbia, South Carolina. If there are no other qualified applicants, members of St. Andrew By-The-Sea UMC in Hilton Head Island, South Carolina may be considered, regardless of their major or college location.

Financial data Stipends generally range from $500 to $1,500. Funds are disbursed directly to the recipient's college.

Duration 1 year.

Number awarded 1 or more each year.

Deadline April of each year.

[353]
STUDENT OPPORTUNITY SCHOLARSHIPS FOR ETHNIC MINORITY GROUPS

Presbyterian Church (USA)
Attn: Office of Financial Aid for Studies
100 Witherspoon Street, Room M-052
Louisville, KY 40202-1396
(502) 569-5224   Toll Free: (888) 728-7228, ext. 5224
Fax: (502) 569-8766   E-mail: finaid@pcusa.org
Web: www.pcusa.org

Summary To provide financial assistance to upper-division college students who are Presbyterians, especially those of racial/ethnic minority heritage majoring in designated fields.

Eligibility This program is open to members of the Presbyterian Church (USA), especially those from racial/ethnic minority groups (Asian American, African American, Hispanic American, Native American, Alaska Native). Applicants must be able to demonstrate financial need, be entering their junior or senior year of college as full-time students, and have a GPA of 2.5 or higher. Preference is given to applicants who are majoring in the following fields of interest to missions of the church: education, health services and sciences, religious studies, sacred music, social services, and social sciences.

Financial data Stipends range up to $3,000 per year, depending upon the financial need of the recipient.

Duration 1 year; may be renewed for up to 3 additional years if the recipient continues to need financial assistance and demonstrates satisfactory academic progress.

Number awarded Varies each year.

Deadline June of each year.

[354]
SUSANNAH WESLEY SCHOLARSHIP

United Methodist Church-California-Pacific Annual Conference
Attn: Conference Council on Youth Ministries
110 South Euclid Avenue
P.O. Box 6006
Pasadena, CA 91102-6006
(626) 568-7360   Toll Free: (800) 244-8622
Fax: (626) 796-7297   E-mail: youngpeople@cal-pac.org
Web: calpacyoungpeople.org/events/youthday

Summary To provide financial assistance to high school seniors who are members of United Methodist Churches in the California-Pacific Annual Conference and interested in attending college in any state.

Eligibility This program is open to high school seniors who are members of churches within the area of the United Methodist California-Pacific Annual Conference and planning to attend college in any state. Applicants must be able to demonstrate financial need. Along with their application, they must submit an essay, up to 4 pages in length, describing their participation in the following areas of involvement and ministry: school, community, local church, district, conference, and other connectional activities.

Financial data The stipend is $1,000. Funds are paid directly to the recipient's college.

Duration 1 year; nonrenewable.

Additional information The California-Pacific Annual Conference includes churches in southern California, Hawaii, Guam, and Saipan.

Number awarded 1 or more each year.

Deadline May of each year.

[355]
SYNOD OF THE COVENANT ETHNIC STUDENT SCHOLARSHIPS

Synod of the Covenant
Attn: Ministries in Higher Education
1911 Indianwood Circle, Suite B
Maumee, OH 43537-4063
(419) 754-4050
Toll Free: (800) 848-1030 (within MI and OH)
Fax: (419) 754-4051
Web: www.synodofthecovenant.org

Summary To provide financial assistance to ethnic students working on an undergraduate degree (with priority given to Presbyterian applicants from Ohio and Michigan).

Eligibility This program is open to ethnic minority students working full or part time on a baccalaureate degree or certification at a college, university, or vocational school in any state. Applicants must have a GPA of 3.0 or higher and be able to demonstrate participation in a Presbyterian church. Priority is given to Presbyterian applicants from the states of Michigan and Ohio. Financial need is considered in the selection process.

Financial data The maximum amount allowed within a calendar year is $600 (for full-time students in their first year), $800 (for renewals to full-time students), or $400 (for part-time students). Funds are made payable to the session for distribution.

Duration Students are eligible to receive scholarships 1 time per year, up to a maximum of 5 years. Renewals are granted, provided 1) the completed application is received before the deadline date, 2) the recipient earned at least a 2.0 GPA last year, and 3) the application contains evidence of Presbyterian church participation and continued spiritual development.

Number awarded Varies each year.

Deadline August of each year for fall semester; January of each year for spring semester.

[356]
SYNOD OF THE TRINITY EDUCATIONAL SCHOLARSHIPS

Synod of the Trinity
Attn: Scholarships
3040 Market Street
Camp Hill, PA 17011-4599
(717) 737-0421, ext. 233
Toll Free: (800) 242-0534, ext. 233
Fax: (717) 737-8211   E-mail: mhumer@syntrinity.org
Web: www.syntrinity.org

Summary To provide financial assistance members of Presbyterian churches within the Synod of the Trinity who are interested in attending college in any state.

Eligibility This program is open to 1) members of Presbyterian churches within the Synod of the Trinity (which covers all of Pennsylvania; West Virginia except for the counties of

Berkeley, Grant, Hampshire, Hardy, Jefferson, Mineral, Morgan, and Pendleton; and the Ohio counties of Belmont, Harrison, Jefferson, Monroe, and the southern sector of Columbiana), or 2) students who are actively involved in the ministry of such a church. Applicants must be enrolled or planning to enroll full time at an accredited college or vocational school in any state. They must have total income of less than $85,000 for a family of 4. U.S. citizenship or permanent resident status is required.

Financial data Awards range from $100 to $1,000 per year, depending on the need of the recipient.

Duration 1 year; recipients may reapply.

Number awarded Varies each year.

Deadline April of each year.

[357]
TENNESSEE ACTEENS SCHOLARSHIP

Tennessee Baptist Convention
Attn: WMU Scholarships
5001 Maryland Way
P.O. Box 728
Brentwood, TN 37024-9728
(615) 373-2255   Toll Free: (800) 558-2090, ext. 2038
Fax: (615) 371-2014   E-mail: jferguson@tnbaptist.org
Web: www.tnbaptist.org/page.asp?page=92

Summary To provide financial assistance to members of Baptist churches in Tennessee who have been active in the Acteens program for girls and plan to attend college in any state.

Eligibility This program is open to high school seniors who are members and active participants in mission programs and ministry of a Tennessee Baptist church. Applicants must be able to demonstrate active involvement in Acteens in at least 2 of the following ways: 1) participation in local ministry for at least 2 years; 2) completion of at least 2 levels of MissionsQuest or an approved individual achievement plan; 3) selection as a state or national Acteen advisory panelist or Top Teen; or 4) participation on 2 Acteens Activator Teams. They must have a GPA of 2.6 or higher and be planning to enroll full time at a college or university in any state.

Financial data A stipend is awarded (amount not specified).

Duration 1 year.

Number awarded 1 or more each year.

Deadline January of each year.

[358]
TENNESSEE BAPTIST FOUNDATION COLLEGE AND MEDICAL SCHOLARSHIPS

Tennessee Baptist Foundation
5001 Maryland Way
P.O. Box 728
Brentwood, TN 37024-9728
(615) 371-2029   Toll Free: (800) 552-4644
Fax: (615) 371-2049   E-mail: TBF@tnbaptist.org
Web: www.tbfoundation.org/tbfcat.asp?cat=edu

Summary To provide financial assistance to members of Southern Baptist churches in Tennessee who are attending college in any state to work on an undergraduate degree in any field or a doctoral degree in designated medical fields.

Eligibility This program is open to members of churches cooperating with the Tennessee Baptist Convention who have been residents of Tennessee for at least 1 year prior to applying. Applicants must have completed at least 24 semester hours of collegiate study and have a GPA of 2.3 or higher. They must be working full time on either 1) an undergraduate degree in any field at an accredited college or university in any state, or 2) a doctoral degree at an accredited dental, medical, or pharmacy school in any state. Their household income must be less than $100,000 per year (or $125,000 for families with 2 children in college or $150,000 for families with 3 children in college). Along with their application, they must submit a 2-page summary of their Christian conversion, highlights of their Christian growth, involvement in their church and/or Baptist collegiate ministries, and their goals for life and vocation. Selection is based on academic performance, financial need, and involvement in church and Baptist collegiate ministries.

Financial data A stipend is awarded (amount not specified).

Duration 1 year; may be renewed as long as the recipient maintains a minimum GPA of 2.3 as a sophomore, 2.5 as a junior, or 2.7 as a senior.

Number awarded Varies each year. Recently, the foundation awarded 239 scholarships and grants for all of its programs.

Deadline April of each year.

[359]
TENNESSEE BAPTIST FOUNDATION EDUCATIONAL GRANTS

Tennessee Baptist Foundation
5001 Maryland Way
P.O. Box 728
Brentwood, TN 37024-9728
(615) 371-2029   Toll Free: (800) 552-4644
Fax: (615) 371-2049   E-mail: TBF@tnbaptist.org
Web: www.tbfoundation.org/tbfcat.asp?cat=edu

Summary To provide financial assistance to high school seniors who are members of Southern Baptist churches in Tennessee and planning to attend college in any state.

Eligibility This program is open to members of churches cooperating with the Tennessee Baptist Convention who have been residents of Tennessee for at least 1 year prior to applying. Applicants must be high school seniors planning to enroll full time at an accredited college or university in any state. They must have a GPA of 2.0 or higher, an ACT score of 18 or higher, or an SAT score of 860 or higher. Along with their application, they must submit a 1-page summary of their Christian conversion, highlights of their growth as a Christian, and their involvement in their church. Selection is based on academic performance, family income and/or extenuating circumstances, and involvement in their church.

Financial data A stipend is awarded (amount not specified).

Duration 1 year.

Number awarded Varies each year. Recently, the foundation awarded 239 scholarships and grants for all of its programs.

Deadline April of each year.

[360]
TENNESSEE EAGLE SCOUT OF THE YEAR SCHOLARSHIP

American Legion
Department of Tennessee
215 Eighth Avenue North
Nashville, TN 37203-3583
(615) 254-0568   Fax: (615) 255-1551
E-mail: tnleg@bellsouth.net
Web: www.tennesseelegion.org/youthprograms.shtml

Summary To recognize and reward, with scholarships for college in any state, Eagle Scouts who are members of a troop associated with the American Legion in Tennessee or a son or grandson of a member of the Legion in the state.

Eligibility The Tennessee nominee for American Legion Scout of the Year receives this scholarship. Applicants must be 1) registered, active members of a Boy Scout Troop or Varsity Scout Team sponsored by an American Legion Post in Tennessee or Auxiliary Unit in Tennessee, or 2) registered, active members of a duly chartered Boy Scout Troop or Varsity Scout Team and the sons or grandsons of American Legion or Auxiliary members. Candidates must also 1) be active members of their religious institution and have received the appropriate religious emblem; 2) have demonstrated practical citizenship in church, school, Scouting, and community; and 3) be at least 15 years of age and enrolled in high school. They must be planning to attend college in any state.

Financial data The award is a $1,500 scholarship.

Duration The award is presented annually.

Number awarded 1 each year.

Deadline Deadline not specified.

[361]
TEXAS BAPTIST FINANCIAL ASSISTANCE FOR MINISTRY STUDENTS

Baptist General Convention of Texas
Attn: Theological Education
333 North Washington
Dallas, TX 75246-1798
(214) 828-5254   Fax: (214) 828-5284
E-mail: ministertraining@bgct.org
Web: texasbaptists.org

Summary To provide financial assistance to members of Baptist churches in Texas who are preparing for a career in ministry at a Texas Baptist institution.

Eligibility This program is open to members of Baptist churches in Texas who can present a certificate of license or ordination, or letter of certification of call from a Baptist church. Applicants must demonstrate "a life style of commitment to the principles of the Christian life" and certification by their pastor that they are involved in, supportive of, and committed to the local cooperating church. They must be working on, or planning to work on, a certificate, undergraduate, graduate, or postgraduate program approved by the Theological Education Committee of the Baptist General Convention of Texas (BGCT) at a Bible college, university, or seminary in Texas. Applications must be submitted through the school.

Financial data The amount of support is established by the school.

Duration 1 year; may be renewed if the recipients reaffirm their sense of call to church-related ministry and furnish evidence of their continuing involvement and commitment to a local BGCT church.

Additional information The eligible schools include 1 Bible college (Baptist University of the Americas in San Antonio); 8 universities (Baylor University, Dallas Baptist University, East Texas Baptist University, Hardin-Simmons University, Houston Baptist University, Howard Payne University, University of Mary Hardin-Baylor, and Wayland Baptist University); and 2 seminaries (George W. Truett Seminary at Baylor University and Logsdon School of Theology at Hardin-Simmons University).

Number awarded Varies each year.

Deadline Each school establishes its own deadline.

[362]
TEXAS DISTRICT LUTHERAN WOMEN'S MISSIONARY LEAGUE SCHOLARSHIP

Lutheran Women's Missionary League-Texas District
c/o Carolyn Culbertson, Scholarship Committee Chair
1615 Allison Drive
New Braunfels, TX 78130
(830) 606-1477   E-mail: schirm007@satx.rr.com
Web: www.lwmltxdist.org/officers/schol.html

Summary To provide financial assistance to female members of the Lutheran Church-Missouri Synod (LCMS) in Texas who are interested in preparing for a career within the denomination.

Eligibility This program is open to women who are communicant members of a congregation of the Texas District of the LCMS. Applicants must be full-time undergraduate students enrolled or planning to enroll at a recognized institution of higher learning in a course of study leading to full-time professional church work in the LCMS. Selection is based primarily on overall aptitude for professional church work. Financial need is also considered.

Financial data A stipend is awarded (amount not specified).

Duration 1 year.

Additional information This program was established in 1990.

Number awarded 1 or more each year.

Deadline March of each year.

[363]
TEXAS STATE COUNCIL EDUCATIONAL GRANTS

Knights of Columbus-Texas State Council
Attn: Aid to Education Committee
6633 Highway 290 East, Suite 204
Austin, TX 78723-1157
(512) 442-1492   Fax: (512) 326-1492
E-mail: info@tkofc.org
Web: www.tkofc.org

Summary To provide financial assistance to members of the Knights of Columbus in Texas and their families who are interested in attending college in any state.

Eligibility This program is open to members of the Knights of Columbus in Texas and their wives, children, and grandchildren. Special consideration is given to members of Columbian Squires. Applicants must be attending or planning to attend a college, university, junior college, technical school, business school, or seminary in any state. They must submit an essay, up to 250 words, on their personal reasons for applying and how the receipt of the grant will affect their decision to continue with their education.

Financial data The stipend is $1,000.

Duration 1 year.

Number awarded 17 each year: 1 to an applicant from each of the 15 Catholic archdioceses and dioceses in Texas plus 2 to members of Columbian Squires.

Deadline February of each year.

[364]
THE DOCTORS' LESKO MEDICAL MEMORIAL SCHOLARSHIP

Slovak Catholic Sokol
Attn: Membership Memorial Scholarship Fund
205 Madison Street
P.O. Box 899
Passaic, NJ 07055-0899
(973) 777-2605   Toll Free: (800) 886-7656
Fax: (973) 779-8245 E-mail: life@slovakcatholicsokol.org
Web: www.slovakcatholicsokol.org

Summary To provide financial assistance to members of the Slovak Catholic Sokol who are working on a degree in nursing or another medically-related field at a college or graduate school in any state.

Eligibility This program is open to members of the Slovak Catholic Sokol who have completed at least 1 semester of college and are currently enrolled full time as an undergraduate or graduate student at an accredited college, university, or professional school in any state. Applicants must have been a member for at least 5 years, have at least $3,000 permanent life insurance coverage, and have at least 1 parent who is a member and is of Slovak ancestry. They must be working on a degree in nursing or a medical program.

Financial data The stipend is $1,000 per year.

Duration 1 year; may be renewed 1 additional year.

Additional information Slovak Catholic Sokol was founded as a fraternal benefit society in 1905. It is licensed to operate in the following states: Connecticut, Illinois, Indiana, Massachusetts, Michigan, New Jersey, New York, Ohio, Pennsylvania, and Wisconsin. This program was established in 2003.

Number awarded 1 each year.

Deadline March of each year.

[365]
THEODORE AND MARY JANE RICH MEMORIAL SCHOLARSHIPS

Slovak Catholic Sokol
Attn: Membership Memorial Scholarship Fund
205 Madison Street
P.O. Box 899
Passaic, NJ 07055-0899
(973) 777-2605   Toll Free: (800) 886-7656
Fax: (973) 779-8245 E-mail: life@slovakcatholicsokol.org
Web: www.slovakcatholicsokol.org

Summary To provide financial assistance to members of the Slovak Catholic Sokol who are working on a medically-related degree at a college or graduate school in any state.

Eligibility This program is open to members of the Slovak Catholic Sokol who have completed at least 1 semester of college and are currently enrolled full time as an undergraduate or graduate student at an accredited college, university, or professional school in any state. Applicants must have been a member for at least 5 years, have at least $3,000 permanent life insurance coverage, and have at least 1 parent who is a member and is of Slovak ancestry. They must be enrolled in a medical program. Males and females compete for scholarships separately.

Financial data The stipend is $2,500 per year.

Duration 1 year; may be renewed 1 additional year.

Additional information Slovak Catholic Sokol was founded as a fraternal benefit society in 1905. It is licensed to operate in the following states: Connecticut, Illinois, Indiana, Massachusetts, Michigan, New Jersey, New York, Ohio, Pennsylvania, and Wisconsin. This program was established in 2003.

Number awarded 2 each year: 1 for a male and 1 for a female.

Deadline March of each year.

[366]
THOMAS M. HRICIK MEMORIAL SCHOLARSHIP AWARD FOR FEMALES

First Catholic Slovak Union of the United States and
    Canada
Jednota Benevolent Foundation, Inc.
Attn: Scholarship Program
6611 Rockside Road, Suite 300
Independence, OH 44131
(216) 642-9406   Toll Free: (800) JEDNOTA
Fax: (216) 642-4310   E-mail: FCSU@aol.com
Web: www.fcsu.com

Summary To provide financial assistance for college to female high school seniors who are of Slovak descent and the Catholic faith.

Eligibility This program is open to women graduating from high schools in the United States and Canada and planning to attend an approved institution of higher education. Applicants must be of Slovak descent and the Catholic faith. Along with their application, they must submit 1) a transcript of grades that includes ACT or SAT scores; 2) a list of volunteer community activities in which they have participated; 3) a list of awards received for academic excellence and leadership ability; 4) a description of their career objectives; 5) an essay on why they think they should receive this scholarship; and 6) information on their financial need.

Financial data The stipend is $1,000. The winner also receives a $3,000 single premium life insurance policy upon proof of graduation from college.

Duration 1 year; nonrenewable.

Number awarded 1 each year.

Deadline September of each year.

[367]
THOMAS M. HRICIK MEMORIAL SCHOLARSHIP AWARD FOR MALES

First Catholic Slovak Union of the United States and
    Canada
Jednota Benevolent Foundation, Inc.
Attn: Scholarship Program
6611 Rockside Road, Suite 300
Independence, OH 44131
(216) 642-9406   Toll Free: (800) JEDNOTA
Fax: (216) 642-4310   E-mail: FCSU@aol.com
Web: www.fcsu.com

Summary To provide financial assistance for college to male high school seniors who are of Slovak descent and Catholic faith.

Eligibility This program is open to men graduating from high schools in the United States and Canada and planning to attend an approved institution of higher education. Applicants must be of Slovak descent and Catholic faith. Along with their application, they must submit 1) a transcript of grades that includes ACT or SAT scores; 2) a list of volunteer community activities in which they have participated; 3) a list of awards received for academic excellence and leadership ability; 4) a description of their career objectives; 5) an essay on why they think they should receive this scholarship; and 6) information on their financial need.

Financial data The stipend is $1,000. The winner also receives a $3,000 single premium life insurance policy upon proof of graduation from college.

Duration 1 year; nonrenewable.

Number awarded 1 each year.

Deadline September of each year.

[368]
THOMAS M. HRICIK NURSING SCHOLARSHIPS

First Catholic Slovak Union of the United States and
    Canada
Jednota Benevolent Foundation, Inc.
Attn: Scholarship Program
6611 Rockside Road, Suite 300
Independence, OH 44131
(216) 642-9406   Toll Free: (800) JEDNOTA
Fax: (216) 642-4310   E-mail: FCSU@aol.com
Web: www.fcsu.com

Summary To provide financial assistance to high school seniors who are interested in working on a nursing degree and are of Slovak descent and the Catholic faith.

Eligibility This program is open to seniors graduating from high schools in the United States and Canada and planning to attend an approved 3- or 4-year hospital nursing program or an accredited college or school of nursing. Applicants must be of Slovak descent and the Catholic faith. Along with their application, they must submit 1) a transcript of grades that includes ACT or SAT scores; 2) a list of volunteer community activities in which they have participated; 3) a list of awards received for academic excellence and leadership ability; 4) a description of their career objectives; 5) an essay on why they think they should receive this scholarship; and 6) information on their financial need.

Financial data The stipend is $500. Each winner also receives a $3,000 single premium life insurance policy upon proof of graduation from college.

Duration 1 year; nonrenewable.

Number awarded 3 each year.

Deadline September of each year.

[369]
THORNBOROUGH UNITED METHODIST HIGHER EDUCATION FOUNDATION LOAN FUND

United Methodist Church
Attn: General Board of Higher Education and Ministry
Office of Loans and Scholarships
1001 19th Avenue South
P.O. Box 340007
Nashville, TN 37203-0007
(615) 340-7346   Fax: (615) 340-7367
E-mail: umloans@gbhem.org
Web: www.gbhem.org/loansandscholarships

Summary To loan money for college to United Methodist undergraduate students.

Eligibility Applicants must 1) have been active, full members of the United Methodist Church for at least 1 year prior to application (members of other "Methodist" denominations are not eligible); 2) be a citizen or permanent resident of the United States; 3) be enrolled at a United Methodist-related college or university as a second-year or sophomore student; and 4) have a GPA of 3.0 or higher. Loan forms required for application include a promissory note, co-signer's pledge, notice to co-signer form, financial statement, and certificate of enrollment.

Financial data The maximum annual loan is $5,000 for full-time students or $2,500 for students taking at least half the requirements for full-time status. The interest rate charged is 5%. Payments begin no later than 6 months after the borrower withdraws or graduates from school. Final payment is due no later than 120 months from the date the first payment is due. There are no prepayment penalties.

Duration Loans are made annually, on a calendar year basis.

Additional information This program, established in 2000, is funded by the United Methodist Higher Education Foundation and administered by the Office of Loans and Scholarships.

Number awarded Varies each year.

Deadline Deadlines may apply if funds are limited.

[370]
TOM AND JEAN ROBB SCHOLARSHIP

Iowa United Methodist Foundation
2301 Rittenhouse Street
Des Moines, IA 50321
(515) 974-8927
Web: www.iumf.org/otherscholarships.html

Summary To provide financial assistance for college to Christian students in Iowa.

Eligibility This program is open to Christian students in Iowa interested in attending an accredited college, university, or community college in any state. Preference is given to members of Grace United Methodist Church in Moravia, Iowa. Applicants must submit 250-word essays on 1) an explanation of how their Christian values guide them in their lives; and 2) a description of their leadership roles in school, church, and community. Selection is based on academic potential, Christian values, leadership, and financial need.

Financial data The stipend is $500.

Duration 1 year.

Number awarded 1 each year.

Deadline March of each year.

[371]
T.R. AND HELEN BRAMLETT SCHOLARSHIP

Order of the Eastern Star-Grand Chapter of Texas
Attn: Education Committee
1503 West Division Street
Arlington, TX 76012
(817) 265-6263
Web: www.grandchapteroftexasoes.org/scholar_forms.asp

Summary To provide financial assistance to residents of Texas interested in attending college or graduate school in any state to prepare for a career in religious service.

Eligibility This program is open to residents of Texas who are high school seniors or graduates already enrolled at an accredited college, university, or seminary in any state. Applicants must be interested in working on an undergraduate or graduate degree to prepare for a full-time career as a minister, missionary, director of religious education, Christian youth worker, or church music director. Along with their application, they must submit an essay describing their plans for the future, reasons for applying for the scholarship, and financial status. Undergraduates must be enrolled full time.

Financial data The stipend is $1,000.

Duration 1 year; nonrenewable.

Number awarded 1 or more each year.

Deadline February of each year.

[372]
ULLERY CHARITABLE TRUST FUND

First Presbyterian Church
Attn: Scholarship Fund Program
709 South Boston Avenue
Tulsa, OK 74119-1629
(918) 584-4701   Fax: (918) 584-5233
E-mail: TBriscoe@firstchurchtulsa.org
Web: www.firstchurchtulsa.org/scholarship.htm

Summary To provide financial assistance to Presbyterian students interested in preparing for a career of Christian work.

Eligibility To be eligible for this program, students must be communicant members of the Presbyterian Church (USA), be preparing for a career in full-time Christian ministry within the denomination, and have at least a 2.0 GPA. Priority is given first to members of the First Presbyterian Church (in Tulsa), second to applicants in the Presbytery of Eastern Oklahoma, third to applicants in the Synod of the Sun (Arkansas, Louisiana, Oklahoma, and Texas), and fourth to members of the Presbyterian Church at large. Selection is based on academic merit, academic or career intent, church or religious involvement, and financial need.

Financial data Stipends range from $500 to $2,000. Funds are paid directly to the recipient's school.

Duration 1 year; recipients may reapply.

Additional information This program was established in 1972.

Number awarded Varies each year. Recently, 12 scholarships were awarded from this fund.

Deadline April of each year.

[373]
UNDERGRADUATES EXPLORING MINISTRY PROGRAM

The Fund for Theological Education, Inc.
Attn: Partnership for Excellence
825 Houston Mill Road, Suite 250
Atlanta, GA 30329
(404) 727-1450   Fax: (404) 727-1490
E-mail: fte@thefund.org
Web: www.thefund.org

Summary To provide financial assistance to undergraduate students who are considering the ministry as a career.

Eligibility This program is open to rising juniors and seniors in accredited undergraduate programs at North American colleges and universities. Applicants must be considering ministry as a career. They must be nominated by a college faculty member, administrator, campus minister or chaplain, or current pastor. Nominees must have a GPA of 3.0 or higher, a love of God and church, imagination, creativity, compassion, a capacity for critical thinking, leadership skills, personal integrity, spiritual depth, dedication to a faith tradition, and an ability to understand and to serve the needs of others. U.S. or Canadian citizenship is required.

Financial data The stipend is $2,000.

Duration 1 year.

Additional information This program began in 1999. Fellows also receive an additional stipend to cover travel and expenses to attend the sponsor's summer Conference on Excellence in Ministry, where they spend several days engaged in lectures, worship, forums, workshops, recreational activities, and informal time together with other students, theological leaders, and pastors. Students unable to attend the conference should not apply for the fellowship.

Number awarded Up to 50 each year.

Deadline Nominations must be submitted by January of each year.

[374]
UNITED CHURCH OF CHRIST UNDERGRADUATE SCHOLARSHIPS

United Church of Christ
Local Church Ministries
Attn: Parish Life and Leadership Team
700 Prospect Avenue East
Cleveland, OH 44115-1100
(216) 736-3839   Toll Free: (866) 822-8224, ext. 3839
Fax: (216) 736-3783   E-mail: scholars@ucc.org
Web: www.ucc.org/higher-education/scholarships

Summary To provide financial assistance to undergraduate students who are members of United Church of Christ (UCC) congregations.

Eligibility This program is open to members of UCC congregations who are younger than 25 years of age. Applicants must be entering their sophomore, junior, or senior year at a 4-year accredited college or university in the United States.

Entering sophomores must have a GPA of 2.0 or higher; entering juniors or seniors must have a GPA of 3.0 or higher. Financial need is considered in the selection process.

Financial data Stipends range from $500 to $1,000. Funds are remitted to the recipient's college or university to cover tuition expenses.

Duration 1 year; recipients may reapply.

Additional information This fund was established in 1994.

Number awarded Varies each year.

Deadline May of each year.

[375]
UNITED METHODIST ETHNIC MINORITY SCHOLARSHIPS

United Methodist Church
Attn: General Board of Higher Education and Ministry
Office of Loans and Scholarships
1001 19th Avenue South
P.O. Box 340007
Nashville, TN 37203-0007
(615) 340-7344   Fax: (615) 340-7367
E-mail: umscholar@gbhem.org
Web: www.gbhem.org/loansandscholarships

Summary To provide financial assistance to undergraduate Methodist students who are of ethnic minority ancestry.

Eligibility This program is open to full-time undergraduate students at accredited colleges and universities in the United States who have been active, full members of a United Methodist Church for at least 1 year prior to applying. Applicants must have at least 1 parent who is African American, Hispanic, Asian, Native American, Alaska Native, or Pacific Islander. They must have a GPA of 2.5 or higher and be able to demonstrate financial need. U.S. citizenship, permanent resident status, or membership in a central conference of the United Methodist Church is required. Selection is based on church membership, involvement in church and community activities, GPA, and financial need.

Financial data A stipend is awarded (amount not specified).

Duration 1 year; recipients may reapply.

Number awarded Varies each year.

Deadline April of each year.

[376]
UNITED METHODIST GENERAL SCHOLARSHIP PROGRAM

United Methodist Church
Attn: General Board of Higher Education and Ministry
Office of Loans and Scholarships
1001 19th Avenue South
P.O. Box 340007
Nashville, TN 37203-0007
(615) 340-7344   Fax: (615) 340-7367
E-mail: umscholar@gbhem.org
Web: www.gbhem.org/loansandscholarships

Summary To provide financial assistance to undergraduate and graduate students who are members of United Methodist Church congregations.

Eligibility This program includes a number of individual scholarships that were established by private donors through wills and annuities. The basic criteria for eligibility include 1) U.S. citizenship or permanent resident status; 2) active, full membership in a United Methodist Church for at least 1 year prior to applying (some scholarships require 3-years' membership); 3) GPA of 2.5 or higher (some scholarships require 3.0 or higher); 4) demonstrated financial need; and 5) full-time enrollment in an undergraduate or graduate degree program at an accredited educational institution in the United States. Students from the Central Conferences must be enrolled at a United Methodist-related institution. Most graduate scholarships are designated for persons working on a degree in theological studies (M.Div., D.Min., Ph.D.) or higher education administration. Some scholarships stipulate that the applicant meet more than the basic eligibility criteria (e.g., resident of specific conference, majoring in specified field).

Financial data The funding is intended to supplement the students' own resources.

Duration 1 year; renewal policies are set by participating universities.

Number awarded Varies each year.

Deadline May of each year.

[377]
UNITED METHODIST HIGHER EDUCATION FOUNDATION NATIVE ALASKAN FUND

United Methodist Higher Education Foundation
Attn: Scholarships Administrator
1001 19th Avenue South
P.O. Box 340005
Nashville, TN 37203-0005
(615) 340-7385　　　　　Toll Free: (800) 811-8110
Fax: (615) 340-7330
E-mail: umhefscholarships@gbhem.org
Web: www.umhef.org/receive.php?id=endowed_funds

Summary To provide financial assistance to Native Alaskan Methodist undergraduate and graduate students at Methodist-related colleges and universities.

Eligibility This program is open to Native Alaskans enrolling as full-time undergraduate or graduate students at United Methodist-related colleges and universities. Preference is given to United Methodist students at Alaska Pacific University. Applicants must have been active, full members of a United Methodist Church for at least 1 year prior to applying. They must have a GPA of 3.0 or higher and be able to demonstrate financial need. Along with their application, they must submit a 200-word essay on their involvement and/or leadership responsibilities in their church, school, and community within the last 3 years. U.S. citizenship or permanent resident status is required.

Financial data The stipend is at least $1,000 per year.

Duration 1 year; nonrenewable.

Number awarded Varies each year. Recently, 2 of these scholarships were awarded.

Deadline May of each year.

[378]
UNITED METHODIST STUDENT LOAN PROGRAM

United Methodist Church
Attn: General Board of Higher Education and Ministry
Office of Loans and Scholarships
1001 19th Avenue South
P.O. Box 340007
Nashville, TN 37203-0007
(615) 340-7346　　　　　Fax: (615) 340-7367
E-mail: umloans@gbhem.org
Web: www.gbhem.org/loansandscholarships

Summary To loan money for college to United Methodist undergraduate and graduate students.

Eligibility Applicants must 1) have been active, full members of the United Methodist Church for at least 1 year prior to application (members of other "Methodist" denominations are not eligible); 2) be a citizen or permanent resident of the United States; 3) have been admitted to a degree program (undergraduate or graduate) in an accredited college/university or graduate/professional school; and 4) have a GPA of 2.0 or higher. Loan forms required for application include a promissory note, co-signer's pledge, notice to co-signer form, financial statement, and certificate of enrollment.

Financial data The maximum annual loan is $5,000 for full-time students or $2,500 for students taking at least half the requirements for full-time status. The interest rate charged is 5%. Payments begin no later than 6 months after the borrower withdraws or graduates from school. Final payment is due no later than 120 months from the date the first payment is due. There are no prepayment penalties.

Duration Loans are made annually, on a calendar year basis.

Number awarded Varies each year.

Deadline Deadlines may apply if funds are limited.

[379]
URBAN MINISTRY SCHOLARSHIP PROGRAM

United Methodist City Society
475 Riverside Drive, Room 1922
New York, NY 10115
(212) 870-3084　　　　　Fax: (212) 870-3091
E-mail: bshillady@umcitysociety.org
Web: www.nyac.com/pages/detail/1725

Summary To provide financial assistance to undergraduate and graduate students who belong to the United Methodist Church in New York and are preparing for ordained ministry in an urban context at a college in any state.

Eligibility This program is open to persons studying in an undergraduate or graduate program at a college or university in any state approved by the United Methodist City Society. Applicants must be members of a United Methodist Church in the New York Annual Conference and planning to enter full-time ordained ministry in the United Methodist Church, with a special interest in urban ministry. Financial need is considered in the selection process. Scholarship monies are distributed in the following order: undergraduate degree program, graduate first degree program (e.g., M,Div.), special training in urban ministry and, finally, courses in English as a second language.

Financial data Stipends range from $500 to $2,000. Funds are paid directly to the recipient's school.

Duration 1 year; recipients may reapply.

Number awarded Varies each year.

Deadline May of each year.

[380]
VERA DUENO SCHOLARSHIP

Wisconsin United Methodist Foundation
750 Windsor Street, Suite 305
P.O. Box 620
Sun Prairie, WI 53590-0620
(608) 837-9582   Toll Free: (888) 903-9863
Fax: (608) 837-2492   E-mail: wumf@wumf.org
Web: www.wumf.org/grantsFF/grantsScholars.html

Summary To provide financial assistance to Methodists from Wisconsin who are interested in attending college in any state.

Eligibility This program is open to members of United Methodist Churches affiliated with the Wisconsin Conference who are enrolled or planning to enroll at a 4-year college or university in any state. Applicants must submit an essay that describes their personal situation and vocational goals, church-related activities and involvement, school and community involvement, and financial plan for funding their education, including any special financial needs.

Financial data Stipends range from $500 to $1,000.

Duration 1 year.

Additional information This program was established in 2001.

Number awarded 1 or more each year.

Deadline March of each year.

[381]
VERDE DICKEY MEMORIAL SCHOLARSHIP

United Methodist Higher Education Foundation
Attn: Scholarships Administrator
1001 19th Avenue South
P.O. Box 340005
Nashville, TN 37203-0005
(615) 340-7385   Toll Free: (800) 811-8110
Fax: (615) 340-7330
E-mail: umhefscholarships@gbhem.org
Web: www.umhef.org/receive.php?id=endowed_funds

Summary To provide financial assistance to upper-division students at schools affiliated with the United Methodist Church who are preparing for a career as a teacher or coach.

Eligibility This program is open to full-time students entering their junior or senior year at a United Methodist-related college or university. Applicants must have been active, full members of a United Methodist Church for at least 1 year prior to applying. They must 1) be majoring in education or physical education; 2) be planning to become teachers or coaches; 3) have a GPA of 3.0 or higher; 4) be able to demonstrate financial need; and 5) be a citizen or permanent resident of the United States.

Financial data The stipend is $7,500.

Duration 1 year.

Number awarded 2 each year.

Deadline May of each year.

[382]
VERMONT KNIGHTS OF COLUMBUS SCHOLARSHIPS

Knights of Columbus-Vermont State Council
c/o James P. Candon II
21 Williams Street
Rutland, VT 05701
(802) 747-7936   E-mail: jcandon2@yahoo.com
Web: www.vtkofc.org

Summary To provide financial assistance to high school seniors in Vermont who have a connection to the Knights of Columbus and plan to attend college in any state.

Eligibility This program is open to seniors graduating from high schools in Vermont who are the child of a member of the Knights of Columbus in a subordinate council of the Vermont jurisdiction, the child of a deceased member in good standing at the time of death, or a member of the Knights of Columbus or a Columbian Squires Circle in the Vermont jurisdiction. Applicants must be interested in attending a college or university in any state. Along with their application, they must submit a letter on their chief interests in school, participation in school activities, chief out-of-school interests and hobbies, summer or part-time employment, and plans for the future. Selection is based on that letter, academic achievement, and financial need.

Financial data The stipend is $600.

Duration 1 year.

Number awarded 8 each year.

Deadline February of each year.

[383]
VIOLET MANN BONHAM PARISH NURSE SCHOLARSHIP

Woman's Missionary Union of Virginia
2828 Emerywood Parkway
Richmond, VA 23294
(804) 915-5000, ext. 8267
Toll Free: (800) 255-2428 (within VA)
Fax: (804) 672-8008   E-mail: wmuv@wmuv.org
Web: wmuv.org/developing-future-leaders/scholarships

Summary To provide financial assistance to nurses in Virginia interested in obtaining further education in order to serve as a Parish Nurse within the Baptist General Association of Virginia (BGAV).

Eligibility This program is open to Virginia Baptists who have a current Virginia state nursing license. Applicants must be interested in obtaining additional education in order to provide nursing and Christian ministerial services within Virginia to persons in need of nursing and/or health and wellness care. Along with their application, they must submit essays of 250 words or more on 1) their life's Christian testimony or mission statement, and 2) how receipt of this scholarship will impact their life. An interview is required.

Financial data A stipend is awarded (amount not specified). Funds may only be used for the costs of instruction, text books, and materials.

Duration 1 year.

Additional information This program was established in 2004.

Number awarded 1 each year.

Deadline Applications may be submitted any time.

[384]
VIRGINIA BAPTIST FOUNDATION SCHOLARSHIPS

Virginia Baptist Foundation, Inc.
2828 Emerywood Parkway
Richmond, VA 23294
(804) 672-8862   Toll Free: (800) 868-2464
Fax: (804) 672-3747
Web: www.vbfinc.org/Scholarships/ProgramDescription.htm

Summary   To provide financial assistance to members of Southern Baptist churches in Virginia who are interested in attending college, graduate school, medical school, pharmacy school, or seminary in any state.

Eligibility   This program is open to active members of churches cooperating with the Baptist General Association of Virginia. Applicants must be enrolled full time in a basic degree program at a college, university, medical school, pharmacy school, or seminary in any state. They must have a GPA of at least 2.5 as a high school senior, 2.0 as a college freshman or sophomore, 2.3 as a college junior, 2.5 as a college senior, or 2.0 as a seminary student. They must be recommended by their pastor and approved by the church of which they are a member. Most of the funds offered by this sponsor stipulate that students must attend Baptist colleges, universities, or seminaries in Virginia, but others allow attendance at any institution in any state. Doctoral candidates, except those in pharmacy or medicine, are not eligible. Along with their application, students must submit a 500-word summary of their life, including a Christian testimony, life goals, expected vocation, and school selection process. Financial need is considered in the selection proves.

Financial data   A stipend is awarded (amount not specified).

Duration   1 year; may be renewed up to 3 additional years, provided the recipient maintains a grade point average of "C" or higher.

Number awarded   Varies each year.

Deadline   March of each year.

[385]
WASENA F. WRIGHT JR. CONFERENCE MERIT AWARDS

United Methodist Church-Virginia Conference
Attn: Higher Education Ministries
10330 Staples Mill Road
P.O. Box 5060
Glen Allen, VA 23058-5606
(804) 521-1135   Toll Free: (800) 768-6040, ext. 135
Fax: (804) 521-1179   E-mail: AngieWilliams@vaumc.org
Web: www.vaumc.org/Page.aspx?pid=1029

Summary   To provide financial assistance to Methodist high school seniors in Virginia who are interested in attending a Methodist college or university in any state.

Eligibility   This program is open to high school seniors in Virginia who are nominated by their local United Methodist Church, district Council on Ministries, or district Youth Council. Applicants must be planning to attend a United Methodist college or university in any state. They must submit information on their service to their local church, local community, district, or conference.

Financial data   Stipends range from $500 to $1,000.

Duration   1 year.

Number awarded   Varies each year; in the first 24 years of this program, it awarded 174 of these scholarships.

Deadline   February of each year.

[386]
WASHINGTON EASTERN STAR TRAINING AWARDS FOR RELIGIOUS LEADERSHIP

Order of the Eastern Star-Grand Chapter of Washington
c/o Kay Schroeder, ESTARL Committee
1500A East College Way, 466
Mount Vernon, WA 98273
Web: washingtoneos.org/Scholarships.htm

Summary   To provide financial assistance to residents of Washington who are attending college in any state to prepare for a career in Christian service.

Eligibility   This program is open to residents of Washington currently enrolled at a college or university in any state. Applicants must be preparing for a career in Christian service, including ministry, religious education, mission work, religious music, or youth work. Along with their application, they must submit an essay on their religious philosophy, including their ideas on the need for Christianity in present-day living, how the church can become more effective in the community, and how the church can be made to serve the needs of young people more effectively. Financial need is considered in the selection process.

Financial data   A stipend is awarded (amount not specified).

Duration   1 year; recipients may reapply.

Number awarded   Varies each year.

Deadline   April of each year.

[387]
WEST VIRGINIA EASTERN STAR TRAINING AWARDS FOR RELIGIOUS LEADERSHIP

Order of the Eastern Star-Grand Chapter of West Virginia
c/o Jo Ann Harman, Education Committee Chair
HC 84 Box 26
Lahmansville, WV 26731
(304) 749-7322   E-mail: jsharman@frontiernet.net
Web: www.wveasternstar.org

Summary   To provide scholarship/loans to residents of West Virginia who are interested in attending a college or seminary in any state to prepare for a career in full-time Christian service.

Eligibility   This program is open to students enrolled or planning to enroll full time at a college or seminary in any state to prepare for a career as a ministry or missionary or for other full-time Christian service. Applicants must be at least 16 years of age and have been residents of West Virginia for at least 3 years. They must have a GPA of 2.5 or higher. Along with their application, they must submit a letter explaining why they should be selected for this scholarship. Selection is based on that letter (10 points), academic achievement (35 points), leadership (10 points), service in school and community organizations (10 points), and financial need (35 points). An interview may be required. Applicants must commit to serve at least 5 years in their chosen field of full-time Christian service.

Financial data A stipend is awarded (amount not specified). If recipients leave their field of preparation prior to completing 5 years of service, they must repay all funds received at a specified rate of interest (currently 6%).

Duration 1 year; may be renewed, provided the recipient maintains a GPA of 2.5 or higher.

Number awarded Varies each year.

Deadline May of each year.

[388]
WESTMAR SCHOLARSHIPS

Iowa United Methodist Foundation
2301 Rittenhouse Street
Des Moines, IA 50321
(515) 974-8927
Web: www.iumf.org/westmar.html

Summary To provide financial assistance for college to students who are attending or planning to attend a United Methodist college in Iowa.

Eligibility This program is open to students who are attending or planning to attend a college in Iowa that is affiliated with the United Methodist Church. High school seniors must have a GPA of 3.0 or higher; students already enrolled in college must have a GPA of 2.5 or higher. Selection is based on academic achievement, participation in high school or college activities, 2 letters of recommendation, and financial need. Preference is given to applicants from the following counties in northwestern Iowa: Cherokee, Ida, Lyon, O'Brien, Osceola, Plymouth, Sioux, and Woodbury.

Financial data The stipend is $2,000.

Duration 1 year.

Additional information These scholarships are supported with funds remaining after the closing of Westmar College, which was affiliated with the Iowa Annual Conference of the United Methodist Church.

Number awarded 12 each year.

Deadline March of each year.

[389]
WILLIAM G. AND MARGARET B. FRASIER CHARITABLE FOUNDATION SCHOLARSHIP

Center for Scholarship Administration, Inc.
Attn: Wachovia Accounts
4320 Wade Hampton Boulevard, Suite G
Taylors, SC 29687
Toll Free: (866) 608-0001
E-mail: wachoviascholars@bellsouth.net
Web: www.wachoviascholars.com/frsr/index.php

Summary To provide financial assistance to undergraduate and graduate students from North Carolina who are preparing for a career in the Baptist ministry.

Eligibility This program is open to residents of North Carolina who are studying for the Baptist ministry. Applicants must be full-time students working on a recognized undergraduate or graduate degree at an accredited college, theological seminary, or other institution of higher learning in any state. Selection is based on academic merit, financial need, and community service.

Financial data A stipend is awarded (amount not specified).

Duration 1 year; recipients may reapply.

Number awarded Several each year.

Deadline April of each year.

[390]
WILLIAM R. STANITZ SCHOLARSHIP

Romanian Orthodox Episcopate of America
Attn: Scholarship Committee
P.O. Box 309
Grass Lake, MI 49240-0309
(517) 522-4800   Fax: (517) 522-5907
E-mail: chancery@roea.org
Web: www.roea.org/scholarships.htm

Summary To provide financial assistance for college to active members of American Romanian Orthodox Youth (AROY).

Eligibility To qualify for this scholarship, applicants must be active AROY members, high school graduates, and currently enrolled or planning to enroll in college. The application packet submitted should include a biographical history, educational background and grades, AROY and church activities, extracurricular interests and achievements, reasons why they are applying for the scholarship, a photograph, and a letter of recommendation from a parish priest or AROY adviser regarding parish/AROY activities. Recipients are selected in a random drawing.

Financial data The stipend is $1,000.

Duration 1 year.

Additional information This fund was established in 1971.

Number awarded At least 2 each year.

Deadline June of each year.

[391]
WILLIAM STEARNS LOAN FUND

United Methodist Church-Wisconsin Conference
Attn: Director of Finance and Administration
750 Windsor Street
P.O. Box 620
Sun Prairie, WI 53590-0620
(608) 837-7328   Toll Free: (888) 240-7328
Fax: (608) 837-8547
Web: www.wisconsinumc.org

Summary To provide academic loans to members of United Methodist churches in Wisconsin attending any institution within the University of Wisconsin system.

Eligibility This program is open to members of congregations of the United Methodist Church (UMC) in Wisconsin. Applicants must have been admitted into full membership; mere attendance at church or participation in its activities does not qualify. They must be enrolled in a degree program at the University of Wisconsin system. Financial need must be demonstrated.

Financial data Total loans per student may not exceed $10,000. Loan repayment begins 6 months after the borrower discontinues at least half time enrollment or a maximum of 7 years from the date of the note, whichever occurs first. The repayment period may extend 5 years. The interest rate is 1 point below the prime rate on the date of taking out the loan.

Duration 1 year; recipients may reapply.

Number awarded 1 or more each year.

Deadline Applications may be submitted at any time.

[392]
WILLIE J. WILLIAMS SCHOLARSHIP

African Methodist Episcopal Church
Attn: Eleventh Episcopal District Lay Organization
101 East Union Street, Suite 301
Jacksonville, FL 32202
(904) 355-8262   Fax: (904) 356-1617
E-mail: eedlo@eedlo.org
Web: www.eedlo.org/scholarships.html

Summary To provide financial assistance to members of African Methodist Episcopal (AME) churches in Florida who are interested in studying music at a college in any state.

Eligibility This program is open to seniors graduating from public or private high schools in Florida who are members of AME churches. Applicants must be planning to enroll full time at an institution of higher learning in any state: an AME-supported college, a Predominantly Black College or University, or an accredited trade school. They must have a GPA of 2.5 or higher and be planning to major in music. Along with their application, they must submit a 1-page essay on why a college education is important and a statement regarding their financial need.

Financial data A stipend is awarded (amount not specified).

Duration 1 year.

Number awarded 1 or more each year.

Deadline April of each year.

[393]
WISCONSIN EAGLE SCOUT OF THE YEAR SCHOLARSHIP

American Legion
Department of Wisconsin
2930 American Legion Drive
P.O. Box 388
Portage, WI 53901-0388
(608) 745-1090   Fax: (608) 745-0179
E-mail: info@wilegion.org
Web: www.wilegion.org/programs/scholarships/?Id=228

Summary To recognize and reward, with scholarships for college in any state, Eagle Scouts who are members of a troop associated with the American Legion in Wisconsin or a son or grandson of a member of the Legion in the state.

Eligibility The Wisconsin nominee for American Legion Scout of the Year receives this scholarship. Applicants must be 1) a registered, active members of a Boy Scout Troop, Varsity Scout Team, or Explorer Post chartered to an American Legion Post in Wisconsin or Auxiliary Unit in Wisconsin, or 2) a registered, active member of a Boy Scout Troop, Varsity Scout Team, or Venturing Crew and the son or grandson of an American Legion or Auxiliary member. They must have received the Eagle Scout award; be an active member of their religious institution and have received the appropriate Boy Scout religious emblem; have demonstrated practical citizenship in church, school, Scouting, and community; have reached their 15th birthday; be enrolled in high school; and be planning to attend college in any state.

Financial data The award is a $1,000 scholarship.

Duration The award is presented annually.

Number awarded 1 each year.

Deadline February of each year.

[394]
WISCONSIN UNITED METHODIST FOUNDATION HISPANIC SCHOLARSHIP

Wisconsin United Methodist Foundation
750 Windsor Street, Suite 305
P.O. Box 620
Sun Prairie, WI 53590-0620
(608) 837-9582   Toll Free: (888) 903-9863
Fax: (608) 837-2492   E-mail: wumf@wumf.org
Web: www.wumf.org/grantsFF/grantsScholars.html

Summary To provide financial assistance to Methodists from Wisconsin who are of Hispanic heritage and interested in attending college in any state.

Eligibility This program is open to Hispanic members of United Methodist Churches affiliated with the Wisconsin Conference who are enrolled or planning to enroll at a college or vocational school in any state. Applicants must submit an essay that describes their personal situation and vocational goals, church-related activities and involvement, school and community involvement, and financial plan for funding their education, including any special financial needs.

Financial data Stipends range from $500 to $1,000.

Duration 1 year.

Number awarded 1 or more each year.

Deadline March of each year.

[395]
WISCONSIN UNITED METHODIST FOUNDATION SCHOLARS AWARD

Wisconsin United Methodist Foundation
750 Windsor Street, Suite 305
P.O. Box 620
Sun Prairie, WI 53590-0620
(608) 837-9582   Toll Free: (888) 903-9863
Fax: (608) 837-2492   E-mail: wumf@wumf.org
Web: www.wumf.org/grantsFF/grantsScholars.html

Summary To provide financial assistance to Methodists from Wisconsin who are interested in attending college in any state.

Eligibility This program is open to members of United Methodist Churches affiliated with the Wisconsin Conference who are enrolled or planning to enroll at a 4-year college or university in any state. Applicants must submit an essay that describes their personal situation and vocational goals, church-related activities and involvement, school and community involvement, and financial plan for funding their education, including any special financial needs.

Financial data Stipends range from $500 to $1,000.

Duration 1 year.

Number awarded 1 or more each year.

Deadline March of each year.

[396]
WISCONSIN UNITED METHODIST MERIT SCHOLARSHIP

United Methodist Church-Wisconsin Conference
Attn: Board of Higher Education and Campus Ministry
750 Windsor Street
P.O. Box 620
Sun Prairie, WI 53590-0620
(608) 837-7328   Toll Free: (888) 240-7328
Fax: (608) 837-8547
Web: www.wisconsinumc.org

Summary To provide financial assistance to members of United Methodist churches in Wisconsin who plan to attend a college in any state affiliated with the denomination.

Eligibility This program is open to members of United Methodist Churches affiliated with the Wisconsin Conference who are high school seniors or college freshmen, sophomores, or juniors. Applicants must be working or planning to work full time on a bachelor's degree at a college or university in any state that is recognized as United Methodist by the University Senate. They must have a GPA of 3.0 or higher. Selection is based primarily on academic standing and service to the church; financial need is not considered.

Financial data A stipend is awarded (amount not specified).

Duration 1 year.

Number awarded 1 or more each year.

Deadline April of each year.

[397]
WOMAN'S MISSIONARY UNION OF GEORGIA SEMINARY SCHOLARSHIPS

Georgia Baptist Convention
Attn: Woman's Missionary Union
6405 Sugarloaf Parkway
Duluth, GA 30097
(770) 455-0404   Toll Free: (800) 746-4422, ext. 320
Fax: (770) 452-6572
Web: www.gabaptist.org

Summary To provide financial assistance to women from Georgia who are attending a Baptist seminary.

Eligibility This program is open to women who are residents of Georgia or the daughters of Southern Baptist missionaries from Georgia. Applicants must currently be attending a Baptist seminary. Along with their application, they must submit an autobiography that includes their salvation experience, their call to ministry, any involvement in Women's Missionary Union or missions, and their plans for Christian vocational service. Selection is based on academic ability, commitment to Christian service, character, health, personal references, and financial need.

Financial data The stipend is $600 per year.

Duration 1 year; may be renewed up to 2 additional years.

Additional information This program includes the following named scholarships: the Dorothy Pryor Scholarship, the Janice Singleton Scholarship, and the Lillian D. Gerrard Memorial Scholarship.

Number awarded Varies each year. Recently, 7 of these scholarships were awarded.

Deadline February of each year.

[398]
WOMAN'S MISSIONARY UNION OF MARYLAND/DELAWARE CENTENNIAL SCHOLARSHIPS

Baptist Convention of Maryland/Delaware
Attn: Woman's Missionary Union of Maryland/Delaware
10255 Old Columbia Road
Columbia, MD 21046
(410) 290-5290   Toll Free: (800) 466-5290
E-mail: gparker@bcmd.org
Web: bcmd.org/wmu

Summary To provide financial assistance to members of Southern Baptist churches affiliated with the Baptist Convention of Maryland/Delaware and interested in attending a college or seminary in any state.

Eligibility This program is open to active members of a Southern Baptist church/mission or Baptist student ministry affiliated with the Baptist Convention of Maryland/Delaware. Applicants must be enrolled or planning to enroll full time at 1) an accredited college or university in any state, or 2) a Southern Baptist seminary. They must have a grade point average of "C" or higher and be able to demonstrate financial need. Along with their application, they must submit a brief essay that includes a testimony of their salvation experience; their involvement in church, school, and community activities; and the kind of work God has called them to do after completing their education, how they have come to believe God wants them in this work, and their plans to fulfill His call. Priority is given to applicants who are preparing for missionary service under the North American Mission Board or International Mission Board of the Southern Baptist Convention, career service with the Woman's Missionary Union (WMU), or work with the Men's Ministries.

Financial data The stipend is $375 per semester ($750 per year). Funds are paid directly to the recipient's school.

Duration 1 year; may be renewed for a total of 8 semesters of undergraduate study or 6 semesters of seminary master's degree work.

Number awarded Varies each year.

Deadline February of each year for fall semester or August of each year for spring semester.

[399]
WOMAN'S MISSIONARY UNION OF MARYLAND/DELAWARE SCHOLARSHIPS FOR WOMEN

Baptist Convention of Maryland/Delaware
Attn: Woman's Missionary Union of Maryland/Delaware
10255 Old Columbia Road
Columbia, MD 21046
(410) 290-5290   Toll Free: (800) 466-5290
E-mail: gparker@bcmd.org
Web: bcmd.org/wmu

Summary To provide financial assistance to women who are members of Southern Baptist churches affiliated with the Baptist Convention of Maryland/Delaware and interested in attending a college or seminary in any state.

Eligibility This program is open to women who are active members of a Southern Baptist church/mission or Baptist student ministry affiliated with the Baptist Convention of Maryland/Delaware. Applicants must be enrolled or planning to enroll full time at 1) an accredited college or university in any state, or 2) a Southern Baptist seminary. They must have a grade point average of "C" or higher and be able to demonstrate financial need. Along with their application, they must submit a brief essay that includes a testimony of their salvation experience; their involvement in church, school, and community activities; and the kind of work God has called them to do after completing their education, how they have come to believe God wants them in this work, and their plans to fulfill His call. Priority is given to applicants who are preparing for missionary service under the North American Mission Board or International Mission Board of the Southern Baptist Convention, career service with the Woman's Missionary Union (WMU), or work with the Men's Ministries.

Financial data The stipend is $375 per semester ($750 per year). Funds are paid directly to the recipient's school.

Duration 1 year; may be renewed for a total of 8 semesters of undergraduate study or 6 semesters of seminary master's degree work.

Additional information This program includes the Business Women's Circles Scholarship, the Captain and Mrs. John T. Willing Scholarship, and the Hattie Wilson Norwood Scholarship.

Number awarded Varies each year.

Deadline February of each year for fall semester or August of each year for spring semester.

[400]
WOMEN OF THE ELCA SCHOLARSHIP PROGRAM

Women of the Evangelical Lutheran Church in America
Attn: Scholarships
8765 West Higgins Road
Chicago, IL 60631-4101
(773) 380-2736   Toll Free: (800) 638-3522, ext. 2736
Fax: (773) 380-2419   E-mail: emily.hansen@elca.org
Web: www.elca.org

Summary To provide financial assistance to lay women who are members of Evangelical Lutheran Church of America (ELCA) congregations and who wish to take classes on the undergraduate, graduate, professional, or vocational school level.

Eligibility This program is open to ELCA lay women who are at least 21 years of age and have experienced an interruption of at least 2 years in their education since high school. Applicants must have been admitted to an educational institution to prepare for a career in other than the ordained ministry. They may be working on an undergraduate, graduate, professional, or vocational school degree. U.S. citizenship is required.

Financial data The maximum stipend is $1,000.

Duration Up to 2 years.

Additional information These scholarships are supported by several endowment funds: the Cronk Memorial Fund, the First Triennial Board Scholarship Fund, the General Scholarship Fund, the Mehring Fund, the Paepke Scholarship Fund, the Piero/Wade/Wade Fund, and the Edwin/Edna Robeck Scholarship.

Number awarded Varies each year, depending upon the funds available.

Deadline February of each year.

[401]
WORLD WIDE BARACA PHILATHEA UNION SCHOLARSHIP

World Wide Baraca Philathea Union
610 South Harlem Avenue
Freeport, IL 61032-4833

Summary To provide financial assistance to students preparing for Christian ministry, Christian missionary work, or Christian education.

Eligibility Eligible to apply for this support are students enrolled in an accredited college or seminary who are majoring in Christian ministry, Christian missionary work, or Christian education (e.g., church youth pastor, writer of Sunday school curriculum).

Financial data Stipends are paid directly to the recipient's school upon receipt of the first semester transcript and a letter confirming attendance.

Duration 1 year; may be renewed.

Deadline March of each year.

[402]
W.Z. STULTZ STUDENT SCHOLARSHIP FUND

Synod of the Mid-Atlantic
Attn: Finance and Scholarship Committee
3218 Chamberlayne Avenue
P.O. Box 27026
Richmond, VA 23261-7026
(804) 342-0016   Toll Free: (800) 743-7670
Fax: (804) 355-8535
Web: www.synatlantic.org/scholarships/right.html

Summary To provide financial assistance to high school seniors who are members of churches within the Synod of the Mid-Atlantic of the Presbyterian Church (USA) and interested in attending college in any state.

Eligibility This program is open to high school seniors who are active communicant members of congregations in the Synod of the Mid-Atlantic (Delaware, Maryland, North Carolina, and Virginia) planning to attend a Presbyterian-related college or university in any state. Selection is based on academic achievement, community and school service activities, other extracurricular activities, and financial need.

Financial data The stipend recently was $1,900 per year. Funds are paid directly to the college or university.

Duration 1 year; may be renewed upon recommendation of the college.

Number awarded Varies each year. Recently, 3 of these scholarships were awarded.

Deadline February of each year.

[403]
YELLOWSTONE CONFERENCE MERIT SCHOLARSHIPS

United Methodist Church-Yellowstone Conference
1220 Avenue C, Suite C
P.O. Box 20335
Billings, MT 59104-0335
(406) 256-1385   Fax: (406) 256-4948
Web: www.yacumc.org

Summary To provide financial assistance to members of United Methodist churches in its Yellowstone Conference who are interested in attending a college in any state that is affiliated with the denomination.

Eligibility This program is open to members of congregations of the United Methodist Church (UMC) in its Yellowstone Conference (which serves Montana and Wyoming). Applicants must be attending or planning to attend a UMC college or university in any state. Along with their application, they must submit essays providing information on their financial need and their request in general.

Financial data The stipend is 10% of what the conference receives in the United Methodist Student Sunday offering; recently, that was $660.

Duration 1 year.

Number awarded 1 or 2 each year.

Deadline May of each year.

[404]
YOUNG STATESMAN SCHOLARSHIP

Kentucky Baptist Convention
Attn: Men's Department
13420 Eastpoint Centre Drive
P.O. Box 43433
Louisville, KY 40253-0433
(502) 489-3527   Toll Free: (800) 489-3527 (within KY)
Fax: (502) 489-3199
Web: www.kybaptist.org

Summary To recognize and reward, with college scholarships, high school senior members of the Kentucky Baptist Convention who deliver outstanding speeches on their participation in On Mission Youth.

Eligibility This program is open to seniors at public, private, and home schools who are actively living an On Mission lifestyle and involved in mission education at their local Kentucky Baptist Convention affiliated church. Applicants must give a 6- to 8-minute speech on an On Mission topic. Selection is based on delivery (15 points), evidence of research (15 points), development of ideas (50 points), use of gestures (10 points), and conclusion (10 points).

Financial data The stipend is $1,000 per year.

Duration 1 year; may be renewed up to 3 additional years, provided the recipients remain enrolled in college and supplies written evidence that they continue to be leaders in living an On Mission lifestyle, in mission efforts, and in spiritual development.

Number awarded 1 each year.

Deadline Deadline not specified.

Graduate Students

Listed alphabetically by program title are 446 fellowships, grants, loans, loans-for-service, awards, and other funding opportunities open to Christian students that support graduate study, training, research, and creative activities in secular and religious fields.

[405]
ABC DOCTORAL STUDY GRANTS

American Baptist Churches USA
National Ministries
Attn: Office of Financial Aid for Studies
P.O. Box 851
Valley Forge, PA 19482-0851
(610) 768-2067   Toll Free: (800) ABC-3USA, ext. 2067
Fax: (610) 768-2453
E-mail: Financialaid.Web@abc-usa.org
Web: www.nationalministries.org

Summary To provide financial assistance to American Baptist students who are working on a Ph.D. degree.

Eligibility This program is open to American Baptist students who have completed 1 year of Ph.D. studies in the United States or Puerto Rico. Applicants must plan to teach in a college or seminary, in a field of study directly related to preparing American Baptist ministerial leaders. Selection is based, at least in part, on academic achievement. D.Min. students are not eligible to apply. Students must have been members of an American Baptist church for at least 1 year before applying for assistance. U.S. citizenship is required.

Financial data The grant is $3,000.

Duration 1 year; nonrenewable.

Number awarded Varies each year.

Deadline May of each year.

[406]
ADULT WOMEN SEMINARY SCHOLARSHIP

American Baptist Women's Ministries of Wisconsin
c/o Lois A. Horsman, Scholarship Committee Chair
P.O. Box 68
Wyocena, WI 53969
(608) 429-2483
Web: www.abcofwi.org/abwinfo.htm

Summary To provide financial assistance to female members of American Baptist Churches in Wisconsin who are interested in attending a seminary in any state that is affiliated with the denomination.

Eligibility This program is open to adult women who are residents of Wisconsin and attending or planning to attend an American Baptist seminary in any state. Applicants must have been an active member of an American Baptist Church in Wisconsin for the preceding 3 years. They must have graduated from a college affiliated with the American Baptist Churches USA.

Financial data A stipend is awarded (amount not specified).

Duration 1 year.

Number awarded 1 or more each year.

Deadline Deadline not specified.

[407]
AFRICAN AMERICAN SCHOLARSHIP FUND OF DISCIPLES HOME MISSIONS

Christian Church (Disciples of Christ)
Attn: Disciples Home Missions
130 East Washington Street
P.O. Box 1986
Indianapolis, IN 46206-1986
(317) 713-2652   Toll Free: (888) DHM-2631
Fax: (317) 635-4426   E-mail: mail@dhm.disciples.org
Web: www.discipleshomemissions.org

Summary To provide financial assistance to African Americans interested in preparing for a career in the ministry of the Christian Church (Disciples of Christ).

Eligibility This program is open to African American ministerial students who are members of the Christian Church (Disciples of Christ). Applicants must plan to prepare for the ordained ministry, have at least a "C+" GPA, provide evidence of financial need, be enrolled full time in an accredited school or seminary, provide a transcript of academic work, and be under the care of a regional Commission on the Ministry or in the process of coming under care.

Financial data A stipend is awarded (amount not specified).

Duration 1 year; may be renewed.

Additional information This program began in 1939 as the Negro Student Scholarship Fund of the United Christian Missionary Society. Its current name was adopted in 2008.

Number awarded 1 each year.

Deadline March of each year.

[408]
AHEPA GRADUATE SCHOLARSHIPS

American Hellenic Educational Progressive Association
Attn: AHEPA Educational Foundation
1909 Q Street, N.W., Suite 500
Washington, DC 20009
(202) 232-6300   Fax: (202) 232-2140
E-mail: Admin@ahepa.org
Web: ahepa.org

Summary To provide financial assistance to graduate students who have been active in Greek Orthodox youth activities, have a connection to the American Hellenic Educational Progressive Association (AHEPA), and are working on a degree in any field.

Eligibility This program is open to 1) active members of the AHEPA family (the Order of AHEPA, Daughters of Penelope, Sons of Pericles, or Maids of Athena); or 2) children of members of those organizations and of Greek descent. Applicants must be enrolled or planning to enroll as full-time graduate students at a college or university in any state and work on a degree in any field. Selection is based primarily on academic achievement, although consideration is also given to AHEPA affiliation, extracurricular activities, community service, and Greek Orthodox youth activities; special consideration is given to applicants who can demonstrate financial need.

Financial data Stipends range up to $2,000.

Duration 1 year.

Additional information This program includes the following named scholarships: the Dr. John C. Yavis Scholarship, the Archbishop Demetrios Scholarship, the P.A. Margaronis Scholarship, the Nick Cost Scholarship, and the Spiro and Cleo Millios Scholarship.

Number awarded   Varies each year.

Deadline   March of each year.

[409]
AL SHACKLEFORD AND DAN MARTIN GRADUATE SCHOLARSHIP

Baptist Communicators Association
Attn: Scholarship Committee
1519 Menlo Drive
Kennesaw, GA 30152
(770) 425-3728 E-mail: office@baptistcommunicators.org
Web: www.baptistcommunicators.org/about/scholarship.cfm

Summary   To provide financial assistance to graduate students who are working on a degree to prepare for a career in Baptist communications.

Eligibility   This program is open to students who are working on a graduate degree in communications, English, journalism, or public relations. Applicants must have a GPA of 2.5 or higher. Their vocational objective must be in Baptist communications. Along with their application, they must submit a statement explaining why they want to receive this scholarship.

Financial data   The stipend is $500.

Duration   1 year; recipients may reapply.

Additional information   This program was established in 1988.

Number awarded   1 each year.

Deadline   December of each year.

[410]
ALABAMA-WEST FLORIDA CONFERENCE MINISTERIAL EDUCATION FUND

United Methodist Church-Alabama-West Florida
  Conference
Attn: Board of Ordained Ministry
100 Interstate Park Drive, Suite 120
Montgomery, AL 36109
(334) 356-8014   Toll Free: (888) 873-3127
Fax: (334) 356-8029   E-mail: awfcrc@awfumc.org
Web: www.awfumc.org

Summary   To provide forgivable loans to ministry candidates from the Alabama-West Florida Conference of the United Methodist Church (UMC).

Eligibility   This program is open to certified candidates for ministry from the Alabama-West Florida Conference of the UMW. Applicants must submit documentation of financial need and intent to serve in the conference following graduation and ordination.

Financial data   The maximum loan is $1,500 per semester for full-time students or a prorated amount for part-time students. Loans are forgiven if the recipient serves an appointment within the conference for 5 years or equivalent in part-time service. Recipients who transfer to another annual conference must repay the loan in full.

Duration   1 semester; may be renewed up to 3 additional semesters for students in 2-year programs or up to 5 additional semesters for students in 3-year programs. The maximum loan is $9,000 for the total academic career of a student.

Number awarded   Varies each year.

Deadline   July of each year for fall semester; November of each year for spring semester.

[411]
ALABAMA-WEST FLORIDA UNITED METHODIST FOUNDATION SCHOLARSHIP FUND

Alabama-West Florida United Methodist Foundation, Inc.
170 Belmont Drive
P.O. Box 8066
Dothan, AL 36304
(334) 793-6820   Fax: (334) 794-6480
E-mail: foundation@alwfumf.org
Web: www.alwfumf.org

Summary   To provide financial assistance to ministerial students from the Alabama-West Florida Conference of the United Methodist Church.

Eligibility   This program is open to members of United Methodist Churches within the Alabama-West Florida Conference. Applicants must be attending an approved seminary and preparing for full-time ordained pastoral ministry in the Conference. Selection is based on financial need and promise for ministry.

Financial data   The stipend varies each year.

Duration   1 year.

Additional information   Recipients must serve at least 1 year in the Alabama-West Florida Conference.

Number awarded   1 or more each year.

Deadline   June of each year.

[412]
ALBERT BAKER FUND STUDENT FINANCIAL AID

Albert Baker Fund
777 Campus Commons Road, Suite 165
Sacramento, CA 95825-8309
(916) 643-9999   Toll Free: (800) 269-0388
Fax: (916) 568-1372 E-mail: admin@albertbakerfund.org
Web: www.albertbakerfund.org/financial-aid/us-canada

Summary   To provide financial aid and loans to undergraduate, graduate, and vocational students in the United States and Canada who are Christian Scientists.

Eligibility   This program is open to students who are Christian Scientists and members of The Mother Church (the First Church of Christ, Scientist in Boston, Massachusetts) or a branch church. Applicants must be enrolled or planning to enroll at least half time as an undergraduate or graduate student at an accredited college, university, or accredited vocational school in the United States or Canada. They must have a GPA of 2.5 or higher and be able to demonstrate financial need. U.S. or Canadian citizenship is required.

Financial data   Financial aid is provided in the form of grants and loans (amount not specified). For loans, interest rates are fixed at 3%; they must be repaid within 10 years.

Duration   1 year; may be renewed.

Number awarded   Varies each year. Recently, the program awarded $370,000 in grants and $515,000 in loans to 557 North American students (including 407 undergraduates, 71 graduate students, and 79 vocational students).

Deadline   February, May, September, or November of each year.

[413]
ALBERT R. MURDOCH MINISTERIAL SCHOLARSHIP

Nebraska United Methodist Foundation
100 West Fletcher Avenue, Suite 100
Lincoln, NE 68521-3848
(402) 323-8844   Toll Free: (877) 495-5545
Fax: (402) 323-8840   E-mail: info@numf.org
Web: www.numf.org/special_programs/scholarships.html

Summary To provide financial assistance to upper-division and seminary students at schools in any state who are preparing for Methodist ministry in Nebraska.

Eligibility This program is open to full-time students in the junior or senior year of undergraduate study or the first year of seminary at a college, university, or theological school in any state accredited by the United Methodist Board of Higher Education. Applicants must be planning to become pastors in the Nebraska Annual Conference of the United Methodist Church. They must have a cumulative GPA of 2.5 or higher. Along with their application, they must submit a 1-page statement of their career plans and financial need, a current academic transcript, and 2 letters of recommendation.

Financial data The stipend is approximately $700.

Duration 1 year; may be renewed.

Number awarded 1 each year.

Deadline June of each year.

[414]
ALEXANDER CHRISTIAN FOUNDATION OF INDIANA SCHOLARSHIPS

Alexander Christian Foundation of Indiana
312 East Main Street, Suite B
P.O. Box 246
Greenfield, IN 46140-0246
(317) 467-1223   E-mail: Judith@acfindiana.org
Web: www.acfindiana.org/awards.html

Summary To provide financial assistance to members of the Christian Church or Church of Christ (Independent) in Indiana who are preparing for a church-related vocation at a school in any state.

Eligibility This program is open to members of the Christian Church or Church of Christ (Independent) in Indiana who are candidates for a church-related vocation or currently working full time on an appropriate undergraduate or graduate degree. Applicants must be attending or planning to attend a college or seminary in any state affiliated with the Christian Churches/Churches of Christ. Students currently enrolled at Christian colleges must have a GPA of 3.0 or higher. Along with their application, they must submit an essay of 500 to 1,000 words on "Why I Desire to Serve Christ in a Church-Related Vocation." Selection is based on that essay, evaluations of the applicant's character and motivation by their home church minister and an elder of their church, and transcripts.

Financial data Stipends range from $1,250 to $2,000 per year.

Duration 1 year; may be renewed for 3 additional years of undergraduate study or 1 additional year of graduate study, provided the recipient remains enrolled full time, continues to attend an approved college or seminar, maintains a GPA of 3.0 or higher, and pursues a church-related vocation.

Additional information This program was established in 1964. Church-related vocations include preaching ministry, youth ministry, missions ministry, music ministry, and children's ministry.

Number awarded Varies each year.

Deadline February of each year.

[415]
ALICE KRUSE MINISTERIAL SCHOLARSHIP FUND

Nebraska United Methodist Foundation
100 West Fletcher Avenue, Suite 100
Lincoln, NE 68521-3848
(402) 323-8844   Toll Free: (877) 495-5545
Fax: (402) 323-8840   E-mail: info@numf.org
Web: www.numf.org/special_programs/scholarships.html

Summary To provide financial assistance to students at designated United Methodist seminaries in Nebraska who plan to become a pastor in the state.

Eligibility This program is open to members of Nebraska United Methodist Churches who are ministerial students at 1 of the following seminaries accredited by the Nebraska United Methodist Board of Ordained Ministry: Saint Paul School of Theology (Kansas City, Missouri and Oklahoma City, Oklahoma), Garrett-Evangelical Theological Seminary (Evanston, Illinois), Iliff School of Theology (Denver, Colorado), or Perkins School of Theology (Dallas, Texas). Applicants must plan to become a pastor in the Nebraska Annual Conference and have at least 30 years of eligibility to serve as a minister upon graduation from seminary. They must have completed at least 2 semesters of seminary studies and have a cumulative GPA of 2.5 or higher. Along with their application, they must submit a 1-page description of their calling and career plans for ministry, a current academic transcript, documentation of financial need, and 2 letters of recommendation.

Financial data The stipend is approximately $2,000 per year.

Duration 1 year; may be renewed.

Number awarded 1 each year.

Deadline June of each year.

[416]
ALICE KRUSE SEMINARY SCHOLARSHIP FUND

Nebraska United Methodist Foundation
100 West Fletcher Avenue, Suite 100
Lincoln, NE 68521-3848
(402) 323-8844   Toll Free: (877) 495-5545
Fax: (402) 323-8840   E-mail: info@numf.org
Web: www.numf.org/special_programs/scholarships.html

Summary To provide financial assistance to students at designated United Methodist seminaries who plan to become a pastor in Nebraska.

Eligibility This program is open to members of Nebraska United Methodist Churches who are ministerial students at 1 of the following seminaries accredited by the Nebraska United Methodist Board of Ordained Ministry: Saint Paul School of Theology (Kansas City, Missouri and Oklahoma City, Oklahoma), Garrett-Evangelical Theological Seminary (Evanston, Illinois), Iliff School of Theology (Denver, Colorado), or Perkins School of Theology (Dallas, Texas). Applicants must plan to become a pastor in the Nebraska Annual Conference and have at least 30 years of eligibility to serve as a minister upon graduation from seminary. They must have completed at least 2 semesters of seminary studies and have a cumulative GPA of 2.5 or higher. Along with their application, they must submit a 1-page description of their calling and career plans for ministry, a current academic transcript, documentation of financial need, and 2 letters of recommendation.

Financial data   The stipend is approximately $700 per year.

Duration   1 year; may be renewed.

Number awarded   1 each year.

Deadline   June of each year.

[417]
ALICE W. LOCKMILLER SCHOLARSHIPS

Florida United Methodist Foundation
Attn: Scholarship Committee
450 Martin Luther King Jr. Avenue
P.O. Box 3549
Lakeland, FL 33802-3549
(863) 904-2970, ext. 7103
Toll Free: (866) 363-9673, ext. 7103
Fax: (863) 904-0169   E-mail: Foundation@fumf.org
Web: www.fumf.org

Summary   To provide financial assistance to students who have a connection to the United Methodist Church (UMC) in Florida and are currently attending college, university, or seminary.

Eligibility   This program is open to students currently enrolled full time at a junior college, senior college, university, seminary, or other institution for educational or occupational training beyond the high school level. Applicants must be members or the children of members of a UMC church within the boundaries of the Florida Annual Conference. First consideration is given to students attending institutions related to the UMC in Florida. Second consideration is given to students attending institutions related to the UMC outside Florida. Third consideration is given to students attending all other institutions. Along with their application, they must submit an essay describing their church, community, and school leadership and involvement and their educational plans and goals. Selection is based on academic achievement, church involvement, and community service; financial need is not considered.

Financial data   A stipend is awarded (amount not specified).

Duration   1 year.

Number awarded   1 or more each year.

Deadline   March of each year.

[418]
ALLIE L. SILLS MEMORIAL FUND

Synod of the Northeast
Attn: Student Loan/Scholarship Programs
5811 Heritage Landing Drive
East Syracuse, NY 13057-9360
(315) 446-5990, ext. 215
Toll Free: (800) 585-5881, ext. 215
Fax: (315) 446-3708   E-mail: SynodOffice@Synodne.org
Web: www.synodne.org

Summary   To provide interest-free loans for college or graduate school to Presbyterian students.

Eligibility   This program is open to Presbyterians who are or will be attending a postsecondary institution in the United States or Canada on a full-time basis. Institutions may include but are not limited to: 2-year and 4-year colleges, community colleges and other 2-year programs, nondegree professional or technical training programs, or seminary studies leading to an M.Div. or master's of religious education. Graduate work, other than for those 2 master's degrees, is not supported. Applicants must submit an essay of 400 to 500 words on why they should be considered for a loan, their reasons for wanting to pursue a college or seminary education, their extracurricular activities and interests (school, church, and community), and the role their faith will take in fulfilling their academic goals. Preference is given to applicants from Jefferson County, New York and then to the areas that make up the Northern New York Presbytery.

Financial data   Loans are normally made in the $500 to $2,500 range; there is an individual lifetime maximum of $10,000 for undergraduate students or $20,500 for seminary students. No interest is charged.

Duration   1 year; may be renewed. Loans must be repaid as soon as the student is financially able to do so.

Number awarded   Varies each year.

Deadline   March of each year.

[419]
ALLISON SMITH MEMORIAL FUND

Kansas-Nebraska Convention of Southern Baptists
Attn: Kansas-Nebraska Southern Baptist Foundation
5410 S.W. Seventh Street
Topeka, KS 66606-2398
(785) 228-6800   Toll Free: (800) 984-9092
Fax: (785) 273-4992   E-mail: beckyholt@kncsb.org
Web: www.kncsb.org/ministry/article/foundation_funds

Summary   To provide financial assistance to Southern Baptists from Kansas and Nebraska who are attending a seminary in any state.

Eligibility   This program is open to members of churches in the Kansas-Nebraska Convention of Southern Baptists. Applicants must be attending a Southern Baptist seminary in any state in preparation for full-time Christian service.

Financial data   A stipend is awarded (amount not specified).

Duration   1 year.

Number awarded   1 or more each year.

Deadline   February of each year.

[420]
ALVIN BRIGGS SEMINARY SCHOLARSHIP

Wisconsin United Methodist Foundation
750 Windsor Street, Suite 305
P.O. Box 620
Sun Prairie, WI 53590-0620
(608) 837-9582   Toll Free: (888) 903-9863
Fax: (608) 837-2492   E-mail: wumf@wumf.org
Web: www.wumf.org/grantsFF/grantsScholars.html

Summary To provide financial assistance to Methodists from Wisconsin who are interested in attending a seminary in any state.

Eligibility This program is open to members of United Methodist Churches affiliated with the Wisconsin Conference who are interested in attending local pastor training or a seminary in any state. Applicants must submit an essay that describes their personal situation and vocational goals, church-related activities and involvement, school and community involvement, and financial plan for funding their education, including any special financial needs.

Financial data Stipends range from $500 to $1,000.

Duration 1 year.

Additional information This program was established in 2006.

Number awarded 1 or more each year.

Deadline June of each year.

[421]
AMELIA KEMP MEMORIAL SCHOLARSHIP

Women of the Evangelical Lutheran Church in America
Attn: Scholarships
8765 West Higgins Road
Chicago, IL 60631-4101
(773) 380-2736   Toll Free: (800) 638-3522, ext. 2736
Fax: (773) 380-2419   E-mail: emily.hansen@elca.org
Web: www.elca.org

Summary To provide financial assistance to lay women of color who are members of Evangelical Lutheran Church of America (ELCA) congregations and who wish to study on the undergraduate, graduate, professional, or vocational school level.

Eligibility This program is open to ELCA lay women of color who are at least 21 years of age and have experienced an interruption of at least 2 years in their education since high school. Applicants must have been admitted to an educational institution to prepare for a career in other than a church-certified profession. U.S. citizenship is required.

Financial data The maximum stipend is $1,000.

Duration Up to 2 years.

Number awarded Varies each year, depending upon the funds available.

Deadline February of each year.

[422]
AMERICAN BAPTIST CHURCHES INDIVIDUAL SEMINARIAN GRANTS

American Baptist Churches USA
National Ministries
Attn: Office of Financial Aid for Studies
P.O. Box 851
Valley Forge, PA 19482-0851
(610) 768-2067   Toll Free: (800) ABC-3USA, ext. 2067
Fax: (610) 768-2453
E-mail: Financialaid.Web@abc-usa.org
Web: www.nationalministries.org

Summary To provide financial assistance to American Baptist students attending a seminary not related to American Baptist Churches USA.

Eligibility This program is open to American Baptist students who are attending a seminary in the United States or Puerto Rico that is not related to American Baptist Churches USA. Seminarians must be enrolled at least two-thirds time in 1 of the following first professional degree programs: M.Div., M.C.E., M.A.C.E., or M.R.E. (D.Min. students are not eligible). Applicants must have been members of an American Baptist church for at least 1 year before applying for assistance. U.S. citizenship is required.

Financial data The stipend is $750 per year.

Duration 1 year; recipients may reapply for 2 additional years.

Number awarded Varies each year.

Deadline May of each year.

[423]
AMERICAN BAPTIST CHURCHES OF NEW JERSEY SEMINARIAN SCHOLAR AWARDS

American Baptist Churches of New Jersey
Attn: Scholar Awards Committee
3752 Nottingham Way, Suite 101
Trenton, NJ 08690-3802
(609) 587-8700   Fax: (609) 587-7474
Web: www.abcnj.net

Summary To provide financial assistance to students at seminaries in any state who are members of American Baptist Churches of New Jersey (ABCNJ).

Eligibility This program is open to members of churches that are in covenant with ABCNJ. Applicants must be working on or planning to work on an M.Div., master's of Christian education (M.C.E), or master's of religious education (M.R.E.) degree at a seminary in any state. Along with their application, they must submit a 1-page essay on the topic, "God's Call-My Response." Financial need is not considered in the selection process.

Financial data The stipend is $500.

Duration 1 year.

Number awarded 12 each year.

Deadline July of each year.

[424]
AMERICAN BAPTIST CHURCHES OF WISCONSIN SEMINARIAN SCHOLARSHIPS

American Baptist Churches of Wisconsin
c/o Rev. Arlo Reichter
15330 Watertown Plank Road
Elm Grove, WI 53122-2340
(262) 782-3140   Toll Free: (800) 311-3140
Fax: (262) 782-7573   E-mail: email@abcofwi.org
Web: www.abcofwi.org

Summary To provide financial assistance for seminary education to Wisconsin members of the American Baptist Church.

Eligibility Eligible to apply for this support are seminarians from an American Baptist Church of Wisconsin who are attending an AATS-accredited seminary as a part-time or full-time student. Applicants should be pursuing the M.Div. degree. Students working on a D.Min. degree are not eligible.

Financial data The stipend is $1,000 per semester for full-time students or $500 per semester for part-time students.

Duration 1 semester; may be renewed.

Number awarded Several each year.

Deadline June of each year.

[425]
AMERICAN BAPTIST CHURCHES SEMINARIAN SUPPORT PROGRAM

American Baptist Churches USA
National Ministries
Attn: Office of Financial Aid for Studies
P.O. Box 851
Valley Forge, PA 19482-0851
(610) 768-2067   Toll Free: (800) ABC-3USA, ext. 2067
Fax: (610) 768-2453
E-mail: Financialaid.Web@abc-usa.org
Web: www.nationalministries.org

Summary To provide financial assistance to students attending American Baptist-related seminaries.

Eligibility This program is open to students who are attending American Baptist-related seminaries. Seminarians must be enrolled at least two-thirds time in 1 of the following first professional degree programs: M.Div., M.C.E., M.A.C.E., or M.R.E. (D.Min. students are not eligible). Applicants must have been members of an American Baptist church for at least 1 year before applying for assistance. U.S. citizenship is required.

Financial data Pledges from local churches or organizations will be matched up to $1,000 per academic year. Pledges are sent to the seminary and credited to the student's account. These funds may be used to pay for tuition, fees, and books.

Duration 1 year.

Number awarded Varies each year.

Deadline July of each year.

[426]
AMERICAN BAPTIST WOMEN'S MINISTRIES OF COLORADO STUDENT GRANTS

American Baptist Churches of the Rocky Mountains
Attn: American Baptist Women's Ministries
9085 East Mineral Circle, Suite 170
Centennial, CO 80112
(303) 988-3900   E-mail: web@abcrm.org
Web: www.abcrm.org

Summary To provide financial assistance to women who are members of churches affiliated with the American Baptist Churches (ABC) USA in Colorado, New Mexico, and Utah and interested in attending an ABC college or seminary in any state.

Eligibility This program is open to women older than 26 years of age who are active members of churches cooperating with ABC in Colorado, New Mexico, or Utah. Applicants must be enrolled or planning to enroll at an ABC college, university, or seminary in any state. Along with their application, they must submit a personal letter describing their Christian experience; their participation in the life of their church, school, and community; and their goals for the future. Selection is based on academic performance, Christian participation in church and school, and financial need.

Financial data A stipend is awarded (amount not specified). Funds are sent directly to the recipient's school.

Duration 1 year; recipients may reapply.

Number awarded 1 or more each year.

Deadline March of each year.

[427]
AMERICAN BAPTIST WOMEN'S MINISTRIES OF MASSACHUSETTS SCHOLARSHIP PROGRAM

American Baptist Women's Ministries of Massachusetts
c/o Penny Mulloy, Scholarship Committee Chair
27 Ox Road
Billerica, MA 01821-4439
(978) 667-7496   E-mail: pennymulloy@gmail.com
Web: www.abwmofma.org

Summary To provide financial assistance to American Baptist women in Massachusetts interested in church-related vocations.

Eligibility This program is open to women who intend to offer Christian service in their chosen vocation, have been active members of an American Baptist Church in Massachusetts for at least 1 year prior to submitting an application, and are able to supply satisfactory references. They must be nominated by their pastor. Applicants should include a written statement of faith and a separate letter of life purpose that clearly indicates how they intend to serve in the Christian community after their education is completed. Selection is based on dedication, need, and scholastic ability.

Financial data A stipend is awarded (amount not specified).

Duration 1 year; may be renewed.

Additional information Of the scholarships awarded, 2 are designated as the Lenore S. Bigelow Scholarships, for graduate study at Andover Newton Theological School in Newton Centre, Massachusetts and/or Colgate-Rochester Divinity School in Rochester, New York. An interview with the committee or designated members is required of first-time applicants.

Number awarded Varies each year.

Deadline April of each year.

[428]
AMERICAN BAPTIST WOMEN'S MINISTRIES OF MICHIGAN SCHOLARSHIP GIRLS

American Baptist Churches of Michigan
Attn: American Baptist Women's Ministries of Michigan
4578 South Hagadorn Road
East Lansing, MI 48823-5355
(517) 332-3594   Toll Free: (800) 632-2953
Fax: (517) 332-3186   E-mail: mawilliams@abc-mi.org
Web: www.abc-mi.org/?q=node/38

Summary To provide financial assistance to female members of American Baptist Churches of Michigan who interested in attending a college or seminary in any state.

Eligibility This program is open to female members of American Baptist Churches of Michigan who are entering or attending an accredited college, nursing school, or seminary in any state. The school does not need to have an affiliation with American Baptist Churches, but applicants must be able to demonstrate that their lives and chosen vocations will glorify God as they minister in this world.

Financial data Stipends range from $700 to $800.

Duration 1 year.

Number awarded Varies each year; recently, 2 of these scholarships were awarded.

Deadline February of each year.

[429]
AMERICAN BAPTIST WOMEN'S MINISTRIES OF NEW YORK STATE SCHOLARSHIPS

American Baptist Women's Ministries of New York State
Attn: Scholarship Committee
5865 East Seneca Turnpike
Jamesville, NY 13078
(315) 469-4236   Fax: (315) 492-2369
E-mail: isingram@rochester.rr.com
Web: www.abwm-nys.org/M_M/scholarship.html

Summary To provide financial assistance to women who are members of American Baptist Churches in New York and interested in attending college in any state.

Eligibility This program is open to women who are residents of New York and active members of an American Baptist Church. Applicants must be enrolled or planning to enroll full time at a college or university in any state. While in college, they must maintain Christian fellowship, preferably with the American Baptist Church (although any Protestant church or campus ministry is acceptable). Along with their application, they must submit a 1-page essay on an event that occurred in their life during the past year and how it has impacted their faith. Women may be of any age; graduate students are considered on an individual basis. Financial need is considered in the selection process.

Financial data A stipend is awarded (amount not specified).

Duration 1 year.

Number awarded Varies each year.

Deadline February of each year.

[430]
AMERICAN BAPTIST WOMEN'S MINISTRIES OF PENNSYLVANIA AND DELAWARE STUDENT LOANS

American Baptist Churches of Pennsylvania and
  Delaware
Attn: American Baptist Women's Ministries
106 Revere Lane
Coatesville, PA 19320
Toll Free: (800) 358-6999   Fax: (610) 466-2013
Web: www.abcopad.com/abwm/ABWMOPADIndexnew.htm

Summary To provide loans to students who are members of churches affiliated with the American Baptist Churches of Pennsylvania and Delaware and interested in attending college, seminary, or graduate school in any state.

Eligibility This program is open to members of churches affiliated with the American Baptist Churches of Pennsylvania and Delaware or the Philadelphia Baptist Association. Applicants must be enrolled or planning to enroll full time at a college, graduate school, or special vocational training institution in any state; study at a seminary is eligible if it prepares students for church-related vocations in American Baptist Churches. They may be of any age.

Financial data The maximum loan is $1,500 per year.

Duration 1 year; may be renewed, to a maximum $5,250 in loans to each student. Loans must be repaid within 5 years, with interest of 1% during the first year, 2% during the second year, 3% during the third year, 4% during the fourth year, and 5% during the fifth year.

Additional information This program was established in 1959.

Number awarded Varies each year; recently, approximately 30 students were receiving loans through this program.

Deadline Applications may be submitted at any time.

[431]
AMERICAN BAPTIST WOMEN'S MINISTRIES OF THE PACIFIC NORTHWEST SCHOLARSHIPS

American Baptist Women's Ministries of the Pacific
  Northwest
601 South Ross Point Road
Post Falls, ID 83854-7726
(208) 773-2733   Fax: (208) 773-1687
E-mail: office@abcnw.org
Web: www.abcnw.org

Summary To provide financial assistance to Baptists, particularly women from the Pacific Northwest, who are preparing for Christian service.

Eligibility This program is open to members of an American Baptist church who are college seniors or graduate students. Applicants must be preparing for full-time Christian service through American Baptist Churches/USA. Preference is given to female residents of the Pacific Northwest who are attending an American Baptist institution.

Financial data The stipend is $500.

Duration 1 year.

Number awarded 3 each year.

Deadline March of each year.

[432]
AMOS GENTRY BULLARD FAMILY FUND SCHOLARSHIP

North Carolina Baptist Foundation, Inc.
Attn: Denominational Relations Committee
201 Convention Drive
Cary, NC 27511-4257
(919) 380-7334   Toll Free: (800) 521-7334
Fax: (919) 460-6334
Web: www.ncbaptistfoundation.org

Summary To provide financial assistance to children of members of churches affiliated with the North Carolina Baptist State Convention who are interested in attending a college or seminary in any state.

Eligibility This program is open to residents of North Carolina who are members or children of members of churches affiliated with the Baptist State Convention. Applicants must have been accepted for enrollment at an accredited college, university, or seminary in any state to prepare for a career in full-time Christian ministry. Along with their application, they must submit a 100-word essay on why they should be chosen for this scholarship, including their reasons and ambitions for wishing to continue their education. Financial need is also considered in the selection process.

Financial data A stipend is awarded (amount not specified).

Duration 1 year.

Number awarded 1 or more each year.

Deadline January of each year.

[433]
ANN E. DICKERSON SCHOLARSHIPS

Christian Church (Disciples of Christ)
Attn: Higher Education and Leadership Ministries
11477 Olde Cabin Road, Suite 310
St. Louis, MO 63141-7130
(314) 991-3000   Fax: (314) 991-2957
E-mail: helm@helmdisciples.org
Web: www.helmdisciples.org/aid/dickerson.htm

Summary To provide financial assistance to female members of the Christian Church (Disciples of Christ) who are working on a Ph.D. degree in religion.

Eligibility This program is open to women working on a Ph.D. degree in religion. Applicants must members of the Christian Church (Disciples of Christ). Along with their application, they must submit a 300-word essay describing their vocational goals, their academic interests, and how they envision being of service to the church.

Financial data The stipend is $2,000.

Duration 1 year.

Number awarded 3 each year.

Deadline April of each year.

[434]
ANNE KUMPURIS SCHOLARSHIP

St. Mark's Episcopal Church
Attn: Endowment Committee
1000 North Mississippi Avenue
Little Rock, AR 72207
(501) 225-4203   Fax: (501) 225-9542
E-mail: office_manager@st-marks.com
Web: st-marks.com/community/anne-kumpuris-scholarship

Summary To provide financial assistance to students attending accredited Episcopal seminaries.

Eligibility This program is open to students entering their second or third year at an accredited Episcopal seminary in the United States. Applicants must be seeking holy orders in the Episcopal Church of the USA or in a sister church in the Anglican communion. Along with their application, they must submit essays on 1) a moment in their life in which an experience has exposed their mind to facts and their heart to feelings, thus allowing them to come to realize a deeper understanding; and 2) where they feel most comfortable and why. Financial need is considered in the selection process.

Financial data A stipend is awarded (amount not specified).

Duration 1 year; may be renewed for up to 1 additional year.

Additional information This program was established following the death of Anne Kumpuris in 1957.

Deadline May of each year.

[435]
APOLLOS PROGRAM SCHOLARSHIP AWARDS

Omaha Presbyterian Seminary Foundation
7101 Mercy Road, Suite 216
Omaha, NE 68106-2616
(402) 397-5138   Toll Free: (888) 244-6714
Fax: (402) 397-4944 E-mail: opsf@omaha-sem-found.org
Web: www.omahapresbyterianseminaryfoundation.org

Summary To provide financial assistance to students at Presbyterian theological seminaries.

Eligibility Applicants must be members of a Presbyterian Church, under the care of a presbytery as a candidate/inquirer, and accepted or enrolled to work on an M.Div. at 1 of the following 10 theological institutions: Austin Presbyterian Theological Seminary (Austin, Texas); Columbia Theological Seminary (Decatur, Georgia); University of Dubuque Theological Seminary (Dubuque, Iowa); Johnson C. Smith Theological Seminary (Atlanta, Georgia); Louisville Presbyterian Theological Seminary (Louisville, Kentucky); McCormick Theological Seminary (Chicago, Illinois); Pittsburgh Theological Seminary (Pittsburgh, Pennsylvania); Princeton Theological Seminary (Princeton, New Jersey); San Francisco Theological Seminary (San Anselmo, California); or Union Theological Seminary and Presbyterian School of Christian Education (Richmond, Virginia). Along with their application, they must submit answers to questions on the college or seminary subjects they have enjoyed the most and why, the college or seminary subjects they have enjoyed the least and why, the organizations they have belonged to and the leadership positions they have held, their employment experience, what attracts them to a calling as a minister of word and sacrament, who has seen pastoral skills in them, what they see as the major problem confronting the church today, how they will contribute to the solution of that problem, their present devotional life, how they have been active in the church, a brief description of their spiritual pilgrimage, and how they would describe themselves. Financial need is also considered in the selection process.

Financial data Stipends are $6,000 or $3,000 per year.

Duration 1 year; may be renewed for up to 2 additional years, provided the recipient makes satisfactory educational progress in a qualifying Presbyterian theological institution.

Additional information There are 4 named scholarships under this program: Eugene C. Dinsmore, Robert K. Adams, Silas G. Kessler, and Howard B. Dooley.

Number awarded Varies each year: the 4 named scholarships at $6,000, plus a varying number of scholarships at $3,000.

Deadline April of each year.

[436]
ARFORA/MARTHA GAVRILA SCHOLARSHIP FOR WOMEN

Association of Romanian Orthodox Ladies Auxiliaries of North America
Attn: Scholarship Committee
222 Orchard Park Drive
New Castle, PA 16105
(724) 652-4313   E-mail: adelap@verizon.net
Web: www.arfora.org/scholarships.htm

Summary To provide financial assistance to women who are members of a parish of the Romanian Orthodox Episcopate of America and interested in working on a graduate degree.

Eligibility This program is open to women who have been voting communicant members of a parish of the Romanian Orthodox Episcopate of America for at least 1 year. Applicants must have completed a baccalaureate degree and been accepted as a graduate student at a college or university in any state. Along with their application, they must submit a 300-word statement describing their personal goals; high school, university, church, and community involvement; honors and awards; and why they should be considered for this award. Selection is based on academic achievement, character, worthiness, and participation in religious life.

Financial data The stipend is $1,000.

Duration 1 year.

Additional information This scholarship was first awarded in 1985. The Association of Romanian Orthodox Ladies Auxiliaries (ARFORA) was established in 1938 as a women's organization within the Romanian Orthodox Episcopate of America.

Number awarded 1 each year.

Deadline May of each year.

[437]
ARIZONA EASTERN STAR TRAINING AWARDS FOR RELIGIOUS LEADERSHIP

Order of the Eastern Star-Grand Chapter of Arizona
4600 North 24th Street
Phoenix, AZ 85016
(602) 954-9413
Web: azoes.com

Summary To provide financial assistance to residents of Arizona who are attending a college or seminary in any state to prepare for a career in Christian or Jewish religious service.

Eligibility This program is open to residents of Arizona who are members of a Christian church or of the Jewish faith. Applicants must have declared their intention to devote their life to full-time religious service as a minister, missionary, director of religious education, director of church music, or youth director. They must have completed at least 2 full years of study at a college or seminary in any state. Selection is based primarily on financial need, although GPA (at least 3.0) and courses taken for credit instead of for grade (at least 75% of courses must have been taken for grade).

Financial data A stipend is awarded (amount not specified).

Duration 1 year.

Number awarded Varies each year.

Deadline June or December of each year.

[438]
ARKANSAS BAPTIST FOUNDATION MEDICAL MISSIONS SCHOLARSHIP

Arkansas Baptist Foundation
10117 Kanis Road
Little Rock, AR 72205-6220
(501) 376-0732   Toll Free: (800) 798-0969
Fax: (501) 376-3831   E-mail: info@abf.org
Web: www.abf.org/individuals_scholarships.htm

Summary To provide financial assistance to members of Southern Baptist churches in Arkansas who are interested in attending a college, seminary, or medical school in any state to prepare for a career as a medical missionary.

Eligibility This program is open to members of Southern Baptist churches in Arkansas who are attending or planning to attend a college, seminary, or medical school in any state. Applicants must be preparing for a vocation or an appointment with the International Mission Board or North American Mission Board of the Southern Baptist Convention as a medical missionary.

Financial data A stipend is awarded (amount not specified).

Duration 1 year; recipients may reapply.

Number awarded Varies each year.

Deadline February of each year.

[439]
ARKANSAS BASIC SEMINARY DEGREE FINANCIAL AID PROGRAM

United Methodist Church-Arkansas Conference
Attn: Board of Ordained Ministry
800 Daisy Bates Drive
Little Rock, AR 72202
(501) 324-8033   Toll Free: (877) 646-1816
Fax: (501) 324-8021   E-mail: conference@arumc.org
Web: www.arumc.org/bom_financial_assistance.php

Summary To provide loans-for-service to Methodist students from Arkansas attending a seminary in any state to work on a basic degree in preparation for ministry.

Eligibility This program is open to seminary students who are active members of local congregations affiliated with the

Arkansas Conference of the United Methodist Church (UMC). Applicants must be a certified candidate enrolled at a seminary in any state approved by the UMC University Senate. They may not have received a scholarship from the United Methodist Foundation.

Financial data Loans provide up to 40% of the cost of tuition, to a maximum of $7,000 per year for students at UMC seminaries or $5,000 per year for students at other seminaries. Loans are forgiven if the recipient provides service to a United Methodist church in Arkansas at the rate of 1 year of service for 2 semesters of aid. Otherwise, interest of 4% per year is charged.

Duration 1 year; may be renewed.

Number awarded 1 or more each year.

Deadline January, July, or September of each year.

[440]
ARKANSAS CONFERENCE ETHNIC LOCAL CHURCH CONCERNS SCHOLARSHIPS

United Methodist Church-Arkansas Conference
Attn: Committee on Ethnic Local Church Concerns
800 Daisy Bates Drive
Little Rock, AR 72202
(501) 324-8045   Toll Free: (877) 646-1816
Fax: (501) 324-8018   E-mail: mallen@arumc.org
Web: www.arumc.org

Summary To provide financial assistance to ethnic minority Methodist students from Arkansas who are interested in attending college or graduate school in any state.

Eligibility This program is open to ethnic minority undergraduate and graduate students who are active members of local congregations affiliated with the Arkansas Conference of the United Methodist Church (UMC). Applicants must be currently enrolled in an accredited institution of higher education in any state. Along with their application, they must submit a transcript (GPA of 2.0 or higher) and documentation of participation in local church activities. Preference is given to students attending a UMC-affiliated college or university.

Financial data The stipend is $500 per semester ($1,000 per year) for undergraduates or $1,000 per semester ($2,000 per year) for graduate students.

Duration 1 year; may be renewed.

Number awarded 1 or more each year.

Deadline September of each year.

[441]
ARKANSAS GRADUATE THEOLOGICAL STUDIES FINANCIAL AID PROGRAM

United Methodist Church-Arkansas Conference
Attn: Board of Ordained Ministry
800 Daisy Bates Drive
Little Rock, AR 72202
(501) 324-8033   Toll Free: (877) 646-1816
Fax: (501) 324-8021   E-mail: conference@arumc.org
Web: www.arumc.org/bom_financial_assistance.php

Summary To provide loans-for-service to Methodist students from Arkansas attending a seminary in any state to work on an advanced degree.

Eligibility This program is open to seminary students who are active members of local congregations affiliated with the Arkansas Conference of the United Methodist Church (UMC).

Applicants must have completed the basic course of study and be interested in a program of graduate theological studies to become provisional members by the alternate route. Deacon candidates on the professional certificate route toward ordination are also eligible.

Financial data Loans provide up to 45% of the cost of tuition, to a maximum of $5,000 per year. Loans are forgiven if the recipient provides service to a United Methodist church in Arkansas at the rate of 1 year of service for 2 semesters of aid. Otherwise, interest of 4% per year is charged.

Duration Loans support up to 32 hours of graduate theological studies.

Number awarded 1 or more each year.

Deadline January, July, or September of each year.

[442]
ARKANSAS UNITED METHODIST SCHOLARSHIP FOR SEMINARY STUDENTS

United Methodist Foundation of Arkansas
Attn: Vice President
5300 Evergreen Drive
Little Rock, AR 72205-1814
(501) 664-8632   Toll Free: (877) 712-1107
Fax: (501) 664-6792   E-mail: jmarshall@umfa.org
Web: www.umfa.org

Summary To provide financial assistance to students from Arkansas who will be attending a United Methodist seminary in any state.

Eligibility This program is open to Arkansas students who have been accepted by a United Methodist seminary in any state as a full-time graduate student. Applicants must submit a statement describing their call to ministry, a copy of their certificate of candidacy, their most recent college transcript, a recommendation from someone currently and directly involved with their ministry or leadership, and an agreement to serve (upon graduation) under appointment of the Bishop and Cabinet of the Arkansas area of the United Methodist Church for either 6 years or 2 years for each year of support. Financial need is considered in the selection process.

Financial data A stipend is awarded (amount not specified).

Duration 1 year; may be renewed up to 2 additional years.

Additional information This program was established in 2001.

Number awarded 9 each year.

Deadline February of each year.

[443]
ARNE ADMINISTRATIVE LEADERSHIP SCHOLARSHIP

Women of the Evangelical Lutheran Church in America
Attn: Scholarships
8765 West Higgins Road
Chicago, IL 60631-4101
(773) 380-2736   Toll Free: (800) 638-3522, ext. 2736
Fax: (773) 380-2419   E-mail: emily.hansen@elca.org
Web: www.elca.org

Summary To provide financial assistance to women members of congregations of the Evangelical Lutheran Church of America (ELCA) who wish to train for administrative positions.

Eligibility This program is open to women members of the ELCA who have completed a bachelor's degree or its equivalent and have taken some academic or professional courses since completing that degree. Applicants must have been admitted to an academic institution as a full-time student to take regular classes, night courses, or summer session. U.S. citizenship is required. Selection is based on records of graduate academic or professional courses, examples of being a decision-maker, and evidence of ability and willingness to study.

Financial data The maximum stipend is $1,000.

Duration Up to 2 years.

Additional information This program was established in 1998.

Number awarded Varies each year.

Deadline February of each year.

[444]
ARNOLD W. "JEFF" AND MABEL RENSINK ENDOWMENT FOR SEMINARY SCHOLARSHIP

Iowa United Methodist Foundation
2301 Rittenhouse Street
Des Moines, IA 50321
(515) 974-8927
Web: www.iumf.org/seminaryscholarships.html

Summary To provide financial assistance to United Methodist seminary students from Iowa.

Eligibility This program is open to students who have completed at least a bachelor's degree and are enrolled in studies at the graduate or professional level at an approved United Methodist seminary. Applicants must be members of an Iowa United Methodist Church and have a "personal relationship with Jesus Christ." They must exhibit a call to the ministry and include a statement in their application that describes that call. Preference is given to applicants from the Mason City district. Financial need is considered in the selection process.

Financial data The stipend is $1,000.

Duration 1 year.

Number awarded 1 each year.

Deadline March of each year.

[445]
ASSOCIATION OF BRETHREN CARING MINISTRIES NURSING SCHOLARSHIPS

Church of the Brethren
Attn: Caring Ministries
1451 Dundee Avenue
Elgin, IL 60120-1694
(847) 742-5100, ext. 300   Toll Free: (800) 323-8039
Fax: (847) 742-6103
Web: www.brethren.org

Summary To provide financial assistance to members of the Church of the Brethren working on an undergraduate or graduate degree in nursing.

Eligibility This program is open to students who are members of the Church of the Brethren or employed in a Church of the Brethren agency. Applicants must be enrolled in a L.P.N., R.N., or graduate program in nursing. Along with their application, they must submit 1) a statement describing their reasons for wanting to enter nursing or continue their nursing education, including something of their aspirations for service

in the profession; and 2) a description of how the scholarship will assist them in reaching their educational and career goals.

Financial data The stipend is $2,000 for R.N. and graduate nurse candidates or $1,000 for L.P.N. candidates.

Duration 1 year. Recipients are eligible for only 1 scholarship per degree.

Number awarded Varies each year.

Deadline March of each year.

[446]
ATHANASIOS AND EKATERINI BACKUS SCHOLARSHIP

American Hellenic Educational Progressive Association
Attn: AHEPA Educational Foundation
1909 Q Street, N.W., Suite 500
Washington, DC 20009
(202) 232-6300   Fax: (202) 232-2140
E-mail: Admin@ahepa.org
Web: ahepa.org

Summary To provide financial assistance to medical students who have a connection to the American Hellenic Educational Progressive Association (AHEPA).

Eligibility This program is open to 1) active members of the AHEPA family (the Order of AHEPA, Daughters of Penelope, Sons of Pericles, or Maids of Athena); or 2) children of members of those organizations and of Greek descent. Applicants must be enrolled or planning to enroll as full-time medical students at a school in any state. Selection is based primarily on academic achievement, although consideration is also given to AHEPA affiliation, extracurricular activities, community service, and Greek Orthodox youth activities; special consideration is given to applicants who can demonstrate financial need.

Financial data Stipends range up to $2,000.

Duration 1 year.

Number awarded 1 or more each year.

Deadline March of each year.

[447]
BALDWIN F. AND AMY L. KRUSE TRUST FUND

Nebraska United Methodist Foundation
100 West Fletcher Avenue, Suite 100
Lincoln, NE 68521-3848
(402) 323-8844   Toll Free: (877) 495-5545
Fax: (402) 323-8840   E-mail: info@numf.org
Web: www.numf.org/special_programs/scholarships.html

Summary To provide financial assistance to students at United Methodist seminaries who plan to become a pastor in Nebraska.

Eligibility This program is open to members of Nebraska United Methodist Churches who are ministerial students at seminaries accredited by the Nebraska United Methodist Board of Ordained Ministry. Applicants must be working on an advanced degree, beyond the bachelor's degree, as preparation for ordained ministry in the Nebraska Annual Conference of the United Methodist Church. Along with their application, they must submit a current resume, current academic transcript, description of calling and plans for ministry, letter of recommendation from the Nebraska Annual Conference

Board of Ordained Ministry, 2 additional letters of recommendation, and documentation of financial need.

Financial data The stipend is approximately $700 per year.

Duration 1 year; may be renewed.

Number awarded 1 each year.

Deadline May of each year.

[448]
BAPTIST FOUNDATION OF ALABAMA SCHOLARSHIPS

Baptist Foundation of Alabama
Attn: Client Services
7650 Halcyon Summit Drive
P.O. Box 241227
Montgomery, AL 36124-1227
(334) 394-2000   Fax: (334) 394-2039
E-mail: scholarship@tbfa.og
Web: www.tbfa.org/scholarship.html

Summary To provide financial assistance to members of Baptist churches in Alabama who are interested in attending a college or seminary in any state.

Eligibility This program is open to full-time students who are affiliated with a Southern Baptist church in Alabama. Applicants must be attending or planning to attend a college or seminary in any state and have a GPA of 2.0 or higher.

Financial data A stipend is awarded (amount not specified).

Duration 1 year.

Number awarded 1 or more each year.

Deadline March of each year.

[449]
BAPTIST FOUNDATION OF COLORADO SCHOLARSHIPS

Colorado Baptist General Convention
Attn: Baptist Foundation of Colorado
7393 South Alton Way
Centennial, CO 80112-2302
(303) 771-2480, ext. 224
Toll Free: (888) 771-2480, ext. 224
E-mail: dlohrey@cbgc.org
Web: www.baptistfoundationofcolorado.org

Summary To provide financial assistance to members of Southern Baptist churches in Colorado who are interested in attending a college or seminary in any state to prepare for a career in ministry.

Eligibility This program is open to students who are members of Colorado Baptist General Convention home churches. Applicants must be enrolled full time at a Southern Baptist college, university, or seminary in any state to prepare for a church-related vocation. They must have a GPA of 3.0 or higher and be able to demonstrate financial need. Undergraduates must be at least sophomores; seminary students must have completed at least 15 credit hours of study. Along with their application, they must submit 1-paragraph statements that 1) describe their salvation experience, and 2) describe the church-related vocation they are pursuing and why they feel God's call to that vocation.

Financial data A stipend is awarded (amount not specified).

Duration 1 year; may be renewed.

Number awarded Varies each year.

Deadline March of each year.

[450]
BAPTIST FOUNDATION OF ILLINOIS SCHOLARSHIPS

Illinois Baptist State Association
Attn: Baptist Foundation of Illinois
3085 Stevenson Drive
P.O. Box 19247
Springfield, IL 62794-9247
(217) 391-3123   Fax: (217) 585-1029
E-mail: dougmorrow@ibsa.org
Web: www.ibsa.org/ministries/baptistfoundation

Summary To provide financial assistance to Southern Baptists from Illinois who are interested in attending a college or seminary in any state.

Eligibility This program is open to students enrolled or planning to enroll full time at an accredited college, university, or seminary in any state. Applicants must have been an active member for at least 1 year of a church affiliated with the Illinois Baptist State Association. They must be able to demonstrate financial need and the potential for Christian leadership and service. Along with their application, they must submit a statement of personal Christian testimony, including a description of their life and attitudes before they met Christ, how they realized they needed Christ in their life, how they became a Christian, what being a Christian means to them today, and how they might use their vocation as a means to share a Christian witness. Selection is based on academic ability; leadership and participation in church, school, and community activities; vocational clarity; character; and financial need.

Financial data Recently, stipend amounts averaged approximately $1,500.

Duration 1 year.

Number awarded Varies each year. Recently, 33 of these scholarships, with a total value of $49,000, were awarded.

Deadline February of each year.

[451]
BAPTIST GENERAL ASSOCIATION OF VIRGINIA MINISTERIAL EDUCATION FUNDS

Baptist General Association of Virginia
Virginia Baptist Missionary Board
Attn: Shared Ministry Assistant
2828 Emerywood Parkway
Richmond, VA 23294
(804) 915-2439   Toll Free: (800) ALL-BGAV, ext. 6225
Fax: (804) 672-2051   E-mail: scholarships@vbmb.org
Web: www.vbmb.org/Services/Scholarship/default.cfm

Summary To provide financial assistance to Baptist residents of Virginia interested in attending a college or seminary in any state to prepare for a career in ministry.

Eligibility This program is open to students enrolled or planning to enroll at an accredited college, university, or seminary in any state. Applicants must have been active members of a cooperating church of the Baptist General Association of Virginia (BGAV) for at least 1 year. They must be called and committed to religious service as a local church minister, missionary, chaplain, or denominational servant. Preference is given to applicants from Virginia Baptist backgrounds and who plan their ministries in and through Virginia Baptist channels. Students working on an advanced degree beyond the master's level are not eligible. Selection is based on academic ability, Christian service, community service, vocational clarity, BGAV commitment, and financial need.

Financial data The stipend ranges up to $5,000 per year.

Duration 1 year. Full-time students are eligible for up to 4 years of undergraduate study and up to 4 years at the graduate level. Part-time students are eligible for up to 6 years of undergraduate study and up to 6 years at the graduate level.

Additional information Recipients are expected to participate in a practical ministry experience of approximately 2 to 6 hours per week under a mentor approved by the BGAV.

Number awarded 1 or more each year.

Deadline March of each year.

[452]
BAPTIST GENERAL ASSOCIATION OF VIRGINIA NONTRADITIONAL MINISTERIAL EDUCATION SCHOLARSHIPS

Baptist General Association of Virginia
Virginia Baptist Missionary Board
Attn: Shared Ministry Assistant
2828 Emerywood Parkway
Richmond, VA 23294
(804) 915-2439   Toll Free: (800) ALL-BGAV, ext. 6225
Fax: (804) 672-2051   E-mail: scholarships@vbmb.org
Web: www.vbmb.org/Services/Scholarship/default.cfm

Summary To provide financial assistance to Baptist pastors and lay elders in Virginia who are interested in attending designated seminaries for continuing education related to ministry in the local church.

Eligibility This program is open to pastors and lay elders in Virginia who are enrolled or planning to enroll part time at 1 of 6 designated seminaries. Applicants must be active members of a cooperating church of the Baptist General Association of Virginia (BGAV) and their church must contribute financially to the Virginia portion of the Cooperative Missions budget. They must be seeking continuing education for ministry in the local church through a nondegree program of study. Financial need is considered in the selection process.

Financial data Funding covers up to one-third of the cost of a course.

Duration Participants may enroll in up to 3 courses per semester or 6 courses per year. They must reapply each semester.

Additional information The partner institutions are Baptist Theological Seminary at Richmond, John Leland Center for Theological Studies (Falls Church, Virginia), Bluefield College (Bluefield, Virginia), Clear Creek Baptist Bible College (Pineville, Kentucky), or Virginia Intermont College (Bristol, Virginia).

Number awarded Varies each year.

Deadline Applications may be submitted at any time.

[453]
BAPTIST LIFE SCHOLARSHIP GRANTS

Baptist Life Association
Attn: Scholarship Committee
8555 Main Street
Buffalo, NY 14221-7494
(716) 633-4393   Toll Free: (800) 227-8543
Fax: (716) 633-4916
E-mail: memberservice@baptistlife.org
Web: www.baptistlife.org/benefits.html

Summary To provide financial assistance for college or graduate school to insured members of Baptist Life.

Eligibility This program is open to full-time undergraduate and graduate students who have been insured members of Baptist Life for at least 2 years. Applicants must submit a pastoral reference and a statement of personal testimony that provides information about their interests, hobbies, strengths, or any other item that will help the committee get to know them and their walk with God. Selection is based on those submissions, academic achievement, and financial need.

Financial data The stipend is $1,000.

Duration 1 year; may be renewed up to 3 additional years.

Number awarded Several each year.

Deadline May of each year.

[454]
BAPTIST WOMEN IN MINISTRY OF NORTH CAROLINA STUDENT SCHOLARSHIPS

Baptist Women in Ministry of North Carolina
Attn: Geneva Metzger
2604 Overbrook Drive
Greensboro, NC 27408-5313
(336) 288-1877   E-mail: mizzometzger@yahoo.com
Web: www.bwimnc.org/Scholarships.html

Summary To provide financial assistance to women ministerial students enrolled at North Carolina Baptist institutions.

Eligibility This program is open to women working on a graduate degree in theological education at North Carolina Baptist institutions. Applicants must be able to demonstrate a clear call and commitment to vocational Christian ministry, academic excellence, leadership skills, and expressed support of inclusiveness in all dimensions of life.

Financial data The stipend is $1,000.

Duration 1 year.

Additional information The eligible schools include Duke Divinity School, Campbell University Divinity School, M. Christopher White School of Divinity at Gardner-Webb University, and the Wake Forest University Divinity School.

Number awarded 4 each year: 1 at each of the eligible schools.

Deadline Deadline not specified.

[455]
BARBER EDUCATION FUND

Onarga United Methodist Church
Attn: Scholarship Committee
109 East Seminary Avenue
Onarga, IL 60955-1240
(815) 268-4320   Fax: (815) 268-4725
E-mail: oumc109@yahoo.com

Summary To provide financial assistance to students in theological schools, especially Methodists from Illinois, preparing for full-time service to the church.

Eligibility This program is open to students at theological schools working on a degree related to ordained ministry, Christian education, youth ministry, or other specialized ministries within the church. Preference is given to United Methodist students, especially those with roots in the area of Onarga United Methodist Church (Iroquois County, Illinois).

Financial data The stipend ranges from $500 to $1,200.

Duration 1 year.

Number awarded 1 or more each year.

Deadline May of each year.

[456]
BEAVER UNITED METHODIST MEN'S SEMINARY SCHOLARSHIP

Beaver United Methodist Church
Attn: Men's Scholarship Committee
201 Avenue F
P.O. Box 309
Beaver, OK 73932-0309
(580) 625-4514

Summary To provide loans-for-service to members of United Methodist Churches (UMC) in Oklahoma who are attending a seminary in any state to prepare for a career in UMC ministry in Oklahoma.

Eligibility This program is open to students enrolled full time in an accredited and approved seminary or graduate school of theology and working on a degree that qualifies them for ordination in the UMC. Applicants must have been a member of a UMC congregation in Oklahoma for at least 2 years and have been certified as a candidate for ordination, including completion of the psychological assessment and the background check. Selection is based on availability of funding, number of credit hours carried, financial need, and willingness to return to the Oklahoma Annual Conference of the UMC to serve in the ministry.

Financial data The stipend is $2,000 per semester ($4,000 per year). After graduation, recipients are expected to return to the Oklahoma Annual Conference of the UMC to serve in the ministry for at least 3 years. If they fail to fulfill that obligation, they are expected to repay the scholarship money on a pro-rata basis.

Duration 1 semester; may be renewed up to 3 additional semesters.

Number awarded 1 or more each year.

Deadline July of each year.

[457]
BERNICE F. ELLIOTT MEMORIAL SCHOLARSHIP

Baptist Convention of New Mexico
Attn: Missions Mobilization Team
5325 Wyoming Boulevard, N.E.
P.O. Box 94485
Albuquerque, NM 87199-4485
(505) 924-2315   Toll Free: (800) 898-8544
Fax: (505) 924-2320   E-mail: cpairett@bcnm.com
Web: www.bcnm.com

Summary To provide financial assistance to women who are Southern Baptists from New Mexico and interested in attending a college or seminary in any state.

Eligibility This program is open to women college and seminary students who are members of churches affiliated with the Baptist Convention of New Mexico. Preference is given to applicants who are committed to full-time Christian service, have a background in the Woman's Missionary Union, and can demonstrate financial need.

Financial data A stipend is awarded (amount not specified).

Duration 1 year; may be renewed.

Number awarded 1 or more each year.

Deadline March of each year.

[458]
BESSIE BELLAMY PARKER SCHOLARSHIPS

South Carolina United Methodist Foundation
P.O. Box 5087
Columbia, SC 29250-5087
(803) 771-9125   Fax: (803) 771-9135
E-mail: scumf@bellsouth.net
Web: www.umcsc.org/scholarships.html

Summary To provide financial assistance to female Methodist seminary students from South Carolina.

Eligibility This program is open to women from South Carolina who are certified candidates for ministry in the United Methodist Church. Applicants must have completed at least 1 year of full-time enrollment in an approved United Methodist seminary with a grade point average of "C" or higher. They must be planning to work in a local church setting. Selection is based (in descending order of importance) on self-understanding of ministry and intended future direction, promise for ministry, financial need, and academic performance in seminary.

Financial data A stipend is awarded (amount not specified).

Duration 1 year.

Additional information This scholarship was established by the South Carolina Conference of the United Methodist Church in 1986.

Number awarded 1 or more each year.

Deadline April of each year.

[459]
BISHOP CHARLES F. GOLDEN SCHOLARSHIP

United Methodist Church-California-Pacific Annual
  Conference
Attn: Board of Ordained Ministry
1720 East Linfield Street
Glendora, CA 91740
(626) 335-6629   Fax: (626) 335-5750
E-mail: cathy.adminbom@gmail.com
Web: www.calpacordainedministry.org/523451

Summary To provide loans-for-service to ministerial candidates under the care of the California-Pacific Annual Conference of the United Methodist Church (UMC) who are attending a seminary in any state.

Eligibility This program is open to certified ministerial candidates and probationary members in good standing in the UMC California-Pacific Annual Conference who are under the care of its Board of Ordained Ministry or related to a District Committee. Applicants must be attending a seminary in any state approved by the UMC University Senate. They must be able to demonstrate financial need.

Financial data The award is $550 per semester for full-time students or a pro-rated amount for part-time students. Awards are issued as interest-free loans but convert to a grant after 2 years of full-time service under a UMC District Superintendent.

Duration 1 semester; recipients may reapply.

Additional information The California-Pacific Annual Conference includes churches in southern California, Hawaii, Guam, and Saipan.

Number awarded Varies each year.

Deadline August of each year for fall term; December of each year for spring term.

[460]
BISHOP CHARLES P. GRECO GRADUATE FELLOWSHIPS

Knights of Columbus
Attn: Committee on Fellowships
P.O. Box 1670
New Haven, CT 06507-0901
(203) 752-4332   Fax: (203) 772-2696
E-mail: info@kofc.org
Web: www.kofc.org/un/en/scholarships/greco.html

Summary To provide financial assistance to members of the Knights of Columbus and their families who are interested in working on a graduate degree to prepare for a career as a teacher of people with intellectual disabilities.

Eligibility This program is open to members as well as to their wives, sons, and daughters and to the widows and children of deceased members. Applicants must be working full time on a master's degree to prepare for a career as a teacher of people with intellectual disabilities. They must be at the beginning of their graduate program. Special consideration is given to applicants who select a Catholic graduate school.

Financial data The stipend is $500 per semester ($1,000 per year), payable to the university.

Duration 1 semester; may be renewed for up to 3 additional semesters.

Additional information This program was established in 1973.

Deadline April of each year.

[461]
BISHOP FRANK MURPHY SCHOLARSHIP FOR WOMEN IN MINISTRY

Women's Ordination Conference
Attn: Scholarship Committee
P.O. Box 15057
Washington, DC 20003
(202) 675-1006   Fax: (202) 675-1008
E-mail: woc@womensordination.org
Web: www.womensordination.org/content/view/38/66

Summary To provide financial assistance to members of the Women's Ordination Conference (WOC) who are working on a graduate degree to prepare for Catholic ministry.

Eligibility This program is open to women who are members of the WOC. Applicants must be enrolled or accepted in a graduate program at a seminary or a diocesan certificate program preparing for Catholic priestly ministry. They must submit a letter of recommendation from a mentor who can testify to their commitment to WOC's goals, a personal statement of how their future ministry supports WOC's mission, a resume or curriculum vitae, and proof of enrollment.

Financial data The stipend is $1,000. Funds must be used for educational expenses.

Duration 1 year.

Additional information The WOC is an organization "working locally and nationally in collaboration with the world-wide movement for women's ordination." In pursuit of its goals, it "works for justice and equality for women in our church; strives to eliminate all forms of domination and discrimination in the Catholic church; advocates inclusive church structures; supports and affirms women's talents, gifts and calls to ministry." Recipients are required to submit a report at the end of the grant period explaining how the award impacted their study and growth.

Number awarded 2 or more each year.

Deadline January of each year.

[462]
BISHOP JAMES C. BAKER AWARD

United Methodist Church
Attn: General Board of Higher Education and Ministry
Office of Loans and Scholarships
1001 19th Avenue South
P.O. Box 340007
Nashville, TN 37203-0007
(615) 340-7344   Fax: (615) 340-7367
E-mail: umscholar@gbhem.org
Web: www.gbhem.org/loansandscholarships

Summary To provide financial assistance to United Methodist campus ministers who are interested in a program of advanced study.

Eligibility This program is open to campus ministers in higher education who have at least 3 years of experience in campus ministry and expect to remain in the profession. Applicants must have been active, full members of a United Methodist Church for at least 3 years prior to applying. They must have an M.Div. degree and be interested in a program of advanced study. U.S. citizenship or permanent resident status is required.

Financial data The stipend is $5,000.

Duration 1 year; recipients may reapply.

Number awarded Varies each year. Recently, 2 of these scholarships were awarded.

Deadline January of each year.

[463]
BISHOP THOMAS HOYT, JR. FELLOWSHIP

St. John's University
Attn: Collegeville Institute for Ecumenical and Cultural Research
14027 Fruit Farm Road
Box 2000
Collegeville, MN 56321-2000
(320) 363-3366   Fax: (320) 363-3313
E-mail: staff@CollegevilleInstitute.org
Web: collegevilleinstitute.org/res-fellowships

Summary   To provide funding to students of color who wish to complete their doctoral dissertation while in residence at the Collegeville Institute for Ecumenical and Cultural Research of St. John's University in Collegeville, Minnesota.
Eligibility   This program is open to people of color completing a doctoral dissertation in ecumenical and cultural research. Applicants must be interested in a residency at the Collegeville Institute for Ecumenical and Cultural Research of St. John's University. Along with their application, they must submit a 1,000-word description of the research project they plan to complete while in residence at the Institute.
Financial data   The stipend covers the residency fee of $2,000, which includes housing and utilities.
Duration   1 year.
Additional information   Residents at the Institute engage in research, publication, and education on the important intersections between faith and culture. They seek to discern and communicate the meaning of Christian identity and unity in a religiously and culturally diverse world.
Number awarded   1 each year.
Deadline   October of each year.

[464]
BISHOP THOMAS V. DAILY VOCATIONS SCHOLARSHIPS

Knights of Columbus
Attn: Department of Scholarships
P.O. Box 1670
New Haven, CT 06507-0901
(203) 752-4332   Fax: (203) 772-2696
E-mail: info@kofc.org
Web: www.kofc.org/un/en/vocations/scholarships.html

Summary   To provide financial assistance to seminary students preparing for a vocation as a Catholic priest.
Eligibility   This program is open to students enrolled in approved seminaries in the United States and Canada. Applicants must be preparing for a vocation in the Catholic priesthood. Selection is based on merit. Preference is given to seminarians who are members of the Knights of Columbus or whose fathers are members, but all qualified applicants are considered.
Financial data   The stipend is $2,500 per year; funds must be used for tuition, room, and board.
Duration   1 year; may be renewed up to 3 additional years.
Additional information   This program was established in 1992.
Number awarded   Varies each year. Recently, 11 new scholarships (9 to students at U.S. seminaries and 2 to students at Canadian seminaries) were awarded.
Deadline   May of each year.

[465]
B.J. DEAN SCHOLARSHIP

Community Foundation of Middle Tennessee
Attn: Scholarship Committee
3833 Cleghorn Avenue, Suite 400
Nashville, TN 37215-2519
(615) 321-4939   Toll Free: (888) 540-5200
Fax: (615) 327-2746   E-mail: mail@cfmt.org
Web: www.cfmt.org/scholarships

Summary   To provide financial assistance to women from Tennessee or Texas preparing for a career in the ministry at a seminary in any state.
Eligibility   This program is open to women from Tennessee or Texas interested in entering the ministry; students enrolled at Yale Divinity School are also eligible. Applicants must be preparing for full-time ministry but not necessarily seeking ordination. They must be planning to enroll full time at a seminary in any state. There are no denominational restrictions. Along with their application, they must submit an essay describing their educational plans and how those plans will help them reach their career goals. Financial need is considered in the selection process.
Financial data   Stipends range from $500 to $2,500 per year. Funds are paid to the recipient's school and must be used for tuition, fees, books, supplies, room, board, or miscellaneous expenses.
Duration   1 year; recipients may reapply.
Additional information   This fund was established in 1995.
Number awarded   1 or more each year.
Deadline   March of each year.

[466]
BOARD HIGHER EDUCATION ON CAMPUS MINISTRY SCHOLARSHIP

United Methodist Church-Oklahoma Conference
Attn: Campus Ministry Office
1501 N.W. 24th Street
Oklahoma, OK 73106-3635
(405) 530-2013   Toll Free: (800) 231-4166, ext. 2013
Fax: (405) 525-4164   E-mail: lmachalek@okumc.org
Web: www.okumcministries.org

Summary   To provide financial assistance to undergraduate and graduate Methodist students from Oklahoma who plan to attend college, graduate school, or seminary in any state.
Eligibility   This program is open to undergraduate and graduate students who are members of congregations affiliated with the Oklahoma Conference of the United Methodist Church. Applicants must be enrolled or planning to enroll as a full-time student at a college, university, graduate school, or seminary in any state. Selection is based on academic excellence, participation in church activities, and financial need.
Financial data   The stipend is $500.
Duration   1 year.
Number awarded   1 or more each year.
Deadline   April of each year.

[467]
BOHNETT MEMORIAL FOUNDATION SCHOLARSHIPS

Violet R. and Nada V. Bohnett Memorial Foundation
Attn: Jamie Bohnett, Director
7981 168th Avenue, N.E., Suite 220
Redmond, WA 98052
(425) 883-0208   Fax: (425) 883-2729
E-mail: jnbohnett@aol.com
Web: www.bohnettmemorialfoundation.org

Summary To provide financial assistance for college or graduate school in any field to students in selected western states who are "people of faith."

Eligibility This program is open to undergraduate and graduate students who "profess a genuine faith in Jesus Christ" and are interested in addressing the needs of fragile families today. Applicants must have demonstrated a pattern of volunteer service in their church or community. Preference is given to residents of western Washington, but residents of California, Colorado, and Hawaii are also eligible.

Financial data Stipends range from $1,000 to $1,500.

Duration 1 year.

Number awarded Several each year.

Deadline Deadline not specified.

[468]
BONNIE RUTH HOLLEY MEMORIAL SCHOLARSHIP

United Methodist Church-Louisiana Conference
Attn: Coordinator, Conference Board of Ordained Ministry
527 North Boulevard
Baton Rouge, LA 70802-5700
(225) 346-1646, ext. 230
Toll Free: (888) 239-5286, ext. 230
Fax: (225) 383-2652   E-mail: johneddd@bellsouth.net
Web: www.la-umc.org

Summary To provide financial assistance to Methodists from Louisiana who are attending a seminary in any state to prepare for a career in ordained ministry.

Eligibility This program is open to members of United Methodist Churches in Louisiana who are enrolled or planning to enroll full time at a seminary in any state. Applicants must be able to demonstrate promise for ordained ministry and articulate vocational goals in service to the church. Along with their application, they must submit an essay on their vocational goals and plans for ministry.

Financial data The stipend is $2,500.

Duration 1 year.

Number awarded 1 each year.

Deadline February of each year.

[469]
BOTKIN FOUNDATION AWARDS

United Methodist Church-California-Pacific Annual
  Conference
Attn: Board of Ordained Ministry
1720 East Linfield Street
Glendora, CA 91740
(626) 335-6629   Fax: (626) 335-5750
E-mail: cathy.adminbom@gmail.com
Web: www.calpacordainedministry.org/523451

Summary To provide financial assistance to ministerial candidates under the care of the California-Pacific Annual Conference of the United Methodist Church (UMC) who are attending a seminary in any state.

Eligibility This program is open to certified ministerial candidates and probationary members in good standing in the UMC California-Pacific Annual Conference who are under the care of its Board of Ordained Ministry or related to a District Committee. Applicants must be enrolled full time at a semi-nary in any state approved by the UMC University Senate. They must be able to demonstrate financial need.

Financial data The stipend is $2,000.

Duration 1 year.

Additional information The California-Pacific Annual Conference includes churches in southern California, Hawaii, Guam, and Saipan.

Number awarded Varies each year.

Deadline August of each year.

[470]
BOWEN CHARITABLE TRUST SCHOLARSHIPS

West Virginia Baptist Convention
1019 Juliana Street
P.O. Box 1019
Parkersburg, WV 26102-1019
(304) 422-6449   Fax: (304) 485-0940
Web: bowentrust.org

Summary To provide financial assistance to undergraduate and graduate students from West Virginia who are preparing for a career of vocational ministry within the American Baptist Church USA.

Eligibility This program is open to undergraduate and graduate students who are preparing to dedicate their lives to Christian service in vocational ministry, including as a pastor, associate/assistant pastor, minister of Christian education, music, worship, youth, pastoral care, or family life, Christian counselor, or chaplain. Scholarships are granted in the following order of priority: 1) members of Calvary Baptist Church in Charleston, West Virginia and/or First Baptist Church of Clendenin, West Virginia; 2) members of other churches in the Kanawha Valley Association of the West Virginia Baptist Convention; 3) members of other churches in the West Virginia Baptist Convention; 4) members of the Mount Lebanon Baptist Church in Mount Lebanon, Pennsylvania; and 5) members of other American Baptist USA churches. Preference is also given to students at Alderson Broaddus College (Philippi, West Virginia) and Eastern University or Palmer Seminary (Philadelphia, Pennsylvania). Applicants must submit documentation of financial need and an essay on their call to ministry.

Financial data A stipend is awarded (amount not specified). Funding does not exceed the cost of tuition, housing, meals, books, and fees for a student living on campus in campus housing.

Duration 1 year; may be renewed for the maximum number of years for the course of study.

Number awarded Varies each year.

Deadline Applications may be submitted at any time, but they must be received at least 90 days prior to the beginning of the school term for which funding is requested.

[471]
CALIFORNIA EASTERN STAR TRAINING AWARDS FOR RELIGIOUS LEADERSHIP

Order of the Eastern Star-Grand Chapter of California
Attn: Scholarship Committee
16960 Bastanchury Road, Suite E
Yorba Linda, CA 92886-1711
(714) 986-2380   Fax: (714) 986-2385
Web: www.oescal.org/CESF/applications.htm

Summary To provide financial assistance to residents of California, especially those with a Masonic connection, interested in attending a seminary or theological college in any state.
Eligibility This program is open to California residents who are college graduates desiring to enter or continue in a theological college or seminary in any state. Applicants must be U.S. citizens and have a GPA of 3.0 or higher. Along with their application, they must submit 150-word essays on their educational goals, reasons for choice of school, and how this scholarship will help them with their education. Applications are encouraged from members of Masonic organizations (such as Eastern Star, DeMolay, Job's Daughters, and Rainbow Girls). Selection is based on academic record; honors and awards; extracurricular and community activities; service to church, synagogue, and/or religious organization; and financial need.
Financial data A stipend is awarded (amount not specified).
Duration 1 year; may be renewed.
Number awarded Varies each year.
Deadline February of each year.

[472]
CALIFORNIA-NEVADA ANNUAL CONFERENCE STUDENT SCHOLARSHIP GRANTS

United Methodist Church-California-Nevada Annual
 Conference
Attn: Board of Ordained Ministry
1276 Halyard Drive
P.O. Box 980250
West Sacramento, CA 95798-0250
(916) 374-1500   Fax: (916) 372-5544
Web: www.cnumc.org/forms/detail/275

Summary To provide financial assistance to students at seminaries in any state who are under care of a United Methodist Church (UMC) local church in its California-Nevada Annual Conference.
Eligibility This program is open to UMC students who are declared or certified candidates for ministry in the California-Nevada Annual Conference (which serves northern California and Nevada). Applicants must be enrolled at a seminary in any state that is recognized by the UMC Academic Senate. They must have met at least once with their district committee on ordained ministry. Selection is based on financial need, missional priorities, and evidence of sound personal financial practices.
Financial data Stipends range up to $3,000.
Duration 1 year.
Number awarded Varies each year.
Deadline March of each year.

[473]
CALIHAN ACADEMIC FELLOWSHIPS

Acton Institute for the Study of Religion and Liberty
161 Ottawa N.W., Suite 301
Grand Rapids, MI 49503
(616) 454-3080   Toll Free: (800) 345-2286
Fax: (616) 454-9454   E-mail: scholarships@acton.org
Web: www.acton.org

Summary To provide financial assistance to seminarians and graduate students who have an interest in the relationship between religious and classical liberal ideas.
Eligibility This program is open to seminarians and graduate students working on a degree in theology, philosophy, religion, economics, or related fields at an institution in the United States. Applicants must be able to demonstrate strong academic performance, an interest in the relationship between religious and classical liberal ideas, and the potential to contribute to the advancement of a free and virtuous society. Along with their application, they must submit a 2-page essay on their intellectual development, future plans, and career goals, including the source and development of their interest in religion and its relationship to liberty and how they expect to contribute to an understanding of those ideas. Selection is based on that essay, 2 letters of reference, transcripts, and other academic funding.
Financial data The maximum stipend is $3,000.
Duration 1 year; recipients may reapply.
Number awarded 1 or more each year.
Deadline July or October of each year.

[474]
CALIHAN TRAVEL GRANTS

Acton Institute for the Study of Religion and Liberty
161 Ottawa N.W., Suite 301
Grand Rapids, MI 49503
(616) 454-3080   Toll Free: (800) 345-2286
Fax: (616) 454-9454   E-mail: scholarships@acton.org
Web: www.acton.org/programs/students/calihan_travel.php

Summary To provide funding to seminarians and graduate students who have been selected either to present, at an academic conference, research related to integrating religious ideas with principles of the classical liberal tradition or to conduct research on such a topic.
Eligibility This program is open to seminarians and graduate students working on a degree in theology, philosophy, religion, economics, or related fields at an institution in the United States. Applicants must have been selected to present, at an academic conference, a paper on their research that contributes to an understanding or application of the relationship between religion and liberty. Students who need to travel to, and conduct research at, archives or libraries are also eligible. The proposal should include 2 academic references, an estimate of expenses, and information on other sources of funding for the conference and/or travel.
Financial data The maximum grant is $3,000.
Duration This is a 1-time grant.
Number awarded 1 or more each year.
Deadline Applications may be submitted at any time.

[475]
CAMPBELL TRUST STUDENT LOAN PROGRAM

Florida United Methodist Foundation, Inc.
Attn: Scholarship Committee
450 Martin Luther King Jr. Avenue
P.O. Box 3549
Lakeland, FL 33802-3549
(863) 904-2970   Toll Free: (866) 363-9673
Fax: (863) 904-0169   E-mail: Foundation@fumf.org
Web: www.fumc.org/InfoForIndividuals/StudentLoans

Summary To provide educational loans to Methodist college and seminary students from Florida.

Eligibility This program is open to Methodist students enrolled full time at a junior college, senior college, university, seminary, or other postsecondary institution for educational or occupational training. First priority is given to Florida residents attending institutions related to the United Methodist Church in Florida. Second priority is given to Florida residents attending institutions related to the United Methodist Church outside of Florida. Third priority is given to Florida residents attending non-church-related institutions. Final priority is given to non-Florida residents attending church-related institutions.

Financial data The amount of the loan depends on the availability of funds and the number of approved applicants.

Duration 1 year.

Number awarded Varies each year.

Deadline July of each year for fall term; November of each year for spring term.

[476]
CANNON ENDOWMENT SCHOLARSHIP

United Church of Christ
Parish Life and Leadership Ministry Team
Attn: Grants, Scholarships, and Resources
700 Prospect Avenue East
Cleveland, OH 44115-1100
(216) 736-3839   Toll Free: (866) 822-8224, ext. 3839
Fax: (216) 736-3783   E-mail: jeffersv@ucc.org
Web: www.ucc.org/seminarians/ucc-scholarships-for.html

Summary To provide financial assistance to seminary students who are interested in becoming a military chaplain.

Eligibility This program is open to students at accredited seminaries who are affiliated with the Christian Church (Disciples of Christ), Presbyterian Church (USA), United Church of Christ, or United Methodist Church. Applicants must be planning to become military chaplains.

Financial data The stipend is approximately $2,500.

Duration 1 year.

Additional information This program was established in 1992.

Number awarded Varies each year. Recently, 3 of these scholarships were awarded.

Deadline Deadline not specified.

[477]
CARDINAL BERNARD F. LAW SCHOLARSHIP

Knights of Columbus-Missouri State Council
c/o J.Y. Miller, Scholarship Committee Chair
322 Second Street
Glasgow, MO 65254
(660) 338-2105   E-mail: j.y.miller@sbcglobal.net
Web: www.mokofc.org/youth.htm

Summary To provide financial assistance to Catholic residents of Missouri who plan to prepare for a religious vocation by attending seminary in any state.

Eligibility This program is open to residents of Missouri who are enrolled or planning to enroll at an accredited seminary in any state. Applicants must be preparing for a religious vocation with the approval of a Missouri Catholic diocese or a religious order in the state. Along with their application, they must submit a 200-word statement explaining their goals for the future, their professional ambitions, and how this scholarship will help them to achieve their goals. Selection is based on Catholic citizenship, community service, scholarship, and financial need.

Financial data The stipend is $1,000.

Duration 1 year.

Additional information This program was established in 1984.

Number awarded 1 each year.

Deadline February of each year.

[478]
CARL H. BOSSMAN SCHOLARSHIPS

Presbytery of the Twin Cities Area
Attn: Committee on Preparation for Ministry
122 West Franklin Avenue, Suite 508
Minneapolis, MN 55404
(612) 871-7281, ext. 18
Toll Free: (888) 323-4714, ext. 18
Fax: (612) 871-0698   E-mail: pamm@ptcaweb.org
Web: www.ptcaweb.org

Summary To provide financial assistance to Presbyterians in selected areas of Minnesota and Wisconsin who are interested in working on a master's degree in divinity or religious education.

Eligibility Applicants must be candidates or inquirers who are in a covenant relationship with the Presbytery of the Twin Cities Area (which serves western Wisconsin and southeastern Minnesota). They must be working on an academic degree in divinity or religious education at a seminary approved by the presbytery. Preference is given to applicants from St. Croix County, Wisconsin, and to applicants who are inclined to serve smaller congregations. Selection is based primarily on financial need.

Financial data Stipends depend on the availability of funds and the number of potential recipients. Recently, approximately $5,200 has been available for scholarships each year.

Duration 1 year.

Number awarded 1 or more each year.

Deadline January of each year.

[479]
CARL J. SANDERS MINISTERIAL SCHOLARSHIP FUND

Alabama-West Florida United Methodist Foundation, Inc.
170 Belmont Drive
P.O. Box 8066
Dothan, AL 36304
(334) 793-6820   Fax: (334) 794-6480
E-mail: foundation@alwfumf.org
Web: www.alwfumf.org

Summary To provide financial assistance to ministerial students from the Alabama-West Florida Conference of the United Methodist Church.

Eligibility This program is open to members of United Methodist Churches within the Alabama-West Florida Conference. Applicants must be enrolled in the third year at an approved seminary and demonstrate a clear intent to return to the conference in service as ordained United Methodist clergy. They must be younger than 32 years of age. Financial need is considered in the selection process.

Financial data The stipend depends on the need of the recipient and the number of applicants but does not exceed the actual cost of tuition and books.

Duration 1 year.

Number awarded 1 or more each year.

Deadline June of each year.

[480]
CAROLYN WEATHERFORD SCHOLARSHIP FUND

Woman's Missionary Union
Attn: WMU Foundation
100 Missionary Ridge
Birmingham, AL 35242
(205) 408-5525   Toll Free: (877) 482-4483
Fax: (205) 408-5508   E-mail: wmufoundation@wmu.org
Web: www.wmufoundation.com

Summary To provide an opportunity for women to work on a graduate degree or an internship so they can engage in activities of the Woman's Missionary Union (WMU).

Eligibility This program is open to women who are members of the Baptist Church and are attending or planning to attend a Southern Baptist seminary or divinity school at the graduate level or participate in an internship. Applicants must be interested in 1) field work experience as interns or in women's missionary work in the United States; or 2) service in women's missionary work in the United States. They must arrange for 3 letters of endorsement, from a recent professor, a state or associational WMU official, and a recent pastor. Selection is based on current active involvement in WMU, previous activity in WMU, plans for long-term involvement in WMU and/or home missions, academic strength, leadership skills, and personal and professional characteristics.

Financial data A stipend is awarded (amount not specified).

Duration 1 year.

Number awarded 1 or more each year.

Deadline February of each year.

[481]
CATHOLIC BIBLICAL ASSOCIATION OF AMERICA ARCHAEOLOGY RESEARCH STIPENDS

Catholic Biblical Association of America
Attn: Executive Secretary
Catholic University of America
433 Caldwell Hall
Washington, DC 20064
(202) 319-5519   Fax: (202) 319-4799
E-mail: cua-cathbib@cua.edu
Web: cba.cua.edu/archstipends.cfm

Summary To provide funding to members of the Catholic Biblical Association of America (CBA) interested in conducting doctoral or postdoctoral research in archaeology at a dig in any country.

Eligibility This program is open to active and associate members of CBA who either are full-time doctoral students in biblical studies or related areas or have received a doctorate in those areas. Applicants must have been accepted, at least provisionally, for a specific, high-quality dig in any country.

They must submit a description of the area of inquiry they intend to pursue in conjunction with the dig or at least a description of what they expect to find. Financial need is considered in the selection process.

Financial data The grant is $3,000.

Duration 1 archaeological season; may be renewed for a second season.

Number awarded 3 each year.

Deadline February of each year.

[482]
CATHOLIC BIBLICAL ASSOCIATION OF AMERICA MEMORIAL STIPENDS

Catholic Biblical Association of America
Attn: Executive Secretary
Catholic University of America
433 Caldwell Hall
Washington, DC 20064
(202) 319-5519   Fax: (202) 319-4799
E-mail: cua-cathbib@cua.edu
Web: cba.cua.edu/memstip.cfm

Summary To provide financial assistance to doctoral candidates, especially members of the Catholic Biblical Association of America (CBA), interested in working on a degree in biblical studies.

Eligibility This program is open to students who hold a tuition scholarship in a doctoral program involving biblical studies. Preference is given to actual or prospective CBA members. Selection is based on achievement, promise in biblical studies, and financial need.

Financial data The stipend is $4,000 per year.

Duration 1 year; may be renewed up to 4 additional years.

Number awarded 12 each year.

Deadline November of each year.

[483]
CATHOLIC BIBLICAL ASSOCIATION OF AMERICA SCHOLARSHIP GRANTS

Catholic Biblical Association of America
Attn: Executive Secretary
Catholic University of America
433 Caldwell Hall
Washington, DC 20064
(202) 319-5519   Fax: (202) 319-4799
E-mail: cua-cathbib@cua.edu
Web: cba.cua.edu/scholar.cfm

Summary To provide financial assistance to members of the Catholic Biblical Association of America (CBA) interested in working on a doctoral degree at designated institutions.

Eligibility This program is open to associate members of CBA who are enrolled or planning to enroll full time at Catholic University of America, the Graduate Theological Union at Berkeley, the University of Notre Dame, or Fordham University. Applicants must be planning to work on a doctoral degree in biblical studies. They must be nominated by their university.

Financial data The program provides full payment of tuition to the institution and a stipend of $15,500 per year to the student.

Duration 1 year; may be renewed up to 4 additional years.

Additional information This program consists of the Patrick W. Skehan and Louis F. Hartman, C.Ss.R. Scholarship at Catholic University of America, the Raymond F. Brown, S.S. Scholarship at the Graduate Theological Union, the Bruce Vawter, C.M. Scholarship at Notre Dame, and the Roland E. Murphy, O.Carm. Scholarship at Fordham.

Number awarded Up to 4 each year.

Deadline Deadline not specified.

[484]
CENTENNIAL UNITED METHODIST CHURCH DIVINITY SCHOLARSHIP

Centennial United Methodist Church
Attn: Foundation Scholarship Committee
1524 West County Road C-2
Roseville, MN 55113-1600
(651) 633-7644   Fax: (651) 633-2715
E-mail: cumc@centennialumc.org
Web: www.centennialumc.org

Summary To provide financial assistance to seminary students who plan to serve in the Minnesota Annual Conference of the United Methodist Church.

Eligibility This program is open to students enrolled in a seminary or graduate school approved by the University Senate of the United Methodist Church. Applicants must be planning to serve in the Minnesota Annual Conference of the United Methodist Church after graduation as a full-time minister. They must already have a relationship with that conference, as an inquiring candidate, exploring candidate, declared candidate for licensing or ordination, or certified candidate. Selection is based on professional promise and financial need.

Financial data Stipends range from $500 to $2,000.

Duration 1 year.

Additional information This program was established in 1971 as the Johnson-Kitts Scholarship. It now includes the Rosa Krogh Christian Education Scholarship and the Eileen Tichenor Scholarship.

Number awarded Varies each year. Recently, 6 of these scholarships were awarded.

Deadline October of each year.

[485]
CHAMPIONS FOR CHRIST SCHOLARSHIPS

Champions for Christ Foundation, Inc.
P.O. Box 786
Greenville, SC 29602-0786
(864) 294-0800   E-mail: contact@championsforchrist.us
Web: www.championsforchrist.us

Summary To provide financial assistance to students interested in working on an undergraduate or graduate degree to prepare for full time Christian ministry.

Eligibility This program is open to high school seniors, undergraduates, and graduate students "who have surrendered their lives to full-time Christian service." Applicants must submit a letter of recommendation from their pastor, a personal statement of their salvation experience and call to the ministry, and a statement of doctrinal beliefs. Financial need is considered in the selection process.

Financial data A stipend is awarded (amount not specified).

Duration 1 year; may be renewed.

Number awarded Varies each year.

Deadline June of each year for fall term; October of each year for winter or spring term; March of each year for summer term.

[486]
CHARLES AND PAMELA AVERY SCHOLARSHIP TRUST

Alabama-West Florida United Methodist Foundation, Inc.
170 Belmont Drive
P.O. Box 8066
Dothan, AL 36304
(334) 793-6820   Fax: (334) 794-6480
E-mail: foundation@alwfumf.org
Web: www.alwfumf.org

Summary To provide financial assistance to ministerial students and local pastors from the Alabama-West Florida Conference of the United Methodist Church.

Eligibility This program is open to members of United Methodist Churches within the Alabama-West Florida Conference who are either ministerial students or licensed full-time local pastors. Applicants must be attending an approved seminary with the clear intent to remain in, or return to, the Conference for the purpose of ministry to its churches. Financial need is considered in the selection process.

Financial data The stipend varies each year.

Duration 1 year.

Number awarded 1 or more each year.

Deadline June of each year.

[487]
CHARLES B. KEESEE EDUCATIONAL FUND MINISTERIAL STUDENT GRANTS

Charles B. Keesee Educational Fund, Inc.
P.O. Box 431
Martinsville, VA 24114
(276) 632-2229   Fax: (276) 632-8826
E-mail: cbkeesee@earthlink.net
Web: www.cbkeesee.net

Summary To provide financial assistance to residents of North Carolina, South Carolina, and Virginia who attend designated Southern Baptist seminaries.

Eligibility This program is open to U.S. citizens who have been residents of North Carolina, South Carolina, or Virginia for at least 12 months prior to entering college. Applicants must be working on or planning to work on a master's degree at 1 of the following Southern Baptist seminaries: Southeastern Baptist Theological Seminary (Wake Forest, North Carolina); Southern Baptist Theological Seminary (Louisville, Kentucky); Southwestern Baptist Theological Seminary (Fort Worth, Texas); New Orleans Baptist Theological Seminary (New Orleans, Louisiana); Midwestern Baptist Theological Seminary (Kansas City, Missouri); Golden Gate Baptist Theological Seminary (Mill Valley, California); Baptist Theological Seminary at Richmond (Richmond, Virginia), Campbell University Divinity School (Buies Creek, North Carolina), The Leland Center (Arlington, Virginia), or M. Christopher White School of Divinity at Gardner-Webb University (Boiling Springs, North Carolina). Applicants must be preparing for a career in full-time ministry or religious work in the Baptist denomination. Along with their application, they must submit a brief statement that covers their most recent class grades for the term or session, seminary or other school activities, church activities, efforts at self-help, and life plans and purposes. They must also be able to document financial need. Spouses of Baptist ministers who are not employed in secular work and devote their lives to assisting with their spouses' ministry are also eligible.

Financial data The stipend is $4,500 per year.

Duration 1 year; may be renewed up to 3 additional years.

Additional information This program was established in 1941. Full-time religious work may include preaching, pastoral duties, local church music and youth ministry, teaching Bible and religion, missionary work, or similar activities. Eligible programs include a M.Div. degree, as well as a master of arts in Christian education, missiology, intercultural studies, church music, Biblical languages, Islamic studies, worship, or international church planting. Recipients who do not enter full-time religious work in the Baptist denomination are morally obligated to return all grants they have received.

Number awarded Approximately 700 of these grants, worth more than $3 million, are awarded each year.

Deadline March of each year for fall and spring semesters; September of each year for spring semester only.

[488]
CHARLES ZARIGIAN, ESQ. MEMORIAL AWARD

Armenian Students' Association
Attn: Scholarship Committee
333 Atlantic Avenue
Warwick, RI 02888
(401) 461-6114　　　　　　　　Fax: (401) 461-6112
E-mail: headasa@aol.com
Web: www.asainc.org/national/scholarships.shtml

Summary To provide financial assistance to students of Armenian ancestry, especially those working on an undergraduate or graduate degree in law, teaching, or Christian ministry.

Eligibility This program is open to undergraduate and graduate students of Armenian descent who have completed at least the first year of college; preference is given to those working on a degree in law, teaching, or Christian ministry. Applicants must be enrolled full time at a 4-year college or university or a 2-year college and planning to transfer to a 4-year institution in the following fall. They must be a U.S. citizen or have appropriate visa status to study in the United States. Along with their application, they must submit a 300-word essay about themselves, including their future plans. Financial need is considered in the selection process.

Financial data The stipends range from $500 to $2,500.

Duration 1 year.

Additional information There is a $15 application fee.

Number awarded 1 each year.

Deadline March of each year.

[489]
CHARLESTON HEIGHTS BAPTIST CHURCH SCHOLARSHIP

Woman's Missionary Union
Attn: WMU Foundation
100 Missionary Ridge
Birmingham, AL 35242
(205) 408-5525　　　　　　　　Toll Free: (877) 482-4483
Fax: (205) 408-5508　　　E-mail: wmufoundation@wmu.org
Web: www.wmufoundation.com

Summary To provide financial assistance for undergraduate or graduate study to the dependent children of Southern Baptist missionaries, especially those from South Carolina.

Eligibility This program is open to Southern Baptist students who are working on an undergraduate or graduate degree in any field. Applicants must be dependents of international missionaries who are under appointment of the North American Mission Board (NAMB) of the Southern Baptist Convention. Preference is given to missionaries from South Carolina.

Financial data A stipend is awarded (amount not specified).

Duration 1 year.

Number awarded Varies each year.

Deadline January of each year.

[490]
CHARLOTTE BRENT MEMORIAL SCHOLARSHIP

United Methodist Church-Louisiana Conference
Attn: Coordinator, Conference Board of Ordained Ministry
527 North Boulevard
Baton Rouge, LA 70802-5700
(225) 346-1646, ext. 230
Toll Free: (888) 239-5286, ext. 230
Fax: (225) 383-2652　　　E-mail: johneddd@bellsouth.net
Web: www.la-umc.org

Summary To provide financial assistance to women from Louisiana who are attending a Methodist seminary in any state to prepare for a career in ordained ministry.

Eligibility This program is open to female members of United Methodist Churches in Louisiana who are enrolled or planning to enroll full time at a Methodist seminary in any state. Applicants must be beginning a second career as an ordained minister. Along with their application, they must submit an essay on their vocational goals and plans for ministry.

Financial data The stipend is $1,000.

Duration 1 year.

Number awarded 1 each year.

Deadline February of each year.

[491]
CHILDREN OF MISSIONARIES SCHOLARSHIPS

Presbyterian Church (USA)
Attn: Office of Financial Aid for Studies
100 Witherspoon Street, Room M-052
Louisville, KY 40202-1396
(502) 569-5224　　　Toll Free: (888) 728-7228, ext. 5224
Fax: (502) 569-8766　　　　　　E-mail: finaid@pcusa.org
Web: www.pcusa.org

Summary To provide financial assistance for college or graduate school to children of Presbyterian missionaries.

Eligibility This program is open to students whose parents are engaged in active service as foreign missionaries for the Presbyterian Church (USA). Applicants must be full-time undergraduate or graduate students at an accredited institution in the United States and have a GPA of 2.5 or higher. They must be able to demonstrate financial need. U.S. citizenship or permanent resident status and membership in the PCUSA are also required.

Financial data Stipends range up to $1,500 per year, depending upon the financial need of the recipient.

Duration 1 year; may be renewed up to 3 additional years.

Number awarded Varies each year.

Deadline June of each year.

[492]
CHRISTIAN CONNECTOR SEMINARY/ CHRISTIAN GRADUATE SCHOOL SCHOLARSHIP

Christian Connector, Inc.
627 24 1/2 Road, Suite D
Grand Junction, CO 81501
(970) 256-1610   Toll Free: (800) 667-0600
Web: www.christianconnector.com

Summary To provide financial assistance to students interested in attending a Christ-centered seminary or Christian graduate school.

Eligibility This program is open to students planning to enroll for the first time at a Christ-centered seminary or Christian graduate school. Schools that are members of the CCCU, NACCAP, or AABC automatically qualify. Students currently enrolled at a seminary or Christian graduate school are not eligible. Applicants enter the competition by registering online with the sponsoring organization, providing personal information and indicating the seminary or graduate school they are considering attending. The recipient of the scholarship is selected in a random drawing.

Financial data The award is $1,000. Funds are sent directly to the winner's school.

Duration The award is presented annually.

Number awarded 1 each year.

Deadline May of each year.

[493]
CHRISTIAN VOCATION/WALLINGFORD SCHOLARSHIPS

First Presbyterian Church
Attn: Scholarship Fund Program
709 South Boston Avenue
Tulsa, OK 74119-1629
(918) 584-4701   Fax: (918) 584-5233
E-mail: TBriscoe@firstchurchtulsa.org
Web: www.firstchurchtulsa.org/scholarships.htm

Summary To provide financial assistance to Presbyterian students interested in preparing for a religion-related career.

Eligibility To be eligible for this program, students must be communicant members of the Presbyterian Church (USA), be pursuing a Christian vocation field of study at an accredited institution, and have a GPA of 2.0 or higher. Priority is given first to members of the First Presbyterian Church (in Tulsa), second to applicants in the Presbytery of Eastern Oklahoma, third to applicants in the Synod of the Sun (Arkansas, Louisiana, Oklahoma, and Texas), and fourth to mem-

bers of the Presbyterian Church at large. Selection is based on academic merit, academic or career intent, church or religious involvement, and financial need.

Financial data Stipends range from $500 to $2,000. Funds are paid directly to the recipient's school.

Duration 1 year; recipients may reapply.

Additional information This program was established in 1988.

Number awarded Several each year.

Deadline April of each year.

[494]
CHURCH TRAINING AND DEACONESS HOUSE SCHOLARSHIP

Episcopal Diocese of Pennsylvania
Attn: Church Training and Deaconess House Scholarship Fund
240 South Fourth Street
Philadelphia, PA 19106
(215) 627-6434, ext. 101   Fax: (215) 627-7550
E-mail: diopa@libertynet.org
Web: www.diopa.org/leadership/transition/deaconess

Summary To provide financial assistance for graduate school to women preparing for a career in religious or benevolent work for the Episcopal Church.

Eligibility This program is open to women at the graduate level who are training for religious and benevolent work for the Episcopal Church. Preference is given to women in the Diocese of Pennsylvania. Applicants must have an earned bachelor's degree and acceptance into 1) a seminary; 2) an accredited college or university advanced degree program in education, religion, social work, medicine, or allied fields; or 3) a degree credit program of continuing education in their present field of work. Along with their application, they must submit a 250-word essay on how they expect to use this graduate educational training to advance their ordained or lay ministry within the Episcopal Church or the church at large. Selection is based on the quality of the essay, academic record, and financial need.

Financial data Stipends range from $2,000 to $3,000.

Duration 1 year; may be renewed up to 2 additional years.

Number awarded 1 or more each year.

Deadline March of each year.

[495]
CLINICAL EDUCATOR SCHOLARSHIPS

Evangelical Lutheran Church in America
Division for Ministry
Attn: Ministries in Chaplaincy, Pastoral Counseling, and Clinical Education
8765 West Higgins Road
Chicago, IL 60631-4195
(773) 380-2876   Toll Free: (800) 638-3522, ext. 2876
Fax: (773) 380-2829   E-mail: Theresa.Duty@elca.org
Web: www.elca.org

Summary To provide financial assistance to members of the Evangelical Lutheran Church in America (ELCA) interested in preparing for certification as educators in pastoral care and counseling ministries.

Eligibility This program is open to active members of ELCA congregations (either lay or ordained) who are preparing to become CPE supervisors, pastoral counseling educators, or other certified clinical ministry educators. Applicants must be ecclesiastically endorsed or in the process of seeking Ministries in Chaplaincy, Pastoral Counseling, and Clinical Education (MCPCCE) endorsement. All training positions/programs must comply with the Inter-Lutheran Coordinating Committee (ILCC) document, "Ministries in Chaplaincy, Pastoral Counseling and Clinical Education, Endorsement Standards and Procedures, Call Criteria and Program Guidelines" (2006 edition). They must submit 1) a statement of the nature of the training program and how it fits into both long- and short-range goals for their ministry; 2) a statement of acceptance and contract from a training supervisor; 3) a statement explaining financial need; 4) supervisory and self-evaluations from previous clinical education programs, including units of CPE and/or pastoral counseling training experiences; and 5) if presently serving in a ministry under call, a letter stating the extent to which financial support and/or compensatory time will be provided by the congregation or employing organization for this training.

Financial data   Grants up to $3,000 per year are awarded.

Duration   1 year; may be renewed.

Number awarded   Varies each year.

Deadline   March or September of each year.

[496]
COLEMAN TYSON SIEKMAN PRISON CHAPLAIN SCHOLARSHIP ENDOWMENT

United Methodist Higher Education Foundation
Attn: Scholarships Administrator
1001 19th Avenue South
P.O. Box 340005
Nashville, TN 37203-0005
(615) 340-7385   Toll Free: (800) 811-8110
Fax: (615) 340-7330
E-mail: umhefscholarships@gbhem.org
Web: www.umhef.org/receive.php?id=endowed_funds

Summary   To provide financial assistance to Methodist elders and seminarians interested in preparing for a career as a criminal justice chaplain.

Eligibility   This program is open to ordained elders in the United Methodist Church (UMC) and to United Methodist seminary students on the elder track. Applicants must be committed to becoming a criminal justice chaplain. They must be younger than 33 years of age.

Financial data   A stipend is awarded (amount not specified).

Duration   1 year.

Number awarded   1 or more each year.

Deadline   Deadline not specified.

[497]
COLORADO EASTERN STAR TRAINING AWARDS FOR RELIGIOUS LEADERSHIP

Order of the Eastern Star-Grand Chapter of Colorado
2445 South Quebec Street, Suite B
Denver, CO 80231
(303) 759-5936   Fax: (303) 759-3924
E-mail: grchapcoestar@qwestoffice.net
Web: www.oes-colorado.org/estarl.html

Summary   To provide financial assistance to residents of Colorado who are attending college in any state to prepare for a career in religious service.

Eligibility   This program is open to residents of Colorado who have completed at least 2 years of college and are enrolled full time at a college, university, or seminary in any state. Applicants must be preparing for a career in religious service as a minister, missionary, director of church music, director of religious education, or youth leadership.

Financial data   The stipend is $1,000 per year.

Duration   1 year; recipients may reapply.

Number awarded   Varies each year. Recently, 6 of these scholarships were awarded.

Deadline   April of each year.

[498]
COMMITTEE ON ETHNIC MINORITY RECRUITMENT SCHOLARSHIP

United Methodist Church-California-Pacific Annual
  Conference
Attn: Board of Ordained Ministry
1720 East Linfield Street
Glendora, CA 91740
(626) 335-6629   Fax: (626) 335-5750
E-mail: cathy.adminbom@gmail.com
Web: www.calpacordainedministry.org/523451

Summary   To provide financial assistance to members of ethnic minority groups in the California-Pacific Annual Conference of the United Methodist Church (UMC) who are attending a seminary in any state to qualify for ordination as an elder or deacon.

Eligibility   This program is open to members of ethnic minority groups in the UMC California-Pacific Annual Conference who are enrolled at a seminary in any state approved by the UMC University Senate. Applicants must have been approved as certified candidates by their district committee and be seeking Probationary Deacon or Elder's Orders. They may be seeking 1 or more types of assistance: tuition scholarships, grants for books and school supplies (including computers), or emergency living expense grants.

Financial data   Tuition stipends are $1,000 per year; books and supplies grants range up to $1,000 per year; emergency living expense grants depend on need and the availability of funds.

Duration   1 year; may be renewed up to 2 additional years.

Additional information   The California-Pacific Annual Conference includes churches in southern California, Hawaii, Guam, and Saipan.

Number awarded   Varies each year.

Deadline   August of each year for fall term; December of each year for spring term.

[499]
CONNECTICUT EASTERN STAR TRAINING AWARDS FOR RELIGIOUS LEADERSHIP

Order of the Eastern Star-Grand Chapter of Connecticut
c/o Nancy A. Watson, Scholarship Committee Chair
48 Elderkin Crossing
Norwich, CT 06360
(860) 887-1128   E-mail: nawatson@snet.net
Web: www.ctoes.com/CT_OES/oes_info.htm

Summary To provide financial assistance to residents of Connecticut who are attending college or graduate school in any state to work on a degree related to religious leadership or religious music.

Eligibility This program is open to residents of Connecticut who are preparing for a career in religion as a minister, missionary, church musician or organist, director of religious education, director of youth leadership, or other related position. Applicants must be enrolled at a college or university in any state and working on an associate, bachelor's, master's, or doctoral degree. They must be able to demonstrate financial need (family adjusted gross income less than $50,000 per year). Along with their application, they must submit a brief statement or summary of their plans as those relate to their educational and religious leadership career objectives and long-term goals.

Financial data A stipend is awarded (amount not specified).

Duration 1 year.

Number awarded 1 or more each year.

Deadline February of each year.

[500]
COOK SCHOLARSHIP AWARDS

South Carolina United Methodist Foundation
P.O. Box 5087
Columbia, SC 29250-5087
(803) 771-9125   Fax: (803) 771-9135
E-mail: scumf@bellsouth.net
Web: www.umcsc.org/scholarships.html

Summary To provide financial assistance to Methodist students from South Carolina who are attending college or graduate school in any state to prepare for a career in Christian service.

Eligibility This program is open to members of United Methodist Churches in South Carolina and to persons affiliated with the South Carolina Conference of the United Methodist Church (UMC). Applicants must be enrolled in an undergraduate, graduate, or professional degree program at an accredited college, university, or theological school in any state approved by the UMC University Senate. They must be preparing for a career in full-time Christian service. Selection is based on their understanding of their ministry and its future direction, promise for ministry in the church, and financial need.

Financial data The stipend is at least $500.

Duration 1 year.

Additional information This scholarship was established by the South Carolina Conference of the United Methodist Church in 1989.

Number awarded 1 or more each year.

Deadline March of each year.

[501]
COOPER FUND GRANTS

United Methodist Church-Mississippi Conference
Attn: Office of Ministerial Services
321 Mississippi Street
Jackson, MS 39201
(601) 354-0515, ext. 32   Toll Free: (866) 647-7486
E-mail: scumbest@mississippi-umc.org
Web: www.mississippi-umc.org/pages/detail/779

Summary To provide financial assistance to upper-division and graduate students from Mississippi who are preparing for full-time professional ministry within the United Methodist Church (UMC) at a school in any state.

Eligibility This program is open to residents of Mississippi who are either 1) juniors or seniors at an accredited college or university in any state, or 2) enrolled at an accredited seminary in any state. Applicants must be planning to enter the full-time professional ministry (ordained, elder, deacon, music, education) of the UMC. They must be able to demonstrate financial need.

Financial data The stipend is $1,000.

Duration 1 year.

Additional information This program was established in 1906.

Number awarded 4 each year: 2 to undergraduates and 2 to seminary students.

Deadline May of each year.

[502]
COOPERATIVE BAPTIST FELLOWSHIP LEADERSHIP SCHOLARSHIPS

Cooperative Baptist Fellowship
2930 Flowers Road South, Suite 133
Atlanta, GA 30341
(770) 220-1600   Toll Free: (800) 352-8741
Fax: (770) 220-1685   E-mail: contact@thefellowship.info
Web: www.thefellowship.info

Summary To provide financial assistance to students enrolled at seminaries affiliated with the Cooperative Baptist Fellowship (CBF).

Eligibility This program is open to students enrolled at the 15 theology schools (14 in the United States and 1 abroad) that cooperate with the CBF network of ministry partners. Applicants must demonstrate a commitment to vocational ministry. Selection is based on financial need, commitment to serve in Baptist life in keeping with the mission statement of the CBF, and potential success in theological education and ministry.

Financial data The stipend is $4,000 per year.

Duration 1 year.

Additional information The cooperating institutions are Baptist Seminary of Kentucky (Georgetown, Kentucky), Baptist Theological Seminary at Richmond (Richmond, Virginia), Baptist University of the Americas (San Antonio, Texas), Brite Divinity School at Texas Christian University (Fort Worth, Texas), Campbell University Divinity School (Buies Creek, North Carolina), Candler School of Theology at Emory University (Atlanta, Georgia), Central Baptist Theological Seminary (Shawnee, Kansas), Duke University Divinity School (Durham, North Carolina), International Baptist Theological Seminary of the European Baptist Federation (Prague, Czech

Republic), M. Christopher White School of Divinity at Gardner-Webb University (Boiling Springs, North Carolina), Logsdon School of Theology at Hardin-Simmons University (Abilene, Texas), Lutheran Theological Southern Seminary (Columbia, South Carolina), McAfee School of Theology at Mercer University (Atlanta, Georgia), George W. Truett Theological Seminary at Baylor University (Waco, Texas), and Wake Forest University Divinity School (Winston-Salem, North Carolina).

Number awarded   Varies each year. Recently, 77 of these scholarships were awarded.

Deadline   Deadline not specified.

[503]
COOPERATIVE BAPTIST FELLOWSHIP OF FLORIDA SCHOLARSHIPS

Cooperative Baptist Fellowship of Florida
Attn: Chair, Scholarship Team
217 Hillcrest Street
P.O. Box 2556
Lakeland, FL 33806-2556
(863) 682-6802   Toll Free: (888) 241-CBFF
Fax: (863) 683-5797   E-mail: contact@floridacbf.org
Web: www.floridacbf.org/fl/scholarships.htm

Summary   To provide financial assistance for college, seminary, or graduate school to members of the Cooperative Baptist Fellowship (CBF) of Florida.

Eligibility   This program is open to CBF members in Florida, including both clergy and laity. Applicants must be proposing to participate in an official educational endeavor that will enhance their ministry. The activity may be overtly religious or secular as long as the recipient will use the education to enhance a ministry within the Baptist community of faith. Applications are accompanied by 2 brochures, entitled "Where Do I Belong?" and "Why It Matters Where You Serve the Lord." Applicants must submit their reaction to those brochures. They must also demonstrate financial need. Priority is given to students in master's or doctoral programs at accredited institutions.

Financial data   A stipend is awarded (amount not specified).

Duration   1 year.

Number awarded   1 or more each year.

Deadline   April of each year.

[504]
COOPERATIVE BAPTIST FELLOWSHIP OF GEORGIA SEMINARY SCHOLARSHIPS

Cooperative Baptist Fellowship of Georgia
Attn: Scholarship
P.O. Box 4343
Macon, GA 31208-4343
(478) 742-1191, ext. 28   Toll Free: (877) 336-6426
Fax: (478) 742-6150   E-mail: lwheeler@cbfga.org
Web: www.cbfga.org/51/Scholarships

Summary   To provide financial assistance to seminary students who have a connection to the Cooperative Baptist Fellowship (CBF) of Georgia.

Eligibility   This program is open to students working on a master's degree at an accredited seminary. Applicants are not required to be attending a Baptist institution, but they

must have a connection to CBF of Georgia. They must show potential for leadership within CBF. Along with their application, they must submit a 3-page essay on their faith journey and vocational calling, ministry goals, and current relationship to CBF.

Financial data   A stipend is awarded (amount not specified).

Duration   1 year; nonrenewable.

Number awarded   Varies each year. Recently, 16 of these scholarships were awarded.

Deadline   March of each year.

[505]
COOPERATIVE BAPTIST FELLOWSHIP OF NORTH CAROLINA SCHOLARSHIPS

Cooperative Baptist Fellowship of North Carolina
Attn: Scholarship Review Committee
8025 North Point Boulevard, Suite 205
Winston-Salem, NC 27106
(336) 759-3456   Toll Free: (888) 822-1944
Fax: (336) 759-3459   E-mail: cbfnc@cbfnc.org
Web: www.cbfnc.org/CareersandCalling/Scholarships.aspx

Summary   To provide financial assistance to members of churches affiliated with the Cooperative Baptist Fellowship of North Carolina (CBFNC) who are interested in attending a divinity school that is outside of North Carolina or not in a partnership relationship with the Fellowship.

Eligibility   This program is open to residents of North Carolina who are members of a church affiliated with the CBFNC. Applicants must be interested in attending a divinity school in a state other than North Carolina or that is not a CBFNC partner institution. Along with their application, they must submit a 2-page narrative that describes their call to faith and to vocational ministry, their hopes or goals, their commitment to CBFNC's values and principals, and their financial need.

Financial data   Stipends range from $1,000 to $2,000 per year.

Duration   1 year; may be renewed.

Number awarded   Varies each year; recently, 13 of these scholarships were awarded.

Deadline   June of each year.

[506]
COOPERATIVE BAPTIST FELLOWSHIP OF SOUTH CAROLINA SCHOLARSHIPS

Cooperative Baptist Fellowship of South Carolina
Attn: Inheritors Committee
1314 Lincoln Street, Suite 308
P.O. Box 11159
Columbia, SC 29211
(803) 779-1888   Fax: (803) 779-2242
E-mail: info@cbfofsc.org
Web: www.cbfofsc.org

Summary   To provide financial assistance to South Carolina residents who are associated with the Cooperative Baptist Fellowship (CBF) and attending designated seminaries in the United States and abroad.

Eligibility   This program is open to South Carolina seminary students who are members of churches that are CBF-friendly or who attend CBF-friendly institutions. Applicants must submit a 2-page statement on their faith journey and calling, including their goals for ministry, whether or not they hope to serve in South Carolina, and their current relationship with the CBF of South Carolina.

Financial data The stipend is $600.

Duration 1 year.

Additional information The seminaries with a relationship to the CBF of South Carolina are Baptist Seminary of Kentucky (Georgetown, Kentucky), Baptist Theological Seminary at Richmond (Richmond, Virginia), Baptist University of the Americas (San Antonio, Texas), Brite Divinity School at Texas Christian University (Fort Worth, Texas), Campbell University Divinity School (Buies Creek, North Carolina), Candler School of Theology at Emory University (Atlanta, Georgia), Central Baptist Theological Seminary (Shawnee, Kansas), Baptist House of Studies at Duke University Divinity School (Durham, North Carolina), George W. Truett Theological Seminary at Baylor University (Waco, Texas), International Baptist Theological Seminary of the European Baptist Federation (Prague, Czech Republic), Logsdon School of Theology at Hardin-Simmons University (Abilene, Texas), Baptist Studies Program at Lutheran Theological Southern Seminary (Columbia, South Carolina), M. Christopher White School of Divinity at Gardner-Webb University (Boiling Springs, North Carolina), McAfee School of Theology at Mercer University (Atlanta, Georgia), and Wake Forest University Divinity School (Winston-Salem, North Carolina).

Number awarded Varies each year. Recently, 11 of these scholarships were awarded.

Deadline April of each year for fall term; October of each year for spring term.

[507]
COWLES UNITED METHODIST CHURCH MEMORIAL SCHOLARSHIP FUND

Nebraska United Methodist Foundation
100 West Fletcher Avenue, Suite 100
Lincoln, NE 68521-3848
(402) 323-8844   Toll Free: (877) 495-5545
Fax: (402) 323-8840   E-mail: info@numf.org
Web: www.numf.org/special_programs/scholarships.html

Summary To provide financial assistance to students at United Methodist seminaries in any state who plan to become a pastor in Nebraska.

Eligibility This program is open to members of Nebraska United Methodist Churches who are ministerial students at seminaries in any state accredited by the Nebraska United Methodist Board of Ordained Ministry. Applicants must plan to become a pastor in the Nebraska Annual Conference and have at least 30 years of eligibility to serve as a minister upon graduation from seminary. They must have a cumulative GPA of 2.5 or higher. Along with their application, they must submit a 1-page statement of their calling and career plans for ministry, documentation of financial need, a current academic transcript, and 2 letters of recommendation.

Financial data The stipend is approximately $2,500 per year.

Duration 1 year; may be renewed.

Number awarded 1 or more each year.

Deadline June of each year.

[508]
CRAIG HOLBROOK PARHAM SCHOLARSHIP FUND

First Baptist Church
722 Grace Street
Greenwood, SC 29649-2133
(864) 229-5557   Fax: (864) 229-2561
E-mail: info@fbcgwd.com
Web: www.fbcgwd.com

Summary To provide financial assistance to Baptist seminary students from South Carolina, especially those from Greenwood.

Eligibility This program is open to members of the Baptist faith who are attending a seminary in any state to prepare for full-time Christian service. Applicants must have a connection with upper South Carolina or the state of South Carolina. Preference is given to members of First Baptist Church in Greenwood. Selection is based on academic achievement and financial need.

Financial data Stipends range from $250 to $1,000.

Duration 1 year.

Number awarded Approximately 15 each year.

Deadline April of each year.

[509]
D. GLENN HILTS SCHOLARSHIP

Association of Seventh-Day Adventist Librarians
c/o Cynthia Mae Helms, Scholarship Committee Chair
Andrews University
James White Library, Room 221
Berrien Springs, MI 49104-1400
(269) 471-6260   E-mail: helmsc@andrews.edu
Web: www.asdal.org/hilts/index.html

Summary To provide financial assistance to members of the Seventh-Day Adventist Church interested in working on a graduate degree in librarianship.

Eligibility This program is open to full-time students in graduate library science programs at ALA-accredited institutions who are members of Seventh-Day Adventist churches. Applicants not attending a library school in the United States or Canada must be accepted into an overseas graduate library school recognized by the International Federation of Library Associations. All applicants must submit a 600-word essay describing their interest in librarianship, their professional goals, and the contributions they feel they might make to Seventh-Day Adventist libraries and information centers.

Financial data The stipend is $1,200; one half is paid at the beginning of the recipient's first term and the other half after successful completion of that term.

Duration 1 year.

Additional information This scholarship was first awarded in 1985. Recipients are encouraged to seek employment in a Seventh-Day Adventist library.

Number awarded 1 each year.

Deadline July of each year.

[510]
DANIEL E. PHILLIPS MEMORIAL SCHOLARSHIP

United Methodist Church-New Mexico Conference
Attn: Board of Ordained Ministry
11816 Lomas Boulevard, N.E.
Albuquerque, NM 87112
(505) 255-8786, ext. 101   Toll Free: (800) 678-8786
Fax: (505) 265-6184 E-mail: mridgeway@nmconfum.com
Web: www.nmconfum.com

Summary To provide financial assistance to Methodists from New Mexico who are interested in attending a seminary in any state to prepare for ordained ministry as a second career.

Eligibility This program is open to students who are enrolled or planning to enroll at a seminary in any state and who have an affiliation with a congregation of the New Mexico Conference of the United Methodist Church (UMC). Applicants must be preparing for ordained ministry to local churches in the New Mexico Conference as a second career. Along with their application, they must submit brief essays on their current financial situation, how their sense of calling to ministry has changed or grown during the past year, the areas of ministry in which they are currently interested, what they believe to be their greatest spiritual gifts, how they believe God is calling them to use those gifts in the local church, and their earlier career and the values they believe that they bring to ministry because of that experience.

Financial data A stipend is awarded (amount not specified).

Duration 1 year.

Number awarded 1 or more each year.

Deadline April of each year.

[511]
DANIEL E. WEISS FUND FOR EXCELLENCE

American Baptist Churches USA
National Ministries
Attn: Office of Financial Aid for Studies
P.O. Box 851
Valley Forge, PA 19482-0851
(610) 768-2067   Toll Free: (800) ABC-3USA, ext. 2067
Fax: (610) 768-2453
E-mail: Financialaid.Web@abc-usa.org
Web: www.nationalministries.org

Summary To provide financial assistance to American Baptist college students who are interested in attending a seminary but not for theological studies.

Eligibility This program is open to American Baptist students who are currently enrolled as juniors or seniors at a college or university in the United States or Puerto Rico. They must be nominated by a pastor, campus minister, or college faculty member as a student who displays commitment to the Gospel and church life, is growing as a disciple of Christ, shows maturity and integrity of character, and demonstrates outstanding academic ability. Nominees must be planning to enroll at a seminary following graduation from college. They do not need to undertake theological studies, but they must possess gifts and skills for ministry. U.S. citizenship is required.

Financial data The stipend is $3,000.

Duration 1 year (the first year of seminary); nonrenewable.

Number awarded Varies each year.

Deadline Nominations must be submitted by October of each year.

[512]
DAVID AND MARY CROWLEY SCHOLARSHIP

Baptist Convention of New York
Attn: BCNY Foundation
6538 Baptist Way
East Syracuse, NY 13057
(315) 433-1001   Toll Free: (800) 552-0004
Fax: (315) 433-1026   E-mail: cmeyer@bcnysbc.org
Web: www.bcnysbc.org/bcnyfoundation.html

Summary To provide financial assistance to members of churches in the Baptist Convention of New York who are interested in additional education.

Eligibility This program is open to members in good standing of churches in the Baptist Convention of New York. Applicants must be seeking education through the Southern Baptist Convention schools associated with the Cooperative Program. Along with their application, they must submit 1) an essay in which they share their goals for the future and how a degree in higher education will help them achieve those goals; and 2) an autobiography that includes their conversion experience, call to Christian service (for those planning a religious vocation), and plans to fulfill this calling. Financial need is also considered in the selection process.

Financial data A stipend is awarded (amount not specified).

Duration 1 year; may be renewed up to 3 additional years.

Number awarded 1 or more each year.

Deadline February of each year.

[513]
DAVID H.C. READ PREACHER/SCHOLAR AWARD

Madison Avenue Presbyterian Church
921 Madison Avenue
New York, NY 10021-3595
(212) 288-8920   Fax: (212) 249-1466
Web: www.mapc.com/outreach/scholarship

Summary To recognize and reward excellence among graduating seminarians who show outstanding promise as preachers and scholars.

Eligibility Candidates must be in the final year of an M.Div. degree program at a member school of the Association of Theological Schools in the United States and Canada. They must be scheduled to receive the degree by June of the application year, be nominated by their seminary (only 2 nominations per school), and be committed to the parish pulpit. Along with their application, they must submit a curriculum vitae, an official transcript, letters of recommendation, copies and audio tapes of 2 sermons (1 on the Old Testament, 1 on the New Testament) preached before live audiences, concise exegetical papers (not more than 1,000 words in length) on the biblical text on which each sermon is based, a brief biographical statement, and a statement of commitment to the parish ministry. Based on these materials, 4 finalists are selected; 1 winner is chosen from that group. Selection is based on merit, not need, and the award is granted without regard to race, color, sex, age, national or ethnic origin, or disability.

Financial data The winner receives $20,000 and the finalists receive $1,000 each.

Duration The award is presented annually.

Additional information David H.C. Read was the senior minister at Madison Avenue Presbyterian Church from 1956 to 1989. The church established this award in 1990.

Number awarded 3 finalists and 1 winner are selected each year.

Deadline January of each year.

[514]
DEMPSTER GRADUATE FELLOWSHIP

United Methodist Church
Attn: General Board of Higher Education and Ministry
Division of Ordained Ministry
1001 19th Avenue South
P.O. Box 340007
Nashville, TN 37203-0007
(615) 340-7388   Fax: (615) 340-7377
E-mail: dcheatham@gbhem.org
Web: www.gbhem.org/loansandscholarships

Summary To provide financial assistance to United Methodist students working on a doctoral degree to prepare for an academic career.

Eligibility This program is open to members of the United Methodist Church working on a Ph.D. degree. Applicants must have an M.Div. degree from a United Methodist seminary or be enrolled in such a seminary at the time of applying. They must be planning to teach in a seminary or to teach religion and related subjects in a college or university. Selection is based on intellectual competence, academic achievement, promise of usefulness in teaching careers, personal qualities, clarity of purpose, and commitment to Christian ministry and the preparation of pastoral leadership for the church. Candidacy for ordination as an elder in an annual conference of the United Methodist Church is preferred.

Financial data The stipend is $10,000 for single students or $11,000 for married recipients. Renewals are limited to $5,000 per year.

Duration 1 year; may be renewed for up to 4 additional years, but only for a maximum lifetime award of $30,000.

Number awarded Up to 5 each year.

Deadline October of each year.

[515]
DESERT SOUTHWEST UNITED METHODIST FOUNDATION SCHOLARSHIPS

Desert Southwest United Methodist Foundation
Attn: Executive Director
1550 East Meadowbrook Avenue
Phoenix, AZ 85014-4040
(602) 266-6956, ext. 203   Toll Free: (800) 229-8622
Fax: (602) 265-1524   E-mail: Lucille@dsumf.org
Web: www.dsumf.org/scholarships.htm

Summary To provide financial assistance for college or graduate school to members of Methodist Churches within the Desert Southwest Conference.

Eligibility This program is open to active members of congregations that are affiliated with the United Methodist

Church Desert Southwest Conference, which serves Arizona and southern Nevada. Applicants must be 1) enrolled in a seminary or school of religion that is accredited by the United Methodist Church University Senate; 2) enrolled in a college or university within the boundaries of the Desert Southwest Conference; or 3) majoring in elementary education. They must submit essays on 1) their recent past, current, and anticipated future non-ordained involvement in their church; 2) their immediate and long-term goals; 3) their plan for their ordained or licensed Christian ministry; and 4) their financial need.

Financial data A stipend is awarded (amount not specified).

Duration 1 year.

Number awarded Varies each year.

Deadline June of each year for fall semester; December of each year for spring semester.

[516]
DEVELOPMENT DISABILITIES SCHOLASTIC EXCELLENCE AWARD FOR LUTHERAN SEMINARIANS

Bethesda Lutheran Communities
Attn: Coordinator, Bethesda Institute
600 Hoffmann Drive
Watertown, WI 53094
(920) 261-3050   Toll Free: (800) 369-4636, ext. 4449
Fax: (920) 262-6513
E-mail: Bethesda.institute@mailblc.org
Web: bethesdalutherancommunities.org/youth/scholarships

Summary To provide financial assistance to Lutheran seminarians who are interested in preparing for a career in the field of developmental disabilities.

Eligibility Applicants must be active communicant members of a Lutheran congregation; be classified as a first- or second-year student or a vicar at a seminary affiliated with the Wisconsin Evangelical Lutheran Synod (WELS), the Lutheran Church-Missouri Synod (LCMS), or the Evangelical Lutheran Synod (ELS); and have a commitment to inclusion of persons with developmental disabilities within the local parish. Along with their application, they must submit 1) an essay of 250 to 300 words on the career they are planning in the field of developmental disabilities and how that career choice would impact the lives of people with developmental disabilities; 2) 4 letters of recommendation; 3) an official college transcript; and 4) documentation that they have completed at least 100 hours of volunteer and/or paid service to people who are developmentally disabled within the past 2 calendar years. Financial need is not considered in the selection process.

Financial data The stipend is $3,000.

Duration 1 year.

Number awarded 1 each year.

Deadline April of each year.

[517]
DINGUS FUND GRANTS

United Methodist Church-Kentucky Annual Conference
Attn: Board of Ordained Ministry
7400 Floydsburg Road
Crestwood, KY 40014-8202
(502) 425-3884　　　　　Toll Free: (800) 530-7236
Fax: (502) 426-5181
Web: www.kyumc.org/pages/detail/985

Summary To provide financial assistance to students from Kentucky who are preparing for ordination as a deacon in the United Methodist Church (UMC).

Eligibility This program is open to seminary students who are certified as candidates for ordained ministry by their district committee within the UMC Kentucky Annual Conference. Applicants must be able to demonstrate financial need. Priority is given to first-time applicants.

Financial data A stipend is awarded (amount not specified).

Duration 1 term; may be renewed.

Number awarded 1 or more each year.

Deadline February of each year for terms beginning April through June; May of each year for terms beginning July through September; August of each year for terms beginning October through December; November of each year for terms beginning January through March.

[518]
DISCIPLE CHAPLAINS' SCHOLARSHIP

Christian Church (Disciples of Christ)
Attn: Disciples Home Missions
130 East Washington Street
P.O. Box 1986
Indianapolis, IN 46206-1986
(317) 713-2652　　　　　Toll Free: (888) DHM-2631
Fax: (317) 635-4426　　　E-mail: mail@dhm.disciples.org
Web: www.discipleshomemissions.org

Summary To provide financial assistance to first-year seminarians interested in preparing for a career in the ministry of the Christian Church (Disciples of Christ).

Eligibility This program is open to first-year seminary students who are members of the Christian Church (Disciples of Christ). Applicants must plan to prepare for the ordained ministry, have at least a "C+" GPA, provide evidence of financial need, be enrolled full time in an accredited school or seminary, provide a transcript of academic work, and be under the care of a regional Commission on the Ministry or in the process of coming under care.

Financial data The stipend is $1,500.

Duration 1 year; may be renewed.

Number awarded Varies each year.

Deadline March of each year.

[519]
DISTANCE LEARNING SCHOLARSHIP

Christian Connector, Inc.
627 24 1/2 Road, Suite D
Grand Junction, CO 81501
(970) 256-1610　　　　　Toll Free: (800) 667-0600
Web: www.christianconnector.com

Summary To provide financial assistance to students interested in working on an undergraduate or graduate degree from a Christ-centered distance learning program.

Eligibility This program is open to students planning to enroll through a distance learning program at a Christ-centered Christian college, Bible college, seminary, or Christian graduate school. Schools that are members of the CCCU, NACCAP, or AABC automatically qualify. Applicants enter the competition by registering online with the sponsoring organization, providing personal information and information about the distance learning program they are considering. The recipient of the scholarship is selected in a random drawing.

Financial data The award is $1,000. Funds are sent directly to the winner's school.

Duration The award is presented annually.

Number awarded 1 each year.

Deadline May of each year.

[520]
DISTRICT OF COLUMBIA BAPTIST FOUNDATION SCHOLARSHIPS

District of Columbia Baptist Convention
Attn: District of Columbia Baptist Foundation
1628 16th Street, N.W., Suite 403
Washington, DC 20009
(202) 234-7194　　　　　Fax: (202) 234-8196
E-mail: Ellen.teague@dcbaptist.org
Web: www.dcbaptist.org/dcbcfoundation.php

Summary To provide financial assistance to members of churches cooperating with the District of Columbia Baptist Convention (DCBC) who are interested in attending seminary in any state.

Eligibility This program is open to active members of cooperating DCBC churches who are preparing for a career in full-time ministry. Applicants must be planning to enroll full time at a Baptist seminary or a seminary with a Baptist studies program to work on a first graduate degree in theology. They must have a GPA of 2.75 or higher and be able to demonstrate financial need. Along with their application, they must submit a brief summary of their Christian experience and call to ministry.

Financial data The current maximum stipend is $1,600 per semester ($3,200 per year). Funds are sent directly to the recipient's educational institution.

Duration 1 year; may be renewed up to 4 additional years, although the maximum lifetime support an individual may receive is $10,000.

Number awarded Varies each year.

Deadline April of each year for fall semester; August of each year for spring semester.

[521]
DOLLARS FOR SCHOLARS PROGRAM

United Methodist Higher Education Foundation
Attn: Scholarships Administrator
1001 19th Avenue South
P.O. Box 340005
Nashville, TN 37203-0005
(615) 340-7385   Toll Free: (800) 811-8110
Fax: (615) 340-7330
E-mail: umhefscholarships@gbhem.org
Web: www.umhef.org/receive.php?id=dollars_for_scholars

Summary To provide financial assistance to students at Methodist colleges, universities, and seminaries whose home churches agree to contribute to their support.

Eligibility The Double Your Dollars for Scholars program is open to students attending or planning to attend a United Methodist-related college, university, or seminary as a full-time student. Applicants must have been an active, full member of a United Methodist Church for at least 1 year prior to applying. Their home church must nominate them and agree to contribute to their support. Many of the United Methodist colleges and universities have also agreed to contribute matching funds for a Triple Your Dollars for Scholars Program, and a few United Methodist conference foundations have agreed to contribute additional matching funds for a Quadruple Your Dollars for Scholars Program. Awards are granted on a first-come, first-served basis. Some of the awards are designated for Hispanic, Asian, and Native American (HANA) students funded by the General Board of Higher Education and Ministry.

Financial data The sponsoring church contributes $1,000 and the United Methodist Higher Education Foundation (UMHEF) contributes a matching $1,000. Students who attend a participating United Methodist college or university receive an additional $1,000 for the Triple Your Dollars for Scholars Program, and those from a participating conference receive a fourth $1,000 increment for the Quadruple Your Dollars for Scholars Program.

Duration 1 year; may be renewed as long as the recipients maintain satisfactory academic progress as defined by their institution.

Additional information Currently, participants in the Double Your Dollars for Scholars program include 2 United Methodist seminaries and theological schools, 1 professional school, 19 senior colleges and universities, and 1 2-year college. The Triple Your Dollars for Scholars program includes an additional 11 United Methodist seminaries and theological schools, 73 senior colleges and universities, and 5 2-year colleges (for a complete list, consult the UMHEF). The conference foundations participating in the Quadruple Your Dollars for Scholars Program are limited to the Alabama-West Florida United Methodist Foundation, the Mississippi United Methodist Foundation (for students at Millsaps College or Rust College), the Missouri United Methodist Foundation (for students at Saint Paul School of Theology or Central Methodist University), the Nashville Area United Methodist Foundation, the North Carolina United Methodist Foundation (for students at Louisburg College, Methodist University, or North Carolina Wesleyan College), the North Georgia United Methodist Foundation, the Oklahoma United Methodist Foundation (for students at Oklahoma City University) the United Methodist Foundation of Arkansas (for students at Hendrix College or

Philander Smith College), the United Methodist Foundation of South Indiana, and the United Methodist Foundation of Western North Carolina.

Number awarded 350 each year, including 25 designated for HANA students.

Deadline Local churches must submit applications in March of each year for senior colleges, universities, and seminaries or May of each year for 2-year colleges.

[522]
DORA AMES LEE LEADERSHIP DEVELOPMENT FUND

United Methodist Church
General Board of Global Ministries
Attn: United Methodist Committee on Relief
475 Riverside Drive, Room 1522
New York, NY 10115
(212) 870-3871   Toll Free: (800) UMC-GBGM
E-mail: jyoung@gbgm-umc.org
Web: gbgm-umc.org/health/doralee.cfm

Summary To provide financial assistance to Methodists and other Christians of Asian or Native American descent who are preparing for a career in a health-related field.

Eligibility This program is open to undergraduate and graduate students who are U.S. citizens of Asian American or Native American descent. Applicants must be professed Christians, preferably United Methodists. They must be attending a college or university to enter or continue in a health-related field. Financial need is considered in the selection process.

Financial data The stipend is $2,000.

Duration 1 year.

Additional information This program was established in 1980.

Number awarded 5 each year.

Deadline June of each year.

[523]
DOREENE CATER SCHOLARSHIP

First United Methodist Church of the Saint Cloud Region
Attn: Scholarship Committee
302 Fifth Avenue South
St. Cloud, MN 56301
(320) 251-0804   Fax: (320) 251-0878
E-mail: fumc@fumc-stcloud.org
Web: www.fumc-stcloud.org/education

Summary To provide financial assistance to members of United Methodist Churches in the Minnesota Conference who are interested in preparing for a career in an area that will benefit people and the environment.

Eligibility This program is open to members of United Methodist Churches in the Minnesota Conference who are interested in a career in such areas as education, medicine, environmental sciences, seminary education, and social service. Applicants must be entering at least their sophomore year. They must submit 2 letters of reference and transcripts of previous work.

Financial data Stipends range from $500 to $1,500, depending on the need of the recipient and the number of applicants.

Duration 1 year; may be renewed.

Number awarded   Varies each year.
Deadline   May of each year.

[524]
DORIS AND ARTHUR MANDEVILLE SCHOLARSHIP

United Methodist Church-Greater New Jersey Conference
Conference Board of Higher Education and Ministry
Attn: Scholarship Committee
1001 Wickapecko Drive
Ocean, NJ 07712-4733
(732) 359-1040   Toll Free: (877) 677-2594, ext. 1040
Fax: (732) 359-1049   E-mail: Lperez@gnjumc.org
Web: www.gnjumc.org/grants_loans_and_scholarship

Summary   To provide financial assistance to New Jersey
Methodists who are attending graduate school in any state to
prepare for a career in service to the church.

Eligibility   This program is open to full-time graduate students who are members of congregations affiliated with the
Greater New Jersey Conference of the United Methodist
Church. Applicants must be preparing for a career in
ordained ministry or Christian education in the United Methodist Church. Along with their application, they must submit a
video (VHS or DVD) on why they feel they deserve this scholarship, including information on their Christian commitment
and plans to serve the Methodist Church after they graduate.
Financial need is also considered in the selection process.

Financial data   A stipend is awarded (amount not specified).

Duration   1 year.

Additional information   This program is jointly administered by the Greater New Jersey Conference Board of Higher
Education and the Epworth United Methodist Church of Palmyra, New Jersey.

Number awarded   1 or more each year.

Deadline   March of each year.

[525]
DR. AND MRS. ERNEST STEURY MEDICAL STUDENT SCHOLARSHIP

Christian Medical & Dental Associations
2604 Highway 421
P.O. Box 7500
Bristol, TN 37621-7500
(423) 844-1000   Toll Free: (888) 230-2637
Fax: (423) 844-1005   E-mail: main@cmda.org
Web: www.cmda.org

Summary   To provide scholarship/loans to medical students who are committed to a career in foreign or domestic
Christian medical missions.

Eligibility   This program is open to U.S. citizens entering
their first or second year at an accredited medical school or
college of osteopathic medicine in the United States and
working towards an M.D. or D.O. degree. Applicants must be
candidates with or under care of a recognized mission board;
usually, that means they have gone through a screening process before a mission board and are tentatively accepted as
career missionaries based upon the completion of their medical education. If the applicant is married, both partners must
have this status. Applicants must have experienced a sincere
call into career medical missions and be willing to serve for an
extended period of time on a foreign or domestic mission
field. Along with their application, they must submit a 2- to 3-
page personal statement on how they came to know Christ as
their savior, their call to medical missions, where they hope to
serve, the kind of medical ministry in which they hope to be
involved, their reasons for entering the field of medicine, the
opportunities they have had to impact other people for Christ
and whether they have ever led someone to Christ, and their
involvement with Christian Medical & Dental Associations
(CMDA), including when they became a member and activities in which they are involved. Financial need is considered
in the selection process.

Financial data   This is a scholarship/loan. The maximum
award is $25,000 per year. The total amount is written off at
the rate of 14% for each year of service in the mission field, or
a total of approximately 86 months. If a recipient 1) decides
not to serve on a foreign mission field; 2) is delayed in arriving
on the mission field for more than 2 years beyond completion
of medical or osteopathic training; or 3) does not complete
the full 86 months of service on the mission field, repayment
must begin with interest at 8.25% and be completed within 10
years.

Duration   1 year; may be renewed up to 3 additional years.

Additional information   Recipients serving in domestic or
foreign missions must spend at least 75% of their professional time in indigent care. Up to 25% of their time may be
spent in personal income-generating activities that are
approved by their mission board.

Number awarded   Varies each year.

Deadline   March of each year.

[526]
DR. ANTHONY P. BAGATELOS MEDICAL SCHOLARSHIP

Greek Orthodox Cathedral of the Annunciation
245 Valencia Street
San Francisco, CA 94103-2320
(415) 864-8000   Fax: (415) 431-5860
E-mail: office@annunciation.org
Web: www.annunciation.org

Summary   To provide financial assistance to students of
Greek descent or the Greek Orthodox faith who are interested in attending medical school.

Eligibility   This program is open to students who are of
Greek descent or of the Greek Orthodox faith who 1) matriculate at and attend medical school, preferably at Stanford
University, and 2) intend to practice medicine within the 9-
county area surrounding San Francisco Bay, preferably in
San Francisco. Along with their application, they must submit
an official transcript and 2 letters of recommendation.

Financial data   Stipends up to $1,000 are provided. Funds
are paid to the recipient's school.

Duration   1 year; normally, the scholarship is renewed until
the recipient graduates from medical school.

Number awarded   1 each year.

Deadline   May of each year.

[527]
DR. CHESTER A. MCPHEETERS SCHOLARSHIP

United Methodist Higher Education Foundation
Attn: Scholarships Administrator
1001 19th Avenue South
P.O. Box 340005
Nashville, TN 37203-0005
(615) 340-7385   Toll Free: (800) 811-8110
Fax: (615) 340-7330
E-mail: umhefscholarships@gbhem.org
Web: www.umhef.org/receive.php?id=endowed_funds

Summary   To provide financial assistance to undergraduate and graduate Methodist students who are preparing for ministry.

Eligibility   This program is open to full-time undergraduate and graduate students who are preparing for a career as a minister in the United Methodist Church. Applicants must have been active, full members of a United Methodist Church for at least 1 year prior to applying and be attending or planning to attend a seminary or theological school affiliated with that denomination. They must have a GPA of 3.0 or higher and be able to demonstrate financial need. Along with their application, they must submit a 200-word essay on their involvement and/or leadership responsibilities in their church, school, and community within the last 3 years. U.S. citizenship or permanent resident status is required.

Financial data   The stipend is at least $1,000 per year.

Duration   1 year; recipients may reapply.

Number awarded   Varies each year. Recently, 4 of these scholarships were awarded.

Deadline   May of each year.

[528]
DR. CLAUDE AND JEANNIE CONE CENTURY FUND

New Mexico Baptist Foundation
5325 Wyoming Boulevard, N.E.
P.O. Box 16560
Albuquerque, NM 87191-6560
(505) 332-3777   Toll Free: (877) 841-3777
Fax: (505) 332-2777   E-mail: foundation@nmbf.com
Web: www.bcnm.com

Summary   To provide financial assistance to members of Southern Baptist churches in New Mexico who are interested in attending designated Baptist institutions.

Eligibility   This program is open to members of Southern Baptist churches in New Mexico who are enrolled at Wayland Baptist University (Plainview, Texas), Southwestern Baptist Theological Seminary (Fort Worth, Texas), or Golden Gate Baptist Theological Seminary (Mill Valley, California). Applicants must have a GPA of 2.5 or higher and be able to demonstrate financial need.

Financial data   A stipend is awarded (amount not specified).

Duration   1 year.

Number awarded   1 or more each year.

Deadline   June of each year.

[529]
DR. GEORGE AND EMMA J. TORRISON SCHOLARSHIP FUND

Evangelical Lutheran Church in America
Attn: Vocation and Education
8765 West Higgins Road
Chicago, IL 60631-4195
(773) 380-2843   Toll Free: (800) 638-3522, ext. 2843
Fax: (773) 380-2750   E-mail: Gina.Autenrieth@elca.org
Web: www.elca.org

Summary   To provide financial assistance to members of the Evangelical Lutheran Church in America (ELCA) who are working on or planning to work on a medical degree.

Eligibility   This program is open to active members of the ELCA who are either graduating college seniors accepted in a medical school or current medical school students. Students must be nominated for these scholarships. Applicants from ELCA colleges and universities must be nominated by the president of the institution; applicants at public colleges and universities must be nominated by the ELCA campus pastor; applicants at colleges and universities without a Lutheran campus ministry must be nominated by the pastor of the ELCA church in which they hold membership. Selection is based on stated career goals; financial need is not considered. Preference is given to applicants whose careers would lead them toward working to alleviate currently incurable diseases.

Financial data   The stipend is $5,000.

Duration   1 year; nonrenewable.

Additional information   This program was established in 1988.

Number awarded   Up to 4 each year.

Deadline   March of each year.

[530]
DWAIN MARROW SCHOLARSHIP

New Mexico Baptist Foundation
5325 Wyoming Boulevard, N.E.
P.O. Box 16560
Albuquerque, NM 87191-6560
(505) 332-3777   Toll Free: (877) 841-3777
Fax: (505) 332-2777   E-mail: foundation@nmbf.com
Web: www.bcnm.com

Summary   To provide financial assistance to members of Southern Baptist churches in New Mexico who are interested in attending a college or seminary in any state.

Eligibility   This program is open to members of Southern Baptist churches in New Mexico who are enrolled at an accredited a college or seminary in any state in response to a call to full-time ministry. Applicants must have a GPA of 2.0 or higher and be able to demonstrate financial need.

Financial data   A stipend is awarded (amount not specified).

Duration   1 year.

Number awarded   1 or more each year.

Deadline   June of each year.

[531]
E. CRAIG BRANDENBURG SCHOLARSHIP

United Methodist Church
Attn: General Board of Higher Education and Ministry
Office of Loans and Scholarships
1001 19th Avenue South
P.O. Box 340007
Nashville, TN 37203-0007
(615) 340-7344   Fax: (615) 340-7367
E-mail: umscholar@gbhem.org
Web: www.gbhem.org/loansandscholarships

Summary To provide financial assistance to mature Methodist students who are working on an undergraduate or graduate degree to change their profession or continue study after interruption.

Eligibility This program is open to full-time undergraduate and graduate students who are 35 years of age or older. Applicants must have been active, full members of a United Methodist Church for at least 1 year prior to applying. They must 1) be able to demonstrate special need because of a change of profession or vocation, interruption of study, or resumption of education; 2) have a GPA of 2.5 or higher; and 3) be U.S. citizens or permanent residents. Preference is given to applicants attending United Methodist colleges, universities, or seminaries.

Financial data Stipends range from $500 to $2,000.

Duration 1 year; recipients may reapply.

Number awarded Varies each year.

Deadline February of each year.

[532]
ECIM SCHOLARSHIPS

Episcopal Church Center
Attn: Domestic and Foreign Missionary Society
Episcopal Council of Indian Ministries
815 Second Avenue, Seventh Floor
New York, NY 10017-4503
(212) 716-6175   Toll Free: (800) 334-7626
Fax: (212) 867-0395   E-mail: dcoy@episcopalchurch.org
Web: www.episcopalchurch.org/native_american.htm

Summary To provide financial assistance to Native Americans interested in theological education within the Episcopal Church in the United States of America (ECUSA).

Eligibility Applicants must be seminarians of American Indian/Alaska Native descent attending an accredited Episcopal institution. They must submit documentation of tribal membership, diocesan endorsement from the bishop stating that the applicant is on track for ordination, and a signed statement that the applicant intends to serve in Indian ministry upon completion of study.

Financial data The amount of the award depends on the needs of the recipient and the availability of funds, to a maximum of $2,000 per year.

Additional information The Episcopal Council of Indian Ministries (ECIM) also awards the David Oakerhater Merit Fellowship to a middler with outstanding achievement and the Oakerhater Award of $2,500 to a seminarian pursuing a Ph.D. This program relies on funds established as early as 1879 and includes the Episcopal Legacy Fund for Scholarships Honoring the Memory of the Rev. Dr. Martin Luther King, Jr., established in 1991.

Number awarded Varies each year.

Deadline May of each year for fall semester or October of each year for spring semester.

[533]
ED E. AND GLADYS HURLEY FOUNDATION GRANTS

Ed E. and Gladys Hurley Foundation
Bank of America, N.A., Trustee
Attn: Jenae Guillory
901 Main Street, 19th Floor
Dallas, TX 75202-3714

Summary To provide financial assistance to undergraduate and graduate students in Texas who are interested in becoming Protestant ministers or who wish to pursue religious education.

Eligibility This program is open to undergraduate and graduate students who are preparing for a career as a Protestant minister, missionary, or other religious worker. Applicants may be residents of any state, but they must be attending a college or university in Texas. They must be able to demonstrate financial need and above-average grades.

Financial data The stipend is $1,000 per year.

Duration 1 year.

Number awarded Varies each year. Recently, 87 of these grants were awarded.

Deadline April of each year.

[534]
EDITH M. ALLEN SCHOLARSHIPS

United Methodist Church
Attn: General Board of Higher Education and Ministry
Office of Loans and Scholarships
1001 19th Avenue South
P.O. Box 340007
Nashville, TN 37203-0007
(615) 340-7344   Fax: (615) 340-7367
E-mail: umscholar@gbhem.org
Web: www.gbhem.org/loansandscholarships

Summary To provide financial assistance to Methodist students who are African American and working on an undergraduate or graduate degree in specified fields.

Eligibility This program is open to full-time undergraduate and graduate students at Methodist colleges and universities (preferably Historically Black United Methodist colleges) who have been active, full members of a United Methodist Church for at least 3 years prior to applying. Applicants must be African Americans working on a degree in education, social work, medicine, and/or other health professions. They must have at least a "B+" average and be recognized as a person whose academic and vocational contributions will help improve the quality of life for others.

Financial data A stipend is awarded (amount not specified).

Duration 1 year; recipients may reapply.

Number awarded Varies each year.

Deadline April of each year.

[535]
EDITH SEVILLE COALE SCHOLARSHIPS

Zonta Club of Washington, D.C.
c/o Diana Garcia, President
230 North Royal Street
Alexandria, VA 22314
Web: www.zontawashingtondc.org

Summary To provide financial assistance to Protestant women in the Washington, D.C. area who have completed the first year of medical school.

Eligibility Protestant women from any state who are in the second, third, or fourth year of medical school in the Washington, D.C. area are eligible to apply. Selection is based on financial need and scholastic achievement.

Financial data The amount awarded varies; recently, stipends averaged $4,155.

Duration 1 year.

Additional information The trust fund contains limited funds. Awards are not made for the first year of medical school. Preference is given to women students nominated by medical school faculty members.

Number awarded Varies each year. Recently, 8 of these scholarships were awarded.

Deadline December of each year.

[536]
EDWIN WHITNEY TRUST FUND AWARDS

Edwin Whitney Trust Fund
c/o Storrs Congregational Church
2 North Eagleville Road
Storrs, CT 06268-1710
(860) 429-6558   Fax: (860) 429-9693
E-mail: info@storrscongchurch.org
Web: www.storrscongchurch.org

Summary To provide financial assistance to Connecticut residents interested in preparing for ministry in the United Church of Christ.

Eligibility This program is open to Connecticut residents who are members of the United Church of Christ and accepted at or presently enrolled in a theological seminary recognized by the American Association of Theological Schools. They must be interested in preparing for the United Church of Christ ministry. Preference is given to residents from Mansfield, Connecticut. Financial need is considered in the selection process.

Financial data Up to $2,000 per year; the exact amount depends upon the financial needs of the recipient.

Duration 1 year; recipients may reapply, but no recipient will be awarded more than a lifetime total of $2,000.

Number awarded Varies each year.

Deadline June each year.

[537]
EIICHI MATSUSHITA MEMORIAL SCHOLARSHIP FUND

Evangelical Lutheran Church in America
Association of Asians and Pacific Islanders
8765 West Higgins Road
Chicago, IL 60631
(630) 416-6476   Toll Free: (800) 638-3522, ext. 2575
Fax: (773) 380-2588   E-mail: jykmoy@wavecable.com
Web: archive.elca.org/asian/fund.html

Summary To provide financial assistance to Asian/Pacific Islanders who wish to receive seminary training to become ordained Lutheran pastors or certified lay teachers.

Eligibility This program is open to students who are of Asian or Pacific Islander background and are attending a Lutheran seminary, have been endorsed by the appropriate synodical or district commissions, have demonstrated financial need, and have received partial financial support from their home congregations. Applicants must include a 250-word statement on their commitment to Asian/Pacific Islander ministry.

Financial data The stipend is $750.

Duration 1 year; may be renewed.

Additional information The scholarship was established by Asian Lutherans in North America. It is administered by Tierrasanta Lutheran Church on behalf of all the seminaries of the 3 Lutheran churches that united in 1988 to form the Evangelical Lutheran Church in America: the Association of Evangelical Lutheran Churches, the American Lutheran Church, and the Lutheran Church in America.

Number awarded 2 each year.

Deadline September of each year.

[538]
ELCA FUND FOR LEADERS IN MISSION

Evangelical Lutheran Church in America
Division for Ministry
Attn: Fund for Leaders in Mission
8765 West Higgins Road
Chicago, IL 60631-4195
(773) 380-2749   Toll Free: (800) 638-3522, ext. 2749
Fax: (773) 380-2829   E-mail: paul.hanson@elca.org
Web: www.elca.org

Summary To provide financial assistance to members of the Evangelical Lutheran Church in America (ELCA) who are entering a seminary.

Eligibility This program is open to students entering ELCA seminaries who plan to study full time. Candidates must be nominated by their seminary on the basis of their promise for leadership ministry and financial need. Nominees then complete an application that includes a 500-word essay.

Financial data The program provides full payment of tuition at ELCA seminaries.

Duration 3 years.

Additional information This program was established in 2000.

Number awarded Varies each year. Recently, 122 students were receiving full tuition scholarship support from this fund.

Deadline Deadline not specified.

[539]
ELEANOR HURLEY MEMORIAL SCHOLARSHIP

United Methodist Church-Louisiana Conference
Attn: Coordinator, Conference Board of Ordained Ministry
527 North Boulevard
Baton Rouge, LA 70802-5700
(225) 346-1646, ext. 230
Toll Free: (888) 239-5286, ext. 230
Fax: (225) 383-2652   E-mail: johneddd@bellsouth.net
Web: www.la-umc.org

Summary   To provide financial assistance to Methodists from Louisiana who are attending specified seminaries to prepare for a career in ordained ministry.

Eligibility   This program is open to members of United Methodist Churches in Louisiana who are enrolled or planning to enroll full time at 1 of the following seminaries: Perkins School of Theology of Southern Methodist University (Dallas, Texas), St. Paul School of Theology (Kansas City, Missouri and Oklahoma City, Oklahoma), Yale Divinity School (New Haven, Connecticut), or Union Theological Seminary (New York, New York). Applicants must be beginning a second career as an ordained minister. Along with their application, they must submit an essay on their vocational goals and plans for ministry.

Financial data   The stipend is $1,500.

Duration   1 year.

Additional information   This program was established in 2000.

Number awarded   2 each year.

Deadline   February of each year.

[540]
ELENA LUCREZIA CORNARO PISCOPIA SCHOLARSHIP FOR GRADUATE STUDIES

Kappa Gamma Pi
10215 Chardon Road
Chardon, OH 44024-9700
(440) 286-3764   Fax: (440) 286-4379
E-mail: cornarokgp@yahoo.com
Web: www.kappagammapi.org/_cornaro.html

Summary   To provide financial assistance for graduate school to members of Kappa Gamma Pi (the national Catholic college graduate honor society).

Eligibility   This program is open to members of the society who have been accepted by an accredited graduate school. Applicants must have graduated from a participating Catholic college or university. Along with their application, they must submit 200-word statements on 1) their volunteer work and leadership experience; 2) their career aspirations and personal goals; and 3) their financial situation.

Financial data   The stipend is $3,000, to be used as needed for graduate expenses at any accredited college or university.

Duration   1 year; nonrenewable.

Additional information   This program, established in 1984, is named for the first woman in the world to receive a university degree (in 1678).

Number awarded   Varies each year. Recently, 5 of these scholarships were awarded.

Deadline   April of each year.

[541]
ELIZABETH ALLISON HYNSON MEMORIAL SCHOLARSHIP FUND

Episcopal Church Center
Attn: Domestic and Foreign Missionary Society
Convenor of the Scholarship Committee
815 Second Avenue
New York, NY 10017-4503
(212) 922-6175   Toll Free: (800) 334-7626, ext. 6175
Fax: (212) 867-0395   E-mail: dcoy@episcopalchurch.org
Web: arc.episcopalchurch.org/ministry/hynsonfnd.htm

Summary   To provide financial assistance to candidates and postulants at seminaries of the Episcopal Church in the United States of America (ECUSA).

Eligibility   This program is open to young (under 30 years of age) postulants and candidates preparing for Holy Orders at any of the 11 accredited Episcopal seminaries who intend to serve in parish ministry. Preference is given to applicants from the dioceses of east Carolina, Minnesota, Atlanta, and southwest Florida.

Financial data   The stipend is $2,000. Funds are paid to the seminary.

Duration   1 year.

Number awarded   1 each year.

Deadline   April of each year.

[542]
ELLA TACKWOOD FUND

United Methodist Higher Education Foundation
Attn: Scholarships Administrator
1001 19th Avenue South
P.O. Box 340005
Nashville, TN 37203-0005
(615) 340-7385   Toll Free: (800) 811-8110
Fax: (615) 340-7330
E-mail: umhefscholarships@gbhem.org
Web: www.umhef.org/receive.php?id=endowed_funds

Summary   To provide financial assistance to Methodist undergraduate and graduate students at Historically Black Colleges and Universities of the United Methodist Church.

Eligibility   This program is open to students enrolling as full-time undergraduate and graduate students at the Historically Black Colleges and Universities of the United Methodist Church. Applicants must have been active, full members of a United Methodist Church for at least 1 year prior to applying. They must have a GPA of 2.5 or higher and be able to demonstrate financial need. Along with their application, they must submit a 200-word essay on their involvement and/or leadership responsibilities in their church, school, and community within the last 3 years. U.S. citizenship or permanent resident status is required.

Financial data   The stipend is at least $1,000 per year.

Duration   1 year; nonrenewable.

Additional information   This program was established in 1985. The qualifying schools are Bennett College for Women, Bethune-Cookman College, Claflin University, Clark Atlanta University, Dillard University, Huston-Tillotson College, Meharry Medical College, Paine College, Philander Smith College, Rust College, and Wiley College.

Number awarded Varies each year. Recently, 3 of these scholarships were awarded.

Deadline May of each year.

[543]
ELLEN CUSHING SCHOLARSHIPS

American Baptist Churches USA
National Ministries
Attn: Office of Financial Aid for Studies
P.O. Box 851
Valley Forge, PA 19482-0851
(610) 768-2067   Toll Free: (800) ABC-3USA, ext. 2067
Fax: (610) 768-2453
E-mail: Financialaid.Web@abc-usa.org
Web: www.nationalministries.org

Summary To provide financial assistance to Baptist women interested in working on a graduate degree in human service fields.

Eligibility This program is open to female Baptists in graduate programs who are preparing for a human service career in the secular world. Applicants must be U.S. citizens who have been a member of a church affiliated with American Baptist Churches USA for at least 1 year. M.Div. and D.Min. students are not eligible. Preference is given to students active in their school, church, or region.

Financial data The stipend is $2,000.

Duration 1 year.

Number awarded Up to 3 each year.

Deadline May of each year.

[544]
EMIL SLAVIK MEMORIAL SCHOLARSHIP

Slovak Catholic Sokol
Attn: Membership Memorial Scholarship Fund
205 Madison Street
P.O. Box 899
Passaic, NJ 07055-0899
(973) 777-2605   Toll Free: (800) 886-7656
Fax: (973) 779-8245 E-mail: life@slovakcatholicsokol.org
Web: www.slovakcatholicsokol.org

Summary To provide financial assistance to members of the Slovak Catholic Sokol who are working on a degree in specified fields at a college or graduate school in any state.

Eligibility This program is open to members of the Slovak Catholic Sokol who have completed at least 1 semester of college and are currently enrolled full time as an undergraduate or graduate student at an accredited college, university, or professional school in any state. Applicants must have been a member for at least 5 years, have at least $3,000 permanent life insurance coverage, have both parents who are members, and have at least 1 parent who is of Slovak descent. They must be working on a degree in the liberal arts, the sciences, pre-law, pre-medicine, or business.

Financial data The stipend is $2,500 per year.

Duration 1 year; may be renewed 1 additional year.

Additional information Slovak Catholic Sokol was founded as a fraternal benefit society in 1905. It is licensed to operate in the following states: Connecticut, Illinois, Indiana, Massachusetts, Michigan, New Jersey, New York, Ohio, Pennsylvania, and Wisconsin.

Number awarded 1 each year.

Deadline March of each year.

[545]
EPISCOPAL ASIAMERICA MINISTRY COMMISSION CONTINUING EDUCATION SCHOLARSHIPS AND FELLOWSHIPS

Episcopal Church Center
Attn: Office of Asian American Ministries
815 Second Avenue
New York, NY 10017-4594
(212) 922-5344   Toll Free: (800) 334-7626
Fax: (212) 867-7652
E-mail: wvergara@episcopalchurch.org
Web: www.episcopalchurch.org/asian.htm

Summary To provide financial assistance to Asian Americans interested in seeking ordination and serving in a ministry involving Asians in the Episcopal Church.

Eligibility This program is open to Asian students pursuing theological education, including diocesan programs as well as seminary education. Applicants must be a member of an Asian constituency in the Episcopal Church and have begun the process of seeking ordination through a local Episcopal diocese. Scholarships are presented only for full-time study.

Financial data The maximum scholarship is $4,000 per semester for seminary study and $2,500 per semester for diocesan theological study programs.

Duration 1 semester; renewable.

Additional information This program was established in 1991 as part of the Episcopal Legacy Fund for Scholarships Honoring the Memory of the Rev. Dr. Martin Luther King, Jr. Applications must include an essay indicating an understanding of the life and ministry of Dr. King.

Number awarded Varies each year.

Deadline April of each year for the fall semester; August of each year for the spring semester.

[546]
EPISCOPAL CHURCH FOUNDATION FELLOWSHIP PARTNERS PROGRAM

Episcopal Church Center
Attn: Episcopal Church Foundation
815 Second Avenue, Room 400
New York, NY 10017-4564
(212) 697-2858   Toll Free: (800) 697-2858
Fax: (212) 297-0142
E-mail: Kelly@episcopalfoundation.org
Web: www.episcopalfoundation.org

Summary To provide financial assistance to graduate students in fields of importance to the Episcopal Church and to ministers seeking training in "transformational ministry."

Eligibility This program provides both academic fellowships and transformational ministry fellowships. Both fellowships are available to members, lay and clergy, of the Episcopal Church in the United States and the global Anglican Communion. Academic fellowships are open to graduate students (except those in first professional degree programs, such as M.Div., J.D., or M.D.) whose program of study has the potential to impact congregations, address a recognized shortage area, or provide expertise in an area of need for the Episcopal Church. Recent fellowships were in the areas of mission, theological developments within the Anglican Communion, and religious conflict and peace. Applicants may be enrolled in a master's or doctoral program or engaged in clinical study or training at the post-undergraduate level. They must be nominated by the dean or director of their current or former degree program. Transformational ministry fellowships are available to candidates engaged in ministries at the grassroots or congregational level that will change individuals, groups, or communities in positive ways, impacting their ability to see and use God's gifts, bringing them into a closer relationship with God. Applicants must demonstrate how their ministry has the potential to transform community at the grassroots level. They must be nominated by the rector or vicar of an Episcopal or Anglican congregation or the director of an Episcopal organization or ministry. The nomination must be endorsed by a bishop of the Episcopal Church or Anglican Communion. Special consideration is given to programs in locations with limited resources or among underserved communities.

Financial data   Grants are $15,000 for the first year or $10,000 for each renewal year.

Duration   1 year; may be renewed for up to 2 additional years, depending on continued need and impact.

Additional information   This program began more than 40 years ago as the Episcopal Church Foundation Doctoral Fellowships, limited to scholars planning teaching careers in theological education. It was revised and expanded in 2006.

Number awarded   3 each year.

Deadline   March of each year.

[547]
ESTHER EDWARDS GRADUATE SCHOLARSHIP

United Methodist Church
Attn: General Board of Higher Education and Ministry
Office of Loans and Scholarships
1001 19th Avenue South
P.O. Box 340007
Nashville, TN 37203-0007
(615) 340-7344   Fax: (615) 340-7367
E-mail: umscholar@gbhem.org
Web: www.gbhem.org/loansandscholarships

Summary   To provide financial assistance to female graduate students who are working on a degree in higher education administration to prepare for a career with a United Methodist school.

Eligibility   This program is open to women who are working on a graduate degree to prepare for an executive management career in higher education administration with a United Methodist school, college, or university. Applicants must have been active, full members of a United Methodist Church for at least 1 year prior to applying. They must have a GPA of 2.5 or higher. First preference is given to students currently employed by a United Methodist school, college, or university and to full-time students.

Financial data   The stipend is $5,000.

Duration   1 year; nonrenewable.

Number awarded   1 each year.

Deadline   February of each year.

[548]
ETHEL COLQUITT MARTIN SCHOLARSHIP FUND

Alabama-West Florida United Methodist Foundation, Inc.
170 Belmont Drive
P.O. Box 8066
Dothan, AL 36304
(334) 793-6820   Fax: (334) 794-6480
E-mail: foundation@alwfumf.org
Web: www.alwfumf.org

Summary   To provide financial assistance to ministerial students from the Alabama-West Florida Conference of the United Methodist Church.

Eligibility   This program is open to members of United Methodist Churches within the Alabama-West Florida Conference. Applicants must be enrolled in the third year at an approved seminary and demonstrate a clear intent to return to the conference in service as ordained United Methodist clergy. They must be younger than 32 years of age. Financial need is considered in the selection process.

Financial data   The stipend depends on the need of the recipient and the number of applicants, but the amount awarded does not exceed the actual cost of tuition and books.

Duration   1 year.

Number awarded   1 or more each year.

Deadline   June of each year.

[549]
EULA MAE HENDERSON SCHOLARSHIPS

Baptist General Convention of Texas
Attn: Woman's Missionary Union of Texas
333 North Washington, Suite 160
Dallas, TX 75246-1716
(214) 828-5150   Toll Free: (888) 968-6389
Fax: (214) 828-5179   E-mail: wmutx@bgct.org
Web: www.bgct.org/texasbaptists/Page.aspx?&pid=2975

Summary   To provide financial assistance to women members of Baptist churches in Texas who are preparing for a career in ministry at a Texas Baptist institution.

Eligibility   This program is open to women who are active members of Southern Baptist churches in Texas. Applicants must be full-time students in at least their second semester of graduate work in preparation for a career in vocational Christian ministry through the International Mission Board, the North American Mission Board, or the Woman's Missionary Union (all of the Southern Baptist Convention). Along with their application, they must submit brief statements on when they became a Christian, their call to vocational Christian ministry, the field of Christian mission they plan to enter following graduation, the factors and influences that led them to select that field, and their involvement in Women's Missionary Union organizations. They must have a GPA of 3.0 or higher and be able to document financial need.

Financial data   The stipend is $500 per semester ($1,000 per year).

Duration   1 semester; may be renewed up to 7 additional semesters if the recipient continues to meet the requirements.

Additional information   This program was established in 1986. The eligible schools are Southwestern Baptist Theological Seminary, George W. Truett Seminary at Baylor University, Logsdon School of Theology at Hardin-Simmons University, and Baylor University's School of Social Work.

Number awarded Varies each year. Recently, 3 of these scholarships were awarded.

Deadline February of each year.

[550]
EVANGELICAL LUTHERAN CHURCH IN AMERICA GRANTS FOR ADVANCED THEOLOGICAL STUDY

Evangelical Lutheran Church in America
Division for Ministry
Attn: Department for Theological Education
8765 West Higgins Road
Chicago, IL 60631-4195
(773) 380-2885   Toll Free: (800) 638-3522, ext. 2885
Fax: (773) 380-2829
E-mail: Jonathan.Strandjord@elca.org
Web: www.elca.org

Summary To provide financial assistance to members of the Evangelical Lutheran Church in America (ELCA) who wish to work on a doctoral degree.

Eligibility Applicants must be active members of an ELCA congregation (either lay or ordained) who are pursuing advanced academic theological education degrees (Ph.D., Th.D., or Ed.D.) with the intent of teaching in the field of theological education. Financial need is considered in the selection process.

Financial data Grants up to $4,000 per year are awarded. Dissertation grants are $2,000.

Duration Up to 4 years. Prior grantees may receive a fifth year of support as a dissertation grant.

Number awarded Approximately 50 each year.

Deadline April of each year.

[551]
EVANGELISM FOR THE 21ST CENTURY GRANTS

Evangelical Education Society of the Episcopal Church
P.O. Box 3674
Arlington, VA 22203
(703) 807-1862   E-mail: office@ees1862.org
Web: www.ees1862.org/05-grants/index.html

Summary To provide funding for projects that strengthen the evangelical witness of the Episcopal Church.

Eligibility This program is open to Episcopal students, faculty, administrators, staff, and families at institutions accredited by the Association of Theological Schools. Applicants must be proposing projects that raise up lay and ordained ministers to bring new evangelical vigor to parish churches; help believers understand and articulate the Christian faith and to live accordingly; and take the Gospel to the unchurched. Special consideration is given to projects that foster fresh initiatives and methodologies; connect the academic world of the seminaries to the work carried out by lay and ordained ministers in surrounding communities; may result in pilot programs or models that others can adopt or adapt; state clearly how funds will be used and how the project's results can be evaluated; and present well-defined goals.

Financial data Grants range from $500 to $5,000.

Duration 1 year.

Number awarded Varies each year. Recently, 31 of these grants were awarded.

Deadline January or September of each year.

[552]
FAIRMONT PRESBYTERIAN CHURCH DEACONS' SCHOLARSHIP FOR POSTGRADUATE DEGREES

Fairmont Presbyterian Church
Attn: Scholarship Committee
3705 Far Hills Avenue
Kettering, OH 45429
(937) 299-3539   Fax: (937) 299-5974
E-mail: office@fairmontchurch.org
Web: www.fairmontchurch.org

Summary To provide financial assistance to students interested in preparing for the Presbyterian ministry or another church-related vocation at a seminary in any state.

Eligibility This program is open to graduate students interested in preparing for the Presbyterian ministry or another church-related vocation. Applicants must be enrolled or planning to enroll at a seminary in any state. They must submit 3 letters of recommendation and a 750-word essay on what they believe God is calling them to do in the ministry, including what has motivated them to prepare for a vocation in the ministry. Priority is given to applicants in the following order: 1) members of the Fairmont Presbyterian Church; 2) members of the Miami of Ohio Presbytery; and 3) students affiliated with the Presbyterian Church (USA). Selection is based on merit and financial need.

Financial data Stipends range from $300 to $1,000 per year.

Duration 1 year; may be renewed up to 2 additional years.

Additional information This program was established in 1955.

Number awarded Varies each year.

Deadline June of each year.

[553]
FANNIE V. WARD SCHOLARSHIP

Order of the Eastern Star-Grand Chapter of Texas
Attn: Education Committee
1503 West Division Street
Arlington, TX 76012
(817) 265-6263
Web: www.grandchapteroftexasoes.org/scholar_forms.asp

Summary To provide financial assistance to residents of Texas interested in attending college or graduate school in any state, especially those planning to prepare for a career in religious service.

Eligibility This program is open to residents of Texas who are high school seniors or graduates already enrolled at an accredited college, university, or seminary in any state. Applicants must be interested in working on an undergraduate or graduate degree in any field, although the program especially encourages applications from those planning to prepare for a full-time career as a minister, missionary, director of religious education, Christian youth worker, or church music director. Along with their application, they must submit an essay describing their plans for the future, reasons for applying for the scholarship, and financial status. Undergraduates must be enrolled full time.

Financial data The stipend is $1,000.

Duration 1 year; nonrenewable.

Number awarded 1 or more each year.

Deadline February of each year.

[554]
FATHER LEONARD BACHMANN GRADUATE SCHOLARSHIPS

Catholic Daughters of the Americas
Attn: Scholarship Chair
10 West 71st Street
New York, NY 10023
(212) 877-3041   Fax: (212) 724-5923
E-mail: CDofANatl@aol.com
Web: www.catholicdaughters.org

Summary To provide financial assistance to Catholic graduate students in any field, especially members of the Catholic Daughters of the Americas (CDA).

Eligibility Eligible to apply for this support are U.S. citizens of the Catholic faith who are interested in working on a graduate degree. Applicants must submit a transcript, a letter of academic reference, a statement of their reason for applying for this scholarship, and an autobiography. Preference is given to applicants who are members or the relatives of members of the Catholic Daughters of the Americas. Financial need is not considered in the selection process.

Financial data The stipend is either $3,000 or $1,000.

Duration 1 year.

Number awarded 2 each year: 1 at $3,000 and 1 at $1,000.

Deadline April of each year.

[555]
FATHER MICHAEL J. MCGIVNEY VOCATIONS SCHOLARSHIPS

Knights of Columbus
Attn: Department of Scholarships
P.O. Box 1670
New Haven, CT 06507-0901
(203) 752-4332   Fax: (203) 772-2696
E-mail: info@kofc.org
Web: www.kofc.org/un/en/vocations/scholarships.html

Summary To provide financial assistance to seminary students preparing for a vocation as a Catholic priest.

Eligibility This program is open to students enrolled in approved seminaries in the United States and Canada. Applicants must be preparing for a vocation in the Catholic priesthood. Selection is based on financial need. Preference is given to seminarians who are members of the Knights of Columbus or whose fathers are members, but all qualified applicants are considered.

Financial data The stipend is $2,500 per year; funds must be used for tuition, room, and board.

Duration 1 year; may be renewed up to 3 additional years.

Additional information This program was established in 1992.

Number awarded Varies each year. Recently, 34 new scholarships (28 to students at U.S. seminaries and 6 to students at Canadian seminaries) were awarded.

Deadline May of each year.

[556]
FAYE AND ROBERT LETT SCHOLARSHIP

American Baptist Churches of Ohio
Attn: Ohio Baptist Education Society
136 Galway Drive North
P.O. Box 288
Granville, OH 43023-0288
(740) 587-0804   Fax: (740) 587-0807
E-mail: pastorchris@neo.rr.com
Web: www.abc-ohio.org

Summary To provide funding to African American upper-division and graduate students from Ohio who are interested in preparing for the Baptist ministry at a college or seminary in any state.

Eligibility This program is open to African American residents of Ohio who have completed at least 2 years of study at an accredited college or university in any state and are interested in continuing their education as an upper-division or seminary student. Applicants must 1) hold active membership in a church affiliated with the American Baptist Churches of Ohio or a church dually-aligned with the American Baptist Churches of Ohio; 2) be in the process of preparing for a professional career in Christian ministry (such as a local church pastor, church education, youth or young adult ministries, church music, specialized ministry, chaplaincy, ministry in higher education, or missionary service); 3) be committed to working professionally within the framework of the American Baptist Churches USA; and 4) acknowledge a personal commitment to the Gospel of Jesus Christ, an understanding of the Christian faith, and a definite call to professional Christian ministry as a life work. Financial need must be demonstrated.

Financial data Stipends generally range from $1,000 to $1,500 a year.

Duration 1 year.

Additional information This program was established in 1990.

Number awarded 1 or more each year.

Deadline March of each year.

[557]
FELLOWSHIP OF UNITED METHODISTS IN MUSIC AND WORSHIP ARTS SCHOLARSHIPS

The Fellowship of United Methodists in Music and
   Worship Arts
Attn: Executive Director
P.O. Box 24787
Nashville, TN 37202-4787
(615) 749-6875   Toll Free: (800) 952-8977
Fax: (615) 749-6874   E-mail: fummwa@aol.com
Web: fummwa.affiniscape.com

Summary To provide financial assistance to Methodist and other selected Christian students who are working on an academic degree in music or the worship arts.

Eligibility This program is open to full-time students entering or enrolled at an accredited college, university, or school of theology. Applicants must be studying sacred music, worship, or the arts related to worship. They must have been members of the United Methodist Church (UMC) for at least 1 year immediately before applying. Members of other Christian denominations are also eligible if they have been employed in the UMC for at least 1 year. Applicants must be able to demonstrate exceptional artistic or musical talents, leadership abilities, and outstanding promise of future usefulness to the church in an area of worship and/or music.

Financial data The stipend is $1,000.

Duration 1 year.

Number awarded 1 or more each year.

Deadline February of each year.

[558]
FIRST CATHOLIC SLOVAK LADIES ASSOCIATION GRADUATE SCHOLARSHIPS

First Catholic Slovak Ladies Association
Attn: Director of Fraternal Scholarship Aid
24950 Chagrin Boulevard
Cleveland, OH 44122-5634
(216) 464-8015   Toll Free: (800) 464-4642
Fax: (216) 464-9260   E-mail: info@fcsla.com
Web: www.fcsla.com/scholarship.shtml

Summary To provide financial assistance to graduate students who are members of the First Catholic Slovak Ladies Association.

Eligibility This program is open to full-time graduate students at accredited colleges and universities in the United States or Canada. Applicants must have been beneficial members of the First Catholic Slovak Ladies Association for at least 3 years on a $1,000 legal reserve certificate, a $5,000 term certificate, or an annuity certificate. Along with their application, they must submit an autobiographical essay of approximately 500 words that includes a statement of their goals and objectives. Selection is based on academic standing (50%), financial need (20%), family membership in the association (15%), leadership (10%), and extenuating circumstances (5%).

Financial data The stipend is $1,750.

Duration 1 year.

Additional information This program includes 2 awards designated as Theresa Sajan Scholarships for Graduate Students.

Number awarded 16 each year.

Deadline February of each year.

[559]
FIRST PRESBYTERIAN CHURCH OF SHREVEPORT SEMINARY SCHOLARSHIPS

First Presbyterian Church
Attn: Scholarship Committee
900 Jordan Street
Shreveport, LA 71101-4378
(318) 222-0604   Fax: (318) 221-8589
E-mail: swhaley@fpcshreveport.com
Web: www.fpcshreveport.org/776394

Summary To provide financial assistance to students at seminaries affiliated with the Presbyterian Church (USA).

Eligibility This program is open to students at PCUSA theological seminaries. First priority is given to members of the First Presbyterian Church of Shreveport, Louisiana. Applicants must have a GPA of 3.0 or higher and be able to demonstrate financial need. Along with their application, they must submit a 1-page personal statement that describes their relationship to First Presbyterian Church of Shreveport or, if they have no relationship to that church, how they came to

faith, their relationship with PCUSA, and their career goals and plans.

Financial data The stipend is $500 per semester ($1,000 per year).

Duration 1 semester; may be renewed.

Additional information This fund began in 1957 as the Hotson Trust Fund. Since then, several other named funds have also been established: Bell-McGuire Memorial Scholarship Fund, Ruth Grey Knighton Jackson Memorial Scholarship Fund, Staman Scholarship Fund, Johnette Kirby Educational Fund, Files Educational Funds, and Hicks-Ray Trust Scholarship Fund.

Number awarded Several each year. To date, more than 200 students have received funds through this program and are now pastors, seminary professors, and college teachers.

Deadline April of each year.

[560]
FIRST PRESBYTERIAN CHURCH SCHOLARSHIP FUND

First Presbyterian Church
Attn: Scholarship Fund Program
709 South Boston Avenue
Tulsa, OK 74119-1629
(918) 584-4701   Fax: (918) 584-5233
E-mail: TBriscoe@firstchurchtulsa.org
Web: www.firstchurchtulsa.org/scholarships.htm

Summary To provide financial assistance to Presbyterian students interested in working on an undergraduate or graduate degree in any field.

Eligibility To be eligible for this program, students must be communicant members of the Presbyterian Church (USA), be working on an undergraduate or graduate degree at an accredited institution, and have at least a 2.0 GPA. Priority is given first to members of the First Presbyterian Church (in Tulsa), second to applicants in the Presbytery of Eastern Oklahoma, third to applicants in the Synod of the Sun (Arkansas, Louisiana, Oklahoma, and Texas), and fourth to members of the Presbyterian Church at large. Selection is based on academic merit, academic or career intent, church or religious involvement, and financial need.

Financial data Stipends range from $500 to $2,000. Funds are paid directly to the recipient's school.

Duration 1 year; recipients may reapply.

Additional information This program was established in 1988. It includes the following named funds (each of which includes additional restrictions): the Harry Allen Scholarship Fund, the Ethel Frances Crate Scholarship Fund, the Elsa Everett Scholarship Fund, the Cydna Ann Huffstetler Scholarship Fund, and the Clarence Warren Scholarship Fund.

Number awarded Varies each year. Recently, this program awarded 12 unrestricted scholarships and another 14 scholarships with various restrictions.

Deadline April of each year.

[561]
FLEMING FAMILY FOUNDATION SCHOLARSHIPS

Fleming Family Foundation
Attn: Randy Fleming, President
P.O. Box 410
Springfield, NE 68059
(402) 210-4885   Fax: (402) 253-2208
E-mail: auctioneer_32@msn.com
Web: www.umcneb.org/pages/detail/114

Summary To provide financial assistance to Methodists from Nebraska interested in entering full-time Christian service by working on an undergraduate or graduate degree at a school in any state.

Eligibility This program is open to residents of Nebraska who are members of a congregation of the United Methodist Church (UMC). Applicants must be attending or planning to attend a college or university in any state to work on an undergraduate or graduate degree as preparation for a career in full-time Christian service. Along with their application, they must submit brief essays on 1) their participation in the life of their school, community, church, and similar organizations; 2) what influenced them in selecting their college and their career goals; 3) where they see themselves professionally after graduation; and 4) their financial need.

Financial data The stipend is $1,000.

Duration 1 year.

Number awarded Varies each year.

Deadline May of each year.

[562]
FLETCHER MAE HOWELL SCHOLARSHIP

Woman's Missionary Union of Virginia
2828 Emerywood Parkway
Richmond, VA 23294
(804) 915-5000, ext. 8267
Toll Free: (800) 255-2428 (within VA)
Fax: (804) 672-8008   E-mail: wmuv@wmuv.org
Web: wmuv.org/developing-future-leaders/scholarships

Summary To provide financial assistance to African American women from Virginia who are working on a graduate degree in Christian education.

Eligibility This program is open to African American women from Virginia who are interested in full-time graduate study in Christian education. An interview is required.

Financial data The stipend is $1,000.

Duration 1 year.

Number awarded Up to 2 each year.

Deadline January of each year.

[563]
FLORENCE LILLIAN DRUSE MISSIONARY SCHOLARSHIP FUND

United Methodist Church-Wisconsin Conference
Attn: Board of Higher Education and Campus Ministry
750 Windsor Street
P.O. Box 620
Sun Prairie, WI 53590-0620
(608) 837-7328   Toll Free: (888) 240-7328
Fax: (608) 837-8547
Web: www.wisconsinumc.org

Summary To provide forgivable loans for training as a missionary, especially to members of United Methodist churches in Wisconsin interested in graduate study.

Eligibility This program is open to students interested in a program of college or university training in preparation for work in the missionary field, whether foreign, domestic, or medical. Preference is given to members of United Methodist Churches in Wisconsin and to applicants who already have a bachelor's degree. Applicants must be likely to serve in a missionary field for at least 5 years. They must be able to demonstrate financial need. U.S. citizenship or permanent resident status is required.

Financial data A loan of $2,500 per academic year is offered. After 5 years of verified missionary service, the loan is forgiven.

Duration 1 year. Recipients may reapply. The maximum lifetime loan amount available to each individual is $7,500.

Number awarded 1 or more each year.

Deadline April of each year.

[564]
FLORIDA BAPTIST FOUNDATION STUDENT LOANS

Florida Baptist Foundation
Attn: Student Loan Committee
1320 Hendricks Avenue, Suite 2
Jacksonville, FL 32207
(904) 346-0325, ext. 221
Toll Free: (800) 780-0325, ext. 221
Fax: (904) 346-0414   E-mail: info@floridabaptist.org
Web: www.floridabaptist.org/studentloans

Summary To provide academic loans for college or seminary to members of Southern Baptist churches in Florida.

Eligibility This loan program is open to residents of Florida who are members of a Southern Baptist church. Applicants must be enrolled (or planning to enroll) full time at 1) an accredited college or university in any state, or 2) a Southern Baptist seminary. They must submit a 1-page statement about themselves, their family, and their future plans. Selection is based on financial need, academic performance, Christian character, and church participation.

Financial data The maximum loan is $2,500 per year or $6,000 in a lifetime. Interest payments, at a rate based on the outstanding principal balance, are due monthly while the student is in school. Principal payments begin 6 months after completion of or leaving school and must be repaid within 48 months.

Duration 1 year; may be renewed.

Additional information Loans to selected seminary students are made from the Gross Loan Fund. Loans to other seminary students and undergraduates are made from the Cunningham Loan Fund.

Number awarded Varies each year. The Gross Loan Fund provides loans to 6 seminary students each year. The number of loans from the Cunningham Loan Fund varies.

Deadline Deadline not specified.

[565]
FLORIDA EASTERN STAR TRAINING AWARDS FOR RELIGIOUS LEADERSHIP

Order of the Eastern Star-Grand Chapter of Florida
Attn: Grand Secretary
P.O. Box 97
Bonifay, FL 32425-0097
(850) 547-9199 Fax: (850) 547-9299
E-mail: grandsecretary@floridaoes.org
Web: www.floridaoes.org

Summary To provide financial assistance to residents of Florida who are attending a college or seminary in any state to prepare for a career in religious leadership.

Eligibility This program is open to residents of Florida who are currently enrolled full time at an accredited college or seminary in any state. Applicants must be taking classes that will lead to a degree in a field of religious leadership, as a minister, missionary, director of religious education, Christian youth worker, or church music director. They must have a GPA of 2.0 or higher and a record of good moral character. Selection is based on academic record, character, leadership in Christian activities, citizenship, and financial need. Preference is given to students who are at least a junior in college.

Financial data A stipend is awarded (amount not specified).

Duration 1 year.

Number awarded 1 or more each year.

Deadline May of each year for fall semester; November of each year for spring semester.

[566]
FRED E. AND JANET SMITH PLYLER SCHOLARSHIP

South Carolina United Methodist Foundation
P.O. Box 5087
Columbia, SC 29250-5087
(803) 771-9125 Fax: (803) 771-9135
E-mail: scumf@bellsouth.net
Web: www.umcsc.org/scholarships.html

Summary To provide financial assistance to residents of South Carolina preparing for Methodist ministry at a school in any state.

Eligibility This program is open to residents of South Carolina preparing for ordained ministry in the United Methodist Church (UMC). Applicants must be enrolled full time at a seminary, graduate school, or theological school in any state that is approved by the University Senate of the UMC. Selection is based on financial need and promise for ministry.

Financial data A stipend is awarded (amount not specified).

Duration 1 year.

Additional information This scholarship was established by the South Carolina Conference of the United Methodist Church in 2002.

Number awarded 1 or more each year.

Deadline April of each year.

[567]
FUND FOR THEOLOGICAL EDUCATION CONGREGATIONAL FELLOWSHIPS

The Fund for Theological Education, Inc.
Attn: Partnership for Excellence
825 Houston Mill Road, Suite 250
Atlanta, GA 30329
(404) 727-1450 Fax: (404) 727-1490
E-mail: fellowships@thefund.org
Web: www.thefund.org

Summary To provide matching funding to students who are planning to enter a seminary to prepare for a career in the ministry and who are receiving support from their congregation.

Eligibility This program is open to students entering their first year of full time study for an M.Div. degree at an accredited seminary. They must be nominated by a congregation that has already committed to provide them with financial support. Nominees must be Canadian or U.S. citizens under 35 years of age and have a GPA of 3.0 or higher in their undergraduate work. Along with their application, they must submit a 3-page essay discussing their understanding of what God is calling the church to be and to do in this time and place and how their own gifts, struggles, and commitments offer a response to the call as a future leader of a congregation.

Financial data This program provides matching funding, to a maximum of $5,000, that the nominating congregation commits toward the student's first year.

Duration 1 year.

Additional information Fellows also receive an additional stipend to cover travel and expenses to attend the sponsor's summer Conference on Excellence in Ministry, where they spend several days engaged in lectures, worship, forums, workshops, recreational activities, and informal time together with other students, theological leaders, and pastors. Students unable to attend the conference should not apply for the fellowship.

Number awarded Up to 40 each year.

Deadline March of each year.

[568]
FUND FOR THEOLOGICAL EDUCATION MINISTRY FELLOWSHIPS

The Fund for Theological Education, Inc.
Attn: Partnership for Excellence
825 Houston Mill Road, Suite 250
Atlanta, GA 30329
(404) 727-1450 Fax: (404) 727-1490
E-mail: fellowships@thefund.org
Web: www.thefund.org/programs/ministry_fellowships.phtml

Summary To provide financial assistance to students enrolled at a seminary and preparing for a career in the ministry.

Eligibility This program is open to full-time students completing their first year of an M.Div. program at an accredited seminary. Each seminary may nominate up to 5 students. Nominees must be Canadian or U.S. citizens under 35 years of age and have a GPA of 3.0 or higher in their undergraduate work and 3.3 or higher in their seminary studies. They must 1) be able to document excellent abilities for ministry and a deep commitment to ministry as a career, as well as a record of high academic achievement; 2) have a relationship with and dedication to a particular denomination of the Christian church; 3) have a drive to understand others' needs and act on their behalf; and 4) bring imagination, creativity, compassion, vision, a capacity for critical thinking, leadership, personal integrity, and good communication skills to their work.

Financial data Fellows receive a stipend of $10,000 for educational and living expenses and for a self-designed ministry project.

Duration 1 year.

Additional information This program began in 1999. Fellows also receive an additional stipend to cover travel and expenses to attend the sponsor's summer Conference on Excellence in Ministry, where they spend several days engaged in lectures, worship, forums, workshops, recreational activities, and informal time together with other students, theological leaders, and pastors. Students unable to attend the conference should not apply for the fellowship.

Number awarded Up to 20 each year.

Deadline February of each year.

[569]
GARRETT TRUST FUND

United Church of Christ
Parish Life and Leadership Ministry Team
Attn: Grants, Scholarships, and Resources
700 Prospect Avenue East
Cleveland, OH 44115-1100
(216) 736-3839   Toll Free: (866) 822-8224, ext. 3839
Fax: (216) 736-3783   E-mail: jeffersv@ucc.org
Web: www.ucc.org/seminarians/ucc-scholarships-for.html

Summary To provide financial assistance to seminary students who are interested in becoming a pastor in the United Church of Christ (UCC).

Eligibility This program is open to students at accredited seminaries who have been members of a UCC congregation for at least 1 year. Applicants must 1) have a GPA of 3.0 or higher, 2) be enrolled in a course of study leading to ordained ministry, and 3) be in care of an association or conference at the time of application. They must demonstrate leadership ability through participation in their local church, association, conference, or academic environment. Along with their application, they must sign a faith statement. Financial need is considered in the selection process.

Financial data Stipends range from $600 to $1,000, depending on the need of the recipient.

Duration These are 1-time, nonrenewable grants.

Additional information This fund was established in 1946.

Number awarded 1 or more each year.

Deadline Applications may be submitted at any time.

[570]
GENE ROGER AND MILDRED WIMBERLY KIZER SCHOLARSHIP

South Carolina United Methodist Foundation
P.O. Box 5087
Columbia, SC 29250-5087
(803) 771-9125   Fax: (803) 771-9135
E-mail: scumf@bellsouth.net
Web: www.umcsc.org/scholarships.html

Summary To provide financial assistance to Methodist students from South Carolina who are attending college or graduate school in any state to prepare for a career in Christian service.

Eligibility This program is open to residents of South Carolina who are preparing for full-time Christian service in the United Methodist Church (i.e., those ministries of the Church for which ordination, consecration, or certification is required). Applicants must be enrolled at a college, seminary, theological school, or graduate school in any state approved by the University Senate of the United Methodist Church. Preference is given to members of Indian Field, St. George, North, or Saint Andrews (Orangeburg) United Methodist Churches. Financial need is a significant factor in the selection process.

Financial data A stipend is awarded (amount not specified).

Duration 1 year.

Additional information This scholarship was established by the South Carolina Conference of the United Methodist Church in 1998.

Number awarded 1 or more each year.

Deadline April of each year.

[571]
GEORGE MERCER, JR. MEMORIAL SCHOLARSHIP

Episcopal Diocese of Long Island
Attn: Mercer Scholarship Committee
36 Cathedral Avenue
P.O. Box 510
Garden City, NY 11530-4435
(516) 248-4800   Fax: (516) 248-1616
Web: www.dioceselongisland.org

Summary To provide financial assistance to students at Episcopal seminaries.

Eligibility This program is open to students enrolled in accredited seminaries of the Episcopal Church in the United States of America. Applicants must be recommended by the faculty of their school. Preference is given in the following order: residents of Long Island (New York), seniors, middlers, ordained doctoral candidates, students with great financial need, foreign exchange students, juniors, and 1-year students. Selection is based on financial need, leadership potential, and promise for ministry.

Financial data The stipend is $2,500 per year.

Duration 1 year; may be renewed.

Number awarded Varies each year. Recently, $350,000 was allocated for this program.

Deadline October of each year.

[572]
GEORGIA BAPTIST FOUNDATION SEMINARY SCHOLARSHIPS

Georgia Baptist Foundation, Inc.
6405 Sugarloaf Parkway
Duluth, GA 30097
(770) 452-8338   Toll Free: (800) 452-9064
E-mail: gbaptist@bellsouth.net
Web: www.gbfoundation.org

Summary To provide financial assistance to Georgia Baptists who are attending or planning to attend a Baptist seminary.

Eligibility This program is open to members of churches that are affiliated with the Georgia Baptist Convention. Applicants must be enrolled, or planning to enroll, as full-time students at Baptist seminaries to work on a master's or doctoral degree.

Financial data The stipend depends on the need of the recipient and availability of funds.

Duration 1 year; may be renewed.

Number awarded Varies each year.

Deadline August of each year for fall semester; February of each year for spring semester.

[573]
GEORGIA HARKNESS SCHOLARSHIP AWARDS

United Methodist Church
Attn: General Board of Higher Education and Ministry
Division of Ordained Ministry
1001 19th Avenue South
P.O. Box 340007
Nashville, TN 37203-0007
(615) 340-7409   Fax: (615) 340-7367
E-mail: gharkness@gbhem.org
Web: www.gbhem.org/loansandscholarships

Summary To provide financial assistance to women over 35 years of age who are preparing for a second career in ordained ministry as an elder in the United Methodist Church.

Eligibility This program is open to women over 35 years of age who have a bachelor's degree. Applicants must be enrolled full time in a school of theology approved by the University Senate of the United Methodist Church and working on a M.Div. degree. They must be currently certified as candidates for ordained ministry as an elder in the United Methodist Church. The award is not available for undergraduate, D.Min., or Ph.D. work. Selection is based on financial need, academic scholarship, spiritual leadership, and commitment to social justice.

Financial data The stipend is $5,000.

Duration 1 year; recipients may reapply.

Number awarded Varies each year.

Deadline February of each year.

[574]
GERALD A. WIEWEL VOCATION SCHOLARSHIP

Western Catholic Union
510 Maine Street
P.O. Box 410
Quincy, IL 62306-0410
(217) 223-9721   Toll Free: (800) 223-4WCU
Fax: (217) 223-9726   E-mail: info@wculife.com
Web: www.westerncatholicunion.org/benefits.htm

Summary To provide financial assistance to members of Western Catholic Union (WCU) who are preparing for a religious vocation.

Eligibility This program is open to WCU members who are enrolled in a seminary or convent to prepare for a religious vocation. Applicants must submit a 500-word essay on why they are qualified to receive this grant, including a statement of their future goals and aspirations. Selection is based on that essay, academic achievement, religious activities, community involvement, and financial need.

Financial data The stipend is $1,000.

Duration 1 year.

Additional information Western Catholic Union was established in 1877 as a fraternal benefit society.

Number awarded 3 each year.

Deadline February of each year.

[575]
GERNENZ-SHURTLEFF SCHOLARSHIP

American Baptist Churches of the Great Rivers Region
Attn: Scholarship Committee
3940 Pintail Drive
P.O. Box 3786
Springfield, IL 62708
(217) 726-7366   Fax: (888) 922-2477
E-mail: grrabc@abcgrr.org
Web: www.abcgrr.org/ministries/scholarshipinformation.htm

Summary To provide financial assistance for college or seminary to members of American Baptist Churches in Illinois and Missouri.

Eligibility This program is open to members of American Baptist Churches of the Great Rivers Region, which covers Missouri and all of Illinois except for Cook, DuPage, and Lake counties. Applicants must be nominated by their pastor or other professional leader of their church and attending or planning to attend an accredited college, university, or seminary. College students may be majoring in any field, but all applicants must show evidence of potential for Christian service in the world today, regardless of their vocation. Financial need and potential for service are more important factors in the selection process than present academic standing.

Financial data The amount of the stipend varies each year.

Duration 1 year.

Number awarded Varies each year.

Deadline March of each year.

[576]
GERTRUDE BOYD CRANE SCHOLARSHIP

United Methodist Church-Oregon-Idaho Conference
Attn: United Methodist Women
1505 S.W. 18th Avenue
Portland, OR 97201-2524
(503) 226-7031   Toll Free: (800) J-WESLEY
Web: www.umoi.org/pages/detail/45

Summary   To provide financial assistance to female Methodists from Oregon and Idaho who are interested in attending seminary in any state to prepare for a church-related career.

Eligibility   This program is open to women who are members of congregations affiliated with the Oregon-Idaho Conference of the United Methodist Church (UMC). Applicants must be enrolled or planning to enroll at an accredited graduate school or seminary in any state to prepare for a church-related vocation within the Conference. Selection is based primarily on financial need.

Financial data   The stipend, which depends on the availability of funds, generally ranges from $200 to $1,900.

Duration   1 year.

Number awarded   1 each year.

Deadline   April of each year.

[577]
GERTRUDE COOPER SCHOLARSHIP ENDOWMENT

United Methodist Church-New Mexico Conference
Attn: Board of Ordained Ministry
11816 Lomas Boulevard, N.E.
Albuquerque, NM 87112
(505) 255-8786, ext. 101   Toll Free: (800) 678-8786
Fax: (505) 265-6184 E-mail: mridgeway@nmconfum.com
Web: www.nmconfum.com

Summary   To provide financial assistance to Methodists from New Mexico who are interested in attending a seminary in any state that is affiliated with the denomination.

Eligibility   This program is open to students who have an affiliation with a congregation of the New Mexico Conference of the United Methodist Church (UMC). Applicants must be enrolled or planning to enroll at a UMC seminary in any state. They must be preparing for a career in pastoral appointment to local churches in the New Mexico Conference. Along with their application, they must submit brief essays on their current financial situation, how their sense of calling to ministry has changed or grown during the past year, the areas of ministry in which they are currently interested, what they believe to be their greatest spiritual gifts, and how they believe God is calling them to use those gifts in the local church.

Financial data   A stipend is awarded (amount not specified).

Duration   1 year.

Number awarded   1 or more each year.

Deadline   April of each year.

[578]
GLADYS EICKHOFF MEMORIAL SCHOLARSHIP

Baptist Convention of New Mexico
Attn: Missions Mobilization Team
5325 Wyoming Boulevard, N.E.
P.O. Box 94485
Albuquerque, NM 87199-4485
(505) 924-2315   Toll Free: (800) 898-8544
Fax: (505) 924-2320   E-mail: cpairett@bcnm.com
Web: www.bcnm.com

Summary   To provide financial assistance to Southern Baptist students from New Mexico who are attending seminary in any state.

Eligibility   This program is open to seminary students who are members of churches affiliated with the Baptist Convention of New Mexico. Applicants must be attending a seminary in any state. Students enrolled in Doctor of Ministry programs may also be eligible.

Financial data   The stipend is $250 per semester ($500 per year).

Duration   1 year; may be renewed.

Number awarded   1 or more each year.

Deadline   June of each year for fall semester; November of each year for spring semester.

[579]
GRANNIS-MARTIN MEMORIAL SCHOLARSHIP

First United Methodist Church of the Saint Cloud Region
Attn: Scholarship Committee
302 Fifth Avenue South
St. Cloud, MN 56301
(320) 251-0804   Fax: (320) 251-0878
E-mail: fumc@fumc-stcloud.org
Web: www.fumc-stcloud.org/education

Summary   To provide scholarship/loans to seminary students who have a Minnesota connection and are planning to enter the service of the United Methodist Church.

Eligibility   This program is open to seminary students who have a Minnesota connection through church, family, or an institution or organization in which they are or have been involved. Applicants must be enrolled or planning to enroll at a seminary to prepare for full-time work in the United Methodist ministry. Transcripts and letters of recommendation are required.

Financial data   All awards are made initially as loans and normally range from $1,000 to $1,500 per year. Each recipient is asked to sign a promissory note with the understanding that upon competition of study, one-third of the outstanding loan will be forgiven for each year of service to the United Methodist Church (i.e., after 3 years of service, the total amount of the loan is forgiven).

Duration   1 year; may be renewed. If the recipient remains in the approved program of study, no additional years of service will be incurred beyond the 3 years required for loan forgiveness.

Number awarded   Several each year.

Deadline   June of each year for current seminary students; July of each for incoming seminary students.

[580]
GREATER NEW JERSEY ANNUAL CONFERENCE EDUCATIONAL SOCIETY SCHOLARSHIPS

United Methodist Church-Greater New Jersey Conference
Conference Board of Higher Education and Ministry
Attn: Scholarship Committee
1001 Wickapecko Drive
Ocean, NJ 07712-4733
(732) 359-1040   Toll Free: (877) 677-2594, ext. 1040
Fax: (732) 359-1049   E-mail: Lperez@gnjumc.org
Web: www.gnjumc.org/grants_loans_and_scholarship

Summary   To provide fellowship/loans to United Methodist graduate and seminary students from New Jersey who are preparing for ministry.

Eligibility   This program is open to active members of United Methodist Churches affiliated with the Greater New Jersey Conference. Applicants must be enrolled as seminary or graduate students at a school in any state and preparing for the ordained or diaconal ministry in the conference. Selection is based on academic achievement, financial need, and participation in church activities.

Financial data   A stipend is awarded (amount not specified). Recipients must agree to serve for at least 5 years as a member of the Conference under appointment by the Bishop.

Duration   1 year.

Number awarded   Varies each year.

Deadline   March of each year.

[581]
GREATER NEW JERSEY CONFERENCE EDUCATIONAL SOCIETY LOANS

United Methodist Church-Greater New Jersey Conference
Conference Board of Higher Education and Ministry
Attn: Scholarship Committee
1001 Wickapecko Drive
Ocean, NJ 07712-4733
(732) 359-1040   Toll Free: (877) 677-2594, ext. 1040
Fax: (732) 359-1049   E-mail: Lperez@gnjumc.org
Web: www.gnjumc.org/grants_loans_and_scholarship

Summary   To provide loans for college to United Methodist undergraduate and seminary students from New Jersey who are preparing for ministry at a school in any state.

Eligibility   This program is open to active members of United Methodist Churches affiliated with the Greater New Jersey Conference. Applicants must be enrolled as undergraduate or seminary students at a school in any state and planning to enter the Christian ministry of the conference. Selection is based on academic achievement, financial need, and participation in church activities.

Financial data   Loans up to $2,000 per year are available.

Duration   1 year; may be renewed.

Number awarded   Varies each year.

Deadline   March of each year.

[582]
HALE DONATION SCHOLARSHIP

First Congregational Church of Coventry
Attn: Hale Donation
1171 Main Street
P.O. Box 355
Coventry, CT 06238-0355
(860) 742-5689

Summary   To provide loans-for-service to students preparing for the Christian ministry.

Eligibility   This program is open to students preparing for the Christian ministry. Priority is given to students in this order: 1) students with financial need; 2) residents of Tolland County, Connecticut (although applications may be submitted by students in any state); and 3) students preparing for the Christian Ministry in the United Church of Christ.

Financial data   The amount awarded varies, depending upon the needs of the recipient. For recipients who complete their seminary training and enter an area of Christian ministry, this is an outright grant. Recipients who fail to enter Christian ministry must repay the funds (but, no interest is charged).

Duration   1 year; may be renewed.

Additional information   This fund was established in 1803, in memory of the grandfather of Captain Nathan Hale.

Number awarded   1 or more each year.

Deadline   April of each year.

[583]
HANA SCHOLARSHIPS

United Methodist Church
Attn: General Board of Higher Education and Ministry
Office of Loans and Scholarships
1001 19th Avenue South
P.O. Box 340007
Nashville, TN 37203-0007
(615) 340-7344   Fax: (615) 340-7367
E-mail: umscholar@gbhem.org
Web: www.gbhem.org/loansandscholarships

Summary   To provide financial assistance to upper-division and graduate Methodist students who are of Hispanic, Asian, Native American, Alaska Native, or Pacific Islander ancestry.

Eligibility   This program is open to full-time juniors, seniors, and graduate students at accredited colleges and universities in the United States who have been active, full members of a United Methodist Church (UMC) for at least 1 year prior to applying. Applicants must have at least 1 parent who is Hispanic, Asian, Native American, Alaska Native, or Pacific Islander. They must be able to demonstrate involvement in their Hispanic, Asian, or Native American (HANA) community in the UMC. Selection is based on that involvement, academic ability (GPA of at least 2.85 for undergraduates or 3.0 for graduate students), and financial need. U.S. citizenship or permanent resident status is required.

Financial data   The maximum stipend is $3,000 for undergraduates or $5,000 for graduate students.

Duration   1 year; recipients may reapply.

Number awarded   50 each year.

Deadline   March of each year.

[584]
HARDING FOUNDATION GRANTS

Harding Foundation
395 West Hidalgo Avenue
P.O. Box 130
Raymondville, TX 78580
(956) 689-2706　　　　　　　　　　Fax: (956) 689-5740

Summary To provide financial assistance to theological students who are working on an M.Div. degree and plan to enter the service of the United Methodist Church.

Eligibility This program is open to students who are enrolled in an M.Div. degree program on a full-time basis. Applicants must plan to enter the ministry of a mainline Protestant church. Special consideration is given to applicants who are willing to serve in the Rio Grande Conference or the Southwest Texas Conference of the United Methodist Church. Students engaged in practice preaching or at-home thesis writing are not eligible. Along with their applications, students must submit a letter of recommendation from a minister, a letter of recommendation from a teacher, and an autobiography (up to 500 words) which explains why they are entering the field and how they intend to serve.

Financial data The maximum stipend is $3,000 per year, paid in 2 equal installments.

Duration Up to 3 years.

Deadline January of each year.

[585]
HAROLD O. LONG SCHOLARSHIP

American Baptist Churches of the Great Rivers Region
Attn: Scholarship Committee
3940 Pintail Drive
P.O. Box 3786
Springfield, IL 62708
(217) 726-7366　　　　　　　　　　Fax: (888) 922-2477
E-mail: grrabc@abcgrr.org
Web: www.abcgrr.org/ministries/scholarshipinformation.htm

Summary To provide financial assistance for college or seminary to members of American Baptist Churches in Illinois and Missouri.

Eligibility This program is open to members of American Baptist Churches of the Great Rivers Region, which covers Missouri and all of Illinois except for Cook, DuPage, and Lake counties. Applicants must be entering or attending an American Baptist-related college, university, or seminary to prepare for full-time Christian ministry in the American Baptist Church. Selection is based on financial need and academic achievement. First priority is given to members of the First Baptist Church of Decatur, Illinois; second preference is given to members of American Baptist Churches in Area II (which covers the Illinois cities of Decatur, Jacksonville, Quincy, and Springfield); third preference is given to applicants from other churches in the Great Rivers region.

Financial data The stipend is at least $1,000 per year.

Duration 1 year; may be renewed if the recipient maintains a GPA of 2.0 or higher.

Number awarded Varies each year.

Deadline March of each year.

[586]
HARRIET ALICEA SCHOLARSHIP FUND

United Methodist Church-Wisconsin Conference
Attn: Board of Higher Education and Campus Ministry
750 Windsor Street
P.O. Box 620
Sun Prairie, WI 53590-0620
(608) 837-7328　　　　　　　Toll Free: (888) 240-7328
Fax: (608) 837-8547
Web: www.wisconsinumc.org

Summary To provide financial assistance to Native American and Hispanic members of United Methodist churches in Wisconsin interested in preparing for ministry at an institution in any state.

Eligibility This program is open to Native American and Hispanic members of congregations of the United Methodist Church (UMC) in Wisconsin. Applicants must be involved in ministry leading toward licensed Local Pastor or Ordained Pastoral Ministry. They must be seeking funding for Lay Speaking School, Course of Studies, college expenses preparatory for seminary education, or seminary. Along with their application, they must submit a letter of recommendation from their pastor.

Financial data The stipend is $500.

Duration 1 year.

Number awarded 1 or more each year.

Deadline Deadline not specified.

[587]
HARRODSBURG BAPTIST FOUNDATION SCHOLARSHIPS

Harrodsburg Baptist Church
Attn: Harrodsburg Baptist Foundation
312 South Main Street
P.O. Box 286
Harrodsburg, KY 40330
(859) 734-2339　　　　　　　　　　Fax: (859) 734-8384
E-mail: hbf1954@harrodsburgbaptistfoundation.org
Web: www.harrodsburgbaptist.org

Summary To provide financial assistance to Baptist upper-division and seminary students, especially those from selected areas of Kentucky.

Eligibility This program is open to members of Baptist churches who are full-time students working on a degree in a Christian vocational studies program, mainly as a Baptist minister or missionary. Students in a non-ministerial school must be classified as a junior or higher; graduate students must be attending an accredited seminary. First preference is given to members of Harrodsburg Baptist Church, second to members of other Baptist churches in Mercer County, Kentucky, third to members of other Kentucky Baptist churches, and fourth to other students. Applicants must submit information on their reasons for seeking this scholarship and their current financial situation. A personal interview is required.

Financial data The normal annual stipend is $1,200.

Duration 1 year; may be renewed until the student has 1) received a total of $4,800 from the fund; 2) completed a master's degree; or 3) received funds for 4 calendar years.

Additional information The foundation was organized in 1954.

Number awarded 1 or more each year.

Deadline Deadline not specified.

[588]
HARRY C. AND REBA C. RICKARD ENDOWMENT FUND SCHOLARSHIPS

Virginia United Methodist Foundation
10330 Staples Mill Road
P.O. Box 5060
Glen Allen, VA 23058-5606
(804) 521-1122   Toll Free: (800) 768-6040, ext. 122
Fax: (804) 521-1121   E-mail: Foundation@vaumc.org
Web: www.vaumc.org/Page.aspx?pid=1033

Summary To provide financial assistance to Methodists in Virginia who are interested in attending a college or university in any state to prepare for a church-related vocation.

Eligibility This program is open to members of United Methodist Churches in Virginia between 17 and 30 years of age who are graduating high school seniors, college undergraduates, or seminary students. Applicants must be attending or planning to attend a college or seminary in any state to prepare for a full-time church vocation. Along with their application, they must submit an essay of 1 to 2 pages on their career plans and their goals and hopes for ministry; the essay should include whether they plan to serve in a local church setting or in a church-related institution or agency.

Financial data The stipend is $1,000.

Duration 1 year.

Additional information This program was established in 2007.

Number awarded 5 each year.

Deadline March of each year.

[589]
HARRY R. KENDALL LEADERSHIP DEVELOPMENT SCHOLARSHIPS

United Methodist Church
General Board of Global Ministries
Attn: United Methodist Committee on Relief
475 Riverside Drive, Room 1522
New York, NY 10115
(212) 870-3871   Toll Free: (800) UMC-GBGM
E-mail: jyoung@gbgm-umc.org
Web: new.gbgm-umc.org/umcor/work/health/scholarships

Summary To provide financial assistance to African Americans who are Methodists or other Christians and preparing for a career in a health-related field.

Eligibility This program is open to undergraduate and graduate students who are U.S. citizens or permanent residents of African American descent. Applicants must be professed Christians, preferably United Methodists. They must be planning to enter a health care field or already be a practitioner in such a field. Financial need is considered in the selection process.

Financial data The stipend is $2,000.

Duration 1 year.

Additional information This program was established in 1980.

Number awarded Varies each year.

Deadline June of each year.

[590]
HARVESTERS SCHOLARSHIPS

Harvesters Scholarship Foundation
3642 Castle Rock Road
Diamond Bar, CA 91765
E-mail: HarvestersScholarship@hotmail.com
Web: www.harvestersscholarship.com

Summary To provide financial assistance to undergraduate and graduate students who are preparing for a career as a Christian missionary.

Eligibility This program is open to full-time students working on an undergraduate or master's degree at a college or university in Canada or the United States. Applicants must be responding to a call to become a missionary upon graduation. They must have a GPA of 3.0 or higher and a family income less than $60,000 per year. Along with their application, they must submit 1) verification that they are a born-again Christian, have accepted Jesus Christ as their personal savior, and have committed their whole life to serving the Lord, Jesus Christ and God, as a loyal servant; 2) a personal statement describing their calling, vision for ministry, and any specific desires (e.g., mission field); 3) letters of reference; and 4) documentation of financial status.

Financial data A stipend is awarded (amount not specified).

Duration 1 year; may be renewed.

Additional information Recipients must agree to participate in sharing or witnessing in events sponsored by the sponsoring foundation.

Number awarded 1 or more each year.

Deadline May of each year.

[591]
HARVEY FELLOWS PROGRAM

Mustard Seed Foundation
Attn: Harvey Fellows Program
7115 Leesburg Pike, Suite 304
Falls Church, VA 22043
(703) 524-5620   Fax: (703) 524-5643
Web: msfdn.org/scholarships

Summary To provide financial aid to Christian students to attend prestigious graduate schools in the United States or abroad and to prepare for careers in "strategic occupations where Christians appear to be underrepresented."

Eligibility This program is open to American and foreign students. The most competitive applicants are those whose intended vocational fields are demonstrated to have a significant impact on society and to be of high priority for Christian involvement. These fields include (but are not limited to) government, corporate, and university research; international economics and finance in public and private sectors; international diplomacy, security, and business; journalism and media; film production and visual and performing arts; public policy and federal, state, and major city government; research, teaching, and administration at premier colleges and universities. Vocations that are not considered a priority for this scholarship include: work within a church or religious organization; civil service; elementary and secondary education; general business; homemaking; farming; nonprofit relief and economic development; military service; private practice law or medicine; clinical psychology or counseling; social work; professional sports; and other fields that traditionally have attracted a higher percentage of Christians. Selection is based on the applicants' description of their Christian faith and evidence of its strength and maturity; demonstrated ongoing commitment and accountability to the local church; articulation of the strategic nature of their vocational arena as a mission field and as a position from which to influence society; argument for the lack of a distinctive Christian voice in that field; demonstrated leadership within the discipline; potential to impact people and systemic structures within the field; and ability to affect the chosen field (often demonstrated by current publishing and research success, professional experiences and exposure, and recommendations). Financial need is not a factor. Preference is given to candidates with at least 2 years of study remaining and to those whose research or project interests are not explicitly Christian in nature.

Financial data Each fellow is awarded an annual $16,000 stipend. Funds must be used at a "premier" graduate degree program, subject to approval by the selection committee. Fellows may use their stipends for tuition, living expenses, research tools or travel, studio space, professional conferences, and interview travel.

Duration 1 year; may be renewed up to 2 additional years.

Additional information This fellowship was first awarded in 1994. A significant component of the program is a 1-week summer institute where fellows meet in Washington, D.C. to explore the integration of faith, learning, and vocation. The sponsor pays program costs; fellows are responsible for transportation to and from the institute. Recipients must attend 1 of the top 5 institutions (anywhere in the world) in their field of study. Christian colleges and small liberal arts schools are excluded, because, according to the sponsors, they "have not yet found" any that are "nationally acknowledged in professional publications or national rankings as top five institutions."

Number awarded Varies each year. Recently, 33 were awarded.

Deadline October of each year.

[592]
HELEN M. VALENTINE SEMINARIAN SCHOLARSHIP

Faith Lutheran Church
Attn: Scholarship Committee
353 North Midland Avenue
Joliet, IL 60435
(815) 725-4213   E-mail: FaithNews1@sbcglobal.net
Web: faithjoliet.com

Summary To provide financial assistance to seminary students preparing for ordained served in the Evangelical Lutheran Church in America (ELCA).

Eligibility This program is open to students currently enrolled in a seminary and preparing for ordained service in the ELCA. First consideration is given to members of Faith Lutheran Church of Joliet, Illinois. Second consideration is given to students attending an ELCA seminary. Financial need is a primary factor in the selection process.

Financial data A stipend is awarded (amount not specified).

Duration 1 year.

Number awarded 1 or more each year.

Deadline May of each year.

[593]
HENRY P. BRIDGES MINISTERS' TRUST

First Presbyterian Church
105 South Boone Street
Johnson City, TN 37604
(423) 926-5108   Fax: (423) 434-2751
E-mail: contact@fpcjc.org
Web: www.fpcjc.org

Summary To provide financial assistance to students intending to go into the Presbyterian ministry who reside in selected areas in the East and Southeast.

Eligibility Bridges scholarships are available to selected students intending to go into the Presbyterian ministry who reside in and are members of a Presbyterian church in the presbyteries located in east Tennessee, western North Carolina, Baltimore, District of Columbia, and New Castle, Delaware. They must attend either 1) Davidson College (Davidson, North Carolina) or Hampden-Sydney College (Hampden-Sydney, Virginia) or 2) 1 of the following Presbyterian theological seminaries: Columbia (Decatur, Georgia), Louisville (Louisville, Kentucky), McCormick (Chicago, Illinois), Princeton (Princeton, New Jersey), or Union (Richmond, Virginia). Selection is based on academic achievement, leadership ability, church involvement, and financial need.

Financial data The fund provides for living expenses, tuition, books, and other related needs.

Duration 1 year; may be renewed.

Additional information Application requests from Tennessee or North Carolina should be sent to the First Presbyterian Church in Johnson City. Application requests from Maryland, District of Columbia, or Delaware should be made to: Bridges Scholarship Committee, Hancock Presbyterian Church, 17 East Main Street, P.O. Box 156, Hancock, MD 21750, (301) 678-5510. Funds have been awarded since 1957.

Number awarded Varies each year.

Deadline March of each year.

[594]
HERBERT W. AND CORRINE CHILSTROM SCHOLARSHIP

Women of the Evangelical Lutheran Church in America
Attn: Scholarships
8765 West Higgins Road
Chicago, IL 60631-4101
(773) 380-2736   Toll Free: (800) 638-3522, ext. 2736
Fax: (773) 380-2419   E-mail: emily.hansen@elca.org
Web: www.elca.org

Summary To provide financial assistance to mature women who are studying for a second career in the ordained ministry in the Evangelical Lutheran Church of America (ELCA).

Eligibility Applicants for this scholarship must be women who have experienced an interruption of at least 5 years in their education since college graduation and are currently entering the final year of an M.Div. program at an ELCA seminary. They must have been endorsed by the Synodical Candidacy Committee. Selection is based on academic achievement, personal commitment and determination to serve as a pastor in the ELCA, and financial need. U.S. citizenship is required.

Financial data The maximum stipend is $2,000.

Duration 1 year.

Additional information This scholarship was established in 1995 to honor Rev. Herbert W. Chilstrom and Rev. Corrine Chilstrom during the 25th anniversary year of the ordination of women in the predecessor bodies of the ELCA. Recipients must agree to serve for at least 3 years as an ELCA pastor after graduation from seminary.

Number awarded 1 each year.

Deadline February of each year.

[595]
HILBURN PRINE STUDENT LOAN PROGRAM

Florida United Methodist Foundation, Inc.
Attn: Scholarship Committee
450 Martin Luther King Jr. Avenue
P.O. Box 3549
Lakeland, FL 33802-3549
(863) 904-2970　　　　　　Toll Free: (866) 363-9673
Fax: (863) 904-0169　　　　E-mail: Foundation@fumf.org
Web: www.fumc.org/InfoForIndividuals/StudentLoans

Summary To provide educational loans to Methodist students from Florida who are preparing for a church-related career at a college or seminary in any state.

Eligibility This program is open to members of congregations affiliated with the Florida Conference of the United Methodist Church. Applicants must be full-time students attending a junior college, senior college, university, seminary, or other postsecondary institution in any state and working on a degree in a Christian educational field. Those fields are not limited to pastoral ministry or directors of Christian education but include children and youth counselors, teachers, youth coordinators, children and youth directors associated with Christian schools, local after-school programs, or camping ministries.

Financial data The amount of the loan depends on the availability of funds and the number of approved applicants.

Duration 1 year.

Number awarded Varies each year.

Deadline July of each year for fall term; November of each year for spring term.

[596]
HILDRETH/ELLISOR SCHOLARSHIP TRUST

Alabama-West Florida United Methodist Foundation, Inc.
170 Belmont Drive
P.O. Box 8066
Dothan, AL 36304
(334) 793-6820　　　　　　Fax: (334) 794-6480
E-mail: foundation@alwfumf.org
Web: www.alwfumf.org

Summary To provide financial assistance to ministerial students from the Alabama-West Florida Conference of the United Methodist Church.

Eligibility This program is open to members of United Methodist Churches within the Alabama-West Florida Conference. Applicants must be attending an approved seminary

and demonstrate a clear intent to return to the conference in service as ordained United Methodist clergy.

Financial data The stipend varies each year.

Duration 1 year.

Number awarded 1 or more each year.

Deadline June of each year.

[597]
HISPANIC LEADERSHIP DEVELOPMENT FUND

United Methodist Church
General Board of Global Ministries
Attn: United Methodist Committee on Relief
475 Riverside Drive, Room 1522
New York, NY 10115
(212) 870-3871　　　　　　Toll Free: (800) UMC-GBGM
E-mail: jyoung@gbgm-umc.org
Web: new.gbgm-umc.org/umcor/work/health/scholarships

Summary To provide financial assistance to Methodists and other Christians of Hispanic descent who are preparing for a career in a health-related field.

Eligibility This program is open to undergraduate and graduate students who are U.S. citizens or permanent residents of Hispanic descent. Applicants must be professed Christians, preferably United Methodists. They must be working on an undergraduate or graduate degree to enter or continue in a health-related field. Financial need is considered in the selection process.

Financial data The stipend is $2,000.

Duration 1 year.

Additional information This program was established in 1986.

Number awarded Varies each year.

Deadline June of each year.

[598]
HISPANIC SCHOLARSHIP FUNDS

American Baptist Churches USA
National Ministries
Attn: Hispanic Ministries
P.O. Box 851
Valley Forge, PA 19482-0851
(610) 768-2421　　　　Toll Free: (800) ABC-3USA, ext. 2421
Fax: (610) 768-2453
E-mail: Salvador.Orellana@abc-usa.org
Web: www.nationalministries.org

Summary To provide financial assistance to Hispanic Americans who are interested in preparing for or furthering a church career in the American Baptist Church (ABC).

Eligibility This program is open to Hispanic American members of the ABC or its recognized institutions who demonstrate financial need. They must be enrolled on at least a two-thirds basis at an accredited institution, working on an undergraduate degree or first professional degree in a seminary. Applicants must be currently serving or planning to serve in a vocation with the church or with its recognized institutions. They must be U.S. citizens who have been a member of an American Baptist Church for at least 1 year.

Financial data The stipends range from $500 to $3,000 per year.

Duration 1 year; may be renewed.

Deadline May of each year.

[599]
HISPANIC SCHOLARSHIP TRUST FUND

Episcopal Church Center
Attn: Latino/Hispanic Ministries
Los Angeles Regional Office
P.O. Box 512164
Los Angeles, CA 90051-0164
(805) 797-3160   Fax: (213) 482-5304
E-mail: aguillen@episcopalchurch.org
Web: www.episcopalchurch.org

Summary To provide financial assistance to Hispanic Americans interested in theological education within the Episcopal Church in the United States of America (ECUSA).

Eligibility This program is open to students of Hispanic descent seeking to complete courses in theological education at an accredited institution in order to fulfill the requirements for ordination in the ECUSA. Applicants must be functionally bilingual and have a proven record in and commitment to Hispanic ministry. Only second-year juniors and middler-year seminarians are eligible.

Financial data The amount of the award depends on the needs of the recipient and the availability of funds.

Additional information This program was established in 1982.

Number awarded Varies each year. Recently, 4 candidates for ordination received support from this fund.

Deadline April of each year.

[600]
HOCUTT MEMORIAL SCHOLARSHIP

Woman's Missionary Union
Attn: WMU Foundation
100 Missionary Ridge
Birmingham, AL 35242
(205) 408-5525   Toll Free: (877) 482-4483
Fax: (205) 408-5508   E-mail: wmufoundation@wmu.org
Web: www.wmufoundation.com

Summary To provide financial assistance to undergraduate or graduate students preparing for a career in Baptist missions.

Eligibility This program is open to Southern Baptist undergraduate and graduate students who are preparing for a career as a chaplain or in U.S. based Baptist missions. Applicants may be seeking funding for academic preparation, internships designed to develop their abilities to serve in the chaplaincy or missions field, or for formal continuing education programs related to the chaplaincy or missions.

Financial data A stipend is awarded (amount not specified).

Duration 1 year.

Number awarded Varies each year.

Deadline January of each year.

[601]
HOLLY ELLIOTT AND LAUREL GLASS SCHOLARSHIP ENDOWMENT

United Methodist Higher Education Foundation
Attn: Scholarships Administrator
1001 19th Avenue South
P.O. Box 340005
Nashville, TN 37203-0005
(615) 340-7385   Toll Free: (800) 811-8110
Fax: (615) 340-7330
E-mail: umhefscholarships@gbhem.org
Web: www.umhef.org/receive.php?id=endowed_funds

Summary To provide financial assistance to students at United Methodist seminaries who are deaf or deaf-blind.

Eligibility This program is open to students enrolled full time at United Methodist theological schools who are culturally deaf, orally deaf, deafened, late deafened, deaf-blind, or hard of hearing. Applicants must be preparing for specialized ministries in the church, including (but not limited to) those wishing to become ordained. They must have been active, full members of a United Methodist Church for at least 1 year prior to applying. Financial need and U.S. citizenship or permanent resident status are required.

Financial data The stipend is at least $1,000 per year.

Duration 1 year; nonrenewable.

Additional information This program was established in 2004.

Number awarded 1 each year.

Deadline May of each year.

[602]
HOLY TRINITY CENTENNIAL SCHOLARSHIP TRUST

Holy Trinity Parish
Attn: Scholarship Selection Committee
515 East Ponce de Leon Avenue
Decatur, GA 30030
(404) 377-2622   Fax: (404) 377-2624
E-mail: christian@htparish.com
Web: www.holytrinitydecatur.org/outreach/scholarship-fund

Summary To provide financial assistance to persons actively involved in or committed to future participation in the ministry of the Episcopal Church.

Eligibility Applicants must be actively involved in or committed to future participation in the ministry, lay or ordained, of the Episcopal Church or within the larger Anglican Communion. They must be interested in initiating, developing, or completing a program of study through an educational institution, seminar, or certification program. Along with their application, they must submit a narrative describing their objective in undertaking the course of study, how they came to be interested in it, and how they intend to apply what they have learned to a ministry within the Episcopal Church/Anglican Communion. Financial need is considered in the selection process.

Financial data Stipends range from $1,000 to $5,000. Funds may be used for registration, books, tuition, or fees.

Duration 1 year.

Additional information This program was established in 1994.

Number awarded 1 or more each year.

Deadline March of each year.

[603]
HOOD MEMORIAL SCHOLARSHIP

United Methodist Church-Arkansas Conference
Attn: Board of Higher Education and Campus Ministry
800 Daisy Bates Drive
Little Rock, AR 72202
(501) 324-8045   Toll Free: (877) 646-1816
Fax: (501) 324-8018   E-mail: conference@arumc.org
Web: www.arumc.org

Summary To provide financial assistance to Methodist students from Arkansas preparing for Christian service in ministry at a college or seminary in any state.

Eligibility This program is open to residents of Arkansas who have been members of a United Methodist Church (UMC) for at least 1 year. Applicants must be full-time undergraduate or graduate students at an accredited college, university, or seminary in any state approved by the UMC University Senate and preparing for full-time Christian service in ministry. They must be able to demonstrate financial need and a record of involvement in their local church, Wesley Foundation, and/or United Methodist campus ministry and with their community. Along with their application, they must submit a statement that includes their philosophy of life, their religious development, and what influenced them in selecting their career goal.

Financial data The stipend is $1,000 per year.

Duration 1 year; may be renewed.

Number awarded 1 or more each year.

Deadline April of each year.

[604]
HUBERT TRUST SCHOLARSHIP

Baptist Medical Dental Fellowship
4209 Royal Avenue
Oklahoma City, OK 73108-2033
(405) 606-7027   Fax: (405) 609-3203
E-mail: bmdf@bmdf.org
Web: www.bmdf.org/scholarships

Summary To provide funding to health professions students interested in conducting a project anywhere in the world under the supervision of a medical missionary affiliated with Baptist Medical Dental Fellowship (BMDF).

Eligibility This program is open to health professions students interested in conducting a short-term mission project in response to global humanitarian needs. Although applicants are not required to be members of BMDF, they are expected to support its goal of sharing the Gospel of Jesus Christ through each of its health care missions projects. Examples of projects they may propose to conduct include assisting hospitals in immunization campaigns, conducting public health seminars, assisting with medical or dental clinics, or establishing nutritional rehabilitation centers. Along with their application, they must submit a description of the proposed project that includes why the project is important to them, how the experience will expand their world awareness, and why the project will enhance their personal and professional life.

Financial data The amount of the grant depends on the merits of the proposal.

Duration Most projects should be completed within 4 months.

Number awarded Varies each year.

Deadline Applications may be submitted at any time.

[605]
IDAHO EASTERN STAR TRAINING AWARDS FOR RELIGIOUS LEADERSHIP

Order of the Eastern Star-Grand Chapter of Idaho
c/o Eleanor Rupp, ESTARL Central Committee Chair
4589 Aspen Way
Post Falls, ID 83854
(208) 773-7650
Web: www.idahooes.org

Summary To provide financial assistance to residents of Idaho who are attending a college or seminary in any state to prepare for a career in religious service.

Eligibility This program is open to residents of Idaho who are entering their junior or senior year at an accredited college or university or a seminary in any state. Applicants must be preparing for a full-time career as a minister, missionary, director of religious education, Christian youth worker, or church music director. Along with their application, they must submit a personal letter explaining their goals and reasons for applying for this award.

Financial data A stipend is awarded (amount not specified).

Duration 1 year.

Number awarded 1 or more each year.

Deadline March of each year.

[606]
ILLINOIS EASTERN STAR TRAINING AWARDS FOR RELIGIOUS LEADERSHIP

Order of the Eastern Star-Grand Chapter of Illinois
P.O. Box 317
Macon, IL 62544
(217) 764-3326   Fax: (217) 764-5462
E-mail: gc@illoes.org
Web: www.illoes.org/Charities.htm

Summary To provide financial assistance to residents of Illinois who are attending a college or seminary in any state to prepare for a career in religious service.

Eligibility This program is open to residents of Illinois who are enrolled at an accredited college, university, or seminary in any state. Applicants must be preparing for a full-time career as a minister, missionary, director of religious education, Christian youth worker, or church music director. Along with their application, they must submit a brief statement on their vocational goals after completion of higher education and their involvement in community services.

Financial data A stipend is awarded (amount not specified).

Duration 1 year.

Number awarded 1 or more each year.

Deadline March of each year.

[607]
INDIANA BAPTIST FOUNDATION SCHOLARSHIPS

State Convention of Baptists in Indiana
Attn: Indiana Baptist Foundation
900 North High School Road
P.O. Box 24189
Indianapolis, IN 46224
(317) 481-2400, ext. 238   Toll Free: (800) 444-5424
Fax: (317) 241-9875   E-mail: ray.barrett@ibflegacy.org
Web: www.inbaptistfoundation.com

Summary   To provide financial assistance for college, seminary, or graduate school in any state to members of Southern Baptist churches in Indiana.

Eligibility   This program is open to Indiana Southern Baptists who are preparing for a religious or other vocation at a college, seminary, or graduate school in any state. Doctoral candidates are not eligible. Applicants must submit an endorsement by an Indiana Southern Baptist church and a statement describing God's leadership in their choice of profession, area of study, or school selection. Financial need is the most important factor considered in the selection process.

Financial data   The stipend is $1,000.

Duration   1 year; may be renewed.

Number awarded   Varies each year.

Deadline   February of each year.

[608]
INDIANA CONFERENCE SEMINARIAN AID FUND

United Methodist Church-Indiana Conference
Attn: Director of Clergy Services
301 Pennsylvania Parkway, Suite 300
Indianapolis, IN 46280
(317) 564-3252   Fax: (317) 735-4228
E-mail: questions@inumc.org
Web: www.inumc.org/pages/detail/246

Summary   To provide financial assistance to members of United Methodist Churches in Indiana interested in attending a seminary in any state.

Eligibility   This program is open to certified candidates under supervision by their District Committee on Ordained Ministry within the Indiana Conference of the United Methodist Church (UMC). Applicants must be enrolled full time at an accredited seminary recognized by the UMC University Senate. They must be willing to complete at least 1 year of full-time service within the conference for each year of aid received. Financial need is considered in the selection process. Students pursuing education beyond the basic seminary degree (M.Div.) are not eligible.

Financial data   The basic stipend is $2,500 per year. For students who attend a United Methodist seminary in a state contiguous to Indiana, the stipend is $3,750 per year. For students who attend a United Methodist seminary outside the contiguous area, the grant is $5,000 per year.

Duration   1 year; may be renewed 2 additional years.

Number awarded   1 or more each year.

Deadline   June of each year.

[609]
INDIANA EASTERN STAR TRAINING AWARDS FOR RELIGIOUS LEADERSHIP

Order of the Eastern Star-Grand Chapter of Indiana
Attn: Jonny Beeler, Grand Secretary
890 Red Skelton Circle
Franklin, IN 46131
(317) 736-4487   E-mail: indianaoes@embarqmail.com
Web: farrandtel.com/oes-indiana/awardmenub.htm

Summary   To provide financial assistance to residents of Indiana who are attending a college or seminary in any state to prepare for a career in Christian service.

Eligibility   This program is open to residents of Indiana who have completed at least 1 year of study at a college, university, or seminary in any state. Applicants must "wish to devote their lives to God's Service" as a minister, missionary, evangelist, director of religious education, director of youth leadership, director of church choir, director of youth choir, or church musician. Selection is based on character, leadership in Christian activities, citizenship, and financial need.

Financial data   A stipend is awarded (amount not specified).

Duration   1 year.

Number awarded   Varies each year.

Deadline   February of each year.

[610]
IOKDS HEALTH CAREERS SCHOLARSHIPS

International Order of the King's Daughters and Sons
Attn: Director, Health Careers Scholarship Department
34 Vincent Avenue
P.O. Box 1040
Chautauqua, NY 14722-1040
(716) 357-4951   Fax: (716) 357-3762
E-mail: iokds5@windstream.net
Web: www.iokds.org/scholarship.html

Summary   To provide financial assistance to Christian and other students preparing for careers in medicine, dentistry, pharmacy, physical and occupational therapy, and selected medical technologies.

Eligibility   This program is open to U.S. or Canadian citizens who are enrolled full time at an accredited college or university and studying medicine, dentistry, nursing, pharmacy, physical or occupational therapy, or medical technology. Applicants in undergraduate programs must be in at least the third year of college. Nursing students must have completed their first year of schooling. Students seeking M.D. or D.D.S. degrees must be in at least the second year of medical or dental school. Pre-med students are not eligible. Preference is given to students of Christian background. Selection is based on personal statistics, educational background, financial statement, and a statement from the applicant describing the reason for choosing the field of training and future plans.

Financial data   The stipend is $1,000 per year.

Duration   1 year; may be renewed up to 2 additional years.

Additional information   This program began in 1976.

Number awarded   Varies each year. Recently, 43 of these scholarships were awarded.

Deadline   March of each year.

[611]
IOWA ANNUAL CONFERENCE GRADUATE STUDIES GRANTS PROGRAM

United Methodist Church-Iowa Annual Conference
Attn: Board of Ordained Ministry
2301 Rittenhouse Street
Des Moines, IA 50321-3101
(515) 283-1991   Fax: (515) 288-1906
Web: www.iaumc.org/forms/detail/291

Summary To provide financial assistance to students preparing for ordained ministry under the Iowa Annual Conference of the United Methodist Church (UMC).

Eligibility This program is open to certified candidates for ministry who are in good standing with their district Committee on Ordained Ministry of the Iowa Conference of the UMC. Applicants must be enrolled at a seminary approved by the UMC University Senate and intending to complete a master's degree (either an M.Div. or a master's degree in specialized ministry), be ordained as a deacon or elder, and serve in ministry in the Iowa Conference.

Financial data The stipend is $1,000 per semester ($2,000 per year).

Duration 1 year; may be renewed for up to 2 additional years.

Number awarded 1 or more each year.

Deadline May or November of each year.

[612]
IOWA EASTERN STAR TRAINING AWARDS FOR RELIGIOUS LEADERSHIP

Order of the Eastern Star-Grand Chapter of Iowa
c/o Nancy L. Niday, Grand Secretary
303 1/2 East Marion Street
P.O. Box 72
Knoxville, IA 50138
(641) 842-2720   Toll Free: (866) 484-2071
Fax: (641) 842-3678   E-mail: iowaoes@iowatelecom.net
Web: www.iowaeasternstar.org/EASTARL.html

Summary To provide financial assistance to residents of Iowa interested in attending a college or seminary in any state to prepare for a religious career.

Eligibility This program is open to residents of Iowa who have completed at least 3 years of postsecondary education at a college or university in any state. Applicants must be interested in continuing their education at their current school or at a postgraduate institution to prepare for a career in full-time Christian service, including minister, missionary, director of church music, church youth leader, and religious educator. They must be able to demonstrate financial need. Along with their application, they must submit a short statement that includes why they should receive this award and what use they expect to make of the training.

Financial data A stipend is awarded (amount not specified).

Duration 1 year.

Number awarded Varies each year.

Deadline April of each year.

[613]
IOWA UNITED METHODIST FOUNDATION GENERAL SCHOLARSHIPS

Iowa United Methodist Foundation
2301 Rittenhouse Street
Des Moines, IA 50321
(515) 974-8927
Web: www.iumf.org/otherscholarships.html

Summary To provide financial assistance to members of United Methodist Church (UMC) congregations in Iowa interested in studying at UMC-affiliated colleges in Iowa or a UMC seminary.

Eligibility This program is open to high school seniors, college students, vocational/technical students, seminarians, and graduate students who are members of Iowa UMC congregations. Applicants must be attending or planning to attend a UMC college in Iowa or a UMC seminary in any state. Financial need is considered in the selection process.

Financial data The stipend is $520.

Duration 1 year.

Additional information This program is supported by small undesignated gifts to the Iowa United Methodist Foundation.

Number awarded 2 each year.

Deadline March of each year.

[614]
IRA L. AND MARY L. HARRISON MEMORIAL SCHOLARSHIP

Baptist Convention of New Mexico
Attn: Missions Mobilization Team
5325 Wyoming Boulevard, N.E.
P.O. Box 94485
Albuquerque, NM 87199-4485
(505) 924-2315   Toll Free: (800) 898-8544
Fax: (505) 924-2320   E-mail: cpairett@bcnm.com
Web: www.bcnm.com

Summary To provide financial assistance to Native American Southern Baptist students from New Mexico who are attending designated colleges or Baptist seminaries.

Eligibility This program is open to undergraduate and seminary students who are Native American members of churches affiliated with the Baptist Convention of New Mexico. Applicants must have a GPA of 2.0 or higher and be able to demonstrate financial need. Undergraduates must be attending Wayland Baptist University at its main campus in Plainview, Texas or at its New Mexico external campuses in Clovis or Albuquerque. Graduate students must be attending 1 of the 6 Southern Baptist seminaries: Southeastern Baptist Theological Seminary (Wake Forest, North Carolina); Southern Baptist Theological Seminary (Louisville, Kentucky); Southwestern Baptist Theological Seminary (Fort Worth, Texas); New Orleans Baptist Theological Seminary (New Orleans, Louisiana); Midwestern Baptist Theological Seminary (Kansas City, Missouri); or Golden Gate Baptist Theological Seminary (Mill Valley, California).

Financial data A stipend is awarded (amount not specified).

Duration 1 year; may be renewed.

Number awarded 1 or more each year.

Deadline June of each year for fall semester; November of each year for spring semester.

[615]
IRCEL HARRISON THEOLOGICAL SCHOLARSHIP

Tennessee Cooperative Baptist Fellowship
Attn: Leadership Development Committee
P.O. Box 399
Murfreesboro, TN 37133-0399
(615) 907-8525   Toll Free: (888) 661-TCBF
Fax: (615) 907-2785   E-mail: nextgen@tncbf.org
Web: www.tncbf.org

Summary To provide financial assistance to members of the Cooperative Baptist Fellowship (CBF) who have a connection to Tennessee and are working on a graduate theological degree.

Eligibility This program is open to students working on a master's or doctoral degree at an ATS-approved theological school other than an institution where tuition is supplemented by the Cooperative Program of the Southern Baptist Convention. Applicants must be a member of a CBF-affiliated congregation or demonstrate support to state and/or national CBF programs, ministries, or missions. They must have a Tennessee connection through birth, residence, college education, or desire to serve in the state. Along with their application, they must submit a resume and cover letter with biographical information, their call to faith in Christ, their sense of vocational calling, their core Baptist beliefs, their relationship to CBF, and their desire for the scholarship.

Financial data The stipend is $1,000.

Duration 1 year.

Additional information This program was established in 2000 and given its current name in 2008.

Number awarded 1 or more each year.

Deadline February of each year.

[616]
IRENE DRINKALL FRANKE/MARY SEELEY KNUDSTRUP SCHOLARSHIP

Women of the Evangelical Lutheran Church in America
Attn: Scholarships
8765 West Higgins Road
Chicago, IL 60631-4101
(773) 380-2736   Toll Free: (800) 638-3522, ext. 2736
Fax: (773) 380-2419   E-mail: emily.hansen@elca.org
Web: www.elca.org

Summary To provide financial assistance to lay women who are members of Evangelical Lutheran Church of America (ELCA) congregations and who wish to pursue graduate studies.

Eligibility This program is open to ELCA lay women who are at least 21 years of age and have experienced an interruption of at least 2 years in their education since high school. Applicants must have been admitted to a graduate program at an academic institution to prepare for a career of Christian service but not in the ordained ministry. U.S. citizenship is required.

Financial data The maximum stipend is $1,000.

Duration Up to 2 years.

Number awarded Varies each year, depending upon the funds available.

Deadline February of each year.

[617]
IRENE S. WISCHER EDUCATIONAL FOUNDATION SCHOLARSHIPS

Irene S. Wischer Educational Foundation
c/o ETS Scholarship & Recognition Programs
P.O. Box 6730
Princeton, NJ 08541
(609) 771-7878   E-mail: SRP-CSR@ets.org
Web: www.frostbank.com

Summary To provide financial assistance to residents of Texas, especially Christians, who are interested in attending college or graduate school in any state.

Eligibility This program is open to U.S. citizens who have been residents of Texas for at least 12 consecutive months. Preference is given to Christians who attend church regularly. Applicants must be attending or planning to attend an accredited college, university, graduate school, vocational/technical school, or trade school in any state. They must be able to demonstrate academic potential and ability, good character, and financial need. Along with their application, they must submit 3 letters of recommendation, including 1 from a member of clergy at their church.

Financial data Stipends range up $10,000 per year, depending on the need of the recipient.

Duration 1 year; may be renewed up to 3 additional years.

Additional information This program, established in 2007, is administered by Frost National Bank, with operational management by ETS Scholarship & Recognition Programs.

Number awarded 1 or more each year.

Deadline January of each year.

[618]
IWALANI CARPENTER SOWA SCHOLARSHIP

Ke Ali'i Pauahi Foundation
Attn: Financial Aid & Scholarship Services
567 South King Street, Suite 160
Honolulu, HI 96813
(808) 534-3966   Toll Free: (800) 842-4682, ext. 43966
Fax: (808) 534-3890   E-mail: scholarships@pauahi.org
Web: www.pauahi.org/scholarships

Summary To provide financial assistance to graduate students, especially Native Hawaiians, who are preparing for a career in Protestant Christian ministry.

Eligibility This program is open to graduate students working full time on a degree that will prepare them for a career in Protestant Christian ministry. Applicants must express a desire to minister in Hawaii. Preference is given to Native Hawaiians (descendants of the aboriginal inhabitants of the Hawaiian Islands prior to 1778), graduates of Kamehameha Schools, and applicants who can demonstrate financial need.

Financial data The stipend is $1,400.

Duration 1 year.

Number awarded 1 each year.

Deadline March of each year.

[619]
J. LAWRENCE AND MARGARET F. MCCLESKEY SCHOLARSHIP

South Carolina United Methodist Foundation
P.O. Box 5087
Columbia, SC 29250-5087
(803) 771-9125   Fax: (803) 771-9135
E-mail: scumf@bellsouth.net
Web: www.umcsc.org/scholarships.html

Summary   To provide financial assistance to residents of South Carolina preparing for ministry at a Methodist seminary in any state.

Eligibility   This program is open to residents of South Carolina who are certified candidates for ordained ministry in the United Methodist Church (UMC). Applicants must be enrolled at a Methodist seminary or theological school in any state. Selection is based on financial need and promise for ministry.

Financial data   Stipends are at least $1,000.

Duration   1 year.

Additional information   This scholarship was established by the South Carolina Conference of the United Methodist Church in 1997.

Number awarded   1 or more each year.

Deadline   April of each year.

[620]
J.A. KNOWLES MEMORIAL SCHOLARSHIP

United Methodist Church
Attn: General Board of Higher Education and Ministry
Office of Loans and Scholarships
1001 19th Avenue South
P.O. Box 340007
Nashville, TN 37203-0007
(615) 340-7344   Fax: (615) 340-7367
E-mail: umscholar@gbhem.org
Web: www.gbhem.org/loansandscholarships

Summary   To provide financial assistance to undergraduate and graduate students attending schools in Texas affiliated with the United Methodist Church.

Eligibility   This program is open to U.S. citizens and permanent residents who have been active, full members of a United Methodist Church in Texas for at least 1 year prior to applying. Applicants must be attending a Texas college or university related to the United Methodist Church. They must have a GPA of 2.5 or higher and be enrolled as a full-time undergraduate or graduate student. Financial need is considered in the selection process.

Financial data   The stipend is $1,000.

Duration   1 year.

Number awarded   50 each year.

Deadline   May of each year.

[621]
JAMES M. PHILPUTT MEMORIAL SCHOLARSHIP/LOAN

Christian Church (Disciples of Christ)
Attn: Disciples Home Missions
130 East Washington Street
P.O. Box 1986
Indianapolis, IN 46206-1986
(317) 713-2652   Toll Free: (888) DHM-2631
Fax: (317) 635-4426   E-mail: mail@dhm.disciples.org
Web: www.discipleshomemissions.org

Summary   To provide scholarship/loans to students at selected seminaries interested in preparing for a career in the ministry of the Christian Church (Disciples of Christ).

Eligibility   This program is open to seminary and graduate ministerial students at University of Chicago Divinity School, Union Theological Seminary, Vanderbilt Divinity School, or Yale Divinity School. Applicants must be members of the Christian Church (Disciples of Christ), plan to prepare for the ordained ministry, have at least a "C+" GPA, provide evidence of financial need, be enrolled full time in an accredited school or seminary, provide a transcript of academic work, and be under the care of a regional Commission on the Ministry or in the process of coming under care.

Financial data   Recipients are awarded funds in the form of a scholarship/loan, with 2 methods of repayment: 1) the amount of the scholarship/loan must be repaid in cash (with 6% interest, beginning 3 months after leaving school) if the recipient does not enter the ministry; or 2) the amount of the scholarship/loan is reduced by one-third for each year of full-time professional ministry performed by the recipient, so that 3 years of service cancels the entire amount.

Duration   1 year; may be renewed.

Additional information   Recipients must sign a promissory note.

Number awarded   Varies each year.

Deadline   March of each year.

[622]
JANE FRYER MCCONAUGHY MEMORIAL SCHOLARSHIP PROGRAM

Elkhart County Community Foundation
Attn: Scholarship Coordinator
101 South Main Street
P.O. Box 2932
Elkhart, IN 46515-2932
(574) 295-8761   Fax: (574) 389-7497
E-mail: shannon@elkhartccf.org
Web: www.elkhartccf.org/scholarships/index.xpl

Summary   To provide financial assistance to undergraduate and graduate students who are Indiana residents or enrolled at colleges in the state and preparing for a career in the ministry, missionary service, or teaching.

Eligibility   This program is open to Indiana residents attending college in any state and residents of any state attending college in Indiana. Applicants must be enrolled as undergraduate or graduate students obtaining training required for the ministry, missionary service, or the teaching profession. Priority is given to seminary students and students training for missionary services. Selection is based on career goals, academic record, and financial need.

Financial data Stipends range from $500 to $1,500.
Duration 1 year.
Number awarded 2 to 6 each year.
Deadline February of each year.

[623]
JANE WALKER SCHOLARSHIP

United Methodist Church-Alabama-West Florida
  Conference
Attn: Commission on the Status and Role of Women
100 Interstate Park Drive, Suite 120
Montgomery, AL 36109
(334) 356-8014   Toll Free: (888) 873-3127
Fax: (334) 356-8029   E-mail: awfcrc@awfumc.org
Web: www.awfumc.org

Summary To provide financial assistance to female residents of the Alabama-West Florida Conference of the United Methodist Church (UMC) who are undergraduate or seminary students preparing for a church-related career.
Eligibility This program is open to women who are residents of the Alabama-West Florida Conference of the UMW and who affirm, represent, and advocate women's leadership in the church. Applicants must be accepted or enrolled at an approved UMC seminary or working on an undergraduate degree in Christian education at an approved UMC institution in any state. They must be a candidate for ministry or preparing for a UMC church-related career. Along with their application, they must submit a 500-word essay on why they are preparing for full-time Christian ministry and how they can promote the cause of women through this ministry. Financial need is also considered in the selection process.
Financial data The stipend is $1,000.
Duration 1 year.
Number awarded 1 each year.
Deadline May of each year.

[624]
JANIE CREE BOSE ANDERSON SCHOLARSHIPS

Kentucky Woman's Missionary Union
Attn: Scholarships
13420 Eastpoint Centre Drive
P.O. Box 436569
Louisville, KY 40253-6569
(502) 489-3534   Toll Free: (866) 489-3534 (within KY)
Fax: (502) 489-3566   E-mail: kywmu@kybaptist.org
Web: kywmu.org/scholarships

Summary To provide financial assistance to female Baptists from Kentucky who are attending a college or seminary in any state to prepare for Christian service.
Eligibility This program is open to women who are active members of churches affiliated with the Kentucky Baptist Convention or the General Association of Baptists in Kentucky. Applicants must be attending an accredited college, university, or seminary in any state as a full-time student. They must have a GPA of 2.7 or higher and be preparing for Christian service. Along with their application, they must submit a brief essay on how they became a Christian and their career goals.
Financial data Stipends range from $400 to $700.
Duration 1 year.

Number awarded 1 or more each year.
Deadline January of each year.

[625]
JEANNE AUDREY POWERS LEADERSHIP FOR CHANGE SCHOLARSHIP

Pacific School of Religion
Attn: Center for Lesbian and Gay Studies in Religion and
  Ministry
1798 Scenic Avenue
Berkeley, CA 94709-1323
(510) 849-8275   Toll Free: (800) 999-0528
E-mail: kmcshane@psr.edu
Web: www.psr.edu

Summary To provide financial assistance to Methodist seminary students who are interested in promoting inclusion of gay and lesbian people in the church.
Eligibility This program is open to United Methodist students who are attending or planning to attend any of the 13 seminaries of the United Methodist Church (UMC) or Pacific School of Religion. Applicants must be preparing for ordination as elders in the UMC. They must be committed to promoting full inclusion of gay and lesbian people in the life of the UMC. Along with their application, they must submit brief essays on 10 topics, such as the formative experiences in their life that have led them toward ordained ministry, the personal experiences that have made them aware of the need for more just systems in the UMC, and how their practice of ministry would be affected if the UMC position on homosexuality is changed.
Financial data The stipend is $3,000 per year.
Duration 1 year; may be renewed up to 2 additional years.
Number awarded 1 or more each year.
Deadline April of each year.

[626]
JEROME J. JUNK MEMORIAL SCHOLARSHIPS

Knights of Columbus-California State Council
15808 Arrow Boulevard, Suite A
Fontana, CA 92335
(909) 434-0460   E-mail: state.office@kofc-ca.org
Web: kofc-ca.org/?t=t_csc_studentscholarships2

Summary To provide financial assistance to members of the Knights of Columbus and their families in California who are interested in attending a religious vocational school in any state.
Eligibility This program is open to 1) members of the Knights of Columbus in a California council; 2) spouses and children of Knights of Columbus members in a California council; 3) spouses and children of deceased members who were in good standing with a California council at the time of death; 4) members of a California Columbian Squires Circle; and 5) former members of a California Columbian Squires Circle who are either current members in good standing or sons of Knights of Columbus members in good standing in a California council. Applicants must be attending or planning to attend a postsecondary school in any state to prepare for a religious vocation. Along with their application, they must submit transcripts, SAT and/or ACT scores, a personal statement, and 3 letters of recommendation.
Financial data The stipend is $1,000.

Duration 1 year.
Number awarded 3 each year.
Deadline February of each year.

[627]
J.K. SASAKI MEMORIAL SCHOLARSHIPS

West Los Angeles United Methodist Church
Attn: Scholarship Committee
1913 Purdue Avenue
Los Angeles, CA 90025
(310) 479-1379   Fax: (310) 478-7756
E-mail: wlaumc@aol.com
Web: www.wlaumc.org

Summary To provide financial assistance to Japanese American and other Asian American seminary students who are preparing for ordained ministry in the United Methodist Church.

Eligibility This program is open to Japanese American and other Asian American students at Protestant seminaries in the United States. Applicants must be planning to serve a Japanese American or Asian American congregation of the United Methodist Church as an ordained minister. They must have a GPA of 2.5 or higher. Along with their application, they must submit 2 essays (of 500 words each) on 1) their motivations for preparing for a career in the United Methodist Church, and 2) their concerns for the local church and the United Methodist Church.

Financial data Stipends range from $250 to $1,000.

Duration 1 year; recipients may reapply.

Additional information This program was established in 1972 and given its current name in 2006.

Number awarded 1 or more each year.

Deadline March of each year.

[628]
JOHN AND FERREL SUTTLE SCHOLARSHIPS

Arkansas Baptist Foundation
10117 Kanis Road
Little Rock, AR 72205-6220
(501) 376-0732   Toll Free: (800) 798-0969
Fax: (501) 376-3831   E-mail: info@abf.org
Web: www.abf.org/individuals_scholarships.htm

Summary To provide scholarship/loans to members of Southern Baptist churches in Arkansas who are attending or planning to attend designated Baptist seminaries.

Eligibility This program is open to members of Southern Baptist churches in Arkansas who are attending or planning to attend 1 of the following seminaries: Southwestern Baptist Theological Seminary (Fort Worth, Texas); Southern Baptist Theological Seminary (Louisville, Kentucky); Southeastern Baptist Theological Seminary (Wake Forest, North Carolina); Golden Gate Baptist Theological Seminary (Mill Valley, California); New Orleans Baptist Theological Seminary (New Orleans, Louisiana); or Midwestern Baptist Theological Seminary (Kansas City, Missouri). Applicants must be full-time students preparing for a full-time church-related vocation or an appointment with the International Mission Board or North American Mission Board of the Southern Baptist Convention in preaching, religious education, or music ministry. Preference is given to applicants who can demonstrate financial

need and to members of First Baptist Church in Sheridan, Arkansas.

Financial data The stipend is $1,200 per year. Recipients must execute a promissory note evidencing an intent and obligation to reimburse the sponsor if they fail to pursue a career with a Southern Baptist church, denominational institution, or denominational agency within 3 years after completing their seminary training.

Duration 1 year; recipients may reapply.

Number awarded Varies each year.

Deadline February of each year.

[629]
JOHN C. WRIGHT SCHOLARSHIP

United Methodist Higher Education Foundation
Attn: Scholarships Administrator
1001 19th Avenue South
P.O. Box 340005
Nashville, TN 37203-0005
(615) 340-7385   Toll Free: (800) 811-8110
Fax: (615) 340-7330
E-mail: umhefscholarships@gbhem.org
Web: www.umhef.org/receive.php?id=endowed_funds

Summary To provide financial assistance to undergraduate and graduate Methodist students from Virginia who are interested in preparing for a career in ministry.

Eligibility This program is open to undergraduate and graduate students who are studying theology to prepare for United Methodist ministry. Applicants must have been active, full members of a United Methodist Church in Virginia for at least 1 year prior to applying. They must have a GPA of 3.0 or higher and be able to demonstrate financial need. Along with their application, they must submit a 200-word essay on their involvement and/or leadership responsibilities in their church, school, and community within the last 3 years. U.S. citizenship or permanent resident status is required. Priority is given to Virginia residents who are enrolled or planning to enroll at 1) a United Methodist-related seminary or theological school; 2) a United Methodist-related liberal arts school and study theology; or 3) Virginia Wesleyan College in Norfolk, Virginia.

Financial data The stipend is at least $1,000 per year.

Duration 1 year; recipients may reapply.

Additional information The donor of this scholarship intended that recipients should repay it if they decide not to become ordained and give service in the United Methodist Church.

Number awarded Varies each year. Recently, 2 of these scholarships were awarded.

Deadline May of each year.

[630]
JOHN HARRISON NESS MEMORIAL AWARD

United Methodist Church
General Commission on Archives and History
Attn: General Secretary
36 Madison Avenue
P.O. Box 127
Madison, NJ 07940
(973) 408-3189   Fax: (973) 408-3909
E-mail: gcah@gcah.org
Web: www.gcah.org

Summary To recognize and reward outstanding papers on aspects of United Methodist history written by a student in an M.Div. program.

Eligibility This competition is open to students enrolled in the M.Div. program (or its equivalent) in United Methodist or other seminaries accredited by the Association of Theological Schools. They are eligible to submit a paper on an aspect of United Methodist history. The paper should be between 3,000 and 5,000 words, be properly footnoted, and use the annotation standards accepted at the seminary. A bibliography must be included.

Financial data First prize is $500 and second prize is $300. The winning paper(s) may be published in *Methodist History.*

Duration The competition is held annually.

Additional information No prize is awarded if the judges decide there are no suitable submissions.

Number awarded 2 each year.

Deadline January of each year.

[631]
JOHN, KARL, ELIZABETH WURFFEL MEMORIAL FUND

Synod of the Northeast
Attn: Student Loan/Scholarship Programs
5811 Heritage Landing Drive
East Syracuse, NY 13057-9360
(315) 446-5990, ext. 215
Toll Free: (800) 585-5881, ext. 215
Fax: (315) 446-3708   E-mail: SynodOffice@Synodne.org
Web: www.synodne.org

Summary To provide financial assistance to Presbyterians in the Synod of the Northeast who are interested in attending college or graduate school in any state.

Eligibility This program is open to members of Presbyterian churches in the Synod of the Northeast (Connecticut, Maine, Massachusetts, New Hampshire, New Jersey, New York, Rhode Island, and Vermont) who are entering into a program in any state leading to 1) a 4-year baccalaureate degree, 2) a 3-year M.Div. degree, or 3) a 2-year Christian education degree. Applicants must submit an essay of 400 to 500 words on why they should be considered for this assistance, their reasons for wanting to pursue a college or seminary education, their extracurricular activities and interests (school, church, and community), and the role their faith will take in fulfilling their academic goals. Selection is based on financial need, academic potential, church and campus ministry involvement, community and mission involvement, and continued academic improvement.

Financial data The stipend is $2,000 per year.

Duration 1 year; may be renewed up to 3 additional years.

Additional information This program was established in 2000.

Number awarded 3 each year.

Deadline March of each year.

[632]
JOHN Q. SCHISLER GRADUATE AWARDS

United Methodist Church
Attn: General Board of Higher Education and Ministry
Office of Loans and Scholarships
1001 19th Avenue South
P.O. Box 340007
Nashville, TN 37203-0007
(615) 340-7344   Fax: (615) 340-7367
E-mail: umscholar@gbhem.org
Web: www.gbhem.org/loansandscholarships

Summary To provide financial assistance to United Methodist graduate students preparing for a career as a professional Christian educator.

Eligibility This program is open to full-time graduate students at theological seminaries approved by the University Senate of the United Methodist Church who are preparing for a career as a professional Christian educator in the local church. Applicants must have been active, full members of the United Methodist Church for at least 3 years prior to applying. They must be planning to become a lay professional, ordained deacon in full connection, or diaconal minister; students planning to become an ordained elder are not eligible. U.S. citizenship or permanent resident status is required. Selection is based on academic standing (GPA of 2.85 or higher), leadership ability, character, vocational goals in Christian education, commitment to Christ and the mission of the church, and financial need.

Financial data The stipend ranges from $500 to $2,000.

Duration 1 year.

Number awarded Varies each year. Recently, 10 of these scholarships were awarded.

Deadline January of each year.

[633]
JOHN TRACY ELLIS DISSERTATION AWARD

American Catholic Historical Association
c/o Catholic University of America
Mullen Library, Room 320
Washington, DC 20064
(202) 319-5079   Fax: (202) 319-5079
E-mail: acha@achahistory.org
Web: www.achahistory.org/awards

Summary To provide funding to doctoral students working on a dissertation that deals with an aspect of the history of the Catholic Church.

Eligibility This program is open to graduate students who have completed all degree requirements for the doctorate except the dissertation and have received approval for work on a dissertation topic dealing with the history of the Catholic Church. Applicants must submit the following: certification from their chair or director of graduate studies that they have completed all degree requirements except the dissertation, a statement (up to 1,000 words) by the applicant describing the dissertation project and the way in which the award would be used to further its completion, and 2 letters of recommendation. They must be citizens, permanent residents, or student visa holders of the United States or Canada.

Financial data The grant is $1,200.

Duration The grant is awarded annually.

Additional information This award was first presented in 1998.

Number awarded 1 each year.

Deadline September of each year.

[634]
JOHN WESLEY FELLOWSHIPS

A Foundation for Theological Education
c/o Paul Ervin, Executive Director
P.O. Box 238
Lake Junaluska, NC 8745
(828) 456-9901   Fax: (828) 456-9433
E-mail: paulervin@prodigy.net
Web: www.johnwesleyfellows.org

Summary To provide financial assistance to United Methodists who are working on a doctoral degree.

Eligibility This program is open to members of United Methodist Churches who are working on a Ph.D. or Th.D. degree. Applicants must submit a 20-page statement that covers 1) the theological affirmations they believe to be essential to the Christian faith and life; 2) the principal issues, leading scholars, and primary schools of thought in their propose field; 3) the Wesleyan distinctives that they regard as especially important, and how those relate to current theological issues and trends; 4) their feelings about and present involvement in the United Methodist Church; and 5) their spiritual autobiography, including their present areas of growth and struggle. Selection is based on that statement, college and seminary transcripts, GRE scores, reference letters, and financial need.

Financial data The stipend averages $10,000 per year.

Duration Normally 4 years.

Additional information This program was established in 1977.

Number awarded Up to 5 each year.

Deadline January of each year.

[635]
JOHN-ELIZABETH BLAHO MILLER FUND

Pittsburgh Foundation
Attn: Scholarship Coordinator
Five PPG Place, Suite 250
Pittsburgh, PA 15222-5414
(412) 394-2649   Fax: (412) 391-7259
E-mail: turnerd@pghfdn.org
Web: www.pittsburghfoundation.org

Summary To provide financial assistance to seminary students, especially those of Hungarian descent, who are preparing for the Lutheran ministry.

Eligibility This program is open to students attending or planning to attend a seminary to prepare for the Lutheran ministry. Preference is given to students who are from Hungary and of Hungarian ancestry. Applicants must be able to demonstrate financial need. Along with their application, they must submit a description of any activities or volunteer work in which they participate or have participated over the past 3 years that relate to the Lutheran Church or their Hungarian heritage.

Financial data A stipend is awarded (amount not specified).

Duration 1 year.

Number awarded 2 each year.

Deadline June of each year.

[636]
JONATHAN M. DANIELS MEMORIAL FELLOWSHIP

Episcopal Divinity School
Attn: Manager of Student Records
99 Brattle Street
Cambridge, MA 02138-3494
(617) 868-3450   Toll Free: (866) 4EDS-NOW
Fax: (617) 864-5385
Web: www.eds.edu/sec.asp?pageID=10

Summary To provide funding to seminarians seeking to strengthen their theological education by participating in social programs concerned with important human needs.

Eligibility This funding is available to students at accredited theological schools in the United States or Canada. They must be interested in being set free from their academic life and commitments to engage directly in some area of social concern, such as civil rights, anti-racism, fair housing, community organizing, or environmental issues. Funds are not available to support research, supervised field education, existing nonprofit organizations, or any activity that is primarily based on the school curriculum. There is no restriction on the place of the proposed project.

Financial data Grants up to $3,000 are available. Exceptional proposals may be considered for larger amounts.

Duration The fellowships are awarded annually. The proposed project should be for a summer, a semester, a year, or a combination of these.

Additional information The funded project must be completed before the recipient graduates.

Number awarded Varies each year; recently, 3 of these fellowships were awarded.

Deadline February of each year.

[637]
JONES DAVIS SCHOLARSHIPS

United Methodist Church-Louisiana Conference
Attn: Coordinator, Conference Board of Ordained Ministry
527 North Boulevard
Baton Rouge, LA 70802-5700
(225) 346-1646, ext. 230
Toll Free: (888) 239-5286, ext. 230
Fax: (225) 383-2652   E-mail: johneddd@bellsouth.net
Web: www.la-umc.org

Summary To provide financial assistance to Methodists from Louisiana who are attending seminary in any state to prepare for a career in vocational service to the church.

Eligibility This program is open to members of United Methodist Churches in Louisiana who are enrolled or planning to enroll full time at a seminary in any state. Applicants must be able to articulate vocational goals in service to the church. That may include ministry as an elder in full connection, deacon in full connection, licensed local pastor, diaconal minister, or certified lay professional in Christian education, music, youth, evangelism, camping/retreat ministries, spiritual formation, or older adult ministry. Along with their application, they must submit an essay on their vocational goals and plans for ministry.

Financial data   The stipend is $2,000.

Duration   1 year.

Additional information   This program was established in 2003.

Number awarded   2 each year.

Deadline   February of each year.

[638]
JOSEPHINE CAMPBELL HUFFER SCHOLARSHIP

United Methodist Church-Indiana Conference
Attn: Commission on the Status and Role of Women
301 Pennsylvania Parkway, Suite 300
Indianapolis, IN 46280
(317) 924-1321   Fax: (317) 735-4228
E-mail: questions@inumc.org
Web: www.inumc.org/pages/detail/190

Summary   To provide financial assistance to Methodist women from Indiana who are attending a seminary in any state.

Eligibility   This program is open to women seminarians who are preparing for the ordained ministry in the Indiana Conference of the United Methodist Church (UMC) at a seminary in any state. Applicants must submit 1) a 1-page autobiography; 2) a 1-page summary of their understanding of their call to ministry and the impact that has on their professional goals; and 3) a financial statement. Selection is based on financial need (50%), clarity of call (20%), recommendations (20%), and academic honors and awards (10%).

Financial data   The stipend is $500. Funds are sent directly to the seminary attended by the recipient.

Duration   1 year.

Additional information   This scholarship was established in 1984 by the Southern Indiana Conference of the UMC, which merged with the Northern Indiana Conference in 2008.

Number awarded   1 each year.

Deadline   April of each year.

[639]
JOSEPHINE CARROLL NORWOOD MEMORIAL SCHOLARSHIPS

Baptist Convention of Maryland/Delaware
Attn: United Baptist Women of Maryland, Inc.
10255 Old Columbia Road
Columbia, MD 21046
(410) 290-5290   Toll Free: (800) 466-5290
E-mail: gparker@bcmd.org
Web: bcmd.org/wmu

Summary   To provide financial assistance to women who are members of Baptist churches associated with an affiliate of United Baptist Women of Maryland and interested in attending seminary or graduate school in any state to prepare for a Christian vocation.

Eligibility   This program is open to women who are enrolled or planning to enroll full time at a seminary or graduate school in any state to prepare for a Christian vocation. Applicants must be a member in good standing of a Baptist church associated with an affiliate of United Baptist Women of Maryland. They must have a grade point average of "C" or higher and be able to demonstrate financial need. Along with their application, they must submit brief statements on their

Christian experience, school activities, church and community activities, and career goals.

Financial data   A stipend is awarded (amount not specified).

Duration   1 year.

Number awarded   Varies each year.

Deadline   June of each year.

[640]
JOSEPHINE RUDY SMITH SCHOLARSHIP

United Methodist Church-Kentucky Annual Conference
Attn: Office of Ministerial Services
7400 Floydsburg Road
Crestwood, KY 40014-8202
(502) 425-3884   Toll Free: (800) 530-7236
Fax: (502) 426-5181
Web: www.kyumc.org/pages/detail/985

Summary   To provide forgivable loans to students at United Methodist seminaries who are interested in preaching in Kentucky following ordination.

Eligibility   This program is open to seminary students at theological schools related to the United Methodist Church. Applicants must be in good standing with the Kentucky Annual Conference and willing to agree to preach in Kentucky following ordination.

Financial data   The award is $2,200 for juniors, $2,400 for middlers, and $2,600 for seniors, plus $800 for each summer session. Recipients must commit to accept a preaching assignment in Kentucky or a missionary assignment under Episcopal control for 5 years following completion of seminary. If they fail to fulfill that service obligation, they must repay all funds received with 6% interest.

Duration   1 year; may be renewed up to 2 additional years.

Number awarded   1 or more each year.

Deadline   August of each year for fall semester; November of each year for spring semester.

[641]
JOSEPHUS DANIEL PELL FOUNDATION GRANTS

United Methodist Church-Virginia Conference
Attn: Office of Ministerial Services
10330 Staples Mill Road
P.O. Box 5060
Glen Allen, VA 23058-5606
(804) 521-1126   Toll Free: (800) 768-6040, ext. 126
Fax: (804) 521-1179   E-mail: BethDowns@vaumc.org
Web: www.vaumc.org/Page.aspx?pid=761

Summary   To provide financial assistance to Methodist seminary students from Virginia.

Eligibility   This program is open to full-time students at United Methodist seminaries who are on the elder track for ordained ministry within the Virginia Conference. Applicants must have the recommendation of their district committee on ordained ministry, their district superintendent, and the conference Board of Ordained Ministry. They must be able to demonstrate financial need.

Financial data   Grant amounts depend on the need of the recipient and the availability of funds.

Duration   1 year.

Additional information This program is supported by the Josephus Daniel Pell Foundation.

Number awarded Varies each year.

Deadline June or September of each year.

[642]
J.S. REESE SHANKLIN SCHOLARSHIP

Baptist Convention of Maryland/Delaware
Attn: Woman's Missionary Union of Maryland/Delaware
10255 Old Columbia Road
Columbia, MD 21046
(410) 290-5290 Toll Free: (800) 466-5290
E-mail: gparker@bcmd.org
Web: bcmd.org/wmu

Summary To provide financial assistance to men who are members of Southern Baptist churches affiliated with the Baptist Convention of Maryland/Delaware and interested in attending a college or seminary in any state.

Eligibility This program is open to men who are active members of a Southern Baptist church/mission or Baptist student ministry affiliated with the Baptist Convention of Maryland/Delaware. Applicants must be enrolled or planning to enroll full time at 1) an accredited college or university in any state, or 2) a Southern Baptist seminary. They must have a grade point average of "C" or higher and be able to demonstrate financial need. Along with their application, they must submit a brief essay that includes a testimony of their salvation experience; their involvement in church, school, and community activities; and the kind of work God has called them to do after completing their education, how they have come to believe God wants them in this work, and their plans to fulfill His call. Priority is given to applicants who are preparing for missionary service under the North American Mission Board or International Mission Board of the Southern Baptist Convention, career service with the Woman's Missionary Union (WMU), or work with the Men's Ministries.

Financial data The stipend is $375 per semester ($750 per year). Funds are paid directly to the recipient's school.

Duration 1 year; may be renewed for a total of 8 semesters of undergraduate study or 6 semesters of seminary master's degree work.

Number awarded Varies each year.

Deadline February of each year for fall semester or August of each year for spring semester.

[643]
JUDGE S. LEE VAVURIS LEGAL SCHOLARSHIP

Greek Orthodox Cathedral of the Annunciation
245 Valencia Street
San Francisco, CA 94103-2320
(415) 864-8000 Fax: (415) 431-5860
E-mail: office@annunciation.org
Web: www.annunciation.org

Summary To provide financial assistance to students of Greek descent or the Greek Orthodox faith who are interested in attending law school.

Eligibility This program is open to students who are of Greek descent or of the Greek Orthodox faith who 1) matriculate at and attend law school, preferably at the University of San Francisco, and 2) intend to practice law within the 9-county area surrounding San Francisco Bay, preferably in San Francisco. Along with their application, they must submit an official transcript and 2 letters of recommendation.

Financial data Stipends up to $1,000 are provided. Funds are paid to the recipient's school.

Duration 1 year.

Number awarded 1 each year.

Deadline May of each year.

[644]
JULIA C. PUGH SCHOLARSHIP

Woman's Missionary Union
Attn: WMU Foundation
100 Missionary Ridge
Birmingham, AL 35242
(205) 408-5525 Toll Free: (877) 482-4483
Fax: (205) 408-5508 E-mail: wmufoundation@wmu.org
Web: www.wmufoundation.com

Summary To provide financial assistance for undergraduate or graduate study to the dependent children of Southern Baptist missionaries.

Eligibility This program is open to Southern Baptist undergraduate and graduate students in any field who have significant financial need and do not qualify for regular scholarships. Applicants must be dependents of North American or international missionaries who are under appointment of the North American Mission Board (NAMB) of the Southern Baptist Convention.

Financial data A stipend is awarded (amount not specified).

Duration 1 year.

Number awarded Varies each year.

Deadline February of each year.

[645]
JULIETTE M. ATHERTON SCHOLARSHIPS FOR ORDAINED PROTESTANT MINISTERS

Hawai'i Community Foundation
Attn: Scholarship Department
827 Fort Street Mall
Honolulu, HI 96813
(808) 537-6333 Toll Free: (888) 731-3863
Fax: (808) 521-6286
E-mail: scholarships@hcf-hawaii.org
Web: www.hawaiicommunityfoundation.org/scholarships

Summary To provide financial assistance to Protestant ministers in Hawaii who are interested in working on an advanced degree at an institution in any state.

Eligibility This program is open to ordained Protestant ministers in an established denomination in Hawaii planning to work on an advanced degree (usually a doctorate) related to their ministerial profession. Applicants must have already attended and graduated from seminary. Along with their application, they must submit a brief statement on how their studies furthers their work in Hawaii.

Financial data The amounts of the awards depend on the availability of funds and the need of the recipient. Recently, the average value of all scholarships awarded by the foundation was $2,041.

Duration 1 year.

Number awarded Varies each year. Recently, 3 of these scholarships were awarded.

Deadline February of each year.

[646]
JULIETTE M. ATHERTON SCHOLARSHIPS FOR SEMINARY STUDIES

Hawai'i Community Foundation
Attn: Scholarship Department
827 Fort Street Mall
Honolulu, HI 96813
(808) 537-6333   Toll Free: (888) 731-3863
Fax: (808) 521-6286
E-mail: scholarships@hcf-hawaii.org
Web: www.hawaiicommunityfoundation.org/scholarships

Summary To provide financial assistance to residents of Hawaii who are attending a seminary in any state to prepare for the Protestant ministry.

Eligibility This program is open to residents of Hawaii who are planning to attend an accredited graduate school of theology in any state with the goal of being ordained in an established Protestant denomination. Applicants must be able to demonstrate academic achievement (GPA of 2.7 or higher), good moral character, and financial need. Along with their application, they must submit a short statement indicating their reasons for attending college, their planned course of study, their career goals, and what community service means to them.

Financial data The amounts of the awards depend on the availability of funds and the need of the recipient. Recently, the average value of all scholarships awarded by the foundation was $2,041.

Duration 1 year.

Number awarded Varies each year. Recently, 14 of these scholarships were awarded.

Deadline February of each year.

[647]
JULIETTE MATHER SCHOLARSHIP

Woman's Missionary Union
Attn: WMU Foundation
100 Missionary Ridge
Birmingham, AL 35242
(205) 408-5525   Toll Free: (877) 482-4483
Fax: (205) 408-5508   E-mail: wmufoundation@wmu.org
Web: www.wmufoundation.com

Summary To provide financial assistance to Southern Baptist undergraduate or graduate students preparing for a career in Christian ministry.

Eligibility This program is open to Southern Baptist undergraduate and graduate students who are preparing for a career in Christian ministry and service. They must be interested in preparing to become the Baptist leaders of the future.

Financial data A stipend is awarded (amount not specified).

Duration 1 year.

Number awarded Varies each year.

Deadline January of each year.

[648]
JUSTIN HARUYAMA MINISTERIAL SCHOLARSHIP

Japanese American United Church
Attn: Haruyama Scholarship Committee
255 Seventh Avenue
New York, NY 10001
(212) 242-9444   Fax: (212) 242-5274
E-mail: infojauc@gmail.com
Web: www.jauc.org/haruyama_e.html

Summary To provide financial assistance to Protestant seminary students who are interested in serving Japanese American congregations.

Eligibility This program is open to students of Japanese ancestry who are enrolled full time at an accredited Protestant seminary in the United States. Applicants must be working on a ministerial degree in order to serve Japanese American congregations. Along with their application, they must submit 2 letters of recommendation, a transcript of grades, information on their financial situation, and a brief statement of their spiritual journey.

Financial data The stipend is $500.

Duration 1 year; may be renewed.

Number awarded 1 or more each year.

Deadline May of each year.

[649]
KANSAS-NEBRASKA CHRISTIAN HIGHER EDUCATION FUND

Kansas-Nebraska Convention of Southern Baptists
Attn: Kansas-Nebraska Southern Baptist Foundation
5410 S.W. Seventh Street
Topeka, KS 66606-2398
(785) 228-6800   Toll Free: (800) 984-9092
Fax: (785) 273-4992   E-mail: beckyholt@kncsb.org
Web: www.kncsb.org/ministry/article/foundation_funds

Summary To provide financial assistance to Southern Baptists from Kansas and Nebraska who are entering a college or seminary in any state affiliated with the denomination.

Eligibility This program is open to members of churches in the Kansas-Nebraska Convention of Southern Baptists. Applicants must be entering their first year at a Southern Baptist college, university, or seminary in any state.

Financial data A stipend is awarded (amount not specified).

Duration 1 year. Seminary students may reapply.

Number awarded 1 or more each year.

Deadline February of each year.

[650]
KATHARINE C. BRYAN GRADUATE SCHOLARSHIP

Tennessee Baptist Convention
Attn: WMU Scholarships
5001 Maryland Way
P.O. Box 728
Brentwood, TN 37024-9728
(615) 373-2255   Toll Free: (800) 558-2090, ext. 2038
Fax: (615) 371-2014   E-mail: jferguson@tnbaptist.org
Web: www.tnbaptist.org/page.asp?page=92

Summary To provide financial assistance to female members of Baptist churches in Tennessee who are interested in attending graduate school in any state.

Eligibility This program is open to women who are members of Tennessee Baptist churches or have Tennessee Baptist ties. Applicants must be active in missions and ministries of their local church. They must be enrolled in full-time graduate study and have a GPA of 2.6 or higher.

Financial data A stipend is awarded (amount not specified).

Duration 1 year; may be renewed if the recipient maintains a GPA of 3.5 or higher.

Number awarded 1 or more each year.

Deadline January of each year.

[651]
KATHERINE J. SCHUTZE MEMORIAL SCHOLARSHIP

Christian Church (Disciples of Christ)
Attn: Disciples Home Missions
130 East Washington Street
P.O. Box 1986
Indianapolis, IN 46206-1986
(317) 713-2652   Toll Free: (888) DHM-2631
Fax: (317) 635-4426   E-mail: mail@dhm.disciples.org
Web: www.disciileshomemissions.org

Summary To provide financial assistance to female seminary students affiliated with the Christian Church (Disciples of Christ).

Eligibility This program is open to female seminary students who are members of the Christian Church (Disciples of Christ). Applicants must plan to prepare for the ordained ministry, have at least a "C+" GPA, provide evidence of financial need, be enrolled full time in an accredited school or seminary, provide a transcript of academic work, and be under the care of a regional Commission on the Ministry or in the process of coming under care.

Financial data A stipend is awarded (amount not specified).

Duration 1 year; may be renewed.

Number awarded 1 or more each year.

Deadline March of each year.

[652]
KENTUCKY ANNUAL CONFERENCE MINISTERIAL EDUCATION FUND SERVICE LOAN

United Methodist Church-Kentucky Annual Conference
Attn: Office of Ministerial Services
7400 Floydsburg Road
Crestwood, KY 40014-8202
(502) 425-3884   Toll Free: (800) 530-7236
Fax: (502) 426-5181
Web: www.kyumc.org/pages/detail/985

Summary To provide forgivable loans to students at United Methodist seminaries who are interested in preaching in Kentucky following ordination.

Eligibility This program is open to seminary students at theological schools related to the United Methodist Church. Applicants must be in good standing with the Kentucky Annual Conference and willing to commit to preaching in Kentucky following ordination.

Financial data The award is $220 per credit hour. Applicants must agree to accept a preaching assignment in Kentucky for 5 years following completion of seminary. If they fail to fulfill that service obligation, they must repay all funds received.

Duration 1 semester; may be renewed.

Number awarded 1 or more each year.

Deadline September of each year for fall semester; January of each year for spring semester.

[653]
KENTUCKY BAPTIST FELLOWSHIP SCHOLARSHIPS

Kentucky Baptist Fellowship
Attn: Scholarship Coordinator
225 South Hurstbourne Parkway, Suite 205
Louisville, KY 40222
(502) 426-1931   Fax: (502) 426-1612
E-mail: john@kybf.org
Web: www.kybf.org/scholarships

Summary To provide financial assistance for seminary to members of churches cooperating with the Kentucky Baptist Fellowship.

Eligibility This program is open to residents of Kentucky who are members of local churches that cooperate with the Kentucky Baptist Fellowship. Applicants must be enrolled or planning to enroll at a seminary to prepare for a career in ministry. Along with their application, they must submit an essay of 3 to 5 pages that addresses their faith in Christ, their sense of vocational calling, their core Baptist beliefs, their relationship to Cooperative Baptist Fellowship, and their desire for this scholarship. In the selection process, first priority is given to applicants who have served as a Kentucky Baptist Fellowship summer missionary, second to students attending or planning to attend Baptist Seminary of Kentucky, and finally to students accepted at a Cooperative Baptist Fellowship partnering theological school.

Financial data The stipend is $1,000.

Duration 1 year; nonrenewable.

Number awarded 1 or more each year.

Deadline March of each year.

[654]
KJT RELIGIOUS SCHOLARSHIPS

KJT Memorial Foundation
214 East Colorado
P.O. Box 297
La Grange, TX 78945
(979) 968-5877   Toll Free: (800) 245-8182
E-mail: info@kjtnet.org
Web: www.kjtnet.org/benefits.htm

Summary To provide financial assistance to members of the Catholic Union of Texas (KJT) who are preparing for the priesthood.

Eligibility This program is open to students who are attending a seminary and preparing for the priesthood. Applicants must have been KJT-insured members for at least 1 year. Even those who are in the advanced years of study may apply, if they are studying for a Texas diocese.

Financial data A maximum of $5,400 is awarded to the seminarian or applicant for religious vocation over a period of

8 years. Upon ordination to priesthood, an additional monetary gift is offered.

Duration Up to 8 years.

Additional information KJT is the symbol for the Catholic Union of Texas. In Czech, it is Katolicka Jednota Texaskaa, hence KJT. This is a Texas fraternal benefit insurance organization.

Number awarded Varies each year.

Deadline June of each year.

[655]
KNIGHTS TEMPLAR OF CALIFORNIA CHRISTIAN MINISTRY SCHOLARSHIP FUND

Knights Templar of California
Attn: Knights Templar Educational Foundation
801 Elm Avenue
Long Beach, CA 90813
(562) 436-8271   Fax: (562) 437-5411
E-mail: ca.yorkrite@verizon.net

Summary To provide financial assistance to students at designated Protestant seminaries in California.

Eligibility This program is open to students at 1 of the following Protestant seminaries: American Baptist Seminary of the West, Church Divinity School of the Pacific, Pacific School of Religion, San Francisco Theological Seminary, and School of Theology at Claremont. Candidates must be nominated by the scholarship committee of their seminary. They must demonstrate financial need, better than average academic achievement, and a desire to prepare for a career in Protestant Christian ministry. Finalists are interviewed.

Financial data The stipend is $1,000.

Duration 1 year.

Additional information This program was established in 1955.

Number awarded 20 each year: 4 at each of the 5 seminaries.

Deadline Deadline not specified.

[656]
LANGDON GARRISON MINISTERIAL SCHOLARSHIP TRUST

Alabama-West Florida United Methodist Foundation, Inc.
170 Belmont Drive
P.O. Box 8066
Dothan, AL 36304
(334) 793-6820   Fax: (334) 794-6480
E-mail: foundation@alwfumf.org
Web: www.alwfumf.org

Summary To provide financial assistance to ministerial students from the Alabama-West Florida Conference of the United Methodist Church.

Eligibility This program is open to members of United Methodist Churches within the Alabama-West Florida Conference. Applicants must be attending an approved seminary and preparing to become an ordained elder with the intention of serving in the Conference. Selection is based on financial need and potential for ministry.

Financial data The stipend varies each year.

Duration 1 year.

Number awarded 1 or more each year.

Deadline June of each year.

[657]
LAWRENCE AND DONNA TAYLOR SCHOLARSHIPS

Boone First United Methodist Church
703 Arden Street
Boone, IA 50036
(515) 432-4660   E-mail: bnfumc@mchsi.com
Web: www.boonefmc.org/TaylorEstateScholarships

Summary To provide financial assistance to members of congregations affiliated with the World Methodist Council who are interested in attending college or graduate school to prepare for a church-related vocation.

Eligibility This program is open to full-time students preparing for the ordained ministry or certification as director of Christian education, minister of Christian education, or associate in Christian education. Applicants must have been an active member of a congregation of a denomination within the World Methodist Council for at least 3 years. Selection is based on academic standing, leadership ability, character, Christian commitment, and financial need. Preference is given to graduate students.

Financial data Stipends range from $375 to $3,000 per year. Payment is made directly to the recipient's school.

Duration 1 year; recipients may reapply.

Number awarded 1 or more each year.

Deadline April of each year.

[658]
LEE FRANCES HELLER MEMORIAL AWARD

International Foundation for Gender Education
Attn: Transgender Scholarship and Education Legacy
    Fund
13 Felton Street
P.O. Box 540229
Waltham, MA 02454-0229
(781) 899-2212   Fax: (781) 899-5703
E-mail: carrie@tself.org
Web: www.tself.org

Summary To provide financial assistance to Christian transgender students who are working on an undergraduate or graduate degree in religious studies.

Eligibility This program is open to undergraduate and graduate students who are living full time in a gender or sex role that differs from that assigned to them at birth and who are "out and proud" about their transgender identity. Applicants must be Christians working on a degree in religious studies. They may be of any age or nationality, but they must be attending or planning to attend a college, university, trade school, or technical college in the United States or Canada. Along with their application, they must submit an essay that identifies their home congregation and indicates how their transgender identity and their involvement in the Christian church have related to each other. Selection is based on affirmation of transgender identity; demonstration of integrity and honesty; participation and leadership in community activities; service as a role model, mentor, colleague, or adviser for the transgender communities; and service as transgender role model, mentor, colleague, or adviser to non-transpeople in religious studies.

Financial data Stipends average $2,000. Funds are paid directly to the student.

Duration 1 year; nonrenewable.

Number awarded 1 each year.

Deadline January of each year.

[659]
LEMUEL C. SUMMERS SCHOLARSHIP

United Methodist Higher Education Foundation
Attn: Scholarships Administrator
1001 19th Avenue South
P.O. Box 340005
Nashville, TN 37203-0005
(615) 340-7385   Toll Free: (800) 811-8110
Fax: (615) 340-7330
E-mail: umhefscholarships@gbhem.org
Web: www.umhef.org/receive.php?id=endowed_funds

Summary To provide financial assistance to undergraduate and graduate Methodist students who are preparing for ministry.

Eligibility This program is open to full-time undergraduate, graduate, and professional students at United Methodist-related colleges, universities, seminaries, and theological schools. Applicants must have been active, full members of a United Methodist Church for at least 1 year prior to applying and be preparing for Christian ministry. They must have a GPA of 3.0 or higher and be able to demonstrate financial need. Along with their application, they must submit a 200-word essay on their involvement and/or leadership responsibilities in their church, school, and community within the last 3 years. U.S. citizenship or permanent resident status is required.

Financial data The stipend is at least $1,000 per year.

Duration 1 year; recipients may reapply.

Number awarded Varies each year. Recently, 5 of these scholarships were awarded.

Deadline May of each year.

[660]
LESTER H. SPENCER MINISTERIAL SCHOLARSHIP FUND

Alabama-West Florida United Methodist Foundation, Inc.
170 Belmont Drive
P.O. Box 8066
Dothan, AL 36304
(334) 793-6820   Fax: (334) 794-6480
E-mail: foundation@alwfumf.org
Web: www.alwfumf.org

Summary To provide financial assistance to ministerial students from the Alabama-West Florida Conference of the United Methodist Church.

Eligibility This program is open to members of United Methodist Churches within the Alabama-West Florida Conference. Applicants must be enrolled in the second or third year at an approved seminary and demonstrate a clear intent to return to the conference in service as ordained United Methodist clergy. Selection is based on financial need and evidence of promise and gifts for the ministry.

Financial data The stipend is $1,000.

Duration 1 year.

Number awarded 1 or more each year.

Deadline June of each year.

[661]
LLOYD AND IVA MATTISON YOUTH MINISTRY SCHOLARSHIP

Christian Church (Disciples of Christ)
Attn: Disciples Home Missions
130 East Washington Street
P.O. Box 1986
Indianapolis, IN 46206-1986
(317) 713-2652   Toll Free: (888) DHM-2631
Fax: (317) 635-4426   E-mail: mail@dhm.disciples.org
Web: www.discipleshomemissions.org

Summary To provide financial assistance to seminarians interested in preparing for a career in youth ministry of the Christian Church (Disciples of Christ).

Eligibility This program is open to ministerial students who are members of the Christian Church (Disciples of Christ). Applicants must plan to prepare for the ordained ministry with an emphasis on youth, have at least a "C+" GPA, provide evidence of financial need, be enrolled full time in an accredited school or seminary, provide a transcript of academic work, and be under the care of a regional Commission on the Ministry or in the process of coming under care.

Financial data A stipend is awarded (amount not specified).

Duration 1 year; may be renewed.

Additional information This program was established in 1993.

Number awarded 1 each year.

Deadline March of each year.

[662]
LORENE L. GERDON SEMINARY SCHOLARSHIP

Iowa United Methodist Foundation
2301 Rittenhouse Street
Des Moines, IA 50321
(515) 974-8927
Web: www.iumf.org/seminaryscholarships.html

Summary To provide financial assistance to students in Iowa who are interested in preparing for a career as a Methodist minister.

Eligibility This program is open to students from the Ottumwa District of the United Methodist Church who are interested in attending a seminary or other institution that will train them for local Methodist ministry or related full-time church work. Financial need is considered in the selection process.

Financial data The stipend is $1,000.

Duration 1 year.

Number awarded 5 each year.

Deadline March of each year.

[663]
LOUISE BAREKMAN MEMORIAL SCHOLARSHIP

Texas Medical Association
Attn: Educational Loans, Scholarships and Awards
401 West 15th Street
Austin, TX 78701-1680
(512) 370-1300   Toll Free: (800) 880-1300, ext. 1600
Fax: (512) 370-1630   E-mail: info@tmaloanfunds.com
Web: www.tmaloanfunds.com/Content/Template.aspx?id=9

Summary To provide financial assistance to members of Protestant churches in Texas who are enrolled in medical school in the state.

Eligibility This program is open to residents of Texas who are members of a Protestant church and have a record of regular attendance at that church. Applicants must be enrolled in the first, second, or third year at a medical school in Texas. They must be able to demonstrate financial need.

Financial data The stipend currently is $630.

Duration 1 year.

Number awarded 1 each year.

Deadline January of each year.

[664]
LOUISE BISHOP SCHOLARSHIP

United Methodist Church-Bowling Green District
Attn: Louise Bishop Ministerial Education Fund
District Supervisor
1123 State Street
P.O. Box 9937
Bowling Green, KY 42102-9937
(270) 842-5075   Fax: (270) 842-1914
E-mail: bgdist@bellsouth.net
Web: www.kyumc.org/pages/detail/1143

Summary To provide financial assistance to seminary students, especially those from the Bowling Green District of Kentucky, who are preparing for ministry in the United Methodist Church (UMC).

Eligibility This program is open to full-time seminary students and local pastors who are attending seminary part time or completing the required course of study. Applicants must intend to serve in the ministry of the UMC. Preference is given to students who are from or serving churches in the Bowling Green District of Kentucky. Financial need is considered in the selection process.

Financial data The stipend is $1,000 per year.

Duration 1 year; may be renewed up to 4 additional years.

Number awarded 1 or more each year.

Deadline Deadline not specified.

[665]
LOUISIANA METHODIST MERIT SCHOLARSHIP

United Methodist Church-Louisiana Conference
Attn: Higher Education and Campus Ministry
527 North Boulevard
Baton Rouge, LA 70802-5700
(225) 346-1646   Toll Free: (888) 239-5286
Fax: (225) 383-2652   E-mail: lcumc@bellsouth.net
Web: www.la-umc.org

Summary To provide financial assistance to undergraduate and graduate students from Louisiana who are attending

or planning to attend a United Methodist college or university in any state.

Eligibility This program is open to undergraduate and graduate students who are members of United Methodist Churches in Louisiana. Applicants must be attending or planning to attend an accredited United Methodist college or university in any state. A letter of nomination from their pastor or chair of higher education and campus ministry is required and must describe their academic achievement; active involvement in church, school, civic, and community activities; and reasons why they merit the scholarship. Applicants must also submit a statement that describes their career goals and financial need.

Financial data The stipend is $1,000.

Duration 1 year.

Number awarded 2 each year.

Deadline March of each year.

[666]
LOUISIANA WMU SCHOLARSHIP FOR AFRICAN-AMERICAN MISSION PASTORS

Louisiana Baptist Convention
Attn: Woman's Missionary Union
P.O. Box 311
Alexandria, LA 71309
(318) 448-3402   Toll Free: (800) 622-6549
E-mail: wmu@lbc.org
Web: www.lbc.org

Summary This provide financial assistance to African American Southern Baptists from Louisiana who are enrolled at a seminary to prepare for a career as a missions pastor.

Eligibility This program is open to African Americans who are endorsed by the director of missions and the pastor of a sponsoring Southern Baptist church in Louisiana. Applicants must be enrolled full time at a seminary or a satellite campus to prepare for a career as a missions pastor and have a GPA of 2.5 or higher. They must be participating in a missions education organization of the church or on campus and must contribute to offerings of the church and other programs. Along with their application, they must submit a brief summary of their Christian beliefs, including what they believe the Lord has called them to do in a church-related vocation.

Financial data The stipend is $1,200 per year.

Duration Up to 3 years.

Number awarded 1 or more each year.

Deadline June of each year.

[667]
LOUISIANA WMU SCHOLARSHIP FOR WOMEN SEMINARY STUDENTS

Louisiana Baptist Convention
Attn: Woman's Missionary Union
P.O. Box 311
Alexandria, LA 71309
(318) 448-3402   Toll Free: (800) 622-6549
E-mail: wmu@lbc.org
Web: www.lbc.org

Summary This provide financial assistance to women from Louisiana who are working on a master's degree at a Southern Baptist seminary.

Eligibility This program is open to women who are active members of a Southern Baptist church in Louisiana. Applicants must be enrolled full time at 1 of the 6 Southern Baptist seminaries, have a GPA of 2.5 or higher, and be working on a master's degree. They must participate in activities of the Woman's Missionary Union (WMU) and be actively involved in missions education of the church or on campus. Along with their application, they must submit a brief summary of their Christian beliefs, including what they believe the Lord has called them to do in a church-related vocation.

Financial data The stipend is $1,600 per year.

Duration Up to 3 years.

Additional information The eligible seminaries are Southeastern Baptist Theological Seminary (Wake Forest, North Carolina); Southern Baptist Theological Seminary (Louisville, Kentucky); Southwestern Baptist Theological Seminary (Fort Worth, Texas); New Orleans Baptist Theological Seminary (New Orleans, Louisiana); Midwestern Baptist Theological Seminary (Kansas City, Missouri); or Golden Gate Baptist Theological Seminary (Mill Valley, California).

Number awarded 1 or more each year.

Deadline June of each year.

[668]
LOUISVILLE INSTITUTE DISSERTATION FELLOWSHIPS

Louisville Institute
Attn: Executive Director
1044 Alta Vista Road
Louisville, KY 40205-1798
(502) 992-5432   Fax: (502) 894-2286
E-mail: info@louisville-institute.org
Web: www.louisville-institute.org/Grants/programs.aspx

Summary To support doctoral research on the character, problems, contributions, and prospects of the historic institutions and stances of American religion.

Eligibility Applicants must be candidates for the Ph.D. or Th.D. degree at a graduate school in North America. They should have finished all pre-dissertation requirements by the time of application and expect to complete their dissertation during the following academic year. Their dissertation proposal must have received official, final faculty approval at the home institution by the application deadline. Preference is given to proposals that attempt to 1) describe more fully how the Christian faith is actually lived by contemporary persons and to bring the resources of the Christian faith into closer relation to their daily lives; 2) help us understand more adequately the institutional reconfiguration of American religion; or 3) explore the nature and challenge of pastoral leadership, with special attention given to the conditions of contemporary Christian ministry in North America and the character of pastoral excellence. Proposals on certain other issues of importance to the churches are also welcome. Proposed dissertations may employ a variety of methodological perspectives, including history, ethics, the social sciences, biblical studies, and historical, systematic, and practical theology. They may also be interdisciplinary in nature.

Financial data The stipend is $19,000.

Duration 12 months; nonrenewable.

Additional information Fellowships are intended to support the final year of dissertation research and writing. The Louisville Institute is located at the Louisville Presbyterian Theological Seminary and is supported by the Lilly Endowment. These fellowships were first awarded in 1991. Recipients are responsible for all tuition, medical insurance, and required fees. Fellows may not accept other awards that provide a stipend during the tenure of this fellowship. In the year of their award, all fellows are expected to participate in 1 conference hosted by the Louisville Institute (the institute will pay the fellows' travel and lodging).

Number awarded Up to 10 each year.

Deadline January of each year.

[669]
LUELLA M. ODELL MEMORIAL SCHOLARSHIP

Wesley United Methodist Church
1385 Oakway Road
Eugene, OR 97401
(541) 343-3665

Summary To provide financial assistance to seminary students preparing for a career as an ordained minister in the United Methodist Church (UMC).

Eligibility This program is open to students completing the first year of study at a seminary accredited by the Association of Theological Schools. Applicants must be a candidate for ordained ministry in the UMC. They must have a vision for serving Jesus Christ and the church and be able to communicate that vision. Selection is based on academic excellence and financial need.

Financial data The stipend is $1,000.

Duration 1 year.

Number awarded 1 or more each year.

Deadline May of each year.

[670]
LUTHER H. BUTLER STUDENT LOAN FUND

North Carolina Baptist Foundation, Inc.
Attn: Denominational Relations Committee
201 Convention Drive
Cary, NC 27511-4257
(919) 380-7334   Toll Free: (800) 521-7334
Fax: (919) 460-6334
Web: www.ncbaptistfoundation.org

Summary To provide educational loans to undergraduate and graduate students at designated Baptist colleges and universities in North Carolina.

Eligibility This loan program is open to students at the following historically-Baptist institutions in North Carolina: Campbell University, Chowan College, Gardner-Webb University, Mars Hill College, Meredith College, or Wingate College. Preference is given to applicants of evangelical Christian faith or background and those seeking a church-related vocation. Selection is based on moral character; dedication to family, church, and community; and financial need. U.S. citizenship or legal resident status is required.

Financial data The maximum loan is $12,000 per year. The interest rate is equal to the prevailing rate charged, plus 2%. No interest is charged and repayment need not begin until 6 months after conclusion of studies. Loans must be repaid within 10 years.

Duration 1 year; may be renewed up to 3 additional years by undergraduates or up to 2 additional years by graduate students.

Additional information There is a $10 application fee.

Number awarded 1 or more each year.

Deadline January of each year.

[671]
LYDIA SCHOLARSHIP

Network of Presbyterian Women in Leadership
Scholarship Coordinator
8134 New LaGrange Road, Suite 227
Louisville, KY 40222-4679
(502) 425-4630   E-mail: npwl@pfrenewal.org
Web: www.npwl.org/Lydia-scholarship

Summary To provide financial assistance to women who are interested in preparing for a career in the Presbyterian Church (USA) ordained pastoral ministry.

Eligibility This program is open to women who are interested in preparing for ordained pastoral ministry in the Presbyterian Church. Applicants must be working on an M.Div. degree and ordination and be involved in the candidate process (or have specified plans to be involved shortly). Along with their application, they must submit essays on their faith story, personal theology, and call to ministry. Those essays should demonstrate their commitment to work for spiritual renewal within the PCUSA, including a willingness to cooperate with the Network of Presbyterian Women in Leadership and Presbyterians for Renewal (its umbrella organization). Financial need is considered in the selection process.

Financial data The stipend is $2,500 per year.

Duration 2 years; may be renewed for 1 additional year.

Number awarded 1 each year.

Deadline February of each year.

[672]
MABEL BOLLE SCHOLARSHIP

American Baptist Churches of the Rocky Mountains
Attn: American Baptist Women's Ministries
9085 East Mineral Circle, Suite 170
Centennial, CO 80112
(303) 988-3900   E-mail: web@abcrm.org
Web: www.abcrm.org

Summary To provide financial assistance to members of churches affiliated with the American Baptist Churches (ABC) USA in Wyoming who are interested in attending an ABC college or seminary in any state.

Eligibility This program is open to active members of churches cooperating with ABC in Wyoming. Applicants must be enrolled or planning to enroll at an ABC college, university, or seminary in any state. They must be committed to full-time Christian service.

Financial data The stipend is $500.

Duration 1 year.

Number awarded 1 or more each year.

Deadline Deadline not specified.

[673]
MABEL D. RUSSELL BLACK COLLEGE FUND

United Methodist Higher Education Foundation
Attn: Scholarships Administrator
1001 19th Avenue South
P.O. Box 340005
Nashville, TN 37203-0005
(615) 340-7385   Toll Free: (800) 811-8110
Fax: (615) 340-7330
E-mail: umhefscholarships@gbhem.org
Web: www.umhef.org/receive.php?id=endowed_funds

Summary To provide financial assistance to Methodist undergraduate and graduate students at Historically Black Colleges and Universities of the United Methodist Church.

Eligibility This program is open to students enrolling as full-time undergraduate and graduate students at the Historically Black Colleges and Universities of the United Methodist Church. Applicants must have been active, full members of a United Methodist Church for at least 1 year prior to applying. They must have a GPA of 3.0 or higher and be able to demonstrate financial need. Along with their application, they must submit a 200-word essay on their involvement and/or leadership responsibilities in their church, school, and community within the last 3 years. U.S. citizenship or permanent resident status is required.

Financial data The stipend is at least $1,000 per year.

Duration 1 year; nonrenewable.

Additional information This program was established in 1978. The qualifying schools are Bennett College for Women, Bethune-Cookman College, Claflin University, Clark Atlanta University, Dillard University, Huston-Tillotson College, Meharry Medical College, Paine College, Philander Smith College, Rust College, and Wiley College.

Number awarded 1 each year.

Deadline May of each year.

[674]
MABEL HEIL SCHOLARSHIP

United Methodist Church-Wisconsin Conference
Attn: Board of Higher Education and Campus Ministry
750 Windsor Street
P.O. Box 620
Sun Prairie, WI 53590-0620
(608) 837-7328   Toll Free: (888) 240-7328
Fax: (608) 837-8547
Web: www.wisconsinumc.org

Summary To provide financial assistance to United Methodist women from Wisconsin who are interested in attending college or graduate school in any state.

Eligibility This program is open to women who are members of congregations affiliated with the Wisconsin Conference of the United Methodist Church and attending or planning to attend college or graduate school in any state. Applicants must submit an essay on why they consider themselves a worthy student and a letter of recommendation from their pastor or the president of the local United Methodist Women. Preference is given to women who are responsible for others and are returning to the employment field.

Financial data A stipend is awarded (amount not specified).

Duration 1 semester; recipients may reapply.

Number awarded 1 or more each year.

Deadline April of each year for the first semester; September of each year for the second semester.

[675]
MADGE TRUEX FUND SEMINARY STUDENT LOANS

Missouri Baptist Convention
Attn: Woman's Missionary Union
400 East High Street
Jefferson City, MO 65101
(573) 636-0400 Toll Free: (800) 736-6227
Fax: (573) 659-7436 E-mail: dwells6779@sbcglobal.net
Web: www.mobaptist.org/home/wmu

Summary To provide forgivable loans to female graduate and seminary students, especially those from Missouri, preparing for a career as a Baptist missionary.

Eligibility This program is open to women enrolled or planning to enroll at a graduate school in any state or a Southern Baptist seminary. Applicants must be training for a full-time, church-related vocation in missions. Preference is given to applicants born in Missouri or those who have spent a major portion of their lives in the state. An interview is required.

Financial data The maximum loan is $800 per year. No interest is charged until after completion of schooling, at which time the rate is 4.5%. Repayment is waived if the recipient enters the missionary field.

Duration 1 year; may be renewed up to 2 additional years.

Number awarded Varies each year.

Deadline Deadline not specified.

[676]
MAE LASSLEY/OSAGE SCHOLARSHIPS

Osage Scholarship Fund
c/o Roman Catholic Diocese of Tulsa
P.O. Box 690240
Tulsa, OK 74169-0240
(918) 294-1904 Fax: (918) 294-0920
E-mail: sarah.jameson@dioceseoftulsa.org
Web: www.osagetribe.com

Summary To provide financial assistance to Osage Indians who are Roman Catholics attending college or graduate school.

Eligibility This program is open to Roman Catholics who are attending or planning to attend a college or university as a full-time undergraduate or graduate student. Applicants must be Osage Indians on the rolls in Pawhuska, Oklahoma and have a copy of their Certificate of Indian Blood (CIB) or Osage tribal membership card. Selection is based on academic ability and financial need.

Financial data The stipend is $1,000 per year.

Duration 1 year; may be renewed if the recipient maintains full-time enrollment and a GPA of 2.5 or higher as an undergraduate or 3.0 or higher as a graduate student.

Number awarded Normally, 10 each year: 2 for students attending St. Gregory's University in Shawnee, Oklahoma as freshmen and 8 for any college or university.

Deadline April of each year.

[677]
MAINE CONFERENCE SEMINARIAN SCHOLARSHIP

United Church of Christ-Maine Conference
Attn: Witness Life Commission
28 Yarmouth Crossing Drive
Yarmouth, ME 04096
(207) 846-5118 Toll Free: (800) 244-0937 (within ME)
Fax: (207) 846-2301 E-mail: conference@maineucc.org
Web: www.maineucc.org

Summary To provide financial assistance to United Church of Christ (UCC) seminary students from Maine.

Eligibility This program is open to seminary students who are under care of a UCC church affiliated with the Maine Conference. Applicants must submit information on their financial need, seminary career, full- or part-time employment, and involvement with their local church, association, and conference.

Financial data Stipends range up to $1,000.

Duration 1 year.

Number awarded Varies each year; recently, 8 of these scholarships were awarded.

Deadline May of each year.

[678]
MAKE A DIFFERENCE! DOCTORAL STUDIES AWARD

United Church of Christ
Parish Life and Leadership Ministry Team
Attn: Grants, Scholarships, and Resources
700 Prospect Avenue East
Cleveland, OH 44115-1100
(216) 736-3839 Toll Free: (866) 822-8224, ext. 3839
Fax: (216) 736-3783 E-mail: jeffersv@ucc.org
Web: www.ucc.org/seminarians/ucc-scholarships-for.html

Summary To provide financial assistance to doctoral students who are interested in preparing for a teaching career at a seminary of the United Church of Christ (UCC).

Eligibility This program is open to students working on a doctoral degree who have been members of a UCC congregation for at least 1 year. Applicants must have a GPA of 3.0 or higher and be enrolled in a course of study leading to a teaching position at a UCC seminary. They must demonstrate leadership ability through participation in their local church, association, conference, or academic environment.

Financial data Stipends are approximately $2,500 per year.

Duration 1 year.

Number awarded Varies each year. Recently, 3 of these awards were presented.

Deadline Deadline not specified.

[679]
MAKE A DIFFERENCE! EDUCATIONAL SUPPORT AWARDS

United Church of Christ
Parish Life and Leadership Ministry Team
Attn: Grants, Scholarships, and Resources
700 Prospect Avenue East
Cleveland, OH 44115-1100
(216) 736-3839   Toll Free: (866) 822-8224, ext. 3839
Fax: (216) 736-3783   E-mail: jeffersv@ucc.org
Web: www.ucc.org/seminarians/ucc-scholarships-for.html

Summary   To provide financial assistance to seminary students who are interested in becoming a pastor in the United Church of Christ (UCC).

Eligibility   This program is open to students at accredited seminaries who have been members of a UCC congregation for at least 1 year. Applicants must 1) have a GPA of 3.0 or higher, 2) be enrolled in a course of study leading to ordained ministry, and 3) be in care of an association or conference at the time of application. Students must be nominated by their association committee on ministry. They must demonstrate leadership ability through participation in their local church, association, conference, or academic environment.

Financial data   Stipends are approximately $500 per year. Funds are paid directly to the seminary, to be applied toward tuition, books, or other educational expenses.

Duration   1 year.

Number awarded   Varies each year. Recently, 9 of these scholarships were awarded.

Deadline   Deadline not specified.

[680]
MAKE A DIFFERENCE! SEMINARIAN SCHOLARSHIP

United Church of Christ
Parish Life and Leadership Ministry Team
Attn: Grants, Scholarships, and Resources
700 Prospect Avenue East
Cleveland, OH 44115-1100
(216) 736-3839   Toll Free: (866) 822-8224, ext. 3839
Fax: (216) 736-3783   E-mail: jeffersv@ucc.org
Web: www.ucc.org/seminarians/ucc-scholarships-for.html

Summary   To provide financial assistance to students at seminaries of the United Church of Christ (UCC).

Eligibility   This program is open to students at the 7 seminaries of the UCC who have been a member of a UCC congregation for at least 1 year. They must 1) have a GPA of 3.0 or higher, 2) be enrolled in a course of study leading to ordained ministry, and 3) be in care of an association or conference at the time of application. Students must be nominated by the president of their seminary. They must demonstrate leadership ability through participation in their local church, association, conference, or academic environment.

Financial data   Stipends range from $1,500 to $2,500 per year. Funds are paid directly to the seminary to be applied toward tuition.

Duration   1 year.

Additional information   The UCC seminaries are Andover Newton Theological School (Newton Centre, Massachusetts), Bangor Theological Seminary (Bangor, Maine), Chicago Theological Seminary (Chicago, Illinois), Eden Theolog-ical Seminary (St. Louis, Missouri), Lancaster Theological Seminary (Lancaster, Pennsylvania), Pacific School of Religion (Berkeley, California), and United Theological Seminary of the Twin Cities (New Brighton, Minnesota).

Number awarded   Varies each year. Recently, 6 of these scholarships were awarded.

Deadline   Deadline not specified.

[681]
MARGARET AND CHARLES E. STEWART SCHOLARSHIP FUND

Philadelphia Foundation
1234 Market Street, Suite 1800
Philadelphia, PA 19107-3794
(215) 563-6417   Fax: (215) 563-6882
E-mail: scholarships@philafound.org
Web: www.philafound.org

Summary   To provide financial aid to graduate students who are preparing for the pastoral ministry in the Black church in any Protestant denomination.

Eligibility   This program is open to M.Div. candidates enrolled full time at an accredited seminary. They must be interested in preparing for the pastorate in the Black church of any Protestant denomination. Financial need is considered in the selection process.

Financial data   The stipend is $500. Funds are to be used to pay tuition.

Duration   1 year; nonrenewable.

Additional information   This fund was established in 1994.

Number awarded   4 each year.

Deadline   April of each year.

[682]
MARGARET MOSER LANDERS SCHOLARSHIP TRUST

Alabama-West Florida United Methodist Foundation, Inc.
170 Belmont Drive
P.O. Box 8066
Dothan, AL 36304
(334) 793-6820   Fax: (334) 794-6480
E-mail: foundation@alwfumf.org
Web: www.alwfumf.org

Summary   To provide financial assistance to ministerial students from the Alabama-West Florida Conference of the United Methodist Church.

Eligibility   This program is open to members of United Methodist Churches within the Alabama-West Florida Conference. Applicants must be studying to become an ordained United Methodist minister and be planning to return for service within the bounds of the Alabama-West Florida Conference. They must be younger than 38 years of age.

Financial data   The amount of the stipend varies each year.

Duration   1 year.

Number awarded   1 or more each year.

Deadline   June of each year.

[683]
MARGUERITE YOUNG ENDOWMENT FUND

Pittsburgh Foundation
Attn: Scholarship Coordinator
Five PPG Place, Suite 250
Pittsburgh, PA 15222-5414
(412) 394-2649   Fax: (412) 391-7259
E-mail: turnerd@pghfdn.org
Web: www.pittsburghfoundation.org

Summary To provide financial assistance to seminary students preparing for a career in Protestant ministry.

Eligibility This program is open to students enrolled at 1 of 9 designated Protestant seminaries who are preparing for full-time ministry and/or currently working as an intern at a Protestant church. Applicants must submit 500-word essays on the following topics: 1) where they see themselves in 10, 20, and 30 years; and 2) their view of the nature and role of scripture in their ministry.

Financial data The amount of the stipend varies; recently, it was more than $7,500.

Duration 1 year.

Additional information The designated seminaries are Bethel Theological Seminary, Dallas Theological Seminary, Gordon-Conwell Theological Seminary, Lutheran Theological Seminary at Philadelphia, Pittsburgh Theological Seminary, Reformed Presbyterian Theological Seminary, Reformed Theological Seminary, Trinity Episcopal School for Ministry, and Trinity Evangelical Divinity School of the Trinity International University.

Number awarded 1 each year.

Deadline April of each year.

[684]
MARJORIE GERALD & GRACE UNITED METHODIST CHURCH SEMINARY SCHOLARSHIP

Iowa United Methodist Foundation
2301 Rittenhouse Street
Des Moines, IA 50321
(515) 974-8927
Web: www.iumf.org/seminaryscholarships.html

Summary To provide financial assistance to United Methodist seminary students from Iowa.

Eligibility This program is open to students who have completed at least a bachelor's degree and are enrolled in studies at the graduate or professional level at an approved United Methodist seminary. Applicants must be preparing for ministry in the local church and must be members of an Iowa United Methodist Church. Financial need is considered in the selection process.

Financial data The stipend is $610.

Duration 1 year.

Number awarded 1 each year.

Deadline March of each year.

[685]
MARTHA WATSON STUDENT LOAN FUND

North Carolina Baptist Foundation, Inc.
Attn: Denominational Relations Committee
201 Convention Drive
Cary, NC 27511-4257
(919) 380-7334   Toll Free: (800) 521-7334
Fax: (919) 460-6334
Web: www.ncbaptistfoundation.org

Summary To provide educational loans to college and seminary students, especially those attending Baptist institutions.

Eligibility This loan program is open to U.S. citizens and legal residents who are attending or planning to attend a college, university, technical school, or seminary. Preference is given to 1) applicants of evangelical Christian faith or background; 2) those seeking a church-related vocation; 3) residents of North Carolina; 4) members of 3 named churches in Robeson County and their children; 5) blood relatives of Mrs. Fawn Watson; and 6) students who can demonstrate financial need.

Financial data The maximum loan is $3,000 per year for students attending a Baptist institution or $1,600 for students attending a non-Baptist institution. The interest rate is equal to the prevailing rate, up to a maximum of 12%. No interest is charged and repayment need not begin until 6 months after conclusion of studies. Loans must be repaid within 15 years.

Duration 1 year; may be renewed up to 3 additional years by undergraduates or up to 2 additional years by graduate students.

Additional information There is a $10 application fee.

Number awarded 1 or more each year.

Deadline January of each year.

[686]
MARY B. RHODES MEDICAL SCHOLARSHIP

Woman's Missionary Union
Attn: WMU Foundation
100 Missionary Ridge
Birmingham, AL 35242
(205) 408-5525   Toll Free: (877) 482-4483
Fax: (205) 408-5508   E-mail: wmufoundation@wmu.org
Web: www.wmufoundation.com

Summary To provide financial assistance to children of Southern Baptist missionaries who are working on a degree in a medical field.

Eligibility This program is open to Southern Baptist students who are working on a degree in a medical field, including nursing, dentistry, or pharmacy. Applicants must be planning to go into international missions work. They must be dependents of international missionaries who are under appointment of the North American Mission Board (NAMB) of the Southern Baptist Convention.

Financial data A stipend is awarded (amount not specified).

Duration 1 year.

Number awarded Varies each year.

Deadline February of each year.

[687]
MARY C. EASTERLING SCHOLARSHIP

SouthTrust Bank of Alabama, N.A.
Attn: Asset Management
P.O. Box 1000
Anniston, AL 36202
(256) 231-4330   Fax: (256) 231-4341

Summary To provide funding to Protestant students beginning or working on a graduate degree who are interested in preparing themselves for a career in Christian work or service.

Eligibility This program is open to the following categories of students (in order of preference): 1) members of a Methodist Church who live in Anniston, Alabama; 2) members of any other Protestant Church who live in Anniston, Alabama; 3) members of the Methodist Church who live outside of Anniston but within Calhoun County, Alabama; 4) members of any Protestant church who live outside of Anniston but within Calhoun County, Alabama; and 5) members of any Protestant Church who are already doing graduate work in a seminary, church school, or state college. Applicants must be attending graduate school with the intention of performing full-time Christian work or service. Selection is based on financial need, moral character, and the likelihood of success as full-time Christian workers.

Financial data The stipend is approximately $500.

Duration 1 year.

Number awarded 1 or more each year.

Deadline May of each year.

[688]
MARY CATHRYN KENNINGTON SCHOLARSHIP

Order of the Eastern Star-Grand Chapter of Texas
Attn: Education Committee
1503 West Division Street
Arlington, TX 76012
(817) 265-6263
Web: www.grandchapteroftexasoes.org/scholar_forms.asp

Summary To provide renewable financial assistance to residents of Texas interested in attending college or graduate school in any state, especially those planning to prepare for a career in religious service.

Eligibility This program is open to residents of Texas who are high school seniors or graduates already enrolled at an accredited college, university, or seminary in any state. Applicants must be interested in working on an undergraduate or graduate degree in any field, although the program especially encourages applications from those planning to prepare for a full-time career as a minister, missionary, director of religious education, Christian youth worker, or church music director. They must have a GPA of 2.0 or higher. Along with their application, they must submit an essay describing their plans for the future, reasons for applying for the scholarship, and financial status. Undergraduates must be enrolled full time.

Financial data The stipend is $1,000 per year.

Duration 1 year; may be renewed, provided the recipient maintains a GPA of 2.0 or higher.

Number awarded 1 or more each year.

Deadline February of each year.

[689]
MARY CROWLEY MEMORIAL SCHOLARSHIP

Baptist Convention of New York
Attn: BCNY Foundation
6538 Baptist Way
East Syracuse, NY 13057
(315) 433-1001   Toll Free: (800) 552-0004
Fax: (315) 433-1026   E-mail: cmeyer@bcnysbc.org
Web: www.bcnysbc.org/bcnyfoundation.html

Summary To provide financial assistance to members of churches in the Baptist Convention of New York who are preparing for a vocation in full-time Christian service or other activities.

Eligibility This program is open to members in good standing of churches in the Baptist Convention of New York. First priority is given to students preparing for full-time Christian service as ministerial students, missionary candidates, or other church-related vocations in music, education, or youth. If funds are available, students not entering full-time Christian vocations are considered. Along with their application, they must submit 1) an essay in which they share their goals for the future and how a degree in higher education will help them achieve those goals; and 2) an autobiography that includes their conversion experience, call to Christian service (for those planning a religious vocation), and plans to fulfill this calling. Financial need is also considered in the selection process.

Financial data A stipend is awarded (amount not specified).

Duration 1 year; may be renewed up to 3 additional years.

Number awarded 1 or more each year.

Deadline February of each year.

[690]
MARY L. CLARK MINISTRY STUDY GRANT

Synod of the Trinity
Attn: Scholarships
3040 Market Street
Camp Hill, PA 17011-4599
(717) 737-0421, ext. 233
Toll Free: (800) 242-0534, ext. 233
Fax: (717) 737-8211   E-mail: mhumer@syntrinity.org
Web: www.syntrinity.org

Summary To provide financial assistance to Presbyterians from Pennsylvania who are studying for the ministry at a school in any state.

Eligibility This program is open to residents of Pennsylvania who are members of the Presbyterian Church (USA). Applicants must be preparing for service in the Presbyterian ministry at a Presbyterian seminary or a seminary approved by their Committee on Preparation for Ministry. They must be under the supervision of a Presbytery within the bounds of the Synod of the Trinity within Pennsylvania.

Financial data Grants normally are limited to $1,000 per year. Funds may be used for 1) programs related to continuing education; 2) costs of traveling overseas for educational purposes; 3) tuition for a degree beyond a baccalaureate degree; or 4) tuition for a church vocational development continuing education program that enhances a skill or proficiency required for vocational responsibilities.

Duration 1 year; may be renewed.

Number awarded Varies each year.

Deadline April of each year.

[691]
MARY MEADE MAXWELL VOCATIONS SCHOLARSHIPS

Synod of the Trinity
Attn: Scholarships
3040 Market Street
Camp Hill, PA 17011-4599
(717) 737-0421, ext. 233
Toll Free: (800) 242-0534, ext. 233
Fax: (717) 737-8211   E-mail: mhumer@syntrinity.org
Web: www.syntrinity.org

Summary To provide financial assistance to Presbyterians who reside within Synod of the Trinity and are preparing for church-related vocations.

Eligibility This program is open to members of congregations and Presbyteries within the bounds of the Synod of the Trinity, which covers all of Pennsylvania; West Virginia (except for the counties of Berkeley, Grant, Hampshire, Hardy, Jefferson, Mineral, Morgan, and Pendleton); and the Ohio counties of Belmont, Harrison, Jefferson, Monroe, and the southern sector of Columbiana. Applicants must be an inquirer or a candidate in a Presbytery of the Synod and preparing for a full-time church-related vocation in the Presbyterian Church (USA). Preference is given to first-time applicants.

Financial data A stipend is paid (amount not specified). Funds may be used for 1) programs related to continuing education, or 2) tuition for a degree or non-degree oriented program other than a baccalaureate degree.

Duration 1 year; may be renewed.

Number awarded Varies each year.

Deadline April of each year.

[692]
MASSACHUSETTS BAPTIST CHARITABLE SOCIETY SCHOLARSHIPS

Massachusetts Baptist Charitable Society
Attn: Executive Director
14 Juniper Point Road
Groton, MA 01450
(978) 448-0451   Fax: (978) 448-2534
E-mail: revdrwright1@verizon.net
Web: www.massbaptistcharitable.org/apply.htm

Summary To provide financial assistance to American Baptist pastors in Massachusetts who are interested in working on an advanced degree at a school in any state.

Eligibility This program is open to pastors who have standing in the American Baptist Church (ABC) in Massachusetts, have a recognized ABC/USA ordination, and are serving at least 19 hours per week in a recognized ministry in Massachusetts. Applicants must be working on or planning to work on a D.Min., Ph.D., Th.D., or S.T.M. degree program in any state that is accredited by the Association of Theological Schools. They must have, or be completing, an M.Div. degree. Along with their application, they must submit an essay of 1 to 2 pages on how they think their studies will enhance their particular ministry as well as their ministry to the wider family of believers. Financial need is considered in

the selection process. Applicants who are attending a graduate school in New England must have an interview with the sponsor's executive director.

Financial data The stipend is $2,000.

Duration 1 year.

Additional information The Massachusetts Baptist Charitable Society was founded in 1794 to provide assistance to widows of deceased clergy. Over the years, it took on additional functions and, in 2000, began awarding these scholarships. The program includes the Ernest H. Hatch Scholarship and the Charles F. Putnam Scholarship.

Number awarded Varies each year.

Deadline July of each year.

[693]
MASTER'S FUND

Order of the Daughters of the King, Inc.
101 Weatherstone Drive, Suite 870
Woodstock, GA 30188
(770) 517-8552   Fax: (770) 517-8066
E-mail: dok1885@doknational.org
Web: www.doknational.org

Summary To provide financial assistance to members of the Daughters of the King who are seeking undergraduate or graduate training at a church-related school in the United States or abroad.

Eligibility This program is open to women who are communicants of the Episcopal church, autonomous churches of the Anglican communion, or churches in communion with the Episcopal church. Applicants must be at least 21 years of age, have at least 2 years of college education or its equivalent, and have letters of recommendation from their bishop/rector, the dean or academic adviser of their school, and 3 church women who know them well. The program gives priority to women preparing for missionary or other church-related work, but applicants may be seeking training at an accredited college, university, or graduate school in the United States or abroad. They must be willing to give at least 2 years' service (at a suitable salary) to the church upon completion of their training. Along with their application, they must submit a 500-word statement on what they believe God is calling them to do. Individuals can apply, but nominations are welcome. Priority is given to members of the Daughters; nominees from the church's Executive Council, bishops, and clergy; and nominees from members of the Daughters.

Financial data Scholarships range from $500 to $700 per year; funds are granted for tuition only and the money is paid directly to the school.

Duration 1 year; may be renewed until completion of studies.

Additional information This program was established in 1922.

Number awarded Varies; up to 15 each year.

Deadline February, May, or September of each year.

[694]
MATTIE J.C. RUSSELL SCHOLARSHIP

Woman's Missionary Union
Attn: WMU Foundation
100 Missionary Ridge
Birmingham, AL 35242
(205) 408-5525   Toll Free: (877) 482-4483
Fax: (205) 408-5508   E-mail: wmufoundation@wmu.org
Web: www.wmufoundation.com

Summary To provide financial assistance for undergraduate or graduate study to the dependent children of Southern Baptist missionaries.

Eligibility This program is open to Southern Baptist students who are working on an undergraduate or graduate degree in any field. Applicants must be dependents of North American missionaries who are under appointment of the North American Mission Board (NAMB) of the Southern Baptist Convention.

Financial data A stipend is awarded (amount not specified).

Duration 1 year.

Number awarded Varies each year.

Deadline February of each year.

[695]
MCA CHAPLAIN CANDIDATE SCHOLARSHIPS

Military Chaplains Association of the United States of
   America
Attn: Chaplain Candidate Scholarship Committee
P.O. Box 7056
Arlington, VA 22207-7056
(703) 533-5890   E-mail: chaplains@mca-usa.org
Web: mca-usa.org/scholarships

Summary To provide financial assistance to seminary students who are serving as chaplain candidates for the U.S. armed forces.

Eligibility This program is open to full-time students in accredited seminaries who are currently approved as and serving as chaplain candidates in the armed forces (Army, Air Force, or Navy). Applicants must be able to demonstrate financial need. Along with their application, they must submit 500-word essays on 1) their sense of call to ministry with particular emphasis on their call to provide pastoral care for military personnel and their families; and 2) their understanding thus far of ministry in a religiously diverse environment (such as the armed forces of the United States).

Financial data The stipend is $2,000.

Duration 1 year.

Additional information This program was established in 1992.

Number awarded Varies each year. Since the program was established, it has awarded 63 scholarships.

Deadline June of each year.

[696]
MCKEAG FUND GRANTS

United Methodist Church-Kentucky Annual Conference
Attn: Board of Ordained Ministry
7400 Floydsburg Road
Crestwood, KY 40014-8202
(502) 425-3884   Toll Free: (800) 530-7236
Fax: (502) 426-5181
Web: www.kyumc.org/pages/detail/985

Summary To provide financial assistance to Methodist students from Kentucky who are enrolled in a seminary as preparation for ordination within the United Methodist Church (UMC).

Eligibility This program is open to seminary students who are certified as candidates for ministry by their district committee within the UMC Kentucky Annual Conference. Applicants must be preparing for ordination as a deacon. Priority is given to first-time applicants.

Financial data A stipend is awarded (amount not specified).

Duration 1 term; may be renewed.

Number awarded 1 or more each year.

Deadline February of each year for terms beginning April through June; May of each year for terms beginning July through September; August of each year for terms beginning October through December; November of each year for terms beginning January through March.

[697]
MEL LARSON JOURNALISM SCHOLARSHIPS

Evangelical Press Association
Attn: Scholarships
P.O. Box 28129
Crystal, MN 55428
(763) 535-4793   Fax: (763) 535-4794
E-mail: director@epassoc.org
Web: www.epassoc.org

Summary To provide financial assistance to upper-division and graduate students interested in preparing for a career in Christian journalism.

Eligibility This program is open to entering juniors, seniors, and graduate students who have at least 1 year of full-time study remaining. Applicants must be majoring or minoring in journalism or communications, preferably with an interest in the field of Christian journalism. They must be enrolled at an accredited Christian or secular college or university in the United States or Canada and have a GPA of 3.0 or higher. Along with their application, they must submit a biographical sketch that includes their birth date, hometown, family, and something about the factors that shaped their interest in Christian journalism; a copy of their academic record; references from their pastor and from an instructor; samples of published writing from church or school publications; and an original essay (from 500 to 700 words) on the state of journalism today.

Financial data Stipends range from $1,000 to $2,500.

Duration 1 year.

Additional information This program includes the Mel Larson Memorial Scholarship.

Number awarded Varies each year: recently, 4 of these scholarships were awarded.

Deadline March of each year.

[698]
MELVIN KELLY AND MAYME DUBOSE MEDLOCK MINISTERIAL SCHOLARSHIP

South Carolina United Methodist Foundation
P.O. Box 5087
Columbia, SC 29250-5087
(803) 771-9125   Fax: (803) 771-9135
E-mail: scumf@bellsouth.net
Web: www.umcsc.org/scholarships.html

Summary To provide financial assistance to residents of South Carolina who are attending college or graduate school in any state to prepare for ordained Methodist ministry.

Eligibility This program is open to residents of South Carolina who are certified candidates for ordained ministry in the United Methodist Church (UMC). Applicants must be enrolled full time either as an undergraduate at an accredited college or university or as a graduate student at a seminary or theological school in any state approved by the University Senate of the United Methodist Church. Financial need may be considered in the selection process.

Financial data A stipend is awarded (amount not specified).

Duration 1 year.

Additional information This scholarship was established by the South Carolina Conference of the United Methodist Church in 2001.

Number awarded 1 or more each year.

Deadline April of each year.

[699]
MEMORIAL BAPTIST CHURCH FOUNDATION MINISTERIAL SCHOLARSHIP

Memorial Baptist Church Foundation, Inc.
Attn: Scholarship Committee
3455 North Glebe Road
Arlington, VA 22207-4399
(703) 538-7000   Fax: (703) 538-6861
E-mail: admin@memorialbaptistchurch.org
Web: www.memorialbaptistchurch.org/foundation.shtml

Summary To provide financial assistance to seminary students preparing for full-time Christian ministry in a Baptist church.

Eligibility This program is open to students in training or ready to enter training for full-time Christian service with the intention of serving as a minister in a Baptist church. Applicants must submit a 1- to 2-page personal statement that addresses how they became a Christian, what faith in Christ means to them, how they came to realize a calling to the ministry, their recent involvement in church activities and ministries, how they believe their gifts might be used in God's service, and the type of ministry to which they currently feel led. Selection is based on that statement, academic record, work experience, participation in church life, and financial need. Preference is given first to members of Memorial Baptist Church in Arlington, Virginia, second to Baptists residing in the NorthStar Church Network, third to Baptists in Virginia,

and fourth to Baptists residing elsewhere in the United States.

Financial data A stipend is awarded (amount not specified).

Duration 1 year; may be renewed, provided the recipient maintains a GPA of 2.5 or higher.

Number awarded Varies each year.

Deadline May of each year.

[700]
METHODIST SEPTEMBER 11 MEMORIAL SCHOLARSHIPS

United Methodist Higher Education Foundation
Attn: Scholarships Administrator
1001 19th Avenue South
P.O. Box 340005
Nashville, TN 37203-0005
(615) 340-7385   Toll Free: (800) 811-8110
Fax: (615) 340-7330
E-mail: umhefscholarships@gbhem.org
Web: www.umhef.org/receive.php?id=sept_11_scholarship

Summary To provide financial assistance to Methodists and undergraduate and graduate students at Methodist institutions whose parent or guardian was disabled or killed in the terrorist attacks on September 11, 2001.

Eligibility This program is open to 1) students attending a United Methodist-related college or university in the United States, and 2) United Methodist students attending a higher education institution in the United States. All applicants must have lost a parent or guardian or had a parent or guardian disabled as a result of the September 11, 2001 terrorist attacks. They must be enrolled as full-time undergraduate or graduate students. U.S. citizenship or permanent resident status is required.

Financial data The stipend depends on the number of applicants.

Duration 1 year; may be renewed as long as the recipients maintain satisfactory academic progress as defined by their institution.

Number awarded Varies each year; a total of $30,000 is available for this program.

Deadline Applications may be submitted at any time.

[701]
METHODIST STUDIES SCHOLARSHIP FOR PART-TIME STUDENTS

United Methodist Church
General Board of Higher Education and Ministry
Attn: Division of Ordained Ministry
1001 19th Avenue South
P.O. Box 340007
Nashville, TN 37203-0007
(615) 340-7375   Fax: (615) 340-7377
E-mail: deacons@gbhem.org
Web: www.gbhem.org

Summary To provide financial assistance to Methodist candidates for ministerial certification who are enrolled on a part-time basis.

Eligibility This program is open to Methodists engaged in 1) professional certification studies in a specialized ministry area (e.g., Christian education, evangelism, older adult ministry, children's ministry, music ministry, spiritual formation, ministry with the poor, camp/retreat ministry, or youth ministry); 2) deacon candidates in the Basic Graduate Theological Studies (BGTS) program; or 3) full-time or part-time local pastors who have completed the course of study, associate members of an annual conference, and ordained ministers transferring in from other denominations in the Advanced Course of Study (ACOS) program. Applicants must be enrolled as a special student or a part-time degree student at a school approved by the United Methodist University Senate; full-time students in seminary degree programs are not eligible.

Financial data The stipend is $200 per semester hour for each required 2-hour or 3-hour course completed.

Duration 1 semester; may be renewed.

Number awarded Varies each year.

Deadline Applications may be submitted at any time, but they must be received after the start date for the named coursed.

[702]
MICHELLE JACKSON SCHOLARSHIP FUND

Christian Church (Disciples of Christ)
Attn: Disciples Home Missions
130 East Washington Street
P.O. Box 1986
Indianapolis, IN 46206-1986
(317) 713-2652   Toll Free: (888) DHM-2631
Fax: (317) 635-4426   E-mail: mail@dhm.disciples.org
Web: www.discipleshomemissions.org

Summary To provide financial assistance to African American women interested in preparing for a career in the ministry of the Christian Church (Disciples of Christ).

Eligibility This program is open to female African American ministerial students who are members of the Christian Church (Disciples of Christ). Applicants must plan to prepare for the ordained ministry, have at least a "C+" GPA, provide evidence of financial need, be enrolled full time in an accredited school or seminary, provide a transcript of academic work, and be under the care of a regional Commission on the Ministry or in the process of coming under care.

Financial data A stipend is awarded (amount not specified).

Duration 1 year; may be renewed.

Number awarded 1 each year.

Deadline March of each year.

[703]
MICHIGAN BAPTIST SCHOLARSHIP SOCIETY SCHOLARSHIPS

American Baptist Churches of Michigan
Attn: Michigan Baptist Scholarship Society
4578 South Hagadorn Road
East Lansing, MI 48823
(517) 332-3594   Toll Free: (800) 632-2953
Fax: (517) 332-3186   E-mail: mawilliams@abc-mi.org
Web: www.abc-mi.org/?q=node/865

Summary To provide financial assistance to members of American Baptist Churches of Michigan who are preparing for a professional church vocation.

Eligibility This program is open to members of American Baptist Churches of Michigan who are entering or attending an accredited college, university, or seminary. Applicants must be able to provide evidence of 1) God's call to a professional church vocation; 2) spiritual, personal, and academic maturity; and 3) financial need. Along with their application, they must submit an autobiographical essay of 2 to 3 pages describing their Christian experience, call to professional church vocation, and career goals. Preference is given to full-time students at institutions related to the American Baptist Church.

Financial data Stipends are at least $2,000 per year for seminary students and at least $1,000 per year for college students.

Duration 1 year; may be renewed if the recipient maintains full-time enrollment and a GPA of 2.5 or higher.

Number awarded Varies each year.

Deadline June of each year for support beginning in the first academic term; October of each year for support beginning in the second academic term.

[704]
MINISTERIAL EDUCATION FUND OF THE EVANGELICAL METHODIST CHURCH

Evangelical Methodist Church
Attn: General Board of Ministerial Education
P.O. Box 17070
Indianapolis, IN 46217
(317) 780-8017   Fax: (317) 780-8078
E-mail: hq@emchurch.org
Web: emchurch.org/general-boards/ministerial-education

Summary To provide loans-for-service to college, Bible school, and seminary students preparing for ministry service in the Evangelical Methodist Church.

Eligibility This program is open to 1) undergraduate students enrolled in an accredited Christian college in the Wesleyan tradition who are majoring in Bible, pastoral ministry, Christian education, or missions; and 2) students enrolled in an accredited theological seminary in the Wesleyan tradition approved by the Board of Ministerial Education of the Evangelical Methodist Church. Applicants must be in process toward ordination as an Evangelical Methodist Elder as recommended by their home District Superintendent and Board of Ministerial Relations. They must be a member in good standing in an Evangelical Methodist Church. Students working on a degree beyond the M.Div. are not eligible.

Financial data The maximum loan amount varies each year and is greater for seminary students than for undergraduates. Funds are disbursed jointly to the student and the school, for payment of tuition only. For each year of full-time ministry service while under a call to an Evangelical Methodist Church or the Board of World Missions, after being ordained an elder, one-sixth of the debt is cancelled. If the recipient does not complete the process of ordination as an Elder or drops out of school, the loan is repayable at an interest rate of 6%. Years of service as a Member on Trial do not qualify toward repaying the loan debt. If an Elder withdraws or is discontinued from ministerial service, the balance of the unpaid loan becomes due and is repayable at 6% interest.

Duration 1 year; may be renewed, provided the recipient maintains a GPA of 2.0 or higher.

Number awarded Varies each year.

Deadline Deadline not specified.

[705]
MINNESOTA EASTERN STAR TRAINING AWARDS FOR RELIGIOUS LEADERSHIP

Order of the Eastern Star-Grand Chapter of Minnesota
Attn: Grand Secretary
11501 Masonic Home Drive
Bloomington, MN 55437
(952) 948-6800   E-mail: mngrsecoes@hotmail.com
Web: www.mnoes.com

Summary To provide financial assistance to residents of Minnesota who are attending a college or seminary in any state to prepare for a career in religious leadership in any denomination.

Eligibility This program is open to full- and part-time students at colleges, universities, and seminaries in any state who have been residents of Minnesota for at least 1 year. Applicants must be preparing for a full-time religious career, including ordained ministry, missionary, youth ministry, director of religious education, music ministry, or other related profession. Along with their application, they must submit brief personal statements on the role of religion in today's living, how churches can become more effective, the ways in which they feel they can make a difference in people's lives, and their personal religious philosophy. Selection is based on character, scholarship, leadership, citizenship, and financial need.

Financial data Stipends vary; the total award received by any single student may not exceed $10,000.

Duration 1 year; may be renewed.

Number awarded 1 or more each year.

Deadline January of each year.

[706]
MINNESOTA GLBT LUTHERAN STUDENT AWARD

Philanthrofund Foundation
Attn: Scholarship Committee
1409 Willow Street, Suite 210
Minneapolis, MN 55403-3251
(612) 870-1806   Toll Free: (800) 435-1402
Fax: (612) 871-6587   E-mail: info@PfundOnline.org
Web: www.pfundonline.org/scholarships.html

Summary To provide financial assistance to gay, lesbian, bisexual, and transgender students who are Lutherans, residents of Minnesota, and interested in attending college or graduate school in any state.

Eligibility This program is open to Minnesota residents who are Lutherans and attending or planning to attend a Lutheran or other institution (college, university, or graduate school) in any state. Applicants must identify with or be involved with the gay, lesbian, bisexual, or transgender (GLBT) community. They must indicate how their GLBT identity and their involvement in the Lutheran church are related to each other. Selection is based on the applicant's 1) affirmation of GLBT identity or commitment to GLBT communities; 2) evidence of experience and skills in service and leadership; and 3) evidence of service and leadership in GLBT communi-

ties, including serving as a role model, mentor, and/or adviser.

Financial data The stipend is $2,000. Funds must be used for tuition, books, fees, or dissertation expenses.

Duration 1 year.

Number awarded 1 or more each year.

Deadline January of each year.

[707]
MIRIAM HOFFMAN SCHOLARSHIPS

United Methodist Church
Attn: General Board of Higher Education and Ministry
Office of Loans and Scholarships
1001 19th Avenue South
P.O. Box 340007
Nashville, TN 37203-0007
(615) 340-7344   Fax: (615) 340-7367
E-mail: umscholar@gbhem.org
Web: www.gbhem.org/loansandscholarships

Summary To provide financial assistance to undergraduate and graduate Methodist students who are preparing for a career in music (including music education).

Eligibility This program is open to undergraduate and graduate students who are enrolled full time and preparing for a career in music. Applicants must have been active, full members of a United Methodist Church for at least 1 year prior to applying and have a GPA of 2.5 or higher. Preference is given to students interested in music education or music ministry. U.S. citizenship or permanent resident status is required.

Financial data The stipend is $1,000.

Duration 1 year; recipients may reapply.

Additional information This program was established in 2001.

Number awarded Varies each year. Recently, 12 of these scholarships were awarded.

Deadline May of each year.

[708]
MISSISSIPPI BAPTIST FOUNDATION SEMINARY SCHOLARSHIPS

Mississippi Baptist Foundation
Attn: MBF Scholarship Ministry
515 Mississippi Street
P.O. Box 530
Jackson, MS 39205-0530
(601) 292-3210   Toll Free: (800) 748-1651 (within MS)
Fax: (601) 968-0904
Web: www.msbaptistfoundation.org

Summary To provide financial assistance to members of Baptist churches in Mississippi who are interested in attending a Southern Baptist seminary.

Eligibility This program is open to members in good standing of Baptist churches in Mississippi that are cooperating members of the Mississippi Baptist Convention. Applicants must submit a letter of recommendation from their pastor, documentation of financial need, and a brief summary of their life, including their Christian testimony, goals, and ministry pursuits. They must be working on or planning to work on a master's degree at a Southern Baptist seminary: Southeastern Baptist Theological Seminary (Wake Forest, North Carolina); Southern Baptist Theological Seminary (Louisville, Kentucky); Southwestern Baptist Theological Seminary (Fort Worth, Texas); New Orleans Baptist Theological Seminary (New Orleans, Louisiana); Midwestern Baptist Theological Seminary (Kansas City, Missouri); or Golden Gate Baptist Theological Seminary (Mill Valley, California). Doctoral candidates are not eligible.

Financial data   A stipend is awarded (amount not specified).

Duration   1 year; may be renewed if the recipient maintains a GPA of 2.5 or higher.

Additional information   This program consists of a number of individual endowments, many of which specify a particular field of study, institution to be attended, and scholarship amount.

Number awarded   Varies each year.

Deadline   April of each year.

[709]
MISSISSIPPI CONFERENCE MERIT AWARD PROGRAM

United Methodist Church-Mississippi Conference
Attn: Committee on Higher Education and Campus
  Ministry
321 Mississippi Street
Jackson, MS 39201
(601) 354-0515, ext. 32   Toll Free: (866) 647-7486
E-mail: scumbest@mississippi-umc.org
Web: www.mississippi-umc.org/pages/detail/779

Summary   To provide financial assistance to undergraduate and graduate students who are members of United Methodist Church (UMC) congregations in Mississippi and interested in attending an institution affiliated with the denomination in any state.

Eligibility   This program is open to members of UMC congregations affiliated with the Mississippi Conference who are enrolled or planning to enroll at a UMC college or university in any state as an undergraduate or graduate student. Applicants must submit information on their financial need and their participation in organizations, programs, and their school, church, and community, including honors, awards, and leadership roles.

Financial data   The stipend is $500.

Duration   1 year.

Number awarded   4 each year.

Deadline   May of each year.

[710]
MISSISSIPPI UNITED METHODIST FOUNDATION SCHOLARSHIPS

Mississippi United Methodist Foundation
Attn: Executive Director
581 Highland Colony Parkway
P.O. Box 2415
Ridgeland, MS 39158-2415
(601) 948-8845   Toll Free: (800) 496-0975
Fax: (601) 360-0843   E-mail: info@ms-umf.org
Web: www.ms-umf.org

Summary   To provide financial assistance for college or seminary to members of United Methodist Churches in Mississippi.

Eligibility   This program is open to members of United Methodist Churches in Mississippi who are attending or planning to attend a college or seminary. The foundation administers a number of scholarship funds that have been established by particular congregations or individuals within the state. Each fund has different requirements. For further information, contact the foundation.

Financial data   Stipends range up to $1,000.

Duration   1 year.

Number awarded   Varies each year.

Deadline   May of each year.

[711]
MISSOURI CONFERENCE BOARD OF ORDAINED MINISTRY SEMINARY GRANTS

United Methodist Church-Missouri Conference
Attn: Board of Ordained Ministry
3601 Amron Court
Columbia, MO 65202
(573) 441-1770   Toll Free: (877) 736-1806
Fax: (573) 441-1780
E-mail: TMcManus@moumethodist.org
Web: www.moumethodist.org/pages/detail/851

Summary   To provide scholarship/loans to seminary students who are preparing for ministry within the Missouri Conference of the United Methodist Church.

Eligibility   This program is open to full- and part-time students at seminaries approved by the University Senate of the United Methodist Church (UMC). Applicants must intend to be ordained and remain in the Missouri Conference of the UMC. They must have a working relationship with their District Board of Ordained Ministry in Missouri and be certified candidates. Financial need is considered in the selection process.

Financial data   A stipend is awarded (amount not specified). Both full- and part-time grants are available. Funds are paid jointly to the student and the institution. This is a scholarship/loan program; recipients must agree to repay the entire grant if they do not serve in the UMC ministry for 1 year for each year that grant money is received.

Duration   1 year. Full-time grants may be renewed up to 3 additional years; part-time grants may be renewed up to 5 additional years.

Number awarded   Varies each year.

Deadline   June of each year.

[712]
MISSOURI CONFERENCE STUDENT AID GRANTS

United Methodist Church-Missouri Conference
Attn: Board of Ordained Ministry
3601 Amron Court
Columbia, MO 65202
(573) 441-1770   Toll Free: (877) 736-1806
Fax: (573) 441-1780
E-mail: TMcManus@moumethodist.org
Web: www.moumethodist.org/pages/detail/851

Summary   To provide financial assistance to undergraduate and seminary students who are preparing for ministry within the Missouri Conference of the United Methodist Church.

Eligibility This program is open to full- and part-time students at colleges and seminaries approved by the University Senate of the United Methodist Church (UMC). Applicants must have a working relationship with a district committee or team on ordained ministry in the Missouri Conference of the UMC. Undergraduates must be serving under appointment as a local pastor; seminarians must be certified candidates. Financial need is considered in the selection process.

Financial data A stipend is awarded (amount not specified). Both full- and part-time grants are available. Funds are paid jointly to the student and the institution.

Duration 1 year. Full-time grants may be renewed up to 3 additional years; part-time grants may be renewed up to 5 additional years.

Number awarded Varies each year.

Deadline June of each year.

[713]
MISSOURI STATE KNIGHTS OF COLUMBUS VOCATION SCHOLARSHIPS

Knights of Columbus-Missouri State Council
c/o J.Y. Miller, Scholarship Committee Chair
322 Second Street
Glasgow, MO 65254
(660) 338-2105   E-mail: j.y.miller@sbcglobal.net
Web: www.mokofc.org/youth.htm

Summary To provide financial assistance to residents of Missouri who plan to attend a college or seminary in any state to prepare for a religious vocation.

Eligibility This program is open to residents of Missouri who are enrolled or planning to enroll at an accredited college, university, or seminary in any state. Applicants must be preparing for a religious vocation with the approval of a Missouri Catholic diocese or a religious order in the state. Along with their application, they must submit a 200-word statement explaining their goals for the future, their professional ambitions, and how this scholarship will help them to achieve their goals. Selection is based on Catholic citizenship, community service, scholarship, and financial need.

Financial data The stipend is $1,000.

Duration 1 year.

Additional information This program was originally established in 1971. If no applications are received from individuals desiring to attend a seminary or be a postulant in a religious community, these scholarships may be awarded to applicants wishing to attend any accredited college or university, with preference to those attending a Catholic institution.

Number awarded 2 each year.

Deadline February of each year.

[714]
MISSOURI UNITED METHODIST FOUNDATION SEMINARY SCHOLARS GRANT

Missouri United Methodist Foundation
Attn: Scholarships
111 South Ninth Street, Suite 230
P.O. Box 1076
Columbia, MO 66205-1076
(573) 875-4168   Toll Free: (800) 332-8238
Fax: (573) 875-4595   E-mail: foundation@mumf.org
Web: www.mumf.org/view_page.php?page=41

Summary To provide financial assistance to members of United Methodist Churches in Missouri who are preparing for ministry.

Eligibility This program is open to full- and part-time students working on an M.Div. degree at a seminary approved by the University Senate of the United Methodist Church. Applicants must be recognized by a Missouri District Committee on Ordained Ministry and/or a District Superintendent in the Missouri Conference as either a "certified candidate" or a person with appropriate vocational potential and commitment. They must intend to be ordained into the full-time ministry of the United Methodist Church in Missouri and serve at least 5 years.

Financial data The stipend is $3,000 per year for full-time students or $1,500 per year for half-time students.

Duration 1 year; may be renewed up to 2 additional years by full-time students or up to 5 additional years by half-time students.

Number awarded Varies each year. Recently, 27 of these scholarships were awarded.

Deadline June of each year.

[715]
MOORE-SNITKER SCHOLARSHIP ENDOWMENT

United Methodist Church-New Mexico Conference
Attn: Board of Ordained Ministry
11816 Lomas Boulevard, N.E.
Albuquerque, NM 87112
(505) 255-8786, ext. 101   Toll Free: (800) 678-8786
Fax: (505) 265-6184 E-mail: mridgeway@nmconfum.com
Web: www.nmconfum.com

Summary To provide financial assistance to Methodists from New Mexico who are interested in attending seminary in any state to prepare for a career in ordained ministry.

Eligibility This program is open to students who are enrolled or planning to enroll at a seminary in any state and who have an affiliation with a congregation of the New Mexico Conference of the United Methodist Church (UMC). Applicants must be preparing for a career in ordained ministry to local churches in the New Mexico Conference. Along with their application, they must submit brief essays on their current financial situation, how their sense of calling to ministry has changed or grown during the past year, the areas of ministry in which they are currently interested, what they believe to be their greatest spiritual gifts, and how they believe God is calling them to use those gifts in the local church.

Financial data A stipend is awarded (amount not specified).

Duration 1 year.

Number awarded 1 or more each year.

Deadline April of each year.

[716]
MOUNT OLIVET FOUNDATION GRANTS

Mount Olivet United Methodist Church
Attn: Mount Olivet Foundation
1500 North Glebe Road
Arlington, VA 22207-2199
(703) 527-3934   Fax: (703) 524-8613
E-mail: scutshaw@mtolivet-umc.org
Web: www.mountolivetfoundation.org

Summary To provide financial assistance to undergraduate and graduate students, particularly Methodists.

Eligibility This program is open to undergraduate and graduate students, especially those already enrolled in a degree program. In the selection process, first preference is given to individuals connected to Mount Olivet United Methodist Church, second to members of a United Methodist Church in any state, third to residents of Arlington and northern Virginia, fourth to residents of the Washington, D.C. metropolitan area, and finally to residents of other areas. Financial need is considered in the selection process.

Financial data Stipends range from $500 to $1,500.

Duration 1 year.

Number awarded A limited number are awarded each year.

Deadline March, June, September, or December of each year.

[717]
MRS. GEORGE B. EAGER SCHOLARSHIPS

Kentucky Woman's Missionary Union
Attn: Scholarships
13420 Eastpoint Centre Drive
P.O. Box 436569
Louisville, KY 40253-6569
(502) 489-3534   Toll Free: (866) 489-3534 (within KY)
Fax: (502) 489-3566   E-mail: kywmu@kybaptist.org
Web: kywmu.org/scholarships

Summary To provide financial assistance to female Baptists from Kentucky who are attending graduate school or seminary in any state to prepare for a career related to the work of the Woman's Missionary Union (WMU).

Eligibility This program is open to women who are active members of churches affiliated with the Kentucky Baptist Convention or the General Association of Baptists in Kentucky. Applicants must be attending an accredited Christian graduate school or seminary in any state as a full-time student. They must have a GPA of 2.7 or higher and be preparing for a vocational career in missions, social work, or WMU work. Along with their application, they must submit a brief essay on how they became a Christian and their career goals.

Financial data Stipends range from $400 to $600.

Duration 1 year.

Number awarded 1 or more each year.

Deadline January of each year.

[718]
MUNCY FUND GRANTS

United Methodist Church-Kentucky Annual Conference
Attn: Board of Ordained Ministry
7400 Floydsburg Road
Crestwood, KY 40014-8202
(502) 425-3884   Toll Free: (800) 530-7236
Fax: (502) 426-5181
Web: www.kyumc.org/pages/detail/985

Summary To provide financial assistance to seminary students from Kentucky who are enrolled at United Methodist Church (UMC) seminaries.

Eligibility This program is open to seminary students who are certified as candidates for ordained ministry by their district committee within the UMC Kentucky Annual Conference.

Applicants must be attending a UMC seminary. Priority is given to first-time applicants.

Financial data A stipend is awarded (amount not specified).

Duration 1 term; may be renewed.

Number awarded 1 or more each year.

Deadline February of each year for terms beginning April through June; May of each year for terms beginning July through September; August of each year for terms beginning October through December; November of each year for terms beginning January through March.

[719]
NANCY GRISSOM-SELF SCHOLARSHIP AWARD

United Methodist Church-California-Pacific Annual Conference
Attn: Commission on the Status and Role of Women
110 South Euclid Avenue
P.O. Box 6006
Pasadena, CA 91102-6006
(626) 568-7300   Toll Free: (800) 244-8622
Fax: (626) 796-7297   E-mail: sschooley205@ca.rr.com
Web: www.cal-pac.org/news/detail/698

Summary To provide financial assistance to women who are members of United Methodist churches in the California-Pacific Annual Conference and interested in attending graduate school (including seminary) in any state.

Eligibility This program is open to women who are members of churches within the bounds of the United Methodist California-Pacific Annual Conference. Applicants must be attending or planning to attend a graduate school (including seminary) in any state. Along with their application, they must submit a 3-page essay explaining how their academic goals relate to and support the goals of the Commission on the Status and Role of Women (COSROW). Special consideration is given to women who are older than 30 years of age and returning to school. Selection is based on scholarship, leadership potential, and other evidence of potentialities for future service to others.

Financial data The stipend is $500.

Duration 1 year.

Additional information The California-Pacific Annual Conference includes churches in southern California, Hawaii, Guam, and Saipan.

Number awarded 1 each year.

Deadline July of each year.

[720]
NANETTE KIRBY MEMORIAL SCHOLARSHIPS

United Methodist Church-Louisiana Conference
Attn: Coordinator, Conference Board of Ordained Ministry
527 North Boulevard
Baton Rouge, LA 70802-5700
(225) 346-1646, ext. 230
Toll Free: (888) 239-5286, ext. 230
Fax: (225) 383-2652   E-mail: johneddd@bellsouth.net
Web: www.la-umc.org

Summary To provide financial assistance to Methodists from Louisiana who are attending a college or seminary in any state to prepare for a career in vocational service to the church.

Eligibility This program is open to members of United Methodist Churches in Louisiana who are enrolled or planning to enroll full time at a college, graduate school, or seminary in any state. Applicants may be working on an undergraduate degree with plans to enter a seminary or on a graduate or professional degree. They must be able to articulate vocational goals in service to the church. That may include ministry as an elder in full connection, deacon in full connection, licensed local pastor, diaconal minister, or certified lay professional in Christian education, music, youth, evangelism, camping/retreat ministries, spiritual formation, or older adult ministry. Along with their application, they must submit an essay on their vocational goals and plans for ministry.

Financial data The stipend is $1,000.

Duration 1 year.

Additional information This program was established in 2000.

Number awarded 2 each year.

Deadline February of each year.

[721]
NATIONAL KOREAN PRESBYTERIAN WOMEN GRANTS

National Korean Presbyterian Women
c/o Kyo Mo Chung, Moderator
2309 Misty Haven Lane
Plano, TX 75093
(214) 821-8776   E-mail: jungbang@gmail.com
Web: www.pcusa.org/korean/org-nkpw.htm

Summary To provide financial assistance to Korean American women preparing for ministry in the Presbyterian Church.

Eligibility This program is open to second-generation Korean American women who are entering their third semester of full-time study at a Presbyterian seminary. Selection is based on academic ability and leadership skills.

Financial data The stipend is $1,000.

Duration 1 year.

Deadline May of each year.

[722]
NATIONAL TEMPERANCE SCHOLARSHIP

United Methodist Higher Education Foundation
Attn: Scholarships Administrator
1001 19th Avenue South
P.O. Box 340005
Nashville, TN 37203-0005
(615) 340-7385   Toll Free: (800) 811-8110
Fax: (615) 340-7330
E-mail: umhefscholarships@gbhem.org
Web: www.umhef.org/receive.php?id=endowed_funds

Summary To provide financial assistance to undergraduate and graduate Methodist students at Methodist-related colleges and universities.

Eligibility This program is open to full-time undergraduate and graduate students at United Methodist-related colleges and universities. Applicants must have been active, full members of a United Methodist Church for at least 1 year prior to applying. They must have a GPA of 3.0 or higher and be able to demonstrate financial need. Along with their application, they must submit a 200-word essay on their involvement and/

or leadership responsibilities in their church, school, and community within the last 3 years. U.S. citizenship or permanent resident status is required.

Financial data The stipend is at least $1,000 per year.

Duration 1 year; recipients may reapply.

Number awarded 1 each year.

Deadline May of each year.

[723]
NATIVE AMERICAN SEMINARY AWARDS

United Methodist Church
Attn: General Board of Higher Education and Ministry
Office of Loans and Scholarships
1001 19th Avenue South
P.O. Box 340007
Nashville, TN 37203-0007
(615) 340-7344   Fax: (615) 340-7367
E-mail: umscholar@gbhem.org
Web: www.gbhem.org/loansandscholarships

Summary To provide fellowships and fellowship/loans to Native American seminary students preparing for ministry within the United Methodist Church.

Eligibility This program is open to Native Americans accepted and/or enrolled as a full-time student at a school of theology approved by the University Senate of the United Methodist Church. At least 1 parent must be Native American, American Indian, or Alaska Native Applicants must have been active, full members of a United Methodist Church for at least 3 years prior to applying They must be able to demonstrate financial need, a GPA of 2.5 or higher, and involvement in their Native American community.

Financial data The average stipend is $12,000. Half of the funds are provided in the form of a grant and half in the form of a loan that is forgiven if the recipient serves at least 2 years in a Native American congregation or ministry/fellowship that is recognized by the United Methodist Church.

Duration 1 year.

Number awarded Varies each year. Recently, 12 of these scholarships were awarded.

Deadline April of each year.

[724]
NATIVE AMERICAN SUPPLEMENTAL GRANTS

Presbyterian Church (USA)
Attn: Office of Financial Aid for Studies
100 Witherspoon Street, Room M-052
Louisville, KY 40202-1396
(502) 569-5224   Toll Free: (888) 728-7228, ext. 5224
Fax: (502) 569-8766   E-mail: finaid@pcusa.org
Web: www.pcusa.org/financialaid/programs/grants.htm

Summary To provide financial assistance to Native American students interested in preparing for church occupations within the Presbyterian Church (USA).

Eligibility This program is open to Native American and Alaska Native students who are enrolled full time at a PCUSA seminary or accredited theological institution approved by their presbytery's Committee on Preparation for Ministry (CPM). Applicants must be working on 1) an M.Div. degree and enrolled as an inquirer or candidate by a PCUSA presbytery, or 2) an M.A.C.E. degree and preparing for a church occupation. They must be PCUSA members, U.S. citizens or permanent residents, able to demonstrate financial need, and recommended by the financial aid officer at their theological institution. Along with their application, they must submit a 1,000-word essay on what they believe God is calling them to do in ministry.

Financial data Stipends range from $500 to $1,500 per year. Funds are intended as supplements to students who have been awarded a Presbyterian Study Grant but still demonstrate remaining financial need.

Duration 1 year; may be renewed up to 2 additional years.

Number awarded Varies each year.

Deadline June of each year.

[725]
NCEA/CATHOLIC DAUGHTERS OF THE AMERICAS SCHOLARSHIPS FOR TEACHERS OF CHILDREN WITH SPECIAL NEEDS

National Catholic Educational Association
Attn: Department of Elementary Schools
1005 North Glebe Road, Suite 525
Arlington, VA 22201-5792
Toll Free: (800) 711-6232   Fax: (703) 243-0025
E-mail: nceaelem@ncea.org
Web: www.ncea.org/finaid/index.asp

Summary To provide tuition reimbursement to Catholic school teachers working on a graduate degree in special education.

Eligibility This program is open to teachers in a Catholic school who are taking graduate courses in special needs education. The courses must be in 1 or more of the exceptionalities specified in the Individuals with Disabilities Education Act (IDEA). Applicants must have school or individual membership in the National Catholic Educational Association (NCEA) and continue to teach in a Catholic school for at least 1 year after completion of graduate studies.

Financial data Up to $1,000 in tuition reimbursement is available for courses taken on the graduate level. This reimbursement does not cover any fees the college may impose on its students.

Duration The fees for eligible courses taken within the previous 12 months may be reimbursed.

Additional information This program is funded by the Catholic Daughters of the Americas (CDA) and administered by the NCEA.

Number awarded 1 or more each year.

Deadline May of each year.

[726]
NEBRASKA CONFERENCE SEMINARY SCHOLARSHIPS

United Methodist Church-Nebraska Conference
Attn: Board of Ordained Ministry
3333 Landmark Circle
Lincoln, NE 68504-4760
(402) 464-5994   Toll Free: (800) 435-6107
Fax: (402) 464-6203   E-mail: info@umcneb.org
Web: www.umcneb.org/pages/detail/111

Summary To provide financial assistance to Methodist seminary students under the care of a Nebraska Conference District Committee on Ministry.

Eligibility This program is open to students enrolled at a seminary approved by the University Senate of the United Methodist Church. Applicants must be certified candidates under the care of a Nebraska Conference District Committee on Ministry.

Financial data The stipend for students at United Methodist seminaries is $200 per credit hour. The stipend for students at University Senate-approved non-United Methodist seminaries is $100 per credit hour.

Duration 1 semester; may be renewed.

Number awarded Varies each year.

Deadline Applications may be submitted at any time.

[727]
NEBRASKA EASTERN STAR TRAINING AWARDS FOR RELIGIOUS LEADERSHIP

Order of the Eastern Star-Grand Chapter of Nebraska
Attn: ESTARL Program
P.O. Box 156
Fremont, NE 68026-0156
(402) 727-8644   Fax: (402) 727-7729
E-mail: nebraskaoes@msn.com
Web: www.neoes.org/estarl/index.htm

Summary To provide financial assistance to residents of Nebraska who are attending a college or seminary in any state to prepare for full-time Christian service.

Eligibility This program is open to residents of Nebraska who are preparing for a career in full-time Christian service. Applicants must be 1) enrolled at an accredited Bible college with a goal of ordination; 2) enrolled at an accredited seminary with a goal of ordination; 3) currently assigned to a parish and enrolled in a "Course of Study" program at an accredited seminary; or 4) current ordained clergy who are pursuing additional training to enhance their ministry or obtain additional degrees. Along with their application, they must submit a 1-page essay outlining their experiences and goals. There is no requirement of a Masonic affiliation, although preference may be given to Eastern Star members. Some consideration may be given to financial need.

Financial data A stipend is awarded (amount not specified).

Duration 1 year; recipients may reapply.

Number awarded 1 or more each year.

Deadline February of each year.

[728]
NELDA C. SEAL ENDOWED SCHOLARSHIP FOR MISSION PASTORS

Louisiana Baptist Convention
Attn: Woman's Missionary Union
P.O. Box 311
Alexandria, LA 71309
(318) 448-3402   Toll Free: (800) 622-6549
E-mail: wmu@lbc.org
Web: www.lbc.org

Summary This provide financial assistance to mission pastors affiliated with the Louisiana Baptist Convention who are interested in working on a master's degree or diploma in Christian ministry at a Southern Baptist seminary.

Eligibility This program is open to pastors of Louisiana Baptist Convention mission churches. Applicants must be interested in attending 1 of the 6 Southern Baptist seminaries, or their approved extension classes, to work on a master's degree or diploma in Christian ministry. They must agree to participate in Southern Baptist mission activities while enrolled at the seminary. Along with their application, they must submit a brief narrative on their conversion and call to ministry and reasons for attending seminary.

Financial data The stipend is $600 per year.

Duration 1 year.

Additional information The eligible seminaries are Southeastern Baptist Theological Seminary (Wake Forest, North Carolina); Southern Baptist Theological Seminary (Louisville, Kentucky); Southwestern Baptist Theological Seminary (Fort Worth, Texas); New Orleans Baptist Theological Seminary (New Orleans, Louisiana); Midwestern Baptist Theological Seminary (Kansas City, Missouri); or Golden Gate Baptist Theological Seminary (Mill Valley, California).

Number awarded 1 or more each year.

Deadline June of each year.

[729]
NEW ENGLAND CONFERENCE GRADUATE DEGREE PROGRAM FUNDS

United Methodist Church-New England Conference
Attn: Ministerial Education Fund
276 Essex Street
P.O. Box 249
Lawrence, MA 01842-0449
(978) 682-7676   Fax: (978) 682-8227
Web: www.neumc.org/forms/detail/859

Summary To provide financial assistance to ministers of United Methodist Churches within the New England Conference who are interested in working on an advanced degree.

Eligibility This program is open to United Methodist ministers within the New England Conference who are full members, probationary members having completed their basic seminary degree, and diaconal ministers. Applicants must be enrolled in a graduate program for a degree beyond the M.Div. that is directly related to their ministry. Financial need is considered in the selection process.

Financial data The stipend depends on the need of the recipient and the availability of funds, to a maximum of $1,000 per year.

Duration 1 year; may be renewed 2 additional years.

Number awarded Varies each year.

Deadline Applications may be submitted at any time, but they must be received at least 12 weeks prior to the beginning of the program.

[730]
NEW ENGLAND CONFERENCE GRADUATE SCHOLARSHIPS

United Methodist Church-New England Conference
Attn: Board of Ordained Ministry
276 Essex Street
P.O. Box 249
Lawrence, MA 01842-0449
(978) 682-7676   Fax: (978) 682-8227
Web: www.neumc.org/forms/detail/863

Summary To provide financial assistance to members and ministers of United Methodist Churches within the New Eng-

land Conference who are interested in preparing for ordained ministry or another form of full-time Christian service.

Eligibility This program is open to 1) members of United Methodist Church (UMC) congregations in the New England Conference, and 2) clergy members of the conference. Applicants must be enrolled in a graduate program in any state in preparation for ordained ministry or some other form of full-time Christian service in the UMC. Financial need is considered in the selection process.

Financial data A stipend is awarded (amount not specified).

Duration 1 year.

Number awarded Varies each year.

Deadline June of each year.

[731]
NEW ENGLAND CONFERENCE MINISTRY SCHOLARSHIPS

United Methodist Church-New England Conference
Attn: Ministerial Education Fund
276 Essex Street
P.O. Box 249
Lawrence, MA 01842-0449
(978) 682-7676   Fax: (978) 682-8227
Web: www.neumc.org/forms/detail/860

Summary To provide financial assistance to members of United Methodist Churches within the New England Conference who are preparing for ordination.

Eligibility This program is open to candidates for ordained ministry certified by a district committee within the New England Conference of the United Methodist Church (UMC). Applicants must be enrolled in an M.Div. or equivalent degree program that is directly related to their ministry. They must be able to demonstrate financial need.

Financial data The maximum stipend is $2,000 per year.

Duration 1 year; may be renewed up to 2 additional years.

Number awarded Varies each year.

Deadline May of each year for fall semester; October of each year for spring semester.

[732]
NEW HAMPSHIRE CHARITABLE FOUNDATION STATEWIDE STUDENT AID PROGRAM

New Hampshire Charitable Foundation
37 Pleasant Street
Concord, NH 03301-4005
(603) 225-6641   Toll Free: (800) 464-6641
Fax: (603) 225-1700   E-mail: info@nhcf.org
Web: www.nhcf.org/page16960.cfm

Summary To provide scholarships or loans for undergraduate or graduate study in any state to Episcopal and other New Hampshire residents.

Eligibility This program is open to New Hampshire residents who are graduating high school seniors planning to enter a 4-year college or university, undergraduate students between 17 and 23 years of age working on a 4-year degree, or graduate students of any age. Applicants must be enrolled on at least a half-time basis at a school in New Hampshire or another state. Selection is based on financial need, academic merit, community service, school activities, and work experience. Priority is given to students with the fewest financial resources.

Financial data Awards range from $500 to $3,500 and average $1,800. Most are made in the form of grants (recently, 82% of all awards) or no-interest or low-interest loans.

Duration 1 year; approximately one-third of the awards are renewable.

Additional information Through this program, students submit a single application for more than 50 different scholarship and loan funds. Many of the funds have additional requirements, including field of study; residency in region, county, city, or town; graduation from designated high schools; and special attributes (e.g., of Belgian descent, employee of designated firms, customer of Granite State Telephone Company, disabled, suffering from a life-threatening or serious chronic illness, of Lithuanian descent, dependent of a New Hampshire police officer, dependent of a New Hampshire Episcopal minister, of Polish descent, former Sea Cadet or Naval Junior ROTC, or employed in the tourism industry). The Citizens' Scholarship Foundation of America reviews all applications; recipients are selected by the New Hampshire Charitable Foundation. A $20 application fee is required.

Number awarded Varies each year; approximately $700,000 is awarded annually.

Deadline April of each year.

[733]
NEW MEXICO MINISTERIAL SCHOLARSHIP ENDOWMENT

United Methodist Church-New Mexico Conference
Attn: Board of Ordained Ministry
11816 Lomas Boulevard, N.E.
Albuquerque, NM 87112
(505) 255-8786, ext. 101   Toll Free: (800) 678-8786
Fax: (505) 265-6184 E-mail: mridgeway@nmconfum.com
Web: www.nmconfum.com

Summary To provide financial assistance to Methodists from New Mexico who are interested in attending seminary in any state to prepare for a pastoral appointment.

Eligibility This program is open to students who are enrolled or planning to enroll at a seminary in any state and who have an affiliation with a congregation of the New Mexico Conference of the United Methodist Church (UMC). Applicants must be preparing for a career in pastoral appointment to local churches in the New Mexico Conference. Along with their application, they must submit brief essays on their current financial situation, how their sense of calling to ministry has changed or grown during the past year, the areas of ministry in which they are currently interested, what they believe to be their greatest spiritual gifts, and how they believe God is calling them to use those gifts in the local church.

Financial data A stipend is awarded (amount not specified).

Duration 1 year.

Number awarded 1 or more each year.

Deadline April of each year.

[734]
NEW MEXICO SINGING CHURCHMEN SCHOLARSHIP

Baptist Convention of New Mexico
Attn: Leadership Development Team
5325 Wyoming Boulevard, N.E.
P.O. Box 94485
Albuquerque, NM 87199-4485
(505) 924-2313   Toll Free: (800) 898-8544
Fax: (505) 924-2349   E-mail: mrobinson@bcnm.com
Web: www.bcnm.com

Summary To provide financial assistance to Southern Baptist students from New Mexico who are attending a college or seminary in any state to prepare for a career in music.

Eligibility This program is open to college and seminary students who are active members of churches affiliated with the Baptist Convention of New Mexico. Applicants must have experienced a call to vocational music ministry. They must be enrolled full time at the sophomore level or higher, have a GPA of 3.0 or higher, and be majoring in music.

Financial data A stipend is awarded (amount not specified).

Duration 1 year; may be renewed.

Number awarded 1 or more each year.

Deadline April of each year.

[735]
NMBF SCHOLARSHIP

New Mexico Baptist Foundation
5325 Wyoming Boulevard, N.E.
P.O. Box 16560
Albuquerque, NM 87191-6560
(505) 332-3777   Toll Free: (877) 841-3777
Fax: (505) 332-2777   E-mail: foundation@nmbf.com
Web: www.bcnm.com

Summary To provide financial assistance to members of Southern Baptist churches in New Mexico who plan to attend college in any state.

Eligibility This program is open to members of Southern Baptist churches in New Mexico who are enrolled at a college, university, or seminary in any state. Applicants must have a GPA of 2.5 or higher and be able to demonstrate financial need.

Financial data A stipend is awarded (amount not specified).

Duration 1 year.

Number awarded 1 or more each year.

Deadline April of each year.

[736]
NORMAN NICKERSON SCHOLARSHIP

New Mexico Baptist Foundation
5325 Wyoming Boulevard, N.E.
P.O. Box 16560
Albuquerque, NM 87191-6560
(505) 332-3777   Toll Free: (877) 841-3777
Fax: (505) 332-2777   E-mail: foundation@nmbf.com
Web: www.bcnm.com

Summary To provide financial assistance to members of Southern Baptist churches in New Mexico who are attending college in any state to prepare for a career in church music.

Eligibility This program is open to college and seminary students who are preparing for a career in church music. Applicants must have a GPA of 2.5 or higher and be able to demonstrate financial need. They must be members of Southern Baptist churches in New Mexico.

Financial data A stipend is awarded (amount not specified).

Duration 1 year.

Number awarded 1 or more each year.

Deadline April of each year.

[737]
NORTH CAROLINA BAPTIST GRANTS FOR OTHER THEOLOGICAL SCHOOLS

Baptist State Convention of North Carolina
Attn: Scholarship Office
205 Convention Drive
P.O. Box 1107
Cary, NC 27512-1107
Toll Free: (800) 395-5102
E-mail: scholarships@ncbaptist.org
Web: www.ncbaptist.org/index.php?id=826

Summary To provide financial assistance to members of churches cooperating with the Baptist State Convention of North Carolina who are interested in attending a seminary not affiliated with the Southern Baptist Convention and not located in North Carolina.

Eligibility This program is open to residents of North Carolina who are interested in enrolling full time at a seminary or divinity school other than those provided by North Carolina Baptist colleges and universities or by the Southern Baptist Convention. Applicants must have been a member for at least 1 year of a church that contributes to and participates in the Baptist State Convention of North Carolina and that has formally endorsed the student as a candidate for a church-related vocation. They must be working on an approved degree (M.Div., master of church music, master of Christian education).

Financial data The stipend is $500 per semester ($1,000 per year).

Duration 1 semester; may be renewed for up to 5 additional semesters.

Number awarded Varies each year.

Deadline Deadline not specified.

[738]
NORTH DAKOTA EASTERN STAR TRAINING AWARDS FOR RELIGIOUS LEADERSHIP

Order of the Eastern Star-Grand Chapter of North Dakota
1405 Third Street North
Fargo, ND 58102
(701) 364-0335   E-mail: ndoes4us@ndoes.org
Web: www.ndoes.org/Estarl.htm

Summary To provide financial assistance to residents of North Dakota who are attending a college or seminary in any state to prepare for a career in Christian service.

Eligibility This program is open to residents of North Dakota who are preparing for a career in Christian service as a minister, missionary, director of church music, director of religious education, youth leader, or other related position. Applicants must be enrolled full time at an accredited Bible college, university, or seminary in any state. Selection is based on character, scholarship, citizenship, and financial need.

Financial data A stipend is awarded (amount not specified). Funds are sent directly to the student's college or seminary.

Duration 1 year; recipients may reapply.

Number awarded 1 or more each year.

Deadline April of each year.

[739]
NORTHERN BAPTIST EDUCATION SOCIETY GRANTS

Northern Baptist Education Society
c/o Roger H. Spinney, Executive Secretary
P.O. Box 395
East Falmouth, MA 02536
(508) 388-7683   E-mail: rspin6477@aol.com

Summary To provide financial assistance to American Baptist students either from New England or enrolled in New England seminaries.

Eligibility This program is open to American Baptist students enrolled in an M.Div. program. Applicants must be attending divinity school in New England and/or belong to an American Baptist church in Maine, Massachusetts, New Hampshire, or Vermont. They must have the endorsement of their school and their local church. Financial need is considered in the selection process.

Financial data Stipends range from $200 to $1,000 per semester.

Duration 1 semester; may be renewed up to 5 additional semesters.

Number awarded Varies each year.

Deadline March or October of each year.

[740]
NORTHWEST BAPTIST FOUNDATION SEMINARY SCHOLARSHIPS

Northwest Baptist Convention
Attn: Northwest Baptist Foundation
3200 N.E. 109th Avenue
Vancouver, WA 98682
(360) 882-2250   Toll Free: (800) 594-2981
Fax: (360) 882-2252
Web: www.nwbaptistfdn.org/students.html

Summary To provide financial assistance to Southern Baptists from the Northwest who are attending seminary in any state.

Eligibility This program is open to members of churches affiliated with the Northwest Baptist Convention who have completed at least 15 credit hours of study at a Southern Baptist seminary. Applicants must have a GPA of 2.5 or higher. Along with their application, they must submit a current transcript, 2 letters of recommendation (including 1 from their pastor), and a brief statement on why they are seeking assistance and how they feel their course of study is preparing them for their life's work. Financial need is also considered in the selection process.

Financial data A stipend is awarded (amount not specified).

Duration 1 year; may be renewed.

Additional information The Northwest Baptist Convention serves Oregon, Washington, and northern Idaho.

Number awarded 1 or more each year.

Deadline January of each year.

[741]
NOVAK AWARD

Acton Institute for the Study of Religion and Liberty
161 Ottawa N.W., Suite 301
Grand Rapids, MI 49503
(616) 454-3080　　　　　　Toll Free: (800) 345-2286
Fax: (616) 454-9454　　E-mail: scholarships@acton.org
Web: www.acton.org/programs/students/novak.php

Summary To recognize and reward postdoctoral scholars and doctoral candidates who have made outstanding contributions to our understanding of the relationship between religion and economic liberty.

Eligibility This award is available to scholars who have received a doctorate from an accredited domestic or international program in theology, religion, economics, philosophy, or business during the current or previous 5 years. Current doctoral candidates in those fields are also eligible. Candidates must be nominated by professors, university faculty members, and other scholars who have been contacted by the sponsor. Nominees must then submit a 500-word essay that describes their intellectual development, future plans, and career goals; a curriculum vitae; a research paper, refereed published article, or other scholarly work; and 2 letters of reference. Applications from those outside the United States and those studying abroad receive equal consideration.

Financial data The award is $10,000.

Duration The award is presented annually.

Additional information Recipients must present their research in a public forum known as the Calihan Lecture. All travel expenses to deliver the lecture are covered.

Number awarded 1 each year.

Deadline Nominations must be submitted by November of each year. Applications from nominees are due in December.

[742]
OHIO BAPTIST EDUCATION SOCIETY SCHOLARSHIPS

American Baptist Churches of Ohio
Attn: Ohio Baptist Education Society
136 Galway Drive North
P.O. Box 288
Granville, OH 43023-0288
(740) 587-0804　　　　　　Fax: (740) 587-0807
E-mail: pastorchris@neo.rr.com
Web: www.abc-ohio.org

Summary To provide funding to upper-division and graduate Baptist students from Ohio who are interested in attending a college or seminary in any state.

Eligibility This program is open to residents of Ohio who have completed at least 2 years of study at an accredited college or university in any state and are interested in continuing their education as an upper-division or seminary student. Applicants must 1) hold active membership in a church affiliated with the American Baptist Churches of Ohio or a church dually-aligned with the American Baptist Churches of Ohio; 2) be in the process of preparing for a professional career in

Christian ministry (such as a local church pastor, church education, youth or young adult ministries, church music, specialized ministry, chaplaincy, ministry in higher education, or missionary service); 3) be committed to working professionally within the framework of the American Baptist Churches USA; and 4) acknowledge a personal commitment to the Gospel of Jesus Christ, an understanding of the Christian faith, and a definite call to professional Christian ministry as a life work. Financial need must be demonstrated.

Financial data Stipends generally range from $1,000 to $1,500 a year.

Duration 1 year.

Additional information The Ohio Baptist Education Society has been supporting Baptist students since 1831. This program includes the Rev. Dr. Ralph and Joyce Lamb Memorial Scholarship (established in 2002) and the Rev. Robert E. and Gladys Ernst Scholarship (established in 2007).

Number awarded Varies; generally, 8 to 17 each year.

Deadline March of each year.

[743]
OHIO BAPTIST FOUNDATION SCHOLARSHIPS

Ohio Baptist Foundation
Attn: Director
9000 Antares Avenue
Columbus, OH 43240
(614) 827-1781　　　　　　Fax: (614) 827-1860
E-mail: JackHelton@scbo.org
Web: www.ohiobaptistfoundation.org

Summary To provide financial assistance for college or seminary in any state to members of Southern Baptist churches in Ohio.

Eligibility This program is open to members of Southern Baptist churches in Ohio who are attending postsecondary educational institutions in any state. Applicants must be studying to become pastors, missionaries, music and children's ministers, doctors, nurses, or lawyers.

Financial data Stipends depend on the terms of the fund providing assistance.

Duration 1 year.

Additional information This program is comprised of 14 funds that provide assistance for specified programs of study. For details on each fund, contact the foundation.

Number awarded Varies each year.

Deadline Deadline not specified.

[744]
OHIO EASTERN STAR TRAINING AWARDS FOR RELIGIOUS LEADERSHIP

Order of the Eastern Star-Grand Chapter of Ohio
c/o Clifford Houk, ESTARL Committee Chair
12 Northwood Drive
Athens, OH 45701
E-mail: chouk@columbus.rr.com
Web: www.ohoes.org/projects.htm

Summary To provide financial assistance to residents of Ohio interested in attending a college or seminary in any state to prepare for a religious career.

Eligibility This program is open to residents of Ohio who have completed at least 2 years of postsecondary education at a college or university in any state. Applicants must be interested in continuing their education at their current school or at a postgraduate institution to prepare for a career in full-time Christian service as a minister, missionary, director of church music, director of youth leadership, or director of religious education. Students working on a doctoral degree are not eligible. Selection is based on scholarship, character, leadership qualities, evidence of self-help, and financial need. Preference is given to application who are already training in the religious field and need to continue their education.

Financial data A stipend is awarded (amount not specified).

Duration 1 year; recipients may reapply.

Number awarded Varies each year.

Deadline Deadline not specified.

[745]
OKLAHOMA CONFERENCE MERIT SCHOLARSHIPS

United Methodist Church-Oklahoma Conference
Attn: Campus Ministry Office
1501 N.W. 24th Street
Oklahoma, OK 73106-3635
(405) 530-2013   Toll Free: (800) 231-4166, ext. 2013
Fax: (405) 525-4164   E-mail: lmachalek@okumc.org
Web: www.okumcministries.org

Summary To provide financial assistance to undergraduate and graduate Methodist students from Oklahoma who plan to attend a Methodist institution in any state.

Eligibility This program is open to undergraduate and graduate students who are members of congregations affiliated with the Oklahoma Conference of the United Methodist Church. Applicants must be enrolled or planning to enroll as a full-time student at a United Methodist college, university, graduate school, or seminary in any state. Along with their application, they must submit a 1-page essay outlining their career goals. Selection is based on academic excellence, participation in church activities, and financial need.

Financial data The stipend is $600.

Duration 1 year.

Number awarded 1 or more each year.

Deadline April of each year.

[746]
OKLAHOMA CONFERENCE MINISTERIAL EDUCATION FUND SCHOLARSHIPS

United Methodist Church-Oklahoma Conference
Attn: Board of Ordained Ministry
1501 N.W. 24th Street
Oklahoma, OK 73106-3635
(405) 530-2000   Toll Free: (800) 231-4166
Fax: (405) 525-4164
Web: www.okumc.org

Summary To provide financial assistance to seminary students from Oklahoma preparing for ministry within the United Methodist Church (UMC).

Eligibility This program is open to certified candidates for ministry who have been members of UMC congregations in Oklahoma for at least 2 years. Applicants must be enrolled at an approved seminary or graduate school of theology and working on a degree that qualifies them for ordination in the UMC. They must be able to demonstrate financial need.

Financial data For full-time students, the stipend is $850 per semester ($1,700 per year) at UMC seminaries or $625 per semester ($1,250 per year) at non-UMC seminaries. For part-time students at all seminaries, the stipend is $50 per semester hour.

Duration 1 semester; may be renewed up to an additional 7 semesters.

Number awarded Varies each year.

Deadline Deadline not specified.

[747]
OPAL DANCEY MEMORIAL FOUNDATION SCHOLARSHIPS FOR THEOLOGICAL STUDENTS

Opal Dancey Memorial Foundation
P.O. Box 1137
Bath, OH 44210
E-mail: applicants@opaldanceygrants.org
Web: www.opaldanceygrants.org

Summary To provide financial assistance to students from states in the Great Lakes region working on an M.Div. degree.

Eligibility This program is open to students working full time on an M.Div. degree at an accredited theological school or seminary in a state in the Great Lakes region (Illinois, Indiana, Michigan, Minnesota, New York, Ohio, Pennsylvania, and Wisconsin). Residents of that region who plan to attend an accredited theological seminary outside of the region are also eligible. Applicants must intend to serve in pulpit ministry; no grants are available for work on a Ph.D., Master of Christian Education, Master of Christian Music, or any other degree. Financial need is considered in the selection process.

Financial data The stipend is $3,000 per year.

Duration 1 year; may be renewed for up to 3 additional years.

Additional information This program was established in 1975.

Number awarded Several each year.

Deadline April of each year.

[748]
OREGON EASTERN STAR TRAINING AWARDS FOR RELIGIOUS LEADERSHIP

Order of the Eastern Star-Grand Chapter of Oregon
c/o Elena Sipp
P.O. Box 102
Sumpter, OR 97877
(541) 894-2447
Web: www.oregonoes.org/scholarships/index.html

Summary To provide financial assistance to residents of Oregon who are attending college in any state to work on an undergraduate or graduate degree that will prepare them for a career in church service.

Eligibility This program is open to residents of Oregon who are attending a school in any state that is accredited by the Accrediting Association of Bible Colleges, American Association of Schools of Religious Education, American Association of Theological School, National Association of Schools of Music, or similar association. Applicants must be working on an undergraduate or graduate degree that will prepare them for a full-time church vocation. They must submit a letter of reference from a denominational leader who can describe their relationship or prospect for full-time church service. Financial need is considered in the selection process.

Financial data A stipend is awarded (amount not specified).

Duration 1 year.

Number awarded 1 or more each year.

Deadline April of each year.

[749]
OREGON-IDAHO CONFERENCE UMC ETHNIC MINORITY LEADERSHIP AWARDS

United Methodist Church-Oregon-Idaho Conference
Attn: Campus Ministries and Higher Education Ministry
 Team
1505 S.W. 18th Avenue
Portland, OR 97201-2524
(503) 226-7031   Toll Free: (800) J-WESLEY
Web: www.umoi.org/pages/detail/45

Summary To provide financial assistance to ethnic minority Methodists from Oregon and Idaho who are interested in attending a college or graduate school in any state.

Eligibility This program is open to members of ethnic minority groups (African American, Native American, Asian, Pacific Islander, or Hispanic) who have belonged to a congregation affiliated with the Oregon-Idaho Conference of the United Methodist Church (UMC) for at least 1 year. Applicants must be enrolled or planning to enroll full time as an undergraduate or graduate student at a 2- or 4-year college or university in any state. Along with their application, they must submit personal statements on 1) their faith development; and 2) where they sense God is calling the church in the present and future. Selection is based primarily on demonstrated leadership excellence and/or the potential for leadership excellence in the UMC and in community projects or activities, but other factors, including financial need, are also considered.

Financial data The stipend is $750.

Duration 1 year.

Number awarded 1 each year.

Deadline April of each year.

[750]
OREGON-IDAHO CONFERENCE UMC MERIT AWARDS

United Methodist Church-Oregon-Idaho Conference
Attn: Campus Ministries and Higher Education Ministry
 Team
1505 S.W. 18th Avenue
Portland, OR 97201-2524
(503) 226-7031   Toll Free: (800) J-WESLEY
Web: www.umoi.org/pages/detail/45

Summary To provide financial assistance to Methodists from Oregon and Idaho who are interested in attending a college or graduate school affiliated with the denomination in any state.

Eligibility This program is open to members of congregations affiliated with the Oregon-Idaho Conference of the United Methodist Church (UMC). Applicants must be enrolled or planning to enroll full time as an undergraduate or graduate student at a UMC college or university in any state. They must

be nominated by their local church; each church may nominate only 1 member. Along with their application, they must submit a personal statement that includes their philosophy of life, religious development, and what influenced them in selecting their career goal. In the selection process, 35% of the weight is placed on demonstrated leadership excellence and/or the potential for leadership excellence in the UMC and in community projects or activities, but other factors, including financial need, are also considered.

Financial data The stipend is $750.

Duration 1 year.

Number awarded 1 each year.

Deadline April of each year.

[751]
OREGON-IDAHO CONFERENCE UMC SEMINARY SCHOLARSHIPS

United Methodist Church-Oregon-Idaho Conference
Attn: Board of Ordained Ministry
1505 S.W. 18th Avenue
Portland, OR 97201-2524
(503) 226-7031   Toll Free: (800) J-WESLEY
Web: www.umoi.org/pages/detail/97

Summary To provide loans-for-service to Methodists from Oregon and Idaho who are interested in attending a seminary in any state to prepare for a career in ministry.

Eligibility This program is open to certified candidates for ministry through the appropriate District Committee on Ordained Ministry of the Oregon-Idaho Conference of the United Methodist Church (UMC). Applicants must be enrolled or planning to enroll at a seminary in any state that has been approved by the UMC University Senate. They may be entering an M.Div. or other equivalent seminary degree program, currently enrolled in such a program, completing requirements for ordination, or completing studies as a deacon in full connection.

Financial data Stipends are $1,500 per year for full-time M.Div. students, $500 per 9 semester units completed for part-time M.Div. students, or $1,000 per year for candidates for deacons. After completion of academic training, recipients must serve under appointment of an annual conference of the UMC for at least 2 years; if that obligation is not fulfilled within 5 years, the scholarship reverts to a loan that must be repaid with interest.

Duration 1 year; may be renewed up to 2 additional years of full-time study or up to a total of $3,000 in support for part-time study.

Number awarded Varies each year.

Deadline April of each year.

[752]
PAUL AND BETTY HONZIK SCHOLARSHIP

Hawai'i Community Foundation
Attn: Scholarship Department
827 Fort Street Mall
Honolulu, HI 96813
(808) 537-6333   Toll Free: (888) 731-3863
Fax: (808) 521-6286
E-mail: scholarships@hcf-hawaii.org
Web: www.hawaiicommunityfoundation.org/scholarships

Summary To provide financial assistance to residents of Hawaii who are members of a Presbyterian church and interested in attending a college or seminary in any state.

Eligibility This program is open to residents of Hawaii who are members of a Presbyterian church. Applicants must be attending or planning to attend a 4-year college or seminary in any state. They must be able to demonstrate academic achievement (GPA of 3.0 or higher), good moral character, and financial need. Along with their application, they must submit a short statement indicating their reasons for attending college, their planned course of study, their career goals, and what community service means to them.

Financial data The amounts of the awards depend on the availability of funds and the need of the recipient. Recently, the average value of all scholarships awarded by the foundation was $2,041.

Duration 1 year.

Additional information This program was established in 2005.

Number awarded Varies each year.

Deadline February of each year.

[753]
PENNSYLVANIA EASTERN STAR TRAINING AWARDS FOR RELIGIOUS LEADERSHIP

Order of the Eastern Star-Grand Chapter of Pennsylvania
Attn: Grand Secretary
P.O. Box 8
Womelsdorf, PA 19567
(717) 361-5203
E-mail: grand secretary@paeasternstar.org
Web: www.paeasternstar.org/edscholarship.htm

Summary To provide financial assistance to members of the Order of the Eastern Star in Pennsylvania and their families who are interested in attending a college or seminary in any state to prepare for a religious career.

Eligibility This program is open to residents of Pennsylvania who are members of Eastern Star or their spouses, children, stepchildren, grandchildren, parents, or siblings. Applicants must have completed at least 1 year of study at an accredited school offering religious training in any state. They must have a cumulative GPA of 2.5 or higher and be able to demonstrate financial need. Preference is given to juniors and seniors in college and students in theological seminaries. Along with their application, they must submit 4 letters of recommendation, including 2 from ministers or church leaders, 1 from the religious body they wish to serve, and 1 from a professor or other academic person.

Financial data The stipend is $1,000 per year.

Duration 1 year; may be renewed 1 additional year.

Number awarded Varies each year.

Deadline February of each year.

[754]
PETER AND ELLI MALTA PALEOLOGOS GRADUATE SCHOLARSHIP

Greek Orthodox Archdiocese of America
Attn: Office of the Chancellor
8 East 79th Street
New York, NY 10075
(212) 774-0513   Fax: (212) 774-0251
E-mail: scholarships@goarch.org
Web: www.goarch.org

Summary To provide financial assistance to graduate students who are of the Eastern Orthodox faith and are working on a non-theological degree.

Eligibility The program is open to beginning and continuing full-time graduate students at accredited colleges and universities in the United States. Applicants must be of the Eastern Orthodox faith (within a jurisdiction of the member churches of the Standing Conference of Canonical Orthodox Bishops in the Americas) and U.S. citizens or permanent residents. They must be able to demonstrate financial need. Along with their application, they must submit a description of how their current studies will allow them to employ their talents and how this scholarship will help them to use those talents to serve the Church and/or the community at large.

Financial data The stipend is $10,000.

Duration 1 year.

Number awarded At least 1 each year.

Deadline April of each year.

[755]
POLISH ROMAN CATHOLIC UNION OF AMERICA EDUCATION FUND SCHOLARSHIPS

Polish Roman Catholic Union of America
Attn: Education Fund Scholarship Program
984 North Milwaukee Avenue
Chicago, IL 60622-4101
(773) 782-2600   Toll Free: (800) 772-8632
Fax: (773) 278-4595   E-mail: info@prcua.org
Web: www.prcua.org

Summary To provide financial assistance to undergraduate and graduate students of Polish heritage.

Eligibility This program is open to students enrolled full time as sophomores, juniors, and seniors in an undergraduate program or full or part time as a graduate or professional school students. Along with their application, they must submit brief statements on 1) the Polonian organization(s) that benefited from their membership and how; 2) the organized or other group(s) the benefited from their membership or service and how; and 3) how this scholarship will help them in working on their degree. Selection is based on academic achievement, Polonia involvement, and community service.

Financial data A stipend is awarded (amount not specified). Funds are paid directly to the institution.

Duration 1 year.

Additional information As funding is available, this program also provides awards from the following: the Stanley W. Marion Fund (for study of any field), the Jean C. Osajda Fund (for study of education), the Adele Szumilus Sularski Fund (for study of any field), and the Ann Kushel Fund (for study of religion).

Number awarded 1 or more each year.

Deadline May of each year.

[756]
POLISH ROMAN CATHOLIC UNION OF AMERICA STUDENT SCHOLARSHIP GRANTS

Polish Roman Catholic Union of America
Attn: President
984 North Milwaukee Avenue
Chicago, IL 60622-4101
(773) 782-2600   Toll Free: (800) 772-8632
Fax: (773) 278-4595   E-mail: info@prcua.org
Web: www.prcua.org/benefits/scholarship.htm

Summary To provide financial assistance for college or graduate school to members of the Polish Roman Catholic Union of America (PRCUA).

Eligibility This program is open to active PRCUA members who have held at least $5,000 in life insurance for at least 5 years, at least $15,000 in life insurance for at least 4 years, or at least $25,000 in life insurance for at least 3 years. Applicants must be enrolled as a full-time sophomore, junior, or senior in an undergraduate program or as a part- or full-time graduate or professional student. They must have a GPA of 2.5 or higher. Along with their application, they must submit a 500-word essay on "How I can use my degree to benefit my Polish heritage." Selection is based on that essay along with statements on 1) their career goals and how they plan to achieve those goals, 2) their educational and other accomplishments and why those accomplishments were important in their life, 3) educational organizations to which they belong, and 4) extracurricular activities. U.S. citizenship or permanent resident status is required.

Financial data A stipend is awarded (amount not specified). Funds are paid directly to the institution.

Duration 1 year; may be renewed up to 2 additional years.

Number awarded Varies each year.

Deadline June of each year.

[757]
PRESBYTERIAN CHURCH CONTINUING EDUCATION GRANT PROGRAM

Presbyterian Church (USA)
Attn: Office of Financial Aid for Studies
100 Witherspoon Street, Room M-052
Louisville, KY 40202-1396
(502) 569-5224   Toll Free: (888) 728-7228, ext. 5224
Fax: (502) 569-8766   E-mail: finaid@pcusa.org
Web: www.pcusa.org

Summary To provide financial assistance to ministers of the Presbyterian Church (USA) who are interested in working on a D.Min. degree.

Eligibility This program is open to PCUSA ministers who have served a congregation of 150 or fewer members for at least 2 years. Applicants must be enrolled in the first 3 years of a D.Min. program at an ATS-accredited institution in the United States.

Financial data Grants range from $500 to $1,500 per year.

Duration 1 year; may be renewed up to 2 additional years.

Number awarded Up to 20 each year.

Deadline November of each year.

[758]
PRESBYTERIAN CHURCH PARENT LOANS

Presbyterian Church (USA)
Attn: Office of Financial Aid for Studies
100 Witherspoon Street, Room M-052
Louisville, KY 40202-1396
(502) 569-5224   Toll Free: (888) 728-7228, ext. 5224
Fax: (502) 569-8766   E-mail: finaid@pcusa.org
Web: www.pcusa.org

Summary To provide educational loans to parents of students who are members of the Presbyterian Church (USA).

Eligibility This program is open to parents and legal guardians of students enrolled in an accredited institution of higher education. Applicants must be members of the PCUSA, U.S. citizens or permanent residents, able to demonstrate financial need, and able to give satisfactory evidence of financial reliability.

Financial data Loans may not exceed the actual cost of attendance, to a maximum of $5,000 per year. Funds are disbursed in 2 equal payments: first before start of fall semester and second at the beginning of spring semester. The maximum total loan is $20,000 per family. The interest rate varies but recently was 7%. Repayment begins 60 days after the second disbursement of funds and must be completed in 10 years.

Duration 1 year; may be renewed.

Number awarded Varies each year.

Deadline July of each year.

[759]
PRESBYTERIAN CHURCH THEOLOGICAL STUDENT LOAN PROGRAM

Presbyterian Church (USA)
Attn: Office of Financial Aid for Studies
100 Witherspoon Street, Room M-052
Louisville, KY 40202-1396
(502) 569-5224   Toll Free: (888) 728-7228, ext. 5224
Fax: (502) 569-8766   E-mail: finaid@pcusa.org
Web: www.pcusa.org

Summary To loan money to members of the Presbyterian Church (USA) who are preparing for the ministry or another professional church occupation.

Eligibility This program is open to students enrolled full time at a PCUSA seminary or accredited theological institution approved by their Committee on Preparation for Ministry. Applicants must be working on 1) an M.Div. degree and enrolled as an inquirer or candidate by a PCUSA presbytery, or 2) an M.A.C.E. degree and preparing for a church occupation. They must be PCUSA members, U.S. citizens or permanent residents, able to demonstrate financial need, and recommended by the financial aid officer at their theological institution.

Financial data Inquirers may apply for up to $3,000 per year (up to a lifetime maximum of $6,000). Candidates may apply for up to $3,000 for the first year and up to $6,000 for the second and third years (up to a lifetime maximum of $15,000). The interest rate is 5.5%. No interest is charged while the student is enrolled full time. Repayment begins 6 months after graduation or discontinuation of studies.

Duration 1 year; may be renewed.

Number awarded Varies each year.

Deadline September of each year.

[760]
PRESBYTERIAN CHURCH UNDERGRADUATE/ GRADUATE LOAN PROGRAM

Presbyterian Church (USA)
Attn: Office of Financial Aid for Studies
100 Witherspoon Street, Room M-052
Louisville, KY 40202-1396
(502) 569-5224 Toll Free: (888) 728-7228, ext. 5224
Fax: (502) 569-8766 E-mail: finaid@pcusa.org
Web: www.pcusa.org

Summary To provide financial assistance in the form of loans to undergraduate and graduate students who are members of the Presbyterian Church (USA).

Eligibility This program is open to members of the PCUSA who are enrolled full time at an accredited institution. Applicants must be U.S. citizens or permanent residents making satisfactory progress toward an undergraduate or graduate degree. Both the student and a cosigner must give satisfactory evidence of financial reliability and demonstrate financial need.

Financial data Undergraduates may apply for up to $1,500 in the first year, $2,000 in the second year, $2,500 in the third year, or $3,000 in the fourth year. Graduate students may apply for up to $6,000, divided evenly between the number of academic years remaining. The maximum lifetime loans are $9,000 for undergraduates or $6,000 for graduate students. The interest rate varies but recently was 5.5%. No interest accrues while the student remains in school. Repayment begins 6 months after graduation or discontinuation of studies and must be completed in 10 years.

Duration 1 year; may be renewed by undergraduates for up to 4 years and by graduate students until completion of a degree.

Number awarded Varies each year.

Deadline July of each year.

[761]
PRESBYTERIAN STUDY GRANTS

Presbyterian Church (USA)
Attn: Office of Financial Aid for Studies
100 Witherspoon Street, Room M-052
Louisville, KY 40202-1396
(502) 569-5224 Toll Free: (888) 728-7228, ext. 5224
Fax: (502) 569-8766 E-mail: finaid@pcusa.org
Web: www.pcusa.org/financialaid/programs/grant.htm

Summary To provide financial assistance to graduate students who are members of the Presbyterian Church (USA) and preparing for professional church occupations.

Eligibility This program is open to students enrolled full time at a PCUSA seminary or accredited theological institution approved by their Committee on Preparation for Ministry. Applicants must be working on 1) an M.Div. degree and enrolled as an inquirer or candidate by a PCUSA presbytery, or 2) an M.A.C.E. degree and preparing for a church occupation. They must be PCUSA members, U.S. citizens or permanent residents, able to demonstrate financial need, and recommended by the financial aid officer at their theological institution. Along with their application, they must submit a

1,000-word essay on what they believe God is calling them to do in ministry.

Financial data Stipends range from $1,000 to $4,000 per year.

Duration 1 year; may be renewed up to 2 additional years.

Number awarded Varies each year.

Deadline June of each year.

[762]
PRISCILLA R. MORTON SCHOLARSHIPS

United Methodist Higher Education Foundation
Attn: Scholarships Administrator
1001 19th Avenue South
P.O. Box 340005
Nashville, TN 37203-0005
(615) 340-7385 Toll Free: (800) 811-8110
Fax: (615) 340-7330
E-mail: umhefscholarships@gbhem.org
Web: www.umhef.org/receive.php?id=endowed_funds

Summary To provide financial assistance to members of the United Methodist Church who are interested in working on an undergraduate, graduate, or professional degree.

Eligibility This program is open to undergraduate, graduate, and professional students who have been active, full members of a United Methodist Church for at least 1 year prior to applying. Applicants must have a GPA of 3.5 or higher and be able to demonstrate financial need. Along with their application, they must submit a 200-word essay on their involvement and/or leadership responsibilities in their church, school, and community within the last 3 years. U.S. citizenship or permanent resident status is required. Preference is given to students enrolled or planning to enroll full time at a United Methodist-related college, university, seminary, or theological school.

Financial data The stipend is at least $1,000 per year.

Duration 1 year; recipients may reapply.

Number awarded Varies each year. Recently, 21 of these scholarships were awarded.

Deadline May of each year.

[763]
RACE RELATIONS MULTIRACIAL STUDENT SCHOLARSHIP

Christian Reformed Church
Attn: Office of Race Relations
2850 Kalamazoo Avenue, S.E.
Grand Rapids, MI 49560-0200
(616) 241-1691 Toll Free: (877) 279-9994
Fax: (616) 224-0803 E-mail: crcna@crcna.org
Web: www.crcna.org/pages/racerelations_scholar.cfm

Summary To provide financial assistance to undergraduate and graduate minority students interested in attending colleges related to the Christian Reformed Church in North America (CRCNA).

Eligibility Students of color in the United States and Canada are eligible to apply. Normally, applicants are expected to be members of CRCNA congregations who plan to pursue their educational goals at Calvin Theological Seminary or any of the colleges affiliated with the CRCNA. Students who have no prior history with the CRCNA must attend a CRCNA-related college or seminary for a full academic year before they are eligible to apply for this program. Students entering their sophomore year must have earned a GPA of 2.0 or higher as freshmen; students entering their junior year must have earned a GPA of 2.3 or higher as sophomores; students entering their senior year must have earned a GPA of 2.6 or higher as juniors.

Financial data First-year students receive $500 per semester. Other levels of students may receive up to $2,000 per academic year.

Duration 1 year.

Additional information This program was first established in 1971 and revised in 1991. Recipients are expected to train to engage actively in the ministry of racial reconciliation in church and in society. They must be able to work in the United States or Canada upon graduating and must consider working for 1 of the agencies of the CRCNA.

Number awarded Varies each year; recently, 31 students received a total of $21,000 in support.

Deadline March of each year.

[764]
RACIAL ETHNIC PASTORAL LEADERSHIP SCHOLARSHIP PROGRAM

Synod of Southern California and Hawaii
Attn: Racial Ethnic Pastoral Leadership Work Group
3325 Wilshire Boulevard, Suite 850
Los Angeles, CA 90010-1761
(213) 483-3840, ext. 222   Fax: (213) 483-4275
E-mail: LeonFanniel@synod.org
Web: www.synod.org/repl/index.html

Summary To provide financial assistance to members of racial minority groups in the Presbyterian Church (USA) Synod of Southern California and Hawaii who are preparing for a career as a pastor or other church vocation.

Eligibility Applicants must be under care of their church's Session and enrolled with a Presbytery within the Synod of Southern California and Hawaii. They must be members of racial ethnic groups interested in becoming a Presbyterian pastor or other church worker (e.g., commissioned lay pastor, certified Christian educator) and serving in a racial ethnic ministry within the PCUSA. Racial ethnic persons who already have an M.Div. degree, are from another denomination in correspondence with the PCUSA, and are seeking to meet PCUSA requirements for ordination or transfer may also be eligible if they plan to serve in a racial ethnic congregation or an approved specialized ministry. Applicants must submit documentation of financial need, recommendations from the appropriate presbytery committee or session, a current transcript, and essays on their goals and objectives.

Financial data The stipend is $2,000 per year.

Duration 1 year; may be renewed.

Additional information These scholarships were first awarded in 1984.

Number awarded Varies each year.

Deadline April of each year.

[765]
RACIAL ETHNIC SUPPLEMENTAL GRANTS

Presbyterian Church (USA)
Attn: Office of Financial Aid for Studies
100 Witherspoon Street, Room M-052
Louisville, KY 40202-1396
(502) 569-5224   Toll Free: (888) 728-7228, ext. 5224
Fax: (502) 569-8766   E-mail: finaid@pcusa.org
Web: www.pcusa.org/financialaid/programs/grant.htm

Summary To provide financial assistance to minority graduate students who are Presbyterian Church (USA) members interested in preparing for church occupations.

Eligibility This program is open to racial/ethnic graduate students (Asian American, African American, Hispanic American, Native American, or Alaska Native) who are enrolled full time at a PCUSA seminary or accredited theological institution approved by their Committee on Preparation for Ministry. Applicants must be working on 1) an M.Div. degree and enrolled as an inquirer or candidate by a PCUSA presbytery, or 2) an M.A.C.E. degree and preparing for a church occupation. They must be PCUSA members, U.S. citizens or permanent residents, able to demonstrate financial need, and recommended by the financial aid officer at their theological institution. Along with their application, they must submit a 1,000-word essay on what they believe God is calling them to do in ministry.

Financial data Stipends range from $500 to $1,000 per year. Funds are intended as supplements to students who have been awarded a Presbyterian Study Grant but still demonstrate remaining financial need.

Duration 1 year; may be renewed up to 2 additional years.

Number awarded Varies each year.

Deadline June of each year.

[766]
RECRUITMENT, TRAINING AND DEVELOPMENT GRANTS

Episcopal Church Center
Attn: Office of Black Ministries
815 Second Avenue, Eighth Floor
New York, NY 10017-4594
(212) 922-5343   Toll Free: (800) 334-7626
Fax: (212) 867-7652   E-mail: aifill@episcopalchurch.org
Web: www.episcopalchurch.org

Summary To provide financial assistance and work experience to African Americans interested in theological education within the Episcopal Church in the United States of America (ECUSA).

Eligibility Applicants must be African Americans who are postulants and candidates for holy orders, canonically resident in 1 of the 9 provinces of the ECUSA, and attending 1 of the Episcopal Church's accredited seminaries. Selection is based on participation in the Organization of Black Seminarians Conference (OBES), academic achievement, involvement in the Retention, Training and Deployment (RT&D) programs, and service to the Black community. Financial need is also considered.

Financial data The maximum scholarship stipend is $3,000.

Duration Seminarians may apply a maximum of 3 times: in their junior, middler, and senior years.

Additional information These scholarships are offered as part of the RT&D program, which involves 3 components: 1) recruitment, which helps to identify Black Episcopalians as aspirants for Holy Orders and advise them of the availability of these scholarships; 2) training, which is comprised of the OBES, a mentoring program, and the Black Seminarian Summer Internship; and 3) deployment, which assists the newly ordained persons in fulfilling their call to employ ministry.

Number awarded Varies each year. Recently, 17 of these scholarships were awarded.

Deadline March of each year for fall term; September of each year for spring term.

[767]
REV. BEVERLY E. BOND MEMORIAL SCHOLARSHIP

Jefferson United Methodist Church
Attn: Bond Memorial Scholarship
10328 Jefferson Highway
Baton Rouge, LA 70809
(225) 293-4440   Fax: (225) 293-6821
E-mail: staff@jeffersononline.org
Web: www.jeffersononline.org

Summary To provide financial assistance to Methodists in Louisiana who are preparing for a career as a minister, Christian educator, missionary, or other Christian service professional.

Eligibility This program is open to members of United Methodist Churches in Louisiana who are enrolled or planning to enroll at an accredited college or university supported by the United Methodist Church. Applicants must be planning or currently studying to become a minister, Christian educator, missionary, or other Christian service professional.

Financial data A stipend is awarded (amount not specified).

Duration 1 year.

Number awarded Varies each year.

Deadline May of each year.

[768]
REV. MARTHA SINGLETARY SCHOLARSHIP FUND

United Methodist Church-New Mexico Conference
Attn: Board of Ordained Ministry
11816 Lomas Boulevard, N.E.
Albuquerque, NM 87112
(505) 255-8786, ext. 101   Toll Free: (800) 678-8786
Fax: (505) 265-6184 E-mail: mridgeway@nmconfum.com
Web: www.nmconfum.com

Summary To provide financial assistance to female Methodists from New Mexico who are interested in attending seminary in any state to prepare for a career in ordained ministry.

Eligibility This program is open to women who are enrolled or planning to enroll at a seminary in any state and who have an affiliation with a congregation of the New Mexico Conference of the United Methodist Church (UMC). Applicants must be preparing for a career in ordained ministry to local churches in the New Mexico Conference. Along with their application, they must submit brief essays on their current financial situation, how their sense of calling to ministry has changed or grown during the past year, the areas of ministry in which they are currently interested, what they believe to be their greatest spiritual gifts, and how they believe God is calling them to use those gifts in the local church.

Financial data A stipend is awarded (amount not specified).

Duration 1 year.

Number awarded 1 or more each year.

Deadline April of each year.

[769]
REVEREND CHARLES W. TADLOCK SCHOLARSHIP

United Methodist Church
Attn: General Board of Higher Education and Ministry
Office of Loans and Scholarships
1001 19th Avenue South
P.O. Box 340007
Nashville, TN 37203-0007
(615) 340-7344   Fax: (615) 340-7367
E-mail: umscholar@gbhem.org
Web: www.gbhem.org/loansandscholarships

Summary To provide financial assistance to United Methodist seminary students preparing for parish ministry as an ordained elder.

Eligibility This program is open to students who have completed the first year of study for an M.Div. degree at a theological seminary approved by the University Senate of the United Methodist Church with a GPA of 2.85 or higher. Applicants must have been active, full members of the United Methodist Church for at least 1 year prior to applying. They must be a certified candidate for ministry as an ordained elder by an annual conference of the United Methodist Church. Preference is given to candidates from the Missouri East and Missouri West Conferences attending United Methodist seminaries. U.S. citizenship or permanent resident status and financial need are required.

Financial data The stipend ranges up to $3,000.

Duration 1 year.

Number awarded 1 or more each year.

Deadline May of each year.

[770]
RHODA D. HOOD MEMORIAL SCHOLARSHIP

Northwest Baptist Convention
Attn: Woman's Missionary Union
3200 N.E. 109th Avenue
Vancouver, WA 98682
(360) 882-2100   Fax: (360) 882-2295
Web: www.nwbaptist.org

Summary To provide financial assistance to women from the Northwest who are attending a college or seminary in any state to prepare for a career in vocational ministry, preferably with a Southern Baptist Convention church.

Eligibility This program is open to women who have been active members of a church affiliated with the Northwest Baptist Convention and a member of the Woman's Missionary Union within their church. Special consideration is given to children of ministers from the Northwest. Applicants must be attending or planning to attend an accredited college, university, or Southern Baptist seminary in any state with the intention of serving in a vocational ministry position through a church or denomination; priority is given to applicants going into a mission vocation affiliated with the Southern Baptist Convention. Along with their application, they must submit 1) a written account of their conversion experience and their call to vocational ministry; and 2) a written endorsement from their church.

Financial data A stipend is awarded (amount not specified).

Duration 1 year; may be renewed if the recipient maintains a GPA of 2.5 or higher.

Additional information The Northwest Baptist Convention serves Oregon, Washington, and northern Idaho.

Number awarded 1 or more each year.

Deadline May of each year for fall term; October of each year for spring term.

[771]
RHODE ISLAND EASTERN STAR TRAINING AWARDS FOR RELIGIOUS LEADERSHIP

Order of the Eastern Star-Grand Chapter of Rhode Island
c/o Kathryn Newman, Education and ESTARL Committee
19 Preston Drive
Warwick, RI 02886
(401) 921-0317   E-mail: knewman58@cox.net
Web: www.oesri.org/scholarships.html

Summary To provide financial assistance to residents of Rhode Island who are attending college or graduate school in any state to work on a degree related to religious service.

Eligibility This program is open to residents of Rhode Island who are preparing for a career in religious service as a minister, priest, church leader, director of church music, director of religious education, counselor of youth leadership, or other related fields. Applicants must be enrolled at a college or theological school in any state and working on an undergraduate or graduate degree. They must have a GPA of 2.25 or higher and be able to demonstrate financial need. Along with their application, they must submit an essay of 400 to 500 words on the most important issues their field is facing today.

Financial data A stipend is awarded (amount not specified).

Duration 1 year.

Number awarded Varies each year.

Deadline June of each year.

[772]
RICHARD AND HELEN BROWN COREM SCHOLARSHIPS

United Church of Christ
Parish Life and Leadership Ministry Team
Attn: COREM Administrator
700 Prospect Avenue East
Cleveland, OH 44115-1100
(216) 736-2113   Toll Free: (866) 822-8224, ext. 2113
Fax: (216) 736-3783
Web: www.ucc.org/seminarians/ucc-scholarships-for.html

Summary To provide financial assistance to minority seminary students who are interested in becoming a pastor in the United Church of Christ (UCC).

Eligibility This program is open to students at accredited seminaries who have been members of a UCC congregation

for at least 1 year. Applicants must work through 1 of the member bodies of the Council for Racial and Ethnic Ministries (COREM): United Black Christians (UBC), Ministers for Racial, Social and Economic Justice (MRSEJ), Council for Hispanic Ministries (CHM), Pacific Islander and Asian American Ministries (PAAM), or Council for American Indian Ministries (CAIM). They must 1) have a GPA of 3.0 or higher, 2) be enrolled in a course of study leading to ordained ministry, 3) be in care of an association or conference at the time of application, and 4) demonstrate leadership ability through participation in their local church, association, conference, or academic environment.

Financial data Stipends are approximately $10,000 per year.

Duration 1 year.

Number awarded Varies each year. Recently, 4 scholarships were awarded by UBC, 3 by MRSEJ, and 2 by CHM.

Deadline Deadline not specified.

[773]
RICHARD FURMAN SCHOLARSHIPS

South Carolina Baptist Convention
Attn: Collegiate Ministry Group
190 Stoneridge Drive
Columbia, SC 29210-8254
(803) 765-0030, ext. 4400
Toll Free: (800) 723-7242, ext. 4400 (within SC)
Fax: (803) 799-1044   E-mail: CRVS@scbaptist.org
Web: www.scbcm.org/scholarships

Summary To provide financial assistance to South Carolina Baptists who are attending a Southern Baptist seminary.

Eligibility This program is open to residents of South Carolina who are members of a Southern Baptist church and approved by their home church. Applicants must be full-time students at 1 of the following Southern Baptist seminaries: Southeastern Baptist Theological Seminary (Wake Forest, North Carolina); Southern Baptist Theological Seminary (Louisville, Kentucky); Southwestern Baptist Theological Seminary (Fort Worth, Texas); New Orleans Baptist Theological Seminary (New Orleans, Louisiana); Midwestern Baptist Theological Seminary (Kansas City, Missouri); or Golden Gate Baptist Theological Seminary (Mill Valley, California). They must be preparing to serve as members of the ministerial staff of churches cooperating with the Southern Baptist Convention or to serve on the boards, agencies, or institutions of state Baptist Conventions or of the Southern Baptist Convention.

Financial data The stipend depends on the need of the recipient. Funds are sent directly to the school to be applied to tuition and academic fees.

Duration 1 year; recipients may reapply if they maintain full-time enrollment and a GPA of 2.0 or higher.

Number awarded 1 or more each year.

Deadline March of each year.

[774]
RISDEN P. REECE SCHOLARSHIP

Center for Scholarship Administration, Inc.
Attn: Wells Fargo Accounts
4320 Wade Hampton Boulevard, Suite G
Taylors, SC 29687
Toll Free: (866) 608-0001   E-mail: juliecsa@bellsouth.net
Web: www.csascholars.org/ereece/index.php

Summary   To provide financial assistance to students enrolled at a divinity school.

Eligibility   This program is open to students currently enrolled full time at an accredited divinity school in any state. Applicants must be able to demonstrate academic achievement, traits of "high personal character and leadership," and financial need. Selection is based on academic ability, educational goals, career ambitions, and financial need. An interview is also required.

Financial data   A stipend is awarded (amount not specified).

Duration   1 year; may be renewed up to 4 additional years or until completion of a divinity degree, whichever comes first.

Number awarded   Several each year.

Deadline   February of each year.

[775]
RISH FAMILY SCHOLARSHIP TRUST

Alabama-West Florida United Methodist Foundation, Inc.
170 Belmont Drive
P.O. Box 8066
Dothan, AL 36304
(334) 793-6820   Fax: (334) 794-6480
E-mail: foundation@alwfumf.org
Web: www.alwfumf.org

Summary   To provide financial assistance to ministerial students from the Alabama-West Florida Conference of the United Methodist Church.

Eligibility   This program is open to members of United Methodist Churches within the Alabama-West Florida Conference. Applicants must be studying to become an ordained United Methodist minister and be planning to return for service within the bounds of the Alabama-West Florida Conference.

Financial data   The amount of the stipend varies each year.

Duration   1 year.

Number awarded   1 or more each year.

Deadline   June of each year.

[776]
ROBERT WALKER SCHOLARSHIPS IN CHRISTIAN JOURNALISM

Christian Life Missions
600 Rinehard Road
P.O. Box 952248
Lake Mary, FL 32795
(407) 333-0600   E-mail: Amy.condiff@strang.com
Web: www.christianlifemissions.com

Summary   To provide financial assistance to undergraduate and graduate students interested in preparing for a career in Christian journalism.

Eligibility   This program is open to undergraduate and graduate journalism students who have a GPA of 3.5 or higher. Applicants must submit a letter explaining their interest and commitment to Christian journalism, a current resume, an official transcript, and 5 published works.

Financial data   The stipend is $2,000 per year.

Duration   1 year; recipients may reapply.

Number awarded   Up to 5 each year.

Deadline   April of each year.

[777]
ROSA AND ALTO V. LEE SCHOLARSHIP FUND

Alabama-West Florida United Methodist Foundation, Inc.
170 Belmont Drive
P.O. Box 8066
Dothan, AL 36304
(334) 793-6820   Fax: (334) 794-6480
E-mail: foundation@alwfumf.org
Web: www.alwfumf.org

Summary   To provide financial assistance to ministerial students from the Alabama-West Florida Conference of the United Methodist Church.

Eligibility   This program is open to members of United Methodist Churches within the Alabama-West Florida Conference. Applicants must be attending an approved seminary and demonstrate a clear intent to return to the conference in service as ordained United Methodist clergy. Financial need is considered in the selection process.

Financial data   The stipend depends on the need of the recipient and the number of applicants.

Duration   1 year.

Number awarded   1 or more each year.

Deadline   June of each year.

[778]
ROSALIE BENTZINGER SCHOLARSHIP

United Methodist Church
Attn: General Board of Higher Education and Ministry
Office of Loans and Scholarships
1001 19th Avenue South
P.O. Box 340007
Nashville, TN 37203-0007
(615) 340-7344   Fax: (615) 340-7367
E-mail: umscholar@gbhem.org
Web: www.gbhem.org/loansandscholarships

Summary   To provide financial assistance to United Methodist students working on a doctoral degree in Christian education.

Eligibility   This program is open to full-time students working on a Ph.D. degree in Christian education at a graduate theological seminary approved by the University Senate of the United Methodist Church; preference is given to students at United Methodist institutions. Applicants must have been active, full members of a United Methodist Church for at least 3 years prior to applying and have standing as a deacon in full connection, diaconal minister, or deaconess. They must have a GPA of "B+" or higher and be able to document financial need.

Financial data   The stipend is $5,000.

Duration   1 year.

Number awarded 1 each year.

Deadline January of each year.

[779]
ROSE WIMBERLY SPENCER MEMORIAL TRUST

Alabama-West Florida United Methodist Foundation, Inc.
170 Belmont Drive
P.O. Box 8066
Dothan, AL 36304
(334) 793-6820   Fax: (334) 794-6480
E-mail: foundation@alwfumf.org
Web: www.alwfumf.org

Summary To provide financial assistance to ministerial students from the Alabama-West Florida Conference of the United Methodist Church.

Eligibility This program is open to members of United Methodist Churches within the Alabama-West Florida Conference. Applicants must be attending an approved seminary and demonstrate a clear intent to become an ordained United Methodist minister and return for service within the bounds of the conference.

Financial data A stipend is awarded (amount not specified).

Duration 1 year.

Number awarded 1 or more each year.

Deadline June of each year.

[780]
ROWLEY/MINISTERIAL EDUCATION SCHOLARSHIP

Christian Church (Disciples of Christ)
Attn: Disciples Home Missions
130 East Washington Street
P.O. Box 1986
Indianapolis, IN 46206-1986
(317) 713-2652   Toll Free: (888) DHM-2631
Fax: (317) 635-4426   E-mail: mail@dhm.disciples.org
Web: www.discipleshomemissions.org

Summary To provide financial assistance to seminarians interested in preparing for a career in the ministry of the Christian Church (Disciples of Christ).

Eligibility This program is open to seminary students who are members of the Christian Church (Disciples of Christ). Applicants must plan to prepare for the ordained ministry, have at least a "C+" GPA, provide evidence of financial need, be enrolled full time in an accredited school or seminary, provide a transcript of academic work, and be under the care of a regional Commission on the Ministry or in the process of coming under care.

Financial data A stipend is awarded (amount not specified).

Duration 1 year; may be renewed.

Additional information This program began in 1974.

Number awarded Varies each year.

Deadline March of each year.

[781]
RUMPLE MEMORIAL PRESBYTERIAN CHURCH SCHOLARSHIP ENDOWMENT

Watauga Community Foundation
c/o North Carolina Community Foundation
P.O. Box 2851
Hickory, NC 28603
(828) 328-1237   Toll Free: (888) 375-8117
Fax: (828) 328-3948
E-mail: mmanning@nccommunityfoundation.org
Web: www.nccommunityfoundation.org

Summary To provide financial assistance to residents of North Carolina who are preparing for a career of service to Presbyterian churches.

Eligibility This program is open to residents of North Carolina who are 1) candidates for ministry under supervision and care of their Presbytery; 2) enrolled at a Presbyterian school of Christian education to prepare for a career as a director of Christian education or in the mission field; or 3) accepted by a graduate school or seminary in preparation for a church vocation. Preference is given to members of Rumple Church and to graduates of the Blowing Rock Elementary School District. Financial need is considered in the selection process.

Financial data A stipend is awarded (amount not specified).

Duration 1 year.

Number awarded 1 or more each year.

Deadline Deadline not specified.

[782]
SARA OWEN ETHERIDGE STUDENT SCHOLARSHIP

Baptist Women in Ministry of Georgia
c/o Julie Whidden Long, Scholarship Committee Chair
First Baptist Church of Christ
511 High Street
Macon, GA 31210
(478) 742-6485   E-mail: bwimga@gmail.com
Web: www.bwimga.org/scholarship-info.asp

Summary To provide financial assistance to Baptist women from Georgia who are working on a graduate degree in theology at a seminary in any state.

Eligibility This program is open to women who are, or have been, residents of Georgia. Applicants must be Baptists who have completed at least 30 hours of study for a master's or doctoral degree at a seminary in any state. Along with their application, they must submit a brief narrative that includes a summary of their call to ministry, plans for carrying out their ministry, an autobiography, and a description of any ministry experience that illustrates their gifts for ministry.

Financial data The stipend is $1,500.

Duration 1 year.

Number awarded 1 each year.

Deadline March of each year.

[783]
SCAHILL FAMILY SCHOLARSHIP

Nebraska United Methodist Foundation
100 West Fletcher Avenue, Suite 100
Lincoln, NE 68521-3848
(402) 323-8844   Toll Free: (877) 495-5545
Fax: (402) 323-8840   E-mail: info@numf.org
Web: www.numf.org/special_programs/scholarships.html

Summary   To provide financial assistance to students from Nebraska enrolled at a United Methodist seminary in any state who plan to return to Nebraska to serve as a pastor.

Eligibility   This program is open to members of Nebraska United Methodist Churches who are working on a M.Div. degree at 1 of the 13 United Methodist seminaries throughout the country. Applicants must plan to become a pastor in the Nebraska Annual Conference and have grades acceptable for admission to seminary or continuation of theological studies. Along with their application, they must submit a 1-page description of their calling and career plans for ministry, a current academic transcript, documentation of financial need, and 2 letters of recommendation.

Financial data   The stipend is approximately $1,000 per year.

Duration   1 year; may be renewed.

Number awarded   1 each year.

Deadline   June of each year.

[784]
SCHOLARSHIPS FOR CHRISTIAN BRETHREN COMMENDED WORKERS

Stewards Ministries
1101 Perimeter Drive, Suite 600
Schaumburg, IL 60173
(847) 842-0227   Toll Free: (800) 551-6505
Fax: (847) 517-2705
E-mail: info@stewardsministries.com
Web: www.stewardsministries.com/scholarships.html

Summary   To provide funding for additional study to full-time workers commended from Plymouth Brethren (Christian Brethren) assemblies.

Eligibility   This program is open to full-time workers commended from Plymouth Brethren (Christian Brethren) assemblies in the United States and Canada. Applicants must be planning to 1) attend a seminar or conference, or 2) work on a master's or doctoral degree. Applicants must submit a letter of support (both in spirit and financially) of their educational plans from their commending assembly, information on the length and cost of the program, and an essay on how they feel their ministry will be assisted through the proposed program.

Financial data   Grants depend on the cost of the program and other resources available to the recipient.

Duration   Grants for seminars or conferences may be repeated; grants for graduate student are 1-time only.

Number awarded   Varies each year.

Deadline   Deadline not specified.

[785]
SHEPHERDS FOR THE SAVIOR SCHOLARSHIPS

Shepherds for the Savior
19380 Highway 105 West, Suite 516
Montgomery, TX 77356
(936) 448-6239   Fax: (936) 582-2313

Summary   To provide financial assistance to students attending a Bible school to prepare for a career as a pastor or missionary.

Eligibility   This program is open to students enrolled or accepted for enrollment at a Bible school or similar institution of religious instruction. Applicants must be preparing for a career as a pastor or missionary. Along with their application, they must submit brief statements on 1) their area of study and future plans; 2) their extracurricular activities; 3) when they accepted Jesus Christ as their personal savior; and 4) their faith and their goals for continuation of Christian ministry. Financial need is not considered in the selection process.

Financial data   The stipend is $1,000. Funds are paid directly to the recipient's school.

Duration   1 year.

Number awarded   Up to 50 each year.

Deadline   March or October of each year.

[786]
SHERMAN AND LUCILLE TILNEY EULER SCHOLARSHIP

Synod of the Mid-Atlantic
Attn: Finance and Scholarship Committee
3218 Chamberlayne Avenue
P.O. Box 27026
Richmond, VA 23261-7026
(804) 342-0016   Toll Free: (800) 743-7670
Fax: (804) 355-8535
Web: www.synatlantic.org/scholarships/right.html

Summary   To provide financial assistance to members of churches within the Synod of the Mid-Atlantic of the Presbyterian Church (USA) who are interested in working on a master's degree at a Presbyterian seminary.

Eligibility   This program is open to members of Presbyterian Church (USA) congregations, with first preference to members of the Falls Church (Virginia) Presbyterian Church and second preference to members of other churches within the Synod of the Mid-Atlantic (Delaware, Maryland, North Carolina, and Virginia). Applicants must have been accepted at an officially accredited seminary of the PCUSA in a full-time program for 1) an M.Div. degree, 2) a master's degree in Christian education, or 3) an associated dual degree. Along with their application, they must describe their ministry goals, their involvement in the church and community, and their financial need.

Financial data   The stipend is approximately $3,000 per year.

Duration   1 year; may be renewed.

Number awarded   Varies each year. Recently, 15 of these scholarships were awarded.

Deadline   February of each year.

[787]
SHERMAN SCHOLARSHIP FUND

United Methodist Church-Louisiana Conference
Attn: Coordinator, Conference Board of Ordained Ministry
527 North Boulevard
Baton Rouge, LA 70802-5700
(225) 346-1646, ext. 230
Toll Free: (888) 239-5286, ext. 230
Fax: (225) 383-2652   E-mail: johneddd@bellsouth.net
Web: www.la-umc.org

Summary To provide financial assistance to Methodists from Louisiana who are attending seminary in any state to prepare for a career in ordained ministry.

Eligibility This program is open to members of United Methodist Churches in Louisiana who are enrolled or planning to enroll full time at a seminary in any state. Applicants must be preparing for a career in ordained ministry. Along with their application, they must submit an essay on their vocational goals and plans for ministry.

Financial data The stipend is $1,000.

Duration 1 year.

Additional information This program was established in 1982.

Number awarded 1 each year.

Deadline February of each year.

[788]
SIEBERT LUTHERAN FOUNDATION SEMINARY STUDENT TUITION AID

Siebert Lutheran Foundation, Inc.
300 North Corporate Drive, Suite 200
Brookfield, WI 53045
(262) 754-9160   Fax: (262) 754-9162
E-mail: contactus@siebertfoundation.org
Web: www.siebertfoundation.org

Summary To provide financial assistance to members of Lutheran congregations in Wisconsin who are interested in pursuing ordination in the pastoral ministry.

Eligibility This program is open to members of Lutheran congregations in Wisconsin who are enrolled full time at an accredited seminary in any state. Applicants must have been a member of the congregation before they applied to the seminary. They must be planning for ordination in the Lutheran pastoral ministry. Support is not provided to students serving a vicarship or internship. Selection is based on financial need, not academic achievement.

Financial data A stipend is awarded (amount not specified). Funds are sent directly to the seminaries to be used for tuition, fees, books, supplies, and/or equipment required for courses of instruction.

Duration 1 year.

Number awarded A limited number are awarded each year.

Deadline June of each year.

[789]
SILVER-BEAN SEMINARY GRANTS

American Baptist Churches of Vermont and New Hampshire
Attn: Regional Office
One Oak Ridge Road, Building 3, Suite 4A
West Lebanon, NH 03784
(603) 643-4201   Toll Free: (888) 262-3223
Fax: (603) 643-4264   E-mail: abcvnh@abcvnh.org
Web: www.abcvnh.org/?page_id=34

Summary To provide financial assistance to students at seminaries in any state who are church leaders of American Baptist Churches of Vermont and New Hampshire.

Eligibility This program is open to active professional church leaders from American Baptist Churches of Vermont and New Hampshire. Applicants must be enrolled in an ATS-accredited seminary in any state in an M.Div., D.Min., or ministry-related Ph.D. program.

Financial data The stipend is $500 per year.

Duration 2 years.

Number awarded 1 or more each year.

Deadline February of each year.

[790]
SLOVAK CATHOLIC SOKOL COLLEGE SCHOLARSHIP GRANTS

Slovak Catholic Sokol
Attn: Membership Memorial Scholarship Fund
205 Madison Street
P.O. Box 899
Passaic, NJ 07055-0899
(973) 777-2605   Toll Free: (800) 886-7656
Fax: (973) 779-8245   E-mail: life@slovakcatholicsokol.org
Web: www.slovakcatholicsokol.org

Summary To provide financial assistance to members of the Slovak Catholic Sokol who are attending college or graduate school in any state.

Eligibility This program is open to members of the Slovak Catholic Sokol who have completed at least 1 semester of college and are currently enrolled full time as an undergraduate or graduate student at an accredited college, university, or professional school in any state. Applicants must have been a member for at least 5 years, have at least $3,000 permanent life insurance coverage, and have at least 1 parent who is a member.

Financial data The stipend is $1,000 per year.

Duration 1 year; may be renewed 1 additional year.

Additional information Slovak Catholic Sokol was founded as a fraternal benefit society in 1905. It is licensed to operate in the following states: Connecticut, Illinois, Indiana, Massachusetts, Michigan, New Jersey, New York, Ohio, Pennsylvania, and Wisconsin. This program was established in 2003.

Number awarded 30 each year.

Deadline March of each year.

[791]
SOCIETY FOR THE INCREASE OF THE MINISTRY ALTERNATIVE SCHOLARSHIPS

Society for the Increase of the Ministry
Attn: Executive Director
924 Farmington Avenue, Suite 100
West Hartford, CT 06107
(860) 233-1732   Fax: (860) 233-2644
E-mail: info@simministry.org
Web: www.simministry.org

Summary To provide funding to Episcopalian students who are studying to prepare for a career in the ministry at an institution other than an Episcopalian seminary.

Eligibility This program is open to postulants and candidates of the Episcopal Church in the United States who are not full-time students at an Episcopalian seminary. They must have the approval of their diocese to attend an accredited institution in an alternative educational program of study. Financial need is considered in the selection process.

Financial data Stipends range from $1,500 to $3,500.

Duration 1 year; recipients may reapply.

Number awarded Varies each year. Recently, 4 of these scholarships were awarded.

Deadline February of each year.

[792]
SOCIETY FOR THE INCREASE OF THE MINISTRY TRADITIONAL SCHOLARSHIPS

Society for the Increase of the Ministry
Attn: Executive Director
924 Farmington Avenue, Suite 100
West Hartford, CT 06107
(860) 233-1732   Fax: (860) 233-2644
E-mail: info@simministry.org
Web: www.simministry.org

Summary To provide funding to Episcopalian students who are studying at an Episcopalian seminary to prepare for a career in the ministry.

Eligibility This program is open to postulants and candidates of the Episcopal Church in the United States. Only full-time students can apply. Applicants must be attending 1 of the following 11 Episcopal seminaries: Berkeley Divinity School at Yale University (New Haven, Connecticut), Episcopal Divinity School (Cambridge, Massachusetts), General Theological Seminary (New York, New York), University of the South's School of Theology (Sewanee, Tennessee), Trinity Episcopal School for Ministry, (Ambridge, Pennsylvania), Episcopal Theological Seminary of the Southwest (Austin, Texas), Bexley Hall (Rochester, New York and Columbus, Ohio), Nashotah House (Nashotah, Wisconsin), Virginia Theological Seminary (Alexandria, Virginia), Seabury-Western Theological Seminary (Evanston, Illinois), or the Church Divinity School of the Pacific (Berkeley, California). Selection is based on financial need.

Financial data Stipends range from $1,000 to $3,500.

Duration 1 year; recipients may reapply.

Additional information This program began in 1857. Applications should be submitted to the financial aid officer at 1 of the schools listed above, not to the society.

Number awarded Varies each year. Recently, 84 of these scholarships were awarded.

Deadline February of each year.

[793]
SOUTH CAROLINA CONFERENCE SEMINARY STUDENTS SCHOLARSHIP FUND

South Carolina United Methodist Foundation
P.O. Box 5087
Columbia, SC 29250-5087
(803) 771-9125   Fax: (803) 771-9135
E-mail: scumf@bellsouth.net
Web: www.umcsc.org/scholarships.html

Summary To provide financial assistance to students from South Carolina enrolled at Methodist seminaries in any state.

Eligibility This program is open to certified candidates for ministry in the South Carolina Conference of the United Methodist Church (UMC). Applicants must be enrolled full time in a program of study leading to a first professional degree at a seminary or theological school of the UMC in any state. They must also be applying for assistance through the Ministerial Education Fund. Financial need is considered in the selection process.

Financial data A stipend is awarded (amount not specified).

Duration 1 year.

Additional information This scholarship was established by the South Carolina Conference of the United Methodist Church in 1991.

Number awarded 1 or more each year.

Deadline April of each year.

[794]
SOUTH DAKOTA EASTERN STAR TRAINING AWARDS FOR RELIGIOUS LEADERSHIP

Order of the Eastern Star-Grand Chapter of South Dakota
c/o Carol Helms, ESTARL Committee Chair
P.O. Box 143
Buffalo, SD 57720
E-mail: helmscarol@hotmail.com
Web: www.oeshugs.com/ESTARL.html

Summary To provide financial assistance to residents of South Dakota who are interested in attending a college or seminary in any state to prepare for a career in religious service.

Eligibility This program is open to residents of South Dakota who are attending or planning to attend a college or seminary in any state. Applicants must be interested in preparing for a career in fields of religious service as a minister, missionary, director of church music, director of religious education, or counselor of youth leadership.

Financial data A stipend is awarded (amount not specified).

Duration 1 year; may be renewed.

Number awarded Varies each year.

Deadline Deadline not specified.

[795]
SOUTHERN BAPTIST CONSERVATIVES OF VIRGINIA SCHOLARSHIP FUND

Southern Baptist Conservatives of Virginia
Attn: Seminary Financial Aid
4101 Cox Road, Suite 100
Glen Allen, VA 23060
(804) 270-1848   Toll Free: (888) 234-7716
Fax: (804) 270-1834   E-mail: sbcv@sbcv.org
Web: www.sbcv.org

Summary To provide financial assistance to seminary students from Virginia who are preparing for ministry and can demonstrate beliefs consistent with those of the Southern Baptist Conservatives of Virginia (SBCV).

Eligibility This program is open to residents of Virginia who are enrolled or planning to enroll full time at a seminary owned by the Southern Baptist Convention or a Bible college or seminary that "maintains a conservative, evangelical statement of beliefs consistent with those held by the SBCV." Applicants must be a member of a participating SBCV church that has given SBCV Cooperative Program funds during the calendar year. Along with their application, they must submit statements of their beliefs on who they consider Jesus to be, their salvation experience, how they have served Christ since their conversion, how they were called to serve their Lord and Savior, what they believe about the Bible, whether they agree with the Baptist Faith and Message, and a recent witnessing experience they have had. Selection is based on their statement of belief, commitment to the local church, evidence of the call of God in their life, and financial need.

Financial data A stipend is awarded (amount not specified). Funding is limited to tuition and books.

Duration 1 year. Recipients may reapply by submitting essays on the significant spiritual growth they have experienced in the past year, their present ministry in the church they are now attending, if they believe God is calling them in another direction since they first applied, whether their view of the Bible has changed as a result of their year of study, and the teachers or professors that have inspired them. Renewal requires that they have at least a "C" average.

Number awarded Varies each year.

Deadline March of each year.

[796]
SPANISH BAPTIST CONVENTION OF NEW MEXICO SCHOLARSHIP

Baptist Convention of New Mexico
Attn: Missions Mobilization Team
5325 Wyoming Boulevard, N.E.
P.O. Box 94485
Albuquerque, NM 87199-4485
(505) 924-2315   Toll Free: (800) 898-8544
Fax: (505) 924-2320   E-mail: cpairett@bcnm.com
Web: www.bcnm.com

Summary To provide financial assistance to Hispanic Baptist students from New Mexico interested in attending a college or seminary in any state.

Eligibility This program is open to college and seminary students who are active members of churches affiliated with the Baptist Convention of New Mexico. Applicants must be of Hispanic background and committed to full-time Christian

service. They must be attending a college or seminary in any state.

Financial data A stipend is awarded (amount not specified).

Duration 1 year; may be renewed.

Number awarded 1 or more each year.

Deadline April of each year.

[797]
SPECIAL SEMINARY SCHOLARSHIPS

United Methodist Church
Attn: General Board of Higher Education and Ministry
Office of Loans and Scholarships
1001 19th Avenue South
P.O. Box 340007
Nashville, TN 37203-0007
(615) 340-7344   Fax: (615) 340-7367
E-mail: umscholar@gbhem.org
Web: www.gbhem.org/loansandscholarships

Summary To provide financial assistance to students at United Methodist seminaries who are working on an M.Div. degree.

Eligibility This program is open to students at theological seminaries related to the United Methodist Church who are working on an M.Div. degree. Applicants must have been active, full members of the United Methodist Church for at least 3 years prior to applying. They must be under 30 years of age and preparing for a vocation in ordained ministry.

Financial data A stipend is awarded (amount not specified).

Duration 1 year.

Number awarded Varies each year.

Deadline May of each year.

[798]
ST. ANDREW BY-THE-SEA SCHOLARSHIPS

St. Andrew By-The-Sea United Methodist Church
Attn: Scholarship Committee
20 Pope Avenue
Hilton Head Island, SC 29928
(843) 785-4711   Fax: (843) 785-5716
E-mail: standrewbythesea@gmail.com
Web: www.hhiumc.com/scholarships

Summary To provide financial assistance to Methodists who are attending a college or seminary in any state to prepare for a career in religious service.

Eligibility This program is open to members of United Methodist Church (UMC) congregations in any state who have completed at least their freshman year of college. Applicants must be preparing for a career in ministry, Christian education, or church music. Seminary students are eligible if they intend to enter the ministry of the UMC. Selection is based on academic achievement, personal accomplishments, and financial need. Special consideration is given to graduates of Epworth Children's Home of Columbia, South Carolina. If there are no other qualified applicants, members of St. Andrew By-The-Sea UMC in Hilton Head Island, South Carolina may be considered, regardless of their major or college location.

Financial data Stipends generally range from $500 to $1,500. Funds are disbursed directly to the recipient's college.

Duration 1 year.

Number awarded 1 or more each year.

Deadline April of each year.

[799]
STAR SUPPORTER SCHOLARSHIP/LOAN

Christian Church (Disciples of Christ)
Attn: Disciples Home Missions
130 East Washington Street
P.O. Box 1986
Indianapolis, IN 46206-1986
(317) 713-2652   Toll Free: (888) DHM-2631
Fax: (317) 635-4426   E-mail: mail@dhm.disciples.org
Web: www.discipleshomemissions.org

Summary To provide scholarship/loans to African Americans interested in preparing for a career in the ministry of the Christian Church (Disciples of Christ).

Eligibility This program is open to African American seminary students who are members of the Christian Church (Disciples of Christ). Applicants must plan to prepare for the ordained ministry, have at least a "C+" GPA, provide evidence of financial need, be enrolled full time in an accredited school or seminary, provide a transcript of academic work, and be under the care of a regional Commission on the Ministry or in the process of coming under care.

Financial data Recipients are awarded funds in the form of a scholarship/loan, with 2 methods of repayment: 1) the amount of the scholarship/loan must be repaid in cash (with 6% interest, beginning 3 months after leaving school) if the recipient does not enter the ministry; or 2) the amount of the scholarship/loan is reduced by one-third for each year of full-time professional ministry performed by the recipient, so that 3 years of service cancels the entire amount.

Duration 1 year; may be renewed.

Additional information Recipients must sign a promissory note.

Number awarded Varies each year.

Deadline March of each year.

[800]
STELLA KAHRS MEMORIAL SCHOLARSHIP

Missouri United Methodist Foundation
Attn: Scholarships
111 South Ninth Street, Suite 230
P.O. Box 1076
Columbia, MO 66205-1076
(573) 875-4168   Toll Free: (800) 332-8238
Fax: (573) 875-4595   E-mail: foundation@mumf.org
Web: www.mumf.org/view_page.php?page=41

Summary To provide financial assistance to members of United Methodist Churches in Missouri who are preparing for ministry.

Eligibility This program is open to students working on an M.Div. degree at a seminary approved by the University Senate of the United Methodist Church. Applicants must be recognized by a Missouri District Committee on Ordained Ministry and/or a District Superintendent in the Missouri Conference as either a "certified candidate" or a person with appro-

priate vocational potential and commitment. They must intend to be ordained into the full-time ministry of the United Methodist Church in Missouri. Preference is given to students from the Smithton United Methodist Church and the Heartland South District.

Financial data The stipend is $500.

Duration 1 year.

Number awarded 1 or more each year.

Deadline June of each year.

[801]
STEWARDS MINISTRIES GRADUATE SCHOLARSHIPS

Stewards Ministries
1101 Perimeter Drive, Suite 600
Schaumburg, IL 60173
(847) 842-0227   Toll Free: (800) 551-6505
Fax: (847) 517-2705
E-mail: info@stewardsministries.com
Web: www.stewardsministries.com/scholarships.html

Summary To provide scholarship/loans for graduate study to full-time workers and members commended from Plymouth Brethren (Christian Brethren) assemblies.

Eligibility This program is open to 1) full-time workers commended from Plymouth Brethren (Christian Brethren) assemblies in the United States and Canada; 2) full-time staff members at a local assembly; and 3) students in good standing in an assembly. Applicants must be enrolled full time in a graduate program in theology or a discipline related to their field of ministry. They must intend to serve in an assembly, an assembly-related ministry, or on the mission field for at least 2 years following completion of their studies. The Elders of their assembly are required to provide oversight and mentoring during the academic award year. Along with their application, they must submit 1) a brief description of the involvement in their local assembly, assembly-related ministry, or missionary work over the last 3 years; and 2) a statement describing how their graduate education will assist them in serving in their local assembly, assembly-related ministry, or the mission field. Selection is based on prior academic success, selected academic institution, intended graduate degree program, nature and duration of current assembly ministry, nature of intended postgraduate ministry, and willingness of their assembly to provide academic year mentoring.

Financial data The stipend is $4,000. Funds are distributed to the recipient's assembly to pay for tuition and books. This is a scholarship/loan program; applicants must affirm their intention to serve for at least 2 years following completion of their studies; if that commitment is not completed, they must repay scholarship funds.

Duration 1 year.

Number awarded Varies each year.

Deadline Deadline not specified.

[802]
STOODY-WEST FELLOWSHIP FOR GRADUATE STUDY IN RELIGIOUS JOURNALISM

United Methodist Communications
Attn: Communications Resourcing Team
810 12th Avenue South
P.O. Box 320
Nashville, TN 37202-0320
(615) 742-5481   Toll Free: (888) CRT-4UMC
Fax: (615) 742-5485   E-mail: scholarships@umcom.org
Web: crt.umc.org/interior.asp?ptid=44&mid=10270

Summary To provide financial assistance for graduate school to United Methodists interested in preparing for a career in religious journalism.

Eligibility This program is open to United Methodists currently engaged in religious journalism or planning to enter the field. Religious journalism is interpreted to mean news writing for the secular press, church press, and church institutions. It may include print, broadcast, or electronic journalism. Applicants must be interested in working on a graduate degree at an accredited school or department of journalism. Selection is based on Christian commitment and involvement in the life of the United Methodist Church, academic achievement, journalistic experience and/or evidence of journalistic talent, clarity of purpose in plans and goals for the future, and potential professional ability as a religion communicator.

Financial data The stipend is $6,000; half is paid in September after the recipient enrolls full time in a graduate program at an accredited school or department of journalism in the United States and half at the end of the calendar year.

Duration 1 year.

Additional information This program is named for 2 leaders in public relations and Methodist information in the United Methodist Church from 1940 to 1975, Dr. Ralph Stoody and Dr. Arthur West. Grants are not paid for summer sessions.

Number awarded 1 each year.

Deadline March of each year.

[803]
SYNOD OF LAKES AND PRAIRIES RACIAL ETHNIC SCHOLARSHIPS

Synod of Lakes and Prairies
Attn: Committee on Racial Ethnic Ministry
2115 Cliff Drive
Eagen, MN 55122-3327
(651) 357-1140   Toll Free: (800) 328-1880
Fax: (651) 357-1141 E-mail: mkes@lakesandprairies.org
Web: www.lakesandprairies.org

Summary To provide financial assistance to minority residents of the Presbyterian Church (USA) Synod of Lakes and Prairies who are studying for the ministry at a seminary in any state.

Eligibility This program is open to members of Presbyterian churches who reside within the Synod of Lakes and Prairies (Iowa, Minnesota, Nebraska, North Dakota, South Dakota, and Wisconsin). Applicants must be members of ethnic minority groups studying for the ministry in the Presbyterian Church (USA) or a related ecumenical organization. They must be in good academic standing, making progress toward a degree, and able to demonstrate financial need. Along with their application, they must submit essays of 200

to 500 words each on their vision for the church, and either 1) how their school experience will prepare them to work in the church, or 2) the person who most influenced their commitment to Christ.

Financial data Stipends range from $850 to $3,500.

Duration 1 year.

Number awarded Varies each year. Recently, 9 of these scholarships were awarded.

Deadline September of each year.

[804]
SYNOD OF SOUTH ATLANTIC AFRICAN-AMERICAN RECRUITMENT THEOLOGICAL SCHOLARSHIPS

Synod of South Atlantic
Attn: Staff for Scholarships
118 East Monroe Street, Suite 3
Jacksonville, FL 32202-3214
(904) 356-6070   Fax: (904) 356-0051
E-mail: info@synodofsouthatlantic.org
Web: www.synodofsouthatlantic.org/synodprograms.html

Summary To provide financial assistance to African American students from the Presbyterian Church (USA) Synod of South Atlantic who are attending a Presbyterian seminary in any state.

Eligibility This program is open to African American students working on a theological degree at a PCUSA seminary in any state. Applicants must be inquirers or candidates under the care of a presbytery within the Synod of South Atlantic (Florida, Georgia, and South Carolina). Financial need is considered in the selection process.

Financial data The stipend is $500.

Duration 1 year; may be renewed up to 2 additional years.

Number awarded Varies each year.

Deadline January of each year for fall semester; July of each year for spring semester.

[805]
SYNOD OF SOUTH ATLANTIC THEOLOGICAL EDUCATION SCHOLARSHIPS

Synod of South Atlantic
Attn: Staff for Scholarships
118 East Monroe Street, Suite 3
Jacksonville, FL 32202-3214
(904) 356-6070   Fax: (904) 356-0051
Web: www.synodofsouthatlantic.org/synodprograms.html

Summary To provide financial assistance to students from the Presbyterian Church (USA) Synod of South Atlantic who are attending a Presbyterian seminary in any state.

Eligibility This program is open to students working on a theological degree at a PCUSA seminary in any state. Applicants must be inquirers or candidates under the care of a presbytery within the Synod of South Atlantic (Florida, Georgia, and South Carolina). Financial need is considered in the selection process.

Financial data The stipend is $500.

Duration 1 year; may be renewed up to 2 additional years.

Number awarded Varies each year. Recently, 24 of these scholarships were awarded.

Deadline January of each year for fall semester; July of each year for spring semester.

[806]
SYNOD OF THE COVENANT ETHNIC THEOLOGICAL SCHOLARSHIPS

Synod of the Covenant
Attn: Ministries in Higher Education
1911 Indianwood Circle, Suite B
Maumee, OH 43537-4063
(419) 754-4050
Toll Free: (800) 848-1030 (within MI and OH)
Fax: (419) 754-4051
Web: www.synodofthecovenant.org

Summary To provide financial assistance to ethnic students working on a master's degree at an approved Presbyterian theological institution (with priority given to Presbyterian applicants from Ohio and Michigan).

Eligibility This program is open to ethnic individuals enrolled full time in church vocations programs at approved Presbyterian theological institutions. Priority is given to Presbyterian applicants from the states of Michigan and Ohio. Financial need is considered in the selection process.

Financial data Students may be awarded a maximum of $1,500 on initial application. They may receive up to $2,000 on subsequent applications, with evidence of continuing progress. Funds are made payable to the session for distribution.

Duration Students are eligible to receive scholarships 1 time per year, up to a maximum of 5 years.

Number awarded Varies each year.

Deadline August of each year for fall semester; January of each year for spring semester.

[807]
SYNOD OF THE SUN SEMINARY SCHOLARSHIPS

Synod of the Sun
Attn: Synod of the Sun Presbyterian Foundation
6100 Colwell Boulevard, Suite 200
Irving, TX 75039
Toll Free: (866) 381-7075   E-mail: kathyw@synodsun.org
Web: www.sunfound.org

Summary To provide financial assistance to Presbyterian students from the Synod of the Sun who are enrolled in theological seminaries.

Eligibility This program is open to members of Presbyterian Churches (USA) in the 11 presbyteries that make up the Synod of the Sun (in Arkansas, Louisiana, Oklahoma, and Texas). Applicants must be an inquirer or candidate under the care of the Committee on Preparation for Ministry (CPM) in their presbytery and enrolled full time in an accredited Presbyterian or Presbyterian-related theological school approved by their CPM. They must be planning to serve within the Presbyterian Church (USA) following graduation. Selection is based on merit and financial need.

Financial data A stipend is awarded (amount not specified).

Duration 1 year; may be renewed up to 2 additional years.

Additional information This program began in 1973.

Number awarded Varies each year.

Deadline June of each year.

[808]
T. DENNIE SMITH SCHOLARSHIP FUND

United Methodist Church-South Carolina Conference
Attn: Board of Ordained Ministry
4908 Colonial Drive
Columbia, SC 29203-6070
(803) 786-9486   Toll Free: (888) 678-6272
Fax: (803) 691-0220
Web: www.umcsc.org/scholarships.html

Summary To provide financial assistance to Methodist seminary students from South Carolina.

Eligibility This program is open to certified candidates for ordained ministry in the South Carolina Conference of the United Methodist Church. Applicants must be enrolled full time in a program of study leading to a first professional degree at a seminary or theological school of the United Methodist Church with a grade point average of "C" or higher. They must also be applying for assistance through the Ministerial Education Fund. Financial need is considered in the selection process.

Financial data A stipend is awarded (amount not specified).

Duration 1 year.

Number awarded 1 or more each year.

Deadline April of each year.

[809]
TENNESSEE BAPTIST FOUNDATION COLLEGE AND MEDICAL SCHOLARSHIPS

Tennessee Baptist Foundation
5001 Maryland Way
P.O. Box 728
Brentwood, TN 37024-9728
(615) 371-2029   Toll Free: (800) 552-4644
Fax: (615) 371-2049   E-mail: TBF@tnbaptist.org
Web: www.tbfoundation.org/tbfcat.asp?cat=edu

Summary To provide financial assistance to members of Southern Baptist churches in Tennessee who are attending college in any state to work on an undergraduate degree in any field or a doctoral degree in designated medical fields.

Eligibility This program is open to members of churches cooperating with the Tennessee Baptist Convention who have been residents of Tennessee for at least 1 year prior to applying. Applicants must have completed at least 24 semester hours of collegiate study and have a GPA of 2.3 or higher. They must be working full time on either 1) an undergraduate degree in any field at an accredited college or university in any state, or 2) a doctoral degree at an accredited dental, medical, or pharmacy school in any state. Their household income must be less than $100,000 per year (or $125,000 for families with 2 children in college or $150,000 for families with 3 children in college). Along with their application, they must submit a 2-page summary of their Christian conversion, highlights of their Christian growth, involvement in their church and/or Baptist collegiate ministries, and their goals for life and vocation. Selection is based on academic performance, financial need, and involvement in church and Baptist collegiate ministries.

Financial data A stipend is awarded (amount not specified).

Duration 1 year; may be renewed as long as the recipient maintains a minimum GPA of 2.3 as a sophomore, 2.5 as a junior, or 2.7 as a senior.

Number awarded Varies each year. Recently, the foundation awarded 239 scholarships and grants for all of its programs.

Deadline April of each year.

[810]
TENNESSEE BAPTIST FOUNDATION SEMINARY SCHOLARSHIPS

Tennessee Baptist Foundation
5001 Maryland Way
P.O. Box 728
Brentwood, TN 37024-9728
(615) 371-2029   Toll Free: (800) 552-4644
Fax: (615) 371-2049   E-mail: TBF@tnbaptist.org
Web: www.tbfoundation.org/tbfcat.asp?cat=edu

Summary To provide financial assistance to members of Southern Baptist churches in Tennessee who are interested in attending a Southern Baptist seminary.

Eligibility This program is open to members of churches cooperating with the Tennessee Baptist Convention who have been residents of Tennessee for at least 1 year prior to applying. Applicants must be planning to enroll full time at a Southern Baptist seminary to work on an M. Div. degree. They must have a GPA of 2.5 or higher. Along with their application, they must submit a 2-page summary of their Christian conversion, highlights of their Christian growth, involvement in their church and/or Baptist collegiate ministries, their call to vocational Christian ministry, and their life's goals. Selection is based on academic performance, financial need and/or extenuating family circumstances, and testimony of sense of calling and goals in ministry.

Financial data A stipend is awarded (amount not specified).

Duration 1 year; may be renewed as long as the recipient maintains a GPA of 2.5 or higher.

Number awarded Varies each year. Recently, the foundation awarded 239 scholarships and grants for all of its programs.

Deadline April of each year.

[811]
TENNESSEE WMU SEMINARY SCHOLARSHIP

Tennessee Baptist Convention
Attn: WMU Scholarships
5001 Maryland Way
P.O. Box 728
Brentwood, TN 37024-9728
(615) 373-2255   Toll Free: (800) 558-2090, ext. 2038
Fax: (615) 371-2014   E-mail: jferguson@tnbaptist.org
Web: www.tnbaptist.org/page.asp?page=92

Summary To provide financial assistance to members of Baptist churches in Tennessee who are interested in attending a seminary in any state.

Eligibility This program is open to seminary students who are preparing for a career in missions or Woman's Missionary Union (WMU) activities. Applicants must be able to demon-

strate evidence of Tennessee Baptist ties and a record of participation in Tennessee Baptist missions programs, Baptist collegiate ministries, Tennessee Baptist ministry, and active missions while attending seminary. They must have a GPA of 2.6 or higher and be able to demonstrate financial need.

Financial data A stipend is awarded (amount not specified).

Duration 1 year.

Number awarded 1 or more each year.

Deadline January of each year.

[812]
TEXAS BAPTIST FINANCIAL ASSISTANCE FOR MINISTRY STUDENTS

Baptist General Convention of Texas
Attn: Theological Education
333 North Washington
Dallas, TX 75246-1798
(214) 828-5254   Fax: (214) 828-5284
E-mail: ministertraining@bgct.org
Web: texasbaptists.org

Summary To provide financial assistance to members of Baptist churches in Texas who are preparing for a career in ministry at a Texas Baptist institution.

Eligibility This program is open to members of Baptist churches in Texas who can present a certificate of license or ordination, or letter of certification of call from a Baptist church. Applicants must demonstrate "a life style of commitment to the principles of the Christian life" and certification by their pastor that they are involved in, supportive of, and committed to the local cooperating church. They must be working on, or planning to work on, a certificate, undergraduate, graduate, or postgraduate program approved by the Theological Education Committee of the Baptist General Convention of Texas (BGCT) at a Bible college, university, or seminary in Texas. Applications must be submitted through the school.

Financial data The amount of support is established by the school.

Duration 1 year; may be renewed if the recipients reaffirm their sense of call to church-related ministry and furnish evidence of their continuing involvement and commitment to a local BGCT church.

Additional information The eligible schools include 1 Bible college (Baptist University of the Americas in San Antonio); 8 universities (Baylor University, Dallas Baptist University, East Texas Baptist University, Hardin-Simmons University, Houston Baptist University, Howard Payne University, University of Mary Hardin-Baylor, and Wayland Baptist University); and 2 seminaries (George W. Truett Seminary at Baylor University and Logsdon School of Theology at Hardin-Simmons University).

Number awarded Varies each year.

Deadline Each school establishes its own deadline.

[813]
THE DOCTORS' LESKO MEDICAL MEMORIAL SCHOLARSHIP

Slovak Catholic Sokol
Attn: Membership Memorial Scholarship Fund
205 Madison Street
P.O. Box 899
Passaic, NJ 07055-0899
(973) 777-2605   Toll Free: (800) 886-7656
Fax: (973) 779-8245 E-mail: life@slovakcatholicsokol.org
Web: www.slovakcatholicsokol.org

Summary To provide financial assistance to members of the Slovak Catholic Sokol who are working on a degree in nursing or another medically-related field at a college or graduate school in any state.

Eligibility This program is open to members of the Slovak Catholic Sokol who have completed at least 1 semester of college and are currently enrolled full time as an undergraduate or graduate student at an accredited college, university, or professional school in any state. Applicants must have been a member for at least 5 years, have at least $3,000 permanent life insurance coverage, and have at least 1 parent who is a member and is of Slovak ancestry. They must be working on a degree in nursing or a medical program.

Financial data The stipend is $1,000 per year.

Duration 1 year; may be renewed 1 additional year.

Additional information Slovak Catholic Sokol was founded as a fraternal benefit society in 1905. It is licensed to operate in the following states: Connecticut, Illinois, Indiana, Massachusetts, Michigan, New Jersey, New York, Ohio, Pennsylvania, and Wisconsin. This program was established in 2003.

Number awarded 1 each year.

Deadline March of each year.

[814]
THE REV. FRANCENE EAGLE BIG GOOSE MEMORIAL SCHOLARSHIP

United Methodist Church-Arkansas Conference
Attn: Committee on Native American Ministries
800 Daisy Bates Drive
Little Rock, AR 72202
(501) 324-8045   Toll Free: (877) 646-1816
Fax: (501) 324-8018   E-mail: conference@arumc.org
Web: www.arumc.org

Summary To provide book scholarships to Native American Methodist seminary students from Arkansas.

Eligibility This program is open to seminary students of Native American/Indigenous Heritage, including Native Indians, Native Alaskans, Native Hawaiians, and Pacific Island populations. Applicants must be active members of local congregations affiliated with the Arkansas Conference of the United Methodist Church (UMC). If no applications are received from students within Arkansas, the program is open to students from the Oklahoma Indian Missionary Conference. The seminary they are attending must be approved by the UMC University Senate. Along with their application, they must submit brief essays on their educational goals, how they contribute to the Native American community, and a personal accomplishment of which they are particularly proud that

related to their Native American Heritage. They must be able to demonstrate financial need.

Financial data The stipend is $500 per semester ($1,000 per year). Funds are intended to assist in the purchase of books.

Duration 1 semester; may be renewed.

Number awarded 1 or more each year.

Deadline May of each year for fall semester; December of each year for spring semester.

[815]
THEODORE AND MARY JANE RICH MEMORIAL SCHOLARSHIPS

Slovak Catholic Sokol
Attn: Membership Memorial Scholarship Fund
205 Madison Street
P.O. Box 899
Passaic, NJ 07055-0899
(973) 777-2605   Toll Free: (800) 886-7656
Fax: (973) 779-8245 E-mail: life@slovakcatholicsokol.org
Web: www.slovakcatholicsokol.org

Summary To provide financial assistance to members of the Slovak Catholic Sokol who are working on a medically-related degree at a college or graduate school in any state.

Eligibility This program is open to members of the Slovak Catholic Sokol who have completed at least 1 semester of college and are currently enrolled full time as an undergraduate or graduate student at an accredited college, university, or professional school in any state. Applicants must have been a member for at least 5 years, have at least $3,000 permanent life insurance coverage, and have at least 1 parent who is a member and is of Slovak ancestry. They must be enrolled in a medical program. Males and females compete for scholarships separately.

Financial data The stipend is $2,500 per year.

Duration 1 year; may be renewed 1 additional year.

Additional information Slovak Catholic Sokol was founded as a fraternal benefit society in 1905. It is licensed to operate in the following states: Connecticut, Illinois, Indiana, Massachusetts, Michigan, New Jersey, New York, Ohio, Pennsylvania, and Wisconsin. This program was established in 2003.

Number awarded 2 each year: 1 for a male and 1 for a female.

Deadline March of each year.

[816]
THEOLOGICAL AND PROFESSIONAL SCHOOL MERIT SCHOLARS PROGRAM

United Methodist Higher Education Foundation
Attn: Scholarships Administrator
1001 19th Avenue South
P.O. Box 340005
Nashville, TN 37203-0005
(615) 340-7385   Toll Free: (800) 811-8110
Fax: (615) 340-7330
E-mail: umhefscholarships@gbhem.org
Web: www.umhef.org/receive.php?id=foundation_merit

Summary To provide financial assistance to students preparing for ordination at seminaries affiliated with the United Methodist Church.

Eligibility This program is open to first- through third-year students working on a master's degree at the 14 United Methodist-related theological and professional schools. Applicants must be U.S. citizens or permanent residents and active members of the United Methodist Church for at least 1 year prior to application. They must be planning to enroll full time and have a GPA of 3.0 or higher. Financial need is considered in the selection process.

Financial data The stipend is $3,000.

Duration 1 year; nonrenewable.

Additional information Students may obtain applications from their school.

Number awarded 42 each year: 1 to a member of each class at each school.

Deadline Nominations from schools must be received by August of each year.

[817]
THEOLOGICAL EDUCATION SCHOLARSHIPS FOR ASIAN AND PACIFIC ISLAND AMERICANS

Episcopal Church Center
Attn: Office of Asian American Ministries
815 Second Avenue
New York, NY 10017-4594
(212) 922-5344   Toll Free: (800) 334-7626
Fax: (212) 867-7652
E-mail: wvergara@episcopalchurch.org
Web: www.episcopalchurch.org/asian.htm

Summary To provide financial assistance to Asian and Pacific Island Americans interested in seeking ordination and serving in a ministry involving Asians and Pacific Islanders in the Episcopal Church.

Eligibility This program is open to Asian and Pacific Island students pursuing theological education, including diocesan programs as well as seminary education. Applicants must be a member of an Asian or Pacific Island constituency in the Episcopal Church and have begun the process of seeking ordination through a local Episcopal diocese. Scholarships are presented only for full-time study.

Financial data The maximum scholarship is $4,000 per semester for seminary study or $2,500 per semester for diocesan theological study programs.

Duration 1 semester; renewable.

Additional information This program was established in 1983 with a grant from undesignated funds received through the Venture in Mission Project. Additional funding was received from the Diocese of Southern Virginia.

Number awarded Varies each year.

Deadline April of each year for the fall semester; August of each year for the spring semester.

[818]
T.R. AND HELEN BRAMLETT SCHOLARSHIP

Order of the Eastern Star-Grand Chapter of Texas
Attn: Education Committee
1503 West Division Street
Arlington, TX 76012
(817) 265-6263
Web: www.grandchapteroftexasoes.org/scholar_forms.asp

Summary To provide financial assistance to residents of Texas interested in attending college or graduate school in any state to prepare for a career in religious service.

Eligibility This program is open to residents of Texas who are high school seniors or graduates already enrolled at an accredited college, university, or seminary in any state. Applicants must be interested in working on an undergraduate or graduate degree to prepare for a full-time career as a minister, missionary, director of religious education, Christian youth worker, or church music director. Along with their application, they must submit an essay describing their plans for the future, reasons for applying for the scholarship, and financial status. Undergraduates must be enrolled full time.

Financial data The stipend is $1,000.

Duration 1 year; nonrenewable.

Number awarded 1 or more each year.

Deadline February of each year.

[819]
TRICE MINISTERIAL SCHOLARSHIP

United Methodist Church-Louisiana Conference
Attn: Coordinator, Conference Board of Ordained Ministry
527 North Boulevard
Baton Rouge, LA 70802-5700
(225) 346-1646, ext. 230
Toll Free: (888) 239-5286, ext. 230
Fax: (225) 383-2652   E-mail: johneddd@bellsouth.net
Web: www.la-umc.org

Summary To provide financial assistance to Methodists from Louisiana who are working on a professional or graduate degree at a school in any state to prepare for a career in ordained ministry.

Eligibility This program is open to members of United Methodist Churches in Louisiana who are working full time on a professional or graduate degree at a school in any state. Applicants must be able to demonstrate promise for ordained ministry and articulate vocational goals in service to the church. Along with their application, they must submit an essay on their vocational goals and plans for ministry. Preference is given to students involved in the Wesley Foundation at Louisiana State University.

Financial data The stipend is $800.

Duration 1 year.

Additional information This program was established in 1983.

Number awarded 1 each year.

Deadline February of each year.

[820]
UCC/ADRIENNE M. AND CHARLES SHELBY ROOKS FELLOWSHIP FOR RACIAL AND ETHNIC THEOLOGICAL STUDENTS

United Church of Christ
Attn: Local Church Ministries
700 Prospect Avenue East
Cleveland, OH 44115-1100
(216) 736-3865   Toll Free: (866) 822-8224, ext. 3848
Fax: (216) 736-3783   E-mail: lcm@ucc.org
Web: www.ucc.org/seminarians/ucc-scholarships-for.html

Summary To provide financial assistance to minority students who are either enrolled at an accredited seminary preparing for a career of service in the United Church of Christ (UCC) or working on a doctoral degree in the field of religion.

Eligibility This program is open to members of underrepresented ethnic groups (African American, Hispanic American, Asian American, Native American Indian, or Pacific Islander) who have been a member of a UCC congregation for at least 1 year. Applicants must be either 1) enrolled in an accredited school of theology in the United States or Canada and working on an M.Div. degree with the intent of becoming a pastor or teacher within the UCC, or 2) doctoral (Ph.D., Th.D., or Ed.D.) students within a field related to religious studies. Seminary students must have a GPA in all postsecondary work of 3.0 or higher and must have begun the in-care process; preference is given to students who have demonstrated leadership (through a history of service to the church) and scholarship (through exceptional academic performance). For doctoral students, preference is given to applicants who have demonstrated academic excellence, teaching effectiveness, and commitment to the UCC and who intend to become professors in colleges, seminaries, or graduate schools.

Financial data Grants range from $500 to $5,000 per year.

Duration 1 year; may be renewed.

Number awarded Varies each year. Recently, 11 of these scholarships, including 8 for M.Div. students and 3 for doctoral students, were awarded.

Deadline February of each year.

[821]
ULLERY CHARITABLE TRUST FUND

First Presbyterian Church
Attn: Scholarship Fund Program
709 South Boston Avenue
Tulsa, OK 74119-1629
(918) 584-4701   Fax: (918) 584-5233
E-mail: TBriscoe@firstchurchtulsa.org
Web: www.firstchurchtulsa.org/scholarship.htm

Summary To provide financial assistance to Presbyterian students interested in preparing for a career of Christian work.

Eligibility To be eligible for this program, students must be communicant members of the Presbyterian Church (USA), be preparing for a career in full-time Christian ministry within the denomination, and have at least a 2.0 GPA. Priority is given first to members of the First Presbyterian Church (in Tulsa), second to applicants in the Presbytery of Eastern Oklahoma, third to applicants in the Synod of the Sun (Arkansas, Louisiana, Oklahoma, and Texas), and fourth to members of the Presbyterian Church at large. Selection is based on academic merit, academic or career intent, church or religious involvement, and financial need.

Financial data Stipends range from $500 to $2,000. Funds are paid directly to the recipient's school.

Duration 1 year; recipients may reapply.

Additional information This program was established in 1972.

Number awarded Varies each year. Recently, 12 scholarships were awarded from this fund.

Deadline April of each year.

[822]
UNITED METHODIST GENERAL SCHOLARSHIP PROGRAM

United Methodist Church
Attn: General Board of Higher Education and Ministry
Office of Loans and Scholarships
1001 19th Avenue South
P.O. Box 340007
Nashville, TN 37203-0007
(615) 340-7344   Fax: (615) 340-7367
E-mail: umscholar@gbhem.org
Web: www.gbhem.org/loansandscholarships

Summary To provide financial assistance to undergraduate and graduate students who are members of United Methodist Church congregations.

Eligibility This program includes a number of individual scholarships that were established by private donors through wills and annuities. The basic criteria for eligibility include 1) U.S. citizenship or permanent resident status; 2) active, full membership in a United Methodist Church for at least 1 year prior to applying (some scholarships require 3-years' membership); 3) GPA of 2.5 or higher (some scholarships require 3.0 or higher); 4) demonstrated financial need; and 5) full-time enrollment in an undergraduate or graduate degree program at an accredited educational institution in the United States. Students from the Central Conferences must be enrolled at a United Methodist-related institution. Most graduate scholarships are designated for persons working on a degree in theological studies (M.Div., D.Min., Ph.D.) or higher education administration. Some scholarships stipulate that the applicant meet more than the basic eligibility criteria (e.g., resident of specific conference, majoring in specified field).

Financial data The funding is intended to supplement the students' own resources.

Duration 1 year; renewal policies are set by participating universities.

Number awarded Varies each year.

Deadline May of each year.

[823]
UNITED METHODIST HIGHER EDUCATION FOUNDATION NATIVE ALASKAN FUND

United Methodist Higher Education Foundation
Attn: Scholarships Administrator
1001 19th Avenue South
P.O. Box 340005
Nashville, TN 37203-0005
(615) 340-7385   Toll Free: (800) 811-8110
Fax: (615) 340-7330
E-mail: umhefscholarships@gbhem.org
Web: www.umhef.org/receive.php?id=endowed_funds

Summary To provide financial assistance to Native Alaskan Methodist undergraduate and graduate students at Methodist-related colleges and universities.

Eligibility This program is open to Native Alaskans enrolling as full-time undergraduate or graduate students at United Methodist-related colleges and universities. Preference is given to United Methodist students at Alaska Pacific University. Applicants must have been active, full members of a United Methodist Church for at least 1 year prior to applying. They must have a GPA of 3.0 or higher and be able to demonstrate financial need. Along with their application, they must submit a 200-word essay on their involvement and/or leadership responsibilities in their church, school, and community within the last 3 years. U.S. citizenship or permanent resident status is required.

Financial data The stipend is at least $1,000 per year.

Duration 1 year; nonrenewable.

Number awarded Varies each year. Recently, 2 of these scholarships were awarded.

Deadline May of each year.

[824]
UNITED METHODIST MEN'S 100 CLUB SCHOLARSHIPS

United Methodist Men's 100 Club
c/o Randy Fleming, Executive Director of Fund
  Development
P.O. Box 410
Springfield, NE 68059
(402) 210-4885   Fax: (402) 253-2208
E-mail: auctioneer_32@msn.com
Web: www.umcneb.org/pages/detail/106

Summary To provide financial assistance to Methodists from Nebraska who are attending a seminary in any state.

Eligibility This program is open to residents of Nebraska who are members of a congregation of the United Methodist Church (UMC). Applicants must be attending or planning to attend a seminary in any state to prepare for a career in full-time Christian service. Along with their application, they must submit brief essays on 1) their participation in the life of their church and/or community; 2) what influenced them in selecting their college and their career goals; 3) where they see themselves serving in the UMC after graduation; and 4) their religious development.

Financial data Stipends are $1,500 or $1,000.

Duration 1 year.

Number awarded Varies each year. Recently, 7 of these scholarships were awarded: 1 at $1,500 and 6 at $1,000.

Deadline April of each year.

[825]
UNITED METHODIST STUDENT LOAN PROGRAM

United Methodist Church
Attn: General Board of Higher Education and Ministry
Office of Loans and Scholarships
1001 19th Avenue South
P.O. Box 340007
Nashville, TN 37203-0007
(615) 340-7346   Fax: (615) 340-7367
E-mail: umloans@gbhem.org
Web: www.gbhem.org/loansandscholarships

Summary To loan money for college to United Methodist undergraduate and graduate students.

Eligibility Applicants must 1) have been active, full members of the United Methodist Church for at least 1 year prior to application (members of other "Methodist" denominations are not eligible); 2) be a citizen or permanent resident of the United States; 3) have been admitted to a degree program (undergraduate or graduate) in an accredited college/university or graduate/professional school; and 4) have a GPA of 2.0

or higher. Loan forms required for application include a promissory note, co-signer's pledge, notice to co-signer form, financial statement, and certificate of enrollment.

Financial data The maximum annual loan is $5,000 for full-time students or $2,500 for students taking at least half the requirements for full-time status. The interest rate charged is 5%. Payments begin no later than 6 months after the borrower withdraws or graduates from school. Final payment is due no later than 120 months from the date the first payment is due. There are no prepayment penalties.

Duration Loans are made annually, on a calendar year basis.

Number awarded Varies each year.

Deadline Deadlines may apply if funds are limited.

[826]
URBAN MINISTRY SCHOLARSHIP PROGRAM

United Methodist City Society
475 Riverside Drive, Room 1922
New York, NY 10115
(212) 870-3084   Fax: (212) 870-3091
E-mail: bshillady@umcitysociety.org
Web: www.nyac.com/pages/detail/1725

Summary To provide financial assistance to undergraduate and graduate students who belong to the United Methodist Church in New York and are preparing for ordained ministry in an urban context at a college in any state.

Eligibility This program is open to persons studying in an undergraduate or graduate program at a college or university in any state approved by the United Methodist City Society. Applicants must be members of a United Methodist Church in the New York Annual Conference and planning to enter full-time ordained ministry in the United Methodist Church, with a special interest in urban ministry. Financial need is considered in the selection process. Scholarship monies are distributed in the following order: undergraduate degree program, graduate first degree program (e.g., M,Div.), special training in urban ministry and, finally, courses in English as a second language.

Financial data Stipends range from $500 to $2,000. Funds are paid directly to the recipient's school.

Duration 1 year; recipients may reapply.

Number awarded Varies each year.

Deadline May of each year.

[827]
VANCE H. HAVNER PREACHING AWARD

Vance H. Havner Scholarship Fund, Inc.
Attn: Secretary of Scholarship Board
P.O. Box 9946
Greensboro, NC 27429-0946
E-mail: Williams@gladwellinsurance.com
Web: www.vancehavner.org

Summary To provide financial assistance to male seminary students who are planning a career in evangelism and missions.

Eligibility This program is open to third-year male students at Christian seminaries in the United States who are working on their M.Div. degree. Applicants must exhibit exceptional knowledge of God's Word, possess superior skill and giftedness, and aspire to a ministry that emphasizes the preached Word.

Financial data   The stipend is $3,000.

Duration   1 year.

Number awarded   1 each year.

Deadline   May of each year.

[828]
VERRETT SCHOLARSHIPS

United Methodist Church-Louisiana Conference
Attn: Coordinator, Conference Board of Ordained Ministry
527 North Boulevard
Baton Rouge, LA 70802-5700
(225) 346-1646, ext. 230
Toll Free: (888) 239-5286, ext. 230
Fax: (225) 383-2652   E-mail: johneddd@bellsouth.net
Web: www.la-umc.org

Summary   To provide financial assistance to Methodists from Louisiana who are attending a seminary in any state to prepare for a career in ordained ministry.

Eligibility   This program is open to members of United Methodist Churches in Louisiana who are enrolled at a seminary in any state. Applicants must be preparing for a career in ordained ministry. The program is designed for part-time students, but it is also available to those pursuing degree studies. Along with their application, they must submit an essay on their vocational goals and plans for ministry.

Financial data   The stipend is $500.

Duration   1 year.

Additional information   This program was established in 1989.

Number awarded   5 each year.

Deadline   February of each year.

[829]
VIOLET MANN BONHAM PARISH NURSE SCHOLARSHIP

Woman's Missionary Union of Virginia
2828 Emerywood Parkway
Richmond, VA 23294
(804) 915-5000, ext. 8267
Toll Free: (800) 255-2428 (within VA)
Fax: (804) 672-8008   E-mail: wmuv@wmuv.org
Web: wmuv.org/developing-future-leaders/scholarships

Summary   To provide financial assistance to nurses in Virginia interested in obtaining further education in order to serve as a Parish Nurse within the Baptist General Association of Virginia (BGAV).

Eligibility   This program is open to Virginia Baptists who have a current Virginia state nursing license. Applicants must be interested in obtaining additional education in order to provide nursing and Christian ministerial services within Virginia to persons in need of nursing and/or health and wellness care. Along with their application, they must submit essays of 250 words or more on 1) their life's Christian testimony or mission statement, and 2) how receipt of this scholarship will impact their life. An interview is required.

Financial data   A stipend is awarded (amount not specified). Funds may only be used for the costs of instruction, text books, and materials.

Duration   1 year.

Additional information   This program was established in 2004.

Number awarded   1 each year.

Deadline   Applications may be submitted any time.

[830]
VIRGINIA BAPTIST FOUNDATION SCHOLARSHIPS

Virginia Baptist Foundation, Inc.
2828 Emerywood Parkway
Richmond, VA 23294
(804) 672-8862   Toll Free: (800) 868-2464
Fax: (804) 672-3747
Web: www.vbfinc.org/Scholarships/ProgramDescription.htm

Summary   To provide financial assistance to members of Southern Baptist churches in Virginia who are interested in attending college, graduate school, medical school, pharmacy school, or seminary in any state.

Eligibility   This program is open to active members of churches cooperating with the Baptist General Association of Virginia. Applicants must be enrolled full time in a basic degree program at a college, university, medical school, pharmacy school, or seminary in any state. They must have a GPA of at least 2.5 as a high school senior, 2.0 as a college freshman or sophomore, 2.3 as a college junior, 2.5 as a college senior, or 2.0 as a seminary student. They must be recommended by their pastor and approved by the church of which they are a member. Most of the funds offered by this sponsor stipulate that students must attend Baptist colleges, universities, or seminaries in Virginia, but others allow attendance at any institution in any state. Doctoral candidates, except those in pharmacy or medicine, are not eligible. Along with their application, students must submit a 500-word summary of their life, including a Christian testimony, life goals, expected vocation, and school selection process. Financial need is considered in the selection proves.

Financial data   A stipend is awarded (amount not specified).

Duration   1 year; may be renewed up to 3 additional years, provided the recipient maintains a grade point average of "C" or higher.

Number awarded   Varies each year.

Deadline   March of each year.

[831]
VIRGINIA CONFERENCE SERVICE LOANS

United Methodist Church-Virginia Conference
Attn: Office of Ministerial Services
10330 Staples Mill Road
P.O. Box 5060
Glen Allen, VA 23058-5606
(804) 521-1126   Toll Free: (800) 768-6040, ext. 126
Fax: (804) 521-1179   E-mail: BethDowns@vaumc.org
Web: www.vaumc.org/Page.aspx?pid=761

Summary   To provide loans-for-service to Methodist seminary students from Virginia.

Eligibility   This program is open to certified candidates, licensed local pastors, and probationary members for ordained ministry in the Virginia Conference of the United Methodist Church (UMC). Applicants must be attending a school of theology approved by the University Senate of the UMC to seek ordination as a deacon or elder. They must present documentation of financial need and the recommendation of their district committee on ordained ministry and their district superintendent.

Financial data Loan amounts depend on the need of the recipient and the availability of funds. Loans are to be repaid to the Virginia Conference in years of service, at a rate of 1 year per semester or summer of aid.

Duration 1 year.

Number awarded Varies each year.

Deadline June or September of each year.

[832]
VOLUNTEERS EXPLORING VOCATION FELLOWSHIPS

The Fund for Theological Education, Inc.
Attn: Partnership for Excellence
825 Houston Mill Road, Suite 250
Atlanta, GA 30329
(404) 727-1450   Fax: (404) 727-1490
E-mail: fellowships@thefund.org
Web: www.thefund.org/programs/vev_fellowships.phtml

Summary To provide financial assistance to students who are planning to enter a seminary to prepare for a career in the ministry and who have completed a year of service in a cooperating Volunteers Exploring Vocation (VEV) program.

Eligibility This program is open to students entering their first year of full-time study for an M.Div. degree at an accredited seminary. Applicants must be currently participating in a VEV program approved by the sponsor or have completed a year of service within the previous 12 months. They must be Canadian or U.S. citizens under 35 years of age and have a GPA of 3.0 or higher in their undergraduate work. Along with their application, they must submit a 3-page essay discussing their understanding of what God is calling the Church to be and to do in this time and place and how their own gifts, struggles, and commitments offer a response to the call as a future leader of a congregation.

Financial data The stipend is $2,500. Funds must be applied toward educational costs and living expenses during the first year of seminary.

Duration 1 year.

Additional information Fellows also receive an additional stipend to cover travel and expenses to attend the sponsor's summer Conference on Excellence in Ministry, where they spend several days engaged in lectures, worship, forums, workshops, recreational activities, and informal time together with other students, theological leaders, and pastors. Students unable to attend the conference should not apply for the fellowship. The participating VEV programs are: Brethren Volunteer Service, Catholic Volunteers in Florida, DOOR, Episcopal Service Corps, Jesuit Volunteer Corps, Krista Foundation for Global Citizenship, Lutheran Volunteer Corps, Mennonite Voluntary Service, Mission Year, Notre Dame Mission Volunteers, Presbyterian Church (USA) Young Adult Volunteers, and US2 Program of the United Methodist Church.

Number awarded Up to 10 each year.

Deadline March of each year.

[833]
WASHINGTON EPISCOPAL CHURCH WOMEN MEMORIAL SCHOLARSHIP FUND

Episcopal Diocese of Washington
Attn: Episcopal Church Women
Episcopal Church House
Mount St. Alban
Washington, DC 20016-5094
(202) 537-6530   Toll Free: (800) 642-4427
Fax: (202) 364-6605   E-mail: ecw@edow.org
Web: ecw.edow.org/programs.html

Summary To provide financial assistance for graduate school to women who are members of Episcopal churches in Washington, D.C.

Eligibility This program is open to women members of the Episcopal Church who have been a canonical member of the Diocese of Washington for at least 1 year prior to application. Priority is given to members who reside in the Diocese of Washington. Applicants must be enrolled in graduate or professional study and their course of study must be related to church work or activity in preparation for some pertinent field of Christian endeavor. Along with their application, they must submit a statement of purpose for working on a graduate degree and how they plan to use it, letters of recommendation (including 1 from their vicar or rector), financial information, and (if seeking ordination) a letter from their parish intern committee.

Financial data A stipend is awarded (amount not specified); funds are sent directly to the recipient's school.

Duration 1 year; may be renewed.

Additional information This program was established in 1925. The Episcopal Diocese of Washington serves the District of Columbia and the Maryland counties of Charles, St. Mary's, Prince George's, and Montgomery.

Number awarded 1 or more each year.

Deadline May of each year.

[834]
WAUKESHA COUNTY CHAPEL HILL SCHOLARSHIP

Wisconsin United Methodist Foundation
750 Windsor Street, Suite 305
P.O. Box 620
Sun Prairie, WI 53590-0620
(608) 837-9582   Toll Free: (888) 903-9863
Fax: (608) 837-2492   E-mail: wumf@wumf.org
Web: www.wumf.org/grantsFF/grantsScholars.html

Summary To provide financial assistance to Methodists from Wisconsin, especially those from Waukesha County, who are interested in attending seminary in any state.

Eligibility This program is open to members of United Methodist Churches affiliated with the Wisconsin Conference who are preparing for full-time ministry at a seminary in any state. Applicants must submit an essay that describes their personal situation and vocational goals, church-related activities and involvement, school and community involvement, and financial plan for funding their education, including any special financial needs. Priority is given to applicants from Waukesha County.

Financial data Stipends range from $500 to $1,000.

Duration 1 year.

Additional information This program was established with the remaining assets of the Chapel Hill United Methodist Church in Waukesha, Wisconsin.

Number awarded 1 or more each year.

Deadline June of each year.

[835]
WEST VIRGINIA EASTERN STAR TRAINING AWARDS FOR RELIGIOUS LEADERSHIP

Order of the Eastern Star-Grand Chapter of West Virginia
c/o Jo Ann Harman, Education Committee Chair
HC 84 Box 26
Lahmansville, WV 26731
(304) 749-7322   E-mail: jsharman@frontiernet.net
Web: www.wveasternstar.org

Summary To provide scholarship/loans to residents of West Virginia who are interested in attending a college or seminary in any state to prepare for a career in full-time Christian service.

Eligibility This program is open to students enrolled or planning to enroll full time at a college or seminary in any state to prepare for a career as a ministry or missionary or for other full-time Christian service. Applicants must be at least 16 years of age and have been residents of West Virginia for at least 3 years. They must have a GPA of 2.5 or higher. Along with their application, they must submit a letter explaining why they should be selected for this scholarship. Selection is based on that letter (10 points), academic achievement (35 points), leadership (10 points), service in school and community organizations (10 points), and financial need (35 points). An interview may be required. Applicants must commit to serve at least 5 years in their chosen field of full-time Christian service.

Financial data A stipend is awarded (amount not specified). If recipients leave their field of preparation prior to completing 5 years of service, they must repay all funds received at a specified rate of interest (currently 6%).

Duration 1 year; may be renewed, provided the recipient maintains a GPA of 2.5 or higher.

Number awarded Varies each year.

Deadline May of each year.

[836]
WILLIAM FLETCHER AND AGNES DAWSEY ROGERS SCHOLARSHIP

South Carolina United Methodist Foundation
P.O. Box 5087
Columbia, SC 29250-5087
(803) 771-9125   Fax: (803) 771-9135
E-mail: scumf@bellsouth.net
Web: www.umcsc.org/scholarships.html

Summary To provide financial assistance to residents of South Carolina who are attending a graduate or theology school in any state to prepare for a career as a missionary of the United Methodist Church (UMC).

Eligibility This program is open to residents of South Carolina who are preparing for service as missionaries under the General Board of Global Ministries of the UMC. Applicants must be enrolled in a graduate or postgraduate program at a college, university, or theological school in any state

approved by the UMC University Senate. Preference is given to applicants preparing for missionary service in Brazil.

Financial data A stipend is awarded (amount not specified).

Duration 1 year.

Additional information This scholarship was established by the South Carolina Conference of the United Methodist Church in 1995.

Number awarded 1 or more each year.

Deadline April of each year.

[837]
WILLIAM G. AND MARGARET B. FRASIER CHARITABLE FOUNDATION SCHOLARSHIP

Center for Scholarship Administration, Inc.
Attn: Wachovia Accounts
4320 Wade Hampton Boulevard, Suite G
Taylors, SC 29687
Toll Free: (866) 608-0001
E-mail: wachoviascholars@bellsouth.net
Web: www.wachoviascholars.com/frsr/index.php

Summary To provide financial assistance to undergraduate and graduate students from North Carolina who are preparing for a career in the Baptist ministry.

Eligibility This program is open to residents of North Carolina who are studying for the Baptist ministry. Applicants must be full-time students working on a recognized undergraduate or graduate degree at an accredited college, theological seminary, or other institution of higher learning in any state. Selection is based on academic merit, financial need, and community service.

Financial data A stipend is awarded (amount not specified).

Duration 1 year; recipients may reapply.

Number awarded Several each year.

Deadline April of each year.

[838]
WILLIAM GILBERT AND FLORENCE LEONARD JONES SCHOLARSHIP

Christian Church (Disciples of Christ)
Attn: Higher Education and Leadership Ministries
11477 Olde Cabin Road, Suite 310
St. Louis, MO 63141-7130
(314) 991-3000   Fax: (314) 991-2957
E-mail: helm@helmdisciples.org
Web: www.helmdisciples.org/aid/jones.htm

Summary To provide financial assistance to members of the Christian Church (Disciples of Christ) who are working on a Ph.D. degree in religion.

Eligibility This program is open to full-time students working on a Ph.D. degree in religion. Applicants must be preparing for ordination in, or already ordained in, the Christian Church (Disciples of Christ) and be interested in providing leadership to a congregation or other agency of the church. Along with their application, they must submit a 300-word essay describing their vocational goals, academic interests, and how they envision being of service to the church. Financial need is also considered in the selection process.

Financial data The stipend is $2,000.

Duration 1 year.
Number awarded 1 each year.
Deadline April of each year.

[839]
WILLIAM P. WOOD SCHOLARSHIP

First Presbyterian Church of Charlotte
Attn: Scholarship Committee
200 West Trade Street
Charlotte, NC 28202
(704) 332-5123   Fax: (704) 334-4135
Web: www.firstpres-charlotte.org

Summary To provide financial assistance to students at Presbyterian seminaries who are interested in working on an advanced degree.

Eligibility This program is open to seniors graduating from designated Presbyterian seminaries who are interested in working on an advanced degree (Th.M. or Ph.D.). Applicants must be interested in serving as pastor of a church after completing their advanced study. They must be nominated by their seminary. Selection is based on commitment to leading local congregations, preaching, and community leadership.

Financial data The stipend is $15,000.

Duration 1 year.

Additional information This program was established in 2003. The designated seminaries are Union Theological Seminary, Princeton Theological Seminary, and Columbia Theological Seminary. The recipient must spend at least 2 weeks in residence at First Presbyterian Church of Charlotte, North Carolina.

Number awarded 1 each year.

Deadline Deadline not specified.

[840]
WILLIAM R. JOHNSON SCHOLARSHIP

United Church of Christ
Parish Life and Leadership Ministry Team
Attn: Grants, Scholarships, and Resources
700 Prospect Avenue East
Cleveland, OH 44115-1100
(216) 736-3839   Toll Free: (866) 822-8224, ext. 3839
Fax: (216) 736-3783   E-mail: jeffersv@ucc.org
Web: www.ucc.org/seminarians/ucc-scholarships-for.html

Summary To provide financial assistance to gay, lesbian, bisexual, and transgender seminary students who are interested in becoming a pastor in the United Church of Christ (UCC).

Eligibility This program is open to second- and third-year students at accredited seminaries who have been members of a UCC congregation for at least 1 year. Applicants must be gay, lesbian, bisexual, or transgender and be open about their sexual orientation. They must 1) have a GPA of 3.0 or higher, 2) be enrolled in a course of study leading to ordained ministry, 3) be in care of an association or conference at the time of application, and 4) demonstrate leadership ability through participation in their local church, association, conference, or academic environment.

Financial data Stipends are approximately $2,500 per year.

Duration 1 year.

Additional information This program was established in 2000 in honor of the first openly gay man ordained in the UCC.

Number awarded Varies each year. Recently, 6 of these scholarships were awarded.

Deadline Deadline not specified.

[841]
WISCONSIN BOARD OF ORDAINED MINISTRY SEMINARIAN SCHOLARSHIP

United Methodist Church-Wisconsin Conference
Attn: Board of Ordained Ministry
750 Windsor Street
P.O. Box 620
Sun Prairie, WI 53590-0620
(608) 837-7328   Toll Free: (888) 240-7328
Fax: (608) 837-8547
Web: www.wisconsinumc.org

Summary To provide financial assistance for seminary to members of United Methodist Churches in Wisconsin who are preparing for ministry.

Eligibility This program is open to members of United Methodist Churches affiliated with the Wisconsin Conference who are working on a basic degree in ordained ministry at a seminary in any state.

Financial data The stipend is $1,800 per year.

Duration 1 year; may be renewed up to 2 additional years.

Number awarded 1 or more each year.

Deadline July of each year for fall semester; November of each year for winter semester.

[842]
WISCONSIN UNITED METHODIST FOUNDATION SEMINARIAN SCHOLARSHIP

Wisconsin United Methodist Foundation
750 Windsor Street, Suite 305
P.O. Box 620
Sun Prairie, WI 53590-0620
(608) 837-9582   Toll Free: (888) 903-9863
Fax: (608) 837-2492   E-mail: wumf@wumf.org
Web: www.wumf.org/grantsFF/grantsScholars.html

Summary To provide financial assistance to Methodists from Wisconsin interested in attending seminary in any state.

Eligibility This program is open to members of United Methodist Churches affiliated with the Wisconsin Conference who are preparing for full-time ministry at a seminary in any state. Applicants may not currently be receiving assistance from the Board of Ordained Ministry and may not qualify for support from other sources. Along with their application, they must submit an essay that describes their personal situation and vocational goals, church-related activities and involvement, school and community involvement, and financial plan for funding their education, including any special financial needs.

Financial data Stipends range from $500 to $1,000.

Duration 1 year.

Additional information This program was established in the early 1980s.

Number awarded 1 or more each year.

Deadline June of each year.

[843]
WOLFF PROGRAM FOR THEOLOGICAL EDUCATION

United Church of Christ-Ohio Conference
Attn: Wolff Fund for Recruitment and Funding for
  Theological Education
6161 Busch Boulevard, Suite 100
Columbus, OH 43229
(614) 885-0722   Toll Free: (800) 282-0740
Fax: (614) 885-8824   E-mail: ohioucc@ocucc.org
Web: www.ocucc.org/WolffFund/wolff.htm

Summary To provide forgivable loans to seminary students from Ohio, West Virginia, and northern Kentucky who are preparing for a career of service to the United Church of Christ (UCC).

Eligibility This program is open to students who are members of UCC congregations in the Ohio Conference, which serves Ohio, West Virginia, and northern Kentucky. Applicants must be attending 1 of the 13 seminaries associated with the UCC to prepare for a career in the ministry of the church as an ordained or commissioned minister, in Christian education, or in global mission under the sponsorship of the UCC Global Ministries.

Financial data The award is $2,000. Grants are forgiven after 5 years of ministry within the UCC. Recipients who fail to serve for 5 years are required to repay the grant with interest.

Duration 1 year.

Additional information The 13 seminaries associated with the UCC are Andover Newton Theological School in Newton Centre, Massachusetts; Bangor Theological Seminary in Bangor, Maine; Chicago Theological Seminary in Chicago, Illinois; Eden Theological Seminary in St. Louis, Missouri; Lancaster Theological Seminary in Lancaster, Pennsylvania; Pacific School of Religion in Berkeley, California; United Theological Seminary of the Twin Cities in New Brighton, Minnesota; Hartford Seminary in Hartford, Connecticut; Harvard University School of Divinity in Cambridge, Massachusetts; Howard University School of Divinity in Washington, D.C.; Interdenominational Theological Center in Atlanta, Georgia; Union Theological Seminary in New York City; and Vanderbilt Divinity School in Nashville, Tennessee.

Number awarded Varies each year. Recently, 5 of these scholarships were awarded.

Deadline Deadline not specified.

[844]
WOMAN'S MISSIONARY UNION OF MARYLAND/ DELAWARE CENTENNIAL SCHOLARSHIPS

Baptist Convention of Maryland/Delaware
Attn: Woman's Missionary Union of Maryland/Delaware
10255 Old Columbia Road
Columbia, MD 21046
(410) 290-5290   Toll Free: (800) 466-5290
E-mail: gparker@bcmd.org
Web: bcmd.org/wmu

Summary To provide financial assistance to members of Southern Baptist churches affiliated with the Baptist Convention of Maryland/Delaware and interested in attending a college or seminary in any state.

Eligibility This program is open to active members of a Southern Baptist church/mission or Baptist student ministry affiliated with the Baptist Convention of Maryland/Delaware. Applicants must be enrolled or planning to enroll full time at 1) an accredited college or university in any state, or 2) a Southern Baptist seminary. They must have a grade point average of "C" or higher and be able to demonstrate financial need. Along with their application, they must submit a brief essay that includes a testimony of their salvation experience; their involvement in church, school, and community activities; and the kind of work God has called them to do after completing their education, how they have come to believe God wants them in this work, and their plans to fulfill His call. Priority is given to applicants who are preparing for missionary service under the North American Mission Board or International Mission Board of the Southern Baptist Convention, career service with the Woman's Missionary Union (WMU), or work with the Men's Ministries.

Financial data The stipend is $375 per semester ($750 per year). Funds are paid directly to the recipient's school.

Duration 1 year; may be renewed for a total of 8 semesters of undergraduate study or 6 semesters of seminary master's degree work.

Number awarded Varies each year.

Deadline February of each year for fall semester or August of each year for spring semester.

[845]
WOMAN'S MISSIONARY UNION OF MARYLAND/ DELAWARE SCHOLARSHIPS FOR WOMEN

Baptist Convention of Maryland/Delaware
Attn: Woman's Missionary Union of Maryland/Delaware
10255 Old Columbia Road
Columbia, MD 21046
(410) 290-5290   Toll Free: (800) 466-5290
E-mail: gparker@bcmd.org
Web: bcmd.org/wmu

Summary To provide financial assistance to women who are members of Southern Baptist churches affiliated with the Baptist Convention of Maryland/Delaware and interested in attending a college or seminary in any state.

Eligibility This program is open to women who are active members of a Southern Baptist church/mission or Baptist student ministry affiliated with the Baptist Convention of Maryland/Delaware. Applicants must be enrolled or planning to enroll full time at 1) an accredited college or university in any state, or 2) a Southern Baptist seminary. They must have a grade point average of "C" or higher and be able to demonstrate financial need. Along with their application, they must submit a brief essay that includes a testimony of their salvation experience; their involvement in church, school, and community activities; and the kind of work God has called them to do after completing their education, how they have come to believe God wants them in this work, and their plans to fulfill His call. Priority is given to applicants who are preparing for missionary service under the North American Mission Board or International Mission Board of the Southern Baptist Convention, career service with the Woman's Missionary Union (WMU), or work with the Men's Ministries.

Financial data The stipend is $375 per semester ($750 per year). Funds are paid directly to the recipient's school.

Duration 1 year; may be renewed for a total of 8 semesters of undergraduate study or 6 semesters of seminary master's degree work.

Additional information This program includes the Business Women's Circles Scholarship, the Captain and Mrs. John T. Willing Scholarship, and the Hattie Wilson Norwood Scholarship.

Number awarded Varies each year.

Deadline February of each year for fall semester or August of each year for spring semester.

[846]
WOMAN'S MISSIONARY UNION OF VIRGINIA SEMINARY SCHOLARSHIP

Woman's Missionary Union of Virginia
2828 Emerywood Parkway
Richmond, VA 23294
(804) 915-5000, ext. 8267
Toll Free: (800) 255-2428 (within VA)
Fax: (804) 672-8008   E-mail: wmuv@wmuv.org
Web: wmuv.org/developing-future-leaders/scholarships

Summary To provide financial assistance to women from Virginia who are interested in attending a Baptist seminary.

Eligibility This program is open to women from Virginia who are interested in attending a seminary supported through the Baptist General Association of Virginia (BGAV). Applicants must be seeking career missions appointments and/or professional ministry positions in churches, associations, states, or the world. An interview is required.

Financial data The stipend is $500 per year.

Duration 1 year; may be renewed up to 2 additional years.

Number awarded Up to 5 each year.

Deadline June of each year.

[847]
WOMEN OF COLOR SCHOLARS PROGRAM

United Methodist Church
Attn: General Board of Higher Education and Ministry
Office of Loans and Scholarships
1001 19th Avenue South
P.O. Box 340007
Nashville, TN 37203-0007
(615) 340-7344   Fax: (615) 340-7367
E-mail: umscholar@gbhem.org
Web: www.gbhem.org/loansandscholarships

Summary To provide financial assistance to Methodist women of color who are working on a doctoral degree to prepare for a career as an educator at a United Methodist seminary.

Eligibility This program is open to women of color (have at least 1 parent who is African American, African, Hispanic, Asian, Native American, Alaska Native, or Pacific Islander) who have an M.Div. degree. Applicants must have been active, full members of a United Methodist Church for at least 3 years prior to applying. They must be enrolled full time in a degree program at the Ph.D. or Th.D. level to prepare for a career teaching at a United Methodist seminary.

Financial data The maximum stipend is $10,000 per year.

Duration 1 year; may be renewed up to 3 additional years.

Number awarded Varies each year. Recently, 10 of these scholarships were awarded.

Deadline January of each year.

[848]
WOMEN OF THE ELCA SCHOLARSHIP PROGRAM

Women of the Evangelical Lutheran Church in America
Attn: Scholarships
8765 West Higgins Road
Chicago, IL 60631-4101
(773) 380-2736   Toll Free: (800) 638-3522, ext. 2736
Fax: (773) 380-2419   E-mail: emily.hansen@elca.org
Web: www.elca.org

Summary To provide financial assistance to lay women who are members of Evangelical Lutheran Church of America (ELCA) congregations and who wish to take classes on the undergraduate, graduate, professional, or vocational school level.

Eligibility This program is open to ELCA lay women who are at least 21 years of age and have experienced an interruption of at least 2 years in their education since high school. Applicants must have been admitted to an educational institution to prepare for a career in other than the ordained ministry. They may be working on an undergraduate, graduate, professional, or vocational school degree. U.S. citizenship is required.

Financial data The maximum stipend is $1,000.

Duration Up to 2 years.

Additional information These scholarships are supported by several endowment funds: the Cronk Memorial Fund, the First Triennial Board Scholarship Fund, the General Scholarship Fund, the Mehring Fund, the Paepke Scholarship Fund, the Piero/Wade/Wade Fund, and the Edwin/Edna Robeck Scholarship.

Number awarded Varies each year, depending upon the funds available.

Deadline February of each year.

[849]
WORLD COMMUNION SCHOLARSHIPS

United Methodist Church
General Board of Global Ministries
Attn: Scholarship Office
475 Riverside Drive, Room 1351
New York, NY 10115
(212) 870-3787   Toll Free: (800) UMC-GBGM
E-mail: scholars@gbgm-umc.org
Web: new.gbgm-umc.org

Summary To provide financial assistance to foreign students and to U.S. minority students who are interested in attending graduate school to prepare for leadership in promoting the goals of the United Methodist Church.

Eligibility This program is open to 1) students from Methodist churches in nations other than the United States, and 2) members of ethnic and racial minorities in the United States. Applicants must have applied to or been admitted to a master's, doctoral, or professional program at a university or seminary in the United States. They should be planning to return to their communities to work on furthering Christian mission, whether that be in the local church, the neighborhood clinic, the state rural development office, or the national office on education. Financial need must be demonstrated.

Financial data The stipend ranges from $250 to $12,500, depending on the recipient's related needs and school expenses.

Duration 1 year.

Additional information These awards are funded by the World Communion Offering received in United Methodist Churches on the first Sunday in October.

Number awarded 5 to 10 each year.

Deadline November of each year.

[850]
WORLD WIDE BARACA PHILATHEA UNION SCHOLARSHIP

World Wide Baraca Philathea Union
610 South Harlem Avenue
Freeport, IL 61032-4833

Summary To provide financial assistance to students preparing for Christian ministry, Christian missionary work, or Christian education.

Eligibility Eligible to apply for this support are students enrolled in an accredited college or seminary who are majoring in Christian ministry, Christian missionary work, or Christian education (e.g., church youth pastor, writer of Sunday school curriculum).

Financial data Stipends are paid directly to the recipient's school upon receipt of the first semester transcript and a letter confirming attendance.

Duration 1 year; may be renewed.

Deadline March of each year.

Sponsoring Organization Index

The Sponsoring Organization Index makes it easy to identify agencies that offer financial aid specifically to Christian undergraduate and graduate students working on a secular or religious degree. In this index, the sponsoring organizations are listed alphabetically, word by word. In addition, we've used an alphabetical code (within parentheses) to help you identify the focus of the funding offered by the organizations: U = Undergraduates; G = Graduate Students. For example, if the name of a sponsoring organization is followed by (U) 241, a program sponsored by that organization is described in the Undergraduate section, in entry 241. If that sponsoring organization's name is followed by another entry number—for example, (G) 601—the same or a different program sponsored by that organization is described in the Graduate Students section, in entry 601. Remember: the numbers cited here refer to program entry numbers, not to page numbers in the book.

V

Vance H. Havner Scholarship Fund, Inc., (G) 827

Violet R. and Nada V. Bohnett Memorial Foundation, (U) 55, (G) 467

Virginia Baptist Foundation, Inc., (U) 384, (G) 830

Virginia United Methodist Foundation, (U) 157, (G) 588

W

Watauga Community Foundation, (U) 334, (G) 781

Watts Charity Association, Inc., (U) 135

Wesley United Methodist Church, (G) 669

West Los Angeles United Methodist Church, (G) 627

West Virginia Baptist Convention, (U) 56, (G) 470

Western Catholic Union, (U) 143, (G) 574

Wisconsin United Methodist Foundation, (U) 85, 109, 380, 394-395, (G) 420, 834, 842

Woman's Missionary Union, (U) 63, 107, 168, 201, 210, 212, 245, 251, (G) 480, 489, 600, 644, 647, 686, 694

Woman's Missionary Union of Virginia, (U) 383, (G) 562, 829, 846

Women of the Evangelical Lutheran Church in America, (U) 19, 340, 400, (G) 421, 443, 594, 616, 848

Women's Ordination Conference, (G) 461

World Wide Baraca Philathea Union, (U) 401, (G) 850

Z

Zonta Club of Washington, D.C., (G) 535

Residency Index

Some programs listed in this book are restricted to Christian residents of a particular state or region. Others are open to applicants wherever they may live. The Residency Index will help you pinpoint programs available to Christians in your area as well as programs that have no residency restrictions at all (these are listed under the term "United States"). To use this index, look up the geographic areas that apply to you (always check the listings under "United States"), jot down the entry numbers listed for the educational level that applies to you (Undergraduates or Graduate Students), and use those numbers to find the program descriptions in the directory. To help you in your search, we've provided some "see" and "see also" references in the index entries. Remember: the numbers cited here refer to program entry numbers, not to page numbers in the book.

Tenability Index

Some programs listed in this book can be used only in specific cities, counties, states, or regions. Others may be used anywhere in the United States. The Tenability Index will help you locate funding that is restricted to a specific area as well as funding that has no tenability restrictions (these are listed under the term "United States"). To use this index, look up the geographic areas where you'd like to go (always check the listings under "United States"), jot down the entry numbers listed for the educational level that applies to you (Undergraduates or Graduate Students), and use those numbers to find the program descriptions in the directory. To help you in your search, we've provided some "see" and "see also" references in the index entries. Remember: the numbers cited here refer to program entry numbers, not to page numbers in the book.

Subject Index

There are dozens of different subject fields covered in this directory—both secular and religious. Use the Subject Index to identify this focus, as well as the degree level supported (undergraduate or graduate) by the available funding programs. To help you pinpoint your search, weíve included many "see" and "see also" references. In addition to looking for terms that represent your specific subject interest, be sure to check the "General programs" entry; hundreds of funding opportunities are listed there that can be used to support study or research in any subject area (although the programs may be restricted in other ways). Remember: the numbers cited in this index refer to program entry numbers, not to page numbers in the book.

A

Acting. *See* Performing arts

Administration. *See* Business administration; Education, administration; Management; Public administration

American history. *See* History, American

Archaeology: **Graduate Students, 481.** *See also* General programs; History; Social sciences

Arithmetic. *See* Mathematics

Art: **Graduate Students, 591.** *See also* Fine arts; General programs; names of specific art forms

Attorneys. *See* Law, general

B

Biological sciences: **Undergraduates, 244.** *See also* General programs; Sciences; names of specific biological sciences

Botany: **Undergraduates, 244.** *See also* Biological sciences; General programs

Broadcast journalism. *See* Journalism, broadcast

Broadcasting: **Graduate Students, 591.** *See also* Communications; Radio; Television

Business administration: **Undergraduates, 10, 110, 139, 218; Graduate Students, 544, 741.** *See also* General programs; Management

C

Chemistry: **Undergraduates, 244.** *See also* General programs

Church music. *See* Music, church

Civil liberties: **Undergraduates, 123.** *See also* Civil rights; General programs

Civil rights: **Graduate Students, 636.** *See also* General programs

Colleges and universities. *See* Education, higher

Commerce. *See* Business administration

Communications: **Undergraduates, 5-6, 230, 254; Graduate Students, 409, 591, 697.** *See also* General programs

Community colleges. *See* Education, higher

Community services. *See* Social services

Conservation. *See* Environmental sciences

Counseling: **Undergraduates, 56, 70; Graduate Students, 470, 495.** *See also* General programs; Psychology

D

Dentistry: **Undergraduates, 172, 181, 245, 358; Graduate Students, 604, 610, 686, 809.** *See also* General programs; Health and health care; Medical sciences

Developmental disabilities. *See* Disabilities, developmental

Dietetics. *See* Nutrition

Disabilities: **Graduate Students, 460.** *See also* General programs; Rehabilitation; names of specific disabilities

Disabilities, developmental: **Undergraduates, 88-89; Graduate Students, 516.** *See also* Disabilities; General programs

Divinity. *See* Religion and religious activities

Documentaries. *See* Filmmaking

E

Ecology. *See* Environmental sciences

Economic planning. *See* Economics

Economics: **Graduate Students, 473-474, 591, 741.** *See also* General programs; Social sciences

Education: **Undergraduates, 62, 70, 93, 101, 105, 138, 161, 192, 353, 381; Graduate Students, 488, 494-495, 523, 534, 622.** *See also* General programs; Social sciences; names of specific types and levels of education

Education, administration: **Graduate Students, 547.** *See also* Education; General programs; Management

Education, elementary: **Undergraduates, 87; Graduate Students, 515.** *See also* Education; General programs

Education, higher: **Undergraduates, 376; Graduate Students, 547, 822.** *See also* Education; General programs

Education, music: **Undergraduates, 263; Graduate Students, 707.** *See also* Education; General programs; Music

Education, physical: **Undergraduates, 381.** *See also* Education; General programs

Denomination Index

In this book, we have described hundreds of financial aid programs available primarily or exclusively to Christian students interested in working on an undergraduate or graduate degree. For the purpose of this listing, we defined "Christian" to include denominations "professing belief in Jesus as Christ or based on the life and teachings of Jesus." Funding opportunities for students affiliated with denominations that do not accept the core tenets of Christianity (e.g., the Trinity, the Resurrection of Christ) are not covered in this edition. In addition to looking for funding by specific denomination, students should also check for leads under "Protestant" (if appropriate) and "Christianity," where they will find numerous funding programs that are open to students belonging to any Christian denomination (although the programs may be restricted in other ways). Remember: the numbers cited in this index refer to program entry numbers, not to page numbers in the book.

Undergraduates

Roman Catholic
29, 50, 57, 60, 76, 110, 112, 118-119, 122, 131, 133-134, 143, 188, 200, 206, 225, 234, 240, 242, 244, 269-271, 279, 306, 312-317, 343-344, 363-368, 382

United Church of Christ
374

Graduate Students

Baptist
405-406, 409, 419, 422-432, 438, 448-454, 457, 470, 480, 487, 489, 502-506, 508, 511-512, 520, 528, 530, 543, 549, 556, 564, 572, 575, 578, 585, 587, 598, 600, 607, 614-615, 624, 628, 639, 642, 644, 647, 649-650, 653, 666-667, 670, 672, 675, 685-686, 689, 692, 694, 699, 703, 708, 717, 728, 734-737, 739-740, 742-743, 770, 773, 782, 789, 795-796, 809-812, 829-830, 837, 844-846

Christian Science
412

Christianity
437, 463, 465, 467, 471, 473-474, 485, 488, 492, 497, 499, 513, 519, 525, 553, 557, 562, 565, 567-568, 590-591, 604-606, 609-610, 612, 617, 622, 630-631, 636, 658, 668, 688, 695, 697, 705, 727, 738, 741, 744, 747-748, 753, 771, 774, 776, 785, 794, 818, 827, 832, 835, 850

Church of Brethren
445

Church of Christ
414, 536, 582

Disciples of Christ
407, 433, 476, 518, 621, 651, 661, 702, 780, 799, 838

Episcopal
434, 494, 532, 541, 545-546, 551, 571, 599, 602, 693, 732, 766, 791-792, 817, 833

Lutheran
421, 443, 495, 516, 529, 537-538, 550, 592, 594, 616, 635, 706, 788, 848

Methodist
410-411, 413, 415-417, 420, 439-442, 444, 447, 455-456, 458-459, 462, 466, 468-469, 472, 475-476, 479, 484, 486, 490, 496, 498, 500-501, 507, 510, 514-515, 517, 521-524, 527, 531, 534, 539, 542, 547-548, 557, 561, 563, 566, 570, 573, 576-577, 579-581, 583-584, 586, 588-589, 595-597, 601, 603, 608, 611, 613, 619-620, 623, 625, 627, 629-630, 632, 634, 637-638, 640-641, 652, 656-657, 659-660, 662, 664-665, 669, 673-674, 682, 684, 687, 696, 698, 700-701, 704, 707, 709-712, 714-716, 718-720, 722-723, 726, 729-731, 733, 745-746, 749-751, 762, 767-769, 775, 777-779, 783, 787, 793, 797-798, 800, 802, 808, 814, 816, 819, 822-826, 828, 831, 834, 836, 841-842, 847, 849

Orthodox
408, 436, 446, 526, 643, 754

Presbyterian
418, 435, 476, 478, 491, 493, 552, 559-560, 593, 631, 671, 690-691, 721, 724, 752, 757-761, 764-765, 781, 786, 803-807, 821, 839

Protestant
533, 535, 618, 645-646, 648, 655, 663, 681, 683, 687

Reformed
763

Roman Catholic
460-461, 464, 477, 481-483, 540, 544, 554-555, 558, 574, 626, 633, 654, 676, 713, 725, 755-756, 790, 813, 815

Seventh-Day Adventist
509

United Church of Christ
476, 569, 677-680, 772, 820, 840, 843

Calendar Index

Since most funding programs have specific deadline dates, some may have already closed by the time you begin to look for money. You can use the Calendar Index to identify which programs are still open. To do that, go to the educational category (Undergraduates or Graduate Students) that interests you, think about when you'll be able to complete your application forms, go to the appropriate months, jot down the entry numbers listed there, and use those numbers to find the program descriptions in the directory. Keep in mind that the numbers cited here refer to program entry numbers, not to page numbers in the book.